GRE®
GRADUATE RECORD EXAMINATION

PREMIER
2016

KAPLAN

PUBLISHING

New York

ACKNOWLEDGMENTS

Special thanks to the team that made this book possible:

Arthur Ahn, Mikhail Alexeef, Gina Allison, Matthew Belinkie, Kim Bowers, Brian Carlidge, Lauren Challman, Gerard Cortinez, Elisa Davis, Boris Dvorkin, Steve Ferges, Paula Fleming, Dan Frey, Joanna Graham, Adam Grey, Allison Harm, Adam Hinz, Gar Hong, Xandi Kagstrom, Sarah Krentz, Jennifer Land, Edwina Lui, Jenny Lynch, Keith Lubeley, Heather Maigur, Rachel Mason, Jennifer Moore, Jason Moss, Walt Niedner, Robert Reiss, Glen Stohr, Gene Suhir, Lee A. Weiss, and many others who have contributed materials and advice over the years.

Published by Kaplan Publishing, a division of Kaplan, Inc.
395 Hudson Street
New York, NY 10014

10 9 8 7 6 5 4 3 2 1

ISBN: 978-1-62523-132-1

Kaplan Publishing books are available at special quantity discounts to use for sales promotions, employee premiums, or educational purposes. For more information or to order books, please call the Simon & Schuster special sales department at 866-506-1949.

Table of Contents

http://kaptest.com/publishing

The material in this book is up-to-date at the time of publication. However, the Educational Testing Service may have instituted changes in the test or test registration process after this book was published. Be sure to read carefully the materials you receive when you register for the test.

If there are any important late-breaking developments—or changes or corrections to the Kaplan test preparation materials in this book—we will post that information online at **kaptest.com/publishing**. Check to see if any information is posted there regarding this book.

How to Use This Book

WELCOME TO KAPLAN GRE PREMIER 2016

Congratulations on your decision to pursue a graduate degree, and thank you for choosing Kaplan for your GRE preparation. You've made the right choice in acquiring this book—you're now armed with a comprehensive GRE program that is the result of decades of researching the GRE and teaching many thousands of students the skills they need to succeed. You have everything you need to score higher—let's start by walking through what you need to know to take advantage of this book and the Online Center.

YOUR BOOK

There are two main components to your *Kaplan GRE Premier* study package: your book and your Online Center. This book contains the following:

- Detailed instruction covering the essential Verbal Reasoning, Quantitative Reasoning, and Analytical Writing concepts
- Time-tested and effective Kaplan Methods and strategies for every question type
- One full-length practice test and chapter-end practice questions with detailed answer explanations
- A DVD containing instruction and graduate school admission guidance from elite Kaplan faculty

YOUR ONLINE CENTER

Your Online Center lets you access additional instruction and practice materials to reinforce key concepts and sharpen your GRE skills. Resources include the following:

- Five full-length practice tests
- 500-question Quiz Bank you can use to create customized quizzes
- Ten 20-question Quantitative practice sets

- ten 20-question Verbal practice sets
- five Analytical Writing essay prompts
- detailed answer explanations and sample essay responses
- online answer grid for the practice test found in this book
- academic support from Kaplan faculty via our Facebook page: **www.facebook.com/kaplangradprep**

GETTING STARTED

1. Register your Online Center.
2. Take a GRE practice test to identify your strengths and weaknesses.
3. Create a study plan.
4. Learn and practice using this book and your Online Center.

STEP 1: REGISTER YOUR ONLINE CENTER

Register your Online Center using these simple steps:

1. Go to **kaptest.com/booksonline**.
2. Follow the onscreen instructions. Please have a copy of your book available.

Access to the Online Center is limited to the original owner of this book and is nontransferable. Kaplan is not responsible for providing access to the Online Center to customers who purchase or borrow used copies of this book. Access to the Online Center expires one year after you register.

STEP 2: TAKE A GRE PRACTICE TEST

It's essential to take a practice test early on. Doing so will give you the initial feedback and diagnostic information that you need to achieve your maximum score.

Your diagnostic test is Multi-Stage Test (MST) 1, which is found in your Online Center. MST 1, like all of Kaplan's online full-length tests, is a multi-stage test, which is the same format as the actual GRE. The multi-stage test format feels different from a paper-based test and is scored differently, so the more you practice with MSTs, the better off you'll be. However, for your convenience, we've also included a practice test in this book. This practice test, which includes full-length Analytical Writing, Verbal, and Quantitative sections, will give you a chance to familiarize yourself with the various question types. It also allows you to accurately gauge the content you know and identify areas for practice and review. (Use the online answer grid available in your Online Center to enter your answer choices from the practice test in this book to see a detailed breakdown of your performance by question type and topic.)

Review the detailed answer explanations to better understand your performance. Look for patterns in the questions you answered correctly and incorrectly. Were you stronger in some areas than others? This analysis will help you target your practice time to specific concepts.

STEP 3: CREATE A STUDY PLAN

Use what you've learned from your diagnostic test to identify areas for closer study and practice. Take time to familiarize yourself with the key components of your book and Online Center. Think about how many hours you can consistently devote to GRE study. We have found that most students have success with about three months of committed preparation before Test Day.

Schedule time for study, practice, and review. One of the most frequent mistakes in approaching study is to take practice tests and not review them thoroughly—review time is your best chance to gain points. It works best for many people to block out short, frequent periods of study time throughout the week. Check in with yourself frequently to make sure you're not falling behind your plan or forgetting about any of your resources.

STEP 4: LEARN AND PRACTICE

Your book and Online Center come with many opportunities to develop and practice the skills you'll need on Test Day. Read each chapter of this book and complete the practice questions. Depending on how much time you have to study, you can do this work methodically, covering every chapter, or you can focus your study on those question types and content areas that are most challenging for you. You will inevitably need more work in some areas than in others, but know that the more thoroughly you prepare, the better your score will be.

Remember also to take and review the practice sets in your Online Center. These quizzes give you additional test-like questions so you can put into practice the skills you are learning. As always, review the explanations closely.

Initially, your practice should focus on mastering the needed skills and not on timing. Add timing to your practice as you improve fundamental proficiency. As soon as you are comfortable with the question types and Kaplan Methods, take and review the additional full-length practice tests in your Online Center.

If you find that you would like access to more of Kaplan's practice tests and quizzes, as well as in-depth instruction on the question types and strategies, look into the variety of course options available at **kaptest.com/GRE**.

Thanks for choosing Kaplan. We wish you the best of luck on your journey to graduate school.

PART ONE

Getting Started

CHAPTER 1

Introduction to the GRE

This book will explain more than just a few basic strategies. It will prepare you for practically everything that you are likely to encounter on the GRE. This may sound too good to be true, but we mean it. We are able to do this because we don't explain test questions in isolation or focus on particular test problems. Instead, we explain the underlying principles behind *all* of the questions on the GRE. We give you the big picture.

UNDERSTANDING THE GRE

Let's take a look at how the GRE is constructed. The GRE, or Graduate Record Examination, is a computer-based exam required by many graduate schools for admission to a wide variety of programs at the graduate level. You need to know firsthand the way this test is put together if you want to take it apart. In this section, you will learn about the purposes of the GRE and ways you can learn to be successful on it. For up-to-the-minute news about the GRE, visit Kaplan's website at **www.kaptest.com/GRE**.

THE PURPOSES OF THE GRE

The GRE is designed to assess readiness for a wide variety of graduate programs. The ways in which graduate schools use GRE scores vary. Scores are often required as part of the application for entrance into a program, but they also can be used to grant fellowships or financial aid. Each section of the GRE is designed to assess general skills necessary for graduate school. Some of these skills include the ability to read complex informational text and understand high-level vocabulary words in the Verbal Reasoning section, respond to an issue in written form in the Analytical Writing section, and apply general mathematical concepts to a variety of problem types in the Quantitative Reasoning section. Graduate school admissions officers often view the GRE score as an important indicator of readiness for graduate-level studies. In addition, graduate school admissions officers are comparing hundreds or even thousands of applications, and having a quantitative factor, such as a GRE score, makes the job of comparing so many applicants much easier. Just by having this book and making a commitment to yourself to be as well prepared as possible for this exam, you've already taken the crucial first step toward making your graduate school application as competitive as possible.

THE SECRET CODE

Doing well on the GRE requires breaking down the "secret code" upon which each and every test is constructed. Like all of the tests created by the Educational Testing Service (ETS), the GRE is based on psychometrics, the science of creating "standardized" tests. For a test to be standardized, it must successfully do three things. First, the test must be reliable. In other words, a test taker who takes the GRE should get approximately the same score if she takes a second GRE (assuming, of course, that she doesn't study with Kaplan materials during the intervening period). Second—and this is closely related to our first point—it must test the same concepts on each test. Third, it must create a "bell curve" when a pool of test takers' scores are plotted; in other words, some people will do very well on the test and some will do very poorly, but the great majority will score somewhere in the middle.

What all this boils down to is that to be a standardized test, the GRE has to be predictable. And this is what makes the GRE and other standardized tests coachable. Because ETS has to test the same concepts in each and every test, certain vocabulary words appear over and over again, as do variations of the same exact math questions. Moreover, the GRE has to create some questions that most test takers will get wrong—otherwise, it wouldn't be able to create its bell curve. This means that hard questions will usually contain "traps"—wrong answer choices that will be more appealing than the correct answer to a large percentage of test takers. Fortunately, these traps are predictable (this is what we mean by the "secret code"), and we can teach you how to recognize and avoid them. The goal of this comprehensive program is to help you break the code.

ACQUIRE THE SKILLS

It has been argued that the GRE isn't a fair or effective predictor of the skills a person needs for graduate-level study. And you may be concerned that your scores on the GRE will not be a fair or accurate representation of the strong work you will do in your advanced degree program. Take heart: None of the GRE experts who work at Kaplan were *born* knowing how to ace the GRE. No one is. That's because these tests do not measure innate skills; they measure *acquired* skills. People who are good at standardized tests are simply people who've already acquired these skills, whether in math class, or by reading a lot, or by studying logic in college, or—perhaps most efficiently—in one of Kaplan's GRE courses. But they have, perhaps without realizing it, acquired the skills that spell success on tests like the GRE. And if *you* haven't, you have nothing whatsoever to feel bad about. It's time to acquire them now.

SAME PROBLEMS—BUT DIFFERENT

As we noted, the testmakers use some of the same problems on every GRE. We know it sounds incredible, but it's true—only the words and numbers change. They test the same principles over and over. Here's an example.

Quantity A   Quantity B

$2x^2 = 32$

x 4

This is a type of math problem known as a Quantitative Comparison. (Look familiar? It might, if you've taken the SAT. This question type used to appear on the SAT, although this question type was dropped in 2005.) Your job is to examine the relationship and pick **(A)** if Quantity A is bigger, **(B)** if Quantity B is bigger, **(C)** if they're equal, or **(D)** if not enough information is given to solve the problem.

Most people answer **(C)**, that the quantities are equal. They divide both sides of the centered equation by 2 and then take the square root of both sides to get $x = 4$. However, this is incorrect. x doesn't have to be 4. It could be 4 *or* −4; that is, the quantities could be equal *or* Quantity B could be bigger. Both work, so the answer is **(D)** because the answer cannot be determined from the information given. If you just solve for 4, you'll get this problem—and every one like it—wrong. ETS figures that if you get burned here, you'll get burned again next time. Only next time, it won't be $2x^2 = 32$; it will be $y^2 = 36$ or $s^4 = 81$.

The concepts tested on any particular GRE—right triangles, simple logic, word relationships, and so forth—are the underlying concepts at the heart of *every* GRE. ETS makes changes only after testing them exhaustively. This process is called *norming*, which means taking a normal test and a changed test and administering them to a random group of students. As long as the group is large enough for the purposes of statistical validity and the students get consistent scores from one test to the next, then the revised test is just as valid and consistent as any other GRE.

That may sound technical, but norming is actually a straightforward process. We do it at Kaplan all the time—for the tests that we write for our students. The tests in this book and your Online Center, for instance, are normed exams. While the interactive, computer-based test experience of the GRE is impossible to reproduce on paper, the paper-based test in our book is a normed exam that will produce a roughly equivalent score.

HOW THE GRE IS ORGANIZED

The Graduate Record Examination (GRE) is administered on computer and is approximately four hours long, including breaks. The exam consists of six sections, with different amounts of time allotted for you to complete each section.

Basics of the GRE	
Exam Length	4 hours, including breaks
Scoring Scale	130–170 (1-point increments) for Verbal and Quantitative; 0–6 for Analytical Writing
Format	Multi-stage test (MST), a computer-based format that allows students to navigate forward and backward within each section of the test
Number of Test Sections	6 sections, including an experimental or research section
Breaks	One 10-minute break after your third section; 1-minute breaks between all other sections
Analytical Writing	One section with two 30-minute tasks: analyze an issue and analyze an argument
Verbal Reasoning	Two 30-minute sections with approximately 20 questions each
Quantitative Reasoning	Two 35-minute sections with approximately 20 questions each; onscreen calculator available

Your test will also contain an experimental section—an additional Verbal Reasoning or Quantitative Reasoning section that ETS puts on the test so that ETS can norm the new questions it creates for use on future GREs. That means that if you could identify the experimental section, you could doodle for half an hour, guess in a random pattern, or daydream and still get exactly the same score on the GRE. However, the experimental section is disguised to look like a real section—there is no way to identify it. All you will really know on the day of the test is that one of the subject areas will have three sections instead of two. Naturally, many people try to figure out which section is experimental. But because ETS really wants you to try hard on it, it does its best to keep you guessing. If you guess wrong, you could blow the whole test, so we urge you to treat all sections as scored unless you are told otherwise.

Lastly, instead of an experimental section, your test could contain a research section. This section is unscored and will be indicated as such. If you have a research section on the test, it will be the last section. Pay careful attention to the directions at the beginning of the section.

SCORING

The Analytical Writing section is scored on a scale of 0–6 in half-point increments. (See Chapter 15, "Introduction to Analytical Writing," for details on this scoring rubric.) The Verbal Reasoning and Quantitative Reasoning sections each yield a scaled score within a range of 130 to 170 in one-point increments. You cannot score higher than 170 for either the Verbal Reasoning or the Quantitative Reasoning sections, no matter how hard you try. Similarly, it's impossible to score lower than 130 for Verbal Reasoning or Quantitative Reasoning.

But you don't receive *only* scaled scores; you also receive a percentile rank, which rates your performance relative to that of a large sample population of other GRE takers. Percentile scores tell graduate schools just what your scaled scores are worth. For instance, even if everyone got very high scaled scores, universities would still be able to differentiate candidates by their percentile scores. The following tables give a cross section of the percentile ranks[*] that correspond with certain scaled scores on each section of the GRE, based on test takers between August 1, 2011, and April 30, 2014. For the full percentile-to-score conversion tables, see **https://www.ets.org/s/gre/pdf/gre_guide_table1a.pdf**.

Verbal Reasoning		Quantitative Reasoning		Analytical Writing	
Percentile Ranking	Scaled Score	Percentile Ranking	Scaled Score	Percentile Ranking	Score
99	169–170	98	170	99	6.0
95	165	95	168	98	5.5
87	161	86	163	93	5.0
78	158	78	160	80	4.5
63	154	64	156	56	4.0
50	151	52	153	38	3.5
36	148	37	149	15	3.0
22	144	21	145	7	2.5
10	140	10	141	2	2.0

Universities pay great attention to percentile rank. It's important that you do some research into the programs you're thinking about. Admissions officers from many top graduate school programs consider the GRE the most important factor in graduate school admissions. Some schools have cutoff scores below which they don't even consider applicants. But be careful! If a school tells you it looks for applicants scoring an average of 150 per section, that doesn't mean those scores are good enough for immediate acceptance. Some students will be accepted with scores below that average, and some students may be denied admission even with scores that are higher. Consider the score of 150 per section as an initial target score, but also be sure the rest of your application is strong. You owe it to yourself to find out what kinds of scores *impress* the schools you're interested in and to work hard until you get those scores. Every day we see students work hard and achieve their target scores. Work hard, and you can be among them.

A final note about percentile rank: The sample population to which you are compared to determine your percentile is not the group of people who take the test on the same day as you do. ETS doesn't want to penalize an unlucky candidate who takes the GRE on a date when everyone else happens to be a rocket scientist. Instead, it compares your performance with that of test takers from the past three years. Don't worry about how other people do—strive for your best score. We often tell our students, "Your only competition in this classroom is yourself."

CANCELLATION AND MULTIPLE-SCORES POLICY

Unlike many things in life, the GRE allows you a second chance. If at the end of the test, you feel that you've definitely not done as well as you could have, you have the option to cancel your score. Although score cancellation is available, the option to use *ScoreSelect* means there's rarely a good reason to cancel scores. If you cancel, your scores will be disregarded. (You also won't get to see them.) Canceling a score means that it won't count; however, you will not receive any refund for your test fee.

Two legitimate reasons to cancel your score are illness and personal circumstances that may have caused you to perform unusually poorly on that particular day.

But keep in mind that test takers historically underestimate their performance, especially immediately following the test. They tend to forget about all of the things that went right and focus on everything that went wrong. So unless your performance has been terribly marred by unforeseen circumstances, don't cancel your score. Even if you do cancel your score, it is possible to reinstate it within 60 days for a fee. (See **www.ets.org/gre** for details.)

Also, ETS now offers test takers more choices in determining which scores to report to schools. The relatively new *ScoreSelect* option allows GRE test takers to choose— *after* viewing their scores on Test Day—to report their scores from only the most recent test they took or from all of the GRE tests they have taken in the past five years. Additionally, if a student sends score reports after Test Day, the student can have full freedom to report scores from any testing administration(s), not just the most recent. However, test takers cannot report only Quantitative Reasoning scores or only Verbal Reasoning scores from a given test—results from any testing administration must be reported in full. For more on the *ScoreSelect* option, go to **www.ets.org/gre/revised_general/about/scoreselect**.

Requested score reports are sent to schools 10–15 days after the exam. All GRE testing administrations will remain valid (and usable) in your ETS record for five years. If you choose to report multiple scores, most grad schools will consider the highest score you have for each section, although there are a few exceptions. Check with individual schools for their policies on multiple scores.

Lastly, know that schools receiving your scores will have access to photos taken of you at the test center, plus your Analytical Writing essays from each test administration whose scores you choose to report.

TEST REGISTRATION

You should obtain a copy of the *GRE Information and Registration Bulletin*. This booklet contains information on scheduling, pricing, repeat testing, cancellation policies, and more. You can receive the booklet by calling the Educational Testing Service at (609) 771-7670 or (866) 473-4373 or by downloading it from **www.ets.org/gre**.

The computer-based GRE General Test is offered year-round. To register for and schedule your GRE, use one of the following options. (If you live outside the United States, Canada, Guam, the U.S. Virgin Islands, or Puerto Rico, visit **www.ets.org/gre** for instructions on how to register.)

Registering earlier is strongly recommended because spaces often fill quickly.

Register Online

You can register online (if you are paying with a credit or debit card) at **www.ets.org/gre**. Once the registration process is complete, you can print out your voucher immediately (and can reprint it if it is lost). If you register online, you can confirm test center availability in real time.

Register by Phone

Call 1-800-GRE-CALL or 1-800-473-2255. Your confirmation number, reporting time, and test center location will be given to you when you call. Payments can be made with an American Express, Discover, JCB, MasterCard, or Visa credit or debit card.

Register by Mail

Complete the Authorization Voucher Request Form found in the *GRE Information and Registration Bulletin*. Mail the fee and signed voucher request form in the envelope provided to the address printed on the voucher.

ETS advises that you allow up to three weeks for processing before you receive your voucher in the mail. When you receive your voucher, call to schedule an appointment.

Vouchers are valid for one year from the date of issue. When you register, make sure you list a first- and second-choice test center.

GRE Checklist

Before the Test

- Choose a test date.
- Register online at **www.ets.org/gre,** by phone at 1-800-GRE-CALL, or by mail.
- Receive your admission voucher in the mail or online.
- Check out your test center.
  - Know the kind of workstation you'll be using and whether the room is likely to be hot or cold.
  - Know the directions to the building and room where you'll be tested.
- Create a test prep calendar to ensure that you're ready by the day of the test.
  - On a calendar, block out the weeks you have to prepare for the test.
  - Based on your strengths and weaknesses, establish a detailed plan of study and select appropriate lessons and practice. (Don't forget to include some days off!)
- Stick to the plan; as with any practice, little is gained if it isn't methodical. Skills can't be "crammed" at the last minute.
- Reevaluate your strengths and weaknesses from time to time and revise your plan accordingly.

The Day of the Test

- Make sure you have your GRE admission voucher and acceptable ID.
- Leave yourself plenty of time to arrive at the test site stress-free.
- Arrive at the test site at least 30 minutes early for the check-in procedures.
- Don't worry—you're going to do great!

GRE SUBJECT TESTS

Subject Tests are designed to test the fundamental knowledge that is most important for successful graduate study in a particular subject area. To do well on a GRE Subject Test, you must have an extensive background in the particular subject area—the sort of background you would be expected to have if you had majored in the subject. Subject Tests enable admissions officers to compare students from different colleges with different standards and curricula. Not every graduate school or program requires Subject Tests, so check admissions requirements at those schools in which you're interested.

ORGANIZATION, SCORING, AND TEST DATES

All Subject Tests are administered in paper-based format and consist exclusively of multiple-choice questions that are designed to assess knowledge of the areas of the subject that are included in the typical undergraduate curriculum.

On Subject Tests, you'll earn one point for each multiple-choice question that you answer correctly, but you'll lose one-quarter of a point for each incorrectly answered question. Unanswered questions aren't counted in the scoring. Your raw score is then converted into a scaled score, which can range from 200 to 990. The range varies from test to test.

Some Subject Tests also contain subtests, which provide more specific information about your strengths and weaknesses. The same questions that contribute to your subtest scores also contribute to your overall score. Subtest scores, which range from 20 to 99, are reported along with the overall score. For further information on scoring, you should consult the relevant Subject Test Descriptive Booklet, available from ETS. Subject Tests are offered three times a year: in October, November, and April. Note that not all of the Subject Tests are offered on every test date; consult **www.ets.org/gre** for upcoming test dates and registration deadlines.

SUBJECTS

Currently, seven Subject Tests are offered.

Biochemistry, Cell, and Molecular Biology

This test consists of about 175 questions and is divided among three subscore areas: biochemistry, cell biology, and molecular biology and genetics.

Biology

This test consists of about 200 questions divided among three subscore areas: cellular and molecular biology, organismal biology, and ecology and evolution.

Chemistry

This test consists of about 130 questions. There are no subscores, and the questions cover the following topics: analytical chemistry, inorganic chemistry, organic chemistry, and physical chemistry.

Literature in English

This test consists of about 230 questions on literature in the English language. There are two basic types of questions: factual questions that test your knowledge of writers and literary or critical movements typically covered in the undergraduate curriculum, and interpretive questions that test your ability to read various types of literature critically.

Mathematics

This test consists of about 66 questions on the content of various undergraduate courses in mathematics. Most of the test assesses your knowledge of calculus, linear algebra, abstract algebra, and number theory.

Physics

This test consists of approximately 100 questions covering mostly material from the first three years of undergraduate physics. Topics include classical mechanics, electromagnetism, atomic physics, optics and wave phenomena, quantum mechanics, thermodynamics and statistical mechanics, special relativity, and laboratory methods. About 9 percent of the test covers advanced topics, such as nuclear and particle physics, condensed matter physics, and astrophysics.

Psychology

This test consists of approximately 205 questions drawn from courses most commonly included in the undergraduate curriculum. Questions fall into three categories. The experimental or natural science–oriented category includes questions on learning, language, memory, thinking, sensation and perception, and physiological psychology/behavioral neuroscience. The social or social science–oriented category includes questions on clinical and abnormal psychology, lifetime development, social psychology, and personality. Together, these make up about 83 percent of the test, and each of the two categories provides its own subscore. The other 17 percent or so of the questions fall under the "general" category, which includes the history of psychology, tests and measurements, research design and statistics, and applied psychology.

For more information, consult ETS's Subject Test section at **www.ets.org/gre**.

CHAPTER 2

Multi-Stage Test Mechanics

HOW THE MST WORKS

The multi-stage test, or MST, differs in some critical ways from the typical standardized test. An MST is a computer-based test that you take at a special test center at a time you schedule. Below is a chart that highlights some of the key features of the GRE MST:

MST Features
The test adapts one section at a time, altering the difficulty level of your second Quantitative and Verbal sections based on your performance on the first of each.
You may answer questions in any order within a section and change your answers to previously answered questions within a section.
An onscreen calculator is provided for the Quantitative Reasoning sections.
Mark & Review buttons are available to help you keep track of questions you want to revisit.
The MST lasts about 4 hours, including breaks.

Now that you have a sense of the overall format and structure of the GRE MST, let's look more closely at what the term *multi-stage test* means, how the MST adapts to your performance, and how these factors determine your score.

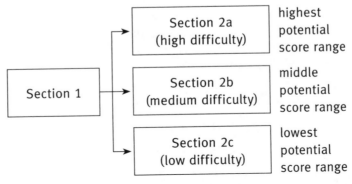

The chart above depicts a simplified version of how adaptivity works on the MST. Depending on your performance on the first Quantitative or Verbal section, you may get channeled into a harder or easier second Quantitative or Verbal section. The difficulty of the second section determines your score range—roughly speaking, the "ceiling" and "floor" of your potential Quantitative or Verbal score. Ultimately, your score will be determined by two factors: (1) the difficulty of the questions you receive and (2) the number of questions you answer correctly.

Therefore, it is important to do as well as possible on the first section since that will put you in the best position to achieve a great score. That said, your performance on the second section is still a crucial determinant of your ultimate score. (Note that the test only adapts within a given subject. In other words, your performance on the Verbal section will not affect the difficulty of a subsequent Quantitative section.)

Understanding the adaptive nature of the MST is interesting and somewhat useful in your prep, but it is actually counterproductive to think too much about it on Test Day. Many test takers try to gauge how they are doing on the exam by assessing the difficulty of the second section they receive. Doing this on Test Day is, at best, a waste of brainpower. At worst, it can cause you to become distracted by counterproductive thoughts ("These questions are too easy! What am I doing wrong?"). Just focus on solving the questions in front of you and do your best.

Simply put, the more questions you get right on the first section, the better off you'll be. The same goes for the second section. Therefore, your goal will be to get as many questions right as possible—not terribly mind-blowing! But how do you do that? Specifically, how can you use the structure of the MST to your advantage as you try to achieve this goal?

Let's now discuss the best ways to navigate the MST and how you can use these functionalities on Test Day to get as many correct answers as possible.

NAVIGATING THE GRE MST INTERFACE

Let's preview the primary computer functions that you will use to move around on the MST. ETS calls them "testing tools." They're basically tabs that you can click with your mouse to navigate through the section. The following screen is typical for a multi-stage test.

Directions: Choose the word or set of words for each blank that best fits the meaning of the sentence as a whole.

```
┌─────────────────────────────────────────────────────────────────────┐
│  Sample Question          Exit  Review  Mark  Help  Back  Next        │
│                          Section                                      │
│                                                                       │
│         1. The task was challenging but not _____;               │
│         the instructor was confident her students would              │
│         rise to the occasion.                                         │
│                                                                       │
│                    ┌──────────────────┐                              │
│                    │   impermeable     │                              │
│                    ├──────────────────┤                              │
│                    │   insuperable     │                              │
│                    ├──────────────────┤                              │
│                    │   implacable      │                              │
│                    ├──────────────────┤                              │
│                    │   invulnerable    │                              │
│                    ├──────────────────┤                              │
│                    │      facile       │                              │
│                    └──────────────────┘                              │
│                                                                       │
│                    Click to select your choice                       │
└─────────────────────────────────────────────────────────────────────┘
```

Here's what the various buttons do:

The Time Button (not pictured)

Clicking on this button turns the time display at the top of the screen on or off. When you have five minutes left in a section, the clock will automatically turn on, and the display will change from hours and minutes to hours, minutes, and seconds.

The Quit Test Button (not pictured)

Hitting this button ends the test prematurely. *Do not* use this button unless you want all of your scores canceled and your test invalidated.

The Exit Section Button

This allows you to exit the section before the time is up. Try not to end the section early—use any extra time to review any problems you flagged or felt concerned about.

The Review Button

This button will allow you to view your progress on all the questions you have looked at so far within the section you're working on. The items you have marked for review will have a check mark next to them. The chart on the screen will also have a column indicating whether or not you have answered a question.

The Mark Button

This button allows you to mark a question for review later. The question will have a check mark next to it in the review section.

The Help Button

This button leads to directions and assistance on how to use the test interface. *But beware:* the test clock won't pause just because you click on Help.

The Back Button

This button allows you to return to previous questions within the section. Note that you may only go back to questions in the section you're currently working on.

The Next Button

Hit this when you want to move on to the next question. You cannot proceed until you have hit this button.

Calculator (not pictured; Quantitative Reasoning section only)

This button opens the onscreen calculator on Quantitative Reasoning sections. It's a pretty basic calculator, and the questions tend to be conceptual in nature, but the calculator still can help you to avoid simple computational errors. Note that you can click on the "Transfer Display" button on the calculator to transfer your answer into a numeric entry box.

MST SECTION MANAGEMENT TECHNIQUES

Section management is an especially important skill to develop for the GRE. The MST allows you to move around within the section you're working on. This can be a great help if you know how to use this functionality to your advantage, but it can also be a source of uncertainty—with the ability to approach each section in whatever order you wish, where should you start? How can you best use the allotted time to rack up as many points as possible? Here are some principles to follow:

Approach the exam as you would a paper-based one. Since it's impossible (and certainly not a good use of your mental effort) to judge the difficulty level of questions while you're working on them, just focus on doing the best you can on each question—as far as you are concerned, they are all of equal importance to your score. Pace yourself so that you can capitalize on all the questions that you are capable of getting correct.

Don't get bogged down on any one question. If you feel that you are getting stuck, mark the question and go to the next one. Use the Mark and Review buttons to tag questions that you wish to return to later in the section. Sometimes when you take a second look at a question, you'll immediately see how to approach those aspects you previously found challenging.

You can also use the Mark button to indicate that you should come back and review the question if you have time at the end of that section. You can do this whether or not you've answered the question. This way, you can better organize your time by keeping track of which questions you are done with and which ones need a second look. Even if you are marking a question to come back to later, you may want to enter an answer the first time through. If you run out of time, you'll be glad that you at least put in a guess.

Use extra time at the end of a section to check your work. This is a major advantage of the MST. Always check the review screen before you finish a section to ensure you haven't forgotten to answer a question.

You may find that it is beneficial to start with some of the question types that take less time to answer. For example, you may find that you score highest on the Verbal section when you answer the Sentence Equivalence questions first. Use the practice sets in this book and your online MSTs to find the approach that works best for you.

There is no penalty for guessing on the GRE. As far as the MST is concerned, leaving an answer blank is the same as selecting an incorrect answer. Therefore, you should guess on every question so you at least have a chance of getting it right. But you should always guess strategically. This book will provide many tools, such as elimination strategies and estimation, that will make you an excellent strategic guesser.

Finally, the onscreen timer can work to your advantage, but if you find yourself looking at it so frequently that it becomes a distraction, you should turn it off for 10 or 15 minutes and try to refocus your attention on the test. You may be concerned about your pacing, but being distracted by the timer can be just as damaging to your score as running out of time. As with a traditional paper-and-pencil test, you don't want to get hung up on clock management.

MST: THE UPSIDE

To sum up, there are many good things about the MST, including the following:

- There will be only a few other test takers in the room with you—it won't be like taking a test in one of those massive lecture halls with distractions everywhere.
- You get a 10-minute break after the third section and a 1-minute break between each of the other sections. The breaks are optional, but you should use them to relax, stretch, and clear your head before the next section.
- You can sign up for the GRE just two days before the test (though we recommend signing up much earlier!), and registration is very easy.
- The MST is convenient to schedule. It's offered at more than 175 centers, three to five days a week (depending on the center), all year long.
- Perhaps the MST's best feature is that it gives you your unofficial Verbal Reasoning and Quantitative Reasoning scores immediately.

MST: THE DOWNSIDE

There are also some less attractive features of the MST:

- The MST is a long test requiring lots of endurance.
- As with any computer-based test, you can't cross off an answer choice to use the process of elimination. Use your scratch paper to avoid reconsidering choices you've already eliminated.
- You have to scroll through Reading Comprehension passages and read them onscreen.
- You'll be given scratch paper to make notes or perform calculations, but if you need more, you'll have to turn in the scratch paper that you've already used before obtaining new paper.
- Many people find that spending considerable time (especially three hours!) in front of a computer screen tires them out and causes eyestrain.
- Having a calculator provided for you on the Quantitative Reasoning sections may seem like a gift, but it comes with a price. The questions on the Quantitative Reasoning section are now more conceptual and less calculation based. Basically, you won't have to worry about doing long division, but the problems will be less straightforward.
- Being able to go back and change your answers may be a plus, but it can lead to pacing issues for some test takers, who will leave questions blank and then either forget to come back to them or run out of time.
- If you wish to take the GRE again, there is a mandatory waiting period: you can only test every 21 calendar days. So if you don't get the scores you need the first time, you need to wait three weeks until you can test again. This can be a problem if you're on a tight deadline.

PAPER-BASED GRE STRATEGIES

If you are located outside of the United States, Canada, Guam, the U.S. Virgin Islands, or Puerto Rico, you may take the paper-based version of the GRE (check **www.ets.org/gre** for test dates). It consists of six sections: two Analytical Writing sections, two Verbal Reasoning sections, and two Quantitative Reasoning sections. There is no experimental or research section on the paper-based GRE.

Note that registration for the paper-based test fills up much more quickly than for the MST. You will need to plan ahead to register for the test.

You have approximately 3 hours and 30 minutes to complete the entire test. The test-taking strategies for the paper-based test are different from those for the MST. One strategy we recommend is to keep track of answers you've eliminated by crossing out wrong answer choices in your test booklet. Here are some targeted strategies for each section of the paper-based GRE.

ANALYTICAL WRITING

For the Analytical Writing section, if you are not using a transcriber, you will have to handwrite your essay, so we suggest you write clearly and legibly. For more tips and strategies for conquering the Analytical Writing section, refer to Chapter 15.

VERBAL REASONING SECTION

Before you start a Verbal Reasoning section, glance over it completely but quickly to familiarize yourself with it. With Reading Comprehension, you can preview the question stems to help guide your reading, but don't try to memorize them or answer the questions without reading the passages. We recommend that you answer the questions you're most comfortable with first. Make sure you set aside at least 15 minutes in each Verbal Reasoning section for Reading Comprehension.

Always try to be aware of how long you're spending on each question; this might require more effort than it does on the MST, since you won't have an onscreen timer. If you find yourself getting hung up on a hard question, move on and come back to it later if you have time. You want to give yourself every opportunity to answer as many questions as you are capable of answering correctly.

The Verbal Reasoning sections on the paper-based test have 25 questions—5 more than each section on the MST. The question types and formats on the paper-based Verbal sections are the same as those on the MST, with one exception: the question format that requires you to highlight a sentence, Select-in-Passage, is not available.

QUANTITATIVE REASONING SECTION

As on the Verbal Reasoning sections, it will behoove you to stay aware of your pacing on the Quantitative Reasoning sections. Calculators are now permitted on the GRE and will be provided at the testing center. Still, don't forget to use your scratch paper for any calculations that are more quickly or accurately performed by hand. Feel free to skip around within this section as well and do all the problems you can do; then come back to the harder ones.

The Quantitative Reasoning sections of the paper-based test have 25 questions—5 more than each section on the MST. The question types and formats on the paper-based Quantitative sections are the same as those on the MST. You will also mark all of your answers directly in the test book, which means you don't have to worry about filling in a separate answer grid!

This chapter has given you an understanding of the GRE MST and paper-based test formats. Let's now turn to the test sections and get you ready for each one.

PART TWO

Verbal Reasoning

CHAPTER 3

Introduction to Verbal Reasoning

OVERVIEW

The Verbal Reasoning section of the GRE tests complex reasoning skills and your ability to analyze the relationships between words and sentences. Vocabulary will be tested contextually, and the reading passages are both dense and written with a sophisticated level of diction. The goal of the test's content, with its emphasis on analytical skills, is to make the test an accurate indicator of your ability to understand what you're reading and apply reasoning skills to the various question types. These skills will translate directly to study at the graduate level.

In this section of the book, we'll take you through all the types of Verbal Reasoning questions you'll see on the GRE and give you the strategies you'll need to answer them quickly and correctly. Also, the vocabulary words you'll most frequently encounter on the test are included in Appendices A–C in the "GRE Resources" section at the back of this book. Think of the glossary and word lists there as building blocks for the questions you will see on the test.

VERBAL REASONING QUESTION TYPES

The GRE contains two Verbal Reasoning sections with approximately 20 questions each. Each section will last 30 minutes and be composed of a consistent, predictable selection of the following question types:

- Text Completion
- Reading Comprehension
- Sentence Equivalence

The Verbal Reasoning portion of the GRE draws heavily upon your vocabulary and assesses your comprehension of written material. Specifically, it evaluates your ability to do the following:

- Analyze sentences and paragraphs
- Derive a word's meaning based upon its context
- Detect relationships among words
- Understand the logic of sentences and paragraphs
- Draw inferences
- Recognize major, minor, and irrelevant points
- Summarize ideas
- Understand passage structure
- Recognize an author's tone, purpose, and perspective

Within each section of Verbal Reasoning questions on the GRE, you will see an assortment of question types.

PACING STRATEGY

The GRE allows you to move freely backward and forward within each section, which can be a big advantage on Test Day. If you get stuck on a particular question, you can flag it and come back to it later when you have time. You only score points for correct answers, so you don't want to get bogged down on one problem and lose time you could have used to answer several other questions correctly. You also are not penalized for incorrect answers, so never leave a question blank.

You will have 30 minutes to work on each Verbal Reasoning section. The approximately 20 questions in each section will be an assortment of Text Completion, Sentence Equivalence, and Reading Comprehension items. However, these types of questions are not distributed equally. The chart below shows how many questions you can expect of each type, as well as the average amount of time you should spend per question type.

	Text Completion	Sentence Equivalence	Reading Comprehension
Number of Questions	approx. 6	approx. 4	approx. 10
Time per Question	1–1.5 minutes, depending on the number of blanks	1 minute	1–3 minutes, depending on the length, to read the passage and 1 minute to answer each question

Use these timing estimates as you work on practice questions and exams. With repetition, you will become comfortable keeping to the same amounts of time on Test Day. Additionally, you will be prepared to use the Mark and Review buttons to your advantage while taking the actual test.

NAVIGATING THE VERBAL REASONING SECTION OF THIS BOOK

The next chapter, Verbal Foundations and Content Review, will review the classic verbal concepts and topics that you will encounter on the GRE. This section of the book also includes individual chapters on Text Completion, Sentence Equivalence, and Reading Comprehension questions. Each of those chapters includes an introduction and definition of the relevant question types, followed by a review and examples of the strategies to follow to answer those questions quickly and correctly. In addition, you'll find a practice set with answers and explanations for each of the question types you'll encounter on the GRE.

Finally, at the end of this section, you'll find the Verbal Reasoning Practice Sets, which include not only practice questions but also answers and explanations. Use the Verbal Reasoning Practice Sets to test your skills and pinpoint areas for more focused study. When you are finished with this section of the book, you will have prepared for every question type you might encounter on the Verbal Reasoning section of the GRE.

CHAPTER 4

Verbal Foundations and Content Review

INTRODUCTION

The GRE tests your mastery of sophisticated language and a wide range of comprehension skills. These concepts include the following:

- Text Completion and Sentence Correction Concepts
  - o Basics of Vocabulary Building
  - o Word Groups
  - o Greek and Latin Roots
  - o Words in Context
  - o Parts of Speech
  - o The Testmaker's Favorite GRE Words
- Reading Comprehension Strategies
  - o Read the First Third of the Passage
  - o Determine the Topic, Scope, and Author's Purpose
  - o Read Strategically

This chapter will cover all these vocabulary concepts as well as specific Reading Comprehension strategies to conquer any questions you might have pertaining to each concept.

KAPLAN'S TIPS FOR STUDYING VOCABULARY

While any word can appear on the GRE, some words are more common than others. Many of the words you'll encounter most often during your prep can be found in an appendix of this book. This handy reference tool contains thousands of the words that you're most likely to find on the GRE. Studying these words is a more effective way to build the kind of vocabulary you need than simply reading the dictionary from *aardvark* to *zygote*.

The vocabulary words found on the GRE are usually members of a very particular class of prefixed and suffixed words that typically are derived from Latin or Greek. You probably remember from middle-school English that prefixes and suffixes are attached to the stem of a word to change its meaning. For instance, *contraindicate*, a verb meaning "to give an indication against," is a great GRE word. So is *contradict*, another verb meaning "to assert the contrary." Recognizing the prefix *contra-*, meaning "against," in one of these words can help you to figure out other words with the same prefix (*contravene*, *contraband*, *contraceptive*, etc.). A solid knowledge of prefixes and suffixes will help you derive the meaning of thousands of words you're not familiar with, especially when they're used in context.

One of the major goals of the verbal portion of the GRE is to test your understanding of vocabulary words in context. This means that on any particular question, you'll always be able to deduce correct answers from contextual clues given.

If you see a word in this book—or anywhere in your reading—that's unfamiliar, take a moment to make a note of it. A good practice for acquiring vocabulary is to keep a vocabulary journal of unfamiliar terms and then practice integrating them into your own working vocabulary.

BASICS OF VOCABULARY BUILDING

Most people build their vocabulary by hearing or reading words in context. Reading is ultimately the best way to increase your vocabulary, but it also takes a great deal of time. There are a couple of techniques you can use to quickly build a more robust vocabulary. In your vocabulary journal, you should be noting words in your reading that aren't familiar to you. As a mental exercise, generate a list of synonyms and antonyms. By compiling such lists, you'll be able to build your vocabulary into an organized structure in your head. It will also be easier to assimilate new words into your active vocabulary if you can easily relate them to other words you already know. For example, if you know what *progressive* means, you'll understand *regressive* immediately if you think of it as the antonym of *progressive*. Making these kinds of cognitive connections will go a long way toward stocking your vocabulary vault.

One final study exercise for vocabulary building is to practice using each unfamiliar word in a sentence. This will help you to internalize the word and its meaning because you'll be using it *in context*.

We'll be going over some of these concepts in more detail later in this chapter, but for now you should be aware of the following tools you can use to build your GRE vocabulary:

- Record and define unfamiliar words.
- Generate synonyms and antonyms.
- Put unfamiliar words in context by using them in sentences.

WORD GROUPS

While it is helpful to have a broad and diverse (but classically rooted) vocabulary, such as you would be likely to encounter in a graduate-level degree program, the GRE does not test whether you know *exactly* what a particular word means. If you have only an idea of what a word means, you have as good a chance of correctly answering a question as you would if you knew the precise dictionary definition of the word. Learning words in groups based upon similar meanings is an excellent way to expand your useful vocabulary. If you have an idea of what a word means, you can use contextual clues to help nail down the nuances of the correct answer choice.

The words in the list below all mean roughly the same thing. Some of them are different parts of speech, but that's OK. They all have something to do with the concept of criticism, which often appears on the GRE. The goal is to be able to identify words that have similar meanings.

CRITICIZE/CRITICISM

ASPERSION	BELITTLE	BERATE
CALUMNY	CASTIGATE	DECRY
DEFAMATION	DENOUNCE	DERIDE/DERISIVE
DIATRIBE	DISPARAGE	EXCORIATE
GAINSAY	HARANGUE	IMPUGN
INVEIGH	LAMBASTE	OBJURGATE
OBLOQUY	OPPROBRIUM	PILLORY
REBUKE	REMONSTRATE	REPREHEND
REPROVE	REVILE	TIRADE
VITUPERATE		

On the test, for instance, you might see a Sentence Equivalence question like this one:

Select the **two** answer choices that, when inserted into the sentence, fit the meaning of the sentence as a whole **and** yield complete sentences that are similar in meaning.

The angry pedestrian _____ the careless driver for his recklessness.

- [A] castigated
- [B] reviled
- [C] atoned
- [D] vouchsafed
- [E] lauded
- [F] reproved

The blank in this Sentence Equivalence question describes how an angry pedestrian would behave toward a careless and reckless driver. The correct answers are *castigated* **(A)** and *reviled* **(B)**. If you know that *castigate* means something like "criticize harshly," that should be enough to know that *reviled* (which means to assail with harsh language) will yield a sentence that means nearly the same thing. *Reproved* is a tempting but deceptive choice. *Reproved* also has a connotation suggestive of criticism. However, the charge of the word *reproved* is far milder than that of the other two words. Therefore, it would produce a sentence that is much less strident in tone. Only *castigated* and *reviled* produce equivalent sentences.

The *criticize* group is not the only group of synonyms whose members appear frequently on the GRE. There are plenty of others. And lists of synonyms are much easier to learn than many words in isolation. Learn them with a thesaurus. Make synonym index cards based on the common groups of GRE words and peruse those lists periodically.

You can certainly add to the word group lists provided in the appendices to this edition, or you can start to generate your own. In addition to synonyms and antonyms, you can put together lists grouped by etymology, similar meaning, and positive and negative connotations.

If you think this suggestion might be fallacious, consider the following: the words in the following list all have something to do with the concept of falsehood. Their precise meanings vary: *erroneous* means "incorrect," whereas *mendacious* means "lying." But the majority of test questions won't require you to know the exact meanings of these words. You will most likely get the question right if you simply know that these words have something to do with the concept of falsehood. If you do have to differentiate between different shades of meaning, that's where contextual clues will help you out.

FALSEHOOD

APOCRYPHAL	CANARD	CHICANERY
DISSEMBLE	DUPLICITY	EQUIVOCATE
ERRONEOUS	ERSATZ	FALLACIOUS
FEIGNED	GUILE	MENDACITY
PERFIDY	PREVARICATE	SPECIOUS
SPURIOUS		

Consider this Text Completion question:

> Though he was prone to _____, the corrupt executive was still capable of moments of honesty.
>
> (A) displeasure
> (B) mendacity
> (C) failure
> (D) levity
> (E) histrionics

The contrast key word "though" indicates that the blank should mean the opposite of "honesty." You might not know the exact denotation of *mendacity,* but because you studied word groups, you'll know that it has the connotation of "false," which will be enough to get the question right.

GREEK AND LATIN ROOTS

Because GRE words are so heavily drawn from Latin and Greek origins, learning word roots can be extremely useful, both in deciphering words with obscure meanings and in guessing intelligently. Studying Latin and Greek roots can allow you to figure out the definitions of words you've never even seen before!

Any individual word root will apply to numerous words, and you'll learn more words in less time if you learn them in groups. For example, once you know that the root PLAC means "to please," you have a hook for remembering the meanings of several words: *placate, implacable, placid, placebo,* and *complacent.*

Sometimes you can use roots to figure out the meaning of an unfamiliar word. Suppose, for example, you come across the word *circumnavigate* and don't know what it means. If you know that the root CIRCUM means "around" and that the root NAV means "ship, sail," then you can guess that *circumnavigate* means "to sail around," as in "*circumnavigate* the globe." Once you've learned the root, you will be able to recognize the meanings of other words with that root, such as *circumvent* or *circuitous.*

Consider the word *panoptic*. It comes from the Greek PAN, meaning "all," and OPTIC, meaning "to see/observe." If you put it all together, you'll arrive at a definition like "everything visible in one view." If you know that, you'll have an advantage in deconstructing other words that incorporate similar constituent parts. You'll have an easier time parsing language with words like _panacea_, _optician_, and _pandemonium_.

Roots offer a common denominator for words thousands of years old—but language changes a lot over time, and words take on new meanings or lose old meanings. Roots don't always give accurate clues about meaning. For example, the word *pediatrician* has PED for a root, and PED has to do with the foot. But a *pediatrician* is a children's doctor. A *podiatrist* is a foot doctor. The reason for this is that PED in regard to feet is a Latin root but PED in regard to children is a Greek root.

The good news is that these aberrations are precisely that: exceptions that prove the rule. More often than not, you should be able to use etymology to your advantage.

WORDS IN CONTEXT

Learning words in context is one of the best ways for the brain to retain word meanings. In GRE Resources at the back of this book, we've not only listed the top 200 GRE words with their definitions, but we've also used all of these words *in context* to help you to remember them. After all, the test is trying to measure how well prepared applicants are for graduate-level academic study. Most graduate students spend much of their time deciphering dense, high-level writing. Given that, your best bet is to read material written for an educated audience, at the graduate level.

As mentioned above, reading is ultimately the best way to increase your vocabulary, although it also takes the most time. Of course, some types of reading material contain more GRE vocabulary words than others. You should get into the habit of reading publications written in a sophisticated register with dense prose, such as the *Wall Street Journal* and the *New York Times*. And because you'll have to read from the computer screen on Test Day, Kaplan recommends that you start reading these publications online, if possible. You might as well start getting accustomed to reading in the testing mode.

This is also a good place to incorporate a technique mentioned earlier: composing practice sentences using the words you're studying. This will ingrain the words in your mind by situating them within a meaningful context.

PARTS OF SPEECH

The GRE never directly tests your ability to classify words by part of speech, but you will get a higher score on Test Day if you can distinguish nouns, adverbs, adjectives, and verbs. If you know how an answer choice must fit into a sentence, you'll be better equipped to narrow down the possible answer choices. Use your understanding of grammar and syntax to help you arrive at the correct answer.

Words with Multiple Meanings

Remember that words can have more than one meaning. They can also function as more than one part of speech. Here's a single word used as a noun, adjective, and verb:

> As the test tube rested overnight, some *precipitate* formed. (noun)
> It would be better to proceed with caution than to take *precipitate* action. (adjective)
> Passage of the resolution could well *precipitate* rebellion. (verb)

The same word, *precipitate*, has vastly different meanings when used in these various forms. As a noun, it means solid matter forming in a solution; as an adjective, it denotes a hasty or rushed action; and, as a verb, it means to force suddenly, often into violence. If you're able to identify the different meanings some words have when they function as different parts of speech, you'll have one more weapon in your arsenal for attacking Sentence Equivalence and Text Completion questions.

Nouns

A noun names a person, place, or thing and answers the questions "Who?" "Where?" or "What?" A noun can function as the subject ("The *eulogy* was eloquent.") or as the object of a verb ("He wrote an eloquent *eulogy*.").

If you know the meaning of a word, you can tell if it's a noun by thinking about the way it would be used in a sentence.

- If the word can function as the subject of a sentence, it's a noun.
- If it can be replaced by a nominative pronoun (*he*, *she*, *it*, or *they*), it's a noun.
- If you can put the word *a*, *an*, or *the* in front of it, it's a noun.
- If you don't know the meaning of a word but it has one of the following suffixes, then it's probably a noun.

–ACY	–AGE	–ANCE
–ANCY	–DOM	–ENCE
–ENCY	–ERY	–HOOD
–ICE	–ICS	–ISM
–IST	–ITY	–MENT
–NESS	–OGY	–OR
–RY	–SHIP	–SION
–TION	–TUDE	–URE

Adjectives and Adverbs

An adjective describes a noun, answering the questions "What kind?" "Which one?" or "How many?" In a sentence, you will generally find adjectives right in front of the nouns they describe ("The book is full of *sophomoric* humor.") or after a form of the verb *to be* or some other verb that links subject and adjective ("The book's humor is *sophomoric*.").

If you know the meaning of a word, you can tell if it's an adjective by thinking about the way the word would be used in a sentence. If the word can be used to describe a noun, it's an adjective. Some adjectives have comparative and superlative forms (for example, *rife, rifer,* and *rifest; sanguine, more sanguine,* and *most sanguine*).

You should also be able to identify adverbs, which function in the same way as adjectives except that they describe verbs, adjectives, whole sentences, or other adverbs. Most adjectives can be turned into adverbs by adding –ly (*harshly*).

If you don't know the meaning of a word but it has one of the following suffixes, then it's probably an adjective.

–ABLE	–AL	–ANE
–ANT	–AR	–ENT
–FUL	–IBLE	–IC
–ILE	–INE	–ISH
–IVE	–LESS	–OSE
–OUS		

Verbs

A verb is a word that represents an action, state, or relationship between two or more things. Every sentence must have at least one verb. The main verb usually comes right after the subject ("They *squander* their fortunes."), but sometimes it is separated from the subject ("The contestant with the second highest vote total *wins* the consolation prize."), and sometimes it even precedes the subject ("Quickly *flow* the years.").

If you don't know the meaning of a word but it has one of the following suffixes, then it's probably a verb.

–EN	–ESCE
–IFY	–IZE

THE TESTMAKER'S FAVORITE GRE WORDS

The research team at Kaplan keeps tabs on GRE vocabulary words and determines which words appear more frequently than others. The following words all turn up time and again on the GRE, so it makes sense to memorize these words if you don't already know them. Of course, some words appear on the GRE more frequently than others.

The top 12 words on the GRE are these:

ANOMALY	ASSUAGE	ENIGMA
EQUIVOCAL	ERUDITE	FERVID
LUCID	OPAQUE	PLACATE
PRECIPITATE	PRODIGAL	ZEAL

The next 20 most popular words are these:

ABSTAIN	ADULTERATE	APATHY
AUDACIOUS	CAPRICIOUS	CORROBORATE
DESICCATE	ENGENDER	EPHEMERAL
GULLIBLE	HOMOGENEOUS	LACONIC
LAUDABLE	LOQUACIOUS	MITIGATE
PEDANT	PRAGMATIC	PROPRIETY
VACILLATE	VOLATILE	

The Top GRE Words in Context section at the end of this book reviews these and 150 other top GRE words. Make sure you spend the time to get to know these words. At least some of them are bound to appear on the GRE you take.

VOCABULARY CONCEPTS PRACTICE SET

Directions: For each sentence below, choose one word for each blank. Select the words that best fit the meaning of the sentence as a whole.

1. Historical biographers do more than merely paraphrase objective assessments and empirical (i) _____. There is an inherently subjective aspect to the genre that (ii) _____ the biographer's claim to objective neutrality.

Blank (i)		Blank (ii)	
A	reminiscences	D	disparages
B	data	E	belies
C	speculations	F	bolsters

2. The aging engineer found it strange that the (i) _____ etching process she pioneered as a graduate student was still considered (ii) _____ after nearly four decades of continual use.

Blank (i)		Blank (ii)	
A	porous	D	antiquated
B	innovative	E	translucent
C	implausible	F	novel

3. Auctions have (i) _____ character: most people only hear about the rare sales in which unique items part for (ii) _____ prices, but there are (iii) _____ auctions where items sell well below their estimates.

Blank (i)		Blank (ii)		Blank (iii)	
A	a prestigious	D	incongruous	G	somber
B	an infamous	E	unprecedented	H	myriad
C	a contradictory	F	pretentious	I	quixotic

Directions: For each of the following questions, choose the **two** answer choices below that, when used to complete the sentence, produce two completed sentences that are similar in meaning.

4. Celebrities who exhibit shameful behavior in public often become the subject of _____.

   A gossip
   B derision
   C provocation
   D scorn
   E commendation
   F prestige

5. Although the scientist was cognizant that such vicissitudes were _____ to the field of quantum mechanics, she was not discouraged.

   A salient
   B salubrious
   C inherent
   D helpful
   E opprobrious
   F endemic

6. High-quality treatment for neuropathic pain is difficult to implement consistently because the scientific research on the subject features strong _____ in the populations studied, especially in children, rendering comparisons impossible.

   A zeal
   B propriety
   C nuance
   D differentials
   E variance
   F justification

VOCABULARY CONCEPTS PRACTICE SET ANSWERS AND EXPLANATIONS

1. B, E

A key phrase in the first sentence is "objective assessments," and the missing word parallels this phrase—this missing word is connected to "objective assessments" with the conjunction "and."

Neither **(A)** *reminiscences* nor **(C)** *speculations* correlates with "objective assessments" as well as **(B)** *data* does. Both *reminiscences* and *speculations* are subjective in nature, whereas "objective assessments" and *data* concern dispassionate evaluation of facts.

Paraphrase the second complex sentence to predict the correct answer: "There is a subjective aspect that _____ their claim to objectivity." A good prediction is "denies." Choice **(E)** *belies* means "to contradict," so it's the correct answer. Choices **(D)** and **(F)**, *disparages* and *bolsters*, have different connotations that are either too negative or too positive, respectively, for the context of this sentence, so they're incorrect.

2. B, F

The key word "still" allows you to understand the relationship between the blanks; both must contain words with similar meanings. An engineer would not have created a **(A)** *porous* (full of holes) or **(C)** *implausible* (difficult to believe) etching process, so the answer for the first blank can only be **(B)** *innovative*. This also corresponds to the word "pioneered" in the sentence. While the word "strange" might at first indicate a direct contrast between the two blanks, such as **(D)** *antiquated*, an aging engineer would actually not find it strange if the etching process she developed as a student were currently considered *antiquated*. She also wouldn't consider it strange for the process to be **(E)** *translucent* (easily understandable). She would, however, find it quite strange if it were still considered **(F)** *novel* (new).

3. C, E, H

The first part of the sentence doesn't have enough information in it for you to fill in the first blank, so you have to read further for clues. Fortunately, it includes a detour road sign ("but") that contrasts "rare" auctions, where unique items sell for certain prices, with auctions whose items sell for less than anticipated. The word in the first blank that best characterizes these dissimilar auctions is choice **(C)** *contradictory*. Choices **(A)** and **(B)**, *prestigious* and *infamous*, would not capture this contrast.

For the second blank, you can paraphrase in order to predict the blank: "There are rare auctions where 'high' prices are paid for unique items, but at other auctions, items sell for below their estimates." If you scan the answer choices, none of the words means exactly that, but **(E)** *unprecedented*, "like nothing that has come before," best completes the meaning of the sentence. A high price for a unique item isn't necessarily **(D)** *incongruous* ("incompatible") or **(F)** *pretentious* ("pompous") because at least one person—the buyer—thought the item was worth what he paid.

Finally, the third blank describes occasions when items sell for less than their estimated value. You know from the detour road sign that this sentence includes a contradiction. Sales where prices are high are described as "rare," so sales where items sell below estimate must be frequent. The answer choice that best matches "frequent" is **(H)** *myriad*, "a great number." Choices **(G)** *somber* ("gloomy") and **(I)** *quixotic* ("foolishly idealistic") make no sense in context.

4. B, D

In this brief sentence, you are not given too many context clues. However, you do know that celebrities are behaving in a "shameful" way that makes them the subject of something. The correct answers will have a negative charge to match "shameful."

Remember, when answering a Sentence Equivalence question, you need to select the two words that complete the sentence in the most similar way. In analyzing the choices, you see that answer choices **(B)** *derision* ("ridicule") and **(D)** *scorn* ("contempt") not only have similar definitions but also give the sentence similar meanings. Do not be tempted by choices **(E)** *commendation* and **(F)** *prestige*. These words may appear similar, but they are not. *Commendation* means "the act of bestowing praise," while *prestige* means "high status or distinction." These two words are not close enough in meaning, and they are too positive. In addition, **(C)** *provocation* does not make sense in the sentence, and **(A)** *gossip*, while appropriate to the context, does not have a matching word to complete the pair.

5. C, F

Paraphrase this sentence: there is something that is discouraging about studying the field of quantum mechanics (i.e., the undefined "vicissitudes" to which it is subject). **(A)** *salient* does not work because there is no other answer choice that means the same thing, and **(B)** *salubrious* and **(D)** *helpful* do not work because they have a positive connotation, which does not make sense with "discouraged." **(C)** *inherent* and **(F)** *endemic* both mean "naturally a part of," and therefore both produce sentences that have the same meaning. Note that **(E)** *opprobrious* yields a sentence that makes sense, but there is no other term that will make a sentence of similar meaning to that one.

6. D, E

This passage is explaining why certain treatment protocols for neuropathy cannot be implemented. The end of the sentence suggests they are not used consistently because the results of studies are very different in the populations studied, making them impossible to compare. Hence, you're looking for two words that have the meaning of "differences" or "divergences." Both will produce sentences that have the meaning of "the results are based on populations with too many differing characteristics to be reliable." Choices **(D)** and **(E)**, *differentials* and *variance*, do that nicely. Note that you didn't need to know the exact definition of either *variance* or *differentials*, but you knew what the correct answers would have to mean, roughly. Knowing the roots of *differentials* and *variance* (*differ* and *vary*) makes the question much easier.

HOW TO APPROACH READING COMPREHENSION

You're going to spend a great deal of your time breaking down dense, complicated prose passages while taking the GRE. These skills, and the ability to wrestle with some very difficult reading, are exactly what you'll need for your work in graduate school. Even engineering and science majors will need to read abstruse technical documents or lab reports, so the best way to excel on the test is to review the skills you'll need to analyze such texts.

BREAKING DOWN THE TEXT

As noted, the texts you'll encounter on the GRE Verbal Reasoning sections are similar to the complex reading you'll encounter in graduate school. These principles hold true for every type of question you'll come across in GRE Reading Comprehension. Keep them in mind as you work through the passages and question sets.

1. Read the first third of the passage.

The first third of a Reading Comprehension passage usually introduces its topic and scope, the author's main idea or primary purpose, and the overall tone. It almost always hints at the structure that the passage will follow. Before diving into the rest of the passage, try to get a handle on the structure of the passage by reading the first third of it carefully. Look for key words such as *however*, *thus*, or *likewise*. These will help to indicate the direction, shape, and thrust of the passage. Pay close attention to how these key words affect the passage's tone and structure.

Structure and Tone. A key strategy for Reading Comprehension is to understand not only the passage's purpose but also its structure and tone. Many question sets will contain a question that concerns how the author organizes or expresses her ideas. Here are some classic GRE passage structures:

- Arguing a position (often a social sciences passage)
- Discussing something specific within a field of study (for example, a passage about Shakespearean sonnets in literature)
- Explaining some significant new findings or research (often a science passage)

Tone refers to an author's attitude toward his topic, or how he expresses a point of view. In passages that cite significant new findings or research, the tone is likely to be academic and detached. In passages that argue a position, the tone may be more forceful and opinionated. In some passages, the author may be describing the opinions of someone else. In this case, the tone might be narrative or descriptive. The tone would be argumentative if the author mentions the opinions of others in order to then debunk them. The correct answer choice for a question about tone will use language similar to that found in the passage; a correct answer choice will not use language more extreme than that used in the passage.

2. Determine the topic, scope, and author's purpose.

Every passage boils down to one or more main ideas. Your job is to cut through the prose and find the main idea. Everything else in the passage supports the main idea. Almost every type of Reading Comprehension question will be easier to answer once you establish the main idea, because correct answer choices will be consistent with it and incorrect choices will not. You can identify the main idea of a passage by determining the topic, scope, and purpose of the passage.

Topic vs. Scope. A topic is broad; its scope is focused. Scope is particularly important because answer choices that go beyond it will always be wrong. The broad topic of James Joyce's *Ulysses*, for example, would be a lot to cover in 200 words. So if you encounter a passage about *Ulysses*, ask yourself, "What aspect of this topic does the author focus on?" Because of length limitations, it must be a narrow aspect. Whatever it is—the author's use of stream of consciousness, the novel's Homeric influences, its aftermath, the principal characters—is the passage's scope. Answer choices that deal with anything outside this narrowly defined aspect of the topic will be wrong.

Author's Purpose. As an author writes a passage, she chooses to develop it by including certain aspects of the topic at hand and excluding others. Those choices reflect the author's purpose and main idea. From the broadly stated topic (for example, solving world hunger), identify the narrower scope (a high-yield farming technique for doing so). That scope leads you to the author's purpose (to describe a new farming technique and its promise) and main idea (that the technology currently exists to solve the problem of world hunger). Once you identify the author's purpose, you will be better able to answer the harder questions associated with a particular passage. Knowing the author's purpose will allow you to more easily answer questions about the author's main idea. It will also help you to make inferences about her reason for including a particular passage or paragraph.

As you read each passage, remember to do the following:

- Identify the topic.
- Narrow it down to its precise scope.
- Identify the author's purpose.

3. Read strategically.

This principle highlights the difference between passive and active reading. Most reading is done passively. For example, you might read a magazine article or novel from beginning to end, without assimilating the details, themes, or connections. That kind of reading is inappropriate for the GRE.

Instead, you'll need to read *actively*. This means you'll have to get good at paraphrasing, looking for key words, and anticipating the direction the author is taking. These strategies help you think carefully about what you read *as you read it*. When you read actively, you don't just absorb the passage—you attack it! You can be an active reader by doing the following:

- Thinking about what you're reading
- Paraphrasing complex ideas
- Asking yourself questions about the passage as you read
- Jotting down notes about the author's arguments and counterarguments

Now that you have a grip on the argument(s) being made in support of the author's position, try to identify the counterarguments. The Verbal Reasoning portion of the GRE obliges you to wrestle a bit with the text. That's part of reading actively, which is exactly what you'll be doing in graduate school. It's not enough just to acknowledge and accept what's presented in the text as received wisdom. Note that how you engage with and analyze a passage will inevitably vary from passage to passage.

Try your hand at a short passage to get the hang of breaking it down. You can use the steps of the process above to help you deconstruct Reading Comprehension passages such as this one:

> The admissions policy at Carver City University stipulates that in considering applications for freshman admission from potential students who meet the entrance requirements, preference will be given to high school graduates who are permanent residents of Carver City. This policy is followed consistently by all admissions officers; however, although over 600 students have graduated from Carver City's high schools in the past year, some slots in the freshman class of 200 are filled by students who are not permanent residents of Carver City.

1. Read the first third of the passage.

The topic here is readily obvious: it's college admissions. The first sentence sets up the basic facts of the situation. The key word to take note of—found in the second sentence—is *however*. It indicates that the author is setting up a conclusion that contradicts what you might expect from the evidence. In a passage this short, the structure is fairly simple as well. The first sentence presents the information you need about the admissions process, and the second presents an outcome that is counterintuitive to that evidence.

2. Determine the topic, scope, and author's purpose.

As noted above, the topic is fairly obvious: college admissions at Carver City University. The specific scope is the university's admissions policy relating to high school graduates from Carver City itself. The author seems to be concerned mostly with the dearth of freshmen at Carver City University who are also permanent residents of Carver City. The author cites the friendly admissions policy for local applicants as part of his argument.

3. Read strategically.

Now, let's nail down what the author is actually saying. Trying to figure out the author's position tests our understanding of the passage's complicated logic. It's a bit tricky with this particular passage because the position is not explicitly stated. There's not a succinct thesis statement (a statement of the author's main idea), so you'll have to unpack things a bit. The author is trying to assert something about the high school graduates who are permanent residents of Carver City. The author makes sure you know that in the last year, 600 students have graduated from Carver City's high schools. If any qualified Carver City resident who wants a slot in the class may have one, but not every slot in the class is filled by a Carver City resident, something must be amiss, as the freshman class consists of only 200 students. Since Carver City high school grads have preference and there are more than enough of them (600 to fill 200 spots), they must either be unqualified in some way or they must not be applying to Carver City University. Remember the admissions policy states that successful applicants must meet entrance requirements. Therefore, some of the slots in the freshman class must have been filled by applicants who both met entrance requirements and were not permanent residents of Carver City. You could paraphrase the position as "There were some slots in the freshman class for which no qualified permanent resident applied."

Now consider what the author is implying. Though the author does not explicitly state it, he is intimating something about the previous year's graduating class. It could be that not enough qualified applicants chose to apply or that those who did apply did not meet entrance requirements. This is the kind of active reading of the text you'll need to do on the Reading Comprehension questions on the GRE.

READING COMPREHENSION STRATEGIES PRACTICE SET

Questions 1 – 3 are based on the passage below.

Among the earliest published literature by African Americans were slave narratives—autobiographical accounts of the lives of slaves who lived primarily in the American South in the early to mid-1800s. These accounts—which included letters, notes, and diaries—often discussed escapes, slave auctions, interactions with plantation owners and abolitionists, and the forced separation of family members, often parents and children. Some of the best-known slave narratives were written by Josiah Henson and Frederick Douglass. In the last three decades, a renewed awareness of the lives of enslaved African Americans has prompted a wave of novels and biographies, sometimes called "neo-slave narratives," in which modern writers such as Toni Morrison and Octavia Butler offer a historical or fictional representation of the lives of slaves.

1. The author would likely consider each of the following a slave narrative EXCEPT:

   (A) an autobiography by a freeborn African American man who lived in New Orleans in the 1830s.

   (B) personal papers of African American field hands who were enslaved in Alabama.

   (C) correspondence between two sisters who were auctioned to different plantation owners in rural Georgia.

   (D) a letter smuggled to an escaped slave from her brother, a slave in South Carolina.

   (E) the diary of a Mississippi slave who was captured while attempting to escape.

2. Consider each of the following choices separately and select all that apply. With which of the following statements would the author be likely to agree?

   A No neo-slave narratives were published later than the early to mid-1800s.

   B Neo-slave narratives are written primarily by women, while most slave narratives were written by men.

   C Some neo-slave narratives are fictional, but all slave narratives are first-hand accounts.

3. The passage provides the most support for which one of the following conclusions?

    Ⓐ The work of abolitionists in the Northern states helped bring about the publication of slave narratives.

    Ⓑ All of the narratives published in the early to mid-1800s were written by slaves living in Southern states.

    Ⓒ Most slave narratives were not published until over a century after they were written.

    Ⓓ In the mid-1900s, fewer people knew about slave narratives than have people in the last ten years.

    Ⓔ Neo-slave narratives such as those by Butler and Morrison have helped to bring attention to slave narratives by earlier writers.

Questions 4 – 6 are based on the passage below.

The problematic relationship between Heidegger's political views and his seminal status as a philosopher is a continuing point of contention in the historical assessment of his achievements. His contributions to Continental philosophy in works such as *Sein und Zeit* have been read, in some circles, through the critical lens of his affiliation with National Socialism in Nazi Germany during the Second World War. His writing during that time covered a broad range of subjects, including philosophy, politics, and aesthetics. His work on ontology directly influenced his contemporary philosophical thinkers, such as Jean-Paul Sartre. Though he is widely regarded within philosophical circles as one of the preeminent luminaries, along with Husserl, in the modern development of ontology, certain scholars and thinkers militate against the value of his thought in its entirety. To regard Heidegger's work highly would be, in their eyes, to absolve him of his support of the politics of Nazism, even though he is being evaluated solely on the basis of his contributions to the study of philosophy and not in any political context.

4. Select the sentence in the passage in which the author summarizes the competing attitudes toward Heidegger within the academic community.

5. Consider each of the following choices separately and select all that apply. The author asserts which of the following about Heidegger?

    Ａ Some academics view him positively for both his political and philosophical work.

    Ｂ His legacy has been affected by opinions he expressed during World War II.

    Ｃ Some academics view him positively, while others cannot countenance him at all.

6. Which conclusion is implied by the author in his description of the status of Heidegger's legacy?

   (A) Heidegger's work should not be given serious recognition due to his political views.

   (B) The Second World War fostered a climate of intellectual innovation in Europe.

   (C) It is possible to critically evaluate Heidegger's contributions to philosophy while not absolving him of responsibility for his political views.

   (D) Scholars should consider the entire body of work of a thinker, in every field to which he or she contributed, when assessing that thinker's legacy in any one field.

   (E) It is impossible to divorce the study of politics from the study of philosophy.

In the chapters that follow this one, you will learn how to approach the three basic types of Verbal Reasoning problems on the GRE. Although the format of these problems—Text Completions, Sentence Equivalence, and Reading Comprehension—varies from problem to problem, one thing is the same: they are all built on the foundations you studied in this chapter.

READING COMPREHENSION STRATEGIES PRACTICE SET ANSWERS AND EXPLANATIONS

1. A

The first two sentences outline defining characteristics of slave narratives and provide examples of the kind of content they might include. Of the answer choices, the only one that falls outside the scope of the question is **(A)**; slave narratives were written by enslaved people, not by free people. Choices **(B)**, **(C)**, **(D)**, and **(E)** all fit the passage's criteria in terms of subject matter, authorship, and geography; choice **(A)** is the only one that deviates.

2. C

The passage's last sentence tells us that neo-slave narratives have been published in the last three decades, so clearly they have been published more recently than the mid-1800s. Choice **(A)** is incorrect. Although the authors of the slave narratives mentioned are both men and the authors of the neo-slave narratives mentioned are both women, there's no basis for us to conclude that this distinction holds true on a broader scale, **(B)**. Only choice **(C)** addresses a distinction the author draws between slave and neo-slave narratives. The passage supports the statement that all slave narratives were autobiographical, whereas neo-slave narratives may be biographical or fictional.

3. D

This question asks us to evaluate which conclusions follow logically from what the author says. The mention of "renewed awareness" implies a previous lapse or reduction in interest, so **(D)** is a reasonable conclusion. The passage doesn't mention abolitionists or the process that led to the narratives' publication, so **(A)** is out of scope. The language of **(B)** is too extreme; you're told that the narratives were primarily, not completely, authored by slaves from the South. Choice **(C)** directly contradicts the first sentence of the passage. Choice **(E)** reverses the order of events presented in the passage; renewed interest in the narratives led to Butler and Morrison's writing, not the other way around.

4. Though he is widely regarded within philosophical circles as one of the preeminent luminaries, along with Husserl, in the modern development of ontology, certain scholars and thinkers militate against the value of his thought in its entirety.

The sentence you're looking for is one that sums up how the intellectual community, as a whole, views Heidegger. This means the sentence should encompass all parties, both those that are receptive to him and those that view him negatively. The second sentence, "His contributions to Continental philosophy in works such as *Sein und Zeit* have been read, in some circles, through the critical lens of his affiliation with National Socialism in Nazi Germany during the Second World War," may be tempting, but this is telling you the way in which his work has been interpreted, not the reactions or attitudes of the academic community. It also doesn't mention any "competing" feelings toward his work. The last sentence provides justification for *why* certain scholars view him as they do, but it does not account for the other schools of thought. The next-to-last sentence, "Though he is widely regarded within philosophical circles as one of the preeminent luminaries, along with Husserl, in the modern development of ontology, certain scholars and thinkers militate against the value of his thought in its entirety," sums up the complete range of reaction to Heidegger across the academic community.

5. B, C

Choice **(A)** is incorrect. The author nowhere explicitly states or implies that anyone has a positive reaction to Heidegger's political views. She only intimates that scholars working in the study of philosophy have been influenced by his work in that field. Choice **(B)** is correct because the author states that Heidegger's work, even in philosophy, has been viewed through this "critical lens." Answer choice **(C)** is also correct. The author cites philosophers, such as Sartre, who have reacted positively to Heidegger's philosophy and asserts that those who view him negatively do so because they cannot abide absolving him of guilt for his support of the Nazis.

6. C

This question asks you to engage the text at a deep level and to infer what the author is suggesting. It is important to pay close attention to the author's tone. The passage's main idea is the evaluation of a thinker's body of work by academic scholars in different fields. The author points out both Heidegger's tremendous accomplishments in the field of philosophy and his less-than-admirable involvement with the Nazi party. Choice **(B)** is dealt with nowhere in the passage. Choice **(E)** goes beyond the scope of the passage. Choice **(A)** is incorrect, because the author emphasizes Heidegger's influence on philosophers like Sartre and makes certain to point out that it is in "their eyes" that Heidegger is so viewed, not the author's own. Choice **(D)** is incorrect because it is the opposite of what the author implies. Choice **(C)** is the correct answer because, in the last sentence of the passage, the author stresses that it is only Heidegger's contributions to philosophy that are being considered, not his political views. The author seems to be suggesting that the two can be judged apart from one another.

CHAPTER 5

Text Completion

INTRODUCTION TO TEXT COMPLETION

In the Text Completion question type, you will be asked to select one entry for each blank from the corresponding column of choices. Each question may include as many as three blanks.

You will find about six Text Completion questions in each Verbal Reasoning section. In each of these questions, one or more words from the sentence will be missing. This question type tests your ability to read critically—to recognize the point of the sentence and find the best word(s) to fit this meaning.

The directions for Text Completion will look like this:

Each sentence below has one or more blanks, each blank indicating that something has been omitted. Beneath the sentence are five words for one-blank questions and sets of three words for each blank for two- and three-blank questions. Choose the word or set of words for each blank that best fits the meaning of the sentence as a whole.

A Text Completion question with one blank will look like this:

Sample Question

| Exit Section | Review | Mark | Help ? | Back ◄ | Next ► |

1. Organic farming is more labor intensive and thus initially more _____, but its long-term costs may be less than those of conventional farming.

| uncommon |
| stylish |
| restrained |
| expensive |
| difficult |

Click to select your choice.

A Text Completion question with two blanks will look like this:

Sample Question

| Exit Section | Review | Mark | Help ? | Back ◄ | Next ► |

1. The sisters could not have been more different; Kate, the older of the two, was (i) _____ and quiet, but Jacie was quick, unpredictable, and well known for her (ii) _____ nature.

Blank (i)

| petulant |
| tempestuous |
| placid |

Blank (ii)

| mercurial |
| boring |
| pliant |

Click to select your choices.

A Text Completion question with three blanks will look like this:

Sample Question

Exit Section	Review	Mark	Help	Back	Next

1. As a result of the (i) _____ pace of life, urban living (ii) _____ many young professionals the opportunity to (iii) _____ their lives with a sense of constant excitement.

Blank (i)	Blank (ii)	Blank (iii)
intrinsic	instigates	eschew
ephemeral	affords	inter
frenetic	arrogates	imbue

Click to select your choices.

THE KAPLAN METHOD FOR TEXT COMPLETION (ONE-BLANK)

STEP 1 Read the sentence, looking for clues.

STEP 2 Predict an answer.

STEP 3 Select the choice that most closely matches your prediction.

STEP 4 Check your answer.

HOW THE KAPLAN METHOD FOR TEXT COMPLETION (ONE-BLANK) WORKS

Now let's discuss how the Kaplan Method will help you answer these questions correctly.

❱❱ STEP 1

Read the sentence, looking for clues.

There are always clues in the sentence that will point you to the right answer. The missing words in Text Completion questions will usually have a relationship with key words in the sentence. Key words and key phrases are descriptors that lead to the meaning of the missing words.

A road sign is a structural key word that signals a connection between ideas; it also determines the direction of the relationship. There are road signs in the GRE that tell you to go straight ahead and those that tell you to take a detour. A semicolon also functions as a road sign, indicating a close connection between two clauses.

"Straight-ahead" road signs are used to make one part of the sentence support or elaborate upon another part. They continue the sentence in the same direction. The positive or negative connotation of what follows is not changed by these clues.

"Detour" road signs change the direction of the sentence. They make one part of the sentence contradict or qualify another part. The positive or negative connotation of an answer is changed by these clues.

Review the following examples of road signs. Interpreting the road sign will help you to determine which way the sentence is going and predict what words will best complete the blanks.

Straight-ahead road signs:	Detour road signs:
And	*But*
Since	*Despite*
Also	*Yet*
Thus	*However*
Because	*Unless*
; (semicolon)	*Rather*
Likewise	*Although*
Moreover	*While*
Similarly	*On the other hand*
In addition	*Unfortunately*
Consequently	*Nonetheless*
	Conversely

❯❯ STEP 2

Predict an answer.

Once you've found the road sign and the key word(s) relevant to the blank, predict an answer for the blank. Your prediction does not have to be a sophisticated or complex word or phrase; it just needs to be a paraphrase that logically fits into the sentence. By predicting, you avoid the temptation of trying every answer choice on its own, which can take up valuable time on Test Day.

❯❯ STEP 3

Select the choice that most closely matches your prediction.

Quickly go through the choices, see which one most closely matches, and eliminate whichever choices do not fit your prediction. If none of the choices match your prediction, reread the question and revisit Steps 1 and 2.

❯❯ STEP 4

Check your answer.

This step is simply double-checking that you did your work correctly and that your answer choice is correct in context. If your answer makes sense when you read your choice back into the sentence, you can confirm and move on. If your choice does not make sense when you read it back into the sentence, you should reread the question and revisit Steps 1–3.

How to Apply the Kaplan Method for Text Completion (One-Blank)

Now let's apply the Kaplan Method to a Text Completion (One-Blank) question:

The yearly financial statement of a large corporation may seem _____ at first, but the persistent reader soon finds its pages of facts and figures easy to decipher.

- (A) bewildering
- (B) surprising
- (C) inviting
- (D) misguided
- (E) uncoordinated

❯❯ STEP 1

Read the sentence, looking for clues.

The sentence contains the detour road sign *but*, which indicates that the correct answer will mean the opposite of another key word or key phrase in the sentence. The key phrase to note in this example is "easy to decipher."

❯❯ STEP 2

Predict an answer.

Knowing that the blank must contrast with the phrase "easy to decipher," you can predict that the missing word will be similar to "difficult to understand."

❯❯ STEP 3

Select the choice that most closely matches your prediction.

Quickly go through the choices and see which one most closely matches "difficult to understand," which in this case is choice **(A)** *bewildering*.

❯❯ STEP 4

Check your answer.

Plugging the word *bewildering* into the sentence fits the context: "The yearly financial statement of a large corporation may seem *bewildering* at first, but the persistent reader soon finds its pages of facts and figures easy to decipher."

Now let's apply the Kaplan Method to a second Text Completion (One-Blank) question:

Although the initial cost of installing solar panels to produce electricity can be _____, the financial benefits are realized for years to come in the form of reduced electric bills.

(A) encouraging
(B) minimal
(C) exciting
(D) misleading
(E) exorbitant

STEP 1
Read the sentence, looking for clues.
The sentence contains the detour road sign *although*, which indicates that the correct answer will mean the opposite of a key word or key phrase in the sentence. The key phrase to note in this example is "reduced electric bills."

STEP 2
Predict an answer.
Knowing that the blank must contrast with the phrase "reduced electric bills," you can predict that the correct answer will be similar to "increased or high payments or costs."

STEP 3
Select the choice that most closely matches your prediction.
Quickly go through the five choices and see which one most closely matches "increased or high payments or costs," which in this case is choice **(E)** *exorbitant*.

STEP 4
Check your answer.
Plugging the word *exorbitant* into the sentence fits the context: "Although the initial cost of installing solar panels to produce electricity can be *exorbitant*, the financial benefits are realized for years to come in the form of reduced electric bills."

THE KAPLAN METHOD FOR TEXT COMPLETION (TWO-BLANK AND THREE-BLANK)

STEP 1 Read the sentence, looking for clues.

STEP 2 Predict an answer for the easier/easiest blank.

STEP 3 Select the choice that most closely matches your prediction.

STEP 4 Predict and select for the remaining blanks.

STEP 5 Check your answers.

HOW THE KAPLAN METHOD FOR TEXT COMPLETION (TWO-BLANK AND THREE-BLANK) WORKS

Now let's discuss how the Kaplan Method for Text Completion changes when there are multiple blanks.

❯ STEP 1

Read the sentence, looking for clues.

This step is the same.

❯ STEP 2

Predict an answer for the easier/easiest blank.

Instead of immediately making a prediction for the first blank, take a moment to identify the easier/easiest blank to work with. Once you've found the road sign and the key word(s) relevant to the easier/easiest blank, predict an answer for that blank.

❯ STEP 3

Select the choice that most closely matches your prediction.

This step is the same.

❯ STEP 4

Predict and select for the remaining blanks.

Once you have completed the easier/easiest blank, you have more context in which to interpret the remaining blanks.

For two-blank Text Completions, use the context to help you choose the answer for the remaining blank. If the answers for the second blank are not working out, you know you need to go back to Step 2.

For three-blank Text Completions, repeat Steps 2 and 3 for the next easiest blank. You now have two completed blanks to provide context for the last, most difficult blank. This way, your approach to two- and three-blank questions is just a logical extension of your approach to one-blank questions.

STEP 5

Check your answers.

This step is the same.

How to Apply the Kaplan Method for Text Completion (Two-Blank and Three-Blank)

Now let's apply the Kaplan Method to a Text Completion (Two-Blank) question:

> Everyone believed the team was favored with athletic talent and a seasoned, successful coaching staff; consequently, it was difficult to (i) _____ why the team was (ii) _____ so badly against one of the worst teams in the division.

Blank (i)		Blank (ii)	
A	fathom	D	elevating
B	interpolate	E	dominating
C	explore	F	floundering

▶ **STEP 1**

Read the sentence, looking for clues.

In this sentence, the straight-ahead road sign "consequently" indicates that the correct answer will support or elaborate on another word or phrase in the text. The key word to note in this example is "badly."

▶ **STEP 2**

Predict an answer for the easier/easiest blank.

Knowing that the second blank must support or elaborate on the phrase "so badly," you can predict that the correct answer will be similar to "not doing very well."

▶ **STEP 3**

Select the answer choice that most closely matches your prediction.

Quickly go through the three choices and see which one most closely matches "not doing very well," which, in this case, is choice **(F)** *floundering*.

▶ **STEP 4**

Predict and select for the remaining blanks.

Once you have completed the easier blank, you have a context in which to interpret the remaining missing word.

For the remaining blank, select the choice that will most logically complete the sentence. The first clause in the sentence indicates that the team should be good. However, the team is doing poorly, and this is "difficult" for everyone because it does not make sense. In other words, it is hard to understand. The answer choice most like "understand" is **(A)** *fathom*.

◆ STEP 5

Check your answers.

Plugging the selected words into the sentence fits the context: "Everyone believed the team was favored with athletic talent and a seasoned, successful coaching staff; consequently, it was difficult to *fathom* why the team was *floundering* so badly against one of the worst teams in the division."

Now let's apply the Kaplan Method to a Text Completion (Three-Blank) question:

> It seemed there would be no resolving the matter since both sides felt they had reached an (i) _____; neither side would (ii) _____, and the resulting (iii) _____ would keep their relationship strained and fragile for years to come.

Blank (i)	Blank (ii)	Blank (iii)
A apogee	**D** capitulate	**G** acrimony
B epiphany	**E** regress	**H** cacophony
C impasse	**F** impugn	**I** sinecure

◆ STEP 1

Read the sentence, looking for clues.

In this sentence, there are clues in the phrases "no resolving the matter" and "strained and fragile," which, along with the straight-ahead road signs "since" and "and," suggest that the correct answers are going to describe or support a conflict between disagreeing parties. In this example, you may already sense the words that complete at least one of the blanks just from the construction of the sentence.

◆ STEP 2

Predict an answer for the easier/easiest blank.

Determine that the answer for the first blank must support or elaborate on the phrase "no resolving the matter."

◆ STEP 3

Select the answer choice that most closely matches your prediction.

Quickly go through the choices and see which one most closely matches "no resolving the matter." You can predict the answer will be **(C)** *impasse*.

STEP 4

Predict and select for the remaining blanks.

For the remaining blanks, select the choice that will most logically complete the sentence. The sentence tells us the sides are at an *impasse*, or blocked path. Predict the answers for the second and third blanks by thinking how groups at an impasse would feel and act. Determine that they are not willing to **(D)** *capitulate*, or give in on their demands, and that the result would be **(G)** *acrimony*, or bitter feelings, between the two sides.

STEP 5

Check your answers.

Plugging the words *impasse*, *capitulate*, and *acrimony* into the sentence fits the context: "It seemed there would be no resolving the matter since both sides felt they had reached an *impasse*; neither side would *capitulate*, and the resulting *acrimony* would keep their relationship strained and fragile for years to come."

KAPLAN'S ADDITIONAL TIPS FOR TEXT COMPLETION QUESTIONS

Look for what's directly implied and not an ambiguous interpretation

The questions you'll encounter are written in sophisticated but still logical and straightforward prose. Therefore, the correct answer is the one most directly implied by the meanings of the words in the sentence. These sentences are constructed to allow you to identify the answer using the inferential strategies you just practiced.

Don't be too creative

Read the sentence literally, not imaginatively. Pay attention to the meaning of the words instead of to any associations or feelings that might come up for you.

Paraphrase long or complex sentences

You may encounter a sentence that, because of its length or structure, is hard to get a handle on. When faced with a complex sentence, slow down and put it in your own words. You could break it into pieces as well and tackle one phrase at a time.

Use word roots

In the GRE Resources section at the back of this book, you can learn the Latin and Greek roots of many common GRE words. If you can't figure out the meaning of a word, take a look at its root to try to get close to its meaning. Etymology can often provide clues to meaning, especially when you couple a root definition with the word in context.

TEXT COMPLETION PRACTICE SET

Try the following Text Completion questions using the Kaplan Method for Text Completion. If you're up to the challenge, time yourself; on Test Day, you'll want to spend only 1 to 1.5 minutes on each question, depending on the number of blanks.

1. The young man always had to have the last word; he would rather be disliked than _____.

   (A) gainsaid
   (B) selfish
   (C) remembered
   (D) praised
   (E) different

2. The giant squid's massive body, adapted for deep-sea life, breaks apart in the reduced pressures of shallower ocean depths, making the search for an intact specimen one of the most _____ quests in all of marine biology.

   (A) meaningful
   (B) elusive
   (C) popular
   (D) expensive
   (E) profitable

3. Although well built and well kept, the little brick house seemed (i) _____ compared to the ornate, almost (ii)_____ new house beside it.

Blank (i)	Blank (ii)
A impressive	D translucent
B dilapidated	E diminutive
C desirable	F ostentatious

4. The (i) _____ gave such an impassioned speech that even the most forlorn members of the crowd were briefly moved to (ii) _____.

Blank (i)	
A	orator
B	miscreant
C	interloper

Blank (ii)	
D	despair
E	duress
F	ebullience

5. His explosive, rude remarks convinced many that he was (i) _____ and of (ii) _____ character, suddenly making his future as a politician seem (iii) _____.

Blank (i)	
A	indifferent
B	charming
C	volatile

Blank (ii)	
D	courageous
E	virtuous
F	ignoble

Blank (iii)	
G	guaranteed
H	precarious
I	facetious

TEXT COMPLETION PRACTICE SET
ANSWERS AND EXPLANATIONS

1. A

The semicolon between these clauses is a straight-ahead road sign; these two ideas are closely related or elaborate upon each other. Since the blank is in the second clause, look to the first for direction. There you discover that this person always has to be right or have the last word in an argument. The second clause will be consistent with this notion; it explains just how much he needs to have the last word. He would rather be disliked than have what happen? A good prediction would be: "He'd rather be disliked than contradicted."

Choice **(A)** *gainsaid* matches the prediction, but look at the others just to be sure. Scanning the other choices quickly, you see that all of the remaining options do not support the first part of the sentence. None of these other choices reinforces the idea that he always has to be right, so even if you aren't familiar with the word *gainsaid*, you can still get the right answer.

2. B

The key word here is "intact," which means that although specimens have been collected, they have rarely (if ever) been in one piece when recovered. You can fairly assume that recovering an intact specimen is difficult. When you look for a synonym for "difficult" in the answer choices, you recognize *elusive* **(B)** as your answer.

3. B, F

In this case, the second blank is easier to predict than the first, so start with that one. The word "almost" before the second blank tells you the correct choice will be a word that means nearly the same as "ornate." Something *ostentatious* is considered showy, excessive, or ornate, so the correct choice is **(F)**.

There are several road signs, key words, and phrases in this sentence that give clues. "Although" with "compared" tells you there is something different about the two houses. The detour road sign "although" allows us to predict that the choice in the first blank will have a meaning opposite to "ornate" and will be close in meaning to "plain." Such a condition is not considered *impressive* **(A)** or *desirable* **(C)**, so the correct choice is **(B)** *dilapidated*.

4. A, F

The key phrase for the first blank is "impassioned speech." You can tell the correct answer for the first blank is someone who can speak expressively. *Miscreants* **(B)** and *interlopers* **(C)** are not necessarily excellent speakers, but *orators* are. The correct choice is **(A)**.

For the second blank, the key words are "impassioned" and "moved," which tell you the speaker's words had a positive effect on the crowd. Since *despair* **(D)** and *duress* **(E)** are not positive, the answer is **(F)** *ebullience*.

5. **C, F, H**

For the first blank, the key phrase is "explosive, rude remarks." Choice **(A)** *indifferent* suggests neutrality, but being explosive and rude is far from being neutral. The second choice, *charming* **(B)**, does not make sense because someone who is "explosive" and "rude" is not seen as being charming. Choice **(C)** *volatile* means "unstable," the same as "explosive."

Since we know the subject of the sentence is explosive, rude, and volatile, we can predict his character will be seen in negative ways. Because *courageous* and *virtuous* have positive connotations, choice **(F)** *ignoble* is the correct choice.

With the information that he is explosive, rude, volatile, and ignoble, predict what kind of "future as a politician" he will have. This is the key phrase for identifying the third blank. His character suggests he is not popular, so we can conclude his future is not **(G)** *guaranteed*. Choice **(I)** *facetious* means "flippant," which does not make sense as a description of the politician's future. Choice **(H)** *precarious* means "uncertain," which fits the context of the sentence and is the correct choice.

CHAPTER 6

Sentence Equivalence

INTRODUCTION TO SENTENCE EQUIVALENCE

Each Verbal Reasoning section features approximately four Sentence Equivalence questions. In each sentence, one word will be missing, and you must identify two correct words to complete the sentence. The correct answer choices, when used in the sentence, will result in the same meaning for *both* sentences. This question type tests your ability to figure out how a sentence should be completed by using the meaning of the entire sentence.

The directions for Sentence Equivalence will look like this:

> Select the **two** answer choices that, when inserted into the sentence, fit the meaning of the sentence as a whole **and** yield complete sentences that are similar in meaning.

A Sentence Equivalence question will look like this:

Sample Question	Exit Section	Review	Mark	Help	Back	Next

1. She volunteered to work in a soup kitchen because of her _____ nature.

- [ ] selfish
- [ ] naive
- [ ] altruistic
- [ ] baneful
- [ ] candid
- [ ] benevolent

Click to select your choices.

THE KAPLAN METHOD FOR SENTENCE EQUIVALENCE

STEP 1   Read the sentence, looking for clues.

STEP 2   Predict an answer.

STEP 3   Select the two choices that most closely match your prediction.

STEP 4   Check your answers to see if the sentence retains the same meaning.

HOW THE KAPLAN METHOD FOR SENTENCE EQUIVALENCE WORKS

Now let's discuss how the Kaplan Method will help you answer these questions correctly.

► STEP 1

Read the sentence, looking for clues.

As you read the sentence, pay attention to the part of speech that the answer choice will be and compare it with the answer choices. Also look for specific words in the sentence that will help you to understand its meaning. These are called "key words" or "road signs"—descriptive phrases or contextual clues that suggest the meaning of the missing word.

Words that connect one part of a sentence to another ("straight-ahead" road signs) include the following:

And	*Likewise*
Since	*Moreover*
Also	*Similarly*
Thus	*In addition*
Because	*Consequently*
; (semicolon)	

Words that indicate one part of the sentence contradicts another part of the sentence ("detour" road signs) include these:

But	*Although*
Despite	*While*
Yet	*On the other hand*
However	*Unfortunately*
Unless	*Nonetheless*
Rather	*Conversely*

Being aware of these road signs will help you to figure out the meaning of the sentence and the relationship of the missing word to other ideas in the sentence.

❯❯ STEP 2

Predict an answer.

Once you have read the sentence and identified clues to words that will complete the sentence, predict an answer. Your prediction should be a word that you choose on your own *before* you look at the answer choices. The prediction word should also be a simple word that logically completes the sentence.

❯❯ STEP 3

Select the two choices that most closely match your prediction.

Quickly review the six answer choices and choose the two words that, when plugged into the sentence, most closely make the intended meaning of the sentence match your prediction. Eliminate the answer choices that do not fit your prediction. Sometimes you will need to adjust your prediction in order to find two answer choices that match each other.

❯❯ STEP 4

Check your answers to see if the sentence retains the same meaning.

Read the sentence with each answer choice plugged in to check that you have selected the correct answers. Make sure that both answer choices make sense in the context of the sentence. Pay close attention to the charge of a word's meaning. For example, "dislike" and "despise" both mean the same thing, but "despise" has a much *stronger* degree of charge to that meaning. Each sentence should have the same meaning. If one or both of your answers do not make sense when you reread the sentence, revisit the question and repeat Steps 1, 2, and 3.

HOW TO APPLY THE KAPLAN METHOD FOR SENTENCE EQUIVALENCE

Now let's apply the Kaplan Method to a Sentence Equivalence question.

1. She volunteered to work in a soup kitchen because of her _____ nature.

   A selfish
   B naive
   C altruistic
   D baneful
   E candid
   F benevolent

❯ STEP 1

Read the sentence, looking for clues.

One way to determine the correct answer in this sentence is to figure out the part of speech of the missing word. The missing word in this sentence is an adjective because it modifies the noun "nature." Another clue in this sentence is the key word "volunteer." A volunteer is someone who offers her time or skills without pay. The blank will be an adjective with a positive connotation that describes the type of person who volunteers.

❯ STEP 2

Predict an answer.

Knowing that the blank must describe someone who offers her time or skills without pay, you can predict that the correct answer will be similar to "helpful."

❯ STEP 3

Select the two choices that most closely match your prediction.

Quickly review the six answer choices to see which two words most closely match "helpful," which in this case are choice **(C)** *altruistic* and choice **(F)** *benevolent*.

❯ STEP 4

Check your answers to see if the sentence retains the same meaning.

Plug each answer choice into the sentence to see if it matches the context. Make sure that each sentence has the same meaning:

"She volunteered to work in a soup kitchen because of her <u>altruistic</u> nature."

"She volunteered to work in a soup kitchen because of her <u>benevolent</u> nature."

Now let's apply the Kaplan Method to a second Sentence Equivalence question.

2. While the first speaker at the conference was confusing and unclear, the second speaker was _____.

   A articulate
   B experienced
   C melancholy
   D ambiguous
   E eloquent
   F vociferous

❯❯ STEP 1

Read the sentence, looking for clues.

In this sentence, the clue word "while" is a detour road sign. "While" indicates that the second part of the sentence will mean the opposite of the first part of the sentence. The first speaker was described as "confusing" and "unclear," which are the key words in this question. The correct answer means the opposite.

❯❯ STEP 2

Predict an answer.

Knowing that the blank will mean the opposite of "confusing" and "unclear," you can predict that correct answers will be similar to "clear."

❯❯ STEP 3

Select the two choices that most closely match your prediction.

Quickly go through the six answer choices and see which two words most closely match "clear" in the context of speaking. In this case, these are choice **(A)** *articulate* and choice **(E)** *eloquent*.

❯❯ STEP 4

Check your answers to see if the sentence retains the same meaning.

Plug each answer choice into the sentence to see if it matches the context. Make sure that each sentence has the same meaning:

> "While the first speaker at the conference was confusing and unclear, the second speaker was <u>articulate</u>."

> "While the first speaker at the conference was confusing and unclear, the second speaker was <u>eloquent</u>."

KAPLAN'S ADDITIONAL TIPS FOR SENTENCE EQUIVALENCE

Consider all answer choices.

Make sure to read and check all answer choices in the sentence before making your final choice. An answer may fit well in the sentence and closely match your prediction, but if there is no other answer choice that also completes the sentence with the same meaning, it isn't correct.

Paraphrase the question.

If you rephrase a difficult or longer sentence into your own words, it will be easier to make a prediction for the answer. Paraphrasing will also make sure that you understand the meaning of the sentence.

Look beyond synonyms.

Simply finding a synonym pair in the answer choices will not always lead you to the correct answer. Answer choices may include a pair of words that are synonyms but do not fit in the context of the sentence. Both of those two choices will be incorrect. The meaning of each sentence must be the same *and* correct. Be sure to try both words in the sentence, checking that each sentence has the same meaning, before making your final choice.

Use prefixes, suffixes, and roots.

Think about the meaning of the prefixes, suffixes, and roots in words that you know if you are struggling to figure out the definition of a word.

SENTENCE EQUIVALENCE PRACTICE SET

Try the following Sentence Equivalence questions using the Kaplan Method for Sentence Equivalence. If you're up to the challenge, time yourself; on Test Day, you'll want to spend only about one minute on each question.

1. He was unable to move his arm after the stroke; in addition, the stroke
   _____ his ability to speak.

   A appeased
   B satisfied
   C impeded
   D helped
   E hindered
   F assisted

2. Although the lab assistant openly apologized for allowing the samples to spoil, her _____ did not appease the research head, and she was let go.

   A insincerity
   B frankness
   C falsehoods
   D candor
   E inexperience
   F hesitation

3. Afterward the deceased man's wife could not stop crying; his daughter was similarly _____.

   A overjoyed
   B morose
   C abashed
   D lucid
   E nonplussed
   F dolorous

4. Her last-minute vacation was _____ compared to her usual trips, which are planned down to the last detail.

    A expensive

    B spontaneous

    C predictable

    D satisfying

    E impulsive

    F atrocious

5. After staying up all night, she felt extremely _____; however, she still ran three miles with her friends.

    A apprehensive

    B lethargic

    C controversial

    D sluggish

    E vigorous

    F energetic

SENTENCE EQUIVALENCE PRACTICE SET ANSWERS AND EXPLANATIONS

1. C, E

The straight-ahead road sign "in addition" in this sentence is a clue that both parts of the sentence are related. Since the missing word is in the second part of the sentence, the first part gives a clue to what your prediction should be. The person had a stroke and was unable to move his arm.

Use this to make a prediction such as "He was unable to move his arm after the stroke; in addition, it <u>prevented</u> his ability to speak."

Quickly review the answer choices, looking for two words that closely match your prediction. Choices **(C)** *impeded* and **(E)** *hindered* both have the meaning "to interfere with" and produce sentences with equivalent meaning. The other four choices do not have meanings anywhere close to "prevented." Choices **(A)** *appeased*, **(B)** *satisfied*, **(D)** *helped*, and **(F)** *assisted* all have too positive a connotation to be correct. *Appeased* has the same meaning as *satisfied*, and *helped* and *assisted* both mean "to aid."

2. B, D

The clue in this sentence is the detour road sign "although," which indicates contrast. Her "open" apology would be expected to "appease" her boss, but she was fired anyway; paraphrasing further, she did something good but suffered bad consequences. The word in the blank will express the good thing she did, so you can predict that the correct answers will be similar to "honesty." Choices **(A)**, **(C)**, **(E)**, and **(F)** are not synonyms for "honesty," leaving choices **(B)** and **(D)**. **(B)** *frankness* and **(D)** *candor* both carry the meaning of "forthright." They're your answers.

3. B, F

The word "similarly" in this sentence is a straight-ahead road sign that you can use to figure out the blank. It indicates that the sentence will continue to move in the same direction. In the sentence, the wife was crying, and her daughter felt the same way.

Use this to make a prediction such as "Afterward, the late man's wife could not stop crying; his daughter was similarly <u>sad</u>."

Quickly review the answer choices, looking for a match. Both **(B)** *morose* and **(F)** *dolorous* fit the sentence and mean the same thing. Choice **(A)** *overjoyed* is the opposite of "sad," so it does not make sense. Someone who feels *abashed*, choice **(C)**, is embarrassed. A *lucid* person, choice **(D)**, is very clearheaded, and *nonplussed* **(E)** means perplexed.

4. B, E

The phrase "compared to her usual trips" is a clue that the first half of the sentence will have an opposite meaning to the second half; that is, her "last-minute" vacation was apparently *not planned in detail*.

You can use this phrase to make a prediction such as: "Her last-minute vacation was <u>unplanned</u> compared to her usual trips, which are planned down to the last detail."

Something that is unplanned is done without much preparation or careful thought. Both choice **(B)** and choice **(E)** match this prediction. Choice **(B)** *spontaneous* means something that happens without planning, and choice **(E)** *impulsive* means doing something without careful thought. Choice **(A)** *expensive* doesn't fit with "unplanned," nor does **(C)** *predictable* (the opposite), **(D)** *satisfying*, or **(F)** *atrocious*.

5. B, D

When someone stays up all night, she is usually very tired. The detour road sign in this sentence is "however" in the second clause. It indicates that the person in the sentence went running, which takes a lot of energy, even though she was up all night.

You can use this clue to make a prediction such as "After staying up all night, she felt extremely <u>tired</u>; however, she still ran three miles with her friends."

Scan the answer choices, looking for a match. You will find it in **(B)** *lethargic* and **(D)** *sluggish*, both of which mean "tired." Choices **(E)** *vigorous* and **(F)** *energetic* are the opposite of "tired." Choice **(A)** *apprehensive* can be used to describe someone who is anxious but not someone who is tired. Choice **(C)** *controversial* can be used to describe something that is open to debate.

CHAPTER 7

Reading Comprehension

INTRODUCTION TO READING COMPREHENSION

Reading Comprehension is the only question type that appears on all major standardized tests, and with good reason. No matter what academic discipline you pursue, you'll have to make sense of dense, complex written material. This means that being able to understand and assess what you read is a critical skill for every graduate student.

To make the test as relevant as possible and to better evaluate your ability to understand graduate-level material, ETS adapts its content from real-world, graduate-level documents. The GRE traditionally takes its topics from four disciplines: social sciences, biological sciences, physical sciences, and the arts and humanities.

The GRE includes roughly 10 reading passages spread between the two Verbal Reasoning sections of the test. Many of these passages are one paragraph in length, although a few are longer. Each passage is followed by one to six questions that relate to that passage. These questions will test your ability to ascertain the author's purpose and meaning, to consider what inferences can properly be drawn from the passage, to research details in the text, and to understand the meaning of words and the function of sentences in context.

A sentence that tells how many questions are based on each passage will appear in boldface before the passage, like this:

Questions 1–3 are based on the passage below.

A Reading Comprehension passage will look like this:

> Many baseball enthusiasts are aware of the story of how Abner Doubleday invented the game of baseball with some friends in 1839 and introduced it to a nation during the Civil War. However, most baseball historians now agree that this story is a convenient fiction, propagated by Albert Spalding, a player, manager, owner, and one of the first manufacturers of sporting equipment. Spalding's desire to distinguish baseball, which so keenly mirrored American interests and pursuits, from similar games played in England, such as cricket and rounders, led Spalding to seek out a purely colonial origin of the sport. Spalding's entire basis for the foundation of baseball history lay in a handwritten letter from 1907 that he said came from a man who claimed to have gone to school with Doubleday and attributed the invention to him. Despite the speculative and dubious claims of the letter, Spalding and other members of his commission were quick to adopt the narrative as gospel and began to market their sport to the masses as a truly American pursuit.

Reading Comprehension questions will take one of three forms. The first will ask you to select the best answer from a set of five possible answers. A Reading Comprehension question of this type will look like this:

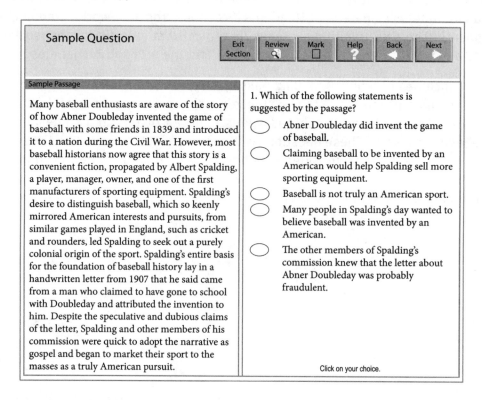

The second type of question gives you three answer choices, one or more of which are true. You will be asked to mark down all correct answers. All correct answers must be selected, and no partial credit will be given for only getting some of the right answers. The directions for this type of question will look like this:

Consider each of the following choices separately and select all that apply.

A Reading Comprehension question of this type will look like this:

Sample Question	Exit Section	Review	Mark	Help	Back	Next

Sample Passage

Many baseball enthusiasts are aware of the story of how Abner Doubleday invented the game of baseball with some friends in 1839 and introduced it to a nation during the Civil War. However, most baseball historians now agree that this story is a convenient fiction, propagated by Albert Spalding, a player, manager, owner, and one of the first manufacturers of sporting equipment. Spalding's desire to distinguish baseball, which so keenly mirrored American interests and pursuits, from similar games played in England, such as cricket and rounders, led Spalding to seek out a purely colonial origin of the sport.

Consider each of the following choices separately and select all that apply.

2. Which of the following statements is true based on the passage?

☐ Abner Doubleday was not a real person.

☐ Albert Spalding had a lot of influence over the business of baseball.

☐ Baseball has a lot in common with the game of cricket.

Click on your choice(s).

A third type of question asks you to select a sentence within the passage that best demonstrates the function or information requested by the question. A Reading Comprehension question of this type will look like this:

Sample Question	Exit Section	Review	Mark	Help	Back	Next

Sample Passage

Many baseball enthusiasts are aware of the story of how Abner Doubleday invented the game of baseball with some friends in 1839 and introduced it to a nation during the Civil War. However, most baseball historians now agree that this story is a convenient fiction, propagated by Albert Spalding, a player, manager, owner, and one of the first manufacturers of sporting equipment. Spalding's desire to distinguish baseball, which so keenly mirrored American interests and pursuits, from similar games played in England, such as cricket and rounders, led Spalding to seek out a purely colonial origin of the sport.

3. Select the sentence in the passage in which the author states that there was only one piece of evidence supporting the Abner Doubleday origin of baseball.

Click on your choice.

THE KAPLAN METHOD FOR READING COMPREHENSION

STEP 1 **Read the passage strategically.**

STEP 2 **Analyze the question stem.**

STEP 3 **Research the relevant text in the passage.**

STEP 4 **Make a prediction.**

STEP 5 **Evaluate the answer choices.**

HOW THE KAPLAN METHOD FOR READING COMPREHENSION WORKS

Now let's discuss how the Kaplan Method will help you answer these questions correctly.

◆ STEP 1

Read the passage strategically.

Reading strategically means identifying the topic, scope, and purpose of a passage, as well as noting the passage's structure and main points. The topic is the general subject matter, and the scope is the specific aspect of the topic that the author focuses on. The topic of the passage above is Abner Doubleday and baseball, but the scope is limited to the myth about his role in creating the sport.

In order to nail down topic, scope, and purpose, you should target the bones of the piece in the form of the passage's main ideas, primary arguments, secondary arguments, supporting statements or evidence, and conclusions. At this point you should start making a passage map. A passage map is a guide to the organization and main points of a passage. For each paragraph, write a one- to two-sentence summary that highlights the main points. For any given passage, you should be able to both summarize the text and identify the main points in your own words before proceeding. It is also important to use the key words and phrases connected to the sentences to identify the important ideas and statements.

With each passage, you need to look for the purpose of the text: Why was it written? While numerous facts will be provided in any given piece, not all passages are purely informative. Each passage will attempt to persuade the reader to some degree, if only to convince you that the subject is important. The key is to identify early on whether the piece is primarily informative or argumentative. This can be done by recognizing the tone the author uses. *Tone*, loosely defined, is the attitude the author has toward his subject. Tone is indispensable in nailing down an author's purpose, especially if that purpose is not entirely explicit. If the author makes use of comparisons (*better, more effective*) or assertions (*should, must, need to*), then the author is likely trying to persuade you. If the author writes in a more straightforward style with no persuasive or judgmental terminology, the piece is likely informative.

Pieces written in that tone are more likely to have the purpose of explanation or description in mind. Purpose is itself important, as it is closely tied to the author's *opinion* on the subject matter. This is of crucial importance for Inference questions.

In general, a social sciences piece is likely to argue a position, as the complex nature of human behavior and interaction is open to wide interpretation. Likewise, a discussion of a piece of art or literature will likely contain arguments as the author asserts an interpretation of these art forms. Scientific articles, on the other hand, will be mainly informative, seeking primarily to explain a scientific concept or discovery. Still, arguments may be advanced or conclusions drawn about the importance of these discoveries or principles in daily application. Therefore, you should pay close attention to tone, as it greatly informs the argument.

⬦ STEP 2

Analyze the question stem.

Many test takers attempt to "shortcut" the process of a Reading Comprehension passage by reading the question stems before reading the passage itself in hopes of giving themselves a "clue" about what to look for as they read. This is almost always a mistake. All Reading Comprehension requires an active awareness and understanding of what is being read, as described in Step 1. The nature of the question stem should not dissuade you from making your own interpretations prior to reading the passage. Therefore, you should be cautious and try not to allow the nature of the stem to influence your interpretation of a passage.

Also, one question stem following the passage may concern itself with a passage's tone, whereas another question may focus on a vocabulary term in context. Trying to read with these questions in mind will affect your sense of priority in interpreting the main ideas of the passage. It is more important for you to be able to use the question stem to know where to look in researching the passage for details than for you to try to use the stem as a road map in advance. Your passage map and/or notes will organize the reading well enough to allow you to find the correct answer(s) quickly.

The purpose of analyzing a question stem is to look for guidance as to the specificity and uniqueness of the answer being sought. Some questions are general questions that you may already have the answer to, such as "What is the purpose of this passage?" or "Which of these mirrors the author's conclusion?" By having followed Step 1, you may already have the information needed to answer this question.

In many cases, however, the question stem indicates a relationship between the answers that should serve as a clue as to how to proceed. If a question asks for the "best" answer or the one that "most closely describes" something in the passage, there may be more than one answer that arguably applies, but only one answer will most closely fit the question stem.

The question stem might also require you to go a step further and make a contrasting judgment against an idea in the passage. A question that asks for the "least likely" answer or the answer that "differs" from the author's perspective would require you to understand the author's conclusions or viewpoints well enough to select the choice that is most opposed to them.

STEP 3

Research the relevant text in the passage.

Once you have analyzed and fully understood the question stem, you should already have an idea of where in the passage the answer will be found, due to your active reading in Step 1. You should not consider more text from the passage than is necessary to answer the specific question. If the question is about vocabulary in context, you should not need to look much further than the sentence in which the word appears, and possibly the preceding sentence, to arrive at the answer.

STEP 4

Make a prediction.

Many of the questions will, by design, test your comprehension of what you have read and not just your ability to go into the passage and mine for the correct details. As such, you will often have the opportunity to formulate a prediction as to the answers of many questions that deal with the main idea, conclusions, arguments, author's meaning, tone, and implications of the information provided. Before moving on to the provided answer choices, try to either form a response in your own mind or, alternatively, target a section in the passage that you think will be most likely to contain the answer.

There will be occasions when you will have to infer an answer based on clues provided in the text that come in the form of details or the author's tone. In these cases, if the question prompts you to consider a particular facet of the passage, you should first create your own hypothesis regarding that facet before moving on to the answers. The relevant sections of the passage for Step 3 are those that provide evidence or details to support (or refute) your conclusion. One note of caution: Making a specific prediction is sometimes not possible for Inference questions. Instead, refer to the passage or your passage map as necessary as you evaluate the answer choices.

STEP 5

Evaluate the answer choices.

Even if there is an answer that clearly matches the prediction you have made, or an answer that jumps out at you as resoundingly correct, it is important to read and consider each answer choice. Eliminating incorrect answers not only helps narrow down options for questions that are hard to answer, it also validates the selection you are considering.

If you are absolutely uncertain, you should begin by identifying answers that are demonstrably incorrect. Eliminating answers can be done using the same steps described above for finding the right answer: by weighing them against the criteria set forth by your own reading and interpretation, the wording of the question stem, the relevant portions of the text, and your predicted response. After eliminating incorrect answers, you can weigh the remaining choices against your criteria and select the best match.

How to Apply the Kaplan Method for Reading Comprehension

Now let's apply the Kaplan Method to a Reading Comprehension passage and questions.

Many baseball enthusiasts are aware of the story of how Abner Doubleday invented the game of baseball with some friends in 1839 and introduced it to a nation during the Civil War. However, most baseball historians now agree that this story is a convenient fiction, propagated by Albert Spalding, a player, manager, owner, and one of the first manufacturers of sporting equipment. Spalding's desire to distinguish baseball, which so keenly mirrored American interests and pursuits, from similar games played in England, such as cricket and rounders, led Spalding to seek out a purely colonial origin of the sport. Spalding's entire basis for the foundation of baseball history lay in a handwritten letter from 1907 that he said came from a man who claimed to have gone to school with Doubleday and attributed the invention to him. Despite the speculative and dubious claims of the letter, Spalding and other members of his commission were quick to adopt the narrative as gospel and began to market their sport to the masses as a truly American pursuit.

1. Which of the following statements is suggested by the passage?

   (A) Abner Doubleday did invent the game of baseball.
   (B) Claiming baseball to be invented by an American would help Spalding sell more sporting equipment.
   (C) Baseball is not truly an American sport.
   (D) Some people in Spalding's day wanted to believe baseball was invented by an American.
   (E) The other members of Spalding's commission knew that the letter about Abner Doubleday was probably fraudulent.

◆ STEP 1

Read the passage strategically.

If you were only to skim the beginning and ending sentences of the passage, you would surmise that the topic is baseball but could get tricked early on into thinking that the passage is about Abner Doubleday in scope. The key word "However" in the second sentence is indicative that it is the following sentence that is of greater importance. Indeed, the sentence does introduce the true point of focus: Albert Spalding and his impact on baseball. You might also note that while there are some judgmental terms (*speculative, dubious*) in the passage, the text's tone is that of an informative passage.

STEP 2

Analyze the question stem.

The key phrase is "suggested by," which tells us that the answer is not explicitly stated in the text but can be discerned by an accurate reading of the text. Each possible answer will have to be considered on its own merits. Remember that the answer has to be evaluated based on the information in the text alone, which must be assumed to be true for the purpose of answering the question, regardless of any outside knowledge.

STEP 3

Research the relevant text in the passage.

In this case, the relevant portions of the text will not become clear until after the answer choices are read, because the question stem does not give us a point of focus. Here we see that the Kaplan Method sometimes requires cycling through the steps in order to arrive at the right answer.

STEP 4

Make a prediction.

Although the question stem does not initially seem to provide enough information about its intent to allow you to make a prediction without seeing the answer choices, if you have been actively reading, it is likely that you have made some conclusions of your own regarding the text, such as to the veracity of the Abner Doubleday story and Albert Spalding's motivations—the unsaid implications of the text. These can serve you well in analyzing the answer choices.

STEP 5

Evaluate the answer choices.

Each given answer reflects a portion of the passage. With each, you should return to Step 3 and target the appropriate sections of the passage that support or refute an answer. Choice **(A)** can immediately be eliminated because it is in direct opposition to the main idea of the piece, stated within the first two sentences. Similarly, choice **(C)** can be eliminated as being in disagreement with the passage. Even if the sport of baseball had its origins in other sports and other countries, the author states that baseball "mirrored American interests and pursuits" and implies that it is firmly embraced by American culture. Remember that you must decide based only on the passage, and even if another author might make the claim of answer choice **(C)**, the author of the passage doesn't. Choices **(B)** and **(E)** can both be eliminated because there is no evidence to support these claims within the text. The speed and willingness of Spalding and his commission to adopt the Doubleday story does provide evidence, however, for the correct answer, **(D)**.

How to Apply the Kaplan Method for Reading Comprehension

Now let's apply the Kaplan Method to a second Reading Comprehension question (based on the previous passage).

Consider each of the following choices separately and select all that apply.

2. Which of the following statements is true based on the passage?

    A Abner Doubleday was not a real person.

    B Albert Spalding influenced the way baseball was perceived.

    C Baseball has a lot in common with the game of cricket.

STEP 1

Read the passage strategically.

One of the first steps in strategic reading is to determine the tone of the passage. In this case, it is informative. You are allowed the use of scratch paper, and creating a passage map is encouraged. With an informative piece, you should be identifying the main ideas and facts of the issue. Doing this will help you to answer a multiple-selection question such as this one.

STEP 2

Analyze the question stem.

The directions for the question remind us that there may be more than one answer. The question stem also mentions "based on the passage," but for the purposes of the test, you are looking for a statement that <u>must be true</u>, even when not explicitly stated. You should eliminate any answer choices that are not clearly confirmed by the text.

STEP 3

Research the relevant text in the passage.

Again, each answer will have to be considered on its own merits, but your outline will tell you where to search for the answer. As you determined from analyzing the question stem, the passage must contain the evidence you need to select each choice, or that choice is not a valid answer.

STEP 4

Make a prediction.

In a way, you have done this with your passage map. In order to answer this question, you must be able to distill the facts from the passage. Your predictions can start with the most important information revealed in the passage and work down in importance. With these facts in mind, you will probably have a gut reaction to the veracity of each possible answer, and you certainly will know where to look in the text to find out.

❯❯ STEP 5

Evaluate the answer choices.

Since each answer choice must be considered independently of the others, let's go in order. Choice **(A)** can quickly be dismissed because the passage concerns itself with Doubleday only as far as his involvement in inventing baseball. The text never disputes his existence. Choice **(A)** is not a correct answer. Choice **(B)** concerns itself with Spalding, the primary figure in the piece. The passage states that he was a player, a manager, an owner, and a sporting goods manufacturer. It says that he appointed a commission. And, above all, the passage states that Spalding was responsible for a pervasive myth. All of these defend choice **(B)** as a valid answer. Choice **(C)** can quickly be confirmed because the author states outright that baseball is similar to cricket. The correct answers are **(B)** and **(C)**.

HOW TO APPLY THE KAPLAN METHOD FOR READING COMPREHENSION

Now let's apply the Kaplan Method to the third example question (based on the previous passage):

3. Select the sentence in the passage in which the author states that there was only one piece of evidence supporting the Abner Doubleday origin of baseball.

❯❯ STEP 1

Read the passage strategically.

Again, making a passage map, or at least a mental one, is critical. Each sentence of the passage has at least some purpose in the text, and your outline and identification of main ideas and supporting details will give you a road map to find the sentence you need for this type of question.

❯❯ STEP 2

Analyze the question stem.

There are several key terms here that will guide your search. The term "states" tells you that the information is clearly given, not implied or suggested, making it easier to find. Because the question, like the passage, must be accepted as true, the phrase "only one piece" means that you only need to find one sentence with such evidence.

❯❯ STEP 3

Research the relevant text in the passage.

With the idea in mind that there is only one piece of evidence to find, and using the passage map created through your critical reading, you should have no trouble finding the section near the end of the passage that begins, "Spalding's entire basis for the foundation of baseball history lay...."

STEP 4
Make a prediction.

For this question, the ability to make a prediction is easier than for the other two questions on this passage, because by using active reading, you would almost certainly recall the letter mentioned in the text and know where to look for it.

STEP 5
Evaluate the answer choices.

For a question of this sort, there are no answer choices per se, but each sentence of the passage is a potential option, so if there is any uncertainty in answering the question, each sentence may have to be considered as a choice. However, if you have been following the previous steps, you will probably not have to evaluate each sentence. Instead, you should be able to quickly find and click on "Spalding's entire basis for the foundation of baseball history lay in a handwritten letter from 1907 that he said came from a man who claimed to have gone to school with Doubleday and attributed the invention to him."

KAPLAN'S ADDITIONAL TIPS FOR READING COMPREHENSION QUESTIONS

Express the main idea in your own words.

Summarizing the main idea of the passage for yourself will not only form the foundation of your comprehension of the passage, it will also be the starting point of all your text evaluation for the questions. While not every passage has a specific main idea, each passage does have a topic and scope, both of which you should discern by the end of the first paragraph. If you are halfway through a passage and still have not identified these elements, you may be reading too fast and not outlining or identifying key words and phrases in the text.

Focus on retaining ideas, not facts.

Unlike in your coursework, you do not have to memorize or retain any of the dates, details, or minutiae of each passage. If you are asked a question about a specific term or detail within the text, such as a date or place, you have the text there to refer back to. In that sense, Reading Comprehension questions are like an open-book test. It is your job to concern yourself with the ideas, arguments, and conclusions the author presents so as to assess the questions accurately and examine them within the context of the passage.

Concentrate on using only what the passage gives you.

In some sense, a passage about a completely foreign topic can serve as a benefit to a smart test taker. Whatever the information is about, it is still presented using familiar systems of information presentation or persuasive writing. This is your guide to Reading Comprehension passages.

A danger occurs when you have pre-existing knowledge of a topic. This knowledge can confuse or muddle your ability to answer a question by clouding or expanding the scope of your reading of the piece beyond what is written. To best handle the questions, you must be concerned only with what can be gleaned from the text itself and not be influenced by outside knowledge that can put you at odds with the correct answer as defined by the passage and the question stem.

Also, during the test, you should surrender the skeptical reading style you would use to evaluate, say, a magazine article or an op-ed piece in a newspaper and, instead, accept the information given in informative passages as true in order to answer the questions. Even with persuasive passages, regardless of your opinion in relation to the author's, you must use only the evidence and arguments given as the groundwork for answering the questions.

Do not approach Highlighted Sentence questions differently.

In Highlighted Sentence questions, two sentences in the passage are highlighted, and you are asked to determine the function of both. Some of the functions a sentence might serve are these:

- Development of an argument
- Conclusion of an argument
- Evidence supporting a conclusion
- Evidence supporting part of a conclusion
- Evidence supporting an objection to the conclusion
- A secondary argument or support for a secondary argument

Your natural instinct may be to focus primarily or only on the highlighted sentences. However, the entire passage should be handled with the same strategy as any other question. As you read the passage, read strategically to determine the position taken by the author. Identify the argument and its conclusion and note how they are supported or refuted. While the highlighted lines are most relevant to answering the question, the surrounding material still provides key context.

Remember to make a prediction before evaluating the answer choices and then move on to evaluating and eliminating obviously incorrect answers. Each answer has two parts, one for each highlighted sentence; both must be correct in order for the answer to be correct. If you are unable to predict an answer, or if your prediction is not among the answer choices, you should be able to eliminate most of the wrong answer choices by looking carefully at the two parts. You may find a mischaracterization of the role of a sentence, a reversal of the sentences' roles, a reference to a sentence not highlighted, or a description of something that does not appear in the passage. Once you have eliminated the obviously incorrect answers, you should more easily be able to identify the answer that best describes the roles of the sentences.

Do not get misled by variations on standard question stems.

While most questions concern themselves with what is true about the passage, some questions will ask you to find the item that is *not* supported by the passage. A question that states that all of the answers EXCEPT one apply may have several "right" answers—choices supported by the text—but if you forget to look for the erroneous answer, you may pick a "right" answer that is, in fact, incorrect for the purposes of the question.

Also, while the passage must be assumed to be true and the question must be assumed to be true, all answer choices are initially to be regarded with suspicion. Any new information that is given only in the context of an answer choice cannot be given the benefit of being true. Answer choices that attempt to insert additional information are almost certainly wrong.

For multiple-choice questions involving highlighted sentences, the standard approach is to ascertain the relationship between the two sentences, but some questions simply ask for the purpose of each sentence within the passage. You must, through your own active reading, be able to discern the purpose of highlighted sentences independently of the question in order to deal most effectively with a Highlighted Sentence question.

READING COMPREHENSION PRACTICE SET

Try the following Reading Comprehension questions using the Kaplan Method for Reading Comprehension. If you're up to the challenge, time yourself; on Test Day, you'll want to spend only 1–3 minutes reading each passage and 1 minute on each question.

Questions 1 and 2 are based on the passage below.

The idea of medical nanotechnology often conjures up the potentially troubling image of tiny machines and devices that both exist and operate far outside the scope of unmagnified human vision. Yet much of what constitutes nanotechnology is purely biological in form and function. For example, strands of DNA and the proteins that make up its structure are mere nanometers thick. Many of the basic functions of life occur on the nanoscale level. Efforts to understand or affect these functions are among the primary fields of nanotechnology. Gene study and gene therapy, two byproducts of medical nanotechnology, have already proven useful for identifying and treating a number of different diseases, sometimes even before symptoms of those diseases present themselves. Even so, genetic nanotechnology and treatments can give as much cause for concern as the idea of microscopic machines at work in the body. The possibility of altering an organism's genetic structure has been a subject of much debate as to what extent such an alteration would be both safe and ethical.

1. In the passage above, what roles do the highlighted sentences serve?

    (A) The first sentence is the main idea, and the second sentence restates the main idea.

    (B) The first sentence makes the central argument of the passage, and the second sentence supports the argument.

    (C) The first sentence provides the primary argument, and the second sentence is the secondary argument.

    (D) The first sentence is a secondary argument, and the second sentence is evidence against that argument.

    (E) The first sentence introduces the topic, and the second sentence is the conclusion.

2. According to the passage, all of the following statements are true EXCEPT:

   Ⓐ Medical nanotechnology is a field of nanotechnology that is entirely biological in practice.

   Ⓑ Nanotechnology has already led to medical practices that are currently in use.

   Ⓒ There are valid concerns regarding the use of nanotechnology.

   Ⓓ Some of what happens on the nanoscale is naturally occurring.

   Ⓔ Gene therapy is a result of medical nanotechnology.

Questions 3–5 are based on the passage below.

Although it is an imperfect model for describing a complex market, the theory of supply and demand is a reasonably accurate method of explaining, describing, and predicting how the quantity and price of goods fluctuate within a market. Economists define supply as the amount of a particular good that producers are willing to sell at a certain price. For example, a manufacturer might be willing to sell 7,000 sprockets if each one sells for $0.45 but would be willing to sell substantially more sprockets, perhaps 12,000, for a higher price of $0.82. Conversely, demand represents the quantity of a given item that consumers will purchase at a set price; in the most efficient market, all buyers pay the lowest price available, and all sellers charge the highest price they are able. The intersection of these occurrences is graphically represented in supply and demand curves that show the prices at which a product becomes too expensive or too readily available.

3. Which one of the following best expresses the main idea of the passage?

   (A) explaining why buyers in a given market tend to seek the lowest price on available goods
   (B) offering a dissenting perspective on an obsolete economic model
   (C) persuading readers that the model of supply and demand is the best method for understanding market forces
   (D) providing an explanation of the two primary elements of an economic model and how they intersect
   (E) analyzing the fluctuation of supply and demand within a market

   Consider each of the following choices separately and select all that apply.

4. If the producer of sprockets nearly doubles its prices as described in the passage, it follows that

   A buyers in the market will be likely to purchase more of the sprockets being sold.
   B the price of sprockets will continue to increase.
   C buyers in the market will be likely to purchase fewer of the sprockets being sold.

5. Select the sentence in the passage that illustrates an abstract concept presented by the author.

READING COMPREHENSION PRACTICE SET ANSWERS AND EXPLANATIONS

1. E

Choice **(E)** is the correct answer. One can arrive at this conclusion not only by the process of elimination but also by understanding that the piece is not truly a persuasive piece. The arguments presented are mainly those of others, not the author. Because this is an informative piece, any answers indicating the existence of arguments are suspect. Only in the second highlighted sentence does the author draw a conclusion or give a slight acknowledgment of people's concerns over medical nanotechnology. **(A)**, **(B)**, and **(C)** can be passed over quickly because the first sentence is not the main idea and its contents are contradicted by the following sentence, which is directed more at the central focus. Choice **(D)** can be dismissed in that the second highlighted sentence to some degree supports people's concerns about nanotechnology and does not refute it, as the choice suggests.

2. A

A careless test taker might be tripped up here because this question is reversed from the standard form. In the answer choices, there are four true statements and one false statement. It is the false one that must be found, so each of the true ones should be evaluated and confirmed in the text. Choice **(A)** is the early favorite for the right answer because the second sentence mentions that much of nanotechnology is biological, but not all, and nothing else in the text gives any indication that this does not apply to medical nanotechnology as well. Choice **(A)** is too extreme, and it is therefore the correct answer. All other choices can be confirmed within the text through explicitly stated or easily inferred information.

3. D

The passage as a whole discusses the basic elements of the model of supply and demand, defining the two terms and describing how they work. That's choice **(D)**. Choice **(A)** is too narrow, focusing on only one of the two forces described. Choice **(B)** is out of scope because there's no mention of the model being obsolete; also, the author simply describes the model—she doesn't dissent from its contentions. Although the passage asserts that the supply and demand model is "reasonably accurate," the passage is primarily concerned with explaining the model, not with persuading readers that it is the "best" model. Therefore, you can rule out **(C)**. Although the theory of supply and demand does allow for the analysis of market forces, **(E)**, the passage itself provides only description, not analysis.

4. C

You are told that producers want to charge as much as possible and buyers want to pay as little as possible, so it makes sense that as prices rise, demand falls, choice **(C)**. Choice **(A)** is the opposite of what the passage implies, which is that demand decreases as prices rise. There's no evidence presented that this change in price will lead to further price increases, so you can rule out **(B)**.

5. For example, a manufacturer might be willing to sell 7,000 sprockets if each one sells for $0.45 but would be willing to sell substantially more sprockets, perhaps 12,000, for a higher price of $0.82.

The abstract concepts addressed in the passage are those of supply and demand, and the only example that illustrates supply and demand occurs in sentence 3. Sentence 1 introduces the supply and demand model. Sentence 2 defines the term *supply*. Sentence 4 explains demand, and sentence 5 describes a graphical representation of the two forces.

CHAPTER 8

Verbal Reasoning Practice Sets

In this section, you will take three practice sections consisting of 20 questions each. This section has been divided into two parts to allow you to check your answers at the halfway mark. You will use a diagnostic tool at that point to help you learn from your mistakes and continue on to the second set with more awareness of the traps you may encounter.

REVIEW OF THE KAPLAN METHODS FOR VERBAL REASONING QUESTION TYPES

Review the steps and strategies you have studied for answering each type of question quickly, efficiently, and correctly before starting your Practice Sets.

THE KAPLAN METHOD FOR TEXT COMPLETION (ONE-BLANK)

STEP 1   Read the sentence, looking for clues.

STEP 2   Predict an answer.

STEP 3   Select the choice that most closely matches your prediction.

STEP 4   Check your answer.

THE KAPLAN METHOD FOR TEXT COMPLETION (TWO-BLANK AND THREE-BLANK)

STEP 1   Read the sentence, looking for clues.

STEP 2   Predict an answer for the easier/easiest blank.

STEP 3   Select the choice that most closely matches your prediction.

STEP 4   Predict and select for the remaining blanks.

STEP 5   Check your answers.

THE KAPLAN METHOD FOR SENTENCE EQUIVALENCE

STEP 1   Read the sentence, looking for clues.

STEP 2   Predict an answer.

STEP 3   Select the two choices that most closely match your prediction.

STEP 4   Check your answers to see if the sentence retains the same meaning.

THE KAPLAN METHOD FOR READING COMPREHENSION

STEP 1   Read the passage strategically.

STEP 2   Analyze the question stem.

STEP 3   Research the relevant text in the passage.

STEP 4   Make a prediction.

STEP 5   Evaluate the answer choices.

VERBAL REASONING PRACTICE SET 1

Directions: Each sentence below has one or more blanks, each blank indicating that something has been omitted. Beneath the sentence are five words for one-blank questions and sets of three words for each blank for two- and three-blank questions. Choose the word or set of words for each blank that best fits the meaning of the sentence as a whole.

1. The patterns of the stock market seem _____ to many beginners, but they can be decoded with dedication and patience.

   Ⓐ unwelcoming

   Ⓑ arcane

   Ⓒ harmonious

   Ⓓ shocking

   Ⓔ lucid

2. In spite of its popularity, *The Merchant of Venice* remains a (i) _____ play, with many critics (ii) _____ the extent of Shakespeare's anti-Semitism.

Blank (i)		Blank (ii)	
A	controversial	D	assuaging
B	celebrated	E	augmenting
C	histrionic	F	debating

3. Considered one of his most (i) _____ works, Mozart's *Requiem in D Minor* has a certain (ii) _____ in Western culture because of its incomplete status at the time of his death, and many (iii) _____ stories have arisen surrounding it; unfortunately, the truth is lost to us.

Blank (i)		Blank (ii)		Blank (iii)	
A	ignominious	D	obscurity	G	fraudulent
B	inconspicuous	E	indifference	H	apocryphal
C	famous	F	mystique	I	verified

4. Although Thomas Paine was most (i) _____ his political pamphlets, he was in fact (ii) _____ writer on many different subjects.

Blank (i)		Blank (ii)	
A	inimical to	D	an abstruse
B	condemned for	E	a prolific
C	famous for	F	a terrible

5. Because he was convinced of his own _____, Adam never acknowledged his mistakes.

A genius

B acclamation

C shrewdness

D infallibility

E popularity

6. St. Elmo's fire is a weather phenomenon that, (i) _____ it has been documented since ancient times, was not (ii) _____ until recently.

Blank (i)		Blank (ii)	
A	because	D	incinerated
B	since	E	reported
C	although	F	understood

Questions 7–10 are based on the passage below.

It has been commonly accepted for some time now that certain scenes in Shakespeare's *Macbeth* are interpolations from the writing of another author; act III, scene 5, and parts of act IV, scene 1, have been determined to be the writing of one of his contemporaries, Thomas Middleton. This can be regarded as both illuminating and problematic, depending upon how the play is being studied. It allows us to infer a great deal about the conventions and practices of writing for the stage at the time. For example, playwriting may have been more collaborative than previously thought, or perhaps Elizabethan notions of plagiarism were different from ours. While historically significant, this does complicate our interpretation of the characters in the play. It is more difficult to assess authorial intention with regard to a character's motives if the text has been redacted by multiple authors.

7. Select the statement or statements that are correct according to the passage.

   [A] The author feels that Shakespeare is guilty of plagiarism.
   [B] The interpolations found in plays such as *Macbeth* make the assessment of authorial intention more straightforward.
   [C] Our current understanding of plagiarism may have arisen after Shakespeare's time.

8. Consider the following choices and select all that apply. Which of the following could aid in the further study of the interpolations discussed in the above passage?

   [A] an investigation into the existence and prevalence of collaborative writing partnerships during Shakespeare's time
   [B] an examination of the themes and techniques of other writers contemporary with Shakespeare
   [C] a search through legal documents of Shakespeare's time for references to plagiarism or intellectual property rights

9. Consider the following choices and select all that apply. Which CANNOT be inferred from the passage?

   A The example of interpolation discussed in the passage would be illegal today.

   B Authors and playwrights in Shakespeare's time might have recruited assistance when composing their works.

   C Shakespeare used Middleton's writing without his consent.

10. In the passage, the two highlighted statements play which of the following roles?

    A The first explains a concept, and the second presents an example of that concept.

    B The first presents an example of the main subject of the passage, and the second is a conclusion based on that example.

    C The first states the conclusion of the argument as a whole, and the second provides support for that conclusion.

    D The first provides evidence for a conclusion that the passage as a whole opposes, and the second presents the objection to that conclusion.

    E The first states the primary conclusion of the passage, and the second states the secondary conclusion.

Directions: For the following questions, select the **two** answer choices that, when inserted into the sentence, fit the meaning of the sentence as a whole **and** yield complete sentences that are similar in meaning.

11. Known to all as having a silver tongue, the orator easily distracts audiences from the meaning of his words with his _____ speech.

    A mellifluous

    B concise

    C stumbling

    D laconic

    E euphonic

    F strident

12. When the underdogs so soundly beat the team favored to win, their victory _____ the entire sports world.

    A horrified

    B estranged

    C shook

    D bored

    E alienated

    F stunned

13. Despite the efforts made by the municipal government to increase public transportation usage, many people of the city continued to drive their own vehicles, complaining that the bus schedules were too _____ to be relied upon.

    A irregular

    B exacting

    C circuitous

    D rigid

    E isolated

    F erratic

14. Word painting is a musical technique in which the progression of the notes _____ the meaning of the lyrics; a famous example of this can be found in Handel's *Messiah*, in which the notes rise with the mention of "mountains" and fall with the mention of "low."

   A affects
   B mimics
   C contrasts
   D reflects
   E opposes
   F renounces

Directions: Each passage in this group is followed by questions based on its content. After reading a passage, choose the best answer to each question. Answer all questions following a passage on the basis of what is stated or implied in that passage.

Questions 15 and 16 are based on the passage below.

In the decades leading up to the 1970s, the primarily French-speaking Canadian province of Québec saw its proportion of native French speakers diminish from year to year. The attrition of French was attributed to the preeminence of English in the workplace, particularly in affluent, "white-collar" jobs. The French-speaking majority was economically marginalized within its own province, as it was left with the choice of either working in lower-paying jobs or teaching its children English as a first language. The latter option would further erase Québec's cultural autonomy and singularity within a country that primarily spoke English. Facing the risk of linguistic extinction, the province passed *Loi 101* (Law 101): The Charter of the French Language. It established French as the only official language of the province, established the primacy of French in the workplace, and led to more economic equity. Since its passage in 1977, the percentage of people in Québec who speak French as a first language has begun to rise.

15. Which of the following is suggested in the passage as a reason for the decline of French in Québec?

    (A) the disparity of economic opportunities available to French and English speakers
    (B) an influx of English-speaking immigrants
    (C) efforts of French Canadians to further integrate themselves with Canadian culture
    (D) the emigration of French Canadians
    (E) the outlawing of French in the other provinces

16. According to the passage, *Loi 101* was significant in that it

    (A) was a final, unsuccessful attempt at enforcing the usage of French in Québec
    (B) curtailed the economic supremacy of English
    (C) restricted the teaching of English in schools
    (D) highlighted the distinctiveness of the cultural identity of Québec from that of the rest of Canada
    (E) provided for bilingual education

Questions 17–19 are based on the paragraph below.

The advent of online education in the first decade of the 21st century was the result of and a response to a number of factors that were both internal and external to the field of higher education. Traditional tertiary institutions, especially those that were privately endowed, raised tuition rates far in excess of the rate of inflation. This, in concert with a larger demand for postsecondary education for working adults, helped facilitate the introduction of online learning. However, it should be acknowledged that the relative simplicity of using the Internet as a platform, as well as its cost-effectiveness, was seized upon by entrepreneurs in the private sector. Online education is largely in the hands of for-profit companies. The question now becomes whether the democratization of higher education is worth the price of removing it from nonprofit, research-based universities.

17. The passage is concerned primarily with

   (A) the advent of online education
   (B) adult-oriented educational systems
   (C) the usefulness of the Internet in postsecondary education
   (D) economic and technological factors that influenced the development and current state of online education
   (E) the advantages and disadvantages of online education

18. The author's use of the term "seized upon" evokes an image of _____ on the part of the entrepreneurs.

   (A) accidental realization
   (B) opportunistic tactics
   (C) violent appropriation
   (D) collusive behavior
   (E) market manipulation

19. The highlighted section refers to

   (A) the cost of online education
   (B) the popularity of online courses
   (C) making education available to a wider range of students
   (D) the role of voting in class selection
   (E) whether or not a democratic society should have online education

Question 20 is based on the passage below.

Thermodynamics is concerned with changes in the properties of matter when we alter the external conditions. An example of this is a gas being compressed by the motion of a piston. The final outcome depends on how the change is made—if the piston is moved in slowly, we say that the compression is "reversible." This means that if we pull the piston back out, we retrace the same sequence of properties but in the reverse order; hence, the temperature of the gas will be the same when the piston has been pulled out as it was before the piston was pushed in. However, if the piston is moved in and out quickly, then the initial state (and temperature) will not be recovered—the gas will always be hotter than it was at the beginning. This is a manifestation, although not a statement, of the second law of thermodynamics. It also makes a difference whether there is a transfer of heat between the cylinder of gas and the external surroundings. If the cylinder is insulated, then the gas will heat on compression and cool on expansion (refrigeration uses this principle). On the other hand, if the cylinder can exchange heat with the surroundings, it will remain at the same temperature if the compression is slow enough.

20. This passage is primarily concerned with

   (A) describing the motion of a piston to demonstrate the laws of thermodynamics
   (B) explaining the conservation of heat during the motion of a piston
   (C) demonstrating how the second law of thermodynamics applies to pistons
   (D) explaining how thermodynamics function
   (E) discussing reversible compression

VERBAL REASONING PRACTICE SET 1 ANSWER KEY

1. B
2. A, F
3. C, F, H
4. C, E
5. D
6. C, F
7. C
8. A, B, C
9. A, C
10. B
11. A, E
12. C, F
13. A, F
14. B, D
15. A
16. B
17. D
18. B
19. C
20. A

DIAGNOSE YOUR RESULTS

Diagnostic Tool

Tally up your score and write your results below.

Total

Total Correct: _____ out of 20 correct

By Question Type

Text Completions (questions 1–6) _____ out of 6 correct
Sentence Equivalence (questions 11–14) _____ out of 4 correct
Reading Comprehension (questions 7–10, 15–20) _____ out of 10 correct

Look back at the questions you got wrong and think about your experience answering them.

❯❯ STEP 1

Find the roadblocks.

If you struggled to answer some questions, then to improve your score, you need to pinpoint exactly what "roadblocks" tripped you up. To do that, ask yourself the following two questions.

Am I weak in the skills being tested?

The easiest way to determine this is to think in terms of what skills are required for each question type. If you're having trouble with Sentence Equivalence or Text Completion, you probably need to review your vocabulary word lists. Maybe you need to brush up on using word etymology to your advantage. If Reading Comprehension questions are bothersome, you need to work on your critical reading skills. If you know you need to brush up on your verbal skills, try the *Kaplan GRE Verbal Workbook*, which contains a focused review of all the verbal reasoning concepts tested on the GRE, as well as practice exercises to build speed and accuracy.

Did the question types throw me off?

Then you need to become more comfortable with them! Sentence Equivalence questions have a unique format, and Reading Comprehension can be daunting with its dense, complex passages. If you struggled, go back to the beginning of this chapter and review the Kaplan principles and methods for the question types you found challenging. Make sure you understand the principles and how to apply the methods. These strategies will help you improve your speed and efficiency on Test Day. Remember, it's not a reading or vocabulary test; it's a critical-reasoning test (even though your reading habits and command of vocabulary are indispensable tools that will help you earn a high score).

Also, get as much practice as you can so that you grow more at ease with the question type formats. For even more practice, try the *Kaplan GRE Verbal Workbook*, which includes practice sets for each question type.

❯❯ STEP 2

Find the blind spots.

Did you answer some questions quickly and confidently but get them wrong anyway?

When you come across wrong answers like these, you need to figure out what you thought you were doing right, what it turns out you were doing wrong, and why that happened. The best way to do that is to **read the answer explanations!**

The explanations give you a detailed breakdown of why the correct answer is correct and why all the other answer choices are incorrect. This helps to reinforce the Kaplan principles and methods for each question type and helps you figure out what blindsided you so it doesn't happen again. Also, just as with your "roadblocks," try to get in as much practice as you can.

❯❯ STEP 3

Reinforce your strengths.

Now read through all the answer explanations for the ones you got right. You should check every answer because if you guessed correctly without actually knowing how to get the right answer, reading the explanations will make sure that whatever needs fixing gets fixed. Work through them one more time. Again, this helps to reinforce the Kaplan principles and methods for each question type, which in turn helps you work more efficiently so you can get the score you want. Keep your skills sharp with more practice.

As soon as you are comfortable with all the GRE question types and Kaplan methods, complete a full-length practice test under timed conditions. In this way, practice tests serve as milestones; they help you to chart your progress. So don't save them all for the final weeks! For even more practice, you can also try the Kaplan GRE Quiz Bank. You get more than 2,500 questions that you can access 24/7 from any Internet browser, each with comprehensive explanations. You can even customize your quizzes based on question type, content, and difficulty level. Take quizzes in Timed Mode to test your stamina or in Tutor Mode to see explanations as you work. Best of all, you also get detailed reports to track your progress.

Visit **http://kaptest.com/GRE** for more details on our Quiz Bank and for more information on our other online and classroom-based options.

VERBAL REASONING PRACTICE SET 1
ANSWERS AND EXPLANATIONS

1. B

The road sign here is "but," which is a detour. The key words "can be decoded" indicate that the contrasting word in the blank means something like "mysterious" or "hard to understand." With that prediction in mind, look for an answer that suggests something incomprehensible, which rules out choices **(C)** *harmonious*, **(D)** *shocking*, and **(E)** *lucid*. Choice **(A)** *unwelcoming* is a possibility, but it refers more to a sense of unpleasantness than to perplexity. Answer choice **(B)** *arcane* is a perfect fit for the sense of something that cannot be easily understood.

2. A, F

Begin by taking note of the phrase "in spite of," which suggests that there will be an opposing idea in the sentence. The sentence describes the play as popular, so you can rule out choices **(B)** *celebrated* and **(C)** *histrionic* for the first blank because you are looking for a word contrasting with popularity. Based on the remaining option, **(A)** *controversial*, you are looking for a solution to the second blank that connotes uncertainty. Choices **(D)** *assuaging* and **(E)** *augmenting* are not possible, since neither means uncertainty. It is therefore answer choice **(F)** *debating* for the second blank. Read the sentence with the blanks filled in: if the play is controversial, it is not universally popular, and it makes sense that critics would debate some aspect of it.

3. C, F, H

When there are so many missing parts, it is often best to begin with whatever complete clause you can find, in this case the final one. This will allow you to fill in the third blank. You are told that we do not know the truth, which allows you to eliminate both choices **(G)** *fraudulent* and **(I)** *verified*, because both indicate that concrete knowledge exists on the matter. Answer choice **(H)** *apocryphal* is the only possible answer. If you know that many apocryphal stories arose surrounding the work, you can make headway into both of the other blanks.

For the first blank, assume that if many stories are made up about something, it is widely talked about—this eliminates choice **(B)** *inconspicuous* without a doubt, and between choices **(A)** *ignominious* and **(C)** *famous*, the choice is fairly straightforward. When you know something is much talked about because it is "incomplete," you can suppose that a neutral synonym of "well-known" is going to be much more likely than a negative synonym of "shameful."

Finally, for the second blank, you can reject choices **(D)** *obscurity* and **(E)** *indifference* because you know the composition is well-known, so answer choice **(F)** *mystique* is the only logical choice (and is supported by the mention of *apocryphal* stories). Let's check our answer: "Considered one of his most *famous* works, Mozart's *Requiem in D Minor* has a certain *mystique* in Western culture, and many *apocryphal* stories have arisen surrounding it; unfortunately, the truth is lost to us." Everything fits in perfectly when you read back the sentence with the correct words filled in.

4. C, E

"Although", a detour road sign, starts off the sentence, indicating that the ideas of the first and second clause will be opposites. While external knowledge might tell you that Paine was, in fact, a famous writer, it is important to remember that the correct answer will be derived from clues in the sentence alone. Also, the key words "political pamphlets" and "many different subjects" tell us what is being contrasted here: one subject (politics) versus many subjects. You might predict that Paine was well-known for his political writing but was actually a good writer on many subjects.

For the first blank, **(C)** *famous for* is a perfect match for your prediction. Choices **(A)** *inimical to* and **(B)** *condemned for* are both negative and, therefore, incorrect. Then for the second blank, neither **(D)** *abstruse* nor **(F)** *terrible* indicate that Paine wrote well. However, **(E)** *prolific* author writes a lot, and it can be presumed that writing comes easily to him. Therefore, **(E)** is the correct answer for the second blank.

Choices **(D)** *abstruse* and **(E)** *terrible* could work in a different sentence, but there is no choice for the first blank that will allow the resulting sentence to make sense. The answer will always be clear and definite—choices **(C)** *famous for* and **(E)** *prolific* create a sentence that makes sense without requiring any other knowledge or qualifications.

5. D

Since Adam "never acknowledged his mistakes," you can assume that Adam does not want to admit to being wrong. Choices **(B)** *acclamation* and **(E)** *popularity* can be immediately discounted because they have nothing to do with being right or wrong. Choices **(A)** *genius* and **(C)** *shrewdness* might work in this sentence (they are both related to mental quickness, and someone convinced of his own intelligence might not want to admit to being wrong). However, answer choice **(D)** *infallibility* directly opposes the notion of being wrong and is, therefore, the correct answer.

6. C, F

Based on the choices, you know that there will be a conjunction between the clauses of the first and second blanks. The contrast of "ancient times" and "recently" tells you to predict a word for the first blank that suggests contrast, which eliminates choices **(A)** *because* and **(B)** *since*, leaving you with answer choice **(C)** *although*.

You know St. Elmo's fire has been documented for a long time, so discount choice **(E)** *reported* for the second blank. Choice **(D)** may be tempting, because *incineration* is related to fire, but it does not make sense in this sentence. That leaves **(F)** *understood*, which does make sense as a contrast with the phenomenon's having been documented.

7. C

This type of question gives you three statements and asks you to select which ones are true. Break it down statement by statement. Statement **(A)** is untrue because the term "plagiarism" is used in the passage in the phrase "perhaps Elizabethan notions of plagiarism were different from ours"—which indicates that one cannot be certain of what might have constituted plagiarism at the time. Statement **(B)** is a 180: the passage does refer to the assessment of authorial intention if the text has been redacted by several authors, but the passage states the exact opposite of statement **(B)**. Statement **(C)** is correct because you are told that our current notion of plagiarism might be different from the notion of plagiarism in Shakespeare's time.

8. A, B, C

This question asks us about where you might direct further study about the interpolations referenced in the passage. This asks us to consider possibilities *based* on what is in the text but not necessarily stated *within* it. **(A)** The passage raises the question of how collaborative writing for the stage may have been during Shakespeare's time. Conducting an investigation into the existence of collaborative writing partnerships would be a good way to determine an answer for this question. **(B)** Familiarizing yourself with the style of other writers who might have helped write or had their work used in the writing of Shakespeare's plays would help in the determination of the actual authorship of passages in *Macbeth* (and other plays), as well as provide insight into authorial intention. Finally, **(C)** is an interesting alternative to a strictly literary study and would help to solve the question posed in the text of what constituted plagiarism in the Elizabethan era. All three are good choices for further study.

9. A, C

This is an exclusion question, so you must select the answers you *cannot* infer from the passage. **(A)**, that this example of interpolation would be illegal today, is impossible to tell, and this is specified by the author's questioning of the difference in notions of plagiarism between now and then; furthermore, it is not specified whether or not Middleton was consciously assisting the composition. **(B)** is suggested within the passage in the supposition that writing such as *Macbeth* might have, in fact, been collaborative—this allows you to eliminate choice **(B)**. **(C)** you know to be also a correct response for the same reason you specified for **(A)**—you do not know precisely Middleton's role in the composition. Answer choices **(A)** and **(C)** are both correct.

10. B

In this question, you are asked to determine the rhetorical roles of the two highlighted statements. The first highlighted statement is used as an example of the interpolations that the first clause in the sentence mentions. The highlighted portion states that parts of Shakespeare's work were in fact written by his peer Middleton. So the first highlighted portion appears to be an example.

The second highlighted statement presents an opinion regarding the impact of interpolations on literary analysis. According to this statement, because others wrote certain parts of Shakespeare's work, it is more difficult to determine a character's motives. Your prediction should be that the first statement is an example, and the second is an opinion or conclusion (remember that in arguments, the words "opinion" and "conclusion" will often be used interchangeably). Answer choice **(B)** matches this prediction perfectly.

The other choices miss the mark completely. For instance, choice **(A)** incorrectly states that the second highlighted portion is the example. Similarly, choice **(C)** indicates that the first statement is the opinion and the second is the evidence, the exact opposite of our prediction. **(D)** states that the passage opposes an argument, but there is no conflict addressed in the passage. Finally, choice **(E)** identifies both statements as conclusions, which is not correct.

11. A, E

The key here is that the sentence tells us that his "silver tongue" makes it hard to concentrate on the meaning of his words. To have a silver tongue is to be noted for the pleasantness of one's speech, so you are looking for a pair of answers that mean "pleasing." **(C)** *stumbling*, **(D)** *laconic*, and **(F)** *strident* all are unrelated to the pleasantness of his tone, and while **(B)** *concise* language may be an attribute of a skilled orator, it will not create a similar sentence to one created by either of the other two possible answers. **(A)** *mellifluous* and **(E)** *euphonic* both mean "to be sweet or pleasing," and both are often used in reference to speech.

12. C, F

For the favorite to lose is a surprise, so you are looking for choices that are synonyms of "surprised." Choice **(A)** *horrified* has a negative connotation not implied in the sentence. Likewise, the emotions conveyed in choices **(B)** *estranged* and **(E)** *alienated* would require more information than you are given to be considered as possible answers. **(D)** *bored* is the opposite of what you are looking for; something surprising is not boring. Answer choice **(C)** *shook* is often used in a metaphorical sense when a surprising event occurs, as is answer choice **(F)** *stunned*, and the two are synonyms of each another and of "surprised."

13. A, F

This is a good example of a sentence in which you are given more information than you need. In fact, the only clue you need lies in the final phrase "to be relied upon." Your answers will be antonyms of "reliable," which eliminates choices **(B)** *exacting*, **(C)** *circuitous* (a tempting choice because of the relationship between bus routes and the root word "circuit," but the meaning is not related to the sentence), **(D)** *rigid*, and **(E)** *isolated*. **(A)** *irregular* and **(F)** *erratic* both suggest that the buses are unreliable and, as is often (but not necessarily) the case with these questions, they are synonyms of each other.

14. B, D

While you might have no background in musical techniques, you never need information from outside the sentence to deduce the correct answer. The example given tells you that the progression of notes in the music seems to imitate the words of the lyrics. So, you need a word that gives the meaning "the progression of the notes mirrors the meaning of the lyrics." Choices **(C)** *contrasts*, **(E)** *opposes*, and **(F)** *renounces* are antonyms of the desired answer. While **(A)** *affects* could work in the sentence, it lacks a synonym and does not properly refer to the desired meaning of "mirrors." Answer choices **(B)** *mimics* and **(D)** *reflects* do, however, and thus you know that they are your desired choices.

15. A

You are asked why the use of the French language declined in Québec. Researching the passage, you see this mentioned in the first few lines. Specifically, you are told that the "preeminence" of the English language in the best jobs forced people to switch. This indicates that in order to take advantage of the best economic opportunities, one had to speak English. The passage suggests that French became an economically unviable language, stating that "the French-speaking majority was economically marginalized." Thus, the two groups had access to significantly different economic and professional opportunities. This is reflected in answer choice **(A)**.

Choices **(B)** and **(D)** are out of scope, as immigrant and emigrant populations are not mentioned. Furthermore, choice **(E)** is also beyond the scope of the passage, as the outlawing of languages is not relevant to the discussion. Finally, choice **(C)** is a 180, as the passage states the French sought to maintain their autonomy, not integrate themselves into other cultures.

16. B

This question asks you to summarize the significance of the law mentioned in the latter part of the passage. Based on the final sentence of the passage (which mentions the rise in French as the primary language), **(A)** is untrue—it was not an unsuccessful attempt. **(B)** is true because the passage specifies that the law "established the primacy of French in the workplace." No mention is made of language in schools, so you can dismiss options **(C)** and **(E)**. Finally, while the cultural identity of Québec is mentioned in the passage, the only results of *Loi 101* specified are the economic equity of the languages and the rise in the usage of French, so you can also reject **(D)** as a possible answer. Answer choice **(B)** is the only option that is based on the information in the passage.

17. D

You must be careful here. Just because **(A)** is a direct quotation of the opening of the passage does not make it the correct answer, and, indeed, the passage moves away from the origins of online education and into other facets of its expansion. **(B)** is not discussed in the passage, even though the author makes note that the demand for adult-oriented education was one of the contributing factors to the rise of online learning. Neither **(C)** nor **(E)** properly describes the entire scope of the passage. Only answer choice **(D)** can be said to encompass the entirety of the passage.

18. B

Here you are called to define a phrase based on its context. What you are looking for is an answer that accurately reflects what is described in the passage: the entrepreneurs saw an untapped potential for profit in the unanswered demand for online learning and "seized upon" it. **(A)** is a poor choice because it implies that their success in capitalizing on the demand was unintentional. **(B)** is a much better solution because it evokes the image of the entrepreneurs taking the opportunity available. **(C)** is highly unlikely because no mention of violence is made in the passage (and, indeed, in reference to online education this would be an unlikely choice to begin with). **(D)** can be eliminated as there is no mention of collusion on the part of for-profit education companies; similarly, **(E)** can be eliminated because those companies are never said to have manipulated the market in order to gain control of the online education market. Answer choice **(B)** is the only possible answer.

19. C

This type of question asks you to define the highlighted phrase based on the context. The key word here is "democratization." While the cost-effectiveness of online education is mentioned earlier in the passage, it is unlikely that **(A)** *the cost of online education* is the correct answer because the sense of the final sentence is that "it remains to be seen whether *making higher education more widely available through online institutions* is worth the price of removing it from nonprofit, research-based universities." Based on this, you can also discount **(B)** *the popularity of online courses* and **(D)** *the role of voting in class selection* because while they may be linked conceptually to the term "democracy," the context tells us this is not what the phrase here concerns. Answer choice **(C)** *making education available to a wider range of students* matches our prediction and properly clarifies the usage of the highlighted phrase in the passage. You can discount **(E)** because it goes well beyond the scope of the passage.

20. A

In a Global question such as this one, the correct answer will reflect the scope and purpose you noted while reading the passage. While the broad topic of the passage is thermodynamics, the bulk of the passage describes the motion of a piston and how the effects of that motion demonstrate the laws of thermodynamics. **(A)** expresses this idea exactly. **(D)** may be tempting since "thermodynamics" is the first word of the passage, but **(D)** is too broad and leaves out any mention of the piston, which plays a key role in the passage as a whole. Choices **(B)**, **(C)**, and **(E)** refer to specific subjects mentioned in the passage but do not refer to the passage as a whole.

VERBAL REASONING PRACTICE SET 2

1. Because she was so _____, Mary was uncomfortable speaking to large groups of people.

   - Ⓐ reticent
   - Ⓑ congenial
   - Ⓒ brusque
   - Ⓓ gregarious
   - Ⓔ scurrilous

2. The band's new album was universally panned by critics, with many _____ their change to a simpler sound.

   - Ⓐ lauding
   - Ⓑ ignorant of
   - Ⓒ tolerating
   - Ⓓ deriding
   - Ⓔ apathetic to

3. The cotton gin played a (i) _____ role in advancing the textile industry, (ii) _____ its negative effects can be seen in the rapid development of slavery as the economic base of the American South.

Blank (i)	Blank (ii)
A negligible	D although
B crucial	E so
C trivial	F plus

4. Although he _____ an image of anti-authoritarianism, Johnny Cash was a frequent visitor to the White House and friends with several presidents during his life.

   - Ⓐ advocated
   - Ⓑ cultivated
   - Ⓒ patronized
   - Ⓓ supported
   - Ⓔ snubbed

5. (i) _____ mushrooms are popular in many cuisines, it is (ii) _____ to eat those found in the wild, as many frequently found mushrooms resemble edible mushrooms but are, in fact, (iii) _____.

Blank (i)	Blank (ii)	Blank (iii)
A Considering	D imprudent	G poisonous
B While	E cheaper	H bland
C Because	F ingenuous	I toothsome

6. Though the poet's work was praised highly by critics, sales of his anthologies were (i) _____; it is possible the poor sales were due to his language being too (ii) _____ to be readily understood.

Blank (i)	Blank (ii)
A scanty	D lucid
B robust	E prosaic
C singular	F abstruse

Question 7 is based on the passage below.

Criticisms of the automaticity model of reading acquisition include a lack of focus on comprehension as the ultimate goal of reading. Too much focus on fluency to the neglect of comprehension is a correlative criticism. Miscue analysis, tracking students' errors or "miscues," has demonstrated that even early readers use prediction as well as translation into dialect as they read, thereby using tools outside of those described in the automaticity model. A third criticism is that dyslexic readers, because of the inherent decoding problems they face, necessarily have trouble following the model and sustaining the reading rates recommended for fluency.

7. The passage suggests that all the following are flaws in the automaticity model of reading acquisition EXCEPT

  Ⓐ failure to consider all the methods commonly used by developing readers

  Ⓑ measuring reading ability by fluency

  Ⓒ prioritizing efficiency in reading over understanding

  Ⓓ insufficient research

  Ⓔ its application in groups of readers who have difficulties decoding reading material

Questions 8–10 are based on the passage below.

Toward the end of the 19th century, many scientists thought that all the great scientific discoveries had already been made and that there was not much left to do beyond some "tidying up." Max Planck, born in 1858, turned this notion upside down with his study of black-body radiation. Even in a vacuum, a hot body will tend to come to thermal equilibrium with a colder body by radiative heat transfer. This is the principle by which we derive energy from the sun. However, measurement of black-body radiation frequencies across a range of temperatures resulted in a parabolic curve, which theory in Planck's time could not explain. After many years of work devoted to this problem, Planck succeeded in quantitatively explaining the experimental data; his key insight was that energy comes in small, discrete packets, called quanta. His theory was the birth of what is called quantum mechanics, the revolutionary theory of matter that is fundamental to the modern understanding of physics, chemistry, and molecular biology.

8. Select the sentence that best describes the importance of Max Planck's work to modern science, as described in the passage.

9. Which of the following would best paraphrase the opening sentence?

   Ⓐ By the late 1800s, much of the scientific community felt it had completed the majority of its work and minor revisions were its only remaining task.

   Ⓑ By 1900, few scientists were still making significant discoveries, and most projects were revising current theories.

   Ⓒ At the end of the 19th century, scientists were concerned that they had run out of discoveries to make and could only perfect already proven theories.

   Ⓓ By 1900, the scientific community had declared that it had come to understand the natural laws of the universe.

   Ⓔ At the end of the 19th century, scientists ceased trying to formulate new theories.

10. Which of the following best describes the relationship between the highlighted portions of the passage?

    Ⓐ topic and scope
    Ⓑ theory and debunking
    Ⓒ problem and solution
    Ⓓ hypothesis and analysis
    Ⓔ thesis and synthesis

11. After naturally occurring smallpox was eradicated, the World Health Organization chose to _____ the remaining samples of the virus in hopes that they might be later used in developing the means to combat other viruses.

    A eliminate

    B duplicate

    C preserve

    D retain

    E extirpate

    F cultivate

12. The *Magna Carta* was one of the most _____ political declarations of the Middle Ages because it declared the monarch's powers to be limited by the law; although its practical effects were not immediate, it is commonly seen as the genesis of constitutional law in England.

    A remarkable

    B immense

    C pivotal

    D recondite

    E ancient

    F momentous

13. Though _____ filled the streets, people seemed unconcerned with the appearance of their city.

    A detritus

    B refuge

    C gaudiness

    D bedlam

    E refuse

    F barrenness

14. G. K. Chesterton's sense of humor is exemplified in his often _____ responses to his friend and rival George Bernard Shaw.

    A punctilious

    B vociferous

    C waggish

    D vicious

    E scathing

    F witty

Directions: Each passage in this group is followed by questions based on its content. After reading a passage, choose the best answer(s) to each question. Answer all questions following a passage on the basis of what is stated or implied in that passage.

Questions 15–18 are based on the passage below.

There is an anthropological theory that states that societies may be divided into one of two broad categories by their cultural motivators: shame or guilt. In a shame-based society, the ethical motivations are primarily external; one's behavior is governed based on potential effects on the social group (such as dishonoring one's family). By contrast, guilt-based societies rely more heavily on internal motivations; one's behavior is governed based on a set of internal guidelines. There is no society where one or the other is entirely absent, but the distinction lies in that, based on the accepted values of the society, one will come to be dominant over the other. It would seem that early Medieval Europe was primarily a shame-based society; indeed, the forms of shame-based motivators in courtly society were extremely highly developed, with express social laws governing various behaviors. This sort of shame may be seen to be divided into many forms, such as positive and negative shame; that is, prospective and retrospective (knowledge of the honor one will accrue or the shame one will avoid through future actions, and humiliation or other punishment after something harmful has been done, respectively), ethical and nonethical (dealing with higher, such as theological and abstract, concepts, and quotidian matters, respectively), and so on. These social structures may also be found in the contemporary tales of the chivalric world. An example of such may be seen in the frequent plot device of the knight committing adultery with the wife of his lord. Adultery with the wife of one's lord is a matter of treason and an explicit moral wrong, and yet the condemnation in these stories seems to focus on the perpetrator's violation of social norms (treason) rather than moral standards (adultery).

15. Read the following statements and select all that apply. Which of the following CANNOT be inferred from the passage?

    [A] Early Medieval Europe was unconcerned with moral codes.

    [B] Some cultures are neither shame-based nor guilt-based.

    [C] Guilt-based societies have few laws.

16. Select the sentence that describes the scope of the passage.

17. Consider the following choices and select all that apply. What can we infer about a society that focuses primarily upon a moral code of right and wrong?

   A It would be guilt-based.
   B It would tolerate adultery.
   C It would not have laws governing behavior.

18. Based on the passage, a society that prizes the harmony of the social group would most likely be

   A guilt-based
   B shame-based
   C extremely permissive
   D governed by a chivalric order
   E bereft of citizens with an internal code of moral right and wrong

Questions 19 and 20 are based on the passage below.

At the atomic scale, all matter exhibits properties commonly associated with both waves and particles. The classic experiment that demonstrates wavelike properties is the double-slit experiment, first performed by Thomas Young at the beginning of the 19th century. If a beam of light passes through two narrow slits and is projected onto a screen behind the slits, a pattern of light and dark fringes can be observed. The explanation for this is based on an analogy with ripples in water. If we drop two stones some distance apart, the ripples start to interfere with each other, sometimes amplifying when two crests or troughs meet, sometimes canceling when a crest meets a trough. A similar explanation holds for interference effects with visible light; the two slits act as independent sources in the same way as do the stones in water. This experiment provided convincing evidence in support of Christian Huygen's wave theory of light, which eventually supplanted the older particle theory of Isaac Newton. However, in the 20th century, Einstein showed that Newton was not entirely wrong. His analysis of the photoelectric effect showed that light could behave as a particle as well as a wave. Surprisingly, electrons, which we tend to think of as particles, also demonstrate interference effects, showing that they too are waves as well as particles.

19. Which of the following best summarizes the findings of Young's experiment, as described in the passage?

    Ⓐ The waves from independent light sources interact with one another in predictable patterns.

    Ⓑ Two light sources can cancel each other out, creating the observed dark fringes.

    Ⓒ Light exhibits properties of both particles and waves.

    Ⓓ Newton's theory was permanently debunked.

    Ⓔ Newton's theory was correct all along.

20. Based on the passage, what would we expect the light fringes in Young's experiment to represent?

   (A) the light particles from both slits landing on the screen
   (B) the amplification created by the combination of both sets of waves of light
   (C) the projection onto the screen where the light is not blocked out by the object with the slits
   (D) the amplification created by light particles
   (E) the projection onto the screen where the light is blocked by the object with the slits

VERBAL REASONING PRACTICE SET 2 ANSWER KEY

1. A
2. D
3. B, D
4. B
5. B, D, G
6. A, F
7. D
8. His theory was the birth of what is called…
9. A
10. C
11. C, D
12. C, F
13. A, E
14. C, F
15. A, B, C
16. It would seem that early Medieval Europe was primarily a shame-based society…
17. A
18. B
19. A
20. B

DIAGNOSE YOUR RESULTS

Diagnostic Tool

Tally up your score and write your results below.

Total

Total Correct: _____ out of 20 correct

By Question Type

Text Completions (questions 1–6) _____ out of 6 correct

Sentence Equivalence (questions 11–14) _____ out of 4 correct

Reading Comprehension (questions 7–10, 15–20) _____ out of 10 correct

Repeat the steps outlined on the Diagnose Your Results page that follows the Verbal Reasoning Practice Set 1 answer key.

VERBAL REASONING PRACTICE SET 2
ANSWERS AND EXPLANATIONS

1. A

Mary is quiet when in groups, so you should look to find a related word. You can thus quickly rule out choices **(B)** *congenial* and **(D)** *gregarious*. Answer choice **(A)** *reticent* properly matches the sense of the second clause, whereas choices **(C)** *brusque* and **(E)** *scurrilous* would require information beyond her being quiet in groups to be good choices.

2. D

The critics do not approve of the band's change, and the word "with" is a straight-ahead road sign here, so look for something that suggests criticism or rejection. This eliminates choices **(A)** *lauding* and **(C)** *tolerating*; furthermore, you know that the reception was strongly negative based on the phrase "universally panned," so you can eliminate choices **(B)** *ignorant of* and **(E)** *apathetic to* because both of these indicate a general lack of interest. This leaves answer choice **(D)** *deriding*, which provides the sense of a strong, negative reaction.

3. B, D

Looking at the sentence and choices, you know that the second word will be some kind of conjunction that connects the two parts of the sentence. You can see from the second part that there were negative effects, while in the first part of the sentence you see mention of industrial advances, suggesting that a contrasting conjunction is likely.

Thus, for the second blank, answer choice **(D)** *although* is an appropriate contrasting conjunction. Choices **(E)** and **(F)** are poor choices because they are contingent on the second clause either being a result of the first or building on the first, rather than contrasting with the first clause.

For the first blank, you can safely rule out choices **(A)** *negligible* and **(C)** *trivial* because we know from the second part of the sentence that the cotton gin had some notable effects. Choice **(B)** *crucial* is the only positive option for the first blank.

4. B

With the road sign "Although," you are given a contrast in this sentence about the way Johnny Cash presented himself—"an image of anti-authoritarianism" versus being closely connected with various U.S. presidents. Judging by the sentence, you would expect a term akin to "promoted," so you can remove **(E)** *snubbed* from the list; furthermore, you know it refers to his own image, not the image of others. Choices **(A)** *advocated*, **(C)** *patronized*, and **(D)** *supported* all imply outward action—to encourage an image of someone or something else. Answer choice **(B)** *cultivated* is the correct choice because it most clearly refers to developing his own image.

5. B, D, G

Three-blank sentences take a little longer to work out. Looking at the choices for the first blank, you can see that it is a conjunction, but you cannot be sure of which until you solve the rest of the sentence. The best place to begin in this sentence is actually at the end—you are given a very useful hint with the detour road sign "but," telling you that blank three will be an antonym to "edible." Looking through the choices, you can see that the correct answer is answer choice **(G)** *poisonous*. While you might not want to eat something **(H)** *bland*, this is not a direct antonym to "edible." Choice **(I)** *toothsome* means "palatable" or "desirable" and is the opposite of what the blank needs.

From here, work backwards to the second blank. Since you now know that you are talking about eating possibly poisonous mushrooms, you can predict that blank two will say that it is "unwise" to do so. Choice **(E)** *cheaper* is irrelevant to the context (and no mention of money is made elsewhere), and choice **(F)** *ingenuous*, meaning "innocent" or "sincere," is unrelated to the sentence. Answer choice **(D)** *imprudent* is a synonym of "unwise" and is therefore the answer you need.

Return to the first blank in the sentence. You are told that mushrooms are popular in many cuisines, and you are looking for an answer that connects the two ideas. Predict roughly "*although* mushrooms are popular in many cuisines, it is imprudent…"; what you are looking for is a conjunction marking this contradicting idea. Answer choice **(B)** *While* is the correct choice. For sentences with three blanks, especially, it is important to reread the sentence with all the blanks filled in: "*While* mushrooms are popular in many cuisines, it is *imprudent* to eat those found in the wild, as many frequently found mushrooms resemble edible mushrooms but are, in fact, *poisonous*." The sentence makes perfect sense.

6. A, F

Within the first half of the sentence, you are given the detour road sign "though" to contrast the high praise with the sales. Thus, choices **(B)** *robust* and **(C)** *singular* cannot be correct because they are too positive. Answer choice **(A)** *scanty*, on the other hand, contrasts appropriately with high praise, and it fits perfectly with "poor sales" later in the sentence.

The second half of the sentence offers a possible explanation for why the sales were poor, suggesting that it was too hard to understand the poet's language, which immediately removes choice **(D)** *lucid*. Choice **(E)** *prosaic* might trip you up; however, answer choice **(F)** *abstruse* is clearly the better choice for the second blank—it is an adjective indicating that the prose is difficult to understand.

7.   D

Reading through the passage, you can determine answer choice **(D)** to be the correct answer, because there is no mention of the amount of research done or needed concerning the automaticity model. Research is out of scope. Choices **(A)**, **(B)**, and **(C)** are explicitly stated in the passage: **(A)** may be found in the description of early readers, and **(B)** and **(C)** may be found in the criticism of focusing on fluency over understanding. Choice **(E)** can be derived from the third criticism about dyslexia, which is that the automaticity model does not account for differences in decoding ability.

8.   His theory was the birth of what is called...

This sentence provides a summary of the importance of his work.

9.   A

While reading the paragraph, paraphrase the text in your head to make sure you understand it. The key aspect of this sentence is that, at the time, there were a number of scientists who believed that the major discoveries had been made and the remaining scientific work was to tweak and perfect current theories. With that in mind, you can look through the options to see which best fits this idea. Answer choice **(A)** is an excellent paraphrase of the sentence. **(B)** is problematic because there is a fundamental difference between scientists believing all the great discoveries to have been made and scientists making few new significant discoveries. You can also reject choices **(C)**, **(D)**, and **(E)** because their description of "scientists" and the "scientific community" as a whole is too broad. The original sentence only states "many scientists," suggesting that there were dissenters, such as Planck.

10.   C

What you must keep in mind here is that you are asked for the relationship between the two highlighted phrases, not their relationship to the passage as a whole. A good way to attack this sort of question is to paraphrase each of the phrases and identify what it is saying on its own. The first phrase states an issue: that the current theory could not explain the parabolic curve scientists observed. The second phrase tells us of Planck's breakthrough discovery of quanta. Thus, you can predict that the answer will tell us the relationship is between the limitations of the current theory and Planck's solution. **(A)** is a trap because it uses words you frequently see elsewhere and are admonished to remember when considering any Reading Comprehension passage. However, *topic and scope* are irrelevant to this question, and choice **(A)** can be dismissed. **(B)** may be tempting because the first highlighted portion does contain the word "theory." However, based on the wording of the first phrase, it is clear that the issue with the current theory was recognized by the scientific community; thus, Planck's solution was not a challenge to a widely accepted belief, and "debunking" is not appropriate. In answer choice **(C)**, you are given *problem and solution*, which matches your prediction and is the correct answer. **(D)** is out of scope; a *hypothesis* is not brought up here, nor is that hypothesis being explained further. **(E)** is incorrect since the first highlighted sentence is not a *thesis*, or summary, of the paragraph, but rather an issue that needs to be addressed.

11. C, D

While you might be tempted to stray toward the answers meaning "destroy" due to the previous mention of eradication and due to the danger of the material (smallpox), you must carefully read through the sentence. It informs us that there is hope that the samples may have further uses, so you know they must be preserved. You can thus reject **(A)** *eliminate* and **(E)** *extirpate*. You are left with two pairs of synonyms, choices **(B)** *duplicate* and **(F)** *cultivate* as well as **(C)** *preserve* and **(D)** *retain*, so you must choose one of the sets. You are able to do this by focusing on what is in the sentence alone—the word "later" suggests saving the samples, not working with them immediately, so answer choices **(C)** and **(D)** are correct.

12. C, F

With strong words like "most," "declarations," and "genesis," the answer will be likewise a word of emphatic meaning. Furthermore, the sentence tells us of the importance of the *Magna Carta*, so you can predict synonyms of "significant" or "revolutionary." Choices **(D)** *recondite* and **(E)** *ancient* are both meaningless in the sentence, and you can eliminate them. Choice **(B)** *immense* can likewise be dismissed because nowhere is the size of the *Magna Carta* described, nor are there any synonyms among the other options. While choice **(A)** *remarkable* may be tempting, both answer choices **(C)** *pivotal* and **(F)** *momentous* connote a significant turning point, which **(A)** does not.

13. A, E

The key here is that the appearance of the city seems to be lacking, so you are looking for words that imply a deficiency in charm or physical beauty. Choice **(D)** *bedlam* could only make sense without the second clause, and choice **(F)** *barrenness* is a lack of something, so it could not fill the streets; furthermore, both are lacking synonyms in the other options. Choice **(C)** *gaudiness* does imply a lack of taste, but it is without a synonym as well. **(A)** *detritus* means "waste" or "debris," which is an excellent option for the blank, and with further investigation you can see it has a synonym in **(E)** *refuse*. **(B)** *refuge* is a trap for the careless, resembling *refuse* and being right below a synonym of *refuse*—be careful when you read the answers!

14. C, F

The words in the blank will describe Chesterton's particular style of humor. You are given a further clue to the answer in the description of Shaw as his "friend and rival." With this description in mind, you can dismiss choices **(B)** *vociferous*, **(D)** *vicious*, and **(E)** *scathing* as behavior unlikely to be shown toward a friend—remember, if the solution would demand further qualification such as "Chesterton was known to be as harsh to his friends as to his critics," then it is highly unlikely to be the correct answer. **(A)** *punctilious* is not a synonym of the remaining two answer choices, **(C)** *waggish* and **(F)** *witty*.

15. A, B, C

You are looking for statements that go beyond what can reasonably be inferred in the passage. **(A)** is a good choice, because while the passage mentions that it was "primarily a shame-based society," there is no mention of a lack of concern with moral codes; further, the passage notes that neither classification of societies is without some influence of the other. **(B)** also cannot be inferred; in fact, it is contradicted in the fourth sentence. As for **(C)**, while the passage mentions the complexity of the social guidelines of shame-based societies, there is no way you can infer that guilt-based societies have few laws. All three of the answers are correct.

16. It would seem that early Medieval Europe was primarily a shame-based society...

This sentence provides us with the particular focus of the passage on Medieval Europe, narrowed down from the topic of shame- and guilt-based societies in general.

17. A

The difference between the two kinds of societies, according to the author, is a matter of internal (guilt) and external (shame) motivators. What you must consider, then, is where a moral code might be placed. You are given one particularly useful clue in the phrase "internal guidelines" in sentence 3, which, even if it lacks the strength of a sense of moral right and wrong, still allows us to classify the society in the question as guilt based. Furthermore, in the example at the end of the passage, it is suggested that "moral standards" are an example of a trait of a guilt based society. The answer is **(A)**. Choice **(B)** is incorrect; don't be distracted by the description at the end of the passage that describes how medieval Europe, a shame-based society, dealt with adultery. Choice **(C)** is beyond the scope of the passage.

18. B

For this question, you must consider the description of the society in the question compared to what you are given in the passage. Early in the passage, you see mention of dishonoring one's family as an example of a damaging effect on the social group. This indicates that the society in the question would be a shame-based society as in the example, and the correct answer is **(B)**. Choice **(C)** is incorrect because there are certainly rules in a shame-based society. Similarly, you can reject **(E)**; it goes beyond the scope of the passage, which does not offer any evidence to suggest that individuals within a society that emphasizes social cohesion do not have an internally regulated morality. **(D)** is incorrect because there is insufficient information to support such an assertion.

19. A

The key to this question lies in the analogy of the ripples in the water, where two troughs or crests amplify each other but one trough and one crest negate each other. Likewise, with the light waves, the two separate light sources produce waves that interact with one another and, like the crests and troughs of the water, have predictable results: the light and dark fringes. Choice **(B)** describes a part of Young's findings, but you must reject it because it does not adequately describe the whole of his findings. Choice **(C)** cannot be the correct answer either, because the passage notes that it was not until Einstein that particle theory was returned to the theory of light. And likewise for choice **(D)**; you are told Einstein proved that Newton's theory was not entirely accurate and so it was not permanently debunked. Similarly, you cannot claim he was entirely correct, so **(E)** is out as well. This leaves choice **(A)**, which matches your prediction.

20. B

The answer, again, comes from the ripple analogy, where two meeting crests are amplified. Thus, choice **(B)** is likely to be the correct answer. You can dismiss **(A)** since Young's experiment is concerned solely with light as a wave, not as a particle, and answer choice **(C)** fails to take into account the purpose of his experiment: separating a single light source into two streams and recombining them on the screen. As for choice **(D)**, amplification of light particles is mentioned as a possibility, but this is out of the scope of the question. Choice **(E)** refers to Huygen's wave theory of light but not Young's experiment. You have a clear answer in choice **(B)**.

VERBAL REASONING PRACTICE SET 3

1. Veteran technical support staff members feel that their services are
_____ by the use of computer programs to do the same work; they claim
that technical support can't be provided procedurally but rather is a case-
by-case effort that requires a skill set built upon training and experience.

   - Ⓐ devalued
   - Ⓑ tarnished
   - Ⓒ ridiculed
   - Ⓓ vituperated
   - Ⓔ impaired

2. The spice saffron is made from the stigma of the *Crocus sativus* plant; the
(i) _____ number of blossoms required to produce saffron and the
(ii) _____ of the flower makes the spice the most expensive in the world.

Blank (i)		Blank (ii)	
A	vast	D	color
B	meager	E	hardiness
C	unique	F	delicacy

3. The field of cryptozoology is the search for animals unknown to science
and those for which we have no scientific attestation; (i) _____ physical
evidence, it relies upon (ii) _____ sightings for proof of creatures such as
the Loch Ness Monster.

Blank (i)		Blank (ii)	
A	ignoring	D	anecdotal
B	lacking	E	imagined
C	needing	F	nominal

4. The humor of Oscar Wilde remains a classic example of _____ wit; his
terse remarks and deadpan delivery belied an acerbic sarcasm and brilliant
insight into the world around him.

   - Ⓐ ostentatious
   - Ⓑ pointed
   - Ⓒ brazen
   - Ⓓ orotund
   - Ⓔ laconic

5. The neglect of the old theater was (i) _____ in the extreme (ii) _____ of the building, which was no longer safe to enter.

Blank (i)	Blank (ii)
A hinted at	D dilapidation
B suggested	E depilation
C manifest	F radiance

6. The countless (i) _____ days left everyone (ii) _____ for the sudden downpour; the deluge brought traffic to a halt as it (iii) _____ the roads.

Blank (i)	Blank (ii)	Blank (iii)
A arid	D waiting	G inundated
B calm	E unprepared	H soaked
C humid	F anxious	I sprayed

Questions 7–10 are based on the passage below.

The origins of the English language can be traced back to the Saxon and other Germanic settlers in Britain beginning in the 5th century CE. The English language's unusual nature can be attributed to the diverse linguistic origins of the groups that contributed to its development and their role in English society. Although English belongs to the Germanic language family and its grammatical and syntactical rules reflect this, English vocabulary can be seen to be from multiple origins. In fact, a large part of the vocabulary was not derived from the Germanic languages at all but is rather of Latin origin. This can be explained by the influence on Old English of Old French and Latin during the Norman Invasion in the 11th century. By the time of the Norman Invasion, Old English was already a language, with both its grammar and vocabulary based in the Germanic language family. However, the establishment of a ruling class who spoke a Romance language caused significant changes in the indigenous tongue. It is also interesting to note that there is a distinct correlation between the length of a word and its origin—most of the shorter words in the English language are derived from the Germanic languages, whereas the longer words are from a Latin background. One theory to explain this is that these more elaborate and complex words were primarily used by the elite after the Norman Invasion—who would have favored a Latin-based (or Romance) vocabulary—whereas words with the same meaning in the Old English were used primarily by the lower classes and thus fell into disuse. Modern English words, then, concerning more complex and theoretical rather than utilitarian ideas (astronomy, poetry, and epistemology), can generally be found to be of Romance origin, whereas more mundane words, such as pronouns and auxiliary verbs, can be traced back to a Germanic origin.

7. Which of the following is implied by the passage?

   Ⓐ English was more heavily influenced by Germanic languages than by Romance languages.

   Ⓑ In the 11th century, English speakers of the lower classes did not discuss abstract, theoretical topics.

   Ⓒ No auxiliary verbs in English can be traced back to a Latin-based origin.

   Ⓓ English owes some of its abnormality to the Norman Invasion.

   Ⓔ Fewer words in English are derived from Latin than from the Germanic languages.

8. Read the following answer choices and select all that apply. The passage suggests that the word "they," a pronoun, would most likely have which of the following origins?

   A Germanic
   B Romance
   C Norse

9. Based on the passage, what is a likely reason why English has not been reclassified as a Romance language?

   (A) It developed as a Germanic language in its first incarnation, Old English.
   (B) The core of the language, its grammar and syntax, is still Germanic.
   (C) A larger portion of the English vocabulary is Germanic rather than Romance.
   (D) The Normans felt an affinity for the local tongue, which was Germanic.
   (E) Neither linguistic heritage has a claim to preeminence.

10. Read the following choices and select all that apply. Which of the following can be inferred from the passage?

    A Searching for meaning based on the Latin root of a word is less likely to be useful in shorter words.
    B The language spoken by the Saxon and Germanic settlers entirely supplanted the indigenous tongue of 5th-century Britain.
    C The discussion of complex ideas during the Norman era in England was primarily the domain of the ruling class.

11. As modern scholarship continues to dim the possibility that Homer was a single historic figure, the question of authorship of his works has been raised; although we might never know who wrote them, scholars still need some way to refer to the author or authors of the *Iliad* and *Odyssey*, so the term "Homeric tradition" has been _____ as a possible new terminology.

    A selected
    B established
    C appropriated
    D bestowed
    E suggested
    F proposed

12. _____ commercial arsenic usage has diminished, its ongoing presence in water and soil continues to be a major public health concern, given the extremely high toxicity of the substance.

     A After
     B Although
     C Inasmuch as
     D Considering
     E While
     F Because

13. Early sewing machines were poorly received by textile workers, who feared the technology would _____ the demand for their skills; despite their protests, the sewing machine became popular both in the factory and in the home.

     A overwhelm
     B diminish
     C obviate
     D mitigate
     E eliminate
     F belittle

14. The protest march quickly turned into a riot, and in the response by police, several people on either side were killed and dozens more wounded; it would later be _____ remembered by both sides as a tragic accident, and no blame would be assigned.

     A indignantly
     B mournfully
     C spitefully
     D bitterly
     E soberly
     F melancholically

Questions 15–17 are based on the passage below.

The term *teleology* refers to the doctrine that things in nature have a final purpose. Thus, an eye is for seeing, a walk for health, a house for shelter, and a book for reading. Little *t* teleology so conceived, though, mustn't be confused with big *t* Teleology, according to which the whole of nature is either progressing, by virtue of some world-historical or cosmic force, toward some overarching purpose or is already the embodiment of some divine plan.

That teleology needn't entail Teleology is a cornerstone of evolutionary theory. From the moment that organic life first appeared on Earth some 4.5 billion years ago, natural selection has been an inexorable, unceasing, and entirely mindless process of winnowing and sifting through a set of design plans. The geological record is littered with plant and animal species falling extinct under the pressures of climatic and geographical changes. Only those designs that natural selection has blindly hit upon and that have worked, designs that are well adapted to the specific environment and that therefore confer upon certain organisms or certain species some ostensible advantage, will be inheritable by their progeny. This implies that there is no Higher End, no Higher Purpose that governs the actions of intelligent and unintelligent life, only local purposes fitting into the materialist picture of "selfish genes" seeking to pass on genetic information to their descendants *ad infinitum*. There is therefore no Teleology from on high, only teleology all the way down.

15. According to the passage, the principal difference between teleology and Teleology could be understood in terms of the difference between

   (A) quality and quantity
   (B) example and concept
   (C) property and object
   (D) cause and effect
   (E) part and whole

16. The primary purpose of the passage is to show how

   Ⓐ new species come into being through a process called natural selection
   Ⓑ evolution represents a change in our comprehension of all forms of life
   Ⓒ evolution through a set of randomly generated, rather than intentional, procedures is possible
   Ⓓ intelligent and sentient creatures are the inevitable results of natural selection
   Ⓔ absolute ignorance works to create living beings much in the same way that absolute wisdom does

17. Read the following choices and select all that apply. Which of the following does the passage cite as a component of evolutionary theory?

   A the fact that Teleology is not necessary for teleology
   B the extinctions of many species
   C the lack of a Higher Purpose for living organisms' behavior

Questions 18–20 are based on the passage below.

John Finnis developed his theory of natural law based on the structure that Thomas Aquinas provided, filling in areas where he felt that Aquinas's theory was lacking; he also amended other aspects of the theory to respond to a world much more culturally diverse than the one in which Aquinas lived. Unlike Aquinas, who gives only a vague account of the first precepts of the natural law, Finnis locates a specific number of basic human goods. Finnis avoids the charge that his theory falls into the "naturalistic fallacy" by asserting that these goods are not moral in themselves but become moral through human participation in them. In addition, these goods are not hierarchical, which allows a much greater range of freedom in choosing actions. Finally, Finnis's theory does not require the presence of God. Though curiosity about the nature of the universe is one of his basic human goods, the actual existence of God is not required by his theory.

Finnis's theory raises as many questions as it answers. While formulating an interesting answer to the "is/ought" problem and giving a much more robust definition of human volition than Aquinas, his solutions create their own problems. His account of the goods is stripped of any method for evaluation. The boundaries of each good are difficult to discern. Further, by asserting that each good is self-evident and equal to all the others, Finnis makes any action taken in furtherance of any of them equivalent morally. Finally, by removing the precepts of natural law from our natural habits and inclinations, placing them instead in self-evident goods, Finnis seems not to be describing our nature at all.

18. Based on the passage, what is the most likely meaning of "good" according to Finnis?

   Ⓐ a physical object, such as foodstuffs or textiles
   Ⓑ morally correct action as determined by God
   Ⓒ an action that helps us achieve a desirable, material end
   Ⓓ something self-evident that we ought to strive to embrace
   Ⓔ something that is naturally occurring

19. Based on the passage, the existence of which of the following would most likely undermine Finnis's definition of "goods"?

   (A) proof of the existence of God
   (B) goods that demand opposing actions
   (C) the demands of our natural desires
   (D) the definition of additional goods
   (E) a method for evaluating goods

20. Read the following answer choices carefully and select all that apply. According to the passage, which of the following is NOT an improvement of Finnis's theory of natural law over Aquinas's?

   [A] avoiding the "naturalistic fallacy"
   [B] removing the necessity of God in his definition of "good"
   [C] curtailing freedom in human actions

VERBAL REASONING PRACTICE SET 3 ANSWER KEY

1. A
2. A, F
3. B, D
4. E
5. C, D
6. A, E, G
7. D
8. A
9. B
10. A
11. E, F
12. B, E
13. C, E
14. B, F
15. C
16. C
17. A, B, C
18. D
19. B
20. C

DIAGNOSE YOUR RESULTS

Diagnostic Tool

Tally up your score and write your results below.

Total

Total Correct: _____ out of 20 correct

By Question Type

Text Completions (questions 1–6) _____ out of 6 correct

Sentence Equivalence (questions 11–14) _____ out of 4 correct

Reading Comprehension (questions 7–10, 15–20) _____ out of 10 correct

Repeat the steps outlined on the Diagnose Your Results page that follows the Verbal Reasoning Practice Set 1 answer key.

VERBAL REASONING PRACTICE SET 3
ANSWERS AND EXPLANATIONS

1. A
The increase in automated support suggests a decline in demand for technical support workers, and the second half of the sentence tells you that you are looking for an answer that indicates that their services are being undervalued. **(B)** *tarnished*, **(C)** *ridiculed*, and **(D)** *vituperated* all suggest, beyond a negative image, a directly hostile one, which is not indicated by the sentence. **(E)** *impaired* might be acceptable from the first part of the sentence alone, but the value of their services implied by the second half can only support **(A)** *devalued*.

2. A, F
The first half of the sentence is just background, so it is from the second half that you must take your clues. It tells us that producing saffron is very costly, so you can anticipate that the number of blossoms required is a large rather than small number. Based on this, you can reject **(C)** *unique* and **(B)** *meager* for the first blank, leaving **(A)** *vast*.

The second blank implies a quality of the flower that makes it rare. The correct choice for the second blank is **(F)** *delicacy*. **(D)** *color* is irrelevant, and **(E)** *hardiness* is the opposite of your prediction.

3. B, D
The hint you are given is that cryptozoology lacks "scientific attestation"; that is, it has no scientific reason to be supported. So for the first blank, you are looking for a word that means "without." **(A)** *ignoring* would mean an intentional rejection of scientific evidence, rather than an absence thereof. **(C)** *needing* would work, but there is no choice for blank (ii) that has to do with physical evidence. Furthermore, "relies upon" points us to a limitation of their evidence. Therefore, **(B)** *lacking* makes the most sense for the first blank.

With regard, again, to scientific attestation, you can infer that the second blank implies that the sightings are not backed by scientific data, so you are looking for a solution that means "unscientific" or "unreliable." **(E)** *imagined* makes little sense, because it implies the sightings are not just inadequate but fictitious. **(D)** *anecdotal* provides us with the sense of unverifiable sightings and completes the first blank with "lacking" for the sense of being without. **(F)** *nominal* does not fit at all, as it means negligible, or in name only.

4. E
Based on the semicolon, you know that the second half of the sentence directly supports the statement made in the first, so you are looking for a word that implies the usage of few words and a dry delivery of his wit. **(A)** *ostentatious* and **(D)** *orotund* can be rejected on the grounds of the terseness and "deadpan delivery" of Wilde's remarks, and the fact that the biting nature of his wit is not readily apparent can

allow us to discount **(B)** *pointed* and **(C)** *brusque*. Checking the remaining option, **(E)** *laconic*, you find that it fits the meaning of the sentence.

5. C, D

The key word here is "extreme," which indicates that you are looking for a word with very strong meaning for the first blank. Furthermore, you know that the building is "no longer safe to enter," so the second blank must refer to some sense of structural decay. Thus, you can expect the full sentence to be something like "The neglect of the old theater was apparent in the extreme deterioration of the building." For the first blank, **(A)** *hinted at* and **(B)** *suggested* can both be eliminated because they are too weak in meaning for "extreme." Furthermore, both words mean the same thing, so neither could be the single correct answer for the first blank. **(C)** *manifest* makes the most sense.

Out of the options for the second blank, **(D)** and **(E)** are very similar-looking words, but only **(D)** *dilapidation* refers to buildings—**(E)** *depilation* refers to hair removal. Always study the words carefully! **(F)** *radiance* is the opposite of what you need.

6. A, E, G

While you expect the final clause, which is preceded by a semicolon, to be related thematically to the rest of the sentence, grammatically it stands on its own. You can therefore figure out the third blank first without needing the other two. The key here is the word "deluge"—you know this is a major rainstorm. Hence, for the third blank, you can reject both **(H)** *soaked* and **(I)** *sprayed* because both are much weaker words than **(G)** *inundated*.

For the second blank, the key clue is "sudden." If it was sudden, then you can assume people were not expecting it—you can thus predict a word synonymous with "not expecting." **(D)** *waiting* and **(F)** *anxious* would both imply people were expecting the downpour; thus, **(E)** *unprepared* is clearly the correct choice.

Finally, for the first blank, this word will be the reason that people were not expecting a sudden storm. **(C)** *humid* doesn't work here, but between **(A)** *arid* and **(B)** *calm*, you may need to pause for a moment. **(B)** *calm* might work—it certainly contrasts with the eventfulness of the weather that followed—but **(A)** *arid* is a better answer because it implies that the weather was specifically very dry—the antithesis of the wetness of the storm. Plugging it all in, "The countless *arid* days left everyone *unprepared* for the sudden downpour; the deluge brought traffic to a halt as it *inundated* the roads." You can see that everything agrees.

7. D

This question is an Inference question. Therefore, we must eliminate the answer choices that don't necessarily follow from the passage. **(A)** is incorrect because we can't say with certainty that Germanic languages had a greater influence than Romance languages did. Yes, the Germanic influence came first and had a greater influence on grammar, but that does not mean its influence on English as a whole is greater. **(B)** is out of scope and extreme. Nothing suggests that the lower classes could *never* discuss abstract theoretical topics. For **(C)**, although we are told most mundane words, like auxiliary verbs, are of Germanic origin, that doesn't mean that *all* auxiliary words must be of Germanic origin. **(E)** is also incorrect because we aren't given any clues as to how many words are derived from each language family. **(D)** is correct because it's directly implied in the passage. The second sentence says that English has an "unusual nature," and the passage goes on to state that this is due to its vocabulary stemming from multiple origins, such as what was brought over by the Norman Invasion.

8.   A

The question states that 'they' is a pronoun, so look in the passage for clues as to where pronouns are likely to be derived. The final sentence explicitly states that English pronouns are of Germanic origin, so you can safely select **(A)** as your answer. Although Old English and Norse are related, this is not mentioned in the passage, and choice **(C)** is meant as a distracter.

9.   B

To answer this question, you are required to make a small inference from the text. The third sentence begins with a detour road sign, "Although," which indicates that the immediately following clause is a fact—in this case that English is a part of the Germanic language family and that the rules governing its structure reflect this. From this you can infer that the structural rules of a language are significant in its classification, which tells you that answer choice **(B)** is correct. **(A)** is factually correct, but there is no indication that the language's first incarnation is related to its current classification, so you cannot accept that as an explanation based on the passage. **(C)** concerns the balance of vocabulary origins between Germanic and Romance, but while the passage does speak of this at length, no mention of number of words as related to the classification of the language is made. **(D)** is not an option, as the Normans regarded English as lower class. **(E)** is incorrect, as the core of the language is noted to be Germanic. **(B)** is the correct choice.

10.   A

As always, you must be careful about what you infer from a passage. For answer choice **(A)**, you would need to find something in the text that would suggest that the shorter the word, the less likely it may be derived from Latin—which you can find in the final two sentences. There is no mention of the indigenous language before the arrival of the Germanic peoples, so you can dismiss **(B)**. **(C)** might seem tempting because the author notes that the words used for complex ideas today are primarily those that were used by the ruling class. However, while discussing complex ideas might seem more likely to be the habit of those with leisure time and education, the passage does not specify anything that would allow us to draw this conclusion, and **(C)** must be rejected.

11. E, F

From the sentence, you learn that scholars are in need of a new "way to refer to the author or authors"; furthermore, judging by the tone and topic of the sentence, you can safely assume that the answers you need will have a neutral tone. While it may seem possible for the solutions to render the phrase "the term *Homeric tradition* has been *rejected*," the straight-ahead road sign "so" renders this unlikely. You can predict that the answers will mean "the term has been put forward." The key to this question is the word "possible" near the end of the sentence. **(A)** *selected* and **(B)** *established* cannot be correct because that would mean the term has been decided upon. **(C)** *appropriated* and **(D)** *bestowed* likewise fail to match our prediction, leaving **(E)** *suggested* and **(F)** *proposed* as the choices that suggest that the term has been offered as an option but no decision has been made. That fits nicely with "possible."

12. B, E

From the meaning of the sentence, you can see that the correct answer choices will render the meaning "commercial arsenic usage has diminished, but its ongoing presence is a major health concern." Because the blank is placed at the start of the first clause, you need a sense of contradiction that gives the meaning "even though." **(A)** *After,* **(C)** *Inasmuch as,* **(D)** *Considering,* and **(F)** *Because* all lack the contradiction you need, leaving only **(B)** *Although* and **(E)** *While,* which are synonyms of each other and match the prediction.

13. C, E

The key to this sentence is to note that the textile workers feared a negative effect on the demand for their skills as a result of the sewing machine. The answer, then, must be indicative of their displeasure with the technology; furthermore, words like "poorly" and "protests" suggest that they felt very strongly about their fear of a decline in their trade, so you must also find words that reflect the strength of their views. **(A)** *overwhelm* is the opposite of what you need and can be rejected. **(B)** *diminish,* **(D)** *mitigate,* and **(F)** *belittle* are all possible choices, but none of these words are strong enough to convey the meaning you are looking for. **(C)** *obviate* and **(E)** *eliminate* suggest an absolute removal of demand for the workers' skills and match both the meaning and the strength of the prediction.

14. B, F

You are told in the final clause that it would be remembered as a "tragic accident" and that no blame was assigned. You are looking for adverbs that reflect this and can expect to find synonyms of "sadly," but you must be careful not to choose answers that suggest vitriol or blame. Based on this, you can see that **(A)** *indignantly,* **(C)** *spitefully,* and **(D)** *bitterly* can all be eliminated. **(B)** *mournfully* is an excellent choice because you often hear about mourning of a tragic accident. **(E)** *soberly,* meaning in this context "clearly," does not have any synonyms among the remaining answers. **(F)** *melancholically* is a direct synonym of **(B)** and matches your predicted answer.

15. C

The difference between teleology and Teleology is mentioned in the first paragraph. To paraphrase, Teleology is the idea that nature is progressing *toward* something, and teleology is the idea that nature progresses *by means of* something. From here you can begin to look at the options for answers. **(A)** *quality and quantity* do not make sense based on your predicted answer—there is no sense of amount in either concept. **(B)** *example and concept* and **(E)** *part and whole* are both inadequate—it may be tempting based on the phrase "teleology so conceived, though, mustn't be confused with." However, this does not suggest that teleology is a type of Teleology. **(C)** *property and object* is a good choice—teleology is something possessed within nature, and Teleology is its goal. **(D)** *cause and effect* also fails to properly describe the relation between the two, suggesting that teleology is a part of a larger Teleology. The passage describes the two as separate ideas, not one as a type of the other.

16. C

As always, begin by examining the passage's topic and scope, the latter of which is the subject of this question. The passage discusses how evolutionary theory rejects the notion of Teleology, instead demonstrating the development of species through the process of natural selection. **(A)** and **(B)** both are part of the description of how evolutionary theory describes the biological history of the world, but neither is the overall scope of the passage. **(C)** states that natural selection, a key part of evolutionary theory, obviates the need for Teleology—which is the focus, that is, the scope, of the passage. **(D)** is an end result but not the overall main argument and thus is incorrect. **(E)** suggests that teleology and Teleology are nearly equivalent, which, according to the passage, is incorrect.

17. A, B, C

This is a Detail question, so each correct answer must be cited somewhere in the passage. Choices **(A)**, **(B)**, and **(C)** are mentioned in the first, fifth, and tenth lines of the second paragraph, respectively, so all three choices are correct.

18. D

Remember, even in weighty passages like these, all the information that you need is in the text. **(A)** *a physical object* is not the right answer because the passage is talking about natural law and human behavior. You can also eliminate **(B)** *morally correct action as determined by God* because the passage specifies that "Finnis's theory does not require the presence of God." **(C)** *action that helps us achieve a desirable, material end* can be rejected for the same reason as **(A)**. Furthermore, you are given an example of one basic human good, according to Finnis: curiosity about the nature of the universe. **(D)** *something self-evident that we ought to strive to embrace* is supported by the text both in the phrase "each good is self-evident" and Finnis's example of how something is made good by human participation. **(E)** *what is naturally occurring* could only be a reasonable possibility based on the repeated usage of the term "natural"; however, "natural law" is a metaphysical concept, and **(E)** is also incorrect.

19. B

The key to answering this question is to bear in mind Finnis's definition of "goods" that you considered in the previous question. You can learn from the passage that they are self-evident and all equal, which points us towards **(B)** *goods that demand opposing actions*—if they are all equally important, then how can we choose between actions that would each further one good while distancing ourselves from the other? **(A)** *proof of the existence of God* is a poor choice, because while his argument does not rely on the existence of God as Aquinas's did, nowhere does the author imply that Finnis's theory hinged on the nonexistence of God. **(C)** *the demands of our natural desires* is likewise incorrect because of the emphasis on human volition and the notion that some actions are inherently "good" and others are not—to give in to your desires would not undermine his definition but simply fail to follow his admonition. **(D)** *the definition of additional goods* would not necessarily weaken his definition so long as the new goods were not in opposition to his already established goods. Similarly, **(E)** *a method for evaluating goods* could help fix a weakness in Finnis's theory rather than undermine it.

20. C

This is a fairly straightforward Reading Comprehension question. It does not require us to make any inferences from the text, just give the text a careful reading to determine whether each answer choice is referred to (and they all are). **(A)** and **(B)** are both listed explicitly under the adaptations Finnis made to strengthen Aquinas's argument, so you can dismiss them. **(C)**, our only remaining option, is correct, as its opposite is one of the adaptations.

PART THREE

Quantitative Reasoning

CHAPTER 9

Introduction to Quantitative Reasoning

OVERVIEW

The Quantitative Reasoning section of the GRE is designed to place most of its emphasis on your ability to reason quantitatively—to read a math problem, understand what it's asking, and solve it. The mathematical concepts tested on the GRE are similar to those tested on the SAT. You will see questions related to arithmetic, algebra, geometry, and data interpretation. There is no trigonometry or calculus on the GRE. The emphasis in the Quantitative Reasoning section is on your ability to reason, using your knowledge of the various topics. The goal is to make the test an accurate indicator of your ability to apply given information, think logically, and draw conclusions. These are skills you will need at the graduate level of study.

In this section of the book, we'll take you through all the types of Quantitative Reasoning questions you'll see on the GRE and give you the strategies you need to answer them quickly and correctly. Also, all of the mathematical concepts you'll encounter on the test are included in the "Math Reference" Appendix at the back of this book. Think of the examples there as building blocks for the questions you will see on the test.

QUANTITATIVE REASONING QUESTION TYPES

The GRE contains two Quantitative Reasoning sections with 20 questions each. Each section will last 35 minutes and be composed of a selection of the following question types:

- Quantitative Comparison
- Problem Solving
- Data Interpretation

The Quantitative Reasoning portion of the GRE draws heavily upon your ability to combine your knowledge of mathematical concepts with your reasoning powers. Specifically, it evaluates your ability to do the following:

- Compare quantities using reasoning
- Solve word problems
- Interpret data presented in charts and graphs

Within each Quantitative Reasoning section on the GRE, you will see an assortment of question types.

PACING STRATEGY

As a multi-stage test, the GRE allows you to move freely backward and forward within each section, which can be a big advantage on Test Day. If you get stuck on a particular question, you can mark it and come back to it later when you have time. You only score points for correct answers, so you don't want to get bogged down on one problem and lose time you could have used to answer several other questions correctly.

You will have 35 minutes to work on each Quantitative Reasoning section. The 20 questions in each section will be an assortment of Quantitative Comparison, Problem Solving, and Data Interpretation items. However, these types are not distributed equally. The chart below shows how many questions you can expect of each question type, as well as the average amount of time you should spend per question type.

	Quantitative Comparison	Problem Solving	Data Interpretation
Number of Questions	approx. 7–8	approx. 9–10	approx. 3
Time per Question	1.5 minutes	1.5–2 minutes	2 minutes

Try to keep these time estimates in mind as you prepare for the test. If you use them as you practice, you will be comfortable keeping to the same amounts of time on Test Day. Additionally, you will be prepared to use the Mark and Review buttons to your advantage while taking the actual test.

To Calculate or Not

An onscreen calculator will be available during the GRE. Numbers can be entered either by clicking on the numbers on the calculator with your mouse or by entering numbers from the keyboard. There are several points to consider about using the calculator on Test Day. A calculator can be a time-saver, and time is immensely important on a standardized test. But while calculators can speed up computations, they can also foster dependence, making it hard for you to spot the shortcuts in GRE questions. Using the calculator for a long, involved computation to answer a question will gobble up your allotted time for that question—and perhaps for several more. You may even make a mistake in your computation, leading to an incorrect answer. Remember, this is a *reasoning* test. The quantitative questions on the GRE are not designed to require lengthy computations.

If that is the case, why is a calculator provided? A calculator can be an asset for the occasional computation that a few questions require. It may prevent an error caused by a freehand calculation. The onscreen calculator provided is a simple four-function calculator. An image of the calculator is provided below, showing the function keys, including the square root key and change-of-sign key.

By not relying on the calculator, you will be free to focus on interpreting numbers and data and using your critical thinking skills. This is the intention of the writers of the test. For example, Problem Solving questions will likely involve more algebra than calculating, and Quantitative Comparison questions will require more reasoning than calculating.

NAVIGATING THE QUANTITATIVE REASONING SECTION OF THIS BOOK

The chapter immediately following this one concerns Math Foundations and Content Review and will review the classic math concepts and topics that you may encounter on the GRE. This section of the book also includes individual chapters on Quantitative Comparison, Problem Solving, and Data Interpretation questions. Each chapter includes an introduction to the relevant question types and then a review with strategies you can follow to answer those questions quickly and correctly. In addition, you'll find a practice set of questions with answers and explanations for each of the question types you'll encounter on the GRE.

Finally, at the end of this section, you'll find the Quantitative Reasoning Practice Sets, three sets of 20 Quantitative Reasoning questions with answers and explanations. Use the Practice Sets to test your skills and pinpoint areas for more focused study. When you are finished with this section of the book, you should be thoroughly prepared for any question you might encounter on the Quantitative Reasoning section of the GRE.

CHAPTER 10

Math Foundations and Content Review

ARITHMETIC

TERMS

Consecutive numbers: Numbers of a certain type, following one another without interruption. Numbers may be consecutive in ascending or descending order. The GRE prefers to test consecutive integers (e.g., −2, −1, 0, 1, 2, 3...), but you may encounter other types of consecutive numbers. For example:

−4, −2, 0, 2, 4, 6... is a series of consecutive even numbers.

−3, 0, 3, 6, 9... is a series of consecutive multiples of 3.

2, 3, 5, 7, 11... is a series of consecutive prime numbers.

Cube: A number raised to the 3rd power. For example $4^3 = (4)(4)(4) = 64$, showing that 64 is the cube of 4.

Decimal: A fraction written in decimal system format. For example, 0.6 is a decimal. To convert a fraction to a decimal, divide the numerator by the denominator. For instance, $\frac{5}{8} = 5 \div 8 = 0.625$.

Decimal system: A numbering system based on the powers of 10. The decimal system is the only numbering system used on the GRE. Each figure, or digit, in a decimal number occupies a particular position, from which it derives its place value.

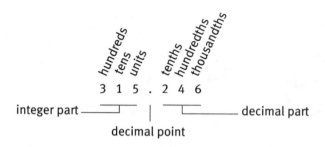

Denominator: The quantity in the bottom of a fraction, representing the whole.

Difference: The result of subtraction.

Digit: One of the numerals 0, 1, 2, 3, 4, 5, 6, 7, 8, or 9. A number can have several digits. For example, the number 542 has three digits: a 5, a 4, and a 2. The number 321,321,000 has nine digits but only four distinct (different) digits: 3, 2, 1, and 0.

Distinct: Different from each other. For example, 12 has three prime factors (2, 2, and 3) but only 2 distinct factors (2 and 3).

Element: One of the members of a set.

Exponent: The number that denotes the power to which another number or variable is raised. The exponent is typically written as a superscript to a number. For example, 5^3 equals (5)(5)(5). The exponent is also occasionally referred to as a "power." For example, 5^3 can be described as "5 to the 3rd power." The product, 125, is "the 3rd power of 5." Exponents may be positive or negative integers or fractions, and they may include variables.

Fraction: The division of a part by a whole. $\dfrac{\text{Part}}{\text{Whole}} = \text{Fraction}.$ For example, $\dfrac{3}{5}$ is a fraction.

Integer: A number without fractional or decimal parts, including positive and negative whole numbers and zero. All integers are multiples of 1. The following are examples of integers: −5, −4, −3, −2, −1, 0, 1, 2, 3, 4, 5.

Number Line: A straight line, extending infinitely in either direction, on which numbers are represented as points. The number line below shows the integers from −3 to 4. Decimals and fractions can also be depicted on a number line, as can irrational numbers, such as $\sqrt{2}$.

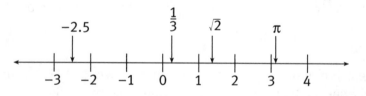

The values of numbers get larger as you move to the right along the number line. Numbers to the right of zero are *positive*; numbers to the left of zero are *negative*.

Zero is neither positive nor negative. Any positive number is larger than any negative number. For example, $-300 < 4$.

Numerator: The quantity in the top of a fraction, representing the part.

Operation: A function or process performed on one or more numbers. The four basic arithmetic operations are addition, subtraction, multiplication, and division.

Part: A specified number of the equal sections that compose a whole.

Product: The result of multiplication.

Sequence: Lists that have an infinite number of terms, in order. The terms of a sequence are often indicated by a letter with a subscript indicating the position of the number in the sequence. For instance, a_3 denotes the third number in a sequence, while a_n indicates the nth term in a sequence.

Set: A well-defined collection of items, typically numbers, objects, or events. The bracket symbols { } are normally used to define sets of numbers. For example, {2, 4, 6, 8} is a set of numbers.

Square: The product of a number multiplied by itself. A squared number has been raised to the 2nd power. For example, $4^2 = (4)(4) = 16$, and 16 is the square of 4.

Sum: The result of addition.

Whole: A quantity that is regarded as a complete unit.

SYMBOLS

$=$	is equal to
$\neq$	is not equal to
$<$	is less than
$>$	is greater than
$\leq$	is less than or equal to
$\geq$	is greater than or equal to
$\div$	divided by
π	pi (the ratio of the circumference of a circle to the diameter)
$\pm$	plus or minus
$\sqrt{}$	square root
$\angle$	angle

RULES OF OPERATION

There are certain mathematical laws governing the results of the four basic operations: addition, subtraction, multiplication, and division. Although you won't need to know the names of these laws for the GRE, you'll benefit from understanding them.

PEMDAS

A string of operations must be performed in proper order. The acronym PEMDAS stands for the correct order of operations:

Parentheses

Exponents

Multiplication

Division
⎫ simultaneously from left to right

Addition

Subtraction
⎫ simultaneously from left to right

If you have trouble remembering PEMDAS, you can think of the mnemonic "Please Excuse My Dear Aunt Sally."

Example:

$$66 (3 - 2) \div 11$$

If you were to perform all the operations sequentially from left to right, without using PEMDAS, you would arrive at an answer of $\dfrac{196}{11}$. But if you perform the operation within the parentheses first, you get $66(1) \div 11 = 66 \div 11 = 6$, which is the correct answer.

Example:

$$30 - 5(4) + \frac{(7 - 3)^2}{8}$$

$$= 30 - 5(4) + \frac{4^2}{8}$$

$$= 30 - 5(4) + \frac{16}{8}$$

$$= 30 - 20 + 2$$

$$= 10 + 2$$

$$= 12$$

Commutative Laws of Addition and Multiplication

Addition and multiplication are both commutative; switching the order of any two numbers being added or multiplied together does not affect the result.

Example:

$$5 + 8 = 8 + 5$$
$$(2)(3)(6) = (6)(3)(2)$$
$$a + b = b + a$$
$$ab = ba$$

Division and subtraction are not commutative; switching the order of the numbers changes the result. For instance, $3 - 2 \neq 2 - 3$; the left side yields a difference of 1, while the right side yields a difference of -1. Similarly, $\frac{6}{2} \neq \frac{2}{6}$; the left side equals 3, while the right side equals $\frac{1}{3}$.

Associative Laws of Addition and Multiplication

Addition and multiplication are also associative; regrouping the numbers does not affect the result.

Example:

$$(3 + 5) + 8 = 3 + (5 + 8) \qquad (a + b) + c = a + (b + c)$$
$$8 + 8 = 3 + 13 \qquad\qquad (ab)c \qquad = a(bc)$$
$$16 = 16$$

The Distributive Law

The distributive law of multiplication allows you to "distribute" a factor over numbers that are added or subtracted. You do this by multiplying that factor by each number in the group.

Example:

$$4(3 + 7) = (4)(3) + (4)(7) \qquad a(b + c) = ab + ac$$
$$4(10) = 12 + 28$$
$$40 = 40$$

The law works for the numerator in division as well.

$$\frac{a + b}{c} = \frac{a}{c} + \frac{b}{c}$$

However, when the sum or difference is in the denominator—that is, when you're dividing by a sum or difference—no distribution is possible.

$\dfrac{9}{4+5}$ is *not* equal to $\dfrac{9}{4} + \dfrac{9}{5}$.

NUMBER PROPERTIES

ADDING AND SUBTRACTING

Numbers can be treated as though they have two parts: a positive or negative sign and a number. Numbers without any sign are understood to be positive.

To add two numbers that have the same sign, add the number parts and keep the sign. Example: To add $(-6) + (-3)$, add 6 and 3 and then attach the negative sign from the original numbers to the sum: $(-6) + (-3) = -9$.

To add two numbers that have different signs, find the difference between the number parts and keep the sign of the number whose number part is larger. Example: To add $(-7) + (+4)$, subtract 4 from 7 to get 3. Because $7 > 4$ (the number part of -7 is greater than the number part of 4), the final sum will be negative: $(-7) + (+4) = -3$.

Subtraction is the opposite of addition. You can rephrase any subtraction problem as an addition problem by changing the operation sign from a minus to a plus and switching the sign on the second number. Example: $8 - 5 = 8 + (-5)$. There's no real advantage to rephrasing if you are subtracting a smaller positive number from a larger positive number. But the concept comes in very handy when you are subtracting a negative number from any other number, a positive number from a negative number or a larger positive number from a smaller positive number.

To subtract a negative number, rephrase as an addition problem and follow the rules for addition of signed numbers. For instance, $9 - (-10) = 9 + 10 = 19$.

To subtract a positive number from a negative number or from a smaller positive number, change the sign of the number that you are subtracting from positive to negative and follow the rules for addition of signed numbers. For example, $(-4) - 1 = (-4) + (-1) = -5$.

MULTIPLICATION AND DIVISION OF POSITIVE AND NEGATIVE NUMBERS

Multiplying or dividing two numbers with the same sign gives a positive result.

Examples:

$$(-4)(-7) = +28$$
$$(-50) \div (-5) = +10$$

Multiplying or dividing two numbers with different signs gives a negative result.

Examples:

$(-2)(+3) = -6$

$8 \div (-4) = -2$

ABSOLUTE VALUE

The absolute value of a number is the value of a number without its sign. It is written as two vertical lines, one on either side of the number and its sign.

Example:

$|-3| = |+3| = 3$

The absolute value of a number can be thought of as the number's distance from zero on the number line. Since both 3 and −3 are 3 units from 0, each has an absolute value of 3. If you are told that $|x| = 5$, x could equal 5 or −5.

PROPERTIES OF ZERO

Adding zero to or subtracting zero from a number does not change the number.

$$x + 0 = x$$
$$0 + x = x$$
$$x - 0 = x$$

Examples:

$5 + 0 = 5$

$0 + (-3) = -3$

$4 - 0 = 4$

Notice, however, that subtracting a number from zero changes the number's sign. It's easy to see why if you rephrase the problem as an addition problem.

Example:

Subtract 5 from 0.

$0 - 5 = -5$. That's because $0 - 5 = 0 + (-5)$, and according to the rules for addition with signed numbers, $0 + (-5) = -5$.

The product of zero and any number is zero.

Examples:

$(0)(z) = 0$

$(z)(0) = 0$

$(0)(12) = 0$

Division by zero is undefined. For GRE purposes, that translates to "It can't be done." Since fractions are essentially division (that is, $\frac{1}{4}$ means $1 \div 4$), any fraction with zero in the denominator is also undefined. So when you are given a fraction that has an algebraic expression in the denominator, be sure that the expression cannot equal zero.

PROPERTIES OF 1 AND −1

Multiplying or dividing a number by 1 does not change the number.

$$(a)(1) = a$$
$$(1)(a) = a$$
$$a \div 1 = a$$

Examples:

$$(4)(1) = 4$$
$$(1)(-5) = -5$$
$$(-7) \div 1 = -7$$

Multiplying or dividing a nonzero number by −1 changes the sign of the number.

$$(a)(-1) = -a$$
$$(-1)(a) = -a$$
$$a \div (-1) = -a$$

Examples:

$$(6)(-1) = -6$$
$$(-3)(-1) = 3$$
$$(-8) \div (-1) = 8$$

FACTORS, MULTIPLES, AND REMAINDERS

Multiples and Divisibility

A *multiple* is the product of a specified number and an integer. For example, 3, 12, and 90 are all multiples of 3: $3 = (3)(1)$; $12 = (3)(4)$; and $90 = (3)(30)$. The number 4 is not a multiple of 3, because there is no integer that can be multiplied by 3 and yield 4.

Multiples do not have to be of integers, but all multiples must be the product of a specific number and an integer. For instance, 2.4, 12, and 132 are all multiples of 1.2: 2.4 = (1.2)(2); 12 = (1.2)(10); and 132 = (1.2)(110).

The concepts of multiples and factors are tied together by the idea of *divisibility*. A number is said to be evenly divisible by another number if the result of the division is an integer with no remainder. A number that is evenly divisible by a second number is also a multiple of the second number.

For example, 52 ÷ 4 = 13, which is an integer. So 52 is evenly divisible by 4, and it's also a multiple of 4.

On some GRE math problems, you will find yourself trying to assess whether one number is evenly divisible by another. You can use several simple rules to save time.

- An integer is divisible by 2 if its last digit is divisible by 2.
- An integer is divisible by 3 if its digits add up to a multiple of 3.
- An integer is divisible by 4 if its last two digits are a multiple of 4.
- An integer is divisible by 5 if its last digit is 0 or 5.
- An integer is divisible by 6 if it is divisible by both 2 and 3.
- An integer is divisible by 9 if its digits add up to a multiple of 9.

Example:

6,930 is a multiple of 2, since 0 is even.

. . . a multiple of 3, since 6 + 9 + 3 + 0 = 18, which is a multiple of 3.

. . . not a multiple of 4, since 30 is not a multiple of 4.

. . . a multiple of 5, since it ends in zero.

. . . a multiple of 6, since it is a multiple of both 2 and 3.

. . . a multiple of 9, since 6 + 9 + 3 + 0 = 18, which is a multiple of 9.

Properties of Odd/Even Numbers

Even numbers are integers that are evenly divisible by 2; *odd* numbers are integers that are not evenly divisible by 2. Integers whose last digit is 0, 2, 4, 6, or 8 are even; integers whose last digit is 1, 3, 5, 7, or 9 are odd. The terms *odd* and *even* apply only to integers, but they may be used for either positive or negative integers. 0 is considered even.

Rules for Odds and Evens

$$\text{Odd} + \text{Odd} = \text{Even}$$
$$\text{Even} + \text{Even} = \text{Even}$$
$$\text{Odd} + \text{Even} = \text{Odd}$$
$$\text{Odd} \times \text{Odd} = \text{Odd}$$
$$\text{Even} \times \text{Even} = \text{Even}$$
$$\text{Odd} \times \text{Even} = \text{Even}$$

Note that multiplying any even number by *any* integer always produces another even number.

It may be easier to use the Picking Numbers strategy in problems that ask you to decide whether some unknown will be odd or even.

Example:

Is the sum of two odd numbers odd or even?

Pick any two odd numbers, for example, 3 and 5: $3 + 5 = 8$. Since the sum of the two odd numbers that you picked is an even number, 8, it's safe to say that the sum of any two odd numbers is even.

Picking Numbers will work in any odds/evens problem, no matter how complicated. The only time you have to be careful is when division is involved, especially if the problem is in Quantitative Comparison format; different numbers may yield different results.

Example:

Integer x is evenly divisible by 2. Is $\frac{x}{2}$ even?

By definition, any multiple of 2 is even, so integer x is even. And $\frac{x}{2}$ must be an integer. But is $\frac{x}{2}$ even or odd? In this case, picking two different even numbers for x can yield two different results. If you let $x = 4$, then $\frac{x}{2} = \frac{4}{2} = 2$, which is even. But if you let $x = 6$, then $\frac{x}{2} = \frac{6}{2} = 3$, which is odd. So $\frac{x}{2}$ could be even or odd—and you wouldn't know that if you picked only one number.

Factors and Primes

The *factors*, or *divisors*, of an integer are the positive integers by which it is evenly divisible (leaving no remainder).

Example:

What are the factors of 36?

36 has nine factors: 1, 2, 3, 4, 6, 9, 12, 18, and 36. We can group these factors in pairs: $(1)(36) = (2)(18) = (3)(12) = (4)(9) = (6)(6)$.

The *greatest common factor*, or greatest common divisor, of a pair of integers is the largest factor that they share.

To find the greatest common factor (GCF), break down both integers into their prime factorizations and multiply all the prime factors they have in common: $36 = (2)(2)(3)(3)$, and $48 = (2)(2)(2)(2)(3)$. What they have in common is two 2s and one 3, so the GCF is $(2)(2)(3) = 12$.

A *prime number* is an integer greater than 1 that has only two factors: itself and 1. The number 1 is not considered a prime, because it is divisible only by itself. The number 2 is the smallest prime number and the only even prime. (Any other even number must have 2 as a factor and therefore cannot be prime.)

Prime Factors

The *prime factorization* of a number is the expression of the number as the product of its prime factors (the factors that are prime numbers).

There are two common ways to determine a number's prime factorization. The rules given above for determining divisibility by certain numbers come in handy in both methods.

Method #1: Work your way up through the prime numbers, starting with 2. (You'll save time in this process, especially when you're starting with a large number, by knowing the first ten prime numbers by heart: 2, 3, 5, 7, 11, 13, 17, 19, 23, and 29.)

Example:

What is the prime factorization of 210?

$$210 = (2)(105)$$

Since 105 is odd, it can't contain another factor of 2. The next smallest prime number is 3. The digits of 105 add up to 6, which is a multiple of 3, so 3 is a factor of 105.

$$210 = (2)(3)(35)$$

The digits of 35 add up to 8, which is not a multiple of 3. But 35 ends in 5, so it is a multiple of the next largest prime number, 5.

$$210 = (2)(3)(5)(7)$$

Since 7 is a prime number, this equation expresses the complete prime factorization of 210.

Method #2: Figure out one pair of factors and then determine their factors, continuing the process until you're left with only prime numbers. Those primes will be the prime factorization.

Example:

What is the prime factorization of 1,050?

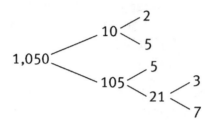

The distinct prime factors of 1,050 are therefore 2, 5, 3, and 7, with the prime number 5 occurring twice in the prime factorization. We usually write out the prime factorization by putting the prime numbers in increasing order. Here, that would be (2)(3)(5)(5)(7). The prime factorization can also be expressed in exponential form: $(2)(3)(5^2)(7)$.

The Least Common Multiple

The *least common multiple* of two or more integers is the smallest number that is a multiple of each of the integers. Here's one quick way to find it:

(1)   Determine the prime factorization of each integer.

(2)   Write out each prime number the maximum number of times that it appears in any one of the prime factorizations.

(3)   Multiply those prime numbers together to get the least common multiple of the original integers.

Example:

What is the least common multiple of 6 and 8?

Start by finding the prime factors of 6 and 8.

$$6 = (2)(3)$$
$$8 = (2)(2)(2)$$

The factor 2 appears three times in the prime factorization of 8, while 3 appears as only a single factor of 6. So the least common multiple of 6 and 8 will be (2)(2)(2)(3), or 24.

Note that the least common multiple of two integers is smaller than their product if they have any factors in common. For instance, the product of 6 and 8 is 48, but their least common multiple is only 24.

In addition to answering questions using the term *least common multiple*, you'll find the concept useful whenever you're adding or subtracting fractions with different denominators.

Remainders

The *remainder* is what is "left over" in a division problem. A remainder is always smaller than the number you are dividing by. For instance, 17 divided by 3 is 5, with a remainder of 2. Likewise, 12 divided by 6 is 2, with a remainder of 0 (since 12 is evenly divisible by 6).

GRE writers often disguise remainder problems. For instance, a problem might state that the slats of a fence are painted in three colors, which appear in a fixed order, such as red, yellow, blue, red, yellow, blue…. You would then be asked something like, "If the first slat is red, what color is the 301st slat?" Since 3 goes into 300 evenly, the whole pattern must finish on the 300th slat and start all over again on the 301st. Therefore, the 301st would be red.

EXPONENTS AND ROOTS

Rules of Operations with Exponents

To multiply two powers with the same base, keep the base and add the exponents together.

Example:

$$2^2 \times 2^3 = (2 \times 2)(2 \times 2 \times 2) = 2^5$$

or

$$2^2 \times 2^3 = 2^{2+3} = 2^5$$

To divide two powers with the same base, keep the base and subtract the exponent of the denominator from the exponent of the numerator.

Example:

$$4^5 \div 4^2 = \frac{(4)(4)(4)(4)(4)}{(4)(4)} = 4^3$$

or

$$4^5 \div 4^2 = 4^{5-2} = 4^3$$

To raise a power to another power, multiply the exponents.

Example:

$$(3^2)^4 = (3 \times 3)^4$$

or

$$(3^2)^4 = (3 \times 3)(3 \times 3)(3 \times 3)(3 \times 3)$$

or

$$(3^2)^4 = 3^{2 \times 4} = 3^8$$

To multiply two powers with different bases but the same power, multiply the bases together and raise to the power.

Example:

$$(3^2)(5^2) = (3 \times 3)(5 \times 5) = (3 \times 5)(3 \times 5) = (3 \times 5)^2 = 15^2$$

A base with a negative exponent indicates the reciprocal of that base to the positive value of the exponent.

Example:

$$5^{-3} = \frac{1}{5^3} = \frac{1}{125}$$

Raising any non-zero number to an exponent of zero equals 1.

Examples:

$$5^0 = 1$$

$$161^0 = 1$$

$$(-6)^0 = 1$$

Commonly Tested Properties of Powers

Many Quantitative Comparison problems test your understanding of what happens when negative numbers and fractions are raised to a power.

Raising a fraction between zero and one to a power produces a smaller result.

Example:

$$\left(\frac{1}{2}\right)^2 = \left(\frac{1}{2}\right)\left(\frac{1}{2}\right) = \frac{1}{4}$$

Raising a negative number to an even power produces a positive result.

Example:

$(-2)^2 = 4$

Raising a negative number to an odd power gives a negative result.

Example:

$(-2)^3 = -8$

Raising an even number to any exponent gives an even number. Raising an odd number to any exponent gives an odd number.

Examples:

$8^5 = 32,768$, an even number

$5^8 = 390,625$, an odd number

Powers of 10

When 10 is raised to an exponent that is a positive integer, that exponent tells how many zeros the number would contain if it were written out.

Example:

Write 10^6 in ordinary notation.

The exponent 6 indicates that you will need six zeros after the 1: 1,000,000. That's because 10^6 means six factors of 10, that is, (10)(10)(10)(10)(10)(10).

To multiply a number by a power of 10, move the decimal point the same number of places to the right as the value of the exponent (or as the number of zeros in that power of 10).

Example:

Multiply 0.029 by 10^3

The exponent is 3, so move the decimal point three places to the right.

$$(0.029)10^3 = 0029. = 29$$

If you had been told to multiply 0.029 by 1,000, you could have counted the number of zeros in 1,000 and done exactly the same thing.

Sometimes you'll have to add zeros as placeholders.

Example:

Multiply 0.029 by 10^6.

Add zeros until you can move the decimal point six places to the right:

$$0.029 \times 10^6 = 0029000. = 29{,}000$$

To divide by a power of 10, move the decimal point the corresponding number of places to the left, inserting zeros as placeholders if necessary.

Example:

Divide 416.03 by 10,000

There are four zeros in 10,000, but only three places to the left of the decimal point. You'll have to insert another zero:

$$416.03 \div 10{,}000 = .041603 = 0.041603$$

By convention, one zero is usually written to the left of the decimal point on the GRE. It's a placeholder and doesn't change the value of the number.

Scientific Notation

Very large numbers (and very small decimals) take up a lot of space and are difficult to work with. So, in some scientific texts, they are expressed in a shorter, more convenient form called *scientific notation*.

For example, 123,000,000,000 would be written in scientific notation as 1.23×10^{11}, and 0.000000003 would be written as 3×10^{-9}. (If you're already familiar with the concept of negative exponents, you'll know that multiplying by 10^{-9} is equivalent to dividing by 10^9.)

To express a number in scientific notation, rewrite it as a product of two factors. The first factor must be greater than or equal to 1 but less than 10. The second factor must be a power of 10.

To translate a number from scientific notation to ordinary notation, use the rules for multiplying and dividing by powers of 10.

Example:

$5.6 \times 10^6 = 5{,}600{,}000$, or 5.6 million

Rules of Operations with Roots and Radicals

A *square root* of any non-negative number x is a number that, when multiplied by itself, yields x. Every positive number has two square roots, one positive and one negative. For instance, the positive square root of 25 is 5, because $5^2 = 25$. The negative square root of 25 is -5, because $(-5)^2$ also equals 25.

By convention, the radical symbol $\sqrt{}$ stands for the positive square root only. Therefore, $\sqrt{9} = 3$ only, even though both 3^2 and $(-3)^2$ equal 9.

When applying the four basic arithmetic operations, radicals (roots written with the radical symbol) are treated in much the same way as variables.

Addition and Subtraction of Radicals

Only like radicals can be added to or subtracted from one another.

Example:

$$2\sqrt{3} + 4\sqrt{2} - \sqrt{2} - 3\sqrt{3} =$$
$$(4\sqrt{2} - \sqrt{2}) + (2\sqrt{3} - 3\sqrt{3}) =$$
$$3\sqrt{2} + (-\sqrt{3}) =$$
$$3\sqrt{2} - \sqrt{3}$$

This expression cannot be simplified any further.

Multiplication and Division of Radicals

To multiply or divide one radical by another, multiply or divide the numbers outside the radical signs, then the numbers inside the radical signs.

Example:

$$(6\sqrt{3})2\sqrt{5} = (6)(2)(\sqrt{3})(\sqrt{5}) = 12\sqrt{15}$$

Example:

$$12\sqrt{15} \div 2\sqrt{5} = \left(\frac{12}{2}\right)\left(\frac{\sqrt{15}}{\sqrt{5}}\right) = 6\sqrt{\frac{15}{5}} = 6\sqrt{3}$$

Simplifying Radicals

If the number inside the radical is a multiple of a perfect square, the expression can be simplified by factoring out the perfect square.

Example:

$$\sqrt{72} = (\sqrt{36})\sqrt{2} = 6\sqrt{2}$$

PROPORTIONS AND MATH FORMULAS

FRACTIONS

The simplest way to understand the meaning of a fraction is to picture the denominator as the number of equal parts into which a whole unit is divided. The numerator represents a certain number of those equal parts.

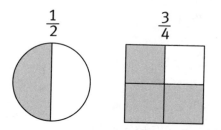

On the left, the shaded portion is one of two equal parts that make up the whole. On the right, the shaded portion is three of four equal parts that make up the whole.

The fraction bar is interchangeable with a division sign. You can divide the numerator of a fraction by the denominator to get an equivalent decimal. However, the numerator and denominator must each be treated as a single quantity.

Example:

Evaluate $\dfrac{5 + 2}{7 - 3}$

You can't just rewrite the fraction as $5 + 2 \div 7 - 3$, because the numerator and the denominator are each considered distinct quantities. Instead, you would rewrite the fraction as $(5 + 2) \div (7 - 3)$. The order of operations (remember PEMDAS?) tells us that operations in parentheses must be performed first.

That gives you $7 \div 4$. Your final answer would be $\dfrac{7}{4}$, $1\dfrac{3}{4}$, or 1.75, depending on the form of the answer choices.

Equivalent Fractions

Since multiplying or dividing a number by 1 does not change the number, multiplying the numerator and denominator of a fraction by the same nonzero number doesn't change the value of the fraction—it's the same as multiplying the entire fraction by 1.

Example:

Change $\dfrac{1}{2}$ into an equivalent fraction with a denominator of 4.

To change the denominator from 2 to 4, you'll have to multiply it by 2. But to keep the value of the fraction the same, you'll also have to multiply the numerator by 2.

$$\frac{1}{2} = \frac{1}{2}\left(\frac{2}{2}\right) = \frac{2}{4}$$

Similarly, dividing the numerator and denominator by the same nonzero number leaves the value of the fraction unchanged.

Example:

Change $\frac{16}{20}$ into an equivalent fraction with a denominator of 10.

To change the denominator from 20 to 10, you'll have to divide it by 2. But to keep the value of the fraction the same, you'll have to divide the numerator by the same number.

$$\frac{16}{20} = \frac{16 \div 2}{20 \div 2} = \frac{8}{10}$$

Reducing (Canceling)

Most fractions on the GRE are in lowest terms. That means that the numerator and denominator have no common factor greater than 1.

For example, the final answer of $\frac{8}{10}$ that we obtained in the previous example was not in lowest terms, because both 8 and 10 are divisible by 2. In contrast, the fraction $\frac{7}{10}$ is in lowest terms, because there is no factor greater than 1 that 7 and 10 have in common. To convert a fraction to its lowest terms, we use a method called reducing, or canceling. To reduce, simply divide any common factors out of both the numerator and the denominator.

Example:

Reduce $\frac{15}{35}$ to lowest terms.

$$\frac{15}{35} = \frac{15 \div 5}{35 \div 5} = \frac{3}{7} \quad \text{(because a 5 cancels out, top and bottom)}$$

The fastest way to reduce a fraction that has very large numbers in both the numerator and denominator is to find the greatest common factor and divide it out of both the top and the bottom.

Example:

Reduce $\dfrac{1,040}{1,080}$ to lowest terms.

$$\frac{1,040}{1,080} = \frac{104}{108} = \frac{52}{54} = \frac{26}{27}$$

Adding and Subtracting Fractions

You cannot add or subtract fractions unless they have the same denominator. If they don't, you'll have to convert each fraction to an equivalent fraction with the least common denominator. Then add or subtract the numerators (not the denominators!) and, if necessary, reduce the resulting fraction to its lowest terms.

Given two fractions with different denominators, the least common denominator is the least common multiple of the two denominators, that is, the smallest number that is evenly divisible by both denominators.

Example:

What is the least common denominator of $\dfrac{2}{15}$ and $\dfrac{3}{10}$?

The least common denominator of the two fractions will be the least common multiple of 15 and 10.

Because $15 = (5)(3)$ and $10 = (5)(2)$, the least common multiple of the two numbers is $(5)(3)(2)$, or 30. That makes 30 the least common denominator of $\dfrac{2}{15}$ and $\dfrac{3}{10}$.

Example:

$$\frac{2}{15} + \frac{3}{10} = ?$$

As we saw in the previous example, the least common denominator of the two fractions is 30. Change each fraction to an equivalent fraction with a denominator of 30.

$$\frac{2}{15}\left(\frac{2}{2}\right) = \frac{4}{30}$$

$$\frac{3}{10}\left(\frac{3}{3}\right) = \frac{9}{30}$$

Then add:

$$\frac{4}{30} + \frac{9}{30} = \frac{13}{30}$$

Since 13 and 30 have no common factor greater than 1, $\dfrac{13}{30}$ is in lowest terms. You can't reduce it further.

Multiplying Fractions

To multiply fractions, multiply the numerators and multiply the denominators.

$$\frac{5}{7}\left(\frac{3}{4}\right) = \frac{15}{28}$$

Multiplying numerator by numerator and denominator by denominator is simple. But it's easy to make careless errors if you have to multiply a string of fractions or work with large numbers. You can minimize those errors by reducing before you multiply.

Example:

Multiply $\left(\dfrac{10}{9}\right)\left(\dfrac{3}{4}\right)\left(\dfrac{8}{15}\right)$.

First, cancel a 5 out of the 10 and the 15, a 3 out of the 3 and the 9, and a 4 out of the 8 and the 4:

$$\left(\frac{\cancel{10}^{2}}{\cancel{9}_{3}}\right)\left(\frac{\cancel{3}^{1}}{\cancel{4}_{1}}\right)\left(\frac{\cancel{8}^{2}}{\cancel{15}_{3}}\right)$$

Then multiply numerators together and denominators together:

$$\left(\frac{2}{3}\right)\left(\frac{1}{1}\right)\left(\frac{2}{3}\right) = \frac{4}{9}$$

Reciprocals

To get the reciprocal of a common fraction, turn the fraction upside-down so that the numerator becomes the denominator, and vice versa. If a fraction has a numerator of 1, the fraction's reciprocal will be equivalent to an integer.

Example:

What is the reciprocal of $\dfrac{1}{25}$?

Inverting the fraction gives you the reciprocal, $\dfrac{25}{1}$. But dividing a number by 1 doesn't change the value of the number.

Since $\dfrac{25}{1}$ equals 25, the reciprocal of $\dfrac{1}{25}$ equals 25.

Dividing Common Fractions

To divide fractions, multiply by the reciprocal of the number or fraction that follows the division sign.

$$\frac{1}{2} \div \frac{3}{5} = \frac{1}{2}\left(\frac{5}{3}\right) = \frac{5}{6}$$

(The operation of division produces the same result as multiplication by the inverse.)

Example:

$$\frac{4}{3} \div \frac{4}{9} = \frac{4}{3}\left(\frac{9}{4}\right) = \frac{36}{12} = 3$$

Comparing Positive Fractions

Given two positive fractions with the same denominator, the fraction with the larger numerator will have the larger value.

Example:

Which is greater, $\frac{3}{8}$ or $\frac{5}{8}$?

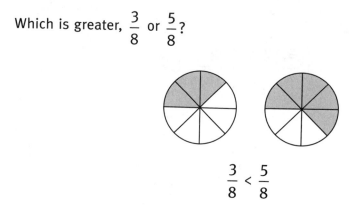

$$\frac{3}{8} < \frac{5}{8}$$

But if you're given two positive fractions with the same numerator but different denominators, the fraction with the smaller denominator will have the larger value.

Example:

Which is greater, $\frac{3}{4}$ or $\frac{3}{8}$?

The diagrams below show two wholes of equal size. The one on the left is divided into 4 equal parts, 3 of which are shaded. The one on the right is divided into 8 equal parts, 3 of which are shaded.

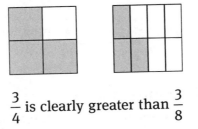

$\frac{3}{4}$ is clearly greater than $\frac{3}{8}$

If neither the numerators nor the denominators are the same, you have three options. You can turn both fractions into their decimal equivalents. Or you can express both fractions in terms of some common denominator and then see which new equivalent fraction has the largest numerator. Or you can cross multiply the numerator of each fraction by the denominator of the other. The greater result will wind up next to the greater fraction.

Example:

Which is greater, $\frac{5}{6}$ or $\frac{7}{9}$?

$$45\,\frac{5}{6}\times\frac{7}{9}\,42$$

Since $45 > 42$, $\frac{5}{6} > \frac{7}{9}$.

Mixed Numbers and Improper Fractions

A *mixed number* consists of an integer and a fraction.

An *improper fraction* is a fraction whose numerator is greater than its denominator. To convert an improper fraction to a mixed number, divide the numerator by the denominator. The number of "whole" times that the denominator goes into the numerator will be the integer portion of the improper fraction; the remainder will be the numerator of the fractional portion.

Example:

Convert $\frac{23}{4}$ to a mixed number.

Dividing 23 by 4 gives you 5 with a remainder of 3, so $\frac{23}{4} = 5\frac{3}{4}$.

To change a mixed number to a fraction, multiply the integer portion of the mixed number by the denominator and add the numerator. This new number is your numerator. The denominator will not change.

Example:

Convert $2\frac{3}{7}$ to a fraction.

$$2\frac{3}{7} = \frac{7(2) + 3}{7} = \frac{17}{7}$$

Properties of Fractions Between −1 and +1

The reciprocal of a fraction between 0 and 1 is greater than both the original fraction and 1.

Example:

The reciprocal of $\frac{2}{3}$ is $\frac{3}{2}$, which is greater than both 1 and $\frac{2}{3}$.

The reciprocal of a fraction between −1 and 0 is less than both the original fraction and −1.

Example:

The reciprocal of $-\frac{2}{3}$ is $-\frac{3}{2}$, or $-1\frac{1}{2}$, which is less than both −1 and $-\frac{2}{3}$.

The square of a fraction between 0 and 1 is less than the original fraction.

Example:

$$\left(\frac{1}{2}\right)^2 = \left(\frac{1}{2}\right)\left(\frac{1}{2}\right) = \frac{1}{4}$$

But the square of any fraction between 0 and −1 is greater than the original fraction, because multiplying two negative numbers gives you a positive product and any positive number is greater than any negative number.

Example:

$$\left(-\frac{1}{2}\right)^2 = \left(-\frac{1}{2}\right)\left(-\frac{1}{2}\right) = \frac{1}{4}$$

Multiplying any positive number by a fraction between 0 and 1 gives a product smaller than the original number.

Example:

$$6\left(\frac{1}{4}\right) = \frac{6}{4} = \frac{3}{2}$$

Multiplying any negative number by a fraction between 0 and 1 gives a product greater than the original number.

Example:

$$(-3)\left(\frac{1}{2}\right) = -\frac{3}{2}$$

DECIMALS

Converting Decimals

It's easy to convert decimals to common fractions, and vice versa. Any decimal fraction is equivalent to some common fraction with a power of 10 in the denominator.

To convert a decimal between 0 and 1 to a fraction, determine the place value of the last nonzero digit and set that value as the denominator. Then use all the digits of the decimal number as the numerator, ignoring the decimal point. Finally, if necessary, reduce the fraction to its lowest terms.

Example:

Convert 0.875 to a fraction in lowest terms.

The last nonzero digit is the 5, which is in the thousandths place. So the denominator of the common fraction will be 1,000. The numerator will be 875: $\frac{875}{1,000}$.

(You can ignore the zero to the left of the decimal point, since there are no nonzero digits to its left; it's just a "placeholder.")

Both 875 and 1,000 contain a factor of 25. Canceling it out leaves you with $\frac{35}{40}$.

Reducing that further by a factor of 5 gives you $\frac{7}{8}$, which is in lowest terms.

To convert a fraction to a decimal, simply divide the numerator by the denominator.

Example:

What is the decimal equivalent of $\frac{4}{5}$?

$$4 \div 5 = 0.8$$

Comparing Decimals

Knowing place values allows you to assess the relative values of decimals.

Example:

Which is greater, 0.254 or 0.3?

Of course, 254 is greater than 3. But $0.3 = \frac{3}{10}$, which is equivalent to $\frac{300}{1,000}$, while 0.254 is equivalent to only $\frac{254}{1,000}$. Since $\frac{300}{1,000} > \frac{254}{1,000}$, 0.3 is greater than 0.254.

Here's the simplest way to compare decimals: add zeros after the last digit to the right of the decimal point in each decimal fraction until all the decimals you're comparing have the same number of digits. Essentially, what you're doing is giving all the fractions the same denominator so that you can just compare their numerators.

Example:

Arrange in order from smallest to largest: 0.7, 0.77, 0.07, 0.707, and 0.077.

The numbers 0.707 and 0.077 end at the third place to the right of the decimal point—the thousandths place. Add zeros after the last digit to the right of the decimal point in each of the other fractions until you reach the thousandths place:

$$0.7 = 0.700 = \frac{700}{1,000}$$

$$0.77 = 0.770 = \frac{770}{1,000}$$

$$0.07 = 0.070 = \frac{70}{1,000}$$

$$0.707 = \frac{707}{1,000}$$

$$0.077 = \frac{77}{1,000}$$

$$\frac{70}{1,000} < \frac{77}{1,000} < \frac{700}{1,000} < \frac{707}{1,000} < \frac{770}{1,000}$$

Therefore, $0.07 < 0.077 < 0.7 < 0.707 < 0.77$.

Estimation and Rounding on the GRE

You should be familiar and comfortable with the practice of "rounding off" numbers. To round off a number to a particular place, look at the digit immediately to the right of that place. If the digit is 0, 1, 2, 3, or 4, don't change the digit that is in the place to which you are rounding. If it is 5, 6, 7, 8, or 9, change the digit in the place to which you are rounding to the next higher digit. Replace all digits to the right of the place to which you are rounding with zeros.

For example, to round off 235 to the tens place, look at the units place. Since it is occupied by a 5, you'll round the 3 in the tens place up to a 4, giving you 240. If you had been rounding off 234, you would have rounded down to the existing 3 in the tens place; that would have given you 230.

Example:

Round off 675,978 to the hundreds place.

The 7 in the tens place means that you will have to round the hundreds place up. Since there is a 9 in the hundreds place, you'll have to change the thousands place as well. Rounding 675,978 to the hundreds place gives you 676,000.

Rounding off large numbers before calculation will allow you to quickly estimate the correct answer.

Estimating can save you valuable time on many GRE problems. But before you estimate, check the answer choices to see how close they are. If they are relatively close together, you'll have to be more accurate than if they are farther apart.

PERCENTS

The word *percent* means "hundredths," and the percent sign, %, means $\frac{1}{100}$.

For example, 25% means $25\left(\frac{1}{100}\right) = \frac{25}{100}$. (Like the division sign, the percent sign evolved from the fractional relationship; the slanted bar in a percent sign represents a fraction bar.)

Percents measure a part-to-whole relationship with an assumed whole equal to 100. The percent relationship can be expressed as $\frac{\text{Part}}{\text{Whole}}(100\%)$. For example, if $\frac{1}{4}$ of a rectangle is shaded, the percent of the rectangle that is shaded is $\frac{1}{4}(100\%) = 25\%$.

Like fractions, percents express the relationship between a specified part and a whole; more specifically, percents express a relationship of a part out of 100. Thus, 25%, $\frac{25}{100}$, and 0.25 are simply different names for the same part-whole relationship.

Translating English to Math in Part-Whole Problems

On the GRE, many fractions and percents appear in word problems. You'll solve the problems by plugging the numbers you're given into some variation of one of the three basic formulas:

$$\frac{\text{Part}}{\text{Whole}} = \textit{Fraction}$$

$$\frac{\text{Part}}{\text{Whole}} = \textit{Decimal}$$

$$\frac{\text{Part}}{\text{Whole}}(100) = \textit{Percent}$$

To avoid careless errors, look for the key words *is* and *of*. *Is* (or *are*) often introduces the part, while *of* almost invariably introduces the whole.

Properties of 100%

Since the percent sign means $\frac{1}{100}$, 100% means $\frac{100}{100}$, or one whole. The key to solving some GRE percent problems is to recognize that all the parts add up to one whole: 100%.

Example:

All 1,000 registered voters in Smithtown are Democrats, Republicans, or independents. If 75% of the registered voters are Democrats and 5% are independents, how many are Republicans?

We calculate that 75% + 5%, or 80% of the 1,000 registered voters, are either Democrats or independents. The three political affiliations together must account for 100% of the voters; thus, the percentage of Republicans must be 100% − 80%, or 20%. Therefore, the number of Republicans must be 20% of 1,000, which is 20% (1,000), or 200.

Multiplying or dividing a number by 100% is just like multiplying or dividing by 1; it doesn't change the value of the original number.

Converting Percents

To change a fraction to its percent equivalent, multiply by 100%.

Example:

What is the percent equivalent of $\frac{5}{8}$?

$$\frac{5}{8}(100\%) = \frac{500}{8}\% = 62\frac{1}{2}\%$$

To change a decimal fraction to a percent, you can use the rules for multiplying by powers of 10. Move the decimal point two places to the right and insert a percent sign.

Example:

What is the percent equivalent of 0.17?

$$0.17 = 0.17 \,(100\%) = 17\%$$

To change a percent to its fractional equivalent, divide by 100%.

Example:

What is the common fraction equivalent of 32%?

$$32\% = \frac{32\%}{100\%} = \frac{8}{25}$$

To convert a percent to its decimal equivalent, use the rules for dividing by powers of 10—just move the decimal point two places to the left.

Example:

What is the decimal equivalent of 32%?

$$32\% = \frac{32\%}{100\%} = \frac{32}{100} = 0.32$$

When you divide a percent by another percent, the percent sign "drops out," just as you would cancel out a common factor.

Example:

$$\frac{100\%}{5\%} = \frac{100}{5} = 20$$

Translation: There are 20 groups of 5% in 100%.

But when you divide a percent by a regular number (not by another percent), the percent sign remains.

Example:

$$\frac{100\%}{5} = 20\%$$

Translation: One-fifth of 100% is 20%.

Common Percent Equivalents

As you can see, changing percents to fractions, or vice versa, is pretty straightforward. But it does take a second or two that you might spend more profitably doing other computations or setting up another GRE math problem. Familiarity with the following common equivalents will save you time.

$$\frac{1}{20} = 5\%$$ $$\frac{1}{2} = 50\%$$

$$\frac{1}{12} = 8\frac{1}{3}\%$$ $$\frac{3}{5} = 60\%$$

$$\frac{1}{10} = 10\%$$ $$\frac{5}{8} = 62\frac{1}{2}\%$$

$$\frac{1}{8} = 12\frac{1}{2}\%$$ $$\frac{2}{3} = 66\frac{2}{3}\%$$

$$\frac{1}{6} = 16\frac{2}{3}\%$$ $$\frac{7}{10} = 70\%$$

$$\frac{1}{5} = 20\%$$ $$\frac{3}{4} = 75\%$$

$$\frac{1}{4} = 25\%$$ $$\frac{4}{5} = 80\%$$

$$\frac{3}{10} = 30\%$$ $$\frac{5}{6} = 83\frac{1}{3}\%$$

$$\frac{1}{3} = 33\frac{1}{3}\%$$ $$\frac{7}{8} = 87\frac{1}{2}\%$$

$$\frac{3}{8} = 37\frac{1}{2}\%$$ $$\frac{9}{10} = 90\%$$

$$\frac{2}{5} = 40\%$$ $$\frac{11}{12} = 91\frac{2}{3}\%$$

Using the Percent Formula to Solve Percent Problems

You can solve most percent problems by plugging the given data into the percent formula:

$$\frac{\text{Part}}{\text{Whole}} (100\%) = \text{Percent}$$

Most percent problems give you two of the three variables and ask for the third.

Example:

Ben spends $30 of his annual gardening budget on seed. If his total annual gardening budget is $150, what percentage of his budget does he spend on seed?

This problem specifies the whole ($150) and the part ($30) and asks for the percentage. Plugging those numbers into the percent formula gives you this:

$$\text{Percent} = \frac{30}{150} \ (100\%) = \frac{1}{5} \ (100\%) = 20\%$$

Ben spends 20% of his annual gardening budget on seed.

Percent Increase and Decrease

When the GRE tests percent increase or decrease, use the formula:

$$\text{Percent increase} = \frac{\text{Increase} \ (100\%)}{\text{Original}}$$

or

$$\text{Percent decrease} = \frac{\text{Decrease} \ (100\%)}{\text{Original}}$$

To find the increase or decrease, just take the difference between the original and the new. Note that the "original" is the base from which change occurs. It may or may not be the first number mentioned in the problem.

Example:

Two years ago, 450 seniors graduated from Inman High School. Last year, 600 seniors graduated. By what percentage did the number of graduating seniors increase?

The original is the figure from the earlier time (two years ago): 450. The increase is 600 − 450, or 150. So the percentage increase is $\frac{150}{450} \ (100\%) = 33\frac{1}{3}\%$.

Example:

If the price of a $120 dress is increased by 25%, what is the new selling price?

To find the new whole, you'll first have to find the amount of increase. The original whole is $120, and the percent increase is 25%. Plugging in, we find that:

$$\frac{\text{Increase}}{120}(100\%) = 25\%$$

$$\frac{\text{Increase}}{120} = \frac{25}{100}$$

$$\frac{\text{Increase}}{120} = \frac{1}{4}$$

$$\text{Increase} = \frac{120}{4}$$

$$\text{Increase} = 30$$

The amount of increase is $30, so the new selling price is $120 + $30, or $150.

Multi-Step Percent Problems

On some difficult problems, you'll be asked to find more than one percent or to find a percent of a percent. Be careful: You can't add percents of different wholes.

Example:

The price of an antique is reduced by 20 percent, and then this price is reduced by 10 percent. If the antique originally cost $200, what is its final price?

The most common mistake in this kind of problem is to reduce the original price by a total of 20% + 10%, or 30%. That would make the final price 70 percent of the original, or 70% ($200) = $140. This is not the correct answer. In this example, the second (10%) price reduction is taken off of the first sale price—the new whole, not the original whole.

To get the correct answer, first find the new whole. You can find it by calculating either $200 − (20% of $200) or 80% ($200). Either way, you will find that the first sale price is $160. That price then has to be reduced by 10%. Either calculate $160 − (10% ($160)) or 90% ($160). In either case, the final price of the antique is $144.

Picking Numbers with Percents

Certain types of percent problems lend themselves readily to the alternative technique of Picking Numbers. These include problems in which no actual values are mentioned, just percents. If you assign values to the percents you are working with, you'll find the problem less abstract.

You should almost always pick 100 in percent problems, because it's relatively easy to find percentages of 100.

Example:

The price of a share of company A's stock fell by 20 percent two weeks ago and by another 25 percent last week to its current price. By what percent of the current price does the share price need to rise in order to return to its original price?

(A) 45%

(B) 55%

(C) $66\frac{2}{3}$%

(D) 75%

(E) 82%

Pick a value for the original price of the stock. Since this is a percent question, picking $100 will make the math easy. The first change in the price of the stock was by 20% of $100, or $20, making the new price $100 − $20 = $80.

The price then fell by another 25%. You know that 25% is the same as $\frac{1}{4}$, and $\frac{1}{4}$ of $80 is $20. Therefore, the current price is $80 − $20 = $60. To return to its original price, the stock needs to rise from $60 to $100, that is, by $100 − $60 = $40. Then $40 is what percent of the current price, $60?

$$\frac{40}{60}\,(100\%) = \frac{2}{3}\,(100\%) = 66\frac{2}{3}\%$$

Percent Word Problems

Percent problems are often presented as word problems. We have already seen how to identify the percent, the part, and the whole in simple percent word problems. Here are some other terms that you are likely to encounter in more complicated percent word problems:

Profit made on an item is the seller's price minus the cost to the seller. If a seller buys an item for $10 and sells it for $12, he has made $2 profit. The percent of the selling price that is profit is as follows:

$$\frac{\text{Profit}}{\text{Original selling price}}\,(100\%) = \frac{\$2}{\$12}\,(100\%) = 16\frac{2}{3}\%$$

A *discount* on an item is the original price minus the reduced price. If an item that usually sells for $20 is sold for $15, the discount is $5. A discount is often represented as a percentage of the original price. In this case, the

$$\text{Percentage discount} = \frac{\text{Discount}}{\text{Original price}} \, (100\%) = \frac{\$5}{\$20} = 25\%$$

The *sale price* is the final price after discount or decrease.

Occasionally, percent problems will involve *interest*. Interest is given as a percent per unit of time, such as 5% per month. The sum of money invested is the *principal*. The most common type of interest you will see is *simple interest*. In simple interest, the interest payments received are kept separate from the principal.

Example:

If an investor invests $100 at 20% simple annual interest, how much does she have at the end of three years?

The principal of $100 yields 20% interest every year. Because 20% of $100 is $20, after three years the investor will have three years of interest, or $60, plus the principal, for a total of $160.

In *compound interest*, the money earned as interest is reinvested. The principal grows after every interest payment received.

Example:

If an investor invests $100 at 20% compounded annually, how much does he have at the end of 3 years?

The first year the investor earns 20% of $100 = $20. So, after one year, he has $100 + $20 = $120.

The second year the investor earns 20% of $120 = $24. So, after two years, he has $120 + $24 = $144.

The third year the investor earns 20% of $144 = $28.80. So, after three years, he has $144 + $28.80 = $172.80.

RATIOS

A *ratio* is the proportional relationship between two quantities. The ratio, or relationship, between two numbers (for example, 2 and 3) may be expressed with a colon between the two numbers (2:3), in words ("the ratio of 2 to 3"), or as a fraction $\frac{2}{3}$.

To translate a ratio in words to numbers separated by a colon, replace *to* with a colon.

To translate a ratio in words to a fractional ratio, use whatever follows the word *of* as the numerator and whatever follows the word *to* as the denominator. For example, if we had to express the ratio *of* glazed doughnuts *to* chocolate doughnuts in a box of doughnuts that contained 5 glazed and 7 chocolate doughnuts, we would do so as $\frac{5}{7}$.

Note that the fraction $\frac{5}{7}$ does not mean that $\frac{5}{7}$ of all the doughnuts are glazed doughnuts. There are $5 + 7$, or 12 doughnuts altogether, so of the doughnuts, $\frac{5}{12}$ are glazed. The $\frac{5}{7}$ ratio merely indicates the proportion of glazed to chocolate doughnuts. For every five glazed doughnuts, there are seven chocolate doughnuts.

Treating ratios as fractions can make computation easier. Like fractions, ratios often require division. And, like fractions, ratios ultimately should be reduced to lowest terms.

Example:

Joe is 16 years old, and Mary is 12 years old. Express the ratio of Joe's age to Mary's age in lowest terms.

The ratio of Joe's age to Mary's age is $\frac{16}{12} = \frac{4}{3}$, or 4:3.

Part:Whole Ratios

In a part:whole ratio, the "whole" is the entire set (for instance, all the workers in a factory), while the "part" is a certain subset of the whole (for instance, all the female workers in the factory).

In GRE ratio question stems, the word *fraction* generally indicates a part:whole ratio. "What fraction of the workers are female?" means "What is the ratio of the number of female workers to the total number of workers?"

Example:

The sophomore class at Milford Academy consists of 15 boys and 20 girls. What fraction of the sophomore class is female?

The following three statements are equivalent:

1. $\frac{4}{7}$ of the sophomores are female.
2. Four out of every seven sophomores are female.
3. The ratio of female sophomores to total sophomores is 4:7.

Ratio vs. Actual Number

Ratios are usually reduced to their simplest form (that is, to lowest terms). If the ratio of men to women in a room is 5:3, you cannot necessarily infer that there are exactly five men and three women.

If you knew the total number of people in the room, in addition to the male-to-female ratio, you could determine the number of men and the number of women in the room. For example, suppose you know that there are 32 people in the room. If the male-to-female ratio is 5 to 3, then the ratio of males to the total is 5:(5 + 3), which is 5:8. You can set up an equation as $\frac{5}{8} = \frac{\text{\# of males in room}}{32}$. Solving, you will find that the number of males in the room is 20.

Example:

The ratio of domestic sales revenues to foreign sales revenues of a certain product is 3:5. What fraction of the total sales revenues comes from domestic sales?

At first, this question may look more complicated than the previous example. You have to convert from a part:part ratio to a part:whole ratio (the ratio of domestic sales revenues to total sales revenues). And you're not given actual dollar figures for domestic or foreign sales. But since all sales are either foreign or domestic, "total sales revenues" must be the sum of the revenues from domestic and foreign sales. You can convert the given ratio to a part:whole ratio because the sum of the parts equals the whole.

Although it's impossible to determine dollar amounts for the domestic, foreign, or total sales revenues from the given information, the 3:5 ratio tells you that of every $8 in sales revenues, $3 comes from domestic sales and $5 from foreign sales.

Therefore, the ratio of domestic sales revenues to total sales revenues is 3:8, or $\frac{3}{8}$.

You can convert a part:part ratio to a part:whole ratio (or vice versa) only if there are no missing parts and no overlap among the parts—that is, if the whole is equal to the sum of the parts.

Example:

In a certain bag, the ratio of the number of red marbles to the number of blue marbles is 3:5. If there are only red and blue marbles in the bag, what is the ratio of the number of red marbles to the total number of marbles?

In this case, you can convert a part-to-part ratio (red marbles to blue marbles) to a part-to-whole ratio (red marbles to all marbles) because you know there are only red and blue marbles in the bag. The ratio of red marbles to the total number of marbles is 3:8.

Example:

Of the 25 people in Fran's apartment building, there are 9 residents who use the roof only for tanning and 8 residents who use the roof only for gardening. The roof is only used by tanners and gardeners.

Quantity A	Quantity B
The ratio of people who use the roof to total residents	17:25

In this question, we do not know if there is any overlap between tanners and gardeners. How many, if any, residents do both activities? Since we don't know, the relationship cannot be determined from the information given.

Ratios of More Than Two Terms

Most of the ratios that you'll see on the GRE have two terms. But it is possible to set up ratios with more than two terms. These ratios express more relationships, and therefore convey more information, than do two-term ratios. However, most of the principles discussed so far with respect to two-term ratios are just as applicable to ratios of more than two terms.

Example:

The ratio of x to y is 5:4. The ratio of y to z is 1:2. What is the ratio of x to z?

We want the y's in the two ratios to equal each other, because then we can combine the x:y ratio and the y:z ratio to form the x:y:z ratio that we need to answer this question. To make the y's equal, we can multiply the second ratio by 4. When we do so, we must perform the multiplication on both components of the ratio. Since a ratio is a constant proportion, it can be multiplied or divided by any number without losing its meaning, as long as the multiplication and division are applied to all the components of the ratio. In this case, we find that the new ratio for y to z is 4:8. We can combine this with the first ratio to find a new x to y to z ratio of 5:4:8. Therefore, the ratio of x to z is 5:8.

RATES

A *rate* is a special type of ratio. Instead of relating a part to the whole or to another part, a rate relates one kind of quantity to a completely different kind. When we talk about rates, we usually use the word *per*, as in "miles per hour," "cost per item," etc. Since *per* means "for one" or "for each," we express the rates as ratios reduced to a denominator of 1.

Speed

The most commonly tested rate on the GRE is speed. This is usually expressed in miles or kilometers per hour. The relationship between speed, distance, and time is given by the formula $\text{Speed} = \dfrac{\text{Distance}}{\text{Time}}$, which can be rewritten two ways: $\text{Time} = \dfrac{\text{Distance}}{\text{Speed}}$ and $\text{Distance} = (\text{Speed})(\text{Time})$.

Anytime you can find two out of the three elements in this equation, you can find the third.

For example, if a car travels 300 miles in 5 hours, it has averaged $\dfrac{300\,\text{miles}}{5\,\text{hours}} = 60\,\text{miles per hour}$. (Note that speeds are usually expressed as averages because they are not necessarily constant. In this example, the car moved at an "average speed" of 60 miles per hour, but probably not at a constant speed of 60 miles per hour.)

Likewise, a rearranged version of the formula can be used to solve for missing speed or time.

Example:

How far do you drive if you travel for 5 hours at 60 miles per hour?

$$\begin{aligned} \text{Distance} &= (\text{Speed})(\text{Time}) \\ \text{Distance} &= (60\,\text{mph})(5\,\text{hours}) \\ \text{Distance} &= 300\,\text{miles} \end{aligned}$$

Example:

How much time does it take to drive 300 miles at 60 miles per hour?

$$\begin{aligned} \text{Time} &= \frac{\text{Distance}}{\text{Speed}} \\ \text{Time} &= \frac{300\,\text{miles}}{60\,\text{mph}} \\ \text{Time} &= 5\,\text{hours} \end{aligned}$$

Other Rates

Speed is not the only rate that appears on the GRE. For instance, you might get a word problem involving liters per minute or cost per unit. All rate problems, however, can be solved using the speed formula and its variants by conceiving of "speed" as "rate" and "distance" as "quantity."

Example:

How many hours will it take to fill a 500-liter tank at a rate of 2 liters per minute?

Plug the numbers into our rate formula:

$$\text{Time} = \frac{\text{Quantity}}{\text{Rate}}$$

$$\text{Time} = \frac{500 \text{ liters}}{2 \text{ liters per minute}}$$

$$\text{Time} = 250 \text{ minutes}$$

Now convert 250 minutes to hours: 250 minutes ÷ 60 minutes per hour = $4\frac{1}{6}$ hours to fill the tank. (As you can see from this problem, GRE Problem Solving questions test your ability to convert minutes into hours and vice versa. Pay close attention to what units the answer choice must use.)

In some cases, you should use proportions to answer rate questions.

Example:

If 350 widgets cost $20, how much will 1,400 widgets cost at the same rate?

Set up a proportion:

$$\frac{\text{Number of widgets}}{\text{Cost}} = \frac{350 \text{ widgets}}{\$20} = \frac{1,400 \text{ widgets}}{\$x}$$

Solving, you will find that $x = 80$.

So, 1,400 widgets will cost $80 at that rate.

Combined Rate Problems

Rates can be added.

Example:

Nelson can mow 200 square meters of lawn per hour. John can mow 100 square meters of lawn per hour. Working simultaneously but independently, how many hours will it take Nelson and John to mow 1,800 square meters of lawn?

Add Nelson's rate to John's rate to find the combined rate.

200 meters per hour + 100 meters per hour = 300 meters per hour.

Divide the total lawn area, 1,800 square meters, by the combined rate, 300 square meters per hour, to find the number of required hours, 6.

Work Problems (Given Hours per Unit of Work)

The work formula can be used to find out how long it takes a number of people working together to complete a task. Let's say we have three people. The first takes a units of time to complete the job, the second b units of time to complete the job, and the third c units of time. If the time it takes all three working together to complete the job is T, then $\frac{1}{a} + \frac{1}{b} + \frac{1}{c} = \frac{1}{T}$.

Example:

John can weed the garden in 3 hours. If Mary can weed the garden in 2 hours, how long will it take them to weed the garden at this rate, working independently?

Set John's time per unit of work as a and Mary's time per unit of work as b. (There is no need for the variable c, since there are only two people.) Plugging in, you find that

$$\frac{1}{3} + \frac{1}{2} = \frac{1}{T}$$
$$\frac{2}{6} + \frac{3}{6} = \frac{1}{T}$$
$$\frac{5}{6} = \frac{1}{T}$$
$$T = \frac{6}{5} \text{ hours}$$

WORK FORMULA FOR TWO

When there are only two people or machines in a combined work problem, we can use a simplified work formula.

$$\frac{1}{a} + \frac{1}{b} = \frac{1}{T}$$
$$(ab)\left(\frac{1}{a} + \frac{1}{b}\right) = \left(\frac{1}{T}\right)(ab)$$
$$\frac{ab}{a} + \frac{ab}{b} = \frac{ab}{T}$$
$$b + a = \frac{ab}{T}$$
$$T(b + a) = \left(\frac{ab}{T}\right)T$$
$$T(b + a) = ab$$
$$T = \frac{ab}{a + b}$$

Here, a = the amount of time it takes person a to complete the job, and b = the amount of time it takes person b to complete the job.

Example:

Let's use the same example from above: John takes 3 hours to weed the garden, and Mary takes 2 hours to weed the same garden. How long will it take them to weed the garden together?

$$\text{Work formula} = \frac{a \times b}{a + b} = \frac{3 \times 2}{3 + 2} = \frac{6}{5}\text{ hours}$$

AVERAGES

The *average* of a group of numbers is defined as the sum of the terms divided by the number of terms.

$$\text{Average} = \frac{\text{Sum of terms}}{\text{Number of terms}}$$

This equation can be rewritten two ways:

$$\text{Number of terms} = \frac{\text{Sum of terms}}{\text{Average}}$$

$$\text{Sum of terms} = (\text{Number of terms})(\text{Average})$$

Thus, any time you have two out of the three values (average, sum of terms, number of terms), you can find the third.

Example:

Henry buys three items costing $2.00, $1.75, and $1.05. What is the average price (arithmetic mean) of the three items? (Don't let the phrase *arithmetic mean* throw you; it's just another term for *average*.)

$$\text{Average} = \frac{\text{Sum of terms}}{\text{Number of terms}}$$

$$\text{Average} = \frac{\$2.0 + \$1.75 + \$1.05}{3}$$

$$\text{Average} = \frac{\$4.80}{3}$$

$$\text{Average} = \$1.60$$

Example:

June pays an average price of $14.50 for 6 articles of clothing. What is the total price of all 6 articles?

$$\text{Sum of terms} = (\text{Average}) (\text{Number of terms})$$
$$\text{Sum of terms} = (\$14.50) (6)$$
$$\text{Sum of terms} = \$87.00$$

Example:

The total weight of the licorice sticks in a jar is 30 ounces. If the average weight of each licorice stick is 2 ounces, how many licorice sticks are there in the jar?

$$\text{Number of terms} = \frac{\text{Sum of terms}}{\text{Average}}$$
$$\text{Number of terms} = \frac{30 \text{ ounces}}{2 \text{ ounces}}$$
$$\text{Number of terms} = 15$$

Using the Average to Find a Missing Number

If you're given the average, the total number of terms, and all but one of the actual numbers, you can find the missing number.

Example:

The average annual rainfall in Boynton for 1976−1979 was 26 inches per year. Boynton received 24 inches of rain in 1976, 30 inches in 1977, and 19 inches in 1978. How many inches of rainfall did Boynton receive in 1979?

You know that total rainfall equals $24 + 30 + 19 +$ (number of inches of rain in 1979).

You know that the average rainfall was 26 inches per year.

You know that there were 4 years.

So, plug these numbers into any of the three expressions of the average formula to find that Sum of terms = (Average)(Number of terms):

$$24 + 30 + 19 + \text{inches in 1979} = (26)(4)$$
$$73 + \text{inches in 1979} = (26)(4)$$
$$73 + \text{inches in 1979} = 104$$
$$\text{inches in 1979} = 31$$

Another Way to Find a Missing Number: The Concept of "Balanced Value"

Another way to find a missing number is to understand that the *sum of the differences between each term and the mean of the set must equal zero.* Plugging in the numbers from the previous problem, for example, we find that:

$$(24 - 26) + (30 - 26) + (19 - 26) + (\text{inches in 1979} - 26) = 0$$
$$(-2) + (4) + (-7) + (\text{inches in 1979} - 26) = 0$$
$$-5 + (\text{inches in 1979} - 26) = 0$$
$$\text{inches in 1979} = 31$$

It may be easier to comprehend why this is true by visualizing a balancing, or weighting, process. The combined distance of the numbers above the average from the mean must be balanced with the combined distance of the numbers below the average from the mean.

Example:

The average of 63, 64, 85, and x is 80. What is the value of x?

Think of each value in terms of its position relative to the average, 80.

63 is 17 less than 80.

64 is 16 less than 80.

85 is 5 greater than 80.

So these three terms are a total of $17 + 16 - 5$, or 28, less than the average. Therefore, x must be 28 greater than the average to restore the balance at 80. So $x = 28 + 80 = 108$.

Average of Consecutive, Evenly Spaced Numbers

When consecutive numbers are evenly spaced, the average is the middle value. For example, the average of consecutive integers 6, 7, and 8 is 7.

If there is an even number of evenly spaced numbers, there is no single middle value. In that case, the average is midway between (that is, the average of) the middle two values. For example, the average of 5, 10, 15, and 20 is 12.5, midway between the middle values 10 and 15.

Note that not all consecutive numbers are evenly spaced. For instance, consecutive prime numbers arranged in increasing order are not evenly spaced. But you can use the handy technique of finding the middle value whenever you have consecutive integers, consecutive odd or even numbers, consecutive multiples of an integer, or any other consecutive numbers that are evenly spaced.

Combining Averages

When there is an equal number of terms in each set, and *only when there is an equal number of terms in each set*, you can average averages.

For example, suppose there are two bowlers and you must find their average score per game. One has an average score per game of 100, and the other has an average score per game of 200. If both bowlers bowled the same number of games, you can average their averages to find their combined average. Suppose they both bowled 4 games. Their combined average will be equally influenced by both bowlers. Hence, their combined average will be the average of 100 and 200. You can find this quickly by remembering that the quantity above the average and the quantity below the average must be equal. Therefore, the average will be halfway between 100 and 200, which is 150. Or, we could solve using our average formula:

$$\text{Average} = \frac{\text{Sum of terms}}{\text{Number of terms}} = \frac{4\,(100) + 4\,(200)}{8} = 150$$

However, if the bowler with the average score of 100 had bowled 4 games and the bowler with the 200 average had bowled 16 games, the combined average would be weighted further toward 200 than toward 100 to reflect the greater influence of the 200 bowler than the 100 bowler upon the total. This is known as a *weighted average*.

Again, you can solve this by using the concept of a balanced average or by using the average formula.

Since the bowler bowling an average score of 200 bowled $\frac{4}{5}$ of the games, the combined average will be $\frac{4}{5}$ of the distance along the number line between 100 and 200, which is 180. Or, you can plug numbers into an average formula to find the following:

$$\text{Average} = \frac{\text{Sum of terms}}{\text{Number of terms}}$$

$$\text{Average} = \frac{4\,(100) + 16\,(200)}{20}$$

$$\text{Average} = \frac{400 + 3{,}200}{20}$$

$$\text{Average} = 180$$

ALGEBRA

ALGEBRAIC TERMS

Variable: A letter or symbol representing an unknown quantity.

Constant (term): A number not multiplied by any variable(s).

Term: A numerical constant; also, the product of a numerical constant and one or more variables.

Coefficient: The numerical constant by which one or more variables are multiplied. The coefficient of $3x^2$ is 3. A variable (or product of variables) without a numerical coefficient, such as z or xy^3, is understood to have a coefficient of 1.

Algebraic expression: An expression containing one or more variables, one or more constants, and possibly one or more operation symbols. In the case of the expression x, there is an implied coefficient of 1. An expression does not contain an equal sign. x, $3x^2 + 2x$, and $\dfrac{7x + 1}{3x^2 - 14}$ are all algebraic expressions.

Monomial: An algebraic expression with only one term. To *multiply monomials*, multiply the coefficients and the variables separately: $2a \times 3a = (2 \times 3)(a \times a) = 6a^2$.

Polynomial: The general name for an algebraic expression with more than one term. An algebraic expression with two terms is called a **binomial**.

Algebraic equation: Two algebraic expressions separated by an equal sign or one algebraic expression separated from a number by an equal sign.

BASIC OPERATIONS

Combining Like Terms

The process of simplifying an expression by adding together or subtracting terms that have the same variable factors is called *combining like terms*.

Example:

Simplify the expression $2x - 5y - x + 7y$.

$2x - 5y - x + 7y = (2x - x) + (7y - 5y) = x + 2y$

Notice that the commutative, associative, and distributive laws that govern arithmetic operations with ordinary numbers also apply to algebraic terms and polynomials.

Adding and Subtracting Polynomials

To *add or subtract polynomials*, combine like terms.

$$(3x^2 + 5x + 7) - (x^2 + 12) = (3x^2 - x^2) + 5x + (7 - 12) = 2x^2 + 5x - 5$$

Factoring Algebraic Expressions

Factoring a polynomial means expressing it as a product of two or more simpler expressions. Common factors can be factored out by using the distributive law.

Example:

Factor the expression $2a + 6ac$.

The greatest common factor of $2a + 6ac$ is $2a$. Using the distributive law, you can factor out $2a$ so that the expression becomes $2a(1 + 3c)$.

Example:

All three terms in the polynomial $3x^3 + 12x^2 - 6x$ contain a factor of $3x$. Pulling out the common factor yields $3x(x^2 + 4x - 2)$.

ADVANCED OPERATIONS

Substitution

Substitution, a process of plugging values into equations, is used to evaluate an algebraic expression or to express it in terms of other variables.

Replace every variable in the expression with the number or quantity you are told is its equivalent. Then carry out the designated operations, remembering to follow the order of operations (PEMDAS).

Example:

Express $\dfrac{a - b^2}{b - a}$ in terms of x if $a = 2x$ and $b = 3$.

Replace every a with $2x$ and every b with 3:

$$\frac{a - b^2}{b - a} = \frac{2x - 9}{3 - 2x}$$

Without more information, you can't simplify or evaluate this expression further.

Solving Equations

When you manipulate any equation, *always do the same thing on both sides of the equal sign*. Otherwise, the two sides of the equation will no longer be equal.

To solve an algebraic equation without exponents for a particular variable, you have to manipulate the equation until that variable is on one side of the equal sign with all numbers or other variables on the other side. You can perform addition, subtraction, or multiplication; you can also perform division, as long as the quantity by which you are dividing does not equal zero.

Typically, at each step of the process, you'll try to isolate the variable by using the reverse of whatever operation has been applied to the variable. For example, in solving the equation $n + 6 = 10$ for n, you have to get rid of the 6 that has been added to the n. You do that by subtracting 6 from both sides of the equation: $n + 6 - 6 = 10 - 6$, so $n = 4$.

Example:

If $4x - 7 = 2x + 5$, what is the value of x?

Start by adding 7 to both sides. This gives us $4x = 2x + 12$. Now subtract $2x$ from both sides. This gives us $2x = 12$. Finally, let's divide both sides by 2. This gives us $x = 6$.

Inequalities

There are two differences between solving an *inequality* (such as $2x < 5$) and solving an *equation* (such as $2x - 5 = 0$).

First, the solution to an inequality is almost always a range of possible values, rather than a single value. You can see the range most clearly by expressing it visually on a number line.

The shaded portion of the number line above shows the set of all numbers between -4 and 0 excluding the endpoints -4 and 0; this range would be expressed algebraically by the inequality $-4 < x < 0$.

The shaded portion of the number line above shows the set of all numbers greater than -1, up to and including 3; this range would be expressed algebraically by the inequality $-1 < x \leq 3$.

The other difference when solving an inequality—and the only thing you really have to remember—is that **if you multiply or divide the inequality by a negative number, you have to reverse the direction of the inequality**. For example, when you multiply both sides of the inequality $-3x < 2$ by -1, you get $3x > -2$.

Example:

Solve for x: $3 - \dfrac{x}{4} \geq 2$

Multiply both sides of the inequality by 4: $12 - x \geq 8$

Subtract 12 from both sides: $-x \geq -4$

Multiply (or divide) both sides by −1 and change the direction of the inequality sign: $x \leq 4$.

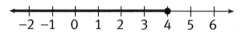

As you can see from the number line, the range of values that satisfies this inequality includes 4 and all numbers less than 4.

Solving for One Unknown in Terms of Another

In general, in order to solve for the value of an unknown, you need as many distinct equations as you have variables. If there are two variables, for instance, you need two distinct equations.

However, some GRE problems do not require you to solve for the numerical value of an unknown. Instead, you are asked to solve for one variable in terms of the other(s). To do so, isolate the desired variable on one side of the equation and move all the constants and other variables to the other side.

Example:

In the formula $z = \dfrac{xy}{a + yb}$, solve for y in terms of x, z, a, and b.

Clear the denominator by multiplying both sides by $a + yb$: $(a + yb)z = xy$

Remove parentheses by distributing: $az + ybz = xy$

Put all terms containing y on one side and all other terms on the other side: $az = xy - ybz$

Factor out the common factor, y: $az = y(x - bz)$

Divide by the coefficient of y to get y alone: $\dfrac{az}{x - bz} = y$

Simultaneous Equations

We've already discovered that you need as many different equations as you have variables to solve for the actual value of a variable. When a single equation contains more than one variable, you can only solve for one variable in terms of the others.

This has important implications for Quantitative Comparisons. To have enough information to compare the two quantities, you usually must have at least as many equations as you have variables.

On the GRE, you will often have to solve two simultaneous equations, that is, equations that give you different information about the same two variables. There are two methods for solving simultaneous equations.

Method 1—Substitution

Step 1: Solve one equation for one variable in terms of the second.

Step 2: Substitute the result back into the other equation and solve.

Example:

If $x - 15 = 2y$ and $6y + 2x = -10$, what is the value of y?

Solve the first equation for x by adding 15 to both sides.

$$x = 2y + 15$$

Substitute $2y + 15$ for x in the second equation:

$$
\begin{aligned}
6y + 2(2y + 15) &= -10 \\
6y + 4y + 30 &= -10 \\
10y &= -40 \\
y &= -4
\end{aligned}
$$

Method 2—Adding to Cancel

Combine the equations in such a way that one of the variables cancels out. To solve the two equations $4x + 3y = 8$ and $x + y = 3$, multiply both sides of the second equation by -3 to get $-3x - 3y = -9$. Now add the two equations; the $3y$ and the $-3y$ cancel out, leaving: $x = -1$.

Before you use either method, make sure you really do have two distinct equations. For example, $2x + 3y = 8$ and $4x + 6y = 16$ are really the same equation in different forms; multiply the first equation by 2, and you'll get the second.

Whichever method you use, you can check the result by plugging both values back into both equations and making sure they fit.

Example:

If $m = 4n - 10$ and $3m + 2n = 26$, find the values of m and n.

Since the first equation already expresses m in terms of n, this problem is best approached by substitution.

Substitute $4n - 10$ for m into $3m + 2n = 26$, and solve for n.

$$
\begin{aligned}
3(4n - 10) + 2n &= 26 \\
12n - 30 + 2n &= 26 \\
14n &= 56 \\
n &= 4
\end{aligned}
$$

Now solve either equation for m by plugging in 4 for n.

$m = 4n - 10$

$m = 4(4) - 10$

$m = 16 - 10$

$m = 6$

So $m = 6$ and $n = 4$.

Example:

If $3x + 3y = 18$ and $x - y = 10$, find the values of x and y.

You could solve this problem by the substitution method. But look what happens if you multiply the second equation by 3 and add it to the first:

$$
\begin{array}{rcl}
3x + 3y & = & 18 \\
+(3x - 3y & = & 30) \\
\hline
6x & = & 48
\end{array}
$$

If $6x = 48$, then $x = 8$. Now you can just plug 8 into either equation in place of x and solve for y. Your calculations will be simpler if you use the second equation: $8 - y = 10$; $-y = 2$; $y = -2$.

Example:

The GRE will sometimes reward you with a shortcut to finding combined value using multiple variables.

If $5x + 5y = 20$, what is the value of $x + y$?

We don't need the value of either variable by itself, but their sum. If we divided both sides by 5, we could find the value of $x + y$.

$5x + 5y = 20$

$5(x + y) = 20$

$x + y = 4$

Example:

If $3x - 5y = 10$ and $6y - 2x = 20$, what is the value of $x + y$?

By aligning the two equations with the same-variable order, you can see a shortcut to adding the two together to find the solution.

$$3x - 5y = 10$$

$$-2x + 6y = 20$$

$$x + y = 30$$

While we don't know the individual values for x or y, we don't need to know them.

Symbolism

Don't panic if you see strange symbols like ★, ✧, and ♦ in a GRE problem.

Problems of this type usually require nothing more than substitution. Read the question stem carefully for a definition of the symbols and for any examples of how to use them. Then, just follow the given model, substituting the numbers that are in the question stem.

Example:

An operation symbolized by ✸ is defined by the equation $x ✸ y = x - \dfrac{1}{y}$. What is the value of $2 ✸ 7$?

The ✸ symbol is defined as a two-stage operation performed on two quantities, which are symbolized in the equation as x and y. The two steps are (1) find the reciprocal of the second quantity and (2) subtract the reciprocal from the first quantity. To find the value of $2 ✸ 7$, substitute the numbers 2 and 7 into the equation, replacing the x (the first quantity given in the equation) with the 2 (the first number given) and the y (the second quantity given in the equation) with the 7 (the second number given). The reciprocal of 7 is $\dfrac{1}{7}$, and subtracting $\dfrac{1}{7}$ from 2 gives you the following:

$$2 - \frac{1}{7} = \frac{14}{7} - \frac{1}{7} = \frac{13}{7}$$

When a symbolism problem involves only one quantity, the operations are usually a little more complicated. Nonetheless, you can follow the same steps to find the correct answer.

Example:

Let $x^\star$ be defined by the equation: $x^\star = \dfrac{x^2}{1-x^2}$. Evaluate $\left(\dfrac{1}{2}\right)^\star$.

$$\left(\frac{1}{2}\right)^\star = \frac{\left(\frac{1}{2}\right)^2}{1-\left(\frac{1}{2}\right)^2} = \frac{\frac{1}{4}}{1-\frac{1}{4}} = \frac{\frac{1}{4}}{\frac{3}{4}} = \frac{1}{4} \times \frac{4}{3} = \frac{1}{3}$$

Every once in a while, you'll see a symbolism problem that doesn't even include an equation. The definitions in this type of problem usually test your understanding of number properties.

Example:

✽x is defined as the largest even number that is less than the negative square root of x. What is the value of ✽81?

(A) −82
(B) −80
(C) −10
(D) −8
(E) 8

Plug in 81 for x and work backward logically. The negative square root of 81 is −9 because $(-9)(-9) = 81$. The largest even number that is less than −9 is −10. (The number part of −8 is smaller than the number part of −9; however, you're dealing with negative numbers, so you have to look for the even number that would be just to the *left* of −9 along the number line.) Thus, the correct answer choice is **(C)** −10.

Sequences

Sequences are lists of numbers. The value of a number in a sequence is related to its position in the list. Sequences are often represented on the GRE as follows:

$$s_1, s_2, s_3, \ldots s_n, \ldots$$

The subscript part of each number gives you the position of each element in the series. s_1 is the first number in the list, s_2 is the second number in the list, and so on.

You will be given a formula that defines each element. For example, if you are told that $s_n = 2n + 1$, then the sequence would be $(2 \times 1) + 1, (2 \times 2) + 1, (2 \times 3) + 1, \ldots$, or 3, 5, 7,…

POLYNOMIALS AND QUADRATICS

The FOIL Method

When two binomials are multiplied, each term is multiplied by each term in the other binomial. This process is often called the *FOIL method*, because it involves adding the products of the First, Outer, Inner, and Last terms. Using the FOIL method to multiply out $(x + 5)(x - 2)$, the product of the first terms is x^2, the product of the outer terms is $-2x$, the product of the inner terms is $5x$, and the product of the last terms is −10. Adding, the answer is $x^2 + 3x - 10$.

Factoring the Product of Binomials

Many of the polynomials that you'll see on the GRE can be factored into a product of two binomials by using the FOIL method backward.

Example:

Factor the polynomial $x^2 - 3x + 2$.

You can factor this into two binomials, each containing an x term. Start by writing down what you know:

$$x^2 - 3x + 2 = (x\ )(x\ )$$

You'll need to fill in the missing term in each binomial factor. The product of the two missing terms will be the last term in the original polynomial: 2. The sum of the two missing terms will be the coefficient of the second term of the polynomial: -3. Find the factors of 2 that add up to -3. Since $(-1) + (-2) = -3$, you can fill the empty spaces with -1 and -2.

Thus, $x^2 - 3x + 2 = (x - 1)(x - 2)$.

Note: Whenever you factor a polynomial, you can check your answer by using FOIL to multiply the factors and obtain the original polynomial.

Factoring the Difference of Two Squares

A common factorable expression on the GRE is the difference of two squares (for example, $a^2 - b^2$). Once you recognize a polynomial as the difference of two squares, you'll be able to factor it automatically, since any polynomial of the form $a^2 - b^2$ can be factored into a product of the form $(a + b)(a - b)$.

Example:

Factor the expression $9x^2 - 1$.

$9x^2 = (3x)^2$ and $1 = 1^2$, so $9x^2 - 1$ is the difference of two squares.

Therefore, $9x^2 - 1 = (3x + 1)(3x - 1)$.

Factoring Polynomials of the Form $a^2 + 2ab + b^2$ or $a^2 - 2ab + b^2$

Any polynomial of this form is the square of a binomial expression, as you can see by using the FOIL method to multiply $(a + b)(a + b)$ or $(a - b)(a - b)$.

To factor a polynomial of this form, check the sign in front of the $2ab$ term. If it's a *plus* sign, the polynomial is equal to $(a + b)^2$. If it's a *minus* sign, the polynomial is equal to $(a - b)^2$.

Example:

Factor the polynomial $x^2 + 6x + 9$.

x^2 and 9 are both perfect squares, and $6x$ is $2(3x)$, which is twice the product of x and 3, so this polynomial is of the form $a^2 + 2ab + b^2$ with $a = x$ and $b = 3$. Since there is a plus sign in front of the $6x$, $x^2 + 6x + 9 = (a + 3)^2$.

Quadratic Equations

A *quadratic equation* is an equation of the form $ax^2 + bx + c = 0$. Many quadratic equations have two solutions. In other words, the equation will be true for two different values of x.

When you see a quadratic equation on the GRE, you'll generally be able to solve it by factoring the algebraic expression, setting each of the factors equal to zero, and solving the resulting equations.

Example:

$x^2 - 3x + 2 = 0$. Solve for x.

To find the solutions, or roots, start by factoring $x^2 - 3x + 2 = 0$ into $(x - 2)(x - 1) = 0$.

The product of two quantities equals zero only if one (or both) of the quantities equals zero. So if you set each of the factors equal to zero, you will be able to solve the resulting equations for the solutions of the original quadratic equation. Setting the two binomials equal to zero gives you this:

$$x - 2 = 0 \text{ or } x - 1 = 0$$

That means that x can equal 2 or 1. As a check, you can plug each of those values in turn into $x^2 - 3x + 2 = 0$, and you'll see that either value makes the equation work.

ALTERNATIVE STRATEGIES FOR MULTIPLE-CHOICE ALGEBRA

Backsolving

On GRE Problem Solving questions, you may find it easier to attack algebra problems by Backsolving. To Backsolve, substitute each answer choice into the equation until you find the one that satisfies the equation.

Example:

If $x^2 + 10x + 25 = 0$, what is the value of x?

Ⓐ 25
Ⓑ 10
Ⓒ 5
Ⓓ −5
Ⓔ −10

The textbook approach to solving this problem would be to recognize the polynomial expression as the square of the binomial $(x + 5)$ and set $x + 5 = 0$. That's the fastest way to arrive at the correct answer of −5.

But you could also plug each answer choice into the equation until you found the one that makes the equation true. Backsolving can be pretty quick if the correct answer is the first choice you plug in, but here, you have to get all the way down to choice **(D)** before you find that $(-5)^2 + 10(-5) + 25 = 0$.

Example:

If $\dfrac{5x}{3} + 9 = \dfrac{x}{6} + 18$, $x =$

Ⓐ 12
Ⓑ 8
Ⓒ 6
Ⓓ 5
Ⓔ 4

To avoid having to try all five answer choices, look at the equation and decide which choice(s), if plugged in for x, would make your calculations easiest. Since x is in the numerators of the two fractions in this equation and the denominators are 3 and 6, try plugging in a choice that is divisible by both 3 and 6. Choices **(A)** and **(C)** are divisible by both numbers, so start with one of them.

Choice **(A)**:

$$20 + 9 = 2 + 18$$
$$29 \neq 20$$

This is not true, so x cannot equal 12.

Choice **(C)**:

$$10 + 9 = 1 + 18$$
$$19 = 19$$

This is correct, so x must equal 6. Therefore, choice **(C)** is correct.

Backsolving may not be the fastest method for a multiple-choice algebra problem, but it's useful if you don't think you'll be able to solve the problem in the conventional way.

Picking Numbers

On other types of multiple-choice algebra problems, especially where the answer choices consist of variables or algebraic expressions, you may want to Pick Numbers to make the problem less abstract. Evaluate the answer choices and the information in the question stem by picking a number and substituting it for the variable wherever the variable appears.

Example:

If $a > 1$, the ratio of $2a + 6$ to $a^2 + 2a - 3$ is

(A) $2a$

(B) $a + 3$

(C) $\dfrac{2}{a - 1}$

(D) $\dfrac{2a}{3(3 - a)}$

(E) $\dfrac{a - 1}{2}$

You can simplify the process by replacing the variable a with a number in each algebraic expression. Since a has to be greater than 1, why not pick 2? Then the expression $2a + 6$ becomes $2(2) + 6$, or 10. The expression $a^2 + 2a - 3$ becomes $2^2 + 2(2) - 3 = 4 + 4 - 3 = 5$.

So now the question reads, "The ratio of 10 to 5 is what?" That's easy enough to answer: 10:5 is the same as $\dfrac{10}{5}$, or 2. Now you can just eliminate any answer choice that doesn't give a result of 2 when you substitute 2 for a. Choice **(A)** gives you 2(2), or 4, so discard it. Choice **(B)** results in 5—also not what you want. Choice **(C)** yields $\dfrac{2}{1}$ or 2. That looks good, but you can't stop here.

If another answer choice gives you a result of 2, you will have to pick another number for a and reevaluate the expressions in the question stem and the choices that worked when you let $a = 2$.

Choice **(D)** gives you $\dfrac{2(2)}{3(3-2)}$ or $\dfrac{4}{3}$, so eliminate choice **(D)**.

Choice **(E)** gives you $\dfrac{2-1}{2}$ or $\dfrac{1}{2}$, so discard choice **(E)**.

Fortunately, in this case, only choice **(C)** works out equal to 2, so it is the correct answer. But remember: When Picking Numbers, always check every answer choice to make sure you haven't chosen a number that works for more than one answer choice.

Using Picking Numbers to Solve for One Unknown in Terms of Another

It is also possible to solve for one unknown in terms of another by Picking Numbers. If the first number you pick doesn't lead to a single correct answer, be prepared to either pick a new number (and spend more time on the problem) or settle for guessing strategically among the answers that you haven't eliminated.

Example:

If $\dfrac{x^2 - 16}{x^2 + 6x + 8} = y$ and $x > -2$, which of the following is an expression for x in terms of y?

(A) $\dfrac{1 + y}{2 - y}$

(B) $\dfrac{2y + 4}{1 - y}$

(C) $\dfrac{4y - 4}{y + 1}$

(D) $\dfrac{2y - 4}{2 + y}$

(E) $\dfrac{y + 4}{y + 1}$

Pick a value for x that will simplify your calculations. If you let x equal 4, then $x^2 - 16 = 4^2 - 16 = 0$, and so the entire fraction on the left side of the equation is equal to zero.

Now, substitute 0 for y in each answer choice in turn. Each choice is an expression for x in terms of y, and since $y = 0$ when $x = 4$, the correct answer will have to give a value of 4 when $y = 0$. Just remember to evaluate all the answer choices, because you might find more than one that gives a result of 4.

Substituting 0 for y in choices **(A)**, **(C)**, and **(D)** yields $\frac{1}{2}$, $-\frac{4}{1}$, and $-\frac{4}{2}$, respectively, so none of those choices can be right. But both **(B)** and **(E)** give results of 4 when you make the substitution; choosing between them will require picking another number.

Again, pick a number that will make calculations easy. If $x = 0$, then $y =$

$$\frac{x^2 - 16}{x^2 + 6x + 8} = \frac{0 - 16}{0 + 0 + 8} = \frac{-16}{8} = -2$$

Therefore, $y = -2$ when $x = 0$. You don't have to try the new value of y in all the answer choices, just in **(B)** and **(E)**. When you substitute -2 for y in choice **(B)**, you get 0. That's what you're looking for, but again, you have to make sure it doesn't work in choice **(E)**. Plugging -2 in for y in **(E)** yields -2 for x, so **(B)** is correct.

STATISTICS

MEDIAN, MODE, AND RANGE

Median: The middle term in a group of terms that are arranged in numerical order. To find the median of a group of terms, first arrange the terms in numerical order. If there is an odd number of terms in the group, then the median is the middle term.

Example:

Bob's test scores in Spanish are 84, 81, 88, 70, and 87. What is his median score?

In increasing order, his scores are 70, 81, 84, 87, and 88. The median test score is the middle one: 84.

If there is an even number of terms in the group, the median is the average of the two middle terms.

Example:

John's test scores in biology are 92, 98, 82, 94, 85, and 97. What is his median score?

In numerical order, his scores are 82, 85, 92, 94, 97, and 98. The median test score is the average of the two middle terms, or $\frac{92 + 94}{2} = 93$.

The median of a group of numbers is often different from its average.

Example:

Caitlin's test scores in math are 92, 96, 90, 85, and 82. Find the difference between Caitlin's median score and the average (arithmetic mean) of her scores.

In ascending order, Caitlin's scores are 82, 85, 90, 92, and 96. The median score is the middle one: 90. Her average score is

$$\frac{82 + 85 + 90 + 92 + 96}{5} = \frac{445}{5} = 89$$

As you can see, Caitlin's median score and her average score are not the same. The difference between them is 90 − 89, or 1.

Mode: The term that appears most frequently in a set.

Example:

The daily temperatures in city Q for one week were 25°, 33°, 26°, 25°, 27°, 31°, and 22°. What was the mode of the daily temperatures in city Q for that week?

Each of the temperatures occurs once on the list, except for 25°, which occurs twice. Since 25° appears more frequently than any other temperature, it is the mode.

A set may have more than one mode if two or more terms appear an equal number of times within the set and each appears more times than any other term.

Example:

The table below represents the score distribution for a class of 20 students on a recent chemistry test. Which score, or scores, are the mode?

Score	# of Students Receiving That Score
100	2
91	1
87	5
86	2
85	1
84	5
80	1
78	2
56	1

The largest number in the second column is 5, which occurs twice. Therefore, there were two mode scores on this test: 87 and 84. Equal numbers of students received those scores, and more students received those scores than any other score.

If every element in the set occurs an equal number of times, then the set has no mode.

COMBINATION

A *combination* question asks you how many unordered subgroups can be formed from a larger group.

Some combination questions on the GRE can be solved without any computation just by counting or listing possible combinations.

Example:

Allen, Betty, and Claire must wash the dishes. They decide to work in shifts of two people. How many shifts will it take before all possible combinations have been used?

It is possible, and not time-consuming, to solve this problem by writing a list. Call Allen "*A*," Betty "*B*," and Claire "*C*." There are three (*AB*, *AC*, *BC*) possible combinations.

The Combination Formula

Some combination questions use numbers that make quick, noncomputational solving difficult. In these cases, use the combination formula $\frac{n!}{k!(n-k)!}$, where n is the number of items in the group as a whole and k is the number of items in each subgroup formed. The ! symbol means factorial (for example, $5! = (5)(4)(3)(2)(1) = 120$).

Example:

The 4 finalists in a spelling contest win commemorative plaques. If there are 7 entrants in the spelling contest, how many possible groups of winners are there?

Plug the numbers into the combination formula, such that n is 7 (the number in the large group) and k is 4 (the number of people in each subgroup formed).

$$\frac{7!}{4!(7-4)!}$$

$$\frac{7!}{4!3!}$$

At this stage, it is helpful to reduce these terms. Since 7 factorial contains all the factors of 4 factorial, we can write 7! as $(7)(6)(5)(4!)$ and then cancel the 4! in the numerator and denominator.

$$\frac{(7)(6)(5)}{(3)(2)(1)} = ?$$

We can reduce further by crossing off the 6 in the numerator and the (3)(2) in the denominator.

$$\frac{(7)(5)}{1} = 35$$

There are 35 potential groups of spelling contest finalists.

When you are asked to find potential combinations from multiple groups, multiply the potential combinations from each group.

Example:

How many groups can be formed consisting of 2 people from room A and 3 people from room B if there are 5 people in room A and 6 people in room B?

Insert the appropriate numbers into the combination formula for each room and then multiply the results. For room A, the number of combinations of 2 in a set of 5 is as follows:

$$\frac{n!}{k!(n-k)!} = \frac{5!}{2!3!} = \frac{(5)(4)(3)(2)(1)}{(2)(1)(3)(2)(1)}$$

Reducing this you get $\frac{(5)(4)}{(2)} = 10$. For room B, the number of combinations of 3 in a set of 6 is as follows:

$$\frac{n!}{k!(n-k)!} = \frac{6!}{3!3!} = \frac{(6)(5)(4)(3)(2)(1)}{(3)(2)(1)(3)(2)(1)}$$

Reducing this, you get $\frac{(6)(5)(4)}{(3)(2)} = 20$.

Multiply these to find that there are (10)(20) = 200 possible groups consisting of 2 people from room A and 3 people from room B.

Sometimes the GRE will ask you to find the number of possible subgroups when choosing one item from a set. In this case, the number of possible subgroups will always equal the number of items in the set.

Example:

Restaurant A has 5 appetizers, 20 main courses, and 4 desserts. If a meal consists of 1 appetizer, 1 main course, and 1 dessert, how many different meals can be ordered at restaurant A?

The number of possible outcomes from each set is the number of items in the set. So there are 5 possible appetizers, 20 possible main courses, and 4 possible desserts. The number of different meals that can be ordered is (5)(20)(4) = 400.

PERMUTATION

Within any group of items or people, there are multiple arrangements, or *permutations*, possible. For instance, within a group of three items (for example: *A*, *B*, *C*), there are six permutations (*ABC*, *ACB*, *BAC*, *BCA*, *CAB*, and *CBA*).

Permutations differ from combinations in that permutations are ordered. By definition, each combination larger than 1 has multiple permutations. On the GRE, a question asking "How many ways/arrangements/orders/schedules are possible?" generally indicates a permutation problem.

To find permutations, think of each place that needs to be filled in a particular arrangement as a blank space. The first place can be filled with any of the items in the larger group. The second place can be filled with any of the items in the larger group except for the one used to fill the first place. The third place can be filled with any of the items in the group except for the two used to fill the first two places, etc.

Example:

In a spelling contest, the winner will receive a gold medal, the second-place finisher will receive a silver medal, the third-place finisher will receive a bronze medal, and the fourth-place finisher will receive a blue ribbon. If there are 7 entrants in the contest, how many different arrangements of award winners are there?

The gold medal can be won by any of 7 people. The silver medal can be won by any of the remaining 6 people. The bronze medal can be won by any of the remaining 5 people. And the blue ribbon can be won by any of the remaining 4 people. Thus, the number of possible arrangements is (7)(6)(5)(4) = 840.

PROBABILITY

Probability is the numerical representation of the likelihood of an event or combination of events. This is expressed as a ratio of the number of desired outcomes to the total number of possible outcomes. Probability is usually expressed as a fraction (for example, "The probability of event A occurring is $\frac{1}{3}$ "), but it can also be expressed in words ("The probability of event *A* occurring is 1 in 3"). The probability of any event occurring cannot exceed 1 (a probability of 1 represents a 100% chance of an event occurring), and it cannot be less than 0 (a probability of 0 represents a 0% chance of an event occurring).

Example:

If you flip a fair coin, what is the probability that it will fall with the "heads" side facing up?

The probability of the coin landing heads up is $\frac{1}{2}$, since there is one outcome you are interested in (landing heads up) and two possible outcomes (heads up or tails up).

Example:

What is the probability of rolling a 5 or a 6 on a six-sided die numbered 1 through 6?

The probability of rolling a 5 or a 6 on a six-sided die numbered 1 through 6 is $\frac{2}{6} = \frac{1}{3}$, since there are 2 desired outcomes (rolling a 5 or a 6) and 6 possible outcomes (rolling a 1, 2, 3, 4, 5, or 6).

The sum of all possible outcomes, desired or otherwise, must equal 1. In other words, if there is a 25% chance that event *A* will occur, then there is a 75% chance that it will not occur. So, to find the probability that an event *will not* occur, subtract the probability that it *will* occur from 1. In the previous example, the probability of not throwing a 5 or a 6 on the die is $1 - \frac{1}{3} = \frac{2}{3}$.

When events are independent, that is, the events do not depend on the other event or events, the probability that several events will all occur is the product of the probability of each event occurring individually.

Example:

A fair coin is flipped twice. What is the probability of its landing with the heads side facing up on both flips?

Multiply the probability for each flip: $\left(\frac{1}{2}\right)\left(\frac{1}{2}\right) = \frac{1}{4}$.

PROBABILITY OF DEPENDENT EVENTS

In some situations, the probability of a later event occurring varies according to the results of an earlier event. In this case, the probability fraction for the later event must be adjusted accordingly.

Example:

A bag contains 10 marbles, 4 of which are blue and 6 of which are red. If 2 marbles are removed without replacement, what is the probability that both marbles removed are red?

The probability that the first marble removed will be red is $\frac{6}{10} = \frac{3}{5}$. The probability that the second marble removed will be red will not be the same, however. There will be fewer marbles overall, so the denominator will be one less. There will also be one fewer red marble. (Note that since we are asking about the odds of picking two red marbles, we are only interested in choosing a second marble if the first was red. Don't concern yourself with situations in which a blue marble is chosen first.) If the first marble removed is red, the probability that the second marble removed will also be red is $\frac{5}{9}$. So the probability that both marbles removed will be red is $\left(\frac{3}{5}\right)\left(\frac{5}{9}\right) = \frac{15}{45} = \frac{1}{3}$.

GEOMETRY

LINES AND ANGLES

A **line** is a one-dimensional geometrical abstraction—infinitely long, with no width. A straight line is the shortest distance between any two points. There is exactly one straight line that passes through any two points.

Example:

In the figure above, $AC = 9$, $BD = 11$, and $AD = 15$. What is the length of BC?

When points are in a line and the order is known, you can add or subtract lengths. Since $AC = 9$ and $AD = 15$, $CD = AD - AC = 15 - 9 = 6$. Now, since $BD = 11$ and $CD = 6$, $BC = BD - CD = 11 - 6 = 5$.

A **line segment** is a section of a straight line of finite length, with two endpoints. A line segment is named for its endpoints, as in segment AB.

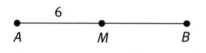

Example:

In the figure above, A and B are the endpoints of the line segment AB, and M is the midpoint ($AM = MB$). What is the length of AB?

Since *AM* is 6, *MB* is also 6, and so *AB* is $6 + 6$, or 12.

Two lines are **parallel** if they lie in the same plane and never intersect regardless of how far they are extended. If line ℓ_1 is parallel to line ℓ_2, we write $\ell_1 \parallel \ell_2$. If two lines are both parallel to a third line, then they are parallel to each other as well.

A **vertex** is the point at which two lines or line segments intersect to form an **angle**. Angles are measured in **degrees** (°).

Angles may be named according to their vertices. Sometimes, especially when two or more angles share a common vertex, an angle is named according to three points: a point along one of the lines or line segments that form the angle, the vertex point, and another point along the other line or line segment. A diagram will sometimes show a letter inside the angle; this letter may also be used to name the angle.

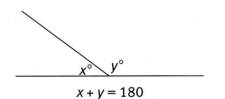

The angle shown in the diagram above could be called $\angle x$, $\angle ABC$, or $\angle B$. (We use a lowercase *x* because *x* is not a point.)

Sum of Angles Around a Point
The sum of the measures of the angles around a point is 360°.

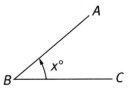

$$a + b + c + d + e = 360$$

Sum of Angles Along a Straight Line
The sum of the measures of the angles on one side of a straight line is 180°. Two angles are *supplementary* to each other if their measures sum to 180°.

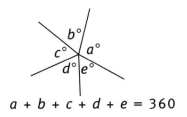

$$x + y = 180$$

Perpendicularity and Right Angles

Two lines are *perpendicular* if they intersect at a 90° angle (a right angle). If line ℓ_1 is perpendicular to line ℓ_2, we write $\ell_1 \perp \ell_2$. If lines ℓ_1, ℓ_2, and ℓ_3 all lie in the same plane, and if $\ell_1 \perp \ell_2$ and $\ell_2 \perp \ell_3$, then $\ell_1 \parallel \ell_3$, as shown in the diagram below.

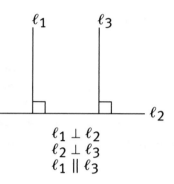

$$\ell_1 \perp \ell_2$$
$$\ell_2 \perp \ell_3$$
$$\ell_1 \parallel \ell_3$$

To find the shortest distance from a point to a line, draw a line segment from the point to the line such that the line segment is perpendicular to the line. Then, measure the length of that segment.

Example:

∠*A* of triangle *ABC* is a right angle. Is side *BC* longer or shorter than side *AB*?

This question seems very abstract, until you draw a diagram of a right triangle, labeling the vertex with the 90° angle as point *A*.

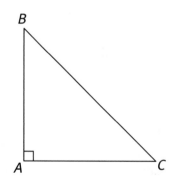

Line segment *AB* has to be the shortest route between point *B* and side *AC*, since side *AB* is perpendicular to side *AC*. If *AB* is the shortest line segment that can join point *B* to side *AC*, *BC* must be longer than *AB*. **Note:** The side opposite the 90° angle, called the *hypotenuse*, is always the longest side of a right triangle.

Two angles are *complementary* to each other if their measures sum to 90°. An *acute angle* measures less than 90°, and an *obtuse angle* measures between 90° and 180°. Two angles are *supplementary* if their measures sum to 180°.

Angle Bisectors

A line or line segment *bisects* an angle if it splits the angle into two smaller, equal angles. Line segment *BD* below bisects ∠*ABC*, and ∠*ABD* has the same measure as ∠*DBC*. The two smaller angles are each half the size of ∠*ABC*.

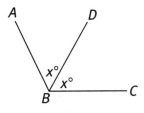

BD bisects ∠*ABC*
∠*ABD* + ∠*DBC* = ∠*ABC*

Adjacent and Vertical Angles

Two intersecting lines form four angles. The angles that are adjacent (next) to each other are *supplementary* because they lie along a straight line. The two angles that are not adjacent to each other are *opposite*, or *vertical*. Opposite angles are equal in measure because each of them is supplementary to the same adjacent angle.

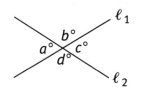

In the diagram above, ℓ_1 intersects ℓ_2 to form angles *a*, *b*, *c*, and *d*. Angles *a* and *c* are opposite, as are angles *b* and *d*. So the measures of angles *a* and *c* are equal to each other, and the measures of angles *b* and *d* are equal to each other. And each angle is supplementary to each of its two adjacent angles.

Angles Around Parallel Lines Intersected by a Transversal

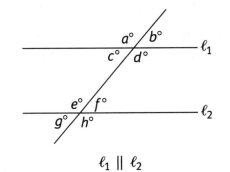

$\ell_1 \parallel \ell_2$

A line that intersects two parallel lines is called a *transversal*. Each of the parallel lines intersects the third line at the same angle. In the figure above, $a = e$.

Since a and e are equal, and since $a = d$ and $e = h$ (because they are opposite angles), $a = d = e = h$. By similar reasoning, $b = c = f = g$.

In short, when two (or more) parallel lines are cut by a transversal, all acute angles formed are equal, all obtuse angles formed are equal, and any acute angle formed is supplementary to any obtuse angle formed.

Example:

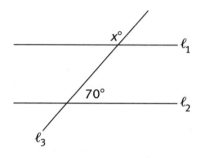

In the diagram above, line ℓ_1 is parallel to line ℓ_2. What is the value of x?

The angle marked $x°$ and the angle adjacent and to the left of the 70° angle on line ℓ_2 are corresponding angles. Therefore, the angle marked $x°$ must be supplementary to the 70° angle. If $70° + x° = 180°$, x must equal 110.

POLYGONS

Important Terms

Polygon: A closed figure whose sides are straight line segments. Families or classes of polygons are named according to their number of sides. A triangle has three sides, a quadrilateral has four sides, a pentagon has five sides, and a hexagon has six sides. Triangles and quadrilaterals are by far the most important polygons on the GRE; other polygons appear only occasionally.

Perimeter: The distance around a polygon; the sum of the lengths of its sides.

Vertex of a polygon: A point where two sides intersect (plural: *vertices*). Polygons are named by assigning each vertex a letter and listing them in order, as in pentagon *ABCDE* below.

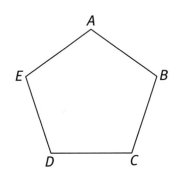

Diagonal of a polygon: A line segment connecting any two nonadjacent vertices.

Regular polygon: A polygon with sides of equal length and interior angles of equal measure.

Small slash marks can provide important information in diagrams of polygons. Sides with the same number of slash marks are equal in length, while angles with the same number of slash marks through circular arcs have the same measure. In the triangle below, for example, $a = b$, and angles X and Z are equal in measure.

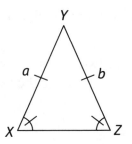

You can figure out the sum of the interior angles of a polygon by dividing the polygon into triangles. Draw diagonals from any vertex to all the nonadjacent vertices. Then, multiply the number of triangles by 180° to get the sum of the interior angles of the polygon. This works because the sum of the interior angles of any triangle is always 180°.

Example:

What is the sum of the interior angles of a pentagon ?

Draw a pentagon (a five-sided polygon) and divide it into triangles, as discussed above.

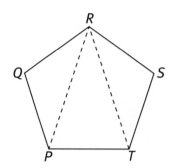

No matter how you've drawn the pentagon, you'll be able to form three triangles. Therefore, the sum of the interior angles of a pentagon is $3 \times 180° = 540°$.

TRIANGLES

Important Terms

Triangle: A polygon with three straight sides and three interior angles.

Right triangle: A triangle with one interior angle of 90° (a right angle).

Hypotenuse: The longest side of a right triangle. The hypotenuse is always opposite the right angle.

Isosceles triangle: A triangle with two equal sides, which are opposite two equal angles. In the figure below, the sides opposite the two 70° angles are equal, so $x = 7$.

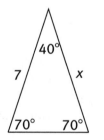

Legs: The two equal sides of an isosceles triangle or the two shorter sides of a right triangle (the ones forming the right angle). **Note:** The third, unequal side of an isosceles triangle is called the *base*.

Equilateral triangle: A triangle whose three sides are all equal in length and whose three interior angles each measure 60°.

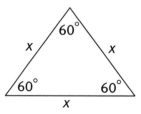

The **altitude,** or **height,** of a triangle is the perpendicular distance from a vertex to the side opposite the vertex. The altitude may fall inside or outside the triangle, or it may coincide with one of the sides.

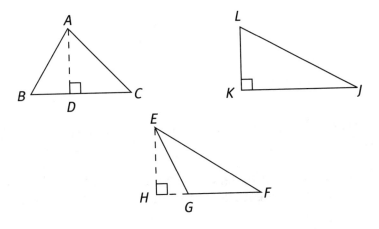

In the diagrams above, AD, EH, *and* LK *are altitudes.*

Interior and Exterior Angles of a Triangle

The sum of the interior angles of any triangle is 180°. Therefore, in the figure below, $a + b + c = 180$.

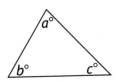

An *exterior angle of a triangle* is equal to the sum of the remote interior angles. The exterior angle labeled $x°$ is equal to the sum of the remote angles: $x = 50 + 100 = 150$.

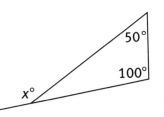

The three exterior angles of any triangle add up to 360°.

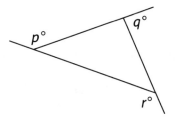

In the figure above, $p + q + r = 360$.

Sides and Angles

The sum of the lengths of any two sides of a triangle is greater than the length of the third side. In the triangle below, $b + c > a$, $a + b > c$, and $a + c > b$.

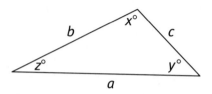

If the lengths of two sides of a triangle are unequal, the greater angle lies opposite the longer side, and vice versa. In the figure above, if $x > y > z$, then $a > b > c$.

Since the two legs of an isosceles triangle have the same length, the two angles opposite the legs must have the same measure. In the figure below, $PQ = PR$, and $\angle Q = \angle R$.

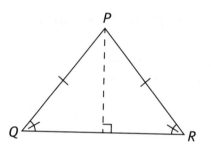

Perimeter and Area of Triangles

There is no special formula for the perimeter of a triangle; it is just the sum of the lengths of the sides.

Example:

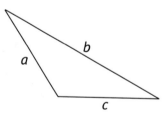

If $b = 2a$ and $c = \dfrac{b}{2}$, find the perimeter of the triangle above in terms of a.

Perimeter $= a + b + c = a + 2a + \dfrac{2a}{2} = 3a + \dfrac{2a}{2} = 3a + a = 4a$.

Incidentally, this is really an isosceles triangle, since $c = \dfrac{b}{2} = \dfrac{2a}{2} = a$.

The area of a triangle is $\left(\dfrac{1}{2}\right)$(Base)(Height).

Example:

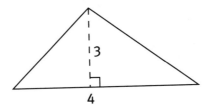

In the diagram above, the base has length 4, and the altitude has length 3. What is the area of the triangle?

$$\text{Area} = \frac{1}{2}bh$$
$$= \frac{bh}{2}$$
$$= \frac{4 \times 3}{2}$$
$$= 6$$

Since the lengths of the base and altitude were not given in specific units, such as centimeters or feet, the area of the triangle is simply said to be 6 square units.

The area of a right triangle is easy to find. Think of one leg as the base and the other as the height. Then the area is one-half the product of the legs, or $\frac{1}{2} \times \text{Leg}_1 \times \text{Leg}_2$.

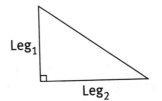

RIGHT TRIANGLES

The right angle is always the largest angle in a right triangle; therefore, the hypotenuse, which lies opposite the right angle, is always the longest side.

Pythagorean Theorem

The *Pythagorean theorem*, which holds for all right triangles and for no other triangles, states that the square of the hypotenuse is equal to the sum of the squares of the legs.

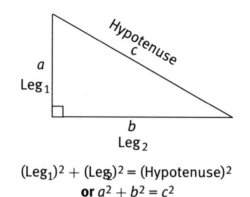

$$(\text{Leg}_1)^2 + (\text{Leg})^2 = (\text{Hypotenuse})^2$$
or $a^2 + b^2 = c^2$

The Pythagorean theorem is very useful whenever you're given the lengths of any two sides of a right triangle; as long as you know whether the remaining side is a leg or the hypotenuse, you can find its length by using the Pythagorean theorem.

Example:

What is the length of the hypotenuse of a right triangle with legs of lengths 9 and 10?

$$
\begin{aligned}
(\text{Hypotenuse})^2 &= (\text{Leg}_1)^2 + (\text{Leg}_2)^2 \\
&= 9^2 + 10^2 \\
&= 81 + 100 \\
&= 181
\end{aligned}
$$

If the square of the hypotenuse equals 181, then the hypotenuse itself must be the square root of 181, or $\sqrt{181}$.

Pythagorean Triples

Certain ratios of integers always satisfy the Pythagorean theorem. You might like to think of them as "Pythagorean triples." One such ratio is 3, 4, and 5. A right triangle with legs of lengths 3 and 4 and a hypotenuse of length 5 is probably the most common kind of right triangle on the GRE. Whenever you see a right triangle with legs of 3 and 4, with a leg of 3 and a hypotenuse of 5, or with a leg of 4 and a hypotenuse of 5, you immediately know the length of the remaining side. In addition, any multiple of these lengths makes another Pythagorean triple; for instance, $6^2 + 8^2 = 10^2$, so a triangle with sides of lengths 6, 8, and 10 is also a right triangle.

The other triple that commonly appears on the GRE is 5, 12, and 13.

Special Right Triangles

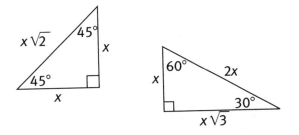

There are two more special kinds of right triangles for which you won't have to use the Pythagorean theorem to find the lengths of the sides. There are special ratios between the lengths of the sides in isosceles right triangles ($45°/45°/90°$ right triangles) and $30°/60°/90°$ right triangles (right triangles with acute angles of $30°$ and $60°$). As you can see in the first drawing above, the sides of an isosceles right triangle are in a ratio of $x : x : x\sqrt{2}$, with the $x\sqrt{2}$ in the ratio representing the hypotenuse. The sides of a $30°/60°/90°$ right triangle are in a ratio of $x : x\sqrt{3} : 2x$, where $2x$ represents the hypotenuse and x represents the side opposite the $30°$ angle. (Remember: The longest side has to be opposite the greatest angle.)

Example:

What is the length of the hypotenuse of an isosceles right triangle with legs of length 4?

You can use the Pythagorean theorem to find the hypotenuse, but it's quicker to use the special right triangle ratios. In an isosceles right triangle, the ratio of a leg to the hypotenuse is $x : x\sqrt{2}$. Since the length of a leg is 4, the length of the hypotenuse must be $4\sqrt{2}$.

Triangles and Quantitative Comparison

All Quantitative Comparison questions require you to judge whether enough information has been given to make a comparison. In geometry, making this judgment is often a matter of knowing the correct definition or formula. For triangles, keep in mind the following:

- If you know two angles, you know the third.
- To find the area, you need the base and the height.
- In a right triangle, if you have two sides, you can find the third. And if you have two sides, you can find the area.
- In isosceles right triangles and $30°/60°/90°$ triangles, if you know one side, you can find everything.

Be careful, though! Be sure you know as much as you think you do.

Example:

Quantity A	Quantity B
Area of right triangle *ABC*, where $\overline{AB} = 5$ and $\overline{BC} = 4$	6

You may think at first that *ABC* must be a 3:4:5 right triangle. Not so fast! We're given two sides, but we don't know which sides they are. If *AB* is the hypotenuse, then it is a 3:4:5 triangle and the area is $\frac{1}{2}(3 \times 4) = 6$, but it's also possible that *AC*, the missing side, is the hypotenuse. In that case, the area would be $\frac{1}{2}(4 \times 5) = 10$. Because Quantity A can either be equal to Quantity B or can be larger than Quantity B, their relationship cannot be determined from the information given.

QUADRILATERALS

A **quadrilateral** is a four-sided polygon. Regardless of a quadrilateral's shape, the four interior angles sum to 360°.

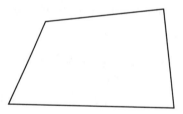

A **parallelogram** is a quadrilateral with two pairs of parallel sides. Opposite sides are equal in length; opposite angles are equal in measure; angles that are not opposite are supplementary to each other (measure of ∠*A* + measure of ∠*D* = 180° in the figure below).

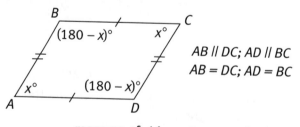

AB ∥ DC; AD ∥ BC
AB = DC; AD = BC

measure of ∠*A* = measure of ∠*C*;
measure of ∠*B* = measure of ∠*D*

A **rectangle** is a parallelogram with four right angles. Opposite sides are equal; diagonals are equal.

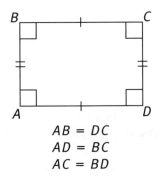

$$AB = DC$$
$$AD = BC$$
$$AC = BD$$

A **square** is a rectangle with equal sides.

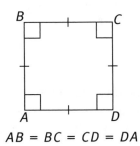

$$AB = BC = CD = DA$$

Perimeters of Quadrilaterals

To find the perimeter of any polygon, you can simply add the lengths of its sides. However, the properties of rectangles and squares lead to simple formulas that may speed up your calculations.

Because the opposite sides are equal, the *perimeter of a rectangle* is twice the sum of the length and the width: Perimeter = 2(Length + Width)

The perimeter of a 5 by 2 rectangle is $2(5 + 2) = 14$.

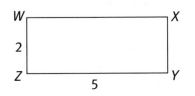

The *perimeter of a square* is equal to the sum of the lengths of the 4 sides. Because all 4 sides are the same length, Perimeter = 4 (Side). If the length of one side of a square is 3, the perimeter is $4 \times 3 = 12$.

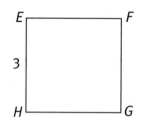

Areas of Quadrilaterals

Area formulas always involve multiplication, and the results are always stated in "square" units. You can see why if you look at the drawing below:

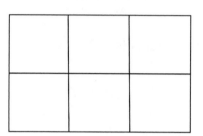

The rectangle is composed of six squares, all equal in size. Let's say that the side of a single small square is 1 unit. Then, we would say that a single square measures "1 by 1." That translates into math as 1×1, or 1^2—in other words, "one square unit."

As you can see from the drawing, there are 6 such square units in the rectangle. That's its area: 6 square units. But you could also find the area by multiplying the number of squares in a row by the number of squares in a column: 3×2, or 6. And since we've defined the length of the side of a square as 1 unit, that's also equivalent to multiplying the length of a horizontal side by the length of a vertical side: again, $3 \times 2 = 6$.

Formulas for Area

To find the area of a rectangle, multiply the **length** by the **width**.

Area of rectangle $= \ell w$

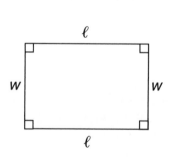

Since the length and width of a square are equal, the area formula for a square just uses the length of a **side:**

$$\text{Area of square} = (\text{Side})^2 = s^2$$

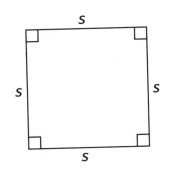

If you're working with a parallelogram, designate one side as the **base.** Then, draw a line segment from one of the vertices opposite the base down to the base so that it intersects the base at a right angle. That line segment will be called the **height.** To find the area of the parallelogram, multiply the length of the base by the length of the height:

$$\text{Area of parallelogram} = (\text{Base})(\text{Height}), \text{ or } A = bh$$

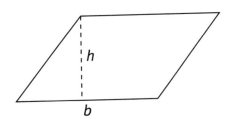

Remember the following:

- In a parallelogram, if you know two adjacent sides, you know all of them; and if you know two adjacent angles, you know all of them.
- In a rectangle, if you know two adjacent sides, you know the area.
- In a square, if you're given virtually any measurement (area, length of a side, length of a diagonal), you can figure out the other measurements.

CIRCLES

Important Terms

Circle: The set of all points in a plane at the same distance from a certain point. This point is called the center of the circle. A circle is labeled by its center point; circle O means the circle with center point O.

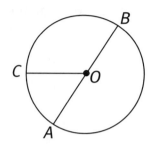

Diameter: A line segment that connects two points on the circle and passes through the center of the circle. *AB* is a diameter of circle *O* above.

Radius: A line segment that connects the center of the circle with any point on the circle (plural: *radii*). The radius of a circle is one-half the length of the diameter. In circle *O* above, *OA*, *OB*, and *OC* are radii.

Central angle: An angle formed by two radii. In circle *O* above, *AOC* is a central angle. *COB* and *BOA* are also central angles. (The measure of *BOA* happens to be 180°.) The total degree measure of a circle is 360°.

Chord: A line segment that joins two points on the circle. The longest chord of a circle is its diameter. *AT* is a chord of circle *P* below.

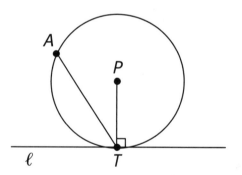

Tangent: A line that touches only one point on the circumference of a circle. A line drawn tangent to a circle is perpendicular to the radius at the point of tangency. In the diagram above, line ℓ is tangent to circle *P* at point *T*.

Circumference and Arc Length

The distance around a polygon is called its **perimeter**; the distance around a circle is called its **circumference**.

The ratio of the circumference of any circle to its diameter is a constant, called **pi** (π). For GRE purposes, the value of π is usually approximated as 3.14.

Since π equals the ratio of the circumference, C, to the diameter, d, we can say that

$$p = \frac{\text{Circumference}}{\text{Diameter}} = \frac{C}{d}.$$

The formula for the circumference of a circle is $C = \pi d$.

The circumference formula can also be stated in terms of the radius, r. Since the diameter is twice the length of the radius, that is, $d = 2r$, then $C = 2\pi r$.

An **arc** is a section of the circumference of a circle. Any arc can be thought of as the portion of a circle cut off by a particular central angle. For example, in circle Q, arc ABC is the portion of the circle that is cut off by central angle AQC. Since arcs are associated with central angles, they can be measured in degrees. The degree measure of an arc is equal to that of the central angle that cuts it off. So in circle Q, arc ABC and central angle AQC would have the same degree measure.

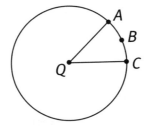

An arc that is exactly half the circumference of its circle is called a **semicircle**.

The length of an arc is the same fraction of a circle's circumference as its degree measure is of 360° (the degree measure of a whole circle). For an arc with a central angle measuring $n°$:

$$\text{Arc length} = \frac{n}{360}(\text{Circumference})$$

$$= \frac{n}{360} \times 2\pi r$$

Example:

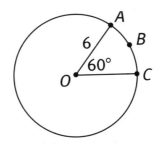

What is the length of arc ABC of circle O above?

$C = 2\pi r$; therefore, if $r = 6$, $C = 2 \times \pi \times 6 = 12\,\pi$. Since AOC measures 60°, arc ABC is $\dfrac{60}{360}$, or $\dfrac{1}{6}$ of the circumference. Thus, the length of arc ABC is $\dfrac{1}{6} \times 12\pi$, or 2π.

Area and Sector Area Formulas

The area of a circle is πr^2.

A **sector** is a portion of a circle's area that is bounded by two radii and an arc. The shaded area of circle X is sector AXB.

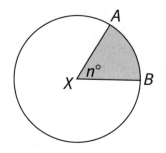

Like arcs, sectors are associated with central angles. And the process and formula used to find the area of a sector are similar to those used to determine arc length. First, find the degree measure of the sector's central angle and figure out what fraction that degree measure is of 360°. Then, multiply the area of the whole circle by that fraction. In a sector whose central angle measures $n°$:

$$\text{Area of sector} = \frac{n}{360}(\text{Area of circle})$$

$$= \frac{n}{360}\pi r^2$$

Example:

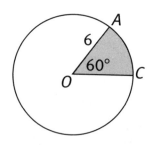

In circle O above, what is the area of sector AOC?

Since $\angle AOC$ measures 60°, a 60° "slice" of the circle is $\dfrac{60°}{360°}$, or $\dfrac{1}{6}$ of the total area of the circle. Therefore, the area of the sector is $\dfrac{1}{6}\pi r^2 = \dfrac{1}{6}(36\pi) = 6\pi$.

Circles and Data Sufficiency

A circle is a regular shape whose area and perimeter can be determined through the use of formulas. If you're given virtually any measurement (radius, diameter, circumference, area), you can determine all the other measurements.

Example:

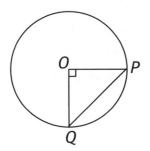

If the length of chord $PQ = 4\sqrt{2}$, what is the circumference of the circle with center O?

    (A)   4

    (A)   8

    (A) 4π

    (A) 8π

    (A) $8\pi\sqrt{2}$

To find the circumference, we need the radius, which is either OP or OQ in this circle. We are given the length of PQ. PQ is a chord of the circle (it connects two points on the circle), but it's also the hypotenuse of right triangle OPQ. Do we know anything else about that triangle? Since OP and OQ are both radii of the circle, they must have the same length, so the triangle is an isosceles right triangle. Using the ratio of the lengths of sides of a 45:45:90 right triangle, with PQ as the hypotenuse, the length of each radius is 4, making the circumference $2\pi r$ or 8π, answer choice (**D**).

COORDINATE GEOMETRY

In coordinate geometry, the locations of points in a plane are indicated by ordered pairs of real numbers.

Important Terms and Concepts

Plane: A flat surface that extends indefinitely in any direction.

x-axis and y-axis: The horizontal (*x*) and vertical (*y*) lines that intersect perpendicularly to indicate location on a coordinate plane. Each axis is a number line.

Ordered pair: Two numbers or quantities separated by a comma and enclosed in parentheses. An example would be (8,7). All the ordered pairs that you'll see in GRE coordinate geometry problems will be in the form (*x,y*), where the first quantity, *x*, tells you how far the point is to the left or right of the *y*-axis, and the second quantity, *y*, tells you how far the point is above or below the *x*-axis.

Coordinates: The numbers that designate distance from an axis in coordinate geometry. The first number is the *x*-coordinate; the second is the *y*-coordinate. In the ordered pair (8,7), 8 is the *x*-coordinate and 7 is the *y*-coordinate.

Origin: The point where the *x*- and *y*-axes intersect; its coordinates are (0,0).

Plotting Points

Here's what a coordinate plane looks like:

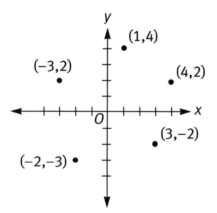

Any point in a coordinate plane can be identified by an ordered pair consisting of its *x*-coordinate and its *y*-coordinate. Every point that lies on the *x*-axis has a *y*-coordinate of 0, and every point that lies on the *y*-axis has an *x*-coordinate of 0.

When you start at the origin and move:

to the right	*x* is positive
to the left	*x* is negative
up	*y* is positive
down	*y* is negative

Therefore, the coordinate plane can be divided into four quadrants, as shown below.

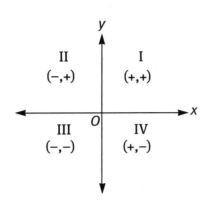

Distances on the Coordinate Plane

The distance between two points is equal to the length of the straight-line segment that has those two points as endpoints.

If a line segment is parallel to the x-axis, the y-coordinate of every point on the line segment will be the same. Similarly, if a line segment is parallel to the y-axis, the x-coordinate of every point on the line segment will be the same.

Therefore, to find the length of a line segment parallel to one of the axes, all you have to do is find the difference between the endpoint coordinates that do change. In the diagram below, the length of AB equals $x_2 - x_1$.

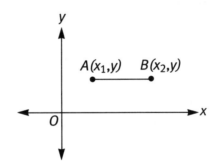

You can find the length of a line segment that is not parallel to one of the axes by treating the line segment as the hypotenuse of a right triangle. Simply draw in the legs of the triangle parallel to the two axes. The length of each leg will be the difference between the x- or y-coordinates of its endpoints. Once you've found the lengths of the legs, you can use the Pythagorean theorem to find the length of the hypotenuse (the original line segment).

In the diagram below, $(DE)^2 = (EF)^2 + (DF)^2$.

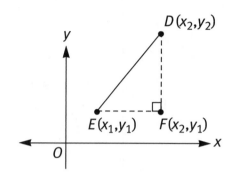

Example:

If the coordinates of point *A* are (3,4) and the coordinates of point *B* are (6,8), what is the distance between points *A* and *B*?

You don't have to draw a diagram to use the method just described, but drawing one may help you to visualize the problem. Plot points *A* and *B* and draw in line segment *AB*. The length of *AB* is the distance between the two points. Now draw a right triangle, with *AB* as its hypotenuse. The missing vertex will be the intersection of a line segment drawn through point *A* parallel to the *x*-axis and a line segment drawn through point *B* parallel to the *y*-axis. Label the point of intersection *C*. Since the *x*- and *y*-axes are perpendicular to each other, *AC* and *BC* will also be perpendicular to each other.

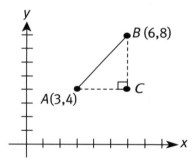

Point *C* will also have the same *x*-coordinate as point *B* and the same *y*-coordinate as point *A*. That means that point *C* has coordinates (6,4).

To use the Pythagorean theorem, you'll need the lengths of *AC* and *BC*. The distance between points *A* and *C* is simply the difference between their *x*-coordinates, while the distance between points *B* and *C* is the difference between their *y*-coordinates. So $AC = 6 - 3 = 3$, and $BC = 8 - 4 = 4$. If you recognize these as the legs of a 3:4:5 right triangle, you'll know immediately that the distance between points *A* and *B* must be 5. Otherwise, you'll have to use the Pythagorean theorem to come to the same conclusion.

Equations of Lines

Straight lines can be described by linear equations.

Commonly:

$$y = mx + b,$$

where m is the slope $\left(\dfrac{\Delta y}{\Delta x}\right)$ and b is the point where the line intercepts the y-axis, that is, the value of y where $x = 0$.

Lines that are parallel to the x-axis have a slope of zero and therefore have the equation $y = b$. Lines that are parallel to the y-axis have the equation $x = a$, where a is the x-intercept of that line.

If you're comfortable with linear equations, you'll sometimes want to use them to find the slope of a line or the coordinates of a point on a line. However, many such questions can be answered without determining or manipulating equations. Check the answer choices to see if you can eliminate any by common sense.

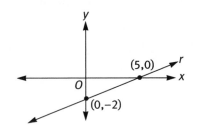

Example:

Line r is a straight line as shown above. Which of the following points lies on line r?

- Ⓐ (6,6)
- Ⓑ (7,3)
- Ⓒ (8,2)
- Ⓓ (9,3)
- Ⓔ (10,2)

Line r intercepts the y-axis at (0,–2), so you can plug –2 in for b in the slope-intercept form of a linear equation. Line r has a rise (Δy) of 2 and a run (Δx) of 5, so its slope is $\dfrac{2}{5}$. That makes the slope-intercept form $y = \dfrac{2}{5}x - 2$.

The easiest way to proceed from here is to substitute the coordinates of each answer choice into the equation in place of x and y; only the coordinates that satisfy the equation can lie on the line. Choice **(E)** is the best answer to start with, because 10 is the only x-coordinate that will not create a fraction on the right side of the equal sign. Plugging in (10,2) for x and y in the slope-intercept equation gives you $2 = \frac{2}{5}(10) - 2$, which simplifies to $2 = 4 - 2$.

That's true, so the correct answer choice is **(E)**.

SOLIDS

Important Terms

Solid: A three-dimensional figure. The dimensions are usually called length, width, and height (ℓ, w, and h) or height, width, and depth (h, w, and d). There are only two types of solids that appear with any frequency on the GRE: rectangular solids (including cubes) and cylinders.

Uniform solid: A solid that could be cut into congruent cross sections (parallel "slices" of equal size and shape) along a given axis. Solids you see on the GRE will almost certainly be uniform solids.

Face: The surface of a solid that lies in a particular plane. Hexagon *ABCDEF* is one face of the solid pictured below.

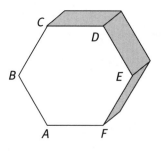

Edge: A line segment that connects adjacent faces of a solid. The sides of hexagon *ABCDEF* are also edges of the solid pictured above.

Base: The "bottom" face of a solid as oriented in any given diagram.

Rectangular solid: A solid with six rectangular faces. All edges meet at right angles. Examples of rectangular solids are cereal boxes, bricks, etc.

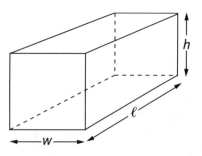

Cube: A special rectangular solid in which all edges are of equal length, *e*, and therefore all faces are squares. Sugar cubes and dice without rounded corners are examples of cubes.

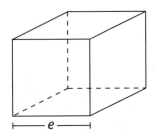

Cylinder: A uniform solid whose horizontal cross section is a circle—for example, a soup can or a pipe that is closed at both ends. A cylinder's measurements are generally given in terms of its radius, *r*, and its height, *h*.

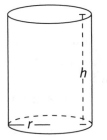

Lateral surface of a cylinder: The "pipe" surface, as opposed to the circular "ends." The lateral surface of a cylinder is unlike most other surfaces of solids that you'll see on the GRE, first because it does not lie in a plane and second because it forms a closed loop. Think of it as the label around a soup can. If you could remove it from the can in one piece, you would have an open tube. If you then cut the label and unrolled it, it would form a rectangle with a length equal to the circumference of the circular base of the can and a height equal to that of the can.

Formulas for Volume and Surface Area

Volume of a rectangular solid = (Area of base) (Height) = (Length × Width) (Height) = *lwh*

Surface area of a rectangular solid = Sum of areas of faces = 2*lw* + 2*lh* + 2*hw*

Since a cube is a rectangular solid for which $l = w = h$, the formula for its volume can be stated in terms of any edge:

- Volume of a cube = *lwh* = (Edge)(Edge)(Edge) = e^3
- Surface area of a cube = Sum of areas of faces = $6e^2$

To find the volume or surface area of a cylinder, you'll need two pieces of information: the height of the cylinder and the radius of the base.

- Volume of a cylinder = (Area of base)(Height) = $\pi r^2 h$
- Lateral surface area of a cylinder = (Circumference of base)(Height) = $2\pi rh$
- Total surface area of a cylinder = Areas of circular ends + Lateral surface area = $2\pi r^2 + 2\pi rh$

MULTIPLE FIGURES

Some GRE geometry problems involve combinations of different types of figures. Besides the basic rules and formulas that you would use on normal geometry problems, you'll need an intuitive understanding of how various geometrical concepts relate to each other to answer these "multiple figures" questions correctly. For example, you may have to revisualize the side of a rectangle as the hypotenuse of a neighboring right triangle or as the diameter of a circumscribed circle. Keep looking for the relationships between the different figures until you find one that leads you to the answer.

Area of Shaded Regions

A common multiple-figures question involves a diagram of a geometrical figure that has been broken up into different, irregularly shaped areas, often with one region shaded. You'll usually be asked to find the area of the shaded (or unshaded) portion of the diagram. Your best bet will be to take one of the following two approaches:

- Break the area into smaller pieces whose separate areas you can find; add those areas together.
- Find the area of the whole figure; find the area of the region(s) that you're *not* looking for; subtract the latter from the former.

Example:

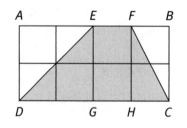

Rectangle *ABCD* above has an area of 72 and is composed of 8 equal squares. What is the area of the shaded region?

The first thing you have to realize is that, for the 8 equal squares to form a total area of 72, each square must have an area of 72 ÷ 8, or 9. Since the area of a square equals the square of the length of a side, each side of a square in the diagram must have a length of $\sqrt{9}$ or 3.

At this point, you choose your approach. Either one will work:

Approach 1:

Break up the shaded area into right triangle *DEG*, rectangle *EFHG*, and right triangle *FHC*.

The area of triangle *DEG* is $\frac{1}{2}(6)(6) = 18$. The area of rectangle *EFHG* is (3)(6), or 18.

The area of triangle *FHC* is $\frac{1}{2}(3)(6)$, or 9. The total shaded area is 18 + 18 + 9, or 45.

Approach 2:

The area of unshaded right triangle *AED* is $\frac{1}{2}(6)(6)$, or 18. The area of unshaded

right triangle *FBC* is $\frac{1}{2}(3)(6)$, or 9. Therefore, the total unshaded area is 18 + 9 = 27.

Subtract the total unshaded area from the total area of rectangle *ABCD*: 72 − 27 = 45.

Inscribed/Circumscribed Figures

A polygon is inscribed in a circle if all the vertices of the polygon lie on the circle. A polygon is circumscribed about a circle if all the sides of the polygon are tangent to the circle.

Square *ABCD* is inscribed in circle *O*. We can also say that circle *O* is circumscribed about square *ABCD*.

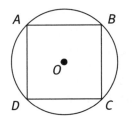

Square *PQRS* is circumscribed about circle *O*. We can also say that circle *O* is inscribed in square *PQRS*.

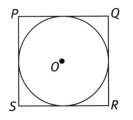

When a triangle is inscribed in a semicircle in such a way that one side of the triangle coincides with the diameter of the semicircle, the triangle is a right triangle.

Example:

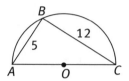

What is the diameter of semicircle *O* above?

AC is a diameter of semicircle *O* because it passes through center point *O*. So triangle *ABC* fits the description given above of a right triangle. Moreover, triangle *ABC* is a special 5:12:13 right triangle with a hypotenuse of 13. Therefore, the length of diameter *AC* is 13.

OTHER TOPICS

DEALING WITH WORD PROBLEMS

The key to solving word problems is translation: turning English into math. Rather than having an equation set up for you, *you* have to decide what arithmetic or algebraic operations to perform on which numbers.

For example, suppose the core of a problem involves working with the equation $3j = s - 4$.

In a word problem, this might be presented as "If John had three times as many macaroons as he has now, he would have four fewer macaroons than Susan would."

Your job is to translate the problem from English into math. A phrase like "three times as many as John has" can be translated as $3j$; the phrase "four fewer than Susan" can be translated as "$s - 4$."

Many people dislike word problems. But on the GRE, the math involved is often easier than in other math problems. Once you've translated the language, most word problems boil down to rather simple mathematical concepts and processes—probably because the testmakers figure that the extra step of translation makes the problem difficult enough.

Here's a general approach to any word problem:

1. Read through the whole question once, without lingering over details, to get a sense of the overall problem.
2. Identify and label the variables or unknowns in a way that makes it easy to remember what they stand for.
3. Translate the problem into one or more equations, sentence by sentence. Be careful of the order in which you translate the terms. For example, consider the phrase "5 less than 4x equals 9." The *correct* way to translate it is "$4x - 5 = 9$."

But many students make the mistake of writing the terms in the order in which they appear in words: "$5 - 4x = 9$."

4. Solve the equation(s).
5. Check your work, if time permits.

Translation Table

This table contains common phrases used in GRE math problems. The left column lists words and phrases that occur frequently; the right column lists the corresponding algebraic symbols.

equals, is, was, will be, has, costs, adds up to, is the same as	$=$
times, of, multiplied by, product of, twice, double, half, triple	$\times$
divided by, per, out of, each, ratio of _ to _	$\div$
plus, added to, sum, combined, and, total	$+$
minus, subtracted from, less than, decreased by, difference between	$-$
what, how much, how many, a number	variable (x, n, etc.)

Example:

Beatrice has three dollars more than twice the number of dollars Allan has.

Translate into $B = 3 + 2A$.

For Word Problems:

Add...

- when you are given the amounts of individual quantities and asked to find the total.

Example:

If the sales tax on a $12.00 lunch is $1.20, what is the total amount of the check?

$$\$12.00 + \$1.20 = \$13.20$$

- when you are given an original amount and an increase and are then asked to find the new amount.

Example:

The bus fare used to be 55 cents. If the fare increased by 35 cents, what is the new fare?

$$55 \text{ cents} + 35 \text{ cents} = 90 \text{ cents}$$

Subtract...

- when you are given the total and one part of the total and you want to find the remaining part or parts.

Example:

If 32 out of 50 children are girls, what is the number of boys?

$$50 \text{ children} - 32 \text{ girls} = 18 \text{ boys}$$

- when you are given two numbers and asked *how much more* or *how much less* one number is than the other. The amount is called the **difference**.

Example:

How much larger than 30 is 38?

$$38 \text{ (larger)} - 30 \text{ (smaller)} = 8$$

Multiply...

- when you are given an amount for one item and asked for the total amount of *many* of these items.

Example:

If 1 book costs $6.50, what is the cost of 12 copies of the same book?

$$12(\$6.50) = \$78.00$$

Divide...

- when you are given a total amount for *many* items and asked for the amount for *one* item.

Example:

If 5 pounds of apples cost $6.75, what is the price of 1 pound of apples?

$$\$6.75 \div 5 = \$1.35$$

- when you are given the size of one group and the total size for many such identical groups and are asked how many of the small groups fit into the larger one.

Example:

How many groups of 30 students can be formed from a total of 240 students?

$$240 \div 30 = 8 \text{ groups of 30 students}$$

SPECIAL WORD PROBLEMS TIP #1
Don't try to combine several sentences into one equation; each sentence usually translates into a separate equation.

SPECIAL WORD PROBLEMS TIP #2
Pay attention to what the question asks for and make a note to yourself if it is not one of the unknowns in the equation(s). Otherwise, you may stop working on the problem too early.

LOGIC PROBLEMS

You won't always have to set up an equation to solve a word problem. Some of the word problems you'll encounter on the GRE won't fall into recognizable text-book categories. Many of these problems are designed to test your analytical and deductive logic. You can solve them with common sense and a little basic arithmetic. Ask yourself how it would be helpful to arrange the information, such as by drawing a diagram or making a table.

In these problems, the issue is not so much translating English into math as simply using your head. The problem may call for nonmath skills, including the ability to organize and keep track of different possibilities, the ability to visualize something (for instance, the reverse side of a symmetrical shape), the ability to think of the exception that changes the answer to a problem, or the ability to deal with overlapping groups.

Example:

If ! and $\int$ are digits and $(!!)(\int\int) = 60\int$, what is the value of $\int$?

Since each of the symbols represents a digit from 0–9, we know that the product of the multiplication equals a value from 600 to 609. We know that the two quantities multiplied each consist of a two-digit integer in which both digits are the same. So list the relevant two-digit integers (00, 11, 22, 33, 44, 55, 66, 77, 88, and 99) and see which two of them can be multiplied evenly into the 600 to 609 range. Only (11)(55) satisfies this requirement. The $\int$ symbol equals 5.

TABLES, GRAPHS, AND CHARTS

Some questions, especially in Data Interpretation, combine numbers and text with visual formats. Different formats are suitable for organizing different types of information. The formats that appear most frequently on GRE math questions are tables, bar graphs, line graphs, and pie charts.

Questions involving tables, graphs, and charts may *look* different from other GRE math questions, but the ideas and principles are the same. The problems are unusual only in the way that they present information, not in what they ask you to do with that information.

Tables

The most basic way to organize information is to create a table. Tables are in some ways the most accurate graphic presentation format—the only way you can misunderstand a number is to read it from the wrong row or column—but they don't allow the reader to spot trends or extremes very readily.

Here's an example of a very simple table.

JOHN'S INCOME: 2007–2011	
Year	Income
2007	$20,000
2008	$22,000
2009	$18,000
2010	$15,000
2011	$28,000

An easy question might ask for John's income in a particular year or for the difference in his income between two years. To find the difference, you would simply look up the amount for both years and subtract the smaller income from the larger income. A harder question might ask for John's average annual income over the five-year period shown; to determine the average, you would have to find the sum of the five annual incomes and divide it by 5.

Bar Graphs

Here's the same information that you saw previously in a table. This time, it's presented as a bar graph.

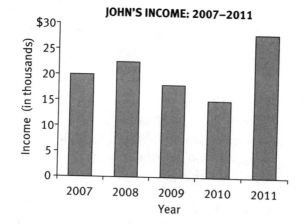

Bar graphs can be used to visually show information that would otherwise appear as numbers in a table. Bar graphs are somewhat less accurate than tables, but that's not necessarily a bad attribute, especially on the GRE, where estimating often saves time on calculations.

What's handy about a bar graph is that you can see which values are larger or smaller without reading actual numbers. Just a glance at this graph shows that John's 2011 income was almost double his 2010 income. Numbers are represented on a bar graph by the heights or lengths of the bars. To find the height of a vertical bar, look for the point where a line drawn across the top of the bar parallel to the horizontal axis would intersect the vertical axis. To find the length of a horizontal bar, look for the point where a line drawn across the end of the bar parallel to the vertical axis would intersect the horizontal axis.

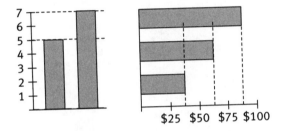

If the height or length of the bar falls in between two numbers on the axis, you will have to estimate.

Line Graphs

Line graphs follow the same general principle as bar graphs, except that instead of using the lengths of bars to represent numbers, they use points connected by lines. The lines further emphasize the relative values of the numbers.

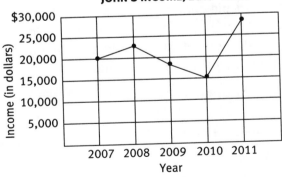

To read John's income for any particular year from this line graph, determine where a line drawn from the appropriate point would intersect the vertical axis.

Pie Charts

Pie charts show how things are distributed. The fraction of a circle occupied by each piece of the "pie" indicates what fraction of the whole that piece represents. In most pie charts, the percentage of the pie occupied by each "slice" will be shown on the slice itself or, for very narrow slices, outside the circle with an arrow or a line pointing to the appropriate slice.

The total size of the whole pie is usually given at the top or bottom of the graph, either as "TOTAL = xxx" or as "100% = xxx." To find the approximate amount represented by a particular piece of the pie, just multiply the whole by the appropriate percent.

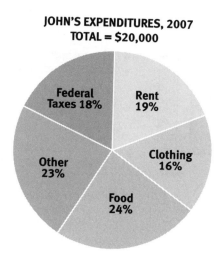

JOHN'S EXPENDITURES, 2007
TOTAL = $20,000

For instance, to find the total tax that John paid to the federal government in 2007, look at the slice of this chart labeled "Federal Tax." It represents 18% of John's 2007 expenditures. Since his total 2007 expenditures were $20,000, he paid 0.18($20,000) = $3,600 in federal taxes in 2007.

One important note about pie charts: If you're not given the whole and you don't know both the percentage and the actual number that at least one slice represents, you won't be able to find the whole. Pie charts are ideal for presenting the kind of information that ratio problems present in words.

CHAPTER 11

Quantitative Comparison

INTRODUCTION TO QUANTITATIVE COMPARISON

In each Quantitative Comparison question, you'll see two mathematical expressions. One is Quantity A, and the other is Quantity B. You will be asked to compare them. Some questions include additional centered information. This centered information applies to both quantities and is essential to making the comparison. Since this type of question is about the relationship between the two quantities, you usually won't need to calculate a specific value for either quantity. Therefore, you do not want to rely on the onscreen calculator to answer these questions.

The directions for a Quantitative Comparison question will look like this:

Directions: Select the correct answer.

Sample Question			Exit Section	Review	Mark	Help ?	Back ◄	Next ►

$$h > 1$$

Quantity A	Quantity B
The number of minutes in h hours	$\dfrac{60}{h}$

    ○ Quantity A is greater.

    ○ Quantity B is greater.

    ○ The two quantities are equal.

    ○ The relationship cannot be determined from the information given.

Click to select your choice.

THE KAPLAN METHOD FOR QUANTITATIVE COMPARISON

STEP 1   Analyze the centered information and quantities.

STEP 2   Approach strategically.

HOW THE KAPLAN METHOD FOR QUANTITATIVE COMPARISON WORKS

Now let's discuss how the Kaplan Method for Quantitative Comparison works.

❱ STEP 1

Analyze the centered information and the quantities.

Notice whether the quantities contain numbers, variables, or both. If there is centered information, decide how it affects the information given in the quantities. Note that a variable has the same value each time it appears within a question.

❱ STEP 2

Approach strategically.

Think about a strategy you could use to compare the quantities now that you've determined the information you have and the information you need. There are a variety of approaches to solving a Quantitative Comparison question, and the practice examples will take you through several of these.

HOW TO APPLY THE KAPLAN METHOD FOR QUANTITATIVE COMPARISON

Now let's apply the Kaplan Method to a Quantitative Comparison question:

Quantity A	Quantity B
$\dfrac{1}{4} + \dfrac{1}{5} + \dfrac{1}{6} + \dfrac{1}{7}$	$\dfrac{1}{\dfrac{1}{4} + \dfrac{1}{5} + \dfrac{1}{6} + \dfrac{1}{7}}$

- Ⓐ Quantity A is greater.
- Ⓑ Quantity B is greater.
- Ⓒ The two quantities are equal.
- Ⓓ The relationship cannot be determined from the information given.

STEP 1

Analyze the centered information and the columns.

This problem would be a nightmare to calculate under timed conditions. But the only thing you need to figure out is whether one quantity is greater than the other. One thing you might notice is that choice **(D)** is not an option here. Because both quantities contain only numbers, there is a definite value for each quantity, and a relationship can be determined. Answer choice **(D)** is never correct when the quantities contain only numbers.

Note that the quantity on the left is the same as the quantity in the denominator of the fraction on the right. You can think about this problem as a comparison of x and $\frac{1}{x}$ (or the reciprocal of x), where x has a definite value. Your job now is to figure out just how to compare them.

STEP 2

Approach strategically.

Before you start to do a long calculation, think about what you already know. While you may not know the sum of the four fractions, you do know two things: $\frac{1}{4} + \frac{1}{4} + \frac{1}{4} + \frac{1}{4} = 1$, and $\frac{1}{5}$, $\frac{1}{6}$, and $\frac{1}{7}$ are each less than $\frac{1}{4}$. Because the reciprocal of any number between 0 and 1 is greater than 1, and Quantity A is a positive number less than 1, its reciprocal in Quantity B is greater than 1. So choice **(B)** is correct. Quantitative Comparisons rarely, if ever, ask for exact values, so don't waste time calculating them.

Now let's apply the Kaplan Method to a second Quantitative Comparison question:

$$w > x > 0 > y > z$$

Quantity A	Quantity B
$w + y$	$x + z$

(A) Quantity A is greater.
(B) Quantity B is greater.
(C) The two quantities are equal.
(D) The relationship cannot be determined from the information given.

▶ STEP 1

Analyze the centered information and the quantities.

In this problem, there are four variables: *w*, *x*, *y*, and *z*. You are asked to compare the values of the sums of pairs of variables. You know the relative values of the different variables, but you don't know the actual amounts. You do know that two of the variables (*w* and *x*) must be positive and two of the variables (*y* and *z*) must be negative numbers.

▶ STEP 2

Approach strategically.

In this case, think about the different sums as pieces of the whole. If every "piece" in one quantity is greater than a corresponding "piece" in the other quantity, and if the only operation involved is addition, then the quantity with the greater individual values will have the greater total value. From the given information, we know the following:

- $w > x$
- $y > z$

The first term, *w*, in Quantity A is greater than the first term, *x*, in Quantity B. Similarly, the second term, *y*, in Quantity A is greater than the second term, *z*, in Quantity B. Because each piece in Quantity A is greater than the corresponding piece in Quantity B, Quantity A must be greater; the answer is **(A)**.

Now let's apply the Kaplan Method to a third Quantitative Comparison question:

The diameter of circle *O* is *d*, and the area is *a*.

Quantity A	Quantity B
$\dfrac{\pi d^2}{2}$	a

   Ⓐ Quantity A is greater.
   Ⓑ Quantity B is greater.
   Ⓒ The two quantities are equal.
   Ⓓ The relationship cannot be determined from the information given.

▶ STEP 1

Analyze the centered information and the quantities.

In this problem, you are given additional information: the sentence that tells you the diameter of circle *O* is *d* and the area is *a*. This is important information because it gives you a key to unlocking this question. Given that information, you can tell that you are comparing the area, *a*, of circle *O* and a quantity that includes the diameter of the same circle. If you're thinking about the formula for calculating area given the diameter, you're thinking right!

❯❯ STEP 2

Approach strategically.

Make Quantity B look more like Quantity A by rewriting a, the area of the circle, in terms of the diameter, d. The area of any circle equals πr^2, where r is the radius. Because the radius is half the diameter, you can substitute $\dfrac{d}{2}$ for r in the area formula to get $a = \pi r^2 = \pi \left(\dfrac{d}{2}\right)^2$ in Quantity B. Simplifying, you get $\dfrac{\pi d^2}{4}$.

Because both quantities contain π, we could compare $\dfrac{d^2}{2}$ to $\dfrac{d^2}{4}$. But let's take it one step further. You know that d is a distance and must be a positive number. That makes it possible to divide both quantities, $\dfrac{d^2}{2}$ and $\dfrac{d^2}{4}$, by d^2 and then just compare $\dfrac{1}{2}$ to $\dfrac{1}{4}$. This makes it easy to see that Quantity A is always greater because $\dfrac{1}{2} > \dfrac{1}{4}$. Choice **(A)** is correct.

KAPLAN'S ADDITIONAL TIPS FOR QUANTITATIVE COMPARISON QUESTIONS

Memorize the answer choices

It is a good idea to memorize what the Quantitative Comparison answer choices mean. This is not as difficult as it sounds. The choices are always the same. The wording and the order never vary. As you work through the practice problems, the choices will become second nature to you, and you will get used to reacting to the questions without reading the four answer choices, thus saving you lots of time on Test Day.

When there is at least one variable in a problem, try to demonstrate two different relationships between quantities

Here's why demonstrating two different relationships between the quantities is an important strategy: if you can demonstrate two different relationships, then choice **(D)** is correct. There is no need to examine the question further.

But how can this demonstration be done efficiently? A good suggestion is to look at the expression(s) containing a variable and notice the possible values of the variable given the mathematical operation involved. For example, if x can be any real number and you need to compare $(x + 1)^2$ to $(x + 1)$, pick a value for x that will make $(x + 1)$ a fraction between 0 and 1 and then pick a value for x that will make $(x + 1)$ greater than 1. By choosing values for x in this way, you are basing your number choices on mathematical properties you already know: a positive fraction less than 1 becomes smaller when squared, but a number greater than 1 grows larger when squared.

Compare quantities piece by piece

Compare the value of each "piece" in each quantity. If every "piece" in one quantity is greater than a corresponding "piece" in the other quantity, and the operation involved is either addition or multiplication, then the quantity with the greater individual values will have the greater total value.

Make one quantity look like the other

When the Quantities A and B are expressed differently, you can often make the comparison easier by changing the format of one quantity so that it looks like the other. This is a great approach when the quantities look so different that you can't compare them directly.

Do the same thing to both quantities

If the quantities you are given seem too complex to compare immediately, look closely to see if there is an addition, subtraction, multiplication, or division operation you can perform on both quantities to make them simpler—provided you do not multiply or divide by zero or a negative number. For example, suppose you have the task of comparing $1 + \dfrac{w}{1 + w}$ to $1 + \dfrac{1}{1 + w}$, where w is greater than 0. To get to the heart of the comparison, subtract 1 from both quantities and you have $\dfrac{w}{1 + w}$ compared to $\dfrac{1}{1 + w}$. To simplify even further, multiply both quantities by $(1 + w)$, and then you can compare w to 1—much simpler.

Don't be tricked by misleading information

To avoid Quantitative Comparison traps, stay alert and don't assume anything. If you are using a diagram to answer a question, use only information that is given or information that you know must be true based on properties or theorems. For instance, don't assume angles are equal or lines are parallel unless it is stated or can be deduced from other information given.

A common mistake is to assume that variables represent only positive integers. As you saw when using the Picking Numbers strategy, fractions or negative numbers often show a different relationship between the quantities.

Don't forget to consider other possibilities

If an answer looks obvious, it may very well be a trap. Consider this situation: a question requires you to think of two integers whose product is 6. If you jump to the conclusion that 2 and 3 are the integers, you will miss several other possibilities.

Not only are 1 and 6 possibilities, but there are also pairs of negative integers to consider: -2 and -3, -1 and -6.

Don't fall for look-alikes

Even if two expressions look similar, they may be mathematically different. Be especially careful with expressions involving parentheses or radicals. If you were asked to compare $\sqrt{5x} + \sqrt{5x}$ to $\sqrt{10x}$, you would not want to fall into the trap of saying the two expressions were equal. Although time is an important factor in taking the GRE, don't rush to the extent that you do not apply your skills correctly. In this case, $\sqrt{5x} + \sqrt{5x} = 2\sqrt{5x}$, which is not the same as $\sqrt{10x}$ unless $x = 0$.

QUANTITATIVE COMPARISON PRACTICE SET

Try the following Quantitative Comparison questions using the Kaplan Method for Quantitative Comparison. If you're up to the challenge, time yourself; on Test Day, you'll want to spend only 1.5 minutes on each question.

1.   <u>Quantity A</u>   <u>Quantity B</u>

$$x^2 + 2x - 2 \qquad\qquad x^2 + 2x - 1$$

   Ⓐ Quantity A is greater.
   Ⓑ Quantity B is greater.
   Ⓒ The two quantities are equal.
   Ⓓ The relationship cannot be determined from the information given.

2. $x = 2y$; y is a positive integer.

            <u>Quantity A</u>   <u>Quantity B</u>
               4^{2y} 2^x

   Ⓐ Quantity A is greater.
   Ⓑ Quantity B is greater.
   Ⓒ The two quantities are equal.
   Ⓓ The relationship cannot be determined from the information given.

3. q, r, and s are positive numbers; $qrs > 12$.

            <u>Quantity A</u>   <u>Quantity B</u>

$$\frac{qr}{5} \qquad\qquad\qquad \frac{3}{s}$$

   Ⓐ Quantity A is greater.
   Ⓑ Quantity B is greater.
   Ⓒ The two quantities are equal.
   Ⓓ The relationship cannot be determined from the information given.

4. In triangle *XYZ* not given, the measure of angle *X* equals the measure of angle *Y*.

<u>Quantity A</u>   <u>Quantity B</u>

The degree measure of angle *Z*   The degree measure of angle *X* plus the degree measure of angle *Y*

   Ⓐ Quantity A is greater.
   Ⓑ Quantity B is greater.
   Ⓒ The two quantities are equal.
   Ⓓ The relationship cannot be determined from the information given.

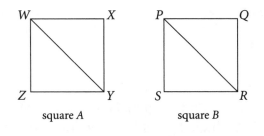

       square *A*   square *B*

5.   <u>Quantity A</u>   <u>Quantity B</u>

$$\frac{\text{Perimeter of square } A}{\text{Perimeter of square } B}$$ $$\frac{\text{Length of } WY}{\text{Length of } PR}$$

   Ⓐ Quantity A is greater.
   Ⓑ Quantity B is greater.
   Ⓒ The two quantities are equal.
   Ⓓ The relationship cannot be determined from the information given.

QUANTITATIVE COMPARISON PRACTICE SET ANSWERS AND EXPLANATIONS

1. B

Comparing the two quantities piece by piece, you find that the only difference is the third piece: -2 in Quantity A and -1 in Quantity B. You don't know the value of x, but whatever it is, x^2 in Quantity A must have the same value as x^2 in Quantity B, and $2x$ in Quantity A must have the same value as $2x$ in Quantity B. Because any quantity minus 2 must be less than that quantity minus 1, Quantity B is greater than Quantity A. The correct choice is **(B)**.

2. A

Replacing the exponent x in Quantity B with the equivalent value given in the centered information, you're comparing 4^{2y} with 2^{2y}. Because y is a positive integer, raising 4 to the exponent $2y$ will result in a greater value than raising 2 to the exponent $2y$. The correct choice is **(A)**.

3. D

Do the same thing to both quantities to make them look like the centered information. When you multiply both quantities by $5s$, you get qrs in Quantity A and 15 in Quantity B. Because qrs could be any integer greater than 12, qrs could be greater than, equal to, or less than 15. Choice **(D)** is correct.

4. D

Because angle $X =$ angle Y, at least two sides of the triangle are equal. You can draw two diagrams with X and Y as the base angles of a triangle. In one diagram, make the triangle tall and narrow so that angle X and angle Y are very large and angle Z is very small. In this case, Quantity B is greater. In the second diagram, make the triangle short and wide so that angle Z is much larger than angle X and angle Y. In this case, Quantity A is greater. Because more than one relationship between the quantities is possible, the correct answer is **(D)**.

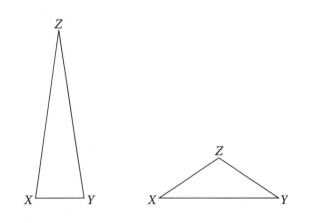

5. C

You don't know the exact relationship between square *A* and square *B*, but it doesn't matter. The problem is actually just comparing the ratios of corresponding parts of two squares. The relationship between the specific side lengths of both squares will also exist between them for any other corresponding length. If a side of one square is twice the length of a side of the second square, the diagonal will also be twice as long. The ratio of the perimeters of the two squares is the same as the ratio of the diagonals.

You can make this abstract relationship concrete by Picking Numbers for the sides of the two squares. Say, for example, that each side of square *A* is 2 and each side of square *B* is 3. Then the ratio of the perimeters is 8:12 or 2:3, and the ratio of the diagonals is $2\sqrt{2} : 3\sqrt{2}$ or 2:3. Therefore, the quantities are equal. Choice **(C)** is correct.

CHAPTER 12

Problem Solving

INTRODUCTION TO PROBLEM SOLVING

Problem Solving can be broken up into several general mathematics categories: algebra, arithmetic, number properties, and geometry.

In a Problem Solving question, you may be asked to solve a pure math problem or a word problem involving a real-world situation. You will be asked to enter your answer into an onscreen box, select one answer, or select one or more options that correctly answer the problem.

The directions for a Problem Solving question requiring a single answer will look like this:

Directions: Click to select your choice.

A Problem Solving question requiring you to select a single answer will look like this, with ovals next to each answer choice:

Sample Question

A health club charges $35 per month plus $2.50 for each aerobics class attended. How many aerobics classes were attended in a certain month if the total monthly charge was $52.50?

○ 7

○ 8

○ 9

○ 10

○ 11

Click to select your choice.

The directions for a Problem Solving question requiring you to select one or more answers will look like this:

Directions: Click to select your choice(s).

If a Problem Solving question asks you to select your choice(s), at least one answer is correct, but as many as all the choices may be correct. You must select all of the correct choices (and none of the incorrect ones) for the question to be counted as correct.

A Problem Solving question requiring you to select one or more answers will look like this, with rectangles next to each answer choice:

Sample Question

If $0 < x < 1$, which of the following *must* be true?

Choose <u>all</u> possible answers.

☐ $2x < x$

☐ $2x < 1$

☐ $2x > 1$

☐ $x^2 < x$

☐ $x^2 < 1$

Click to select your choice(s).

The directions for a Problem Solving question requiring you to make a Numeric Entry will look like this:

Directions: Click in the box and type your numeric answer. Backspace to erase.

Enter your answer as an integer or decimal if there is one box or as a fraction if there are two boxes.

To enter an integer or decimal, type directly in the box or use the Transfer Display button on the calculator.

- Use the backspace key to erase.
- Use a hyphen to enter a negative sign; type a hyphen a second time to remove it. The digits will remain.
- Use a period for a decimal point.
- The Transfer Display button will enter your answer directly from the calculator.
- Equivalent forms of decimals are all correct. (*Example:* 0.14 = 0.140)
- Enter the exact answer unless the question asks you to round your answer.

To enter a fraction, type the numerator and denominator in the appropriate boxes.

- Use a hyphen to enter a negative sign.
- The Transfer Display button does not work for fractions.
- Equivalent forms of fractions are all correct. (*Example:* $\frac{25}{15} = \frac{5}{3}$.) If numbers are large, reduce fractions to fit in boxes.

A Problem Solving question with Numeric Entry will look like this:

Sample Question

| Exit Section | Review | Mark | Help ? | Back | Next |

The health club charges $35 per month plus $2.50 for each aerobics class attended. How many aerobics classes were attended in a certain month if the total monthly charge was $52.50?

[   ] classes

Click in the box and type your numeric answer. Backspace to erase.

THE KAPLAN METHOD FOR PROBLEM SOLVING

STEP 1   Analyze the question.

STEP 2   Identify the task.

STEP 3   Approach strategically.

STEP 4   Confirm your answer.

HOW THE KAPLAN METHOD FOR PROBLEM SOLVING WORKS

Now let's discuss how the Kaplan Method for Problem Solving works:

▶ STEP 1

Analyze the question.

Look at what the question is asking and what area of math is being tested. Also note any particular trends in the answer choices (e.g., numbers/variables, integers/non-integers) and what information is being given. Unpack as much information as possible.

▶ STEP 2

Identify the task.

Determine what question is being asked before solving the problem. Ask yourself, "What does the correct answer represent?" The GRE intentionally provides wrong answers for test takers who get the right answer to the wrong question.

▶ STEP 3

Approach strategically.

Depending on the type of problem, you may use straightforward math—the textbook approach—to calculate your answer, or you may choose one of the following strategies: Picking Numbers, Backsolving, or Strategic Guessing.

When Picking Numbers to substitute for variables, choose numbers that are manageable and fit the description given in the problem. Backsolving is another form of Picking Numbers; you'll start with one of the answer choices and plug that choice back into the question. Lastly, Strategic Guessing can be a great time-saver on the GRE—being able to make a smart guess on a question is preferable to taking too much time and thus compromising your ability to answer other questions correctly.

▶ STEP 4

Confirm your answer.

Check that your answer makes sense. Also check that you answered the question that was asked.

HOW TO APPLY THE KAPLAN METHOD FOR PROBLEM SOLVING

Now let's apply the Kaplan Method to a Problem Solving question:

In a bag of candy, 7 of the candies are cherry flavored, 8 are lemon, and 5 are grape. If a candy is chosen randomly from the bag, what is the probability that the candy is *not* lemon?

❯❯ STEP 1

Analyze the question.

You are given the number of candies in a bag and asked to identify the probability that a randomly selected candy is not lemon flavored. You will have to type your answer into the box.

❯❯ STEP 2

Identify the task.

The probability of an event is defined as $\dfrac{\text{Number of desired outcomes}}{\text{Number of possible outcomes}}$. You will need to find the number of desired outcomes (those in which you don't choose a lemon candy) and the total number of possible outcomes.

❯❯ STEP 3

Approach strategically.

There are 20 candies in the bag, so there are 20 possible outcomes. Of all the candies, 12 are not lemon, so there are 12 desired outcomes. So, the probability of *not* lemon is $\dfrac{12}{20}$. You should avoid reducing fractions for Numeric Entry questions, since all equivalent forms will be counted as correct. Save your time for other questions and limit your risk of committing an error in calculation.

❯❯ STEP 4

Confirm your answer.

Although it might be fun to get a bag of candies and check your answer in a real-world way, it's not practical, especially on Test Day. A more practical check would be to find the probability of choosing a lemon candy at random to be certain that $P(\text{lemon}) = 1 - P(\text{not lemon})$. There are 8 lemon candies out of 20, so this check can be done easily.

$$P(\text{lemon}) \overset{?}{=} 1 - P(\text{not lemon})$$

$$\frac{8}{20} \overset{?}{=} 1 - \frac{12}{20}$$

$$\frac{8}{20} \overset{?}{=} \frac{20}{20} - \frac{12}{20}$$

$$\frac{8}{20} = \frac{8}{20}$$

This check is a way to confirm that the correct numbers have been used in the problem and the correct answer has been found.

Now let's apply the Kaplan Method to a second Problem Solving question:

> When n is divided by 14, the remainder is 10. What is the remainder when n is divided by 7?
>
> Ⓐ 2
> Ⓑ 3
> Ⓒ 4
> Ⓓ 5
> Ⓔ 6

❯ STEP 1

Analyze the question.

In this question, you are asked to compare the relationship between the numbers 14 and 7 used as divisors.

❯ STEP 2

Identify the task.

The task is to use the fact that division of a number, n, by 14 yields a remainder of 10 to identify the remainder when the same number is divided by 7.

❯ STEP 3

Approach strategically.

A good strategy for this question is to pick a number for n that satisfies the condition for division by 14 and then see what happens when it is divided by 7.

Any number divided by itself will give a remainder of zero. So if we need a remainder of 10, we want a number that is 10 more than the number we are dividing by. Be careful; you may be thinking of choosing $14 \div 7 = 2$ or $10 \div 2 = 5$. But these are both trap answer choices because the question also involves using a remainder. Therefore, 24 is a great number to pick here, because when we try 24:

$$24 \div 14 = 1 \text{ Remainder } 10$$

Now that we've confirmed that 24 works, we answer the question that's being asked. Divide 24 by 7:

$$24 \div 7 = 3 \text{ Remainder } 3$$

Answer choice **(B)** is the correct answer.

STEP 4

Confirm your answer.

You can quickly double-check your work, or you can try another number for n that results in a remainder of 10 when divided by 14:

$$38 \div 14 = 2 \text{ Remainder } 10, \text{ and } 38 \div 7 = 5 \text{ Remainder } 3$$

So the remainder is 3 in each case. The correct answer is **(B)**.

Now let's apply the Kaplan Method to a third Problem Solving question:

The line $4x + 6y = 24$ passes through which of the following points?

Indicate <u>all</u> possible answers.

- A   (0,4)
- B   (2,3)
- C   (3,2)
- D   (5,4)
- E   (9,−1)

STEP 1

Analyze the question.

This question is about a line on the coordinate plane. The equation is a function that represents a line. The numbers in the parentheses in the answer choices represent points (x,y) that are mentioned in the equation.

STEP 2

Identify the task.

Your job is to identify which of the given points lie on the line. A line passes through a point if the coordinates of the point make the equation of the line true, so this is the same as saying that you need to find out which point(s), when plugged into the equation, make the equation true.

❖ STEP 3

Approach strategically.

You need to find all correct answers, so test all of them. Substitute the first coordinate for x and the second coordinate for y.

(A) Test $(0,4)$: $4x + 6y = 24 \rightarrow 4(0) + 6(4) = 0 + 24 = 24$. This works.
(B) Test $(2,3)$: $4x + 6y = 24 \rightarrow 4(2) + 6(3) = 8 + 18 \neq 24$. Eliminate.
(C) Test $(3,2)$: $4x + 6y = 24 \rightarrow 4(3) + 6(2) = 12 + 12 = 24$. This works.
(D) Test $(5,4)$: $4x + 6y = 24 \rightarrow 4(5) + 6(4) = 20 + 24 \neq 24$. Eliminate.
(E) Test $(9,-1)$: $4x + 6y = 24 \rightarrow 4(9) + 6(-1) = 36 - 6 \neq 24$. Eliminate.

So choices **(A)** and **(C)** are correct.

❖ STEP 4

Confirm your answer.

Double-check your work to make sure you haven't made any careless errors, such as mistakenly plugging in a value for x when dealing with the variable y.

KAPLAN'S ADDITIONAL TIPS FOR PROBLEM SOLVING

Choose an efficient strategy.

The GRE is not a traditional math test that requires that you show your work in order to get credit, testing the process as well as the answer. The GRE tests only the answer—not how you found it. Because time is often your biggest concern on the GRE, the best way to each solution is often the quickest way, and the quickest way is often not straightforward math. Through practice, you'll become familiar with approaching each question in a more strategic way.

Rely on kaplan math strategies.

Using Kaplan strategies is a way to use reasoning in conjunction with mathematics to answer a question quickly. There may also be cases in which you can combine approaches: for example, using straightforward math to simplify an equation, then picking manageable numbers for the variables to solve that equation.

Picking numbers.

Problems that seem difficult can be good candidates for the Picking Numbers strategy. They include problems where either the question or the answer choices have variables, the problem tests a number property you don't recall, or the problem and the answer choices deal with percents or fractions without using actual values.

Backsolving.

Backsolving is a similar strategy to Picking Numbers, except that you'll use one of the five answer choices as the number to pick. After all, the testmaker gives you the correct answer; it's just mixed in with the wrong answers. Remember, numerical answer choices are always in ascending or descending order. Use that information to your advantage when using Backsolving. Start with either **(B)** or **(D)** first, because you'll have a 40 percent chance of finding the correct answer based on your first round of calculations. If you don't happen to pick the correct answer the first time, reason whether the number you started with was too large or too small. If you test choice **(B)** when the answer choices are in ascending order and **(B)** turns out to be too large, then **(A)** is the correct answer. If **(B)** is too small, then test choice **(D)**. If **(D)** is too large, then **(C)** is the correct answer. If **(D)** is too small, then **(E)** is correct. The opposite would be true if the choices were in descending order. Backsolving allows you to find the correct answer without ever needing to test more than two of the answer choices.

Use strategic guessing.

This is a good strategy if you can eliminate choices by applying number property rules or by estimating because gaps between answer choices are wide.

If some of the choices are out of the realm of possibility, eliminate them and move on.

PROBLEM SOLVING PRACTICE SET

Try the following Problem Solving questions using the Kaplan Method for Problem Solving. If you're up to the challenge, time yourself; on Test Day, you'll want to spend only about 2 minutes on each question.

1. If $r = 3s$, $s = 5t$, $t = 2u$, and $u \neq 0$, what is the value of $\frac{rst}{u^3}$?

   Ⓐ 30
   Ⓑ 60
   Ⓒ 150
   Ⓓ 300
   Ⓔ 600

2. In the diagram, l_1 is parallel to l_2. The measure of angle q is 40 degrees. What is the sum of the measures of the acute angles shown in the diagram?

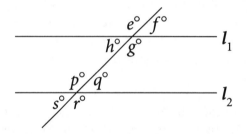

   Note: Figure not drawn to scale.

   [   ] degrees

3. At Central Park Zoo, the ratio of sea lions to penguins is 4:11. If there are 84 more penguins than sea lions, how many sea lions are there?

   Ⓐ 24
   Ⓑ 36
   Ⓒ 48
   Ⓓ 72
   Ⓔ 121

4. Which of the following are prime numbers between $\frac{5}{2}$ and $\frac{43}{5}$? Indicate all possible answers.

   A 3
   B 4
   C 5
   D 7
   E 9

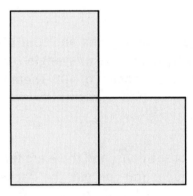

5. The figure above is made up of 3 squares. If the perimeter of the figure is 40 units, what is the area of the figure in square units?

   A 50
   B 75
   C 120
   D 150
   E 200

PROBLEM SOLVING PRACTICE SET
ANSWERS AND EXPLANATIONS

1. E

The other variables all build upon u, so use the Picking Numbers strategy: pick a small number for u and find the values for r, s, and t. For instance, if $u = 1$, then $t = 2u$, so $t = 2$; $s = 5t$, so $s = 10$; and $r = 3s$, so $r = 30$.

So, $\dfrac{rst}{u^3} = \dfrac{30 \times 10 \times 2}{1 \times 1 \times 1} = 600$. The correct answer is (E).

2. 160

In the diagram, there are four acute angles and four obtuse angles created when the parallel lines are cut by the transversal. If angle q has a measure of 40°, then angles s, h, and f each also has a measure of 40°. Therefore, the sum of their degree measures is **160**.

3. C

You need to find the number of sea lions, and there are fewer sea lions than penguins, so starting small is a good idea. You can use the Backsolving strategy; start with choice **(B)**, 36. If there are 36 sea lions, then there are $36 + 84 = 120$ penguins, and the ratio of sea lions to penguins is $\dfrac{36}{120} = \dfrac{3}{10}$. This ratio is less than $\dfrac{4}{11}$, so your answer must be larger. If you try **(D)**, there are 72 sea lions and there are $72 + 84 = 156$ penguins, and the ratio of sea lions to penguins is $\dfrac{72}{156} = \dfrac{6}{13}$. Since this ratio is too large, the correct answer must be **(C)**.

4. A, C, D

You need to find a range of values between two improper fractions. First, change the improper fractions to mixed numbers: $\dfrac{5}{2} = 2\dfrac{1}{2}$ and $\dfrac{43}{5} = 8\dfrac{3}{5}$. Now, a prime number is a positive integer with only two distinct factors, 1 and itself. The prime numbers in the answer choices are 3, 5, and 7, and they are all between $2\dfrac{1}{2}$ and $8\dfrac{3}{5}$. So the correct answers are **(A)**, **(C)**, and **(D)**.

5. B

There are 8 side lengths of the squares that make up the perimeter, which you are told is 40. So, each side of each square must be 5 units. The area of each square can be found by squaring one side, so each square has an area of 25 square units. Since there are three squares, the total area of the figure is 75 square units. The correct answer is **(B)**.

CHAPTER 13

Data Interpretation

INTRODUCTION TO DATA INTERPRETATION QUESTIONS

Data Interpretation questions are based on information located in tables or graphs, and they are often statistics oriented. The data may be located in one table or graph, but you might also need to extract data from two or more tables or graphs. There will be a set of questions for you to answer based on each data presentation.

You may be asked to choose one or more answers from a set of answer choices or to enter your answer in a Numeric Entry field.

The directions for Data Interpretation questions will look like this:

Questions 15–17 are based on the following table.

PERCENT OF SALES PER CLIENT FOR CURTAIN FABRIC OVER THREE MONTHS

	May	June	July
The Home Touch	45%	25%	48%
Curtains Unlimited	30%	23%	23%
Max's Curtain Supply	9%	23%	17%
Valances by Val	13%	20%	8%
Wendy's Windows	3%	9%	4%

A Data Interpretation question that requires you to choose exactly one correct answer will look like this:

Sample Question

| Exit Section | Review | Mark | Help | Back | Next |

If total sales for curtain fabric in July were $150,000, how much revenue did The Home Touch account for?

- ○ 45,000
- ○ 48,000
- ○ 67,500
- ○ 72,000
- ○ 100,000

Click to select your choice.

A Data Interpretation question that requires you to select all the answer choices that apply will look like this:

Sample Question

| Exit Section | Review | Mark | Help | Back | Next |

In the months of June and July, which clients accounted for more than 15% of sales each month?

Choose <u>all</u> that apply.

- ☐ The Home Touch
- ☐ Curtains Unlimited
- ☐ Max's Curtain Supply
- ☐ Valances by Val
- ☐ Wendy's Windows

Click to select your choice(s).

A Data Interpretation question that requires you to enter your numeric answer in a box will look like this:

Sample Question

| Exit Section | Review | Mark | Help | Back | Next |

In May, the two clients representing the greatest percentages of sales accounted for $81,000 in sales. What were the total sales for the month of May?

$ [   ]

Click in the box and type your numeric answer. Backspace to erase.

THE KAPLAN METHOD FOR DATA INTERPRETATION

STEP 1 Analyze the tables and graphs.

STEP 2 Approach strategically.

HOW THE KAPLAN METHOD FOR DATA INTERPRETATION WORKS

Now let's discuss how the Kaplan Method for Data Interpretation works.

◆ STEP 1

Analyze the tables and graphs.

Tables, graphs, and charts often come in pairs that are linked in some way (for example, a manufacturer's total revenue and its revenue by product line). Familiarize yourself with the information in both graphs (or tables) and with how the two are related before attacking the questions. Scan the figures for these components:

- **Title**. Read the charts' titles to ensure you can get to the right chart or graph quickly.
- **Scale**. Check the units of measurement. Does the graph measure miles per minute or hour? Missing the units can drastically change your answer.
- **Notes**. Read any accompanying notes—the GRE will typically give you information only if it is helpful or even critical to getting the correct answer.
- **Key**. If there are multiple bars or lines on a graph, make sure you understand the key so you can match up the correct quantities with the correct items.

◆ STEP 2

Approach strategically.

Data Interpretation questions are designed to test your understanding of fractions and percents and your attention to detail. Taking a split second to make sure you answered the right question can make the difference between a correct answer and the "right" answer to the wrong question.

Questions tend to become more complex as you move through a set. For instance, if a question set contains two graphs, the first question likely refers to just one graph. A later question will most often combine data from both graphs. If you don't use both graphs for this later question, the chances are good you have missed something.

No matter how difficult graph questions appear at first glance, you can usually simplify single-answer multiple-choice questions by taking advantage of their answer-choice format. By approximating the answer rather than calculating it wherever possible, you can quickly identify the right one. As we saw with Problem Solving, estimation can be one of the fastest ways to identify the correct answer in math problems. Data Interpretation questions benefit from this strategy, as they tend to be the most time-consuming questions to answer.

How to Apply the Kaplan Method for Data Interpretation

Now let's apply the Kaplan Method to a Data Interpretation question:

CLIMOGRAPH OF CITY S

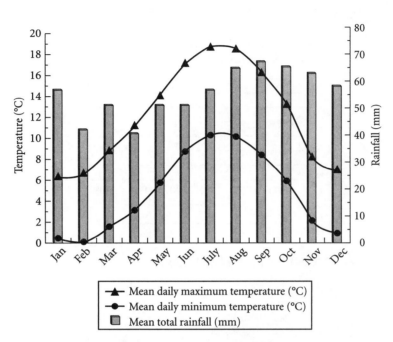

The Tourism Board of City S uses the information provided in the climograph to market the city as a tourist destination. One criterion is that the average monthly rainfall be less than 60 millimeters. What fraction of the months meet this criterion?

❱ STEP 1

Analyze the tables and graphs.

Take the analysis of the graph step-by-step. Start with the title of the graph to verify that the data given are for City S. Then take note of the scale for each type of information—degrees Celsius for temperature and millimeters for rainfall. There are data for each month of the year, which means you will not have to convert the units to answer the question that's being asked.

❱ STEP 2

Approach strategically.

The question asks only about rainfall; those data are given by the bars on the graph. According to the bars, rainfall is greater than 60 mm in August, September, October, and November. That's 4 of 12 months that *do not* meet the criteria, so 8 of 12 months *do* meet it. You may enter the fraction $\frac{8}{12}$ directly into the boxes, and your answer will be accepted. It is *not* required that you reduce it.

Now let's apply the Kaplan Method to a second Data Interpretation question:

**CUSTOMERS WHO SWITCHED SERVICE PROVIDERS
(IN MILLIONS OF CUSTOMERS)**

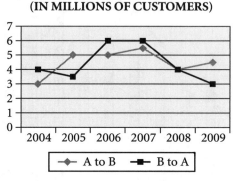

COMPANY A PROFIT 2008

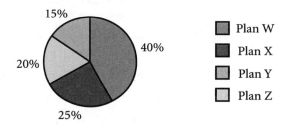

In 2008, Company A had a total profit of $220 million. If half of the customers who switched to Company A were responsible for half of the profit for Plan X, how much did these customers contribute per person toward Company A's profit for the year?

- [A] $1.10
- [B] $13.75
- [C] $20.25
- [D] $27.50
- [E] $55.00

❯ STEP 1

Analyze the tables and graphs.

This question has information about numbers of customers switching service providers for various years. It also has information about one company's profit for the year 2008, so the data in the two graphs will be linked by the year 2008.

STEP 2

Approach strategically.

Approach the question methodically, starting with identifying the number of customers who switched to Company A. The line chart indicates that 4 million customers switched to Company A. This is the only information needed from the top graph.

The pie chart shows the breakdown of profit from the various plans offered and indicates that 25 percent of the profit came from Plan X.

The other information you need to get to the correct answer is given in the question stem:

- Profit of $220 million.
- Half of the customers who switched were responsible for half of Plan X's profits.

Now that your information is organized, all you need to do is the calculation. Plan X accounts for 25 percent of $220 million = $55 million. Half of $55 million is $27.5 million.

If 4 million people switched, then half of the people who switched would be 2 million.

The last step is to divide $27.5 by 2 (you can drop the zeroes in the millions because they will cancel out): $27.5 ÷ 2 = $13.75. The correct choice is **(B)**.

Now let's apply the Kaplan Method to a third Data Interpretation question:

**CUSTOMERS WHO SWITCHED SERVICE PROVIDERS
(IN MILLIONS OF CUSTOMERS)**

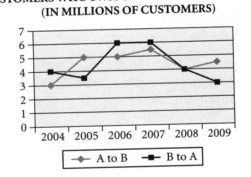

COMPANY A PROFIT 2008

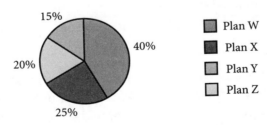

The management of Company B is most interested in the data for the years in which there were at least one million *more* customers who switched from

Company A to Company B than switched from Company B to Company A. In which years did this happen?

Choose <u>all</u> that apply.

[A] 2005

[B] 2006

[C] 2007

[D] 2008

[E] 2009

⮞ STEP 1

Analyze the tables and graphs.

This question asks for a comparison of facts between Company A and Company B. Take time to verify which line in the top graph represents customers switching to Company A and which line represents customers switching to Company B. Confirm that the title states that the data are given in millions and then look at the scale on the line graph.

⮞ STEP 2

Approach strategically.

After examining the line graph carefully, you are ready to gather the information needed to answer the question. The years that satisfy the requirement are those years for which the line representing A to B is at least one full horizontal row above the line representing B to A. Read the graph carefully because you must identify all the correct choices to get credit for a correct answer.

When you are clear what to look for on the graph, start from the left and identify the years 2005 and 2009 as those in which at least one million more customers switched from A to B than switched from B to A. These are choices **(A)** and **(E)**.

KAPLAN'S ADDITIONAL TIPS FOR DATA INTERPRETATION QUESTIONS

Slow Down

There's always a lot going on in Data Interpretation problems—both in the charts and in the questions themselves. If you slow down the first time through, you can avoid calculation errors and having to reread the questions and charts.

Pace Yourself Wisely

To ensure that you score as many points on the exam as possible, use the allotted time for a section wisely. Remember that each question type has the same value. If you must miss a few questions in a section, make them the ones that would take you the longest to answer, not the ones at the end of the section that you could have answered correctly but simply didn't get to. Data Interpretation questions are generally some of the more time-consuming ones to answer, and if answering them isn't one of your strong suits, save them for the end.

DATA INTERPRETATION PRACTICE SET

Try the following Data Interpretation questions using the Kaplan Method for Data Interpretation. If you're up to the challenge, time yourself; on Test Day, you'll want to spend only about 2 minutes on each question.

Questions 1–5 are based on the following graphs.

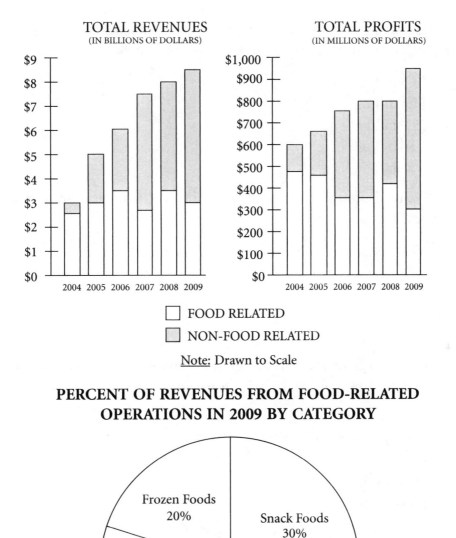

TOTAL REVENUES
(IN BILLIONS OF DOLLARS)

TOTAL PROFITS
(IN MILLIONS OF DOLLARS)

☐ FOOD RELATED
▨ NON-FOOD RELATED

Note: Drawn to Scale

PERCENT OF REVENUES FROM FOOD-RELATED OPERATIONS IN 2009 BY CATEGORY

Frozen Foods 20%

Snack Foods 30%

Alcoholic Beverages 7%

Soft Drinks 43%

1. Approximately how much did total revenues increase from 2004 to 2007?

   (A) $0.5 billion
   (B) $1.5 billion
   (C) $4 billion
   (D) $4.5 billion
   (E) $5 billion

2. For the year in which profits from food-related operations increased over the previous year, total revenues were approximately:

   (A) $3.5 billion
   (B) $4.5 billion
   (C) $5.7 billion
   (D) $6 billion
   (E) $8 billion

3. In 2008, total profits represented approximately what percent of total revenues?

   (A) 50%
   (B) 20%
   (C) 10%
   (D) 5%
   (E) 1%

4. For the first year in which revenues from non-food-related operations surpassed $4.5 billion, total profits were approximately:

   (A) $250 million
   (B) $450 million
   (C) $550 million
   (D) $650 million
   (E) $800 million

5. In 2009, how many millions of dollars were revenues from frozen food operations?

   ⬚ millions of dollars

DATA INTERPRETATION PRACTICE SET ANSWERS AND EXPLANATIONS

1. D

This question asks about total revenues, so you should refer to the left bar graph. Each bar in the graph has two components, but you want to look at the total height of the bars for 2004 and 2007 because the question asks about total revenues. Total revenues for 2004 appear to be $3 billion, and for 2007 they appear to be about $7.5 billion. So the increase is roughly $7.5 billion − $3 billion = $4.5 billion. Answer choice **(D)** is correct.

2. E

You have to refer to both bar graphs to answer this question. First, refer to the right bar graph to find the lone year in which food-related profits increased over the previous year—the only year in which the unshaded portion of the bar increases in size is 2008. Now that you've zeroed in on the year, refer to the left bar graph to determine the total revenues for that year, which appear to be about $8 billion. Answer choice **(E)** is correct.

3. C

This is a percent question, so start with the bar graphs. You need the figures from both food-related and non-food-related sources, so look at the total height of the bars. From the right bar graph, the total profits for 2008 appear to be $800 million; from the left bar graph, total revenues for that year appear to be $8 billion (i.e., $8,000 million). Now, convert the part/whole into a percent:

$$\frac{800\,\text{million}}{8\,\text{billion}} = \frac{800\,\text{million}}{8,000\,\text{million}} = \frac{1}{10} = 10\%$$

4. E

First, find the year for which revenues from non-food-related operations surpassed $4.5 billion on the left bar graph. Finding the correct bar is made more difficult by the fact that you have to deal with the shaded portion, which is at the top of the bar, not at the bottom. Looking carefully, you should then see that 2007 is the year in question. The question asks for total *profits*, so once again refer to the right bar graph, and you'll see the profits for that year are around $800 million. This matches answer choice **(E)**.

5. 600

Finally, you have a question that refers to the pie chart. You are asked about revenues from frozen food operations, and the pie chart tells you that frozen foods represent 20 percent of all food-related revenues for 2009. To convert this into an amount, you need to locate the amount of food-related revenues for 2009. Once again, refer to the left bar graph, where you'll find that food-related revenues in 2009 were $3 billion, or $3,000 million. Then calculate that 20 percent of $3,000 million is **$600** million.

CHAPTER 14

Quantitative Reasoning Practice Sets

In this chapter, you will take three practice sections, composed of 20 questions each. A diagnostic tool is provided after each section to help you learn from your mistakes. Then you can continue to the next set with more awareness of the traps you may encounter.

REVIEW OF THE KAPLAN METHODS FOR QUANTITATIVE REASONING QUESTION TYPES

Before starting your practice sets, review the steps and strategies you have studied for answering each type of Quantitative Reasoning question quickly, efficiently, and correctly before starting your Practice Sets.

THE KAPLAN METHOD FOR QUANTITATIVE COMPARISON

STEP 1 Analyze the centered information and quantities.

STEP 2 Approach strategically.

THE KAPLAN METHOD FOR PROBLEM SOLVING

STEP 1   Analyze the question.

STEP 2   Identify the task.

STEP 3   Approach strategically.

STEP 4   Confirm your answer.

THE KAPLAN METHOD FOR DATA INTERPRETATION

STEP 1   Analyze the tables and graphs.

STEP 2   Approach strategically.

QUANTITATIVE REASONING PRACTICE SET 1

NUMBERS

All numbers are real numbers.

FIGURES

The position of points, lines, angles, and so on may be assumed to be in the order shown; all lengths and angle measures may be assumed to be positive.

Lines shown as straight may be assumed to be straight.

Figures lie in the plane of the paper unless otherwise stated.

Figures that accompany questions are intended to provide useful information. However, unless a note states that a figure has been drawn to scale, you should solve the problems by using your knowledge of mathematics, not by estimation or measurement.

DIRECTIONS

Each of the following questions, 1–8, consists of two quantities, Quantity A and Quantity B. You are to compare the two quantities and choose

(A)   if Quantity A is greater
(B)   if Quantity B is greater
(C)   if the two quantities are equal
(D)   if the relationship cannot be determined from the information given

COMMON INFORMATION

In a question, information concerning one or both of the quantities to be compared is centered above the two quantities. A symbol that appears in both quantities represents the same thing in Quantity A as it does in Quantity B.

1. | Quantity A | Quantity B |
    |---|---|
    | The number of distinct ways to form an ordered line of 3 people by choosing from 6 people | The number of distinct ways to form an unordered group of 3 people by choosing from 10 people |

    (A) Quantity A is greater.
    (B) Quantity B is greater.
    (C) The two quantities are equal.
    (D) The relationship cannot be determined from the information given.

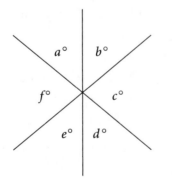

2. | Quantity A | Quantity B |
    |---|---|
    | $a + c + e$ | $b + d + f$ |

    (A) Quantity A is greater.
    (B) Quantity B is greater.
    (C) The two quantities are equal.
    (D) The relationship cannot be determined from the information given.

$$7p + 3 = r$$
$$3p + 7 = s$$

3. | Quantity A | Quantity B |
    |---|---|
    | r | s |

    (A) Quantity A is greater.
    (B) Quantity B is greater.
    (C) The two quantities are equal.
    (D) The relationship cannot be determined from the information given.

The original cost of a shirt is x dollars.

4. | Quantity A | Quantity B |
    |---|---|
    | x | The cost of the shirt if the original cost is first increased by 10% and then decreased by 10% |

    (A) Quantity A is greater.
    (B) Quantity B is greater.
    (C) The two quantities are equal.
    (D) The relationship cannot be determined from the information given.

There were x dictionaries in a bookstore. After $\frac{1}{8}$ of them were purchased, 10 more dictionaries were shipped in, bringing the total number of dictionaries to 52.

5. Quantity A   Quantity B

       x 50

- Ⓐ Quantity A is greater.
- Ⓑ Quantity B is greater.
- Ⓒ The two quantities are equal.
- Ⓓ The relationship cannot be determined from the information given.

There are n people in a room. One-third of them leave the room. Four people enter the room. There are now $\frac{5}{6}$ of the original number of people in the room.

6. Quantity A   Quantity B

       n 20

- Ⓐ Quantity A is greater.
- Ⓑ Quantity B is greater.
- Ⓒ The two quantities are equal.
- Ⓓ The relationship cannot be determined from the information given.

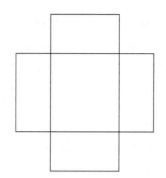

Note: Figure not drawn to scale.

Two rectangles with dimensions 2 meters by 4 meters overlap to form the figure above. All the angles shown measure 90°.

7. Quantity A   Quantity B

The perimeter   16
of the figure,
in meters

- Ⓐ Quantity A is greater.
- Ⓑ Quantity B is greater.
- Ⓒ The two quantities are equal.
- Ⓓ The relationship cannot be determined from the information given.

x is an integer.
$$1 < x < 9$$

8. Quantity A   Quantity B

$(\sqrt{x} + \sqrt{x})^2$ $x + x\sqrt{x}$

- Ⓐ Quantity A is greater.
- Ⓑ Quantity B is greater.
- Ⓒ The two quantities are equal.
- Ⓓ The relationship cannot be determined from the information given.

9. If $\dfrac{x}{y} = \dfrac{2}{3}$ and $x + y = 15$, which of the following is greater than y?

   Indicate **all** possible choices.

   [A] $\sqrt{65}$

   [B] $\sqrt{82}$

   [C] $\sqrt{99}$

   [D] $\sqrt{101}$

   [E] $\sqrt{122}$

10. The product of two integers is 10. Which of the following could be the average (arithmetic mean) of the two numbers?

    Indicate **all** possible choices.

    [A] -5.5

    [B] -3.5

    [C] -1.5

    [D] 1.5

    [E] 3.5

11. Which of the following is greater than the sum of the distinct prime factors of 210?

    Indicate **all** possible choices.

    [A] 12

    [B] 17

    [C] 19

    [D] 21

    [E] 24

12. The average (arithmetic mean) bowling score of n bowlers is 160. The average of these n scores together with a score of 170 is 161. What is the number of bowlers, n?

     bowlers

13. Set T consists of five integers: the first five odd prime numbers when counting upward from zero. This gives set T a standard deviation of approximately 3.71. Which of the following values, if added to the set T, would increase the standard deviation of set T?

    (A) 11

    (B) 9

    (C) 7.8

    (D) 4.15

    (E) 3.7

14.

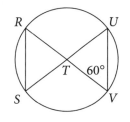

The circle shown has center T. The measure of angle TVU is 60°. If the circle has a radius of 3, what is the length of segment RS?

   (A) 2

   (B) $2\sqrt{2}$

   (C) 3

   (D) $3\sqrt{3}$

   (E) $6\sqrt{2}$

15. What is the probability of rolling a total of 7 with a single roll of two fair six-sided dice, each with the distinct numbers 1–6 on each side?

   Ⓐ $\dfrac{1}{12}$

   Ⓑ $\dfrac{1}{6}$

   Ⓒ $\dfrac{2}{7}$

   Ⓓ $\dfrac{1}{3}$

   Ⓔ $\dfrac{1}{2}$

16. If it takes three days for 10 workers to finish building one house, how many days will it take 15 workers to finish four houses?

 days

Questions 17–20 are based on the following graph and table.

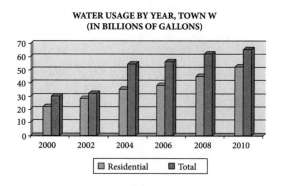

WATER USAGE BY YEAR, TOWN W
(IN BILLIONS OF GALLONS)

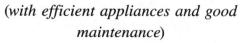

DAILY WATER USAGE STATISTICS

(with efficient appliances and good maintenance)

Use	Gallons per Capita
Showers	9
Clothes washers	10
Toilets	8
Leaks	4
Faucets	11
Other	4

17. Which best describes the range (in billions of gallons) for residential water consumption from 2000 to 2010, inclusive?

   Ⓐ 10
   Ⓑ 20
   Ⓒ 30
   Ⓓ 40
   Ⓔ 50

18. In the year in which total usage exceeded residential usage by the least number of gallons, approximately what percent of total usage was residential usage?

    (A) 68%
    (B) 75%
    (C) 88%
    (D) 95%
    (E) 98%

19. In 2004, only 10,000 residents of town W lived in homes with efficient appliances and good maintenance. How many gallons per day were used by these residents for the three daily household purposes requiring the most water?

    (A) 110,000
    (B) 160,000
    (C) 270,000
    (D) 300,000
    (E) 460,000

20. Households with efficient appliances and good maintenance can reduce water consumption by about 35%. If half of the residential consumption in town W in 2010 was by households with efficient appliances and good maintenance, how many gallons of water (in billions) were saved that year?

    (A) 5
    (B) 14
    (C) 40
    (D) 52
    (E) 65

QUANTITATIVE REASONING PRACTICE SET 1 ANSWER KEY

1. C
2. C
3. D
4. A
5. B
6. A
7. C
8. A
9. B, C, D, E
10. A, B, E
11. C, D, E
12. 9
13. E
14. C
15. B
16. 8
17. C
18. C
19. D
20. B

DIAGNOSE YOUR RESULTS

Diagnostic Tool

Tally up your score and write your results below.

Total

Total Correct: _____ out of 20 correct

By Question Type

Quantitative Comparison (questions 1–8) _____ out of 8 correct

Problem Solving (questions 9–16) _____ out of 8 correct

Data Interpretation (questions 17–20) _____ out of 4 correct

Look back at the questions you got wrong and think about your experience answering them.

❯❯ STEP 1

Find the roadblocks.

If you struggled to answer some questions, then to improve your score, you need to pinpoint exactly what "roadblocks" tripped you up. To do that, ask yourself the following two questions:

Am I weak in the skills being tested?

This will be very easy for you to judge. Maybe you've forgotten how to figure out the area of a triangle or what PEMDAS stands for. If you know you need to brush up on your math skills, try the *Kaplan GRE Math Workbook*, which contains a focused review of all the fundamental math concepts tested on the GRE, as well as practice exercises to build speed and accuracy.

Did the question types throw me off?

Then you need to become more comfortable with them! Quantitative Comparisons have a unique format, and Data Interpretation can be daunting with its charts, graphs, and tables. If you struggled, go back to the beginning of this chapter and review the Kaplan principles and methods for the question types you found challenging. Make sure you understand the principles and how to apply the methods. These strategies will help you improve your speed and efficiency on Test Day. Remember, it's not a math test; it's a critical reasoning test.

Also, get as much practice as you can so that you grow more at ease with the question formats. For even more practice, try the *Kaplan GRE Math Workbook,* which includes practice sets for each question type.

❯❯ STEP 2

Find the blind spots.

Did you answer some questions quickly and confidently but get them wrong anyway?

When you come across wrong answers like these, you need to figure out what you thought you were doing right, what it turns out you were doing wrong, and why that happened. The best way to do that is to **read the answer explanations!**

The explanations give you a detailed breakdown of why the correct answer is correct and why all the other answers choices are incorrect. This helps to reinforce the Kaplan principles and methods for each question type and helps you figure out what blindsided you so it doesn't happen again. Also, just as with your "roadblocks," try to get in as much practice as you can.

❯❯ STEP 3

Reinforce your strengths.

Now read through all the answer explanations for the ones you got right. You should check every answer because if you guessed correctly without actually knowing how to get the right answer, reading the explanations helps you make sure that whatever needs fixing gets fixed. Again, this helps to reinforce the Kaplan principles and methods for each question type, which in turn helps you work more efficiently so you can get the score you want. Keep your skills sharp with more practice.

As soon as you are comfortable with all the GRE question types and Kaplan methods, complete a full-length practice test under timed conditions. Practice tests serve as milestones; they help you to chart your progress! So don't save them all for the final weeks before your Test Day. For even more practice, you can also try the Kaplan GRE Quiz Bank. You get more than 2,500 questions that you can access 24/7 from any Internet browser, and each question comes with a comprehensive explanation. You can even customize your quizzes based on question type, content, and difficulty level. Take quizzes in Timed Mode to test your stamina or in Tutor Mode to see explanations as you work. Best of all, you also get detailed reports to track your progress.

Visit **kaptest.com/GRE** for more details on our Quiz Bank and for more information on our other online and classroom-based options.

QUANTITATIVE REASONING PRACTICE SET 1
ANSWERS AND EXPLANATIONS

1. C

Quantity A is a permutation because order matters. The number of ways 3 people chosen from a group of 6 can be arranged in a line, where order matters, is $6 \times 5 \times 4 = 120$. Quantity B is a combination because order does not matter. The number of ways 3 people can be selected from a group of 10, where order does not matter, is

$$_{10}C_3 = \frac{10!}{3!(10-3)!} = \frac{10 \times 9 \times 8}{3 \times 2 \times 1} = \frac{720}{6} = 120$$

The two quantities are equal.

2. C

There are three sets of vertical angles in this diagram: (a, d), (b, e), and (c, f). In Quantity A, you can substitute b for e because they are vertical angles and therefore equal; this leaves the sum $a + b + c$ in Quantity A. Because these are the three angles on one side of a straight line, they sum to 180°. Similarly, after substituting e for b in Quantity B, $b + d + f$ is the same thing as $d + e + f$, or also 180°. The two quantities are equal.

3. D

Pick a value for p and see what effect it has on r and s. If $p = 1$, $r = (7 \times 1) + 3 = 10$, and $s = (3 \times 1) + 7 = 10$, and the two quantities are equal. But if $p = 0$, $r = (7 \times 0) + 3 = 3$, and $s = (3 \times 0) + 7 = 7$, and Quantity A is less than Quantity B. Because there are at least two different possible relationships, the answer is **(D)**.

4. A

Use the Picking Numbers strategy to answer this question. Suppose the original selling price of the shirt, x, is $100. After a 10% increase in price, the shirt would sell for 110% of $100, which is $110. If there is a 10% decrease next, the shirt would sell for 90% of the current price. That would be 90% of $110: $0.9 \times \$110 = \$99$. This price is less than the original amount, x, so Quantity A is greater.

5. B

Try to set the quantities equal. If x is 50, then the bookstore started out with 50 dictionaries. Then $\frac{1}{8}$ of them were purchased. You can see already that the quantities can't be equal, because $\frac{1}{8}$ of 50 won't yield an integer. But go ahead and see whether the answer is **(A)** or **(B)**. Because $\frac{1}{8}$ of 50 is close to 6, after these dictionaries were purchased, the store would have been left with about $50 - 6$ or 44 dictionaries. Then it received 10 more, giving a total of about 54 dictionaries. But this is more than the store actually ended up with; it only had 52. Therefore, it must have started with *fewer* than 50 dictionaries, and Quantity B is greater. (The last thing you care about is how many dictionaries it really had.)

6. A

There are n people in a room. One-third of them leave the room. So, there are $n - \frac{1}{3}n$ people in the room. Four people enter the room, so you have $n - \frac{1}{3}n + 4$ people. There are now $\frac{5}{6}$ of the original number of people in the room, therefore $n - \frac{1}{3}n + 4 = \frac{5}{6}n$. Now solve for n.

$$n - \frac{1}{3}n + 4 = \frac{5}{6}n$$

$$\frac{2}{3}n + 4 = \frac{5}{6}n$$

$$4 = \frac{5}{6}n - \frac{2}{3}n$$

$$4 = \frac{5}{6}n - \frac{4}{6}n$$

$$4 = \frac{1}{6}n$$

$$24 = n$$

So, $n = 24$ and Quantity A is larger.

7. C

You may have thought this was a choice **(D)** question; after all, you don't know exactly where the boards overlap, whether in the middle of each board, as pictured, or near the end of one of the boards. But that doesn't matter; all you need to know is that they overlap and that all the angles are right angles. If the boards did not overlap, it would be easy to find the perimeter: $2 + 2 + 4 + 4 = 12$ for each board, or 24 for both boards. Now, because the boards do overlap, the perimeter of the figure will be smaller than that, but how much smaller? It will be smaller by the amount of that "lost perimeter" in the middle; the perimeter of the square where the boards overlap. (You know it's a square since all the angles are right angles.) The length of a side of that square is the shorter dimension of each of the boards: 2. Therefore, the perimeter of the square is 4×2 or 8. The perimeter of the figure, then, is $24 - 8$ or 16. The two quantities are equal.

8. A

Start by simplifying the quantity in Quantity A: $\left(\sqrt{x} + \sqrt{x}\right)^2$ is the same as $\left(2\sqrt{x}\right)^2$, which is $4x$. Subtract x from both quantities, and you're left with $3x$ in Quantity A and $x\sqrt{x}$ in Quantity B. Now divide both sides by x, and you're left with 3 in Quantity A and $\sqrt{x}$ in Quantity B. Square both quantities, and you get 9 in Quantity A and x in Quantity B. Since x is an integer between 1 and 9, exclusive, Quantity A is larger. If the algebra seems too abstract, go ahead and use the Picking Numbers strategy. If x equals 4, then Quantity A equals $(2 + 2)^2 = 16$, and Quantity B equals $4 + 8 = 12$.

9. B, C, D, E

If $\dfrac{x}{y} = \dfrac{2}{3}$, then $3x = 2y$ and $y = \dfrac{3x}{2}$. Substitute $y = \dfrac{3x}{2}$ into the equation $x + y = 15$: $x + \dfrac{3x}{2} = 15$, $2x + 3x = 30$, $5x = 30$, $x = 6$. Then, $y = \dfrac{3x}{2} = \dfrac{3(6)}{2} = 9$ and $y^2 = 81$. So any answer with greater than 81 under the radical will be greater than y. Therefore, the correct choices are **(B), (C), (D)**, and **(E)**.

10. A, B, E

The best place to start here is with pairs of positive integers that have a product of 10. The numbers 5 and 2 have a product of 10, as do 10 and 1. But remember that integers may be negative, so -1 and -10 are possible, as well as -2 and -5. The mean of -1 and -10 is -5.5; the mean of -2 and -5 is -3.5. The mean of 2 and 5 is 3.5. The correct answers are **(A), (B)**, and **(E)**.

11. C, D, E

The prime factorization of 210 is $2 \times 3 \times 5 \times 7$. The sum of the prime factors is $2 + 3 + 5 + 7 = 17$. So, the correct choices are **(C), (D)**, and **(E)**.

12. 9

Use the definition of *average* to write the sum of the first n bowlers' scores: $\dfrac{\text{sum of scores}}{n} = \text{average}$; therefore, $n \times \text{average} = \text{sum of scores}$. Substitute the values given in the question, and you have $160n = \text{sum of scores}$ for the initial set of bowlers. Now write the formula for the average again, using the additional score of 170. Now there are $n + 1$ bowlers.

$$\frac{\text{sum of scores}}{n} = \text{average}$$

$$\frac{160n + 170}{n + 1} = 161$$

Cross multiply and use algebra to solve for *n*.

$$160n + 170 = 161(n + 1)$$
$$160n + 170 = 161n + 161$$
$$170 - 161 = 161n - 160n$$
$$9 = n$$

There were **9** bowlers in the original group.

13. E

First, identify the numbers in set *T*: 3, 5, 7, 11, 13. The average of the numbers in set *T* is $\dfrac{3 + 5 + 7 + 11 + 13}{5} = \dfrac{39}{5} = 7.8$. Its standard deviation is given in the question stem as 3.71. In order to increase the standard deviation of a set of numbers, you must add a value that is more than one standard deviation away from the mean. One standard deviation below the mean for set *T* would be $7.8 - 3.71 = 4.09$, and one standard deviation *above* the mean would be $7.8 + 3.71 = 11.51$. Any value outside this range $4.09 \le x \le 11.51$ would increase set *T*'s standard deviation, since it would make the set more "spread out" from the mean than it currently is. The only choice that does that is choice **(E)**.

14. C

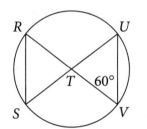

Solving this problem involves several steps, but none is too complicated. The circle has its center at point *T*. Start with the triangle on the right whose vertices are at *T* and two points on the circumference of the circle. This makes two of its sides radii of the circle, which we're told each have a length of 3. Because all radii must have equal length, this makes the triangle an isosceles triangle. In addition, you're told one of the base angles of this triangle has measure 60°. Thus, the other base angle must also have measure 60° (since the base angles in an isosceles triangle have equal measure). The sum of the two base angles is 120°, leaving 180° − 120° or 60° for the other angle, the one at point *T* (making △*TUV* an equilateral triangle with sides of 3).

Now, angle *RTS* is opposite this 60° angle, so its measure must also be 60°. Therefore, $\triangle RST$ is another equilateral triangle, and its sides are 3. Therefore, the length of *RS* is 3, choice **(C)**.

15. B

The probability formula is

$$\text{Probability} = \frac{\text{Number of desired outcomes}}{\text{Number of possible outcomes}}$$

When one die is rolled, there are six possible outcomes. When two dice are rolled, the number of possible outcomes is 6×6, or 36. Getting a total value of 7 can be achieved in the following ways: (1, 6), (2, 5), (3, 4), (4, 3), (5, 2), and (6, 1). There are six possible ways.

So the probability of rolling a total of 7 is $\frac{6}{36}$, which can be reduced to $\frac{1}{6}$, choice **(B)**.

16. 8

In the first scenario, each day $\frac{1 \text{ house}}{3 \text{ days}} = \frac{1}{3}$ of the house will be built. Because there are 10 workers, each person can build $\frac{1}{30}$ of a house each day. In the second scenario, there are 15 workers, so that means $15 \times \frac{1}{30} = \frac{1}{2}$ a house can be built each day. Four houses could, therefore, be built in 8 days:

$$\frac{4 \text{ houses}}{\frac{1}{2} \text{ house}/\text{day}} = 4 \times 2 = 8 \text{ days}$$

17. C

The residential usage (in billions) in 2000 was about 22; the usage was about 52 in 2010. The range is the difference because the residential usage increased over the time period. Therefore, $52 - 22 = 30$, and the range is about 30 billion gallons. The correct answer is **(C)**.

18. C

The two amounts were closest to each other in 2002. The residential amount appears to be about 28; the total appears to be about 32: $28 \div 32 = 0.875$. Choice **(C)** is the closest.

19. D

The three usages with the greatest amounts per person are faucets, washers, and showers, totaling 30 gallons per day. Multiply by 10,000 to get 300,000, choice **(D)**.

20. B

The residential consumption (in billions) in 2010 was approximately 52. Take half of that amount, 26, to represent the amount of water used by households with efficient appliances and plumbing. Let W represent the amount of water these households would have used otherwise.

Set up a percent equation to solve for W. Remember, the savings were 35%, so subtract 35 from 100 to find the percent that would have been used.

$$26 = (100\% - 35\%) \times W$$
$$26 = 65\% \times W$$
$$26 = 0.65 \times W$$
$$\frac{26}{0.65} = W$$

The savings in billions of gallons was $40 - 26 = 14$. The correct answer is **(B)**.

QUANTITATIVE REASONING PRACTICE SET 2

NUMBERS

All numbers are real numbers.

FIGURES

The position of points, lines, angles, and so on may be assumed to be in the order shown; all lengths and angle measures may be assumed to be positive.

Lines shown as straight may be assumed to be straight.

Figures lie in the plane of the paper unless otherwise stated.

Figures that accompany questions are intended to provide useful information. However, unless a note states that a figure has been drawn to scale, you should solve the problems by using your knowledge of mathematics, not by estimation or measurement.

DIRECTIONS

Each of the following questions, 1–10, consists of two quantities, Quantity A and Quantity B. You are to compare the two quantities and choose

- Ⓐ if Quantity A is greater
- Ⓑ if Quantity B is greater
- Ⓒ if the two quantities are equal
- Ⓓ if the relationship cannot be determined from the information given

COMMON INFORMATION

In a question, information concerning one or both of the quantities to be compared is centered above the two quantities. A symbol that appears in both quantities represents the same thing in Quantity A as it does in Quantity B.

1. | Quantity A | Quantity B |
   | --- | --- |
   | The average (arithmetic mean) of 100, 101, and 103 | The median of 100, 101, and 103 |

   Ⓐ Quantity A is greater.
   Ⓑ Quantity B is greater.
   Ⓒ The two quantities are equal.
   Ⓓ The relationship cannot be determined from the information given.

   A and B are points on the circumference of the circle with center O (not shown). The length of chord AB is 15.

2. | Quantity A | Quantity B |
   | --- | --- |
   | Circumference of circle O | 12π |

   Ⓐ Quantity A is greater.
   Ⓑ Quantity B is greater.
   Ⓒ The two quantities are equal.
   Ⓓ The relationship cannot be determined from the information given.

$$x = \frac{4}{3}r^2h^2$$
$$x = 1$$

r and h are positive.

3. | Quantity A | Quantity B |
   | --- | --- |
   | h | $\dfrac{\sqrt{3}}{2r}$ |

   Ⓐ Quantity A is greater.
   Ⓑ Quantity B is greater.
   Ⓒ The two quantities are equal.
   Ⓓ The relationship cannot be determined from the information given.

$\triangle ABC$ lies in the xy-plane with C at (0,0), B at (6,0), and A at (x,y), where x and y are positive. The area of $\triangle ABC$ is 18 square units.

4. | Quantity A | Quantity B |
   | --- | --- |
   | y | 6 |

   Ⓐ Quantity A is greater.
   Ⓑ Quantity B is greater.
   Ⓒ The two quantities are equal.
   Ⓓ The relationship cannot be determined from the information given.

$$\text{For } x \neq y,\ x\,\Phi\,y = \frac{x+y}{x-y}$$
$$p > 0 > q$$

5. | Quantity A | Quantity B |
   | --- | --- |
   | $p\,\Phi\,q$ | $q\,\Phi\,p$ |

   Ⓐ Quantity A is greater.
   Ⓑ Quantity B is greater.
   Ⓒ The two quantities are equal.
   Ⓓ The relationship cannot be determined from the information given.

$$x \neq 0$$

6. Quantity A Quantity B

$$\frac{1}{x} + \frac{1}{x} \qquad \frac{1}{x} \times \frac{1}{x}$$

- Ⓐ Quantity A is greater.
- Ⓑ Quantity B is greater.
- Ⓒ The two quantities are equal.
- Ⓓ The relationship cannot be determined from the information given.

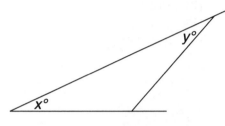

7. Quantity A Quantity B

$$x + y \qquad 180°$$

- Ⓐ Quantity A is greater.
- Ⓑ Quantity B is greater.
- Ⓒ The two quantities are equal.
- Ⓓ The relationship cannot be determined from the information given.

$$4x - 5y = 10$$
$$-3x + 6y = 22$$

8. Quantity A Quantity B

$$33 \qquad x + y$$

- Ⓐ Quantity A is greater.
- Ⓑ Quantity B is greater.
- Ⓒ The two quantities are equal.
- Ⓓ The relationship cannot be determined from the information given.

$$6(10)^n > 60{,}006$$

9. Quantity A Quantity B

$$n \qquad 6$$

- Ⓐ Quantity A is greater.
- Ⓑ Quantity B is greater.
- Ⓒ The two quantities are equal.
- Ⓓ The relationship cannot be determined from the information given.

In a four-digit positive integer y, the thousands digit is 2.5 times the tens digit.

10. Quantity A Quantity B

   The tens digits   4
   of y

- Ⓐ Quantity A is greater.
- Ⓑ Quantity B is greater.
- Ⓒ The two quantities are equal.
- Ⓓ The relationship cannot be determined from the information given.

11. What is the average (arithmetic mean) of $2x + 3$, $5x - 4$, $6x - 6$, and $3x - 1$?

- Ⓐ $2x + 4$
- Ⓑ $3x - 2$
- Ⓒ $3x + 2$
- Ⓓ $4x - 2$
- Ⓔ $4x + 2$

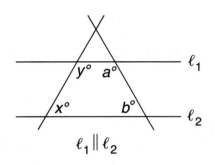

$\ell_1 \parallel \ell_2$

12. Which of the following statements must be true about the figure shown above?

(A) $x = a$

(B) $x = b$

(C) $a = b$

(D) $y = b$

(E) $x + y = a + b$

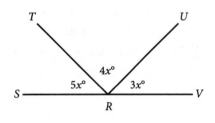

13. What is the degree measure of angle *SRU*?

(A) 15

(B) 45

(C) 105

(D) 135

(E) 180

14. There are at least 200 apples in a grocery store. The ratio of the number of oranges to the number of apples is 9 to 10. How many oranges could there be in the store?

Indicate **all** possible choices.

A 171

B 180

C 216

D 252

E 315

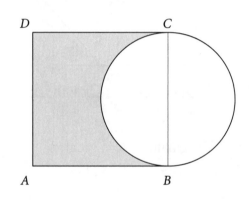

15. Square *ABCD* has a side length of 4. *BC* is the diameter of the circle. Which of the following is greater than or equal to the area of the shaded region, in square units?

Indicate **all** possible choices.

A $16 - 16\pi$

B $16 - 4\pi$

C $16 - 2\pi$

D $16 + \pi$

E $16 + 4\pi$

Questions 16–20 are based on the following graphs.

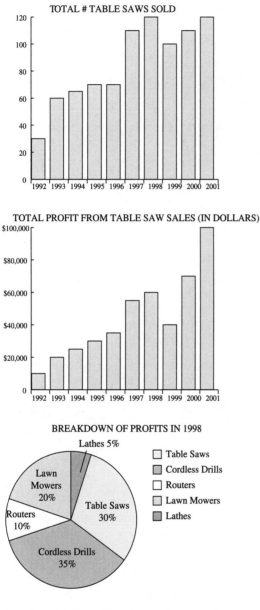

TOTAL # TABLE SAWS SOLD

TOTAL PROFIT FROM TABLE SAW SALES (IN DOLLARS)

BREAKDOWN OF PROFITS IN 1998

16. In 1998, what were the total profits from all hardware tool sales?

$

17. Which year had the greatest percentage increase in number of table saws sold from the previous year?

(A) 1993
(B) 1995
(C) 1997
(D) 2000
(E) 2001

18. Of the following, what is the closest to the percentage change in profits from table saws between 1998 and 1999?

(A) A 50% increase
(B) A 33% increase
(C) A 17% decrease
(D) A 33% decrease
(E) A 50% decrease

19. If the total manufacturing cost of table saws in 1993 was $22,000, what was the price per saw?

$

20. In 1998, what were the approximate profits from sales of cordless drills?

(A) $50,000
(B) $70,000
(C) $80,000
(D) $90,000
(E) $100,000

QUANTITATIVE REASONING PRACTICE SET 2 ANSWER KEY

1. A
2. A
3. C
4. C
5. D
6. D
7. B
8. A
9. D
10. B
11. D
12. E
13. D
14. B, C, D, E
15. C, D, E
16. 200,000
17. A
18. D
19. 700
20. B

Diagnose Your Results

Diagnostic Tool

Tally up your score and write your results below.

Total

Total Correct: _____ out of 20 correct

By Question Type

Quantitative Comparison (questions 1–10) _____ out of 10 correct

Problem Solving (questions 11–15) _____ out of 5 correct

Data Interpretation (questions 16–20) _____ out of 5 correct

Repeat the steps outlined in the Diagnose Your Results page that follows the Quantitative Reasoning Practice Set 1 answer key.

QUANTITATIVE REASONING PRACTICE SET 2 ANSWERS AND EXPLANATIONS

1. A

This question requires no computation but only a general understanding of how averages work and what the word "median" means. The *median* of a group of numbers is the "middle number"; it is the value above which half of the numbers in the group fall and below which the other half fall. If you have an even number of values, the median is the average of the two "middle" numbers; if you have an odd number of values, the median is one of the values. Here, in Quantity B, the median is 101. In Quantity A, if the numbers were 100, 101, and 102, then the average would also be 101, but because the third number, 103, is greater than 102, then the average must be greater than 101. Quantity A is greater than 101, and Quantity B equals 101; Quantity A is larger.

2. A

Start with the information you are given. You know that the length of the chord is 15. What does that mean? Well, because you don't know exactly where A and B are, it doesn't mean too much, but it does tell you that the distance between two points on the circle is 15. That tells you that the diameter must be at least 15. If the diameter were less than 15, then you couldn't have a chord that was equal to 15, because the diameter is always the longest chord in a circle. The diameter of the circle is 15 or greater, so the circumference must be at least 15π. That means that Quantity A must be larger than Quantity B.

3. C

The equation in the centered information looks complicated, but we'll take it one step at a time. Because Quantity A has only h in it, solve the equation for h, leaving h on one side of the equal sign and r on the other side. First, substitute the value for x into the equation; then solve for h in terms of r.

$$x = \frac{4}{3}r^2h^2$$ Substitute 1 for x.

$$1 = \frac{4}{3}r^2h^2$$ Divide both sides by $\frac{4}{3}$.

$$\frac{3}{4} = r^2h^2$$ Take the positive square root of both sides, using the information that r and h are positive.

$$\frac{\sqrt{3}}{2} = rh$$ Divide both sides by r to get h alone.

$$h = \frac{\sqrt{3}}{2r}$$ The two quantities are equal.

4.   C

Draw an *xy*-plane and label the points given to help solve this problem. You know where points *B* and *C* are; they're on the *x*-axis. You don't know where *A* is, however, which may make you think that the answer is choice **(D)**. But you're given more information: you know that the triangle has an area of 18. The area of any triangle is one-half the product of the base and the height. Make side *BC* the base of the triangle; you know the coordinates of both points, so you can find their distance apart, which is the length of that side. *C* is at the origin, the point (0, 0); *B* is at the point (6, 0). The distance between them is the distance from 0 to 6 along the *x*-axis, or just 6. So that's the base. What about the height? Because you know that the area is 18, you can plug what you know into the area formula.

$$\text{Area} = \frac{1}{2} \times \text{base} \times \text{height}$$

$$18 = \frac{1}{2} \times 6 \times \text{height}$$

$$\text{height} = \frac{18}{3}$$

$$\text{height} = 6$$

That's the other dimension of the triangle. The height is the distance between the *x*-axis and point *A*. Now you know that *A* must be somewhere in the first quadrant, since both the *x*- and *y*-coordinates are positive. Don't worry about the *x*-coordinate of the point, because that's not what's being compared; you care only about the value of *y*. You know that the distance from the *x*-axis to the point is 6, because that's the height of the triangle, and that *y* must be positive. Therefore, the *y*-coordinate of the point must be 6. That's what the *y*-coordinate is: a measure of the point's vertical distance from the *x*-axis. (Note that if you hadn't been told that *y* was positive, there would be two possible values for *y*: 6 and −6. A point that's 6 units below the *x*-axis would also give a triangle with height 6.) You still don't know the *x*-coordinate of the point, and in fact you can't figure that out, but you don't care. You know that *y* is 6; therefore, the two quantities are equal.

5.   D

With symbolism problems like this, it sometimes helps to put the definition of the symbol into words. For this symbol, you can say something like "*x* Φ *y* means take the sum of the two numbers and divide that by the difference of the two numbers." One good way to do this problem is to Pick Numbers. You know that *p* is positive and *q* is negative. So suppose *p* is 1 and *q* is −1. Figure out what *p* Φ *q* is first. You start by taking the sum of the numbers, or 1 + (−1) = 0. That's the numerator of the fraction, and you don't really need to go any further than that. Whatever their difference is, because the numerator is 0, the whole fraction must equal 0. (The difference can't be 0 also, since *p* ≠ *q*.) So that's *p* Φ *q*. Now what about *q* Φ *p*? Well, that's going to have the same numerator as $p \, \Phi \, q$: 0. The only thing that changes when you reverse the order of the numbers is the denominator of the fraction. So $q \, \Phi \, p$ has a numerator of 0, and that fraction must equal 0 as well.

So you've found a case where the quantities are equal. Try another set of values and see whether the quantities are always equal. If $p = 1$ and $q = -2$, then the sum of the numbers is $1 + (-2)$ or -1. So that's the numerator of the fraction in each quantity. Now for the denominator of $p \, \Phi \, q$, you need $p - q = 1 - (-2) = 1 + 2 = 3$. Then the value of $p \, \Phi \, q$ is $\dfrac{-1}{3}$. The denominator of $q \, \Phi \, p$ is $q - p = -2 - 1 = -3$. In that case, the value of $q \, \Phi \, p$ is $\dfrac{-1}{-3}$ or $\dfrac{1}{3}$. The quantities are different; therefore, the answer is **(D)**.

6. D

Picking Numbers will help you solve this problem. For $x = 1$, $\dfrac{1}{x} + \dfrac{1}{x} = \dfrac{1}{1} + \dfrac{1}{1} = 2$ and $\dfrac{1}{x} \times \dfrac{1}{x} = \dfrac{1}{1} \times \dfrac{1}{1} = 1$, so Quantity A is larger. For $x = -1$, $\dfrac{1}{x} + \dfrac{1}{x} = \dfrac{1}{-1} + \dfrac{1}{-1} = -2$ and $\dfrac{1}{x} \times \dfrac{1}{x} = \dfrac{1}{-1} \times \dfrac{1}{-1} = 1$, so Quantity B is larger. The quantities are different; therefore, the answer is **(D)**.

7. B

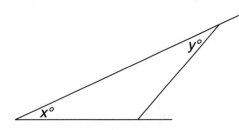

The sum of the three interior angles of a triangle is 180°. Because x and y are only two of the angles, their sum must be less than 180°. Quantity B is greater.

8. A

For the system of equations $4x - 5y = 10$ and $-3x + 6y = 22$, it is not necessary to solve for the values of x and y. Rather, you want to know about the sum of x and y. Notice what happens when you add the two equations.

$$4x - 5y = 10$$
$$-3x + 6y = 22$$
$$\overline{ \quad}$$
$$x + y = 32$$

Because $x + y = 32$ and $33 > 32$, Quantity A is larger.

9.   D

Divide both sides of the inequality by 6. You're left with $(10)^n > 10{,}001$. The number 10,001 can also be written as $10^4 + 1$, so you know that $(10)^n > 10^4 + 1$. Therefore, Quantity A, n, must be 5 or greater. Quantity B is 6. Because n could be less than, equal to, or greater than 6, you need more information.

10.   B

Try to set the quantities equal. Could the tens digit of y be 4? If it is, and the thousands digit is 2.5 times the units digit, then the tens digit must be … 10? That can't be right. A digit must be one of the integers 0–9; 10 isn't a digit. Therefore, 4 is too big to be the tens digit of y. You don't know what the tens digit of y is, but you know that it must be less than 4. Quantity B is greater than Quantity A.

11.   D

To find the average, add the quantities together and divide by 4: $(2x + 3) + (5x - 4) + (6x - 6) + (3x - 1) = 16x - 8$ and $\dfrac{16x - 8}{4} = 4x - 2$. The correct choice is **(D)**.

12.   E

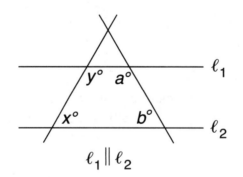

When a transversal cuts a pair of parallel lines, in this case ℓ_1 and ℓ_2, the angles are always supplementary and their sum is 180. So, the sum $(x + y)$ is equal to the sum $(a + b)$. The exact values of the individual angle measures cannot be determined from the figure. The answer is **(E)**.

13.   D

First, find the value of *x*, using the fact that there are 180° in a straight line. Set the sum of the angle measures equal to 180: $5x + 4x + 3x = 180$, $12x = 180$, and $x = 15$. Angle *SRU* equals $4x + 5x = 9x$, which is 135°. Choice **(D)** is correct.

14.   B, C, D, E

You know that the ratio of oranges to apples is 9 to 10 and that there are at least 200 apples. The ratio tells you that there are more apples than oranges. At the minimum, there must be 180 oranges to satisfy the proportion $\frac{9}{10} = \frac{180}{200}$. There could be more than 200 apples, so any number of oranges greater than 180 for which the ratio 9:10 applies is also correct. All of the choices are multiples of 9, so the correct choices are **(B)**, **(C)**, **(D)**, and **(E)**.

15.   C, D, E

The area of the shaded region is the area of the square minus the area of the portion of the circle that is inside the square. The area of a square is its side squared. The area of square *ABCD* is $4^2 = 4 \times 4$, which is 16. Now find the area of the portion of the circle that is inside the square. Because the diameter of the circle is a side of the square, you know that exactly one-half of the circle's area is inside the square. Also, because the diameter of the circle is twice the radius, the radius of the circle is $\frac{4}{2}$ or 2. The area of a circle with a radius *r* is πr^2. The area of the complete circle in this question is $\pi(2)^2$, which is 4π. So half the area of this circle is 2π. Thus, the area of the shaded region is $16 - 2\pi$.

That means that $16 - 4\pi$ and $16 - 16\pi$ are less than $16 - 2\pi$, so they cannot be correct choices. However, the sum of 16 and any positive number is greater than 16 and also greater than $16 - 2\pi$. So, the correct choices are **(C)**, **(D)**, and **(E)**.

16.   200,000

From the second bar graph, the profits from table saws in 1998 were $60,000. From the pie chart, table saws were 30% of the total profits. Let's call the total profits *T* dollars. Then 30% of *T* dollars is $60,000. So $0.3T = 60,000$, and

$$T = \frac{60,000}{0.3} = \frac{60,000}{\frac{3}{10}} = \frac{10 \times 60,000}{3} = \frac{600,000}{3} = 200,000.$$

17.   A

Use the first bar graph to analyze number of table saws sold. The year with the biggest percent increase over the previous year will be the year in which the increase is the biggest fraction of the amount from the previous year. Notice that in 1993, the increase from 1992 was approximately $60 - 30$, or 30. This is approximately a 100% increase, and it is the greatest percent increase over the previous year among all the years from 1993 to 2001. There was a greater increase in number of table saws from 1996 to 1997 than from 1992 to 1993, about $110 - 70 = 40$. However, the *percent* increase from 1996 to 1997 is approximately $\frac{40}{70} \times 100\%$, which is less than 100%, so choice **(A)** is correct.

18. D

In 1998, the profits from table saws were approximately $60,000. In 1999, the profits from table saws were approximately $40,000. From 1998 to 1999, there was a decrease in the profits from table saws. In general,

$$\text{Percent decrease} = \frac{\text{Original value} - \text{New value}}{\text{Original value}} \times 100\%$$

Here, the percent decrease is approximately

$$\frac{\$60{,}000 - \$40{,}000}{\$60{,}000} \times 100\% = \frac{\$20{,}000}{60{,}000} \times 100\% = \frac{1}{3} \times 100\% = 33\frac{1}{3}\%$$

A percent decrease of $33\frac{1}{3}\%$ is closest to **(D)**.

19. 700

In 1993, the profits were $20,000. Using the formula Profit = Revenue − Cost, you can write Revenue = Cost + Profit. The cost was $22,000. So the revenue was $22,000 + $20,000 = $42,000. Because in 1993, 60 table saws were sold, each table saw was sold for $\frac{\$42{,}000}{60}$, which is **$700**.

20. B

In 1998, the profits from table saws were about $60,000, and this profit was 30% of the total profits. Let's call the total profits T dollars. Then 30% of T dollars is $60,000. So $0.3T = 60{,}000$, and

$$T = \frac{60{,}000}{0.3} = 60{,}000 \times \frac{10}{3} = \frac{10 \times 60{,}000}{3} = \frac{600{,}00}{3} = 200{,}000.$$

The total profits in 1998 were approximately $200,000 (you may also have remembered this calculation from question 16). The profits from cordless drills were 35% of the total. So the profits from cordless drills were approximately 0.35($200,000), which is $70,000 or answer choice **(B)**.

QUANTITATIVE REASONING PRACTICE SET 3

NUMBERS

All numbers are real numbers.

FIGURES

The position of points, lines, angles, and so on may be assumed to be in the order shown; all lengths and angle measures may be assumed to be positive.

Lines shown as straight may be assumed to be straight.

Figures lie in the plane of the paper unless otherwise stated.

Figures that accompany questions are intended to provide useful information. However, unless a note states that a figure has been drawn to scale, you should solve the problems by using your knowledge of mathematics, not by estimation or measurement.

DIRECTIONS

Each of the following questions, 1–8, consists of two quantities, Quantity A and Quantity B. You are to compare the two quantities and choose

- Ⓐ if Quantity A is greater
- Ⓑ if Quantity B is greater
- Ⓒ if the two quantities are equal
- Ⓐ if the relationship cannot be determined from the information given

COMMON INFORMATION

In a question, information concerning one or both of the quantities to be compared is centered above the two quantities. A symbol that appears in both quantities represents the same thing in Quantity A as it does in Quantity B.

The diameter of a circle equals the diagonal of a square whose side length is 4.

1. | Quantity A | Quantity B |
    |---|---|
    | The circumference of the circle | $20\sqrt{2}$ |

  (A) Quantity A is greater.
  (B) Quantity B is greater.
  (C) The two quantities are equal.
  (D) The relationship cannot be determined from the information given.

$$x < y < z$$
$$0 < z$$

2. | Quantity A | Quantity B |
    |---|---|
    | x | 0 |

  (A) Quantity A is greater.
  (B) Quantity B is greater.
  (C) The two quantities are equal.
  (D) The relationship cannot be determined from the information given.

3. | Quantity A | Quantity B |
    |---|---|
    | The number of distinct positive integer factors of 96 | The number of distinct positive integer factors of 72 |

  (A) Quantity A is greater.
  (B) Quantity B is greater.
  (C) The two quantities are equal.
  (D) The relationship cannot be determined from the information given.

$$x > 0$$

4. | Quantity A | Quantity B |
    |---|---|
    | $\dfrac{x + 1}{x}$ | $\dfrac{x}{x + 1}$ |

  (A) Quantity A is greater.
  (B) Quantity B is greater.
  (C) The two quantities are equal.
  (D) The relationship cannot be determined from the information given.

$$2^p = 4^q$$

5. | Quantity A | Quantity B |
    |---|---|
    | p | $2q$ |

  (A) Quantity A is greater.
  (B) Quantity B is greater.
  (C) The two quantities are equal.
  (D) The relationship cannot be determined from the information given.

6. | Quantity A | Quantity B |
    |---|---|
    | The number of seconds in 7 hours | The number of hours in 52 weeks |

  (A) Quantity A is greater.
  (B) Quantity B is greater.
  (C) The two quantities are equal.
  (D) The relationship cannot be determined from the information given.

7. <u>Quantity A</u>   <u>Quantity B</u>

     z 20

  Ⓐ Quantity A is greater.
  Ⓑ Quantity B is greater.
  Ⓒ The two quantities are
      equal.
  Ⓓ The relationship cannot be
      determined from the infor-
      mation given.

$$x > 2$$

8. <u>Quantity A</u>   <u>Quantity B</u>

    x^3 $4x$

  Ⓐ Quantity A is greater.
  Ⓑ Quantity B is greater.
  Ⓒ The two quantities are
      equal.
  Ⓓ The relationship cannot be
      determined from the infor-
      mation given.

9. If $A \blacklozenge B = \dfrac{A + B}{B}$, and
$C\clubsuit = C + 3$, what is the
value of $(9\clubsuit) \blacklozenge 3$?

10. Rectangle A has a length of 12
inches and a width of 5 inches.
Rectangle B has a length of 9
inches and a width of 10 inches.
By what number must the area
of rectangle A be multiplied
in order to get the area
of rectangle B?

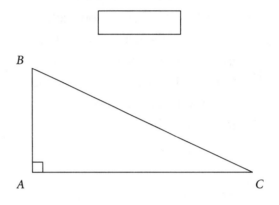

11. In right triangle ABC above, side
AB has a length of 5 units, while
side BC has a length of 13 units.
What is the area of ABC, in
square units?

 square units

12. If the average test score of four
students is 85, which of the
following scores could a fifth
student receive such that the
average of all five scores is
greater than 84 and less than 86?

Indicate <u>all</u> such scores.

  Ⓐ 88
  Ⓑ 86
  Ⓒ 85
  Ⓓ 83
  Ⓔ 80

13. Meg is twice as old as Rolf, but three years ago, she was two years older than Rolf is now. How old is Rolf now?

[   ] years old

14. The cost, in cents, of manufacturing x crayons is $570 + 0.5x$. The crayons sell for 10 cents each. What is the minimum number of crayons that need to be sold so that the revenue received recoups the manufacturing cost?

(A) 50
(B) 57
(C) 60
(D) 61
(E) 95

15. If $xy \neq 0$, $\dfrac{1 - x}{xy} =$

(A) $\dfrac{1}{xy} - \dfrac{1}{y}$

(B) $\dfrac{x}{y} - \dfrac{1}{x}$

(C) $\dfrac{1}{xy} - 1$

(D) $\dfrac{1}{xy} - \dfrac{x^2}{y}$

(E) $\dfrac{1}{x} - \dfrac{1}{y}$

Questions 16–20 refer to the following graphs:

TEAM REVENUES FOR 1997

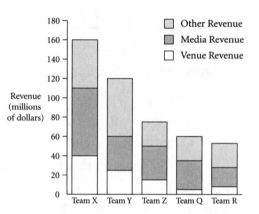

PERCENTAGES OF VENUE
REVENUES FOR TEAM X, 1997

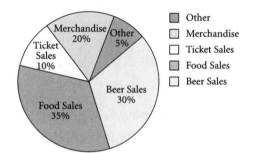

16. For the team with the median venue revenue in 1997, media revenue represented approximately what percent of that team's total revenue?

(A) 25%
(B) 30%
(C) 45%
(D) 70%
(E) 85%

17. Of the following, which is greater than the amount of revenue, in millions of dollars, earned by Team X through food sales in 1997?

    Indicate <u>all</u> such amounts.

    A⃞ 7
    B⃞ 10
    C⃞ 14
    D⃞ 18
    E⃞ 22

18. In 1997, which teams had media revenues of less than $25 million?

    Indicate <u>all</u> such teams.

    A⃞ Team X
    B⃞ Team Y
    C⃞ Team Z
    D⃞ Team Q
    E⃞ Team R

19. If Team Y earned total revenues of at least $150 million in 1998, then Team Y's total revenue could have increased by what percent from 1997 to 1998?

    Indicate <u>all</u> such percents.

    A⃞ 20%
    B⃞ 25%
    C⃞ 30%
    D⃞ 35%
    E⃞ 40%

20. The venue revenues for Team X from merchandise sales and ticket sales were approximately what percent of the venue revenues for Team X from food sales?

    Ⓐ 43%
    Ⓑ 53%
    Ⓒ 67%
    Ⓓ 71%
    Ⓔ 86%

QUANTITATIVE REASONING PRACTICE SET 3 ANSWER KEY

1. B
2. D
3. C
4. A
5. C
6. A
7. C
8. A
9. 5
10. 1.5
11. 30
12. A, B, C, D
13. 5
14. C
15. A
16. C
17. D, E
18. E
19. B, C, D, E
20. E

Diagnose Your Results

Diagnostic Tool

Tally up your score and write your results below.

Total

Total Correct: _____ out of 20 correct

By Question Type

Quantitative Comparison (questions 1–8) _____ out of 8 correct

Problem Solving (questions 9–15) _____ out of 7 correct

Data Interpretation (questions 16–20) _____ out of 5 correct

Repeat the steps outlined in the Diagnose Your Results page that follows the Quantitative Reasoning Practice Set 1 answer key.

QUANTITATIVE REASONING PRACTICE SET 3
ANSWERS AND EXPLANATIONS

1. B

The diagonal of a square of side 4 is $4\sqrt{2}$. The circumference of a circle is π times the diameter. So, the circumference of this circle is $4\sqrt{2}\pi$. Now write Quantity B, $20\sqrt{2}$, as $4(5)\sqrt{2}$ and you can compare the quantities piece by piece. The factors of 4 and $\sqrt{2}$ are the same in both quantities, but π is less than 5. So, Quantity B is larger.

2. D

You could Pick Numbers here or else just use logic. You know that z is positive and that x and y are less than z. But does that mean that x or y must be negative? Not at all—they could be, but they could also be positive. For instance, suppose $x = 1$, $y = 2$, and $z = 3$. Then Quantity A would be larger. However, if $x = -1$, $y = 0$, and $z = 1$, then Quantity B would be larger. You need more information to determine the relationship between the quantities. The answer is **(D)**.

3. C

There are 12 positive integer factors of 96: 1, 2, 3, 4, 6, 8, 12, 16, 24, 32, 48, and 96. There are 12 positive integer factors of 72: 1, 2, 3, 4, 6, 8, 9, 12, 18, 24, 36, and 72. The two quantities are equal.

4. A

If $x > 0$, then $\dfrac{x + 1}{x}$, which also equals $1 + \dfrac{1}{x}$, must be greater than 1. On the other hand, $\dfrac{x}{x + 1}$ must be less than 1. This is because when $x > 0$, the numerator x is smaller than the denominator, so the ratio $\dfrac{x}{x + 1} < 1$. Therefore, $\dfrac{x + 1}{x} > \dfrac{x}{x + 1}$ when $x > 0$, and Quantity A is greater.

5. C

For this question, notice the relationship between the bases, 2 and 4. When comparing exponents, it's easiest to work with equal bases.

You know that $4 = 2^2$. Therefore, $4^q = (2^2)^q = 2^{2q}$. Now you have $2^p = 2^{2q}$, so $p = 2q$. The quantities are equal, choice **(C)**.

6. A

Before you go to the trouble of multiplying the terms, let's see if there's a shortcut. For the GRE, make sure you know the common unit conversions for time. There are 60 seconds in a minute and 60 minutes in an hour, so there are $7 \times 60 \times 60$ seconds in 7 hours. There are 24 hours in a day and 7 days in a week, so there are $7 \times 24 \times 52$ hours in 52 weeks. Let's rewrite the quantities:

Quantity A	Quantity B
$7 \times 60 \times 60$	$7 \times 24 \times 52$

Taking away the common values gives you:

Quantity A	Quantity B
60×60	24×52

You still shouldn't do the math, however. The best strategy is to compare piece by piece, which shows that Quantity A is larger than Quantity B.

7. C

The sum of the measures of the angles on one side of a straight line is 180°. Therefore, $4z + 5z = 180$, so $9z = 180$. Divide both sides by 9 to find $z = 20$. **(C)** is the answer.

8. A

Since $x > 2$, you know $x > 0$ and you can divide both quantities by x without changing their relationship. Quantity A is then x^2 and Quantity B is 4. Since $x > 2$, the least value for x^2 is greater than $2^2 = 4$. Therefore, **(A)** is correct.

9. 5

Let's first find the value of $9\clubsuit$. Then we'll find the value of $(9\clubsuit)\blacklozenge 3$.

Since $C\clubsuit = C + 3$, $9\clubsuit = 9 + 3 = 12$.
Therefore, $(9\clubsuit)\blacklozenge 3 = 12\blacklozenge 3$.
Since $A \blacklozenge B = \dfrac{A + B}{B}$, $12 \blacklozenge 3 = \dfrac{12 + 3}{3} = \dfrac{15}{3}$
Therefore, $(9\clubsuit)\blacklozenge 3 = 5$.

10.   1.5

The area of a rectangle is its length times its width.

The area of rectangle A is $12 \times 5 = 60$.

The area of rectangle B is $9 \times 10 = 90$.

So the area 60 of rectangle A must be multiplied by a number, which you can call x, to obtain the area 90 of rectangle B.

Then $60x = 90$. So $x = \dfrac{90}{60} = \dfrac{3}{2} = 1.5$.

11.   30

Here's a problem where it really pays to have learned the special right triangles. Because one leg of the right triangle is 5 and the hypotenuse is 13, you have a special right triangle, the 5:12:13 right triangle. So the length of AC is 12.

The area of a triangle is $\dfrac{1}{2}$ of the base times the height. The area of a right triangle is $\dfrac{1}{2} \times (\text{leg})_1 \times (\text{leg})_2$, because one leg can be considered to be the base and the other leg can be considered to be the height. So the area of triangle ABC is

$$\frac{1}{2} \times (AC) \times (AB) = \frac{1}{2} \times 12 \times 5 = 6 \times 5 = 30$$

The answer is **30**.

12.   A, B, C, D

The average formula is as follows:

$$\text{Average} = \frac{\text{Sum of the terms}}{\text{Number of terms}}$$

Therefore,

$$\text{Sum of the terms} = \text{Average} \times \text{Number of terms}$$

The sum of the scores of the four students whose average was 85 is $85(4) = 340$. Let's call the fifth student's score x. If the new average is to be greater than 84 and less than 86 and the sum of the scores of all five students is $340 + x$, then $84 < \dfrac{340 + x}{5} < 86$. If you multiply all parts of the inequality by 5, you get $420 < 340 + x < 430$. Subtracting 340 from all parts of the inequality, you get $80 < x < 90$, making **(A)**, **(B)**, **(C)**, and **(D)** the correct choices.

13. 5

This question can be broken into two equations with two unknowns, Meg's age now (M) and Rolf 's age now (R). Equation (i) shows the relationship now; equation (ii) shows the relationship three years ago.

$$\text{(i) } M = 2 \times R \qquad \text{(ii) } M - 3 = R + 2$$

Substitute $2R$ for M in equation (ii) and solve for R:

$$
\begin{aligned}
M - 3 &= R + 2 \\
2R - 3 &= R + 2 \\
2R - R &= 2 + 3 \\
R &= 5
\end{aligned}
$$

Rolf is **5** years old now.

14. C

The cost of manufacturing x crayons is $(570 + 0.5x)$ cents. Because each crayon sells for 10 cents, x crayons will sell for $10x$ cents. You want the smallest value of x such that $10x$ cents is at least $570 + 0.5x$ cents. So you must solve the equation $10x = 570 + 0.5x$ for the value of x that will recoup the investment.

$$
\begin{aligned}
10x &= 570 + 0.5x \\
9.5x &= 570 \\
x &= 60
\end{aligned}
$$

The minimum number of crayons is 60, choice **(C)**.

Alternatively, you could have avoided setting up an algebraic equation by Backsolving, starting with either **(B)** or **(D)**.

15. A

You can write that $\dfrac{1 - x}{xy} = \dfrac{1}{xy} - \dfrac{x}{xy}$. Canceling a factor of x from the numerator and denominator of $\dfrac{x}{xy}$, you have $\dfrac{x}{xy} = \dfrac{1}{y}$.

So, $\dfrac{1 - x}{xy} = \dfrac{1}{xy} - \dfrac{x}{xy} = \dfrac{1}{xy} - \dfrac{1}{y}$. The answer is **(A)**.

16. C

Before you answer any graph question, begin by examining the graphs. Here you have two graphs, a segmented bar graph representing team revenue breakdowns for five teams and a pie chart showing the distribution of venue revenues for Team X.

You're now ready to attack the question, which asks you to find the team with the median venue revenue for 1997 and to determine what percent of that team's total revenue is media revenue. This question must refer to the first graph, and the first part of the question—finding the team with the median venue revenue—is straight-forward. *Median* refers to the number in the middle. Looking at the white portions of the bars in the top graph, you see that Team Z has the median venue revenue. The fastest approach to the answer here (and throughout graph questions generally) is to approximate. The downside to bar graphs is that it's often very hard to get a read on the values. The upside is that if you approximate, often you don't have to read the values. Here you need to determine what percent of Team Z's bar is represented by media revenue (the segment in the middle—always be especially careful to isolate the correct piece of data). By approximating, you can see that the middle segment is about half of the entire bar. Thus the correct answer has to be close to 50%. The only answer choice that works is **(C)**, 45%.

17. D, E
The key to this question is that it involves both graphs. The question asks for the amount Team X earned through food sales, which takes you first to the pie chart, where you see that food sales accounted for 35% of the venue revenues for Team X. But to convert that to a dollar amount, you need a figure for the amount earned in venue revenues by Team X in 1997. According to the bar graph, this is somewhere around $40 million. Now, take 35% of $40 million: $0.35 \times 40 = 14$, so the answer is any amount greater than 14. The answers are **(D)** and **(E)**.

18. E
Look at the bar graph: Team Q had media revenues of $35 - 5 = 30$ million, and Teams X, Y, and Z had media revenues greater than those of team Q. Team R had media revenue of $30 - 10 = 20$ million. The only correct choice is **(E)**.

19. B, C, D, E
Percent change problems are extremely popular graph questions, and as long as you set them up correctly, they are a great opportunity. This question asks for the approximate percent increase in Team Y's total revenue from 1997 to 1998, so you need to figure out (roughly) the amount of increase, place that over the original (or smaller) amount, and then convert the fraction into a percent. You are given the total revenue for 1998 as at least $150 million, so you need to locate the total revenue for 1997 from the bar graph. It looks to be approximately $120 million, so the amount of increase is $30 million (or more), and the original amount is $120 million. Now let's apply the formula:

$$\text{Percent increase} = \frac{\$30 \text{ million}}{\$120 \text{ million}} \times 100\%$$
$$= \frac{1}{4} \times 100\%$$
$$= 25\%$$

So, any percent greater than or equal to 25% is the answer. The answers are **(B)**, **(C)**, **(D)**, and **(E)**.

20. E

Looking at the bar graph, you see from the lowest portion of the bar for Team X that venue revenues of Team X were approximately 40 million dollars (call it 40m, for short). From the pie chart, the venue revenues of Team X from merchandise sales were approximately 20% of 40 million dollars, the venue revenues from ticket sales were approximately 10%, and the venue revenues from food sales were approximately 35%. The venue revenues of Team X from merchandise, in dollars, were approximately $0.2(40m) = 8m$. The venue revenues of Team X from ticket sales, in dollars, were approximately $0.1(40m) = 4m$. So the venue revenues of Team X from merchandise sales and ticket sales, in dollars, were approximately $8m + 4m = 12m$. The venue revenues of Team X from food sales, in dollars, were approximately $0.35(40m) = 14m$. The percent that the venue revenues of Team X that were from merchandise sales and ticket sales, out of the venue revenues of Team X that were from food sales, is approximately $\frac{12m}{14m} \times 100\% = \frac{6}{7} \times 100\% \approx 85.7\%$

To the nearest percent, 85.7% is 86%. Choice **(E)** is correct.

PART FOUR

Analytical Writing

CHAPTER 15

Introduction to Analytical Writing

OVERVIEW

The Analytical Writing section assesses not only how well you write but also the thought processes you employ to formulate and articulate a position. Your analytical and critical thinking skills will be tested by questions that ask you to evaluate complex arguments and form an argument of your own. The goal of the Analytical Writing section is to make the test an accurate indicator of your ability to understand and formulate an argument and to assess your analytical reasoning skills. These skills are exactly those you will need to perform well as a student at the graduate level.

In this section of the book, we'll take you through all the Analytical Writing Essay types you'll see on the GRE and give you the strategies you need to compose a well-written essay quickly and correctly. Also, all of the writing skills you'll need to perform well on the test are reviewed in the Writing Foundations and Content Review chapter.

ANALYTICAL WRITING ESSAY TYPES

The Analytical Writing Section of the GRE contains two different essay types. You'll be given 30 minutes for each essay. You'll be writing essays to address two different tasks:

- The Issue Task will provide a brief quotation on an issue of general interest and instructions on how to respond to the issue. You can discuss the issue from any perspective, making use of your own educational and personal background, examples from current or historical events, things you've read, or even relevant hypothetical situations. In this task, you will be developing your own argument.
- The Argument Task will contain a short argument that may or may not be complete and specific instructions on how to respond to the argument. You will assess the cogency of the argument, analyzing the author's chain of reasoning and evaluating his use of evidence. In this task, you do not develop your own argument but instead critique the argument presented in the prompt.

For each task, you'll be given one topic rather than a choice of several topics.

The Analytical Writing section will allow the graders to evaluate your ability to plan and compose a logical, well-reasoned essay under timed conditions. The essays are written on the computer, using a simple word-processing program. Only a score report is sent to the schools to which you apply.

The Analytical Writing portion of the GRE draws heavily upon your critical thinking abilities and your facility for understanding and analyzing written material. Specifically, it evaluates your ability to do the following:

- articulate and defend a position
- deconstruct and evaluate a complex argument
- develop a cogent argument
- assess the fundamental soundness of an argument
- recognize major, minor, and irrelevant points
- provide evidence and support for an argument
- detect the flaws in an unsound argument
- write articulately and effectively at a high level

HOW THE COMPUTER-BASED ESSAYS ARE ADMINISTERED

You can (and should) outline your essays on scratch paper, but your final answer must be typed into the computer before the end of the timed segment for you to receive a score for your work. At the start of the first Analytical Writing section, you will be given a brief tutorial on how to use the word-processing program. Don't worry. The GRE's word processor is simple and easy to use; the only functions you'll be able to use are *insert text*, *delete text*, *cut text*, *paste text*, and *undo*. You'll be well acquainted with these commands by the time you start writing. When practicing writing essays, turn off any auto-edit functions your word processor has. The GRE's word processor doesn't have these functions, so do your practice essays without them.

PACING STRATEGY

You'll have a limited amount of time to show the essay graders that you can think logically, analyze critically, and express yourself in clearly written English. Consequently, you'll need to know ahead of time how you're going to approach each essay. The Kaplan Method for Analytical Writing will help you plan and execute a clear, organized essay in the amount of time allotted. Note that the timing guidelines below are suggestions for how you should most effectively divide the 30 minutes you'll have for each of the essays. Different writers go through the different steps at their own pace, so don't feel chained to the breakdown below. As you practice, you will get a better sense of the amount of time you need to spend on each step to produce the best essay possible.

	Analyze an Issue	**Analyze an Argument**
Number of Questions	1	1
Time per Question	30 minutes	30 minutes

» **STEP 1**
Take the Issue/Argument Apart: 2 minutes

» **STEP 2**
Select the Points You'll Make: 4 minutes

» **STEP 3**
Organize Your Thoughts: 2 minutes

» **STEP 4**
Write Your Essay: 20 minutes

» **STEP 5**
Proofread: 2 minutes

Try to keep these estimates in mind as you prepare for the test. If you use them as you work through the practice items, you will be comfortable keeping to the same amounts of time on Test Day.

SCORING

The essay scoring for the Analytical Writing sections is *holistic*, which means that the graders base your score on their overall impression of your essay, rather than deducting specific point values for errors. A holistic score emphasizes the inter-relationship of content, organization, and syntax and denotes the unified effect of these combined elements.

The scoring scale is from 0 to 6, with 6 being the highest score. Two graders will read and score each essay. If their scores differ by more than 1 point, a third reader will also score the essay.

Although the Analytical Writing section comprises two separate essays, ETS reports a single score that represents the average of your scores for the two essays, rounded up to the nearest half-point.

You will receive your essay score, along with your official score report, within 10 to 15 days of your test date.

THE SCORING RUBRIC

Each of the two essays requires different reasoning and presentation, so each has slightly different grading criteria. However, the following rubric will give you a general idea of the guidelines graders have in mind when they score Analytical Writing essays.

6: "Outstanding" Essay

- Insightfully presents and convincingly supports an opinion on the issue or a critique of the argument
- Communicates ideas clearly and is generally well organized; connections are logical
- Demonstrates superior control of language: grammar, stylistic variety, and accepted conventions of writing; minor flaws may occur

5: "Strong" Essay

- Presents well-chosen examples and strongly supports an opinion on the issue or a critique of the argument
- Communicates ideas clearly and is generally well organized; connections are logical
- Demonstrates solid control of language: grammar, stylistic variety, and accepted conventions of writing; minor flaws may occur

4: **"Adequate" Essay**

- Presents and adequately supports an opinion on the issue or a critique of the argument
- Communicates ideas fairly clearly and is adequately organized; logical connections are satisfactory
- Demonstrates satisfactory control of language: grammar, stylistic variety, and accepted conventions of writing; some flaws may occur

3: **"Limited" Essay**

- Succeeds only partially in presenting and supporting an opinion on the issue or a critique of the argument
- Communicates ideas unclearly and is poorly organized
- Demonstrates less than satisfactory control of language: contains significant mistakes in grammar, usage, and sentence structure

2: **"Weak" Essay**

- Shows little success in presenting and supporting an opinion on the issue or a critique of the argument
- Struggles to communicate ideas; essay shows a lack of clarity and organization
- Meaning is impeded by many serious mistakes in grammar, usage, and sentence structure

1: **"Fundamentally Deficient" Essay**

- Fails to present a coherent opinion and/or evidence on the issue or a critique of the argument
- Fails to communicate ideas; essay is seriously unclear and disorganized
- Lacks meaning due to widespread and severe mistakes in grammar, usage, and sentence structure

0: **"Unscorable" Essay**

- Completely ignores topic
- Attempts to copy the task
- Written in a language other than English or contains undecipherable text

NAVIGATING THE ANALYTICAL WRITING SECTION OF THIS BOOK

The chapter immediately following this one is on Writing Foundations and Content and will review the classic writing techniques, concepts, and topics that you may encounter on the GRE. This section of the book also includes individual chapters on the Issue essay and the Argument essay questions. Each chapter includes an introduction and definition of the different tasks and a review and examples of the strategies to follow to answer those questions quickly and correctly.

Finally, at the end of this section, you'll find the Analytical Writing Practice. This will consist of two Issue essay prompts and two Argument essay prompts. At the end will be sample essays for each of the prompts. Use the Practice Prompts to test your writing skills and pinpoint areas for more focused study. When you are finished with this section of the book, you should be thoroughly prepared for any task you might encounter on the Analytical Writing section of the GRE.

CHAPTER 16

Analytical Writing Foundations and Content Review

INTRODUCTION TO ANALYTICAL WRITING FOUNDATIONS AND CONTENT REVIEW

The GRE tests your ability to construct a coherent, logical, and well-developed response to a writing prompt. This requires a mastery of grammatical, syntactical, and language concepts, as well as an awareness of audience and command of the writing process. These concepts include:

- Streamlining Wordy Phrases
- Eliminating Redundancy
- Avoiding Excessive Qualification
- Removing Unnecessary Sentences
- Avoiding Needless Self-Reference
- Using Active Voice rather than Passive Voice
- Including Strong Openings
- Avoiding Needlessly Vague Language
- Rewording Clichés
- Avoiding Jargon
- Ensuring Subject-Verb Agreement
- Avoiding Faulty Modification
- Avoiding Unclear Pronoun Reference
- Correctly Using Parallelism
- Using a Consistent Narrative Voice
- Avoiding Slang and Colloquialisms
- Avoiding Sentence Fragments and Run-Ons
- Correctly Using Commas
- Correctly Using Semicolons
- Correctly Using Colons
- Correctly Using Hyphens and Dashes
- Correctly Using Apostrophes

This chapter will cover all these grammatical and writing concepts and provide practice sets to help you conquer the writing task using the clearest, strongest language possible.

STREAMLINING WORDY PHRASES

Why use several words when one will do? Many people make the mistake of writing phrases such as *at the present time* or *at this point in time* instead of the simpler *now*, or *take into consideration* instead of simply *consider*, in an attempt to make their prose seem more scholarly or more formal. It doesn't work. Instead, their prose ends up seeming inflated and pretentious. Don't waste your words or your time.

WORDY: I am of the opinion that the aforementioned managers should be advised that they will be evaluated with regard to the utilization of responsive organizational software for the purpose of devising a responsive network of customers.

CONCISE: We should tell the managers that we will evaluate their use of flexible computerized databases to develop a customer network.

STREAMLINING WORDY PHRASES PRACTICE SET

Read the following sentences and revise the wordy phrases.

1. Government funding cripples the natural relationship of arts enthusiasts and artists by subsidizing work and makes artists less creative and forces the taxpayer to take on the burden of paying for art they don't like.

   _____

   _____

2. There are many reasons why some may believe that the services of one real estate agent are superior in quality to the services of another competing real estate agent or group of agents, including the personal service they provide, the care and quality of the work they do, and the communication lines they set up and keep open.

   _____

   _____

STREAMLINING WORDY PHRASES PRACTICE SET ANSWERS AND EXPLANATIONS

Examples of the revised sentences with explanations:

1   The government should not subsidize artists, because it makes them less creative and forces taxpayers to pay for art they don't like.

The original sentence contained unnecessary repetition. The original sentence does not need to include both "funding" and "subsidizing," as both words refer to the same thing. The clause about "crippling the natural relationship" is also redundant, as that is implied by listing the negative effects government funding will have on both artists and the taxpayers.

2   Reasons for choosing one real estate agent over another include personal service, care, communication, and quality of work.

The revised sentence condenses the two main clauses, i.e. the main idea (choosing one real estate agent over another) and the subsequent list. It also pares down the unnecessary repetition. There is no need to explain that communication lines are set up and kept open, for example.

ELIMINATING REDUNDANCY

Redundancy means that the writer needlessly repeats an idea. For example, it's redundant to speak of *a beginner lacking experience*. The word *beginner* implies lack of experience by itself. You can eliminate redundant words or phrases without changing the meaning of the sentence.

Here are some common redundancies:

REDUNDANT	CONCISE
refer back	refer
few in number	few
small-sized	small
grouped together	grouped
in my own personal opinion	in my opinion
end result	result
serious crisis	crisis
new initiatives	initiatives

REDUNDANT: It is wise to plan ahead for unexpected problems.
CONCISE: It is wise to plan for unexpected problems.

In this example, "plan ahead" is redundant. In what situation would you "plan behind"? "Unexpected problems" is acceptable because, while some problems are unexpected, others are readily anticipated.

ELIMINATING REDUNDANCY PRACTICE SET

Read the following sentences and revise to eliminate redundancy.

1. All of these problems have combined together to create a serious crisis.

   _____

   _____

2. That monument continues to remain a significant tourist attraction.

_____

_____

ELIMINATING REDUNDANCY PRACTICE SET ANSWERS AND EXPLANATIONS

Examples of the revised sentences with explanations:

3   All of these problems have combined to create a crisis.

Crises are inherently serious, and things cannot combine apart. The adverb and adjective are redundant.

4   That monument remains a significant tourist attraction.

There is no need to reinforce "remain" with "continues." The verb "remain" implies that.

AVOIDING EXCESSIVE QUALIFICATION

Because the object of your essay is to convince your reader of your point of view, you will want to adopt a reasonable tone. There will likely be no single, clear-cut "answer" to the essay topic, so don't overstate your case. Occasional use of such qualifiers as *fairly, rather, somewhat,* and *relatively* and of such expressions as *seems to be, a little,* and a *certain amount of* will let the reader know you are reasonable, but overusing such modifiers weakens your argument. Excessive qualification makes you sound hesitant. Like wordy phrases, qualifiers can add bulk without adding substance.

WORDY: This rather serious breach of etiquette may possibly shake the very foundations of the corporate world.
CONCISE: This serious breach of etiquette may shake the foundations of the corporate world.

Just as bad is the overuse of the word *very.* Some writers use this intensifying adverb before almost every adjective in an attempt to be more forceful. If you need to add emphasis, look for a stronger adjective or adverb.

WEAK: Adelaide is a very good flautist.
STRONG: Adelaide is a virtuoso flautist.

OR
Adelaide plays beautifully.

And don't try to qualify words that are already absolute.

WRONG	CORRECT
more unique	unique
the very worst	the worst
completely full	full

AVOIDING EXCESSIVE QUALIFICATION PRACTICE SET

Read the following sentences and revise the excessive qualification(s).

1. She is a fairly excellent teacher.

   _____

   _____

2. It's possible that we might overcome these obstacles.

   _____

   _____

AVOIDING EXCESSIVE QUALIFICATION PRACTICE SET ANSWERS AND EXPLANATIONS

Examples of the revised sentences with explanations:

1   She is an excellent teacher.

The use of the adverb "fairly" unnecessarily weakens the point of the sentence.

2   We might overcome these obstacles.

The word "might" implies that it's possible but not certain, so saying "it's possible" is unnecessary.

REMOVING UNNECESSARY SENTENCES

Brevity is crucial for success on a timed test that emphasizes content over form. Remember, the essays on this test will force you to economize your expression. This principle suggests several things:

- Don't write a sentence that strays from the thesis.
- Don't ask a question only to answer it; rhetorical questions are a no-no.
- Don't merely copy the essay's prompt.
- Don't write a whole sentence only to announce that you're changing the subject.

If you have something to say, say it without preamble. If you need to smooth over a change of subject, do so with a transitional word or phrase rather than with a meaningless sentence.

WORDY: Which idea of the author's is more in line with what I believe? This is a very interesting question.
CONCISE: The author's beliefs are similar to mine.

The author of the wordy example above is just wasting words and time. Get to the point quickly and stay there.

REMOVING UNNECESSARY SENTENCES PRACTICE SET

Read the sentences and rewrite each pair as one concise statement.

1. What's the purpose of getting rid of the chemical pollutants in water? People cannot safely consume water that contains chemical pollutants.

   _____

   _____

2. I do not believe it is necessary to include the telemetry data. The telemetry data adds little of value to the study of stellar drift.

   _____

   _____

REMOVING UNNECESSARY SENTENCES PRACTICE SET ANSWERS AND EXPLANATIONS

Examples of the revised sentences with explanations:

1   People cannot safely consume water that contains chemical pollutants.

The first sentence is an unnecessary rhetorical question.

2   It is not necessary to include the telemetry data, as it adds little of value to the study of stellar drift.

In this situation, there are two different but related thoughts: the merits of the data, and whether or not to include it. It is therefore best to combine the sentences, which can be done elegantly without destroying the flow of the passage.

AVOIDING NEEDLESS SELF-REFERENCE

Avoid such unnecessary phrases as *I believe*, *I feel*, and *in my opinion*. There is no need to remind your reader that what you are writing is your opinion. Self-reference is another—very obvious—form of qualifying what you say.

WEAK: I am of the opinion that air pollution is a more serious problem than most people realize.
FORCEFUL: Air pollution is a more serious problem than most people realize.

AVOIDING NEEDLESS SELF-REFERENCE PRCTICE SET

Eliminate needless self-references in these sentences.

1. It seems to me that nuclear energy is safer and cleaner than burning fossil fuels. I think we should build more nuclear power plants.

   _____

   _____

2. The author, in my personal opinion, is stuck in the past.

   _____

   _____

AVOIDING NEEDLESS SELF-REFERENCE PRCTICE SET ANSWERS AND EXPLANATIONS

Examples of the revised sentences with explanations:

1   Nuclear energy is safer and cleaner than burning fossil fuels, so we should build more nuclear power plants.

"It seems to me" and "I think" hedge unnecessarily and intrude on the argument. (Also note how combining these statements makes the argument flow better.)

2   The author is stuck in the past.

Unless specified otherwise, your writing will always express your opinion.

USING ACTIVE VOICE RATHER THAN PASSIVE VOICE

Using the passive voice is a way to avoid accountability (it's often referred to as the "politician's voice"). Put verbs in the active voice whenever possible. In the active voice, the subject performs the action (e.g., "we write essays"). In the passive voice, the subject is the receiver of the action and is often only implied (e.g., "essays are written by us").

PASSIVE: The estimate of this year's tax revenues was prepared by the General Accounting Office.
ACTIVE: The General Accounting Office prepared the estimate of this year's tax revenues.

The passive voice creates weak sentences and is usually the product of writing before you think. Avoid this by organizing your thoughts before you begin writing. Take a few minutes to find out what you want to say before you say it. To change from the passive to the active voice, ask yourself WHO or WHAT is performing the action. In the sentence above, the General Accounting Office is performing the action; therefore, the General Accounting Office should be the subject of the sentence.

You should avoid the passive voice EXCEPT in the following cases:

- When you do not know who performed the action: *The letter was opened before I received it.*
- When you prefer not to refer directly to the person who performs the action: *An error has been made in computing these data.*

It is rare to have a good reason to use passive voice in either of the Analytical Writing essays on the GRE.

USING ACTIVE VOICE PRACTICE SET

Read the sentences and replace all instances of passive voice with active voice wherever possible.

1. The faulty wiring in the walls went unnoticed by the safety inspectors until it was too late.

   _____

   _____

2. The Spanish-American War was fought by brave but misguided men.

   _____

   _____

USING ACTIVE VOICE PRACTICE SET ANSWERS AND EXPLANATIONS

Examples of the revised sentences with explanations:

1   The safety inspectors did not notice the faulty wiring in the walls until it was too late.

The safety inspectors are the ones doing (or not doing) the action, so they should be the subject of the sentence.

2   Brave but misguided men fought the Spanish-American War.

There is no need for the passive in this situation, as it is absolutely clear who did the fighting.

INCLUDING STRONG OPENINGS

Try not to begin a sentence with *there is, there are,* or *it is.* These roundabout expressions usually indicate that you are trying to distance yourself from the position you are taking. Again, weak openings often result from writing before you think.

INCLUDING STRONG OPENINGS PRACTICE SET

Read the following sentences and revise to improve the openings.

1. There isn't much wilderness left, so we should protect what we have.

   _____

   _____

2. There are several reasons why this plane is obsolete.

   _____

   _____

INCLUDING STRONG OPENINGS PRACTICE SET ANSWERS AND EXPLANATIONS

Examples of the revised sentences with explanations:

1   We should protect what little wilderness we have left.

Notice how this statement takes a forceful position right away.

2   This plane is obsolete for several reasons.

The revised sentence is less timid and states its purpose in a stronger tone.

AVOIDING NEEDLESSLY VAGUE LANGUAGE

Don't just ramble on when writing your GRE essays. Choose specific, descriptive words. Vague language weakens your writing because it forces the reader to guess what you mean instead of concentrating fully on your ideas and style. The essay topics you'll be given aren't going to be obscure. You will be able to come up with specific examples and concrete information about the topics. Your argument will be more forceful if you stick to this approach.

WEAK: Ms. Brown is highly educated.
FORCEFUL: Ms. Brown has a master's degree in business administration.

WEAK: She is a great communicator.
FORCEFUL: She speaks persuasively.

Notice that sometimes, to be more specific and concrete, you will have to use more words than you might with vague language. This principle is not in conflict with the general objective of concision. Being concise may mean eliminating unnecessary words. Avoiding vagueness may mean adding necessary words.

AVOIDING NEEDLESSLY VAGUE LANGUAGE PRACTICE SET

Rewrite these sentences to replace vague language with specific, concrete language. You may need to invent details.

1. There are no boundaries to the age of library patrons, and the installation of vending machines is a scheme that potentially has ill effects where young readers are concerned.

   _____

   _____

2. Living upstairs from the band has been challenging.

   _____

   _____

AVOIDING NEEDLESSLY VAGUE LANGUAGE PRACTICE SET ANSWERS AND EXPLANATIONS

Examples of the revised sentences with explanations:

1   Because the library is open to readers of all ages, including young readers who may overindulge in unhealthy treats, it would be unwise to install vending machines.

The original sentence contains several overwrought phrases and never explains what the "ill effects" of vending machines would be. The rewritten version makes the argument directly.

2   I can never get enough sleep because the band downstairs holds loud practice sessions every night.

You could have rewritten this sentence in many different ways, but the important thing is to change the vague "has been challenging" to a more specific grievance.

REWORDING CLICHÉS

Clichés are overused expressions that may once have seemed colorful and powerful but are now dull and worn out. Time, pressure, and anxiety may make you lose focus; that's when clichés may slip into your writing. A reliance on clichés will suggest you are a lazy thinker. Keep them out of your essay.

WEAK: It began to rain cats and dogs when we arrived at the station.
FORCEFUL: A heavy rain began to fall when we arrived at the station.

Putting a cliché in quotation marks to indicate your distance from the cliché does not strengthen the sentence. If anything, it just makes weak writing more noticeable. If you notice any clichés in your writing, ask yourself if you could replace them with more specific language.

REWORDING CLICHÉS PRACTICE SET

Read the following sentences and remove any clichés.

1. Be positive is my motto!

   _____

   _____

2. Beyond a shadow of a doubt, Jefferson was a great leader.

   _____

   _____

REWORDING CLICHÉS PRACTICE SET ANSWERS AND EXPLANATIONS

Examples of the revised sentences with explanations:

1   I prefer to praise positive actions than to dwell on negative ones.

The unrevised sentence crams two clichés into five words. The revised sentence is both more specific and more original, which will serve you better in writing an analytical essay.

2   Jefferson was a great leader.

The revised sentence makes an equally strong assertion, but has a less histrionic tone.

AVOIDING JARGON

Jargon includes two categories of words that you should avoid. First is the specialized vocabulary of a group, such as that used by doctors, lawyers, or baseball coaches. Second is the overly inflated and complex language that burdens many students' essays. You will not impress anyone with big words that do not fit the tone or context of your essay, especially if you misuse them. If you are not certain of a word's meaning or appropriateness, leave it out. An appropriate word, even a simple one, will add clarity to your argument. As you come across words you are unsure of, ask yourself, "Would a reader in a different field be able to understand exactly what I mean from the words I've chosen? Is there any way I can say the same thing more simply?"

WEAK: The company is not able to bankroll the project.
FORCEFUL: The company is not able to pay for the project.

The following are commonly used jargon words:

assistance	downside	optimize
ballpark	face time	originate
bandwidth	facilitate	parameter
blindside	finalize	prioritize
bottom line	input/output	target
conceptualize	maximize	time frame
cookie-cutter	mutually beneficial	user-friendly
designate	ongoing	utilize

AVOIDING JARGON PRACTICE SET

Revise the following sentences to remove the jargon.

1. When a parent attempts to correct the bad behavior of a child by positively reinforcing good behavior, this classical conditioning can become ineffective due to extinction.

   _____

   _____

2. Foreign diplomats should always interface with local leaders.

   _____

   _____

AVOIDING JARGON PRACTICE SET ANSWERS AND EXPLANATIONS

Examples of the revised sentences with explanations:

1 Attempting to correct a child's bad behavior by rewarding good behavior can become ineffective when the reward is withdrawn.

The first sentence was loaded with jargon not readily understood by the average reader. The revised sentence expresses the exact same thought, but in less technically opaque language.

2 Foreign diplomats should always talk to local leaders.

The verb "interface" is most appropriately used in a technical context. It sounds jarring and pretentious in the unrevised sentence.

ENSURING SUBJECT-VERB AGREEMENT

A verb must agree with its subject regardless of intervening phrases. Do not let the words that come between the subject and the verb confuse you as to the number (singular or plural) of the subject. Usually, one word can be pinpointed as the grammatical subject of the sentence. Find the verb, no matter how far removed, and make sure that it agrees with that subject in number.

INCORRECT: The joys of climbing mountains, especially if one is a novice climber without the proper equipment, escapes me.

CORRECT: The *joys* of climbing mountains, especially if one is a novice climber without the proper equipment, *escape* me.

Watch out for collective nouns like *group, audience, committee,* or *majority.* These take a singular verb unless you are emphasizing the individuals forming the group.

CORRECT: A *majority* of the jury *thinks* that the defendant is guilty. (The collective is being emphasized.)

CORRECT: A *majority* of the committee *have signed* their names to the report. (The individual members of the committee are being emphasized.)

A subject that consists of two or more nouns connected by the conjunction *and* takes the plural form of the verb.

CORRECT: *Karl,* an expert in cooking Hunan chicken, *and George,* an expert in preparing Hunan spicy duck, *have combined* their expertise to start a new restaurant.

However, when the subject consists of two or more nouns connected by *or* or *nor,* the verb agrees with the CLOSEST noun.

CORRECT: Either the senators or the *president is* misinformed.

CORRECT: Either the president or the *senators are* misinformed.

Some connecting phrases look as though they should make a group of words into a plural but actually do not. The only connecting word that can make a series of singular nouns into a plural subject is *and.* In particular, the following connecting words and phrases do NOT result in a plural subject:

along with, as well as, besides, in addition to, together with

INCORRECT: The president, along with the secretary of state and the director of the CIA, are misinformed.

CORRECT: The *president,* along with the secretary of state and the director of the CIA, *is* misinformed.

You can usually trust your ear to give you the correct verb form. However, subject-verb agreement can be tricky in the following instances:

- when the subject and verb are separated
- when the subject is an indefinite pronoun
- when the subject consists of more than one noun

If a sentence that is grammatically correct still sounds awkward, you should probably rephrase your thought.

ENSURING SUBJECT-VERB AGREEMENT PRACTICE SET

Read the sentences below and revise to ensure subject-verb agreement.

1. The arts is a very important topic to discuss at this point in our history.

   _____

   _____

2. The majority of the organization's members is over 60 years old.

   _____

   _____

ENSURING SUBJECT-VERB AGREEMENT PRACTICE SET ANSWERS AND EXPLANATIONS

Examples of the revised sentences with explanations:

1   The arts are a very important topic to discuss at this point in our history.

The verb is plural because the sentence is referring to more than one type of art, even though they collectively form a single topic of discussion

2   The majority of the organization's members are over 60 years old.

The verb must be pluralized because the subject is more than one member.

AVOIDING FAULTY MODIFICATION

Modifiers should be placed as close as possible to what they modify. In English, the position of the word within a sentence often establishes the word's relationship to other words in the sentence. If a modifier is placed too far from the word it modifies, the meaning may be lost or obscured. Notice, in the following sentences, the ambiguity that results when the modifying phrases are misplaced:

UNCLEAR: Gary and Martha sat talking about the problem in the office.

CLEAR: Gary and Martha sat in the office talking about the problem.

UNCLEAR: He only threw the ball eight yards.

CLEAR: He threw the ball only eight yards.

In addition to misplaced modifiers, watch for dangling modifiers: modifiers whose intended referents are not even present.

INCORRECT: Coming out of context, Peter was startled by Julia's perceptiveness.

CORRECT: Julia's remark, coming out of context, startled Peter with its perceptiveness.

AVOIDING FAULTY MODIFICATION PRACTICE SET

Read the following sentences and revise the faulty modification.

1. Inspired by the new love in his life, it took Sam three months only to finish his novel.

   _____

   _____

2. Having been an avid lifelong reader, a bookstore with a café seems like heaven on earth to me.

   _____

   _____

AVOIDING FAULTY MODIFICATION PRACTICE SET ANSWERS AND EXPLANATIONS

Examples of the revised sentences with explanations:

1   Inspired by the new love in his life, Sam finished his novel in only three months.

The original sentence contains two faulty modifiers. First, it is Sam, not "it," who is "inspired," so Sam should appear right after the comma. Second, the point of the sentence is that Sam finished the novel in only three months, not that finishing the novel was the only thing he got done in that time.

2   A bookstore with a café seems like heaven on earth to an avid life-long reader like me.

In the unrevised sentence it is unclear whether it is the author or the bookstore that has been a life-long avid reader.

AVOIDING UNCLEAR PRONOUN REFERENCE

A pronoun is a word that replaces a noun in a sentence. Every time you write a pronoun—such as *he, him, his, she, her, hers, it, its, they, their, that,* or *which*—be sure there can be absolutely no doubt what its antecedent is. (An antecedent is the particular noun to which a pronoun refers.) Careless use of pronouns can obscure your intended meaning.

UNCLEAR: The teacher told the student he was talented. (Does *he* refer to *teacher* or *student*?)

CLEAR: The student was talented, and the teacher told him so.

CLEAR: The teacher considered himself talented and told the student so.

UNCLEAR: Sara knows more about history than Irina because she learned it from her father.

(Does *she* refer to *Sara* or *Irina*?) You can usually rearrange a sentence to avoid ambiguous pronoun references.

CLEAR: Because Sara learned history from her father, she knows more than Irina does.

CLEAR: Because Irina learned history from her father, she knows less about it than Sara does.

If you are worried that a pronoun reference will be ambiguous, rewrite the sentence so that there is no doubt. Don't be afraid to repeat the antecedent if necessary.

UNCLEAR: I would rather settle in Phoenix than in Albuquerque, although it lacks wonderful restaurants.

CLEAR: I would rather settle in Phoenix than in Albuquerque, although Phoenix lacks wonderful restaurants.

A reader must be able to pinpoint the pronoun's antecedent. Even if you think the reader will know what you mean, do not use a pronoun without a clear and appropriate antecedent.

INCORRECT: When you are painting, be sure not to get it on the floor.
(*It* could only refer to the noun *paint*. But do you see the noun *paint* anywhere in the sentence? Pronouns cannot refer to implied nouns.)
CORRECT: When you are painting, be sure not to get any paint on the floor.

AVOIDING UNCLEAR PRONOUN REFERENCE PRACTICE SET

Revise the following sentences to correct unclear pronoun references.

1. Sports enthusiasts' desires should not trump the needs of the river and the quiet enjoyment of the people who live near the river. Their opinions should be taken into account.

   _____

   _____

2. Caroline telephoned her friends in California before going home for the night, which she had not done for weeks.

   _____

   _____

AVOIDING UNCLEAR PRONOUN REFERENCE PRACTICE SET ANSWERS AND EXPLANATIONS

Examples of the revised sentences with explanations:

1   Sports enthusiasts' desires should not trump the needs of the river and the quiet enjoyment of the people who live near the river, whose opinions should be taken into account.

In the original sentences, it is unclear if the pronoun "their" refers the people who live near the river, or the sports enthusiasts. Replacing "their" with "whose" clarifies matters.

2   Caroline telephoned her California friends for the first time in weeks before she went home for the night.

In the unrevised sentence, we do not know whether Caroline had not spent the night at home in weeks or whether she had not telephoned her friends in weeks.

CORRECTLY USING PARALLELISM

It can be rhetorically effective to use a particular construction several times in succession to provide emphasis. The technique is called *parallel construction*, and it is effective only when used sparingly.

Example: *As a* leader, Lincoln inspired a nation to throw off the chains of slavery; *as a* philosopher, he proclaimed the greatness of the little man; *as a* human being, he served as a timeless example of humility.

The repetition of the italicized construction provides the sentence with a strong sense of rhythm and organization and alerts the reader to the multiple aspects of Lincoln's character. Matching constructions must be expressed in parallel form. Writers often use parallel structure incorrectly for dissimilar items.

INCORRECT: They are sturdy, attractive, and cost only a dollar each. (The phrase *They are* makes sense preceding the adjectives *sturdy* and *attractive*, but it cannot be understood before *cost only a dollar each*.)
CORRECT: They are sturdy and attractive, and they cost only a dollar each.

Parallel constructions must be expressed in parallel grammatical form: all nouns, all infinitives, all gerunds, all prepositional phrases, or all clauses.

INCORRECT: All business students should learn word processing, accounting, and how to program computers.
CORRECT: All business students should learn word processing, accounting, and computer programming.

This principle applies to any words that might precede items in a series: either repeat the word before every element in a series or include it only before the first item. (In effect, your treatment of the second element of the series determines the form of all subsequent elements.)

INCORRECT: He invested his money in stocks, in real estate, and a home for retired performers.
CORRECT: He invested his money in stocks, in real estate, and in a home for retired performers.
CORRECT: He invested his money in stocks, real estate, and a home for retired performers.

A number of constructions always call for you to express ideas in parallel form. These constructions include the following:

> X is as _____ as Y.
> X is more _____ than Y.
> X is less _____ than Y.
> Both X and Y . . .
> Either X or Y . . .
> Neither X nor Y . . .
> Not only X but also Y . . .

X and Y can stand for as little as one word or as much as a whole clause, but in any case, the grammatical structure of X and Y must be identical.

INCORRECT: The view from this apartment is as spectacular as from that mountain lodge.

CORRECT: The view from this apartment is as spectacular as the view from that mountain lodge.

INCLUDING PARALLELISM PRACTICE SET

Read these sentences and revise to correct parallelism.

1. Homes sell faster or slowly for a wide variety of reasons.

   _____

   _____

2. The grocery baggers were ready, able, and were quite determined to do a great job.

   _____

   _____

INCLUDING PARALLELISM PRACTICE SET ANSWERS AND EXPLANATIONS

Examples of the revised sentences with explanations:

1   Homes sell faster or slower for all types of reasons.

In order for the parallel construction to work in this sentence, the two thoughts must have identical grammatical form. Therefore, "slower" is correct because it is grammatically similar to "faster."

2   The grocery baggers were ready, able, and quite determined to do a great job.

In this example, there is no need to repeat the verb; the phrase "quite determined to do a great job" can be treated as the final object in the series of terms.

USING A CONSISTENT NARRATIVE VOICE

True, we have advised you to avoid needless self-reference. But an occasional self-reference may be appropriate in your GRE essays. You may even call yourself *I* if you want, as long as you keep the number of first-person pronouns to a minimum. Less egocentric ways of referring to the narrator include *we* and *one*. If these more formal ways of writing seem stilted, stay with *I*.

"In my lifetime, I have seen many challenges to the principle of free speech."

"You can see how a free society can get too complacent when free speech is taken for granted. "

"One must admit that one should not overgeneralize."

The method of self-reference you select is called the *narrative voice* of your essay. Any of the three previous narrative voices is acceptable. Nevertheless, whichever you choose, you must be careful not to shift narrative voice in your essay. If you use *I* in the first sentence, for example, do not use *you* in a later sentence. You can shift narrative voice when presenting someone else's point of view or when speaking hypothetically, but your authorial voice should always be consistent.

INCORRECT: In my lifetime, *I* have seen many challenges to the principle of free speech. *You* can see how a free society can get too complacent when free speech is taken for granted.

It is likewise wrong to shift from *you* to *one*:

INCORRECT: Just by following the news, *you* can readily see how politicians have a vested interest in pleasing powerful interest groups. But *one* should not generalize about this tendency.

USING A CONSISTENT NARRATIVE VOICE PRACTICE SET

Read the sentences below and revise the narrative voice to make it consistent.

1. Not all wilderness areas are similar to the glorious Ansel Adams landscapes that we all imagine. If you've seen pictures of the Arctic National Wildlife Refuge, one would be unimpressed by the "natural beauty" of that massive swamp.

   _____

   _____

2. I am disgusted by the waste we tolerate in this country. One cannot simply stand by without adding to such waste: living here makes you wasteful.

   _____

   _____

USING A CONSISTENT NARRATIVE VOICE PRACTICE SET ANSWERS AND EXPLANATIONS

Examples of the revised sentences with explanations:

1   Not all wilderness areas are similar to the glorious Ansel Adams landscapes that you might imagine. If you were to see pictures of ANWAR, you would be unimpressed by the "natural beauty" of that massive swamp.

The narrative voice of most of the passage is personal and first-person, and does not justify a switch to the more formal third-person "one" in the second sentence.

2   I am disgusted with the waste we tolerate in this country. We cannot simply stand by without adding to such waste: living here makes us wasteful.

Similarly, in this passage the tone and narrative is impassioned and emphatically first person. The reader is directly addressed and exhorted to join in a common cause. Therefore, it should retain both the singular and plural forms of the first-person pronoun.

AVOIDING SLANG AND COLLOQUIALISMS

Conversational speech is filled with slang and colloquial expressions. However, you should avoid slang on the GRE. Slang terms and colloquialisms, or overly casual sayings, can be confusing to the reader, since these expressions are not universally understood. Even worse, such informal writing may give readers the impression that you are poorly educated or arrogant. Always bear in mind the audience for whom your writing is intended. Finally, remember that contractions are not commonly used in formal writing, so try to avoid them altogether in your essays. You should be fine if you keep in mind the differences between *written* and *spoken* English.

INAPPROPRIATE: He is really into gardening.
CORRECT: He is an avid gardener.

INAPPROPRIATE: She plays a wicked game of tennis.
CORRECT: She excels at tennis.

INAPPROPRIATE: Myra has got to go to Memphis for a week.
CORRECT: Myra must go to Memphis for a week.

INAPPROPRIATE: Joan's been doing science for eight years now.
CORRECT: Joan has been a scientist for eight years now.

AVOIDING SLANG AND COLLOQUIALISM PRACTICE SET

Read the sentences below and revise the tone to eliminate slang and colloquialisms.

1. Gertrude has been rockin' the sales floor for almost thirty years now.

    _____

    _____

2. Normal human beings can't cope with repeated humiliation.

    _____

    _____

AVOIDING SLANG AND COLLOQUIALISM PRACTICE SET ANSWERS AND EXPLANATIONS

Examples of the revised sentences with explanations:

1   Gertrude has excelled as a salesperson for almost thirty years.

The tone in the unrevised sentence is too informal. Do not try to make your writing sound like spoken language; the spoken and formal written registers are very different. Always spell out words in their entirety.

2   Normal human beings cannot tolerate repeated humiliation.

Avoid contractions wherever possible.

AVOIDING SENTENCE FRAGMENTS AND RUN-ONS

Every sentence in formal expository writing must have an independent clause: a clause that contains a subject and a predicate. A sentence fragment has no independent clause; a run-on sentence has two or more independent clauses that are improperly connected. As you edit your practice essays, check your sentence constructions, noting any tendency toward fragments or run-on sentences.

FRAGMENT: Global warming. That is what the scientists and journalists are worried about this month.
CORRECT: Global warming is the cause of concern for scientists and journalists this month.

FRAGMENT: Seattle is a wonderful place to live. Mountains, ocean, and forests, all within easy driving distance. If you can ignore the rain.
CORRECT: Seattle is a wonderful place to live, with mountains, ocean, and forests all within easy driving distance. However, it certainly does rain often.

FRAGMENT: Why is the author's position preposterous? Because he makes generalizations that are untrue.
CORRECT: The author's position is preposterous because he makes generalizations that are untrue.

Beginning single-clause sentences with coordinating conjunctions—*for, and, nor, but, or, yet*, and *so*—is acceptable in moderation.

CORRECT: Most people would agree that indigent patients should receive wonderful health care. But every treatment has its price.

Time pressure may also cause you to write two or more sentences as one. When you proofread your essays, watch out for independent clauses that are not joined with any punctuation at all or are only joined with a comma.

RUN-ON: Current insurance practices are unfair they discriminate against the people who need insurance most.

You can repair run-on sentences in any one of three ways. First, you could use a period to make separate sentences of the independent clauses.

CORRECT: Current insurance practices are unfair. They discriminate against the people who need insurance most.

You could also use a semicolon. A semicolon is a weak period. It separates independent clauses but signals to the reader that the ideas in the clauses are related.

CORRECT: Current insurance practices are unfair; they discriminate against the people who need insurance most.

The third method of repairing a run-on sentence is usually the most effective. Use a conjunction to turn an independent clause into a dependent one and to make explicit how the clauses are related. A comma is also called for when using one of the FAN-BOYS (**F**or, **A**nd, **N**or, **B**ut, **O**r, **Y**et, **S**o) coordinating conjunctions. You should insert a comma before one of these conjunctions when it separates two independent clauses.

CORRECT: Current insurance practices are unfair because they discriminate against the people who need insurance most.

CORRECT: Current insurance practices are unfair, for they discriminate against the people who need insurance most.

A common cause of run-on sentences is the misuse of adverbs like *however, nevertheless, furthermore, likewise,* and *therefore.*

RUN-ON: Current insurance practices are discriminatory, furthermore they make insurance too expensive for the poor.

CORRECT: Current insurance practices are discriminatory. Furthermore, they make insurance too expensive for the poor.

AVOIDING SENTENCE FRAGMENTS AND RUN-ONS PRACTICE SET

Read the sentences below and make revisions to correct fragments and run-on sentences.

1. The writer of this letter lays out a cogent argument about why Adams Realty is superior it is organized, has strong points with clear examples, and is convincing.

   _____

   _____

2. Leadership ability. That is the elusive quality that our current government employees have yet to capture.

   _____

   _____

AVOIDING SENTENCE FRAGMENTS AND RUN-ONS PRACTICE SET ANSWERS AND EXPLANATIONS

Examples of the revised sentences with explanations:

1   The writer of this letter lays out a cogent, organized, and convincing argument with strong points and clear examples to illustrate the superiority of Adams Realty.

The unrevised sentence is turgid and unruly. We have two choices: condense the series of nouns and adjectives, or break it into two different sentences. We've gone with concision for this example. By deleting the "it is," which really should indicate the start of a new sentence, we have put the adjectives describing the argument in a series with commas, and put the nouns into a prepositional phrase at the end of the sentence.

2   Leadership ability is the elusive quality that our current government employees have yet to capture.

This pair of sentences is fairly easy to revise. The first is a fragment that can easily be incorporated into the second, as the pronoun "that" refers back to "Leadership ability."

CORRECTLY USING COMMAS

The proper use of commas constitutes one of the trickier points of style and usage. Different editors have different preferences and conventions for how and when to use commas. The guidelines below are ideally suited for use in terse, analytical essays, such as those asked for in the GRE Analytical Writing sections.

Use commas to separate items in a series. If more than two items are listed in a series, they should be separated by commas. The final comma—the one that precedes the word *and*—is optional (but be consistent throughout your essays).

CORRECT: My recipe for buttermilk biscuits contains flour, baking soda, salt, shortening and buttermilk.

CORRECT: My recipe for buttermilk biscuits contains flour, baking soda, salt, shortening, and buttermilk.

Don't place commas before the first element of a series or after the last element.

INCORRECT: My investment adviser recommended that I construct a portfolio of, stocks, bonds, commodities futures, and precious metals.
INCORRECT: The elephants, tigers, and dancing bears, were the highlights of the circus.

Use commas to separate two or more adjectives before a noun but don't use a comma after the last adjective in the series.

INCORRECT: The manatee is a round, blubbery, bewhiskered, creature whose continued presence in American waters is endangered by careless boaters.
CORRECT: The manatee is a round, blubbery, bewhiskered creature whose continued presence in American waters is endangered by careless boaters.

Use commas to set off parenthetical clauses and phrases. (A parenthetical expression is one that is not necessary to the main idea of the sentence.)

CORRECT: Gordon, who is a writer by profession, bakes an excellent cheesecake.

The main idea is that Gordon bakes an excellent cheesecake. The intervening clause merely serves to identify Gordon; thus, it should be set off with commas.

Use commas after introductory, participial, or prepositional phrases.

CORRECT: Having watered his petunias every day during the drought, Harold was very disappointed when his garden was destroyed by insects.
CORRECT: After the banquet, Harold and Martha went dancing.

Use commas to separate independent clauses (clauses that could stand alone as complete sentences) connected by coordinating conjunctions such as *and, but, yet,* and so on.

INCORRECT: Susan's old car has been belching blue smoke from the tailpipe for two weeks, but has not broken down yet.
CORRECT: Susan's old car has been belching blue smoke from the tailpipe for two weeks, but it has not broken down yet.

INCORRECT: Zachariah's pet frog eats 50 flies a day, and never gets indigestion.
CORRECT: Zachariah's pet frog eats 50 flies a day, and it has never gotten indigestion.

USING COMMAS PRACTICE SET

Correct the punctuation errors in the following sentences.

1. Teaching, is not a popularity contest!

   _____

   _____

2. Pushing through the panicked crowd the security guards frantically searched for the suspect.

   _____

   _____

USING COMMAS PRACTICE SET ANSWERS AND EXPLANATIONS

Examples of the revised sentences with explanations:

1   Teaching is not a popularity contest!

The gerund "Teaching" functions as the subject of the main clause, and therefore cannot be set off by a comma.

2   Pushing through the panicked crowd, the security guards frantically searched for the suspect.

The participial phrase "Pushing through the panicked crowd" is not necessary to the main idea of the sentence, and should therefore be set off with a comma.

CORRECTLY USING SEMICOLONS

Use a semicolon without a coordinating conjunction (such as *and, or,* or *but*) to link two closely related independent clauses. Additionally, use semicolons to separate items in a series in which the items contain commas. Be certain that there are complete sentences on both sides of a semicolon unless you are using it to separate items in a series.

INCORRECT: Whooping cranes are an endangered species; and they are unlikely to survive if we continue to pollute.

CORRECT: Whooping cranes are an endangered species; there are only 50 whooping cranes in New Jersey today.

CORRECT: Three important dates in the history of the company are December 16, 1999; April 4, 2003; and June 30, 2007.

Use a semicolon between independent clauses connected by words like *therefore, nevertheless,* and *moreover.*

CORRECT: The staff meeting has been postponed until next Thursday; therefore, I will be unable to get approval for my project until then.

CORRECT: Farm prices have been falling rapidly for two years; nevertheless, the traditional American farm is not in danger of disappearing.

USING SEMICOLONS PRACTICE SET

Correct the punctuation errors in the following sentences.

1. Very few students wanted to take the class in physics, it was only the professor's kindness that kept it from being canceled.

   _____

   _____

2. Marcus has five years' experience in karate; but Tyler has even more.

   _____

   _____

USING SEMICOLONS PRACTICE SET ANSWERS AND EXPLANATIONS

Examples of the revised sentences with explanations:

1   Very few students wanted to take the class in physics; it was only the professor's kindness that kept it from being canceled

The two independent clauses in the sentence have to be separated by a semicolon or a conjunction. Since "only" does not function as a conjunction in this context, a semicolon is required for the sentence to be grammatically correct.

2   Marcus has five years' experience in karate, but Tyler has even more.

When using the coordinating conjunction "but" to separate the two clauses, it should be preceded by a comma, not a semicolon.

CORRECTLY USING COLONS

In formal writing, the colon is used only as a means of signaling that what follows is a list, definition, explanation, or concise summary of what has gone before. The colon usually follows an independent clause, and it will frequently be accompanied by a reinforcing expression like *the following, as follows*, or *namely* or by an explicit demonstrative pronoun like *this*.

CORRECT: Your instructions are as follows: read the passage carefully, answer the questions on the last page, and turn over your answer sheet.
CORRECT: This is what I found in the refrigerator: a moldy lime, half a bottle of stale soda, and a jar of peanut butter.

Be careful not to put a colon between a verb and its direct object.

INCORRECT: I want: a slice of pizza and a small green salad.
CORRECT: This is what I want: a slice of pizza and a small green salad. (The colon serves to announce that a list is forthcoming.)
CORRECT: I don't want much for lunch: just a slice of pizza and a small green salad. (Here what follows the colon defines what *don't want much* means.)

Context will occasionally make clear that a second independent clause is closely linked to its predecessor, developing the previous clause further, even without an explicit expression like those used above. Here, too, a colon is appropriate, although a period will always be correct too.

CORRECT: We were aghast: the "charming country inn" that had been advertised in such glowing terms proved to be a leaking cabin full of mosquitoes.

USING COLONS PRACTICE SET

Correct the punctuation errors in the following sentences.

1. The residents of Mason City do not just enjoy: swimming, boating, and fishing.

   _____

   _____

2. The chef has created a masterpiece, the pasta is delicate yet firm, the mustard greens are fresh, and the medallions of veal are melting in my mouth.

   _____

   _____

USING COLONS PRACTICE SET ANSWERS AND EXPLANATIONS

Examples of the revised sentences with explanations:

1　The residents of Mason City do not just enjoy swimming, boating, and fishing.

The use of a colon is inappropriate in this situation because colons should not separate a verb and its direct object, such as "enjoy" and "swimming."

2　The chef has created a masterpiece: the pasta is delicate yet firm, the mustard greens are fresh, and the medallions of veal are melting in my mouth.

A colon should follow the word "masterpiece" to signal that a list is coming. Note that the list does not have to be single words; it can be composed of independent clauses.

CORRECTLY USING HYPHENS AND DASHES

Use a hyphen with the compound numbers twenty-one through ninety-nine and with fractions used as adjectives.

CORRECT: Sixty-five students constituted a majority.
CORRECT: A two-thirds vote was necessary to carry the measure.

Use a hyphen with the prefixes *ex-*, *all-*, and *self-* and with the suffix *-elect*.

CORRECT: The constitution protects against self-incrimination.
CORRECT: The president-elect was invited to chair the meeting.

Use a hyphen with a compound adjective when it comes before the word it modifies but not when it comes after the word it modifies.

CORRECT: The no-holds-barred argument continued into the night.
CORRECT: The argument continued with no holds barred.

Use a hyphen with any prefix used before a proper noun or adjective.

CORRECT: His pro-African sentiments were heartily applauded.
CORRECT: They believed that his accent was un-Australian.

Use a hyphen to separate component parts of a word to avoid confusion with other words or to avoid the use of a double vowel.

CORRECT: The sculptor was able to re-form the clay after the dog knocked over the bust.
CORRECT: The family re-entered their house after the fire marshal departed.

Use a dash to indicate an abrupt change of thought.

CORRECT: The inheritance must cover the entire cost of the proposal—Gail has no other money to invest.

CORRECT: To get a high score—and who doesn't want to get a high score?— you need to devote yourself to prolonged and concentrated study.

USING HYPHENS AND DASHES PRACTICE SET

Correct the punctuation errors in the following sentences.

1. Harry had every physical advantage—over his opponent—size, speed, strength, but luck was not on his side.

   _____

   _____

2. John and his ex wife remained on friendly terms.

   _____

   _____

USING HYPHENS AND DASHES PRACTICE SET ANSWERS AND EXPLANATIONS

Examples of the revised sentences with explanations:

1   Harry had every physical advantage over his opponent—size, speed, strength—but luck was not on his side.

The original sentence uses dashes to separate "over his opponent" from the rest of the sentence, which is wrong because that phrase is an essential part of the sentence. The list of advantages is a break in thought, so that's what the dashes need to set apart.

2   John and his ex-wife remained on friendly terms.

The prefix "ex" modifies the word "wife," and thus requires a hyphen.

CORRECTLY USING APOSTROPHES

Use an apostrophe in a contraction to indicate that one or more letters have been eliminated. But try to avoid using contractions altogether on the GRE: using the full form of a verb is more appropriate in formal writing.

CONTRACTED: We'd intended to address the question of equal rights, but it's too late to begin the discussion now.

FULL FORM: We had intended to address the question of equal rights, but it is too late to begin the discussion now.

One of the most common errors involving the apostrophe is using it in the contraction *you're* or *it's* to indicate the possessive form of *you* or *it*. When you write *you're*, ask yourself whether you mean *you are*. If not, the correct word is *your*. Similarly, are you sure you mean *it is*? If not, use the possessive form *its*.

INCORRECT: You're chest of drawers is ugly.
CORRECT: *Your* chest of drawers is ugly.

INCORRECT: The dog hurt it's paw.
CORRECT: The dog hurt *its* paw.

Use the apostrophe to indicate the possessive form of a noun.

NOUN	POSSESSIVE
the boy	the boy's
Harry	Harry's
the children	the children's
the boys	the boys'
the bass	the bass's

NOTE: Possessive forms can sometimes look like contractions. The word *boy's*, for example, could have one of three meanings:

- The boy's an expert at chess. (contraction: the boy is ...)
- The boy's left for the day. (contraction: the boy has ...)
- The boy's face was covered with pie. (possessive: the face of the boy)

The word *boys'* can have only one meaning: a plural possessive (the _____ of the boys).

CORRECT: Ms. Fox's office is on the first floor. (One person possesses the office.)
CORRECT: The Foxes' apartment has a wonderful view. (There are several people named Fox living in the same apartment. First you must form the plural; then add the apostrophe to indicate possession.)

Possessive pronouns do not use an apostrophe (with the exception of the neutral *one*, which forms its possessive by adding *'s*).

INCORRECT: The tiny cabin had been our's for many years.
CORRECT: The tiny cabin had been *ours* for many years.

USING APOSTROPHES PRACTICE SET

Read the sentences below and revise for appropriate apostrophe use.

1. People should be allowed to keep their money and use it for the thing's they want.

   _____

   _____

2. The young men were students at the Boy's Latin School.

   _____

   _____

USING APOSTROPHES PRACTICE SET
ANSWERS AND EXPLANATIONS

Examples of the revised sentences with explanations:

1   People should be allowed to keep their money and use it for the things they want.

The word "things" in this sentence is used as a direct object and not as a possessive. There is no need for an apostrophe, as the "s" is simply pluralizing it.

2   The young men were students at the Boys' Latin School.

The apostrophe should follow the "s" in "Boys," as the term refers to more than one boy.

In the chapters that follow, you will learn how to approach the two basic types of Analytical Writing tasks on the GRE. The Argument task will ask you to analyze an incomplete argument, while the Issue task will oblige you to come up with one of your own. Although each type of task requires you to approach an argument in distinctly different ways, both are built on the foundations you studied in this chapter.

CHAPTER 17

The Issue Essay

INTRODUCTION TO THE ISSUE ESSAY

The first of the Analytical Writing essay tasks is the Issue essay. On the Issue essay, you will be given a point of view about which you'll have to form an opinion, and then you'll need to provide a well-supported and justifiable case for that opinion.

The Issue essay requires you to construct your own argument by making claims and providing evidence to support your position on a given issue. The directions will ask you to take a position on the issue, and they'll instruct you to explain your position convincingly, using reasons and/or examples to back up your assertions.

For the assignment topic, expect about one to two sentences that discuss a broad, general issue, sometimes presenting only one point of view and sometimes presenting two conflicting points. Either way, the test will present a statement that could reasonably be either supported or argued against. Your job is to form an opinion on the topic and make a case for that opinion.

The directions for Issue essays will look like this:

> You have 30 minutes to plan and compose a response in which you evaluate the argument passage that appears below. A response to any other argument will receive a score of zero. Make sure that you respond according to the specific instructions and support your evaluation with relevant reasons and/or examples.

An Issue essay will always begin with a statement. It will look something like this:

"The drawbacks to the use of nuclear power mean that it is not a long-term solution to the problem of meeting ever-increasing energy needs."

The second part of the directions, the prompt, will give specific directions for how to approach the essay. An Issue essay prompt will look something like this:

Write a response in which you examine your own position on the statement. Explore the extent to which you either agree or disagree with it and support your reasoning with evidence and/or examples. Be sure to reflect on ways in which the statement might or might not be true and how this informs your thinking on the subject.

The Issue essay prompt may vary. Other prompts you may see for the Issue essay look like this:

- Write your own response to the recommendation in which you discuss why you either agree or disagree with it. Support your response with evidence and/or examples. Use a hypothetical set of circumstances to illustrate the consequences of accepting or rejecting the recommendation and explain how this informs your thinking.
- Develop a response to the claim in which you discuss whether or not you agree with it. Focus specifically on the most powerful or compelling examples that could be used to refute your position.
- Write a response in which you determine which view bears the closest resemblance to your own. In justifying your reasoning and supporting your position, be sure to include your reaction to both of the views presented.
- Develop a response to the claim in which you discuss whether or not you agree with it. Focus specifically on whether or not you agree with the reason upon which the claim is based.
- Write a response discussing your reaction to the policy stated above. Justify your reasoning for the position you take. Explain the potential consequences or implications for implementing such a policy and how this informs your position.

THE KAPLAN METHOD FOR ANALYTICAL WRITING

STEP 1   Take the issue/argument apart.

STEP 2   Select the points you will make.

STEP 3   Organize, using Kaplan's essay templates.

STEP 4   Type your essay.

STEP 5   Proofread your work.

How the Kaplan Method for Analytical Writing Works

Now let's discuss how the Kaplan Method for Analytical Writing works for the Issue essay:

❯❯ STEP 1

Take the issue apart.

Read the assignment and consider both sides of the issue. Use your scratch paper throughout Steps 1–3. Restate the issue in your own words. Consider the other side of the issue and put that into your own words as well.

❯❯ STEP 2

Select the points you will make.

After you consider what both sides of the issue mean, think of reasons and examples for both sides and make a decision as to which side you will support or the extent to which you agree with the stated position.

❯❯ STEP 3

Organize, using Kaplan's essay templates.

Organize your thoughts by outlining what you want to say so that you will be able to approach the actual writing process confidently and focus on expressing your ideas clearly. In the introduction, restate the prompt in your own words, state whether you agree or disagree, and give a preview of the supporting points you plan to make. In the middle paragraphs, give your points of agreement (or disagreement) and provide support. Determine what evidence you will use to support each point. Be sure to lead with your best argument. Think about how the essay as a whole will flow. Conclude by summing up your position on the issue.

STEP 4

Type your essay.

You shouldn't proceed with this step until you've completed the three preceding ones. Graders have a limited amount of time in which to read your essay, so start out and conclude with strong statements. Be emphatic and concise with your prose and link related ideas with transitions. This will help your writing flow and make things easier on the grader. Furthermore, you'll save time and energy by preparing your essay before you start typing it.

STEP 5

Proofread your work.

Save enough time to read quickly through the entire essay. Look for errors you can address quickly: capitalization, paragraph divisions, double-typed words, general typos, and small grammatical errors.

How to Apply the Kaplan Method for Analytical Writing to the Issue Essay

Now let's apply the Kaplan Method for Analytical Writing to an Issue prompt:

> "The drawbacks to the use of nuclear power mean that it is not a long-term solution to the problem of meeting ever-increasing energy needs."

> > Write a response in which you examine your own position on the statement. Explore the extent to which you either agree or disagree with it and support your reasoning with evidence and/or examples. Be sure to reflect on ways in which the statement might or might not be true and how this informs your thinking on the subject.

STEP 1

Take the issue apart.

Your first step is to dissect the issue. Take notes on your scratch paper. Start by restating the issue in your own words: "Although we have a need for alternate sources of energy, we cannot count on nuclear energy as a solution because of its major drawbacks."

Now, consider the other side of the issue—in your own words, this might be "Nuclear power is safe and effective and does not have such serious drawbacks as this statement would suggest."

STEP 2

Select the points you will make.

Your job, as stated in the directions, is to decide whether or not you agree with the statement and then to explain your decision. Some would argue that the use of nuclear power is too dangerous, while others would say that we can't afford not to use it. Which side do you take?

Remember, this isn't about showing the graders what your deep-seated beliefs about energy policy are—it's about showing that you can formulate an argument and communicate it clearly. The position you choose to take for the Issue essay does not have to be one you actually believe in.

Quickly jot down on your scratch paper the pros and cons of each side and choose the side for which you have the most relevant things to say. For this topic, that process might go something like this:

Arguments *for* the use of nuclear power:

- It is inexpensive compared to other forms of energy.
- Fossil fuels will eventually be depleted.
- Solar power is still too problematic and expensive.

Arguments *against* the use of nuclear power:

- It is harmful to the environment.
- It is dangerous to mankind.
- Safer alternatives already exist.
- Better alternatives may lie undiscovered.

Again, it doesn't matter which side you take. Strictly speaking, there is no *right* answer as far as the testmaker is concerned. Let's say that in this case, you decide to argue against nuclear power. Remember, the prompt asks you to argue why the cons of nuclear power outweigh the pros—the inadequacy of this power source is the end toward which you're arguing, so don't list it as a supporting argument.

❯❯ STEP 3

Organize, using Kaplan's essay template.

You should have already begun to think out your arguments—that's how you picked the side you did in the first place. Now's the time to write your arguments out, including those that weaken the opposing side. This step involves your own note taking, so feel free to use abbreviations.

Paragraph 1: Nuclear power is not a viable alternative to other energy sources.

Paragraph 2: Nuclear power creates radioactive waste.

Paragraph 3: Nuclear energy is an industry with related costs to consumers.

Paragraph 4: There are other, more environmentally friendly energy sources.

Paragraph 5: Further investment in nuclear power would be a waste of time and money.

❯❯ STEP 4

Type your essay.

Remember, open up with a general statement indicating that you understand the issue and then assert your position. From there, make your main points. Note: As a basis for comparison, we've included an outstanding essay that deserves a score of 6. The second prompt will include an adequate essay that deserves a score of 4.

Sample Issue Essay 1

Proponents of nuclear energy as "the power source for the future" have long touted its relative economy, "clean-burning" technology, and virtually inexhaustible fuel supply. However, a close examination of the issue reveals that nuclear energy proves more problematic and dangerous than other forms of energy production and thus is not an acceptable solution to the problem of meeting ever-increasing energy needs.

First and foremost, nuclear power production presents the problem of radioactive waste storage. Fuel byproducts from nuclear fission remain toxic for thousands of years, and the spills and leaks from existing storage sites have been hazardous and costly to clean up. This remains true despite careful regulation and even under the best of circumstances. Even more appalling is the looming threat of accidents at the reactor itself: Incidents at the Three Mile Island and Chernobyl power plants and at other production sites have warned us that the consequences of a nuclear meltdown can be catastrophic and felt worldwide.

But beyond the enormous long-term environmental problems and short-term health risks, the bottom-line issue for the production of energy is one of economics. Power production in our society is a business just like any other, and the large companies that produce this country's electricity and gas claim they are unable to make alternatives such as solar power affordable. Yet—largely due to incentives from the federal government—there already exist homes heated by solar power and cars fueled by the sun. If the limited resources devoted to date to such energy alternatives have already produced working models, a more intensive, broadly based and supported effort is likely to make those alternatives less expensive and problematic.

Besides the benefits in terms of both cost and safety, renewable resources such as solar and hydroelectric power represent far better options in the long run for development: These options require money only for the materials needed to harvest the renewable resources. While sunlight and water are free, the innovative technologies and industrial strategies devised to harness them have created a geometric progression of spin-offs affecting fields as diverse as agriculture, real estate, space exploration, and social policy. These options also repeatedly produced secondary economic and social benefits, such as the large recreational and irrigation reservoirs created in the American Southwest behind large hydroelectric dams like the Hoover and Grand Coulee.

While it may now be clear that the drawbacks to the use of nuclear power are too great, it should also be apparent that the long-term benefits of renewable resources would reward investment. If these alternatives are explored more seriously than they have been in the past, safer and less expensive sources of power will undoubtedly live up to their promise. With limited resources at our disposal and a burgeoning global population to consider, further investment in nuclear power would mark an unconscionable and unnecessary waste of time and money.

STEP 5

Proofread your work.

Be sure to allot a few minutes after you have finished writing to review your essay. Though you do not have to write a grammatically flawless essay to score well, you will want to review so that you can catch some of the standout mistakes. You can practice your writing skills in Chapter 16: Analytical Writing Foundations and Content Review.

ASSESSMENT OF SAMPLE ISSUE ESSAY 1: "OUTSTANDING," SCORE OF 6

Now we'll look at how this essay would have been scored on the actual GRE Analytical Writing section:

This essay is carefully constructed throughout, enabling the reader to move effortlessly from point to point as the writer examines the multifaceted implications of the issue. The writer begins by acknowledging arguments for the opposing side and then uses his thesis statement ("a close examination of the issue reveals that nuclear energy proves more problematic and dangerous than other forms of energy production") to explain his own position on the issue. He proceeds to provide compelling reasons and examples to support the premise, and he then takes the argument to an effective conclusion. The writing is clean, concise, and almost error-free. Sentence structure is varied, and diction and vocabulary are strong and expressive.

HOW TO APPLY THE KAPLAN METHOD FOR ANALYTICAL WRITING TO ANOTHER ISSUE ESSAY

Now let's apply the Kaplan Method for Analytical Writing to a second Issue prompt:

"People who hold high expectations for others are rewarded with high performance and respect."

Develop a response to the claim in which you provide specific reasons why you do or do not you agree with it. Focus specifically on the most powerful or compelling examples that could be used to support your position.

STEP 1

Take the issue apart.

Begin by putting the issue in your own words, "If you expect people to do well, they will, and they will respect you for it." Next, consider the other side of the issue, and do the same: "If you expect too much of people, they may get frustrated and perform at a lower level, or you may lose their respect."

STEP 2

Select the points you will make.

Your job, as stated in the directions, is to decide whether or not you agree with the statement and then to explain your decision. Some would argue that high expectations yield high results, while others may think that unrealistic high expectations may destroy confidence. Which side do you take?

Quickly think through the pros and cons of each side and choose the side for which you have the most relevant things to say. For this topic, that process might go something like this:

Arguments *for* holding people to high expectations:

- Without expectations, people don't know how they will be measured or to what level they should perform.
- High expectations convey confidence and trust.
- Striving to meet high expectations improves people's skills, and when these individuals succeed, their success leads to increased confidence and higher performance.

Arguments *against* holding people to high expectations:

- People could give up or lose confidence if they are unable to meet the expectations.
- You may be thought of as someone who is unyielding or only concerned with performance.

Remember, it doesn't matter which side you take. Strictly speaking, there is no *right* answer.

STEP 3

Organize, using Kaplan's essay templates.

Now's the time to write those arguments out, including counterarguments that weaken the opposing side.

Paragraph 1:
High expectations yield high performance and respect in every case, whether the expectations are met or unmet.

Paragraph 2:
Without expectations, people don't know how they will be measured or to what level they should perform. 2nd graders design skyscrapers; retirees train for Olympics.

Paragraph 3:
Challenges from teachers: high expectations convey confidence and trust.

Paragraph 4:
Higher performance improves people's skills and confidence once they meet the expectations. (Challenge office interns example)

Paragraph 5: (opposition)
People fail because others do not value them enough and believe they are capable of less than they actually are.

Paragraph 6: In all cases, high expectations are worth the risk.

STEP 4

Type your essay.

Sample Issue Essay 2

High expectations yield high performance and respect in every case, whether the expectations are met or unmet. Setting expectations allows people to know how they will be measured and to what level they should perform. They also convey confidence and a sense of trust. Once the expectations are met, people feel bolstered by their achievement and have a much stronger sense of self-confidence, leading to even higher performance. These results hold up in a variety of contexts, including in educational, business, and political realms.

The purpose of expectations is often lost in the assignment of a task. The expectations themselves may take the form of the actual tasks to be done, but really, the expectation is the ownership, resourcefulness, and skill of the person assigned the task. Expecting someone to do something overly challenging, such as asking second-graders to design a skyscraper or challenging a retiree to train for the Olympics, may seem egregious, but the stories that intrigue us most are usually about people rising to the challenge. Our own expectations are recalibrated when we learn of people exceeding the expectations we set ourselves to. We look to where the bar is set to see how we measure up. Given a bar, people will usually do what it takes to measure up.

Good teachers are often described as "hard, but fair." This is a good description of someone who holds high expectations for his or her students, and is rewarded by that assessment. A hard but fair teacher is one who challenges the students to exceed their own expectations of themselves, and often others' expectations of them. These are the teachers who assign fourth grade students research papers or ask eighth graders to take a 100-question math test in 100 minutes. Students take up the challenge because it feels good to succeed. They gain confidence and look at tasks unrelated to the classroom in new ways.

High performance breeds higher performance. Once someone has been resourceful or learned a new skill to achieve a task, the person feels empowered to be similarly resourceful achieving different tasks. In fact, a high performer may take on more challenges without prompting. This bears out in business: the neophyte office intern who pulls together a critical report through resourcefulness, skill, and a little luck is a familiar story, but for good reason. This intern with his or her fresh ideas stands out among the drones and is challenged further, rocketing to the proverbial top of the company. If the same expectations were put on the rest of the workforce, would other employees be as resourceful to achieve the expectations? Most likely, as long as the employee is motivated enough by the challenge.

Some people may be frustrated by high expectations, and some may simply ignore those expectations, but being presented with a challenge ultimately builds a person's confidence. No one ever failed because he or she was fairly challenged by a daunting task and supported while tackling it. People fail because others do not value them enough and believe they are capable of less than they actually are. In fact, just being challenged is often enough to shake up people's self-expectations and make them reconsider what they are actually capable of.

In all cases, high expectations are worth the risk. The challenge bolsters self-esteem and self-confidence, and yields high performance. It improves performance in classrooms, on the job, and in other areas where challenges present themselves.

◆ STEP 5
Proofread your work.

Take the last couple of minutes to catch any glaring errors.

ASSESSMENT OF SAMPLE ISSUE ESSAY 2: "ADEQUATE," SCORE OF 4

Now we'll look at how this essay would have been scored on the actual GRE Analytical Writing section:

This essay is, on the whole, well constructed and laid out. The reader can systematically move from point to point as the writer examines the implications of the issue. The writer begins by agreeing with the statement and presenting specific reasons for agreeing. She gives examples to illustrate her point and organizes her essay well. The author's analysis is generally cogent. She asks the reader to take a bit of a leap with some of her claims. For example, claiming that "people will usually do what it takes to measure up" when given a bar is a conclusion not really supported by the paragraph leading us to that conclusion. She asserts that people are inherently encouraged, rather than discouraged, by daunting challenges, but never really justifies that assertion. However, the writing is clean and concise and includes only a few errors. Sentence structure is varied, and the author's diction is strong and expressive. For all these reasons, this essay receives a score of 4.

KAPLAN'S ADDITIONAL TIPS FOR THE ISSUE ESSAY

Don't Overcomplicate Your Prose

The types of issues that the essays use as their subject aren't supposed to be too abstruse or esoteric. Don't worry if you're not extremely familiar with a subject. Similarly, your responses shouldn't be too convoluted. Try to be as clear and linear in your writing as possible when supporting an argument. Bombastic flourishes of rhetoric may seem impressive when you first write them, but the point here is to assert and defend a position, not impress the graders with your vocabulary or wit. Substance will easily outweigh style.

Don't Worry about Whether or Not Your Position Is "Correct"

The purpose of the Issue essay is to develop an argument and defend it. You're going to be scored on how well supported your position is, not on whether it is the "right answer." Indeed, by design most of the topics chosen for this task are not black-and-white issues; they can be argued successfully from very different points of view.

Think about the Issue from Different Perspectives

An important skill you'll need in graduate school (as in life) is the ability to understand an issue or problem from someone else's point of view. Removing your own personal biases from the equation can be a great help, as it will force you to think about an issue logically and not just go with your gut reaction.

ISSUE ESSAY PRACTICE SET

Issue Essay 1

30 Minutes
Length: 1 essay

Directions: You will be given a statement that presents an issue you need to respond to, along with detailed instructions on how to respond to the statement. You have 30 minutes to plan and compose a response in which you develop an argument according to the instructions. A response to any other issue results in a score of zero.

> "The perceived greatness of any political leader has more to do with the challenges faced by that leader than with any of his or her inherent skills and abilities."

Write a response in which you examine your own position on the statement. Explore the extent to which you either agree or disagree with it and support your reasoning with evidence and/or examples. Be sure to reflect on ways in which the statement might or might not be true and how this informs your thinking on the subject.

Issue Essay 2

30 Minutes
Length: 1 essay

Directions:

You will be given a statement that presents an issue you need to respond to, along with detailed instructions on how to respond to the statement. You have 30 minutes to plan and compose a response in which you develop an argument according to the instructions. A response to any other issue results in a score of zero.

> "Progress should be the aim of any great society. People too often cling unnecessarily to obsolete ways of thinking and acting because of both a high comfort level and a fear of the unknown."

Write a response in which you examine your own position on the statement. Explore the extent to which you either agree or disagree with it and support your reasoning with evidence or examples. Be sure to reflect on ways in which the statement might or might not be true and how this informs your thinking on the subject.

ISSUE ESSAY PRACTICE SET ANSWERS AND EXPLANATIONS

Issue Essay Sample Essays and Assessments

What follows are top-scoring sample essays for each of the practice prompts. Note how the authors adhere to the Kaplan Method for Analytical Writing.

Issue Essay 1: "Outstanding," Score of 6

Perceptions of greatness in national and political leaders are largely determined by the seriousness of the problems that they face during their terms in office. Most national histories principally highlight individuals in the context of significant events in which the leaders played important roles. Most political leaders need to have large stores of inherent skill and ability just in order to become a political leader. However, history remembers those who lived in great times more fondly than those who did not. Examples of this are numerous and include the histories of Abraham Lincoln, Woodrow Wilson, and Winston Churchill—all men who are perceived as great leaders largely because of the times in which they lived.

Abraham Lincoln is often considered the greatest of all the American Presidents. He graces two units of the currency and has one of the largest monuments built in his honor in Washington D.C. However, Lincoln is considered great largely because he faced a great challenge—the civil war between the North and the South in the 1860s. Lincoln led the United States to victory over the rebels and reunited the country and is therefore considered great. This is not to say that Lincoln was not skilled. Many know that he was born in a log cabin and progressed to law school and eventually to the presidency. He was also a skilled orator. However another man, James Buchanan, also was born in a log cabin, went to law school, gave good speeches and ascended to the presidency. However there are no monuments to Buchanan in the capital or pictures of his face on the five-dollar bill.

Woodrow Wilson was another talented man who ascended to the presidency of the United States. However his talents are not what make his perceived greatness. In this age, few remember if Wilson was particularly smart, a very good speechmaker, or a good arbitrator. Most remember that he led the United States to victory in the first World War and therefore perceive him as great. At the time, however, Wilson was rather unpopular. In fact, he had so little sway with Congress that he was unable to get the United States to join the League of Nations—a fact that many claim helped lead to the second World War.

Winston Churchill was another man that history views favorably because of the incredible challenges that he faced. However, Churchill was not very popular before the war. When Franklin Roosevelt first met Churchill before either was the leader of his respective country, Roosevelt wrote in his diary that Churchill was full of himself and far too talkative. Early in his term as Prime Minister, Churchill even faced a no-confidence vote in Parliament. However, the events of World War II accorded him the perception of greatness in the eyes of history.

Many might argue that these men and other men and women were already great before history gave them great challenges. While it is impossible to definitely disprove this assertion and it may be true that they had great skill and ability, otherwise they would not have been political leaders, most examples point to the fact that the times make the man or woman. If the presidencies of Buchanan and Lincoln were switched, we would very likely have the Buchanan memorial instead. In summary, it is true that the perceived greatness of a political leader is more due to great challenges than great inherent ability. The historical examples of Lincoln, Wilson, and Churchill bear this out. All were talented, but so too are all political leaders. Only the leaders that live in eventful times are remembered as great.

Assessment of Essay 1

This essay is particularly well constructed; the author begins by acknowledging the arguments for how famous historical leaders should be judged. He asserts his position, "men are perceived as great leaders largely because of the times in which they lived" clearly and effectively. He proceeds to support his position with compelling evidence, drawing on his knowledge of three historical figures who are, by consensus, regarded as great. He contrasts the example of Lincoln with that of Buchanan, who had a similar background but lived under less trying circumstances. The writing is largely clear and direct, with skillful use of diction. For all these reasons, this essay receives a score of 6.

Issue Essay 2: "Outstanding," Score of 6

Keeping up with global progress is, doubtless, a desirable attribute of any society. However, to purport that the reasons certain societies may not progress at the same rate as "great" societies are their reluctance to break from their comfort zones and a fear of the unknown is to present an overly simplistic view. Such a view does not take into consideration the set of economic, political, and cultural constraints that affect every society's ability to progress on a global scale.

Before exploring these constraints, it would be useful to examine the use of the word "great" in the above context. The concept of what makes a society great is highly subjective; some may equate greatness with military might or economic dominance, while others would emphasize cultural achievement or progress in care for less privileged citizens. Whatever one's definition of greatness, however, it is ludicrous to suggest that any society actively rejects the desire to be great. Many societies face the seemingly insurmountable struggle to maintain societal structure in the face of economic need and/or political upheaval; the desire for greatness can only come when a society's basic structure is intact.

Societies facing severe economic challenges are virtually unable to progress in areas like medicine, militia, and agriculture even if they want to do so. Countries like Bolivia use a majority of their limited resources to maintain an agricultural status quo. Bolivian farmers are not afraid of the unknown or passively content with their current situation, but are using all of their resources to maintain a functional economic climate and structure. Given this situation, the luxury of advancements in medicine, economics and military power is simply not possible.

Also, societies embroiled in political upheaval, such as Bangladesh, are unable to send its young and talented members to university where they can spearhead progress; the most viable sectors of the population are required to serve in the military and/or to care for their families through difficult economic and political times. Maintaining a societal structure amid chaotic conditions engenders a lack of globally accepted progress, but as we have seen throughout time, episodes of great drama in any given society can yield important works of art, one such example being Albert Camus' *The Stranger*, written during the French Resistance.

Another point to consider is that, in some cases, an entire society's cultural history, including its artistic contributions, is preserved only through its living members' rich oral tradition and their active rejecting of progress in the worlds of technology, medicine, and science. This is evident when considering such so-called "primitive" societies as the African Masai or certain Native American tribes. The introduction of technology into the world of the Masai would inarguably lead to the demise of the entire society.

In conclusion, to devalue a society that isn't among the most progressive in the world is to discount the contributions a so-called "unprogressive" society can provide, such as artistic and cultural phenomena unique to a given society. Progress is a valuable tool for the advancement of a society, but blindly reaching for greatness can lead to a society's downfall just as much as ignoring it altogether can. The balance between accepting a society's constraints and highlighting its strengths is what will ultimately lead to a society's greatness.

Assessment of Essay 2

This is a particularly insightful essay. The author goes deeper with her argument than you might expect based on the prompt. The argument developed in this essay asks the reader to question his presuppositions and preconceived notions about what constitutes "greatness" as the term is applied to a society. Instead of merely answering the question of whether or not the progress of society is hindered by clinging to traditional views and obsolete ways of thinking, the reader is forced to reconsider what progress actually entails. This elicits the cultural bias of the reader and forces him to confront it. The author challenges the received notions of "great" and "progress" as "an overly simplistic view." From there, she proceeds to defend her position. She examines different cultural contexts and how we might understand "greatness" within those contexts. The essay is well constructed; the author begins by providing examples of how greatness must be understood contextually. She then adds several examples, such as the publication of Camus' *The Stranger*, to illustrate greatness produced under conditions we might think of as making progress impossible. The writing is clear and direct, contains few errors, and reveals skillful use of diction. For all these reasons, this essay receives a score of 6.

CHAPTER 18

The Argument Essay

INTRODUCTION TO THE ARGUMENT ESSAY

The second Analytical Writing task is the Argument essay. In the Argument essay passage, the author will try to persuade you of something—her conclusion—by citing some evidence. On the GRE, always read the argument with a critical eye. Look carefully for *assumptions* in the way the writer moves from evidence to conclusion. You aren't being asked to agree or disagree with the author's *position* or *conclusion*; instead, you must analyze the *chain of reasoning* used in the argument.

The screen directions ask you to decide how convincing you find the argument. Know that every argument presented for this essay on the GRE will be flawed. To make your case, first analyze the argument itself and evaluate its use of evidence; second, explain how a different approach or more information would make the argument better (or possibly worse).

The directions for an Argument essay will look like this:

> You have 30 minutes to plan and compose a response in which you evaluate the argument passage that appears below. A response to any other argument will receive a score of zero. Make sure that you respond according to the specific instructions and support your evaluation with relevant reasons and/or examples.

An Argument task will always begin with a passage containing an author's argument. It will look like this:

> The following is a memorandum from the business manager of a television station:
>
> "Over the past year, our late-night news program has devoted increased time to national news and less time to weather and local news. During this time period, most of the complaints received from viewers were concerned with our station's coverage of weather and local news. In addition, local businesses that used to advertise during our late-night news program have just canceled their advertising contracts with us. Therefore, in order to attract more viewers to the program and to avoid losing any further advertising revenues, we should restore the time devoted to weather and local news to its former level."

The second part of the directions, the prompt, will give specific directions for how to approach the essay. An Argument essay prompt will look like this:

Write a response in which you describe what specific examples or evidence are needed to evaluate the argument and how those examples or evidence would weaken or strengthen the argument.

The Argument essay prompt may vary. Other Argument essay prompts will look like this:

- Write a response in which you explore the assumptions, both implicit and explicit, in the author's argument. Explain how the argument hinges on these assumptions and what the implications are if the assumptions prove unfounded.
- Write a response in which you explain what information would be necessary in order to decide whether the recommendation and the argument on which it is based are reasonable. Be sure to explain how the answers to these questions or pieces of information would help to evaluate the recommendation.
- Write a response in which you discuss what questions would need to be answered to decide how likely the stated recommendation is to yield the predicted result. Be sure to explain how the answers to these questions would help to evaluate the recommendation.
- Write a response in which you discuss what questions would need to be answered in order to assess the reasonableness of both the prediction and the argument upon which it is based. Be sure to explain how the answers to these questions would help to evaluate the prediction.
- Write a response in which you discuss one or more viable alternatives to the proposed explanation. Justify, with support, why your explanation could rival the proposed explanation and explain how your explanation(s) can plausibly account for the facts presented in the argument.

THE KAPLAN METHOD FOR ANALYTICAL WRITING

STEP 1   Take the issue/argument apart.

STEP 2   Select the points you will make.

STEP 3   Organize, using Kaplan's essay templates.

STEP 4   Type your essay.

STEP 5   Proofread your work.

HOW THE KAPLAN METHOD FOR ANALYTICAL WRITING WORKS

Now let's discuss how the Kaplan Method for Analytical Writing works for the Argument essay:

STEP 1

Take the argument apart.

The first step to deconstructing an argument is to identify the conclusion, that is, the author's main point. After you've nailed down the conclusion, your next step is to locate the evidence used to support it. Lastly, identify the unstated assumptions (pieces of evidence that are not explicitly stated but that must be true in order for the argument to be convincing). Note any terms that are ambiguous and need defining.

STEP 2

Select the points you will make.

Identify all the important assumptions between the evidence and the conclusion. Think of additional evidence that might be found that could strengthen or weaken those assumptions.

STEP 3

Organize, using Kaplan's essay template.

Organize your thoughts by outlining what you want to say. Think about how the essay as a whole will flow. In the introduction, show that you understand the argument by putting it into your own words. Point out the author's conclusion and the evidence used to support that conclusion. In each of the middle paragraphs, what you'll do will vary from essay to essay. You might need to reveal the argument's assumptions or flaws, discuss possible ways to strengthen or weaken the argument, identify important questions that would need to be addressed to evaluate the argument, or perform other tasks in accordance with that Argument essay's specific instructions. Regardless of the variation, however, the argument will always be weak, and you should conclude by saying that without additional evidence, you are not persuaded.

❱ STEP 4

Type your essay.

You shouldn't proceed with this step until you've completed the three preceding ones. Graders have a limited amount of time to work with, so start out and conclude with strong statements. Be emphatic and concise with your prose, and use transitions to link related ideas. This will help your writing flow and make things easier on the grader.

❱ STEP 5

Proofread your work.

Save enough time to read through your response in its entirety. As you do so, have a sense of the errors you are likely to make.

Now let's see how these steps work with an Argument assignment by applying the Kaplan Method to the example prompt question provided.

How to Apply the Kaplan Method for Analytical Writing to the Argument Essay

Now let's apply the Kaplan Method for Analytical Writing to a sample Argument prompt:

> "The problem of poor teacher performance that has plagued the state public school system is bound to become a good deal less serious in the future. The state has initiated comprehensive guidelines that oblige state teachers to complete a number of required credits in education and educational psychology at the graduate level before being certified."

Write a response that examines this argument's unstated assumptions. Make sure you explain how this argument depends on those assumptions and what the implications are if the assumptions are wrong.

❱ STEP 1

Take the argument apart.

Conclusion (the point the argument is trying to make): The problem of poorly trained teachers that has plagued the state public school system is bound to become a good deal less serious in the future.

Evidence (facts offered to support the conclusion): The state has initiated comprehensive guidelines that oblige state teachers to complete a number of required credits in education and educational psychology at the graduate level before being certified.

Assumptions (unspoken conditions or beliefs necessary for the conclusion to make sense in light of the evidence):

- Credits in education will improve teachers' classroom performance.
- Current bad teachers haven't already met this standard of training.
- Current bad teachers will not still be teaching in the future or will have to be trained, too.

●❯ STEP 2

Select the points you will make.

Analyze the use of evidence in the argument. Determine whether there's anything relevant that's not discussed, such as the following:

- whether the training will actually address the cause of the problems
- what "poorly performing" means
- how to either improve or remove the bad teachers now teaching

Also determine what types of evidence would make the argument stronger or more logically sound. In this case, we need some new evidence to support the assumptions, such as the following:

- evidence verifying that this training will make better teachers
- evidence making it clear that current bad teachers haven't already had this training
- evidence suggesting why all or many bad teachers won't still be teaching in the future (or why they'll be better trained)

●❯ STEP 3

Organize, using Kaplan's essay template.

For an essay on this topic, your opening sentence might look like this:

> The argument that improved academic training, ensured by requiring credits in education and psychology, will substantially alleviate the current problem of poorly performing teachers may seem logical at first glance.

Paragraph 1: The argument is that improved academic training, ensured by requiring credits in education and psychology, will substantially alleviate the current problem of poorly performing teachers.

Paragraph 2: Will training address the cause of the problem?

Paragraph 3: "Poorly performing" is not precisely defined.

Paragraph 4: Has a similar state instituted similar guidelines and seen results?

Paragraph 5: The author has not presented well-defined terms and relies upon unproven assumptions; for these reasons the argument is not convincing.

Then use your notes as a working outline. In Argument essays, you'll primarily address the ways in which the assumptions seem unsupported. You might also recommend new evidence you'd like to see and explain why. Remember to lead with your best arguments.

❯ STEP 4

Type your essay.

Begin writing your essay now. Your essay for this assignment might look like one of the following sample essays. Note: As bases for comparison, we've included one outstanding essay that deserves a score of 6 and—later in this chapter—one adequate essay that deserves a score of 4.

Sample Argument Essay 1

The argument that improved academic training, ensured by requiring credits in education and psychology, will substantially alleviate the current problem of poorly performing teachers may seem logical at first glance. However, her conclusion relies on assumptions for which there is no clear evidence, and it uses terms that lack definition.

First, the writer assumes that the required courses will produce better teachers. In fact, the courses might be entirely irrelevant to the teachers' failings. Suppose, for example, that the main problem lies in cultural and linguistic gaps between teachers and students; graduate level courses that do not address these issues would be of little use in bridging these gaps and improving educational outcomes. Furthermore, the writer assumes that poorly performing teachers lack this standard of training. In fact, the writer makes no useful correlation between classroom performance and level of training.

Additionally, the writer provides no evidence that poorly performing teachers who are already certified will either stop teaching in the near future or will undergo additional training. In its current form, the argument implies that only teachers seeking certification will receive the specified training. If this is the case, the bright future the writer envisions may be decades away. The argument's conclusion requires the support of evidence demonstrating that all teachers in the system who are identified as having "poor performance" will receive the remedial training and will then change their teaching methods accordingly.

The notion that the coursework will provide better teachers would be strengthened by a clear definition of "poor performance" in the classroom and by additional evidence that the training will address the relevant issues. The author's argument would be strengthened considerably if she provided evidence of a direct relationship between teachers' effectiveness in the classroom and their educational backgrounds.

In conclusion, the writer would not necessarily be wrong to assert that the state's comprehensive guidelines will potentially lead to some improvement in the educational environment in public schools. After all, the additional training will certainly not adversely affect classroom performance. But to support the current conclusion that the guidelines will effectively solve the state's problem, the writer must first define the scope of the problem more clearly and submit more conclusive evidence that the new requirements will, in fact, improve overall teaching performance.

❯ STEP 5
Proofread your work.

Be sure to allot some time after you have finished writing to review your essay. While a few grammatical errors here and there won't harm your score, having enough of them will affect the overall clarity of your essay, and that certainly won't look good. You want to make sure the graders are as favorably disposed to you as possible, and a well-written essay makes their job less tedious.

ASSESSMENT OF SAMPLE ARGUMENT ESSAY 1: "OUTSTANDING," SCORE OF 6

Now we'll look at how this essay would have been scored on the actual GRE Analytical Writing Section:

This outstanding response demonstrates the writer's insightful analytical skills. The introduction notes the prompt's specious reasoning occasioned by unsupported assumptions and a lack of definition and evidence. The writer follows this up with a one-paragraph examination of each of the root flaws in the argument. Specifically, the author exposes these points undermining the argument:

- the assumption that the required courses will produce better teachers
- the assumption that poorly performing teachers currently in the schools have not already had the proposed training
- the complete lack of evidence that ineffective teachers currently working will either stop teaching in the future or will successfully adapt the required training to their classroom work

Each point receives thorough and cogent development (given the time constraints) in a smooth and logically organized discourse. This essay is succinct, economical, and error-free, with sentences that vary in length and complexity, while the diction and vocabulary stand out as both precise and expressive.

How to Apply the Kaplan Method for Analytical Writing to Another Argument Essay

Now let's apply the Kaplan Method for Analytical Writing to a second Argument prompt:

"The commercial airline industry in the country of Freedonia has experienced impressive growth in the past three years. This trend will surely continue in the years to come, since the airline industry will benefit from recent changes in Freedonian society: incomes are rising; most employees now receive more vacation time; and interest in travel is rising, as shown by an increase in media attention devoted to foreign cultures and tourist attractions."

Write a response that examines this argument's unstated assumptions. Make sure you explain how this argument depends on those assumptions and what the implications are if the assumptions are wrong.

❖ STEP 1

Take the argument apart.

Conclusion (the point the argument's trying to make): The upward trend of growth in Freedonia's airline industry will continue.

Evidence (basis offered to support the conclusion): Incomes are rising. Employees have more vacation time. Interest in travel is rising, as shown by increased media attention devoted to foreign cultures and tourist attractions.

Assumptions (unspoken conditions or beliefs necessary for the conclusion to make sense in light of the evidence):

- Incomes will continue to rise in the future.
- Employees will want to spend their vacation time abroad and not at home.
- Those who do wish to travel will want to go somewhere requiring air travel.
- The increased media attention on foreign cultures and tourist attractions is due to public interest in travel.
- The airline industry will directly benefit from these changes.

❖ STEP 2

Select the points you will make.

Analyze the use of evidence in the argument. Determine whether there's anything relevant that's not discussed, such as the following:

- What actually caused the growth in the airline industry?

- The fact that employees may want to spend their increased disposable income and vacation time doing other things
- Whether the increased media attention on foreign cultures is due to other factors besides increased public interest in travel

Also determine what types of evidence would make the argument stronger or more logically sound. In this case, we need some new evidence to support the assumptions, such as the following:

- Evidence verifying that the positive economic changes in Freedonian society will continue
- Evidence suggesting the cause of the increased media coverage of foreign cultures is in fact due to an interest in travel

❯❯ STEP 3

Organize, using Kaplan's essay template.

For an essay on this topic, your opening sentence might look like this:

> The author believes that the recent growth in Freedonia's commercial airline industry will continue for years to come.

Paragraph 1: The conclusion is that the positive growth in Freedonia's commercial airline industry will continue. The evidence is that income, vacation time, and interest in travel are all on the rise.

Paragraph 2: The author assumes that the favorable economic conditions will continue. However, the cause of these conditions is not explained, and neither is the economy's relation to the airline industry.

Paragraph 3: The argument would be strengthened if we knew what caused the media attention and growth in the commercial airline industry.

Paragraph 4: What is the source of the economic conditions, and how do they relate to the airline industry?

Paragraph 5: If the author's assumptions are wrong, Freedonia's airline industry might experience trouble in the future.

Then use your notes as a working outline. In Argument essays, you'll primarily address the ways in which the assumptions seem unsupported. You might also recommend new evidence you'd like to see and explain why. Remember to lead with your best arguments.

⟩⟩ STEP 4

Type your essay.

Sample Argument Essay 2

The author concludes that the positive growth in Freedonia's commercial airline industry will continue for years to come. The evidence is that incomes, vacation time, and interest in travel are all on the rise. While this argument may seem tenable at first glance, the conclusion relies on assumptions for which there is no clear evidence and on undefined terms.

First, the writer assumes that the favorable economic conditions in Freedonia will continue. It is entirely possible that they will not, and that employees will have neither the money nor the vacation time necessary to pay for expensive foreign vacations. Suppose, for example, that incomes do not continue to rise. People would not have the money to spend on expensive vacations. Secondly, do we really know that the citizens of Freedonia will want to spend their money on vacations? Also, how do we know they will want to visit places that necessitate air travel?

The argument would be strengthened considerably if the author provided evidence of a direct relationship between the increased media attention on foreign cultures and tourist attractions and the genuine desire to spend disposable income and vacation time traveling. The author does not explain where this interest comes from. Also, even if people are interested, it does not necessarily follow that they will be either willing or able to indulge that interest with extravagant holidays.

Furthermore, the writer does not explain the source of these economic conditions, nor what relation, if any, they have to the airline industry. What if the changes in Freedonian society that have led to higher incomes and more vacation time do not help the airline industry? Perhaps the economic changes are the result of protective tariffs and trade policies that make it harder for Freedonians to conduct business internationally. Perhaps the government is limiting imports and exports. These possibilities could shrink the growth of the airline industry.

If the writer is wrong about the assumptions he has made regarding Freedonian society, the implications for the commercial airline industry in Freedonia are less rosy. It would mean that there will be less income and no less interest in foreign travel.

⟩⟩ STEP 5

Proofread your work.

Take the last couple of minutes to catch any glaring errors.

ASSESSMENT OF SAMPLE ARGUMENT ESSAY 2: "ADEQUATE," SCORE OF 4

Now we'll look at how this essay would have been scored on the actual GRE Analytical Writing section:

This essay is reasonably well constructed throughout, enabling the reader to move from point to point as the writer examines the multifaceted implications of the issue. The writer correctly identifies and articulates several assumptions that the argument makes but does not justify. The author does an adequate job of pointing out how the argument depends upon those assumptions for its cogency. The essay suffers because the writer jumps around a little bit. The paragraph explaining how the argument could be strengthened should be the second-to-last paragraph, not mixed into the body of the essay. Also, the explication of the economic climate of Freedonia, and its implications for foreign travel, is slight. Finally, the author's conclusion does not do a particularly good job of restating the author's position effectively. The writing itself is direct and includes relatively few errors. Sentence structure is not particularly varied, and the word choice and vocabulary are adequate. For these reasons, the essay earns an "Adequate" score of 4.

KAPLAN'S ADDITIONAL TIPS FOR THE ARGUMENT ESSAY

Try to Keep Things Simple

These essays aren't supposed to be so opaque in their logic that they can't be unpacked on Test Day. Similarly, your responses don't have to be abstruse or convoluted (and shouldn't be!). Try to be as clear and linear in your writing as possible when dissecting an argument.

Don't Worry about Agreeing or Disagreeing with the Argument

This is important. You don't have to agree or disagree with the argument itself. What you (and the graders) are interested in is your ability to *reason*. That means you have to understand the argument and grasp it well enough to be able to point out its assumptions (i.e., where the author takes a leap in logic by assuming, rather than proving, a point). You should not dispute the conclusion or the evidence, only the assumptions. Do not spend any time at all on your personal opinion about the conclusion.

Paraphrase Long or Complex Sentences

You may encounter a sentence that, because of its length or structure, is hard to get a handle on. When faced with a complex sentence, put it into your own words; this will make the argument itself much easier to decipher and wrestle with.

ARGUMENT ESSAY PRACTICE SET

ARGUMENT ESSAY 1

30 Minutes
Length: 1 essay

Directions

You will be given a brief passage that presents an argument, or an argument you need to complete, along with detailed instructions on how to respond to the passage. You have 30 minutes to plan and compose a response in which you analyze the passage according to the instructions. A response to any other argument results in a score of zero.

Note

You are not being asked to present your opinions on the subject. Make sure you respond to the instructions and support your analysis with pertinent reasons and/or examples.

Feel free to take a few minutes to consider the argument and instructions, and to plan your response, before you begin to write. Be certain your analysis is fully developed and logically organized, and make sure you leave enough time to review and revise what you've written.

The following appeared in the City Council Proceedings section of the local newspaper in Smithville:

> "The city council of Smithville has instituted changes to police procedures to improve the visibility of the police force. These changes require that the town hire more police officers, budget more funds for police overtime, and direct officers to patrol significantly more often on foot rather than from their patrol cars. These improvements in visibility will significantly lower the crime rate in Smithville and make its citizens feel safer."

Write a response in which you discuss what questions would need to be answered to decide how likely the stated recommendation is to yield the predicted result. Be sure to explain how the answers to these questions would help to evaluate the recommendation.

ARGUMENT ESSAY 2

30 Minutes
Length: 1 essay

Directions

You will be given a brief passage that presents an argument, or an argument you need to complete, along with detailed instructions on how to respond to the passage. You have 30 minutes to plan and compose a response in which you analyze the passage according to the instructions. A response to any other argument results in a score of zero.

Note

You are not being asked to present your opinions on the subject. Make sure you respond to the instructions and support your analysis with pertinent reasons and/ or examples.

Feel free to take a few minutes to consider the argument and instructions, and to plan your response, before you begin to write. Be certain your analysis is fully developed and logically organized, and make sure you leave enough time to review and revise what you've written.

> "Tusk University should build a new recreational facility, both to attract new students and to better serve the needs of our current student body. Tusk projects that enrollment will double over the next 10 years, based on current trends. The new student body is expected to reflect a much higher percentage of commuter students than we currently enroll. This will make the existing facilities inadequate. Moreover, the cost of health and recreation club membership in our community has increased rapidly in recent years. Thus, students will find it much more advantageous to make use of the facilities on campus. Finally, an attractive new recreation center would make prospective students, especially athletically gifted ones, more likely to enroll at Tusk."

Write a response that examines this argument's unstated assumptions. Make sure you explain how this argument depends on those assumptions and what the implications are if the assumptions are wrong.

ARGUMENT ESSAY PRACTICE SET ANSWERS AND EXPLANATIONS

ARGUMENT ESSAY SAMPLE ESSAYS AND ASSESSMENTS

What follows are top-scoring sample essays for each of the practice prompts. Note how the authors adhere to the Kaplan Method for Analytical Writing.

Argument Essay 1 : "Outstanding," Score of 6

The city council of Smithville believes that increasing the visibility of its police force will reduce crime and increase the safety of its citizens. However, the memo provides no evidence to support this argument, and the city council may not be taking other variables, alternative solutions, or the citizens' desires into consideration.

The Smithville city council assumes that crime persists because the city's police force has too low a profile, but the memo never cites evidence to support this position. The council could do something as simple yet effective as asking the town librarian to review published studies to see if a parallel exists between a high police presence and reduced crime rates. It could also hire an independent research firm to see if a correlation exists between Smithville crime scenes and a lack of police activity.

The council should consider other factors that might account for the current crime rate. The police force may be under-trained or poorly managed. If so, adding more officers or encouraging officers to work longer hours could actually compound the problem. Here again, research could be a vital ally in the council's case: What have other towns with similar problems identified as causal factors? What training do their police forces receive? How are they deployed, on foot or in patrol cars? Answering questions like these might help clarify a solution to the town's problem. The council should also research historic solutions to the problem: How have towns like theirs reduced a growing crime rate? This research could bolster the council's position or provide alternative, less costly solutions that have successfully fought crime.

The council also assumes that a higher police presence automatically reduces citizen concerns over crime, but it doesn't take into consideration the relationship between the residents and the police. Some communities regard police officers with a great deal of distrust, and that attitude may be pronounced in a community where the police force is perceived as unable to cope with crime. Has the community itself, through its elected leaders, the police chief, op-ed pieces in the newspaper, or community groups, expressed a need for a stronger police force? The memo never says.

As it currently stands, the Smithville city council's memo announces a decision that appears to have been made in a vacuum. To convince citizens that bolstering the police force and changing patrol procedures is the way to fight crime, the memo needs to state how the council arrived at this decision. Only then can citizens feel that the council is taking the right course of action.

Assessment of Essay 1

The author successfully identifies and analyzes this argument's recommendation: that the way for Smithville to lower its crime rate and improve citizen safety is to increase police visibility.

In the opening paragraph, the essay restates the argument and then cites its unsupported assumptions. In the following four paragraphs, the author insightfully identifies flaws in the assumptions and perceptively suggests what would need to be known to make such a recommendation and how knowing this information would help in evaluating this recommendation.

Specifically, the author cites these points undermining the argument:

- The assumption that a higher police profile will lower the crime rate
- The assumption that no other cause exists for the high crime rate but low police visibility
- The lack of research into historically successful alternative solutions
- The assumption that the town's citizens will agree that the council's solution is the right one

Throughout the essay, the author uses well-organized paragraphs—each starts with a broad statement followed by supporting statements—and her ideas logically flow from one sentence to the next. She uses succinct, economical diction and rotates complex and simple sentences.

The essay concludes strongly by summarizing the evidence necessary for the council to recommend that higher police visibility will reduce crime and increase citizen safety. The essay remains focused and clear throughout, earning a score of 6.

Argument Essay 2 : "Strong," Score of 5

The author contends that Tusk University should build a new recreational facility to attract new students, and to better serve the needs of its current students. The argument also asserts that this will lead to greater enrollment over the next ten years. While it may prove to be a worthy project, the argument appears to rely on assumptions that lack conclusive supporting evidence. The writer would be well advised to address these issues to make the point of the argument more cogent and convincing.

First and foremost, the writer assumes, without providing any evidence, that recreational facilities will be a significant factor in attracting and serving students interested in Tusk.

This begs the question of the role of recreation and/or athletic facilities in the matriculation and retention of students in institutions of higher learning. In the absence of any reference to the academic mission of the University, or even of the role that the facility might have in attracting, retaining, or helping to fund areas more central to that mission, the writer's conclusion appears unsupported.

Secondly, the writer assumes, again without citing specific evidence, that the projected doubling of enrollment will by itself lead to an increase in demand for the new recreational facilities proposed. Even if the facilities would indeed be attractive relative to those available off campus, the author has provided no proof that a substantial part of the increased or even current enrollment would be inclined to consider the new facilities an asset to their education. Suppose for a moment that this enlarged commuter-based enrollment turns out to be largely made up of part-time students with jobs and family demands away from the campus. Would such a student body see the new facility as a priority? Would the schedules of such students allow them to take advantage of the improvement?

Finally, the author fails to describe what specific services, programs, and amenities the proposed new facility will provide, how and at what cost relative to facilities available elsewhere these will be made available to the university community, and how the financial burden of both building and operating the new center will be offset. Beyond these issues endemic to the campus setting, the writer presents no overview of the environmental, social, and public relations aspects of the project in a larger context, either intra- or extra-collegiate.

The issues raised here could easily be addressed by providing evidence that backs up the author's claim. By assembling sufficient and specific demographic and economic evidence to support the argument's questionable assumptions, the writer may not only be able to overcome the limitations of the current argument, but provide a rationale for the proposal beyond the terms offered here.

Assessment of Essay 2

This essay adequately targets the argument's unstated assumptions and inadequate evidence. The essay identifies and critiques the gaps in the author's chain of logic and reasoning that results from assuming the following:

- that recreational facilities will be a significant factor in attracting and serving students interested in Tusk
- that doubling of enrollment will by itself lead to an increase in demand and presumably in use for the new recreational facilities

The writer clearly grasps the argument's central weaknesses. But although the ideas are clear, the essay lacks transitional phrases and is not well organized. The writing feels rushed and lacks proofreading. While the writer demonstrates a better-than-adequate control of language and ably conforms to the conventions of written English, this 5 essay suffers from turgid prose and a lack of the more thorough development of a typical 6 response.

CHAPTER 19

Analytical Writing Practice Set

In this section, you will take a practice test made up of four analytical writing questions, two Analyze an Issue tasks and two Analyze an Argument tasks. When you complete the set, read the sample essays and analysis to gauge whether your essays are similarly strong and whether they would earn a high score.

REVIEW OF THE KAPLAN METHOD FOR ANALYTICAL WRITING

Before starting your Practice Sets, review the steps and strategies you have studied for answering each type of Analytical Writing task quickly, thoughtfully, and cohesively.

STEP 1   Take the issue/argument apart.

STEP 2   Select the points you will make.

STEP 3   Organize, using Kaplan's essay templates.

STEP 4   Type your essay.

STEP 5   Proofread your work.

ANALYTICAL WRITING PRACTICE PROMPTS

ANALYZE AN ISSUE PRACTICE

You will be given a brief quotation that states or implies an issue of general interest, along with explicit instructions on how to respond to that topic. You have 30 minutes to plan and write an essay that communicates your perspective on the issue according to the instructions.

Respond to the instructions and support your position with relevant reasoning drawn from your academic studies, reading, observation, and/or experience.

Feel free to consider the issue for a few minutes before you begin to write. Be certain your ideas are fully developed and logically organized, and make sure you leave enough time to review and revise what you've written.

Issue Essay 1 Prompt

"Because people increasingly eat at restaurants, all restaurants should be required to display nutritional information about the meals they serve. This knowledge makes it easier for diners to make healthy choices and reduces the risk of diet-related health problems."

Write an essay in which you take a position on the statement above. In developing and supporting your viewpoint, consider ways in which the statement might or might not hold true. (Use a separate sheet of paper or a computer to write your essay.)

Issue Essay 2 Prompt

"All results of publicly funded scientific studies should be made available to the general public free of charge. Scientific journals that charge a subscription or newsstand price are profiting unfairly."

Write an essay in which you take a position on the statement above. In developing and supporting your viewpoint, consider ways in which the statement might or might not hold true. (Use a separate sheet of paper or a computer to write your essay.)

ANALYZE AN ARGUMENT PRACTICE

You will be given a brief passage that presents an argument or an argument you need to complete, along with detailed instructions on how to respond to the passage. You have 30 minutes to plan and compose a response in which you analyze the passage according to the instructions. A response to any other argument results in a score of zero.

Note: You are not being asked to present your opinions on the subject. Make sure you respond to the instructions and support your analysis with pertinent reasons and/or examples.

Feel free to take a few minutes to consider the argument and instructions and to plan your response, before you begin to write. Be certain your analysis is fully developed and logically organized, and make sure you leave enough time to review and revise what you've written.

Argument Essay 1 Prompt

The following appeared as part of a promotional campaign to sell advertising on channels provided by the local cable television company:

> "Advertising with Cable Communications Corp. is a great way to increase your profits. Recently, the Adams Car Dealership began advertising with Cable Communications, and over the last 30 days, sales are up 15% over the previous month. Let us increase your profits, just as we did for Adams Cars!"

Write a response that examines this argument's unstated assumptions. Make sure you explain how this argument depends on those assumptions and what the implications are if the assumptions are wrong. (Use a separate sheet of paper or a computer to write your essay.)

Argument Essay 2 Prompt

The following appeared in the *Ram*, the Altamonte High School student newspaper:

> "Of Altamonte students polled, 65 percent say they participate in either an intramural, varsity, or community sports team. Being a member of a sports team keeps one fit and healthy and promotes an active lifestyle. Since the majority of students are taking care of their physical fitness after or outside of school, Altamonte High should eliminate all physical education classes and put more resources into the development of the intramural and varsity sports teams."

Write a response in which you explain specific evidence needed to evaluate the argument and discuss how the evidence might weaken or strengthen the argument. (Use a separate sheet of paper or computer to write your essay.)

ANALYTICAL WRITING PRACTICE PROMPTS ANSWERS AND EXPLANATIONS

ANALYTICAL WRITING SAMPLE ESSAYS AND ASSESSMENTS

ISSUE ESSAY 1

"Outstanding" Essay (score of 6)

Requiring restaurants to publish the fat and calorie content of their meals has its detractors; they say that disclosing the makeup of meals will alarm diners, driving them away and reducing the restaurants' income. They also balk at the cost of determining these figures in the first place. But the benefits of such a program far outweigh its drawbacks. Disclosure lets people make informed eating choices, an important consideration given what we know about unhealthy diets. In addition, disclosure may end up benefiting the restaurants, both in terms of revenue and public relations.

People are eating in restaurants with increasing frequency, and we know that a healthy diet contributes to better overall health; studies show, for example, that a healthy diet lowers cholesterol and reduces the risk of heart disease. By contrast, a poor diet, one rich in fat and calories, contributes to obesity and diabetes, both of which are on the rise in the United States.

For these reasons, we should require that restaurants post nutritional information on the meals they serve. That way, people can choose the meals they want to eat, whether their desire is to eat healthily or not.

Restaurant owners are understandably concerned that disclosing information perceived as negative could scare people off, but if all restaurants have to comply, no single business should suffer. In addition, disclosure may encourage restaurants to find healthier ways to prepare their meals, which would benefit everyone.

Determining the fat and calorie content of meals will cost restaurants money initially, but such disclosure can benefit them overall; people will appreciate the openness of the disclosure and feel confident that they're in charge of their fat and calorie intake, instilling in them a sense of comfort and control, and making them more likely, rather than less so, to eat at a restaurant that lists fat and calorie contents.

Requiring restaurants to post nutrition information can benefit both owners and patrons. It can have immediate and lasting positive effects on diners who choose to eat healthily, and it can instill a sense of control and confidence in diners who appreciate knowing what they're eating, making them more likely to continue the trend of dining out.

Analyze an Issue Essay 1 Assessment

This essay is well constructed; the author begins by recognizing arguments against restaurant disclosure and then states his opinion ("Disclosure lets people make informed eating choices, an important consideration given what we know about unhealthy diets"). He proceeds to support his position with compelling evidence about health studies, medical trends, business operations, and public relations. The writing is clear and direct, and it reveals skillful use of diction. For all these reasons, this essay receives a score of 6.

ISSUE ESSAY 2

"Outstanding" Essay (score of 6)

Scientific journals that charge a subscription or newsstand price should amend this practice to avail the public of results of publicly funded research. The reasoning here is twofold: first, the public's taxes have paid for all or a part of the research, and second, scientific results should always be readily accessible to all interested parties.

A publicly funded project means, in effect, that the taxpayers own the research and have a right to the results free of charge. Granted, many research projects are funded by a combination of private contributions, institutional grants, and public funding. Even when this is the case, the public should not be punished for being one part of a coalition that may include profit-making groups. Perhaps the research committee will need to include in its duties finding venues to make research results readily available at no charge. The mere fact of public financial support of research, in whole or in part, entitles taxpayers to have access to the fruits of that research.

Another reason to let the public see results at no charge (besides being totally or partially financially responsible for such research) is that from a larger philosophical standpoint, people should be allowed access to scientific information. Innovation in the private sector and the market necessitate access to the latest research and developments. The result of making such research widely available is that the process becomes self-sustaining. New discoveries feed new developments in the private or industrial sector, which in turn fuel further research. Publishers of scientific journals may respond to such an argument by saying that they need to make a profit in order to cover their expenses of reporting, printing, handling, and mailing research results. With that said, shouldn't the government and private sponsors of a project cover these expenses and include them in their overhead, in the same proportion as their support of the research? Additionally, popular science magazines, using their revenues from advertisers and subscribers, might pay journals to reprint research in their magazines. This practice could also provide funds for making the information available for free to parties not interested in an entire slick magazine with multiple subjects.

It is supposed that some scientists and government officials will refuse to allow sensitive or secret scientific information to be available to the public for free. Governments should not disseminate sensitive or secret research publicly, but the scope of research we are talking about is what is already published in scientific journals and available for public consumption. It's also probably true that more transparency will promote more international research and more freedom to experiment. Soviet scientists in the former Soviet Union were not allowed to read about scientific endeavors outside of the USSR. This led to decades of wasted money, effort, and time; errors made that shouldn't have been; and a lot of reinventing of the wheel. Furthermore, other scientists, pharmacists, and pharmaceutical companies need access to professional journals to keep up on the cutting-edge information released post-research. Ethically speaking, they are charged with nurturing scientific debate and keeping the public safe and informed.

In conclusion, scientific journals that charge a subscription or newsstand price are profiting unfairly when they publish wholly or partially publicly funded research results. These journals need to adjust this practice for the benefit of the public and other professionals. The public's taxes have paid for all or a part of the research, and for ethical reasons, research results must always be readily accessible to all interested parties.

Analyze an Issue Essay 2 Assessment

From the very beginning, the author takes a specific position on the issue and supports it, using strong examples and reasons. The author includes counterarguments, such as the potential cost of publication that the scientific journals must foot, but she provides clear rebuttals with powerful supporting evidence. Her inclusion of the Soviet example gives a vivid illustration of the consequences of not freely sharing information, and it appeals to the reader's sense of public justice and safety. The writing is solid, well developed, and error-free, and the writer demonstrates a mastery of rhetorical language. For all these reasons, this essay receives a score of 6.

ARGUMENT ESSAY 1

"Outstanding" Essay (score of 6)

The promotional campaign by Cable Communications Corporation argues that all businesses would benefit from advertising with the cable television company in the form of increased profitability. As evidence to back up this assertion, the promotional campaign notes the experience of the Adams Car Dealership, a recent advertiser with Cable Communications Corporation. Over the last 30 days, Adams Cars has seen a 15% increase in sales over the previous month. The argument as it now stands is unconvincing because it is missing evidence that would make the argument more well reasoned. It also suffers from poorly defined vocabulary, which makes the argument less easy to understand.

The argument presupposes that the example of the Adams Car Dealership is relevant for other businesses. It could be that there is a particular advantage from advertising for car dealerships because car buyers are willing to travel around to buy a car. The same may not be said, for example, of a dry cleaner. In general, people will take their dry cleaning business to the closest dry cleaner because it is a commodity service and a relatively small expenditure. Thus, advertising would be much more effective for a car dealership than a dry cleaner. The statement also presupposes that business owners do not have a better option for advertising. A company may get a higher increase in profits by advertising in print media or online. For business owners to make an informed decision regarding their advertising expenditures, they need to see a comparison between Cable Communication's offering and the offerings of other advertising outlets.

The argument suffers from poorly defined vocabulary. The first piece of such vocabulary is the word "recently." From just this word, it is impossible to tell when the advertising began. If Adams' advertising began three months ago, it would not be very impressive that sales increased 15% between month two and month three of the advertising campaign. Why would there not have been a boost before the most recent month? If the promotional campaign told business owners exactly when Adams began advertising, the owners would have a better ability to evaluate the argument's conclusion. The author should also clarify the phrase "increase your profits." The promotional campaign's argument gives no details on the fees associated with advertising with Cable Communications. If Adams Cars had to develop an ad and pay large sums to Cable Communications to run the ad, the total cost of advertising with the cable company very well may have exceeded the additional profits derived from increased sales. Without additional information in this regard, business owners cannot possibly evaluate the argument's conclusion.

To convince business owners that they should advertise with Cable Communications, the promotional campaign should show additional evidence from a wide variety of businesses that have benefited by advertising with the company. The argument presupposes that the 15% increase in sales at Adams Car Dealership is a direct result of the recent advertising campaign with Cable Communications Corporation. It could be that the dealership had announced a sale for this month or that the previous month's sales were seasonably low—for example sales in March might always be better than sales in February due to some exogenous factor. In order to better believe that Adams benefited from the advertising campaign with Cable Communications, business owners need evidence that there was not some other factor causing the 15% increase. Perhaps evidence could be shown comparing the last 30 days of sales with the same period in the previous year, or the last time the dealership was running the same promotions.

To conclude, the promotional campaign by Cable Communications suffers from poorly defined vocabulary and lack of strong evidence. It turns upon unstated presuppositions, such as assuming that business owners do not have a better alternative for advertising. To better convince business owners of the benefits of advertising with Cable Communications, the company should provide additional details regarding the relevance of cable advertising to multiple business types, the exact nature of Adams' increase in sales, the ability of cable advertising to outperform other forms of advertising, and the true costs of advertising with Cable Communications. With this additional information, the promotional campaign would be much more convincing when it concludes that advertising with Cable Communications is a great way to increase a business's profits.

Analyze an Argument Essay 1 Assessment

The author successfully identifies and analyzes this argument's main contention: that advertising with Cable Communications will increase the profits of every business.

In the opening paragraph, the essay restates the argument and then cites its unsupported assumptions. In the following four paragraphs, the author insightfully identifies flaws in the assumptions and perceptively suggests ways to clarify them.

Specifically, the author cites these points undermining the argument:

1. The one-size-fits-all fallacy of the argument that all businesses would benefit from the exposure
2. The example of 15% profit increase is misleading—not all potential profits would be similar
3. The argument that cable advertising is the best possible option for businesses
4. Vague and misleading language, and not defining key terms

Throughout the essay, the author uses well-organized paragraphs—each starts with a broad statement followed by supporting statements—and his ideas logically flow from one sentence to the next. He uses succinct, economical diction and rotates complex and simple sentences.

The essay concludes strongly by making specific suggestions that would improve the essay's arguments. The essay remains focused and clear throughout, earning it a score of 6.

ARGUMENT ESSAY 2

"Outstanding" Essay (score of 6)

The Ram article falls short of presenting a convincing and logical argument for eliminating all physical education classes at Altamonte High School and putting more resources into the development of intramural and varsity sports. First, the article's statistics are unclear and poorly labeled; they lead to a faulty conclusion. Second, among other things, the article draws conclusions that go beyond what is supported by the evidence, concluding in the drastic recommendation that "Altamonte High should eliminate all physical education classes."

The statistics in the article are not properly labeled and, therefore, have the potential to be misleading: "...65 percent of Altamonte students polled." However, maybe only 100 out of 2,400 students were polled, which is not a legitimate sampling. Maybe only athletes were polled. Maybe only seniors, who tend to have more intramural and varsity members than freshmen, were polled.

The author also overlooks the extent to which the 65 percent of polled students participate in the intramural, varsity, and community teams—some students might be on multiple teams, but others might barely be involved. In any case, this part of the argument is an appeal-to-the-majority fallacy: "A majority of people do such-and-such, so it must automatically be the best way to go." Even if 65% is a completely legitimate statistic, this may not be enough of a majority when one is making decisions about the health and future of all our youth.

In addition, the Ram article draws conclusions beyond what the data supports: "Being a member of a sports team keeps one fit and healthy and promotes an active lifestyle." Just because some members of sports teams are fit and healthy does not logically mean that all are. Or maybe not all sports participants are sufficiently active. For example, perhaps some outfielders of the community sports team rarely get to run, catch, or throw and are never selected by their competitive coach for more challenging positions such as pitcher or catcher. Additionally, the author fails to note if any of these out-of-school activities teach nutrition, how to make healthy choices, how to avoid drug abuse and eating disorders, and other physical education goals beyond competition and teamwork.

In conclusion, the Ram article would be more convincing if the statistics were properly identified and labeled. In addition to data that is properly contextualized and understood, more precise and specific details would bolster the conclusion, such as how active the members of the intramural, varsity, and community teams are ("They stretch for 15 minutes and run for 30 minutes during warm-up"). With such details, the author could support all of the generalizations the article puts forth. Finally, the author of the article needs to justify why 65 percent, if indeed a legitimate sampling, is a sufficient majority for such a major change in school curriculum.

Analyze an Argument Essay 2 Assessment

The author successfully addresses several flaws of the argument in this response, including the potentially faulty or misunderstood statistics and classical reasoning errors, such as the appeal-to-the-majority fallacy and the hasty-generalization fallacy.

The author cites this evidence as potentially flawed:

- The polled students may reflect a sample size or makeup that is skewed, and the inclusion of better labeled or explained statistics would help support the argument.
- The illogical conclusion that what is good for a majority of students would be good for all the students.
- The hasty generalization that students who participate in sports teams are healthier and fitter than those who don't.

Throughout the essay, the paragraphs are well constructed and follow the blueprint of the thesis statement. Every claim is supported by evidence.

The essay concludes by suggesting ways to improve the article, which is what the prompt asks the writer to do. The suggestions are good ones that would definitely strengthen the article writer's argument. The essay remains focused and clear throughout, earning it a score of 6.

PART FIVE

Practice Test

CHAPTER 20

Practice Test

Before taking this practice test, find a quiet place where you can work without interruption for 3 hours and 45 minutes. Make sure you have a comfortable desk, several pencils, and scratch paper. Time yourself according to the time limits shown at the beginning of each section. For the most accurate results, you should go through all five sections in one sitting. Use the online answer grid available in your Online Center to enter your answers to the multiple-choice sections of this test to see a detailed breakdown of your performance by question type and topic. You'll find the answer key and explanations in the next chapter. Good luck!

Note that the time limits and section lengths for this paper-based practice GRE are the same as those for the computer-based GRE. On the actual test, you will have the capability to mark questions within a section to return to them later if time allows. It would be a good idea to use that same approach as you take the practice test. Also, write your essay if you're going to take the paper-based GRE, and type it if you plan to take the computer-based GRE, to better simulate the Test Day experience. You should type it with spell-check and grammar-check off.

ANALYTICAL WRITING 1: ANALYZE AN ISSUE

30 Minutes — 1 Question

Directions: You will be given a brief quotation that states or implies a topic of general interest, along with explicit instructions on how to respond to that topic. Your response will be evaluated according to how well you do the following:

- Respond to the specific directions the task gives you.
- Reflect on the complexities of the issue.
- Organize and develop your thoughts.
- Support your reasoning with relevant examples.
- Express yourself in standard written English.

> "Scientific theories, which most people consider as 'fact,' almost invariably prove to be inaccurate. Thus, one should look upon any information described as 'factual' with skepticism since it may well be proven false in the future."

Write an essay in which you take a position on the statement above. In developing and supporting your viewpoint, consider ways in which the statement might or might not hold true.

ANALYTICAL WRITING 2: ANALYZE AN ARGUMENT

30 Minutes — 1 Question

Directions: You will be presented with a short passage that asserts an argument or position, along with explicit instructions on how to respond to the passage. Your response will be evaluated according to how well you do the following:

- Respond to the specific directions the task gives you.
- Analyze and interpret important elements of the passage.
- Organize and develop your analysis.
- Support your reasoning with relevant examples.
- Express yourself in standard written English.

> The following appeared in a memorandum from the owner of the Juniper Café, a small, local coffee shop in the downtown area of a small American city:
>
> > "We must reduce overhead here at the café. Instead of opening at 6 a.m. weekdays, we will now open at 8 a.m. On weekends, we will only be open from 9 a.m. until 4 p.m. The decrease in hours of operations will help save money because we won't be paying for utilities, employee wages, or other operating costs during the hours we are closed. This is the best strategy for us to save money and remain in business without having to eliminate jobs."

Write a response in which you discuss what questions would need to be answered in order to assess the reasonableness of both the prediction and the argument upon which it is based. Be sure to explain how the answers to these questions would help to evaluate the prediction.

**You have finished this section and now will begin
the next section.**

VERBAL REASONING 1

30 Minutes — 20 Questions

Directions: For each item, select the best answer choice using the directions given.

If a question has answer choices with **ovals,** then the correct answer will be a single choice. If a question's answer choices have **squares,** the correct answer may have more than one choice. Be sure to read all directions carefully.

Select one answer choice for the blank. Fill in the blank in such a way that it best completes the text.

1. Known for their devotion to their masters, dogs were often used as symbols of _____ in Medieval and Renaissance paintings.

   (A) treachery
   (B) opulence
   (C) fidelity
   (D) antiquity
   (E) valor

2. By nature _____, the poet Philip Larkin nonetheless maintained a spirited correspondence with a wide circle of friends.

   (A) voluble
   (B) reclusive
   (C) prolific
   (D) gregarious
   (E) pensive

For each blank, select an answer choice from the corresponding column of choices. Fill all blanks in such a way that they best complete the text.

3. Because the decision-making process was entirely (i) _____, there was no way to predict its outcome. The process was (ii) _____ rolling dice, where there is a finite number of possibilities but no way to accurately predict which two numbers will come up.

Blank (i)	Blank (ii)
A arbitrary	D likened to
B regimented	E belittled by
C unilateral	F dissimilar to

For the following questions, select the **two** answer choices that, when inserted into the sentence, fit the meaning of the sentence as a whole **and** yield complete sentences that are similar in meaning.

4. Although the heralded "variance in taxation bill" at first received much (i) _____, it has had a (ii) _____ impact on the majority of the middle-class population, who are burdened mainly by the relatively unvarying property tax.

Blank (i)		Blank (ii)	
A	commotion	D	negligible
B	acclaim	E	necessary
C	hullabaloo	F	detrimental

5. Critics' practice of making allusions to earlier work when reviewing a new piece is detrimental to the person reading the review prior to seeing the piece, as any (i) _____ viewpoint the reader already holds toward the referenced earlier piece will inevitably (ii) _____ the opinion of the unseen piece, potentially not allowing for (iii) _____ viewing of the new piece.

Blank (i)		Blank (ii)		Blank (iii)	
A	established	D	rebuke	G	biased
B	culpable	E	skew	H	impartial
C	thermic	F	complete	I	enjoyable

6. The shift away from fossil fuels as the world's primary energy source will not be sufficient to stabilize or reduce carbon emissions, and therefore carbon (i) _____ technologies should be implemented to (ii) _____ and store carbon waste.

Blank (i)		Blank (ii)	
A	sequestration	D	incarcerate
B	reduction	E	capture
C	diminution	F	liberate

7. W.C. Handy's self-conferred sobriquet, "The Father of the Blues," is widely _____; although he composed and published the first written blues song, other musicians had been playing the blues for several years.

   A professed
   B deconstructed
   C disputed
   D proven
   E contested
   F demonstrated

8. The expectation of instant gratification engendered by the ease and speed of modern communication can set one up for _____ in personal relationships if one's digital messages are not promptly returned.

   A chagrin
   B endearment
   C recompense
   D vexation
   E elation
   F pacifism

9. Anticipating the arrival of the baby panda, zookeepers _____ the panda exhibit to handle the influx of visitors, scientists, and veterinarians.

   A abridged
   B augmented
   C meliorated
   D maintained
   E truncated
   F neglected

10. Some scientists _____ that by sensing a change in barometric pressure or electricity, certain species of fish may be able to portend seismic events; just before a recent earthquake, several fish were observed leaping into the air from the ocean.

   A repudiate
   B authorize
   C foresee
   D hypothesize
   E question
   F contend

Questions 11 and 12 are based on the passage below.

Modern entomologists are primarily engaged in the research of insects
that provide a direct benefit, or cause direct harm, to human interests. The
benefits of researching and protecting insect life may be immediate, such as
using an insect presence to control pests or diseases, or long-term, such as
protecting native species from unnecessary human intercession in order to
maintain a balanced ecosystem. Research on harmful insect life endeavors
to produce methods of insect control that are reliable and effective, while
minimizing the effect of the control on other species. Although most insect
orders include both pests and beneficial species, a few orders, such as lice
and fleas, provide no benefits to humans and are said to be entirely parasitic.

Consider each of the following choices separately and select all that apply.

11. Which of the following statements is supported by the passage?

    A The majority of insect orders are capable of both advancing and inhibiting
      human interests.

    B An effective insect control method will never cause side effects to insect
      or animal life outside the targeted order.

    C Entomological research has facilitated the development of insect species
      that are considered parasitic.

12. In the context in which it appears, "intercession" most nearly means

    (A) obliteration

    (B) competition

    (C) entreaty

    (D) intrusion

    (E) mediation

Question 13 is based on the passage below.

Instigated primarily by the Irish Republican Brotherhood, the Easter Rising
of 1916 was a landmark event in the battle against English rule. Armed
members of the Brotherhood, in concert with the Irish Volunteers, seized
control of several government buildings in the capital city of Dublin and
issued the Easter Proclamation, a proclamation of Irish independence.
However, the rebels were outnumbered by British forces, which had greater
access to weapons and ammunition.

The siege ended with the unconditional surrender of the militant forces, and sixteen of their leaders were subsequently executed for their roles in the uprising. Those who survived, however, went on with renewed fervor to lobby for Ireland's independence, and the public nature of the uprising changed popular sentiment about British rule. While the Easter Rising was a failure by military and tactical standards, it is viewed as an important milestone in the 1919 establishment of the Republic of Ireland.

13. The two highlighted sentences play which of the following roles in the passage above?

   (A) The first provides support for the passage's conclusion; the second is that conclusion.

   (B) The first is a fact that would seem to contradict the passage's conclusion; the second is that conclusion.

   (C) The first states the main point of the passage; the second is a fact that seems at odds with that point.

   (D) The first provides support for an intermediate conclusion that supports a further conclusion stated in the passage; the second states that intermediate conclusion.

   (E) The first states an outside position that the passage as a whole supports; the second states the main point of the passage.

Questions 14–16 are based on the passage below.

Many Iranian Americans, whether they are immigrants or American born, identify themselves as being of Persian heritage. This descriptor is a frequent cause of confusion among non-Persians who know the country as Iran and understand Persia to be an antiquated name for the empire that encompassed part of Iran as well as parts of modern-day Pakistan and Afghanistan. Opponents of the term argue that because some Afghani and Pakistani groups refer to themselves as being of Persian heritage, the term loses meaning as a signifier of nationality. However, others argue that just as the English language recognizes *Spain* rather than *España*, English speakers should refer to the country as *Persia*, and not as *Iran*, which is the Persian translation of the country's name.

14. The author is primarily concerned with

   Ⓐ arguing that English usage of descriptors of nationality should reflect usage within the native languages of the countries in question

   Ⓑ clarifying how the fall of the Persian Empire has influenced the terminology that modern citizens of Iran use to define their nationality

   Ⓒ distinguishing among three groups that use the same term to describe their national identities

   Ⓓ explaining two opposing positions in an argument about the use of a descriptor of national identity

   Ⓔ persuading readers that in order for the term *Persian* to have a clear relationship to nationality, only Iranians, not Afghanis or Pakistanis, should use the term

Consider each of the following choices separately and select all that apply.

15. Based on the information in the passage, which of the following individuals might describe themselves as Persian?

   A an Afghani-born woman who is a naturalized citizen of Iran

   B an American man born in the United States to Iranian immigrant parents

   C an American woman of English descent who has worked in Pakistan for 15 years

16. The passage cites which one of the following as a source of confusion for some non-Persians?

   Ⓐ the fact that some Afghani and Pakistani groups both refer to themselves as Persian

   Ⓑ the use in English of *Spain* rather than *España*

   Ⓒ the scope of the Persian Empire

   Ⓓ the loss of meaning in a signifier of nationality

   Ⓔ Iranian Americans' decision to self-identify as Persian

Questions 17–19 are based on the passage below.

In Greco-Roman societies, women applied white lead and chalk to their faces to attract attention. Ancient Egyptians wore light foundation to gild their skin, while their kohl eyeliner was only slightly heavier than the eye makeup popular in the mid-1960s. Persians believed that henna dyes, used to stain hair and faces dark, enabled them to summon the majesty of the earth. The European Middle Ages followed the Greco-Roman trend of pale faces. Those rich enough not to work outdoors and acquire a suntan wanted to flaunt their affluence by being pale. To look feminine, fashionable sixth-century women would achieve the same ideal by bleeding themselves. While pale of skin, regal 13th-century Italian women wore bright pink lipstick to show that they could afford makeup.

17. Which of the following statements presents a situation most analogous to that described in the highlighted sentence?

   (A) Contrary to common opinion, zebras are dark animals, with white stripes where the pigmentation is inhibited.
   (B) The frog's brown and yellow coloring, as well as its rough texture, allows it to blend in with tree trunks.
   (C) The short-tailed cricket is known to eat its own wings to survive.
   (D) To look masculine, birds called budgerigars display naturally occurring yellow fluorescent plumage on their crowns.
   (E) The male blue-tailed iguana will chew down some of its spines to appear more masculine.

Consider each of the following choices separately and select all that apply.

18. Which of the following statements is supported by this passage?

   [A] The lightening of women's skin has often, but not always, been preferred.
   [B] A woman's social position could be revealed by her makeup.
   [C] The practice of lightening the skin originated in Greco-Roman societies.

19. The passage cites each of the following reasons for some cultures'
preferring artificially pale skin EXCEPT

    (A) to flaunt affluence
    (B) to look golden
    (C) to call forth the splendor of the earth
    (D) to attract attention
    (E) to look feminine

Question 20 is based on the passage below.

Solipsism is the belief that only oneself and one's own experiences are
real, while anything else—a physical object or another person—is nothing
more than an object of one's consciousness. Thus, in a sense, solipsism
is the concept that nothing "exists" outside of one's own mind. As a
philosophical position, solipsism is usually the unintended consequence of
an overemphasis on the reliability of internal mental states, which provide
no evidence for the existence of external referents.

20. In this passage, the author is primarily concerned with

    (A) discussing the importance of a phenomenon
    (B) refuting a hypothesis advanced by philosophers
    (C) contrasting two schools of thought
    (D) presenting the definition of a concept
    (E) comparing a physical object to a person

You have finished this section and now will begin the next section.

QUANTITATIVE REASONING 1

35 Minutes — 20 Questions

Directions: For each question, indicate the best answer, using the directions given.

You may use a calculator for all the questions in this section.

If a question has answer choices with **ovals**, then the correct answer is a single choice. If a question has answer choices with **squares**, then the correct answer consists of one or more answer choices. Read each question carefully.

Important Facts:

All numbers used are real numbers.

All figures lie in a plane unless otherwise noted.

Geometric figures, such as lines, circles, triangles, and quadrilaterals, **may or may not be** drawn to scale. That is, you should not assume that quantities such as lengths and angle measures are as they appear in a drawing. But you can assume that lines shown as straight are indeed straight, points on a line are in the order shown, and all geometric objects are in the relative positions shown. For questions involving drawn figures, base your answers on geometric reasoning rather than on estimation, measurement, or comparison by sight.

Coordinate systems, such as *xy*-planes and number lines, **are** drawn to scale. Therefore, you may read, estimate, and compare quantities in these figures by sight or by measurement.

Graphical data presentations, such as bar graphs, line graphs, and pie charts, **are** drawn to scale. Therefore, you may read, estimate, and compare data values by sight or by measurement.

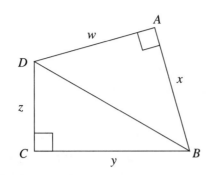

$\triangle ABD$ and $\triangle CDB$ are right triangles.

1. | Quantity A | Quantity B |
    |---|---|
    | $w^2 + x^2$ | $y^2 + z^2$ |

    Ⓐ Quantity A is greater.
    Ⓑ Quantity B is greater.
    Ⓒ The two quantities are equal.
    Ⓓ The relationship cannot be determined from the information given.

2.
$$x + 4y = 6$$
$$x = 2y$$

Quantity A	Quantity B
x	y

Ⓐ Quantity A is greater.
Ⓑ Quantity B is greater.
Ⓒ The two quantities are equal.
Ⓓ The relationship cannot be determined from the information given.

3. In a certain accounting firm, each employee is either a manager, a technician, or an assistant. Twenty-five percent of all employees are managers. Of the remaining employees, one-third are assistants.

Quantity A	Quantity B
The number of managers	Half of the number of technicians

Ⓐ Quantity A is greater.
Ⓑ Quantity B is greater.
Ⓒ The two quantities are equal.
Ⓓ The relationship cannot be determined from the information given.

4. | Quantity A | Quantity B |
    |---|---|
    | $(a + 1)(b + 1)$ | $ab + 1$ |

    Ⓐ Quantity A is greater.
    Ⓑ Quantity B is greater.
    Ⓒ The two quantities are equal.
    Ⓓ The relationship cannot be determined from the information given.

5. In the two-digit number jk, the value of the digit j is twice the value of the digit k.

Quantity A	Quantity B
k	6

Ⓐ Quantity A is greater.
Ⓑ Quantity B is greater.
Ⓒ The two quantities are equal.
Ⓓ The relationship cannot be determined from the information given.

6. Henry purchased x apples, and Jack purchased 10 apples less than one-third of the number of apples Henry purchased.

Quantity A	Quantity B
The number of apples Jack purchased	$\dfrac{x-30}{3}$

    (A) Quantity A is greater.
    (B) Quantity B is greater.
    (C) The two quantities are equal.
    (D) The relationship cannot be determined from the information given.

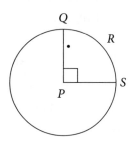

P is the center of a circle with diameter of 8.

7.

Quantity A	Quantity B
The length of arc *QRS*	2

    (A) Quantity A is greater.
    (B) Quantity B is greater.
    (C) The two quantities are equal.
    (D) The relationship cannot be determined from the information given.

8.
$$4 < x < 6$$
$$1 < y < 2$$

Quantity A	Quantity B
The volume of a rectangular solid with a length of 5 feet, a width of 4 feet, and a height of x feet	The volume of a rectangular solid with a length of 10 feet, a width of 8 feet, and a height of y feet

    (A) Quantity A is greater.
    (B) Quantity B is greater.
    (C) The two quantities are equal.
    (D) The relationship cannot be determined from the information given.

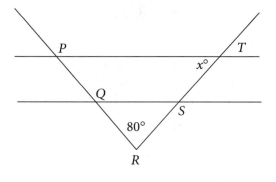

9. In the figure shown above, what is x?

    (A) 40
    (B) 50
    (C) 60
    (D) 70
    (E) 80

10. A producer must select a duo, consisting of one lead actor and one supporting actor, from six candidates. What is the number of possible duos the producer could select?

　　　　　　　　possible duos

11. Jane must select three different items for each dinner she will serve. The items are to be chosen from among five different vegetarian and four different meat selections. If at least one of the selections must be vegetarian, how many different dinners could Jane create?

Ⓐ 30
Ⓑ 40
Ⓒ 60
Ⓓ 70
Ⓔ 80

12. A computer can perform 30 identical tasks in six hours. At that rate, what is the minimum number of computers that should be assigned to complete 80 tasks within three hours?

　　　　　　　　computers

13. Given a positive integer c, how many integers are greater than c and less than $2c$?

Ⓐ $\dfrac{c}{2}$
Ⓑ c
Ⓒ $c - 1$
Ⓓ $c - 2$
Ⓔ $c + 1$

14. If the ratio of $2a$ to b is 8 times the ratio of b to a, then $\dfrac{b}{a}$ could be which of the following? Indicate <u>all</u> possible choices.

A̶ -2
B̶ $-\dfrac{1}{2}$
C̶ $\dfrac{1}{4}$
D̶ $\dfrac{1}{2}$
E̶ 2

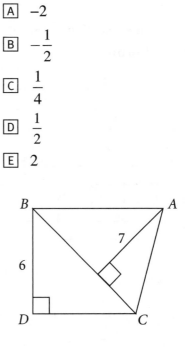

15. In the figure above, the area of $\triangle ABC$ is 35. What is the length of DC?

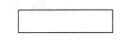

16. If $3^m = 81$, then $m^3 =$

    Ⓐ 4
    Ⓑ 9
    Ⓒ 16
    Ⓓ 64
    Ⓔ 81

17. If $0 < x < 1$, which of the following must be true?

    Indicate <u>all</u> possible choices.

    ▢A $2x < x$
    ▢B $2x < 1$
    ▢C $2x > 1$
    ▢D $x^2 < x$
    ▢E $x^2 < 1$

Questions 18–20 are based on the following graphs.

ENERGY USE BY YEAR, COUNTRY Y, 1980–2010
(IN MILLIONS OF KILOWATT-HOURS)

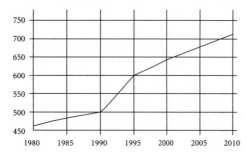

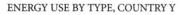

ENERGY USE BY TYPE, COUNTRY Y

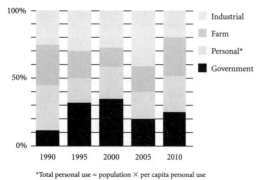

*Total personal use = population × per capita personal use

18. In 1995, how many of the categories shown had energy use greater than 150 million kilowatt-hours?

    Ⓐ None
    Ⓑ One
    Ⓒ Two
    Ⓓ Three
    Ⓔ Four

19. If the population of Country Y in 2005 was 500 million, what was the per capita personal energy use in 2005? (in millions of kilowatt-hours)

    Ⓐ 0.04
    Ⓑ 0.14
    Ⓒ 0.27
    Ⓓ 0.37
    Ⓔ 0.50

20. According to the graphs, total kilowatt-hours of energy for farm use increased between which of the following years?

    Choose <u>all</u> that apply.

    ▢A 1990 and 1995
    ▢B 1995 and 2000
    ▢C 2000 and 2005
    ▢D 2005 and 2010

**You have finished this section and now will begin
the next section.**

VERBAL REASONING 2

30 Minutes — 20 Questions

Directions: For each item, select the best answer choice using the directions given.

If a question has answer choices with **ovals,** then the correct answer will be a single choice. If a question's answer choices have **squares,** the correct answer may be more than one choice. Be sure to read all directions carefully.

Select one answer choice for the blank. Fill in the blank in such a way that it best completes the text.

1. The current need for diversification does not mean the organization should be diverted from its earlier and historical purpose; instead, this diversification should be construed as a means of _____ that purpose.

    Ⓐ undermining
    Ⓑ furthering
    Ⓒ retracting
    Ⓓ classifying
    Ⓔ deterring

For each blank, select an answer choice from the corresponding column of choices. Fill all blanks in such a way that they best complete the text.

2. Animals rely on a combination of internal traits and external behaviors to survive. Bees, for example, have a keen sense of smell that enables them to (i) _____ kin from foe. Their ability to resist (ii) _____, by contrast, is deficient, making them vulnerable to disease. Scientists speculate that the observed extensive grooming among hive mates (iii) _____ various diseases, thus protecting the colony.

Blank (i)	Blank (ii)	Blank (iii)
A promulgate	D pathogens	G minimizes incursions by
B discern	E cold	H implicates replication of
C arbitrate	F poison	I simulates action by

3. A United Nations working group issued a report describing (i) _____ need to draw up valid plans for dealing with the global water crisis. The report emphasizes the critical necessity of galvanizing political efforts to (ii) _____ resources and (iii) _____ international attention on both water and sanitation.

Blank (i)	Blank (ii)	Blank (iii)
A an exigent	D produce ineffable	G foment
B a cretaceous	E retain abundant	H focus
C a specious	F mobilize limited	I ferment

Select one answer choice for the blank. Fill in the blank in such a way that it best completes the text.

4. Although the French general Henri Philippe Pétain was greatly honored for his role as military leader of France during World War I, he incurred _____ for his collaboration during the German occupation of France during World War II.

Ⓐ status
Ⓑ reputation
Ⓒ kudos
Ⓓ recompense
Ⓔ obloquy

For each blank, select an answer choice from the corresponding column of choices. Fill all blanks in such a way that they best complete the text.

5. Cellophane—the transparent, plasticky film used everywhere to wrap food—is actually a paper product. Implausibly, this (i) _____ material is made from the same components as the opaque brown paper bag. Its inventor, Jacques E. Brandenberger, originally conceived of cellophane as a means to prevent stains, but after the wider utility of the product became (ii) _____ to him, he patented cellophane and it became (iii) _____.

Blank (i)	Blank (ii)	Blank (iii)
A diaphanous	D marketable	G amorphous
B standardized	E apparent	H ingenuous
C opaque	F fashionable	I ubiquitous

Select one answer choice for the blank. Fill in the blank in such a way that it best completes the text.

6. Unlike most other philosophers, who try to determine whether an objective reality exists, David Hume felt that the issue was _____.

   Ⓐ pragmatic
   Ⓑ challenging
   Ⓒ theoretical
   Ⓓ insoluble
   Ⓔ esoteric

For the following questions, select the two answer choices that, when inserted into the sentence, fit the meaning of the sentence as a whole and yield complete sentences that are similar in meaning.

7. A portion of the population still disregards warnings about the _____ effects of nicotine and continues to smoke, believing no harm is done to their health, even though a plethora of evidence exists to the contrary.

   Ⓐ deleterious
   Ⓑ addictive
   Ⓒ anemic
   Ⓓ antagonistic
   Ⓔ benign
   Ⓕ pernicious

8. To the public's great shock, the group recently voted into power on a platform of peaceable reform conducted _____ acts against existing branches of government as soon as the election was over.

   Ⓐ contumacious
   Ⓑ endemic
   Ⓒ erratic
   Ⓓ estimable
   Ⓔ irresolute
   Ⓕ seditious

9. Photo retouching and inflated claims are so well concealed in most advertising campaigns that consumers are unaware of the _____ being employed.

   A cabal

   B artifice

   C hegemony

   D chicanery

   E dominance

   F imprecation

10. The performers agreed that the topic of marriage was an excellent theme for their upcoming performance at a conservative organization's charity event; however, the audience was unreceptive to the _____ jokes made during the show.

    A plucky

    B ribald

    C coarse

    D traitorous

    E politic

    F treacherous

Question 11 is based on the passage below.

> Although sharks are classified as fish, they differ significantly in several respects from other freshwater and saltwater fish. Most significantly, a shark's skeleton is composed of lightweight, flexible cartilage, providing an advantage in hunting other marine life; other superclasses of fish have stable calcified skeletons. Additionally, sharks possess no swim bladder, the small organ that allows most fish to control their buoyancy; instead, a substantial liver filled with oil works to keep the sharks afloat.

11. In the argument given, the two highlighted sentences play which of the following roles?

    Ⓐ The first supports the conclusion of the argument; the second summarizes a position that is in opposition to that conclusion.

    Ⓑ The first provides support for the conclusion of the argument; the second provides that conclusion.

    Ⓒ The first states the main point of the argument; the second states an opposing point.

    Ⓓ The first serves as an intermediate conclusion; the second states the ultimate conclusion.

    Ⓔ The first states the conclusion of the argument; the second provides support for that conclusion.

Question 12 is based on the passage below.

The Dewey decimal system provided the first standardized, easily understood method of classifying the items in a library's collection. Classification, in combination with the process of cataloging, meant that patrons could easily identify and locate for themselves items that had a certain title, were written by a certain author, or related to a given subject. Because the system was adopted at most libraries, patrons who learned the system could use it at any library.

12. Based on the information in the passage, it can be inferred that, prior to the implementation of the Dewey decimal system,

Ⓐ libraries were generally small enough that no classification system was needed.

Ⓑ libraries refused to make public the systems they used to classify books.

Ⓒ patrons may have relied heavily on library staff to identify and locate the materials they sought.

Ⓓ more people worked as librarians than after its use became widespread.

Ⓔ library patrons were never able to understand the order in which books were shelved.

Questions 13 and 14 are based on the passage below.

The first smallpox prevention methods were inoculations, intentional infections with active diseased matter that typically caused a mild illness and would later result in immunity. Modern epidemiologists believe that inoculated patients were less likely to contract a fatal case of smallpox because they contracted the disease through skin contact, not inhalation. However, due to extreme disparities in the type and amount of virus used, health practitioners could offer no real prediction of how severe a case a given patient might contract after being inoculated. Inoculation differs from vaccination, which uses a standard dose of dead or weakened virus culture and therefore poses a much lower risk of fatal infection. After a smallpox vaccine was developed in the 1790s, inoculation gradually fell from favor and was eventually banned in numerous jurisdictions.

Consider each of the following choices separately and select all that apply.

13. Which of the following statements is supported by the passage?

[A] Vaccination replaced inoculation because it was a safer method of protecting against disease.

[B] Two random doses of a vaccine are likely to be more similar than two random doses of an inoculum.

[C] Prior to the 1790s, live virus cultures were often used in tuberculosis inoculations.

14. In the context in which it appears, "contracted" most nearly means which of the following?

(A) agreed
(B) shrunk
(C) acquired
(D) shortened
(E) hired

Questions 15–20 are based on the passage below.

Surveying paradigmatic works of tragic literature from antiquity to the present alongside the immense and ever-growing body of secondary literature on the subject, the literary critic Terry Eagleton arrived at the pat judgment that not only had no satisfactory definition of tragedy been offered to date, but also that none besides the admittedly vacuous "very sad" could ever be offered. Overly broad definitions, which for all intents and purposes equate the tragic with seriousness, lead invariably to Scylla; overly narrow ones, such as the Renaissance-inspired struggle theory, to Charybdis. Notwithstanding this definitional dilemma, Eagleton's conclusion, as clear a case of defeatism as any heretofore advanced, leaves much to be desired.

In *A Definition of Tragedy*, Oscar Mandel, who is decidedly more sanguine than Eagleton on this score, discerns in Aristotle's *De Poetica* the rudiments of a substantive definition of the tragic. Following the spirit, albeit not the letter, of Aristotle's text, Mandel sets forth three requirements for any work to be counted as tragic, the third weighing most heavily in his account. First, it must have a protagonist whom we highly (or at least moderately) esteem. Second, it must show how the protagonist comes to suffer greatly. And, third, it must reveal how the protagonist's downfall was inevitably but unwittingly brought about by his or her own action. It is plain to see that, of the three requirements, the third (call this the *inevitability requirement*) is beyond question the most contentious as well as the most dubious. The truth is that the inevitability requirement is entirely too stringent. While it may be a sufficient condition, it is not, Mandel's assertions notwithstanding, the *sine qua non* of tragic literature.

One need look no further than Anton Chekhov's *Three Sisters*, a quintessential work of modern tragedy, to see why this is so. In a provincial capital quite remote from cosmopolitan Moscow, the well-educated, tireless, but spiritually drained sisters are ground down by the inexorable forces of time and fortune. Their failure to leave for Moscow, the childhood home they yearn for, can be understood as their failure to extricate themselves from the tedious and insufferable life brought on by their workaday habits. This suggests a certain acknowledgment on their part of their powerlessness to defy the hands of fate. In the final analysis, the question of whether the protagonist's fate is sealed in consequence of tragic action, as in Greek and Renaissance tragic dramas, or of inaction, as with modern tragedies, has very little to do with one of the absolutely essential ingredients of tragic literature. That ingredient, of course, is the profound sense of insurmountable powerlessness that yields an unnameable, implacable feeling expressing alienation from life itself.

15. While discussing Terry Eagleton's work, the author alludes to Scylla and Charybdis in order to

   - (A) point out the principal faults with Eagleton's ideas about tragedy
   - (B) argue for the importance of understanding myths in our investigation into the nature of tragedy
   - (C) establish that a dilemma pertaining to the essence of tragedy has its origin in myth
   - (D) illustrate how a dilemma common to other intellectual inquiries also applies to our understanding of tragedy
   - (E) delineate the potential problems that lie in wait for anyone who wishes to define tragedy

16. The primary purpose of the passage is to

    (A) criticize Eagleton's view that the most adequate definition of tragedy is "very sad"

    (B) cast doubt on Eagleton's and Mandel's views of tragic literature for failing to enumerate all the necessary conditions for tragedy

    (C) conclude, after analyzing the views of two literary theorists, that tragedy cannot be defined adequately

    (D) criticize Eagleton's view that tragedy cannot be adequately defined and Mandel's view that tragedy requires tragic action and to offer up another condition indispensable for tragedy

    (E) find fault with Eagleton's view that tragedy amounts to what is "very sad" and Mandel's view that tragedy requires great suffering in order to advance a new definition of tragedy in their place

17. The author's attitude toward *Three Sisters* can best be characterized as

    (A) laudatory

    (B) conciliatory

    (C) despondent

    (D) myopic

    (E) diffident

18. It can reasonably be inferred from the author's assessments of Eagleton's and Mandel's views of tragedy that

    (A) Mandel's and Eagleton's conceptions of tragedy can ultimately be dismissed

    (B) both theorists fall short of the mark of what constitutes tragedy, but for different reasons

    (C) the tragic has as much to do with what is very sad as it has to do with the inevitability requirement

    (D) the fact that tragic heroes undergo great suffering is at the center of both accounts

    (E) tragic literature is most fully understood when it combines the insights of many different thinkers

19. The author voices dissatisfaction with Mandel's conception of tragedy by

   - (A) describing in some detail how a particular genre influences the way we think about tragic literature more generally
   - (B) analyzing a work of literature in order to help us appreciate its supreme aesthetic value
   - (C) raising a pointed objection and supporting the objection with a counterexample
   - (D) quibbling with the main criteria, none of which are applicable to a particular work of literature
   - (E) cogently defending conclusions about works of tragedy that, on pain of contradiction, Mandel cannot accept

20. Regarding the passage as a whole, the author's opinion of the first and second requirements spelled out in Mandel's definition of tragedy is most likely that

   - (A) neither the first nor the second requirement fits very easily with the condition of powerlessness that the author defends in the final paragraph
   - (B) the first, but not the second, requirement is essentially at odds with the author's claim that Chekhov's *Three Sisters* is a work that exemplifies the condition of powerlessness
   - (C) the second, but not the first, requirement would have to be rejected on the grounds that it is ostensibly the case that the sisters in *Three Sisters* do not undergo great suffering
   - (D) in light of the condition of powerlessness that the author endorses, it can be concluded that both requirements should not figure prominently in any account of tragedy
   - (E) neither the first nor the second requirement should be necessarily ruled out in our attempt to grasp the essence of tragedy, provided that neither is antithetical to the condition of powerlessness

You have finished this section and now will begin the next section.

QUANTITATIVE REASONING 2

35 Minutes — 20 Questions

Directions: For each question, indicate the best answer, using the directions given.

You may use a calculator for all the questions in this section.

If a question has answer choices with **ovals**, then the correct answer is a single choice. If a question has answer choices with **squares**, then the correct answer consists of one or more answer choices. Read each question carefully.

Important Facts:

All numbers used are real numbers.

All figures lie in a plane unless otherwise noted.

Geometric figures, such as lines, circles, triangles, and quadrilaterals, **may or may not be** drawn to scale. That is, you should not assume that quantities such as lengths and angle measures are as they appear in a drawing. But you can assume that lines shown as straight are indeed straight, points on a line are in the order shown, and all geometric objects are in the relative positions shown. For questions involving drawn figures, base your answers on geometric reasoning, rather than on estimation, measurement, or comparison by sight.

Coordinate systems, such as *xy*-planes and number lines, **are** drawn to scale. Therefore, you may read, estimate, and compare quantities in these figures by sight or by measurement.

Graphical data presentations, such as bar graphs, line graphs, and pie charts, **are** drawn to scale. Therefore, you may read, estimate, and compare data values by sight or by measurement.

1. The perimeter of isosceles $\triangle ABC$ is 40, and the length of side BC is 12.

Quantity A	Quantity B
The length of side AB	14

   Ⓐ Quantity A is greater.
   Ⓑ Quantity B is greater.
   Ⓒ The two quantities are equal.
   Ⓓ The relationship cannot be determined from the information given.

2. $$f(x) = (x + 3)^2$$

Quantity A	Quantity B
$f(0.5)$	9

   Ⓐ Quantity A is greater.
   Ⓑ Quantity B is greater.
   Ⓒ The two quantities are equal.
   Ⓓ The relationship cannot be determined from the information given.

3. | Quantity A | Quantity B |
|---|---|
| The number of miles traveled by a car that traveled for four hours at an average speed of 40 miles per hour | The number of miles traveled by a train that traveled for two and a half hours at an average speed of 70 miles per hour |

- Ⓐ Quantity A is greater.
- Ⓑ Quantity B is greater.
- Ⓒ The two quantities are equal.
- Ⓓ The relationship cannot be determined from the information given.

4. A single cookie weighs between 5 and 15 grams. A single grape weighs exactly 1 gram.

Quantity A	Quantity B
The number of cookies in a bag that weighs 300 grams and contains only cookies	The number of grapes in a bag that weighs 50 grams and contains only grapes

- Ⓐ Quantity A is greater.
- Ⓑ Quantity B is greater.
- Ⓒ The two quantities are equal.
- Ⓓ The relationship cannot be determined from the information given.

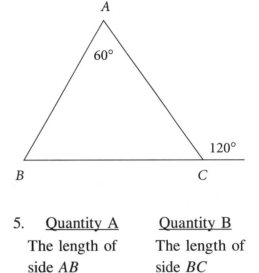

5. | Quantity A | Quantity B |
|---|---|
| The length of side AB | The length of side BC |

- Ⓐ Quantity A is greater.
- Ⓑ Quantity B is greater.
- Ⓒ The two quantities are equal.
- Ⓓ The relationship cannot be determined from the information given

$$8a + 8b = 24$$

6. | Quantity A | Quantity B |
|---|---|
| The length of segment PQ | 2 |

- Ⓐ Quantity A is greater.
- Ⓑ Quantity B is greater.
- Ⓒ The two quantities are equal.
- Ⓓ The relationship cannot be determined from the information given.

7. $$x < y$$

Quantity A	Quantity B
$y - x$	$x - y$

- (A) Quantity A is greater.
- (B) Quantity B is greater.
- (C) The two quantities are equal.
- (D) The relationship cannot be determined from the information given.

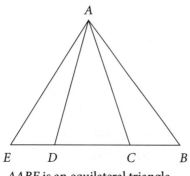

$\triangle ABE$ is an equilateral triangle
The area of $\triangle ACE$ = the area of $\triangle ABD$

8.

Quantity A	Quantity B
The length of side AD	The length of side AC

- (A) Quantity A is greater.
- (B) Quantity B is greater.
- (C) The two quantities are equal.
- (D) The relationship cannot be determined from the information given.

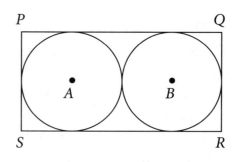

9. The two circles with centers A and B have the same radius, r. If $r = 3$, what is the perimeter of rectangle $PQRS$?

- (A) 12
- (B) 18
- (C) 24
- (D) 36
- (E) 48

10. What is the least integer value of x for which $1 - \left(\dfrac{1}{4}\right)^x$ is greater than 0?

- (A) −2
- (B) −1
- (C) 0
- (D) 1
- (E) 2

11. If $\dfrac{p-q}{p} = \dfrac{2}{7}$, then $\dfrac{q}{p} =$

- (A) $\dfrac{2}{5}$
- (B) $\dfrac{5}{7}$
- (C) 1
- (D) $\dfrac{7}{5}$
- (E) $\dfrac{7}{2}$

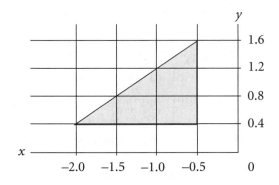

12. What is the area of the shaded region in the figure above?

| | square units

13. Which of the following is 850% greater than 8×10^3?

    Ⓐ 8.5×10^3
    Ⓑ 6.4×10^4
    Ⓒ 6.8×10^4
    Ⓓ 7.6×10^4
    Ⓔ 1.6×10^5

14. Which of the following are divisible by exactly 4 distinct, positive integers?

Indicate <u>all</u> possible numbers.

    Ⓐ   4
    Ⓑ   6
    Ⓒ   8
    Ⓒ   12
    Ⓓ   14

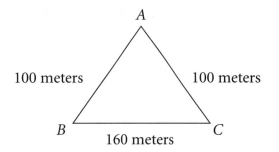

15 The figure above represents a triangular field. What is the minimum distance, in meters, that a person would have to walk to go from point A to a point on side BC?

| | meters

16. If the average of two numbers is $3y$ and one of the numbers is $y - z$, what is the other number, in terms of y and z?

    Ⓐ $y + z$
    Ⓑ $3y + z$
    Ⓒ $4y - z$
    Ⓓ $5y - z$
    Ⓔ $5y + z$

17. Which points lie on the graph of $y = \dfrac{x^2}{x+1}$?

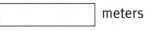

Indicate <u>all</u> possible choices.

    Ⓐ $(-3, -5)$
    Ⓑ $(-2, -4)$
    Ⓒ $(-1, -3)$
    Ⓓ $\left(1, \dfrac{1}{2}\right)$
    Ⓔ $\left(3, 2\dfrac{1}{2}\right)$

Questions 18–20 refer to the charts below.

U.S. PHYSICIANS IN SELECTED SPECIALTIES
BY GENDER, 1986

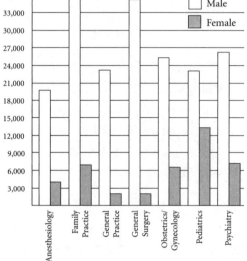

GENERAL SURGERY PHYSICIANS BY AGE, 1986

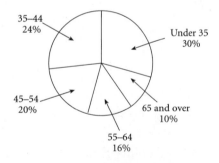

18. Which of the following physician specialties had the lowest ratio of males to females in 1986?

- Ⓐ family practice
- Ⓑ general surgery
- Ⓒ obstetrics/gynecology
- Ⓓ pediatrics
- Ⓔ psychiatry

19. If the number of female general surgery physicians in the under-35 category represented 3.5 percent of all the general surgery physicians, approximately how many male general surgery physicians were under 35 years?

- Ⓐ 9,200
- Ⓑ 9,800
- Ⓒ 10,750
- Ⓓ 11,260
- Ⓔ 11,980

20. Approximately what percent of all general practice physicians in 1986 were male?

- Ⓐ 23%
- Ⓑ 50%
- Ⓒ 75%
- Ⓓ 82%
- Ⓔ 90%

Your Practice Test is now complete.

CHAPTER 21

Practice Test Answers

VERBAL REASONING 1 ANSWER KEY

1. C
2. B
3. A, D
4. B, D
5. A, E, H
6. A, E
7. C, E
8. A, D
9. B, C
10. D, F
11. A
12. D
13. C
14. D
15. A, B
16. E
17. E
18. A, B
19. C
20. D

QUANTITATIVE REASONING 1 ANSWER KEY

1. C
2. A
3. C
4. D
5. B
6. C
7. A
8. D
9. B
10. 30
11. E
12. 6
13. C
14. B, D
15. 8
16. D
17. D, E
18. C
19. C
20. C, D

VERBAL REASONING 2 ANSWER KEY

1. B
2. B, D, G
3. A, F, H
4. E
5. A, E, I
6. D
7. A, F
8. A, F
9. B, D
10. B, C
11. E
12. C
13. A, B
14. C
15. E
16. D
17. A
18. B
19. C
20. E

QUANTITATIVE REASONING 2 ANSWER KEY

1. D
2. A
3. B
4. D
5. C
6. A
7. A
8. C
9. D
10. D
11. B
12. 0.9
13. D
14. B, C, E
15. 60
16. E
17. B, D
18. D
19. B
20. E

Diagnostic Tool

Tally up your score and write the results below.

You can also use the online answer grid available in your Online Center to enter your answers to the multiple-choice sections of this test. If you do so, you will receive a score estimate and a detailed breakdown of your performance by question type and topic. (The score you will receive is only an estimate, however, since a paper-based test, by definition, cannot mimic the adaptive nature and scoring algorithm of the GRE multi-stage test. For practice taking real MSTs, use the tests in your Online Center.)

Total

Total Correct: _____ out of 80

By Section

Verbal Reasoning _____ out of 40
Quantitative Reasoning _____ out of 40

VERBAL REASONING 1 ANSWERS AND EXPLANATIONS

1. C
This particular sentence has no detour road signs. Here the key phrase is "known for their devotion to their masters," so you might predict that the missing word means something like "loyalty" or "devotedness." The correct answer, **(C)** *fidelity*, is a close match for this prediction.

2. B
This sentence contains a detour road sign, "nonetheless," so you can expect the first part of the sentence to contrast with the fact that Larkin "maintained a spirited correspondence with a wide circle of friends." So you might predict that the missing word means something like "withdrawn" or "shy." Choice **(B)** matches this prediction: "By nature *reclusive*, Philip Larkin nonetheless maintained a spirited correspondence with a wide circle of friends." That makes perfect sense.

3. A, D
The road sign "because" in the first half of this sentence tells you that the second half will continue the thought of the first. The second half indicates that there was "no way to predict" the decision-making process's outcome, so a description of the process as "random" makes sense. The prediction matches **(A)** *arbitrary,* meaning "determined by chance, whim, or impulse." Choice **(B)** *regimented*, meaning "rigidly organized," means the opposite of what the sentence requires. Choice **(C)** *unilateral*, meaning "relating to only one side," is also incorrect—the fact that the decision-making process may have been entirely in the hands of one person does not logically lead to there being "no way to predict its outcome." The sentence compares the decision-making process to throwing dice, so a good prediction would be, "making decisions was *similar to* throwing dice." The best match is **(D)** *likened to*. Choice **(E)** *belittled by* doesn't make sense in context, and **(F)** *dissimilar to* means the opposite of what the sentence requires.

4. B, D
Look at blank (ii) first. The tax burden of most of the citizens comes from an "unvarying" tax, so the legislation mentioned earlier in the sentence must have had a *minor* effect on the middle class. **(D)** *negligible* matches perfectly. The road sign "although" indicates contrast, so the bill that produced "negligible" results must have been expected not only to have a significant effect, but a positive one. A prediction is "optimism" or "praise." **(B)** *acclaim* works best. **(C)** *hullabaloo* and **(A)** *commotion* are tempting choices, but they do not have sufficiently strong positive connotations, particularly as the bill is described as having been "heralded."

5. A, E, H

The three blanks are related in this sentence: blank (i) causes blank (ii) and prevents blank (iii). In the first blank, only an **(A)** *established* viewpoint could potentially **(E)** *skew* the reader's opinion, and an **(A)** *established* viewpoint would logically exclude an **(H)** *impartial* viewing. With the information given, only *established, skew,* and *impartial* logically follow each other.

6. A, E

This is a high-difficulty sentence, but elimination and prediction will help you out a great deal. The first clause and then the road sign "therefore" suggest that the clause with the blanks will provide an alternative to the fact that moving away from fossil fuels is insufficient to stabilize carbon emissions. Blank (ii) has a meaning similar to "store," so eliminate **(F)** *liberate*. **(D)** *incarcerate* means to put in prison and refers to people, not substances, so it cannot be correct. **(E)** *capture* matches. For blank (i), notice that the technologies must also be for "storing" carbon waste. Choices **(B)** *reduction* and **(C)** *diminution* can be eliminated. Choice **(A)** *sequestration* matches the prediction of "storing" and is correct.

7. C, E

To figure out what fits in the blank, note the detour road sign "although" between the first and second halves of the sentence. This tells you that what came before will be contradicted by what comes after. The first clause tells you that Handy's nickname is "self-conferred," so you can speculate that not everyone shares Handy's self-assessment. You could paraphrase the sentence this way to predict the blank: "Handy feels he's the father of the blues, but other musicians 'disagree.'" You're looking for a synonym for "disagree." You can eliminate choices **(A)**, **(D)**, and **(F)**, which say that Handy's moniker was *professed, proven,* or *demonstrated*—they mean the opposite of what you want. Choice **(B)**, which states that Handy's nickname was widely *deconstructed*, or "examined," *could* be right since other musicians came up with a different opinion, so keep it as a possibility. Choice **(C)**, *disputed,* has exactly the meaning you need, so keep this, too. That leaves choice **(E)** *contested*, which produces a sentence with the same meaning as choice **(C)**, so **(C)** and **(E)** are the correct answers.

8. A, D

In this sentence, which has no road signs, read for key words and what's implied (i.e., for logic). When an "expectation of instant gratification" isn't fulfilled, a feeling of disappointment would ensue. So the answer choices have to mean "disappointment." You can eliminate choices **(B)** and **(E)**, *endearment* and *elation*, right away since they have the opposite meaning. Choice **(F)** *pacifism*, "an opposition to war of any kind," isn't right for this sentence—an unreturned message would cause *conflict* in a relationship, rather than promote peace. Choice **(C)** *recompense* means "compensation" and can also be eliminated. That leaves **(A)** and **(D)**, *chagrin* and *vexation*, both of which match the prediction and have the right meaning for the sentence.

9. B, C

This is an intriguing sentence since the answer choices include two arcane words, *augmented* and *meliorated*. A good strategy for questions like this is to use the process of elimination on the answer choices. First, look at what the sentence implies, paraphrase it, and predict the answer: "The zookeepers are 'changing' the exhibit to handle more visitors." All the answer choices except **(D)** and **(F)**, *maintained* and *neglected*, express change, so eliminate those two. Of the remaining choices, **(A)** and **(E)**, *abridged* and *truncated*, mean "to make shorter," which, when applied to the sentence, wouldn't help the exhibit accommodate more traffic. The final choices are **(B)** and **(C)**, which are two high-level vocabulary words (meaning "added to" and "improved," respectively) and the correct answers.

10. D, F

Without structural road signs, you need to see if paraphrasing or key words can help you find synonyms. Scientists have observed odd fish behavior that precedes seismic events—the fish jump out of the water. Your paraphrase and prediction might look something like this: "Scientists 'theorize' that fish respond to physical precursors of seismic events." Both choices **(D)** and **(F)**, *hypothesize* and *contend*, fit this definition, and are therefore the correct answers. Choice **(A)** *repudiate* means to reject an idea, not present one. Scientists don't *authorize* information, so choice **(B)** is also incorrect. Choice **(C)** *foresee* does imply prediction, but one based on intuition, not on observed behavior. Finally, it wouldn't make sense for scientists to **(E)** *question* their own prediction in this context.

11. A

You're asked to find the statement or statements that have direct support in the passage. The last sentence in the passage states that most orders are not exclusively beneficial or exclusively parasitic, but include species with both characteristics. That's choice **(A)**. Choice **(B)** is too extreme, since the author speaks of minimizing harm to other species, not eliminating it. Choice **(C)** presents a scenario that's the opposite of what the passage expresses: facilitating the development of parasitic insects isn't in line with the goal of controlling pest species.

12. D

The key phrases "protecting native species" and "maintaining a balanced ecosystem" suggest that entomologists are trying to prevent humans from changing the existing environment. *Intrusion*, choice **(D)**, is a good description of what they're trying to avoid. **(A)** *obliteration* means extinction and is too extreme in this context. There's no suggestion that humans are fighting against insects or asking insects for anything, so rule out **(B)** and **(C)**, respectively. Choice **(E)** *mediation* has a meaning of "intercession," but you are looking for a word with a negative charge.

13. C

In this Function question, you have to characterize the relationship between the two highlighted phrases. The conclusion of this passage is that the Easter Rising was a key turning point in the battle against English rule. Thus, the first phrase, which calls the Easter Rising a "landmark event," is a paraphrase of the author's main conclusion. The second highlighted phrase, which calls the battle a "failure," would seem to contradict the conclusion that the battle was a positive turning point. The contrast key word "while," which precedes the second highlighted phrase, emphasizes the contradictory nature of the Easter Rising. Choice **(C)** matches both halves of the prediction perfectly. Choice **(A)** calls the first phrase evidence, which is incorrect. Choice **(B)** flips the two phrases' roles. Choice **(D)** refers to intermediate conclusions, which neither of the phrases is. Finally, choice **(E)** refers to an "outside position," which the passage does not have.

14. D

This Global question asks you to sum up the passage's purpose. The author's tone is one of explanation rather than argument, so you can rule out **(A)** *arguing that* . . . and **(E)** *persuading readers* . . . right away. The passage explains how the terms *Persian* and *Iranian* intersect and provides two perspectives on why one term might be preferable to the other. That's choice **(D)**. The author does not mention the fall of the Persian Empire, so choice **(B)** is incorrect. Although three groups are mentioned, the author doesn't focus on differentiating among them, so **(C)** isn't the best summary of the passage, either.

15. A, B

To select the correct choices, you must identify the groups to whom the term *Persian* applies according to the passage. Since both Iranian and Afghani people may use the descriptor, the woman in **(A)** could be described as Persian. The first sentence says that both Iranian immigrants and U.S.-born Iranian Americans identify as Persian, so the man in **(B)** also fits the criteria. However, it is clear that the term refers to heritage or citizenship or both, so it would not be accurate to describe someone of English descent who is an American citizen, choice **(C)**, as Persian.

16. E

The verb "cites" indicates that this is a Detail question, so look directly in the passage for the answer. The first two lines of the passage state that Iranian Americans call themselves Persian, and "this descriptor is a frequent cause of confusion among non-Persians." Bingo. Choice **(E)** is a perfect match. Choice **(A)** is a misused detail. It's a reason why some people oppose the use of the term *Persian*, not a reason why non-Persians are confused by the term. Similarly, choices **(B)**, **(C)**, and **(D)** all relate to arguments about whether the term *Persian* should be used; none of them have anything to do with the cause of some non-Persians' confusion, which is what the question asks for.

17. E

The question asks which choice is most analogous in meaning to the highlighted sentence, "To look feminine, fashionable sixth-century women would achieve the same ideal by bleeding themselves." All the choices are about animals, not people, but only **(E)** contains an analogous situation: self-destructive physical harm to (allegedly) produce an image befitting one's gender. Choice **(A)** mentions light and dark coloring, which the passage does discuss, but it's not analogous to the highlighted sentence in meaning. The second choice, **(B)**, concerns camouflage only. While **(C)** includes self-destructive physical harm, that harm is inflicted for survival purposes, not for the sake of appearing more masculine or feminine. The opening phrase of **(D)** sounds like the highlighted sentence, but the remainder of this answer choice discusses a naturally occurring trait, not a self-inflicted one.

18. A, B

The author describes several societies in which women lightened their skin as dictated by the fashion of the time, but she also cites a culture in which darker colors were preferred (Persians with henna dye). Hence, choice **(A)** is correct. The passage states that in 13th-century Italy, the use of makeup was a sign of social status, so choice **(B)** is correct. The passage begins with the Greco-Roman societies, but it doesn't say whether the practice of lightening skin originated there, so **(C)** is incorrect.

19. C

For varied reasons—*to flaunt affluence* **(A)**, *to attract attention* **(D)**, and *to look feminine* **(E)**—most of the societies described in the passage preferred white color or paleness on women's faces. These three choices are thus incorrect. The Egyptians preferred a light foundation also, but of a *golden* hue, so **(B)** is incorrect. In this passage, only the Persians went for a darker look with henna dye in their hair and on their skin to "summon the majesty" of the earth. Choice **(C)** is therefore a reason for preferring artificially darker rather than lighter skin, and it is the correct answer.

20. D

The passage discusses a particular "ism" (a theory or concept) called solipsism, which is the view that oneself is the only object of real knowledge or that nothing but the self exists. The best answer to the question, then, is **(D)**, *presenting the definition of a concept*. Choice **(A)** is close, except that solipsism is a belief, not a *phenomenon*, which is an observable fact or event that can be scientifically described. The author doesn't "refute" anything, so **(B)** is incorrect. Also, there are no key words, such as "conversely" or "on the other hand," to indicate "contrasting" schools of thought, so **(C)** is incorrect. The phrase "a physical object to a person" describes what the author means by "anything else" and is not the basis of any comparison, so **(E)** is incorrect.

QUANTITATIVE REASONING 1 ANSWERS AND EXPLANATIONS

1. C

Right triangles *ABD* and *CDB* share a hypotenuse, segment *DB*. The shared hypotenuse should clue you to use the Pythagorean theorem. See that *w* and *x* are lengths of the legs of right triangle *ABD*; side *AD* has length *w*, side *AB* has length *x*. Also, *y* and *z* are lengths of the legs of right triangle *CDB*; side *CD* has length *z*, side *CB* has length *y*. Where *a* and *b* are lengths of the legs of a right triangle, and *c* is the length of the hypotenuse, $a^2 + b^2 = c^2$. So here $w^2 + x^2 =$ length BD^2; $y^2 + z^2$ also equals length BD^2. The quantities are equal, and the answer is **(C)**.

2. A

You have $x + 4y = 6$ and $x = 2y$, and you want to compare *x* and *y*. Let's start by finding *y*. Substitute $2y$ for *x* in the first equation and get $2y + 4y = 6$ or $6y = 6$. Divide both sides by 6 and get $y = 1$. If $y = 1$ and $x = 2y$, as the second equation states, *x* must equal 2. Because 2 is greater than 1, Quantity A is greater.

3. C

The problem doesn't say how many employees work at the firm, so let's pick a number. Since the problem involves percents, let's pick 100 as the total number of employees.

If there are 100 employees working at the firm, then one quarter of them, or 25, are managers. That leaves 75 employees, one-third of which, or 25, are assistants. Consequently, $100 - 25 - 25 = 50$ employees are left to be technicians. Now check the quantities. Quantity A, the number of managers, is 25. Quantity B, half the number of technicians, is half of 50, which is also 25. Pick **(C)** *the two quantities are equal*.

4. D

To make the quantities look as much alike as you can, use FOIL to multiply out Quantity A. You'll multiply $a \times b$, $1 \times b$, $1 \times a$, and 1×1 and get $ab + a + b + 1$. Quantity B also has $ab + 1$. Quantity A has the additional terms *a* and *b*. There is no information given about possible values for *a* or *b*. Because $a + b$ could be positive, negative, or zero, a relationship cannot be determined, and the answer is **(D)**.

You can also use Picking Numbers; let $a = 1$ and $b = 2$. Then Quantity A is $(1 + 1)(2 + 1) = 6$ and Quantity B is $(1 \times 2) + 1 = 3$. In this case, Quantity A is greater. But if you let $a = -1$ and $b = -2$, you have Quantity A $= (-1 + 1)(-2 + 1) = 0$ and Quantity B $= (-1 \times -2) + 1 = 3$. In this case, Quantity B is greater. You have demonstrated that a definite relationship cannot be determined, leading to answer choice **(D)**.

5.   B

In the two-digit number *jk*, the value of digit *j* is twice the value of digit *k*. You have to compare the value of *k* in Quantity A with 6 in Quantity B. If you plug in 6 for *k*, it is not possible to enter "twice the value of the digit *k*" for the digit *j*. That is because *j* can only be a single digit; it cannot be 12. In other words, *k* has to be something less than 6, so the answer must be **(B)**. The value in Quantity B is greater.

6.   C

Henry purchased *x* apples, and Jack purchased 10 apples less than one-third the number of apples Henry purchased. *One-third of* means the same as *one-third times*, and the number of apples Henry purchased is *x*. Thus, this boils down to $J = \frac{1}{3}x - 10$.

You can plug this in for Quantity A. We have $\frac{1}{3}x - 10$ in Quantity A and $\frac{x-30}{3}$ in Quantity B. Now you can clear the fraction in Quantity B. Let's split Quantity B into two fractions: $\frac{x}{3} - \frac{30}{3}$. Leave the $\frac{x}{3}$ alone and cancel the factor of 3 from the numerator and denominator of $\frac{30}{3}$ and you're left with $\frac{x}{3} - 10$. What's $\frac{x}{3}$? It's one-third of *x*. So Quantity A equals $\frac{1}{3}x - 10$, while Quantity B also equals $\frac{1}{3}x - 10$, and the answer is **(C)**.

7.   A

The figure shows a circle with diameter 8. The circumference of the circle is therefore 8π. Since the 90° central angle cuts a quarter of the circle, the length of arc *QRS* must likewise be a quarter of the circumference. Quantity A is therefore one-quarter of 8π, or 2π. Because π is a positive number, 2π must be greater than 2. Pick **(A)** *Quantity A is greater.*

8.   D

You can suspect **(D)** because there is a range of possible values for the variables. In Quantity A, you have the volume of a rectangular solid with length 5 feet, width 4 feet, and height *x* feet. The formula is length times width times height, so the volume is 5 times 4 times *x*, or 20*x*. The volume of Quantity B is therefore 10 times 8 times *y*, or 80*y*. If $4 < x < 6$, then the range of values for Quantity A is $80 < V < 120$. If $1 < y < 2$, then the range of values for Quantity B is $80 < V < 160$. Since the two ranges overlap, it's possible that the two quantities are equal or that one is greater than the other. So, the correct answer is **(D)**.

9. B

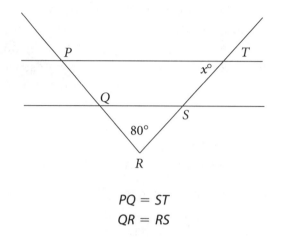

$$PQ = ST$$
$$QR = RS$$

The goal is to find x, the measure of one of the angles formed by the intersection of ST and PT. Now angle QRS is labeled 80°. You also know PQ and ST have the same length and QR and RS have the same length. If you add PQ and QR, you get PR. If you add ST and RS, you get RT. If you add equals to equals, you get equals, so $PQ + QR$ must be the same as $ST + RS$, which means that PR and RT are the same. Thus, you have isosceles triangle PRT, and you're given one angle that has measure 80 and a second angle that has measure x. The angle measuring x is opposite equal side PR. That means the other angle must have the same measure. The sum of the interior angles in a triangle always equals 180°. Thus, $x + x + 80$ must equal 180, $2x = 100$, and $x = 50$. The answer is **(B)**.

10. 30

This is a permutation problem because the order in which the duo is chosen matters. The producer has two slots to fill. For the lead role, there are 6 people to choose from. For the supporting role, there will be 5 people to choose from. So the number of possible duos is $6 \times 5 = $ **30**.

11. E

The question asks for the number of different dinners Jane could make. Since the order of the selections in the dinner doesn't matter, this is a combination problem. But it involves three possible combination types: Veg, Meat, Meat; Veg, Veg, Meat; or Veg, Veg, Veg. We must calculate the possibilities for each type of combination and then add the results to find the total number of different combinations possible.

Let V represent vegetarian and M represent meat.

Then with V, M, M, she has 5 choices for the vegetarian (she must choose 1) × 4 choices for meat (she must choose 2).

For V, V, M, she will choose 2 from among 5 for the vegetarian and 1 among 4 for the meat.

If she goes with V, V, V, the all-vegetarian menu, she will choose a subgroup of 3 from among 5 vegetarian choices.

If n and k are positive integers where $n = k$, then the number of different subgroups consisting of k objects that can be selected from a group consisting of n different objects, denoted by $_nC_k$, is given by the formula

$$_nC_k = \frac{n!}{k!(n-k)!}$$

Here the total number of different possible servings for a plate is $(_5C_1)(_4C_2) + (_5C_2)(_4C_1) + (_5C_3)$.

Now $_5C_1$ represents choosing 1 type of vegetable selection from 5 different types, so $_5C_1 = 5$. (The formula also gives this result.) Now we use the formula to find the next two combinations:

$$_4C_2 = \frac{4!}{2!(4-2)!} = \frac{4!}{2! \times 2!} = \frac{4 \times 3 \times 2 \times 1}{2 \times 1 \times 2 \times 1} = 6$$

$$_5C_2 = \frac{5!}{2!(5-2)!} = \frac{5!}{2! \times 3!} =$$

$$\frac{5 \times \cancel{4}^2 \times \cancel{3} \times \cancel{2} \times \cancel{1}}{\cancel{2} \times 1 \times \cancel{3} \times \cancel{2} \times \cancel{1}} =$$

$$\frac{5 \times 4 \times 3 \times 2 \times 1}{2 \times 1 \times 3 \times 2 \times 1} = 10$$

Here $_4C_1$ corresponds to choosing 1 type of meat selection from 4 different types, so $_4C_1 = 4$. Then we use the formula again:

$$_5C_3 = \frac{5!}{3!(5-3)!} = \frac{5!}{3! \times 2!} =$$

$$\frac{5 \times 4 \times 3 \times 2 \times 1}{3 \times 2 \times 1 \times 2 \times 1} = 10$$

So the number of different possible dinners of these three items is $5 \times 6 + 10 \times 4 + 10 = 80$, choice **(E)**.

12. 6

You could find the number of tasks per hour from one computer, but that would add extra steps, because you want to find out how many computers you need to do a certain number of tasks in three hours. Well, if the computer can do 30 tasks in six hours, it can do 15 tasks in three hours. So, two computers could complete 30 tasks in that time. Three computers could do 45; four could do 60; five could do 75; six could do 90. You can't get by with five computers because you have to get 80 tasks done, so you'll need **6** computers.

13. C

Picking Numbers is the best strategy, since there are variables in the question and the answer choices. If $c = 3$, then $2c = 6$. There are two integers between 3 and 6, so plug $c = 3$ into the answer choices to see which one is equal to 2.

(A) $\dfrac{3}{2} \neq 2$

(B) $3 \neq 2$

(C) $3 - 1 = 2$

(D) $3 - 2 \neq 2$

(E) $3 + 1 \neq 2$

The only answer choice that equals 2 when $c = 3$ is **(C)**, so **(C)** is correct.

14. B, D

You're asked to find what $\dfrac{b}{a}$ *could* be; that tells you there may be more than one possible value for $\dfrac{b}{a}$. You're told the ratio of $2a$ to b is 8 times the ratio of b to a. That's awkward to keep track of in English—it's a little easier to write fractions. The ratio of $2a:b$ equals $8\left(\dfrac{b}{a}\right)$. So, $2\left(\dfrac{a}{b}\right) = 8\left(\dfrac{b}{a}\right)$, or $\dfrac{2a}{b} = \dfrac{8b}{a}$. Cross multiply to get $2a^2 = 8b^2$, or $a^2 = 4b^2$. Multiply each side of the equation by $\dfrac{1}{4a^2} : \dfrac{a^2}{4a^2} = \dfrac{4b^2}{4a^2}$. This is the same as $\dfrac{1}{4} = \dfrac{b^2}{a^2}$. Take the square root of both sides of the equation: $\pm\dfrac{1}{2} = \dfrac{b}{a}$. The ratio of b to a is $\dfrac{1}{2}$ or $-\dfrac{1}{2}$. So, **(B)** and **(D)** are the answers. This problem is also a great candidate for Backsolving, although since this question could have more than one correct answer, you would need to test all answer choices to see which ones work out.

15. 8

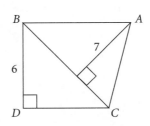

It is given that the area of triangle *ABC* is 35, and in the diagram, you're given a height for triangle *ABC*. If you use *BC* as the base of the triangle, the triangle's height is 7, so you can find the length of *BC*. The length *BC*, which is the base of triangle *ABC*, is also the hypotenuse of right triangle *BDC*. Given the hypotenuse and the length of leg *BD*, which is given in the diagram as 6, you'll be able to find the third leg of the triangle, side *DC*, which is what you're looking for.

Going back to triangle *ABC*, the area is 35 and the height is 7. The area of a triangle is $\frac{1}{2} \times$ base $\times$ height, so $\frac{1}{2} \times$ base $\times$ height is 35. Therefore, $\frac{1}{2} \times 7 \times$ length *BC* is 35. That means $7 \times$ length *BC* is 70, so *BC* must have length 10. Now look at right triangle *BDC*. Here is a right triangle with one leg of length 6, the hypotenuse of length 10, and the third side unknown. That's one of the famous Pythagorean ratios—it's a 3:4:5 triangle. So *DC* must have length 2×4, or **8**.

16. D

First, find the value of *m*. You are told that 3^m is 81. Well, 81 is 9×9 and 9 is 3^2. So you have $3^2 \times 3^2 = 81$ or $3 \times 3 \times 3 \times 3 = 81$. There are four factors of 3 in 81, so *m* has the value 4. Now 4^3 is $4 \times 4 \times 4$ is 64. So **(D)** is correct. Note that **(A)** is a trap—that's the value of *m*, not m^3.

17. D, E

The problem states that *x* is between 0 and 1, so *x* must be a positive fraction (or decimal) less than 1. We can pick a number to get to the correct answer(s) here because both the question and the answer choices have variables. The decimal 0.5 is in the middle of the given range, so it's a good starting point.

(A) Incorrect. Doubling any positive value always produces a greater value, not a lesser value.

(B) Incorrect. $2 \times 0.5 = 1$; a smaller fraction could make this statement true, but our correct answer(s) must always be true.

(C) Incorrect. $2 \times 0.5 = 1$; a larger fraction could make this statement true, but our correct answer(s) must always be true.

(D) Correct. $0.5^2 = 0.25$; the square of any number between 0 and 1 (exclusive) will be less than the original number. This example illustrates that property.

(E) Correct. $0.25 < 1$; the square of any number between 0 and 1 (exclusive) will be less than 1. This is an example of that property. So, the correct answers are **(D)** and **(E)**.

18. C

To find how many categories had energy use greater than 150 million kilowatt-hours, you have to find out how many total kilowatt-hours were used in that year using the line graph. You see that 600 million kilowatt-hours were used in 1995. What is the relationship of 150 million kilowatt-hours to 600 million kilowatt-hours? It's 25% of 600 million kilowatt-hours, so you're looking for categories with more than 25% of the energy use for 1995. How many categories exceeded 25%? Just two, government and industrial. So your answer is **(C)**.

19. C

To find the per capita, or per person, personal energy use in Country Y in 2005, divide the personal energy use by the number of people. Since the question gives you the population—500 million people—you only need to find the personal energy use.

According to the top graph, total energy use in 2005 was about 675 million kilowatt-hours. According to the bottom graph, personal energy use was about 20% of the total, or $675 \times 0.20 = 135$ million kilowatt-hours. Divide this number by the population of Country Y in 2005: 135 million kilowatt-hours divided by 500 million people $= 0.27$ kilowatt-hours per person, or choice **(C)**.

20. C, D

Since this is an all-that-apply question, check each choice systematically.

Choice **(A)**: According to the bottom graph, energy for farm use decreased from 30% to 20% of the total between 1990 and 1995. Since 30 is 50% greater than 20, total energy use would have had to increase by at least 50% to compensate. The top graph shows that it did not, so choice **(A)** is incorrect.

Choice **(B)**: According to the bottom graph, energy for farm use decreased from 20% to 10% of the total between 1995 and 2000. Since 20 is double 10, total energy use would have had to double in order to compensate—that definitely did not happen! Choice **(B)** is out.

The bottom graph shows that energy for farm use, as a percentage of the total, increased from 2000 onward. Since total energy use increased every year, total farm energy use must have increased also. Thus, without any calculation, you know that choices **(C)** and **(D)** must be correct.

VERBAL REASONING 2 ANSWERS AND EXPLANATIONS

1. B

"Instead" is a detour road sign that tells you that the second half of the sentence will say the opposite of the first half. That means diversification shouldn't "divert" the organization, so you're looking for a word that means the opposite of "divert". The answer is **(B)** *furthering*, which means "advancing or promoting." **(A)** *undermining*, **(C)** *retracting*, and **(E)** *deterring* are all the opposite of what you need—they say that diversification will negatively affect the historical purpose. Choice **(D)** *classifying* doesn't make sense in context.

2. B, D, G

The best way to approach the first blank is to consider the logic of this sentence and predict an answer. A "keen" sense of smell is a positive attribute. What should a bee with a keen sense of smell be able to do with regard to kin and foe? To **(A)** *promulgate* is to make known, in the sense of "to announce." **(B)** *discern* means "to perceive or recognize." And **(C)** *arbitrate* means "to decide between disputants." A bee would want to "recognize" friend from foe, whether or not it did either of the other two things, so **(B)** *discern* is the correct choice.

The road sign "by contrast" tells you that some other ability is not as good. Indeed, the bees have a "deficiency" of some kind, specifically one that makes them unable to protect themselves from disease. Which phrase most closely describes the desired response? Any of the three answer choices could work, but, as we said in the strategies section, the question gives you clues. Read the third sentence to see if the answer becomes clear. When you do, you'll note the key words "various diseases" matches one of the second blank's answer choices, *pathogens*. Let's hold on to **(D)** for now.

The third sentence is a bit convoluted, and some of the answer choices are uncommon words, so paraphrase it to put it into simpler terms and predict the answer: "Bees 'protect' their colony through grooming behavior." Only one of the answer choices, **(G)** *minimizes incursions by*, fits our prediction. If you substitute the other terms into the blank and reread the sentence, you can confirm **(G)** as the correct choice; neither **(H)** *implicates replication of* or **(I)** *simulates action by* makes sense in context.

Now that we have two of the blanks filled, we can return to blank (ii). When we read **(D)** *pathogens* into the sentence, the three sentences make sense together, and **(D)** is correct.

3. A, F, H

The key word in this sentence is "crisis." You need adjectives and verbs that play well off of it. If you don't know the meaning of *exigent*, you can use the process of elimination to identify the right answer. **(B)** *cretaceous* means "chalky," and one wouldn't describe a need as chalky.

You can eliminate **(C)** *specious*—it means "false" and is the opposite of what you're looking for. That leaves **(A)** *exigent*, which means "immediate." It is the correct answer.

Which of the actions would be required in a situation of "critical necessity"? Recall that there is a water crisis, so the resource involved is water. The word *ineffable* means "unable to be expressed," so it makes no sense in this context. However, if you didn't know that word, you could use the process of elimination to narrow your choices. If there were a water crisis, water would not be *abundant*, so you can eliminate **(E)**. That leaves **(F)** *mobilize limited* resources. "Limited" makes sense in the context of a crisis, so it is the correct choice and a solid guess if you weren't certain of the meaning of choice **(D)**.

If you're galvanizing political efforts to stave off a crisis, it's likely you would want to **(H)** *focus*, or concentrate, international attention on water use. **(G)** *foment*, "to incite," and **(I)** *ferment*, "to brew," both have connotations about creating; neither makes sense in context, so both are incorrect.

4.   E

The detour road sign "although" contrasts the honor Pétain received for World War I with what he "incurred" during World War II. The sentence's structure implies that the word in the blank will have a negative charge, so you can rule out the positive answer choices **(A)** *status* ("relative rank in a hierarchy") and **(C)** *kudos* ("congratulations"). Choice **(B)** *reputation* doesn't make sense—one earns a reputation; it is not "incurred". Choice **(D)** *recompense* doesn't make sense either, since the French wouldn't compensate someone for a dishonorable action. That leaves you with the correct answer, **(E)** *obloquy*, "disgrace or public censure." One would heap *obloquy* on a person who's done something hateful, like collaborating with the enemy.

5.   A, E, I

This is a long set of sentences, so you should paraphrase them to make the topic easier to get a handle on: "Although people don't think of cellophane as paper, this _____ material is made from the same stuff as paper bags. It was invented to prevent stains, but its usefulness became _____ and resulted in a _____ product."

For the first blank, you're looking for a term that describes cellophane. Even if you don't know what cellophane is, the key words "transparent, plasticky film" provide a great prediction for the blank. The correct answer is **(A)** *diaphanous*, which means "see-through." Choice **(B)** *standardized* has nothing to do with translucency. Choice **(C)** *opaque* means the opposite of what you need.

After Jacques saw how useful cellophane was, he decided to patent it. For the second blank, therefore, predict a word like "visible" or "evident." Choice **(E)** *apparent* is a great match. Choices **(D)** *marketable* and **(F)** *fashionable* may be true of cellophane, but the second blank describes the utility of cellophane, not cellophane itself. It wouldn't make sense to say that cellophane's utility became "marketable to" or "fashionable to" the very person who invented it.

Having filled in the first and second blanks, you quickly test the third. Nothing in the sentences describes cellophane as **(G)** *amorphous*, "shapeless," so eliminate it. Choice **(H)** is a trap—don't confuse *ingenuous*, or "innocent," with "ingenious," or "brilliant." You would expect a product with "overwhelming usefulness" to be **(I)** *ubiquitous*, "available everywhere," and that's the correct answer.

6. D

From the detour road sign "unlike," you can tell that Hume isn't trying to determine whether an objective reality exists. Why wouldn't he do so? Following this logic reveals the right word for the sentence. Hume disregarded objective reality not because he thought the issue was **(A)** *pragmatic*, "practical," or **(B)** *challenging*. That would have made him want to investigate it. He probably didn't try because he felt that the issue was either unverifiable or uninteresting. Choice **(D)** *insoluble*, "not capable of being solved," fits the blank best. It's unclear that Hume would be "unlike most other philosophers" if he thought the issue was **(C)** *theoretical* or **(E)** *esoteric* ("understood only by a select few"), so both are incorrect.

7. A, F

This is a long sentence and the blank occurs in the middle, so paraphrase it. As you do so note that the phrase "even though" is a detour road sign that indicates a contrast. A good paraphrase is, "People smoke, even though nicotine has a _____ effect on their health." You are looking for a pair of synonyms that have a negative tone and mean something like "bad" or "harmful." Choices **(A)** *deleterious* and **(F)** *pernicious* both mean "harmful," so that's the correct pair. Choice **(B)** *addictive* is a property of nicotine, but the sentence deals with nicotine's harmfulness, not its addictiveness. Choices **(C)** *anemic*, meaning "weak," and **(E)** *benign*, meaning "harmless," are contrary to the prediction. Finally, choice **(D)** *antagonistic*, meaning "hostile," is a tempting trap. While "hostile" is a negatively charged word, being hostile is not the same as causing harm.

8. A, F

The phrase "to the public's great shock" is a key phrase—it tells you there's a contrast between what was expected ("peaceable reform") and what really happened. The correct answers must mean something like "violent rebellion." *Contumacious* is a difficult vocabulary word, so we'll use the process of elimination to go through all the answer choices. Choice **(B)** *endemic* means "inherent," which doesn't fit the context of the sentence. Choices **(C)** and **(E)**, *erratic* and *irresolute*, both mean "unpredictable" or "uncertain." If you weren't sure of *irresolute*, consider its root, *resolute*, and think of a similar word, *resolution* in this case. A resolution is something you commit to doing, and irresolute is its opposite, "unsure" or "unable to make a decision." These two words are plausible choices because they imply that the group didn't fulfill its promises, but they don't work in context. You need a contrast with "peaceable reform," something that would result in people's shock—unpredictability and uncertainty aren't shocking.

Choice **(D)** *estimable*, "worthy," means the opposite of what you want. If you didn't know the meaning of this word, you could consider its root, *esti*. Think of words with a similar root that you *can* define, such as *esteem*. Knowing that esteem has a positive tone, you could deduce that *estimable* does as well, making it incorrect. That leaves you with choices **(A)** and **(F)**—*contumacious* and *seditious*—both of which mean "rebellious" and are the correct choices.

9. B, D

Some of the answer choices are fairly difficult words, but you can tell from the key word "concealed" that you want a word negative in tone. Based on that, two words pop out from the answer choices, **(B)** *artifice* and **(D)** *chicanery*, both of which are negative and both of which mean "deception." But you should go through the answer choices one at a time to confirm your selections.

Choice **(A)** *cabal* means "a secret group," and it doesn't work in context.

Choice **(B)** *artifice* sounds a lot like a word you're probably familiar with—"artificial," which means looking like one thing while actually being another. *Artifice* means "trickery." "Photo retouching and inflated claims" are forms of trickery, so this is one of the correct answers.

If you don't know the meaning of the word *hegemony* **(C)**, put it aside until you go through the other answer choices. Choice **(E)** *dominance* means "supremacy" or "domination," and it doesn't make sense in context. Eliminate it. Choice **(D)** *chicanery* also means "deception and trickery," so it's also correct. To determine the meaning of *imprecation*, choice **(F)**, think of a word with a similar root. One is "precarious," which means "dangerous." Are advertising ploys dangerous? No. This word is too extreme to work in context. That leaves you with only *hegemony* outstanding. Even if its meaning is unclear, you have, through the process of elimination, two synonymous answer choices that fit well in context, and you should go with them. *Hegemony* means "influence" or "dominance." If you knew this definition, you'd know that *hegemony* is a synonym for another answer choice, *dominance*, and this is another example of a question with two sets of synonyms in the answer choices.

10. B, C

While this sentence includes a classic detour road sign, "however," its structure is such that you can't identify what "however" is contradicting. As you've learned from

Kaplan's strategies, key words can help you figure out the missing word in a sentence. The key words in this sentence are "conservative" and "unreceptive." You need to predict the kind of joke a conservative audience at a charity event would receive poorly. Choice **(A)** *plucky* means "brave," so eliminate it. Choices **(B)** and **(C)**—*ribald* and *coarse*—both mean "vulgar." These are likely correct, but continue to test the other choices before answering definitively. Choices **(D)** and **(F)**—*traitorous* and *treacherous*—are synonyms that mean "disloyal." Although the performers betrayed the spirit of the event, this is not the meaning of the words needed to describe the jokes. Choice **(E)** *politic* means "diplomatic." This has the opposite meaning of the word you're looking for, so eliminate it. The correct answers are *ribald* and *coarse*.

11. E

The first highlighted sentence expresses the passage's main idea (sharks are different from other fish), and the second highlighted sentence explains one of the ways in which this is true (they have livers, not swim bladders). That's choice **(E)**. Since no opposing perspective is included, you can rule out **(A)**. Choice **(B)** reverses the roles of the two sentences; the second sentence supports the first, not vice versa. No opposing argument is addressed, and the author forms no intermediate conclusion, so **(C)** and **(D)** are incorrect.

12. C

This Inference question asks you to consider the information in the passage and speculate about the events that may have preceded those described. The phrase "for themselves" implies the patrons' ability to locate their own books, so it follows that they would previously have needed assistance from librarians, choice **(C)**. The passage says that Dewey was the first standardized method, but you have no basis to assume that no classification method existed before, **(A)**. Similarly, nothing suggests that libraries kept their methods confidential, **(B)**. Although Dewey helped patrons find materials themselves, no information in the passage implies that this change affected librarians' jobs directly, so you can eliminate **(D)**. As for choice **(E)**, the passage implies that patrons may have had difficulty locating items, but to say that they were never able to understand any given library's system is too extreme.

13. A, B

A lower risk of fatal disease meant that vaccination was safer than inoculation, so **(A)** is correct. Since the passage mentions "enormous variations" between batches of inoculum, the "standard dose" used in vaccines would be more likely to be consistent, so **(B)** is also correct. Choice **(C)** is incorrect because it deals with tuberculosis inoculations, which are beyond the scope of the passage.

14. C

This question refers to the second half of the second sentence, which begins, "Modern epidemiologists believe . . ." This sentence uses both the word "contract" and "contracted," and the meaning in context is the same for both. The passage discusses the process of inoculation: patients are given a mild case of the illness against which they wish to develop immunity. The sentence referred to by the question describes the effectiveness of the procedure in further detail: because the patients got the disease through their skin instead of through inhalation, it was less likely to be fatal. To form a prediction for the answer, you could read the sentence, substituting the simple words "got," "received," or "caught" for the word "contracted." The answer choices all represent possible meanings of the word "contracted," but only choice **(C)** *acquired* matches your prediction for a word that could substitute logically into the sentence as written.

15. E

The passage as a whole is concerned with how to come up with a good definition of tragedy. The author leads into Scylla and Charybdis by mentioning "overly broad definitions" and "overly narrow ones," respectively. Just afterward, she calls this situation a "definitional dilemma." From these clues, you're thus led to infer that Scylla and Charybdis are names for the dangers that may befall anyone who tries to come up with a good definition of tragedy. **(E)** is in line with this inference and is correct. **(A)** cannot be correct because Terry Eagleton begs off providing a good definition in the first place. He seems to think that the task is simply impossible. So broad and narrow definitions, represented by Scylla and Charybdis, respectively, are not signs of Eagleton's principal faults. **(B)** is outside the scope of the passage. The author is making no larger claim about the significance of myth. Similarly, **(C)** is outside the scope. While Scylla and Charybdis are drawn from myth, they in no way establish that Eagleton's dilemma has its origins in myth. Like **(B)** and **(C)**, **(D)** is also outside the scope. Because the author makes no reference to other intellectual inquiries, you have no reason for believing that they are applicable to the case at hand.

16. D

What is the main point of the passage? It is to criticize two authors' views of tragedy (paragraphs 1–2) and to generate a new necessary condition for tragedy (paragraph 3). The answer that most closely matches this understanding is **(D)**. Consider that **(A)** is too narrow: Mandel isn't even mentioned by this choice, despite the fact that he is the "main character" in the passage. The problem with **(B)** is that it includes Eagleton in the author's criticism of Mandel. In other words, the author *does* criticize Mandel for not providing all the necessary conditions for tragedy. But she *does not* have anything explicit to say about whether Eagleton falls prey to the same problem. Consequently, **(B)** is a distortion. Choice **(C)** is the opposite of what the author says. The author implies throughout the passage that tragedy is definable. Though she pokes holes in both theorists' accounts, the author seems, if anything, more sympathetic to Mandel, who thinks that tragedy is definable, than she is to Eagleton, who does not. **(E)**, finally, is too strong because of the bit that follows "in order to." In the final paragraph, the author doesn't provide you with a new definition of tragedy; she simply tells you that there's at least one necessary ingredient in tragedy that Mandel fails to pick up on. Think about the point about necessary and sufficient conditions this way: To make a quiche, it's necessary to use eggs. But eggs aren't enough for something to be a quiche. After all, eggs can be used in a lot of other things—cake and omelets, just to name a few. The author is making the same point about powerlessness in the realm of tragedy: it's necessary (or "absolutely essential") but not sufficient for something to be tragic.

17. A

This question tests your ability to identify GRE vocabulary words within the Reading Comprehension portion of the exam. At the very least, you should be thinking that the author *liked*, *esteemed*, and *pitied* these characters. She says as much when she describes them as being "well-educated, tireless, but spiritually drained" (lines 44–45). The only answer that comes close is **(A)** *laudatory*, meaning "worthy of praise." Choice **(B)**, *conciliatory*, means "intending to placate," so this does not work. Choice **(C)**, *despondent*, means "very sad." You could infer that the characters themselves are despondent, but "the author's attitude" is surely not despondent. Therefore, **(C)** is incorrect. Choice **(D)** *myopic* means "shortsighted," and that has nothing to do with the passage before you, let alone the author's attitude toward the protagonists in this work, so it can be eliminated. And **(E)** *diffident* means "modest" or "timid," and that's not on target. In sum, none but **(A)** rings true.

18. B

This Inference question is essentially asking you to consider not only what Eagleton and Mandel have in common, but also what they do not. What do they have in common? According to the author, they don't give us an adequate conception of tragedy. And now what are the main differences between them? They take different approaches to the task, with Eagleton throwing his hands up and saying, in effect, that tragedy can't be defined and Mandel digging his heels in and saying that it can. **(B)** captures what they share (that is, failure) and what they differ on (that is, the reasons for their respective failures). Regarding **(A)**, the author does not think that their ideas should be dismissed. Why would she have bothered methodically working through their ideas in the first place if this was her attitude toward their ideas? No, clearly she thinks that much can be learned from them. Thus, **(A)** is the opposite of what the passage says. As for choice **(C)**, the author's ultimate assessment is that neither Eagleton's nor Mandel's view will do. What's more, the passage never states whether the first thing about sadness should be weighed as *heavily* as the second thing about inevitability. For both of these reasons, **(C)** can't be inferred. **(D)** is incorrect because you can't validly infer from the fact that a work is very sad that the heroes have necessarily suffered greatly. In Eagleton's view, the fact of great suffering is, at best, probable and not certain. The key word in **(E)** is *combines*. The author does examine different thinkers' ideas, but her strategy is not to combine those ideas; her strategy is to criticize these ideas. Consequently, **(E)** can't be inferred.

19. C

In this question, you should *only* look at paragraph 3. Make sure that "present conception of tragedy" refers to Mandel's view. Think about what the opening sentence is doing: it's making clear to you the author's chief complaint with Mandel. And then consider that the rest of the paragraph is trying to provide evidence for the complaint already mentioned.

Thus, **(C)** is correct. No such luck with **(A)**. Don't be fooled: all talk of genre and influence goes beyond the bounds of the passage. You run into a similar problem with **(B)**. The author has nothing to say about aesthetic value, supreme or otherwise. In sum, **(A)** and **(B)** are outside the scope. On the face of it, **(D)** looks pretty good. True, the author is worrying about something in Mandel's definition. However, she is not taking issue with all three criteria—only with one criterion (the inevitability requirement). Consequently, **(D)** is incorrect. Turning to **(E)**, we don't see much to recommend it. For one thing, the author is not defending conclusions (she is, as the question tells you, simply voicing dissatisfaction). For another, she is not pointing out a trap that Mandel is falling into.

20. E

To begin with, understand the scope of the question squarely before you. The question has to do with the whole passage, not with one of its parts. Now think about the first two requirements. The first is that the protagonist is worthy of esteem; the second that he or she suffers greatly. Ask yourself: What do you think the author's opinion about these two requirements is? Does she like them? Dislike them? It's the first: she most likely thinks that they are good things. Evidence for the first part of this conclusion can be found in paragraph 3 where the author seems to look favorably on the characters in the modern tragedy *Three Sisters*. **(E)** puts this point even more delicately by making us see that both requirements are OK so long as they don't contradict the condition of powerlessness. Therefore, **(E)** is the correct answer.

(A) is the opposite of the correct answer. The author provides no reason to believe that these requirements would not fit with the condition of powerlessness. With respect to **(B)**, the first condition isn't at all at odds with the condition of powerlessness. The author implies as much in paragraph 3 when she shows that good characters in works of tragedy necessarily feel powerless. **(C)** is also incorrect. From all that you read in paragraph 3, you can reasonably conclude that the sisters do suffer a good deal. That leaves you with **(D)** to consider. **(D)** is without question quite tempting. Yet it goes outside the scope of the passage to say that both requirements should not figure prominently. You have reason to believe that they should figure *in some way*, but we can't know for sure *how* prominently they should figure. The answer is **(E)**.

QUANTITATIVE REASONING 2 ANSWERS AND EXPLANATIONS

1. D

The perimeter of *ABC* is 40 and the length of *BC* is 12, and you want to compare the length of *AB* with 14. In an isosceles triangle, there are two sides with equal length, but you don't know whether side *BC* is one of those sides or not. If side *BC* is the unequal side, there are two unknown sides plus 12, and they have a sum of 40, the perimeter. The two remaining sides have a sum of 28, so each is 14. That would mean that *AB* and *AC* would have length 14. Then the answer would be **(C)**. If *BC* is one of the equal sides, however, there are two sides with length 12 and a third unknown side, and the sum is 40. Because 12 + 12 is 24, the third side has length 16. *AB* could be one of the sides of length 12 or the side of length 16. There are three possible lengths for side *AB*—16, 14, and 12—so the answer is **(D)**.

2. A

Plug 0.5 in for *x* and solve. $f(0.5) = (0.5+3)^2 = 3.5^2 = 12.25$. This is greater than 9, so the answer is **(A)**.

3. B

In both quantities, use the basic formula: rate × time = distance. In Quantity A, 40 mph × 4 hours traveled gives you 160 miles. In Quantity B, 70 mph × $2\frac{1}{2}$ hours = 175 miles.

As 175 is greater than 160, the answer is **(B)**.

4. D

Quantity A cannot be precisely defined, but Quantity B can. The grape bag weighs 50 grams, and each grape weighs exactly 1 gram, so there must be 50 grapes in the bag. Quantity B is 50.

Now consider Quantity A. If every cookie in the bag is on the lighter end, weighing only 5 grams, then the number of cookies in the bag is 300 divided by 5, or 60. If, contrarily, the bag is full of the heaviest cookies in town, each weighing 15 grams, then there are 300 divided by 15, or 20, cookies in the bag. Thus, Quantity A is somewhere between 20 and 60, which means it could be less than, equal to, or greater than Quantity B. You have no idea which is the case, so pick **(D)**.

5. C

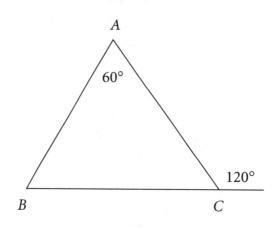

Here you have triangle *ABC*—base *BC* has been extended on one side and there is an exterior angle drawn in and labeled 120°. You want to compare side lengths *AB* and *BC*. In any triangle, the largest side will be opposite the largest angle, so you want to see which of these sides is opposite a larger angle. Angle *A* is labeled 60°, but is angle *C* less than, equal to, or greater than 60? Notice that the adjacent angle is 120°—the two together form a straight line, so their sum is 180°. And 180 − 120 = 60, so angle *C* is a 60° angle. Since the angles are equal, the sides are equal, and the answer is **(C)**.

6. A

Notice the way the diagram is set up: $a + b$ is the same as *PQ*. The equation is $8a + 8b = 24$. Divide both sides by 8. You end up with $a + b = 3$. *PQ* is 3 and because 3 is greater than 2, the answer is **(A)**. Note that you did not have to solve for *a* or *b* individually.

7. A

All you know is that *x* is less than *y*, but even though you don't know their values, you know enough to determine a relationship. In Quantity A, you have $y - x$, the larger number minus the smaller number, so you must get a positive difference, even if both numbers are negative. In Quantity B, you have the smaller number minus the larger number—this time the difference is negative. So you can determine a relationship—you know the answer is **(A)**, Quantity A is always greater than Quantity B.

8. C

The area of a triangle equals $\frac{1}{2} \times$ base $\times$ height. Triangles *ACE* and *ABD* have the same height, because they have the same apex point *A*. The problem states that their areas are equal, so they must have the same base, too. Thus, *EC* = *DB* and *ED* = *CB*. Since triangle *ABE* is equilateral, you also know that *AE* = *AB*. This means that sides *AD* and *AC* are equal as well. If they weren't, one of *ED* or *CB* would have to be longer than the other, and you already know they're equal. The answer is **(C)**.

9. D

If the radius of each circle is 3, then the diameter of each circle is 6. Then *PS* and *QR* = 6, and *PQ* and *SR* = 12. The perimeter of rectangle *PQRS* = 6 + 12 + 6 + 12 = 36. The answer is **(D)**.

10. D

In this question, you have a fraction as a base and must consider various values for *x*, the exponent. Consider what happens when $x = -1$. We know that $\left(\dfrac{1}{4}\right)^{-1} = \dfrac{1}{\left(\dfrac{1}{4}\right)^{1}} = 4.$

Putting that into the full equation, we get $1 - \left(\dfrac{1}{4}\right)^{x} = 1 - 4 = -3.$ This is not greater than zero, and if $x = -2$, the result will be even lower, so choices **(A)** and **(B)** are out. Next, consider what happens when $x = 0$. Any base to the zero power equals 1; then $1 - \left(\dfrac{1}{4}\right)^{x} = 1 - 1 = 0.$ You want the value of *x* that makes the expression greater than 0, so try $x = 1$: $1 - \left(\dfrac{1}{4}\right)^{x} = 1 - \left(\dfrac{1}{4}\right) = \dfrac{3}{4}.$ The answer is **(D)**.

11. B

Begin with cross multiplication and use algebra to isolate $\dfrac{q}{p}$:

$$\dfrac{p - q}{p} = \dfrac{2}{7}$$

$7(p - q) = 2p$	Cross multiply.
$7p - 7q = 2p$	Remove parentheses.
$5p = 7q$	Add *7q*; subtract *2p* on both sides.
$\dfrac{5}{7} = \dfrac{q}{p}$	Divide both sides by *7p*.

Choice **(B)** is correct.

12. 0.9

The shaded region is a right triangle. So, use the numbers on the grid to calculate the base and height of the triangle. The length horizontally is $(-2.0) - (-0.5) = -2.0 + 0.5 = -1.5$. Distances are always positive, so use 1.5 as the base of the triangle. The height of the triangle is $1.6 - 0.4 = 1.2$. Use the equation for the area of a triangle:

$$A = \frac{1}{2}bh = \frac{1}{2} \times 1.5 \times 1.2 = 0.9$$

The area is **0.9**.

13. D

The question asks for the number that is 850% greater than 8×10^3. First, determine the value of 8×10^3. That number is 8,000. To 8,000, you need to add 850% of 8,000. Here's what the math looks like:

$8{,}000 + (850\% \times 8{,}000) = 8{,}000 + (8.5 \times 8{,}000) = 8{,}000 + 68{,}000 = 76{,}000$

In scientific notation, this is 7.6×10^4, choice **(D)**.

14. B, C, E

List the factors for each number to check for all correct choices.

Number	Factors	Number of Factors
4	1, 2, 4	3
6	1, 2, 3, 6	4
8	1, 2, 4, 8	4
12	1, 2, 3, 4, 6, 12	6
14	1, 2, 7, 14	4

So the correct choices are **(B)**, **(C)**, and **(E)**.

15. 60

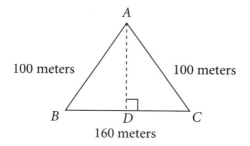

You're trying to find the shortest distance in meters a person would walk to go from point A to a point on side BC of the triangular field represented in the diagram. To get the shortest distance from point A to side BC, draw a perpendicular line from point A to side BC. Call the new vertex point D. Now two smaller right triangles, ADC and ADB have been created.

From the diagram, length BC is 160 meters, AB is 100 meters, and AC is 100 meters. Each of the two right triangles formed has 100 meters as the length of its hypotenuse.

What does that tell you about triangle *ABC*? *AB* and *AC* have the same length, so this is an isosceles triangle. That means that when you drew in the perpendicular distance from *A* down to *D*, you split the isosceles triangle *ABC* into two identical right triangles. Length *BD* is the same as length *CD*. So each of them is half of 160 meters, or 80 meters. Each right triangle has an hypotenuse of 100 meters and one leg of 80 meters. This is a 3:4:5 right triangle, with each member of the ratio multiplied by 20. So *AD* must have length **60**, and the minimum distance is 60 meters.

16. E

The average is $\dfrac{\text{The sum of terms}}{\text{The number of terms}}$. Here you have $y - z$ and the other number, which

you can call x. The average of x and $y - z$ is $3y$, so $3y = \dfrac{x + y - z}{2}$. Multiplying both

sides by 2 gives $6y = x + y - z$. Subtracting $y - z$ from both sides gives $5y + z = x$. So the other number, x, is $5y + z$, answer choice **(E)**.

17. B, D

Test each point. Substitute a value for x and compare the result to the given value for y in the ordered pair.

Let $x = -3$.

$$y = \frac{x^2}{x+1} = \frac{(-3)^2}{-3+1} = \frac{9}{-2} \neq -5$$

Let $x = -2$.

$$y = \frac{x^2}{x+1} = \frac{(-2)^2}{-2+1} = \frac{4}{-1} = -4$$

Let $x = -1$.

$$y = \frac{x^2}{x+1} = \frac{(-1)^2}{-1+1} = \frac{1}{0} \neq -3$$

Let $x = 1$.

$$y = \frac{x^2}{x+1} = \frac{1^2}{1+1} = \frac{1}{2}$$

Let $x = 3$.

$$y = \frac{x^2}{x+1} = \frac{3^2}{3+1} = \frac{9}{4} \neq 2\frac{1}{2}$$

So, the correct answers are **(B)** and **(D)**.

18. D

You're looking for the lowest ratio of males to females. In the double bar graph, the males outnumber females in each double bar, so you want the specialty in which the numbers of males and females are closest. Skimming the bar graphs, you can see that in pediatrics, the female graph and the male graph are closer than any of the others. **(D)** *pediatrics* is the correct answer.

19. B

How many male general surgery physicians were under 35 years old? The pie chart breaks down general surgery physicians by age, so work with that. And because you're looking for a number of general surgery physicians, you know that you're going to have to find the total number of general surgery physicians and then break it down according to the percentages on the pie chart.

The number of female general surgery physicians in the under-35 category represented 3.5% of all the general surgery physicians. What this does is break that slice of the pie for under-35 into two smaller slices, one for men under 35 and one for women under 35. Now the whole slice for under-35-year-olds is 30% of the total, and the question states that the number of females under 35 is 3.5% of the total. So the difference between 30% and 3.5% (26.5%) must be the men in the under-35 category.

From the top graph, estimate the total number of general surgery physicians as 37,000 (35,000 male plus 2,000 female). Multiply 37,000 by 26.5%: 0.265 × 37,000 = 9,805, which is very close to **(B)**, the correct answer.

20. E

The bar graph doesn't give the total number of general practice physicians, but if you add the number of males to the number of females, you get the total number of GP physicians. To find the percent who are male, take the number of males and put it over the total number. There are about 2,000 women and about 23,000 men, making the total about 25,000. Well, if there are around 25,000 GP physicians altogether and 2,000 of them are female, that's around 8%. About 92% are male, which is closest to 90%, **(E)**.

ANALYTICAL WRITING 1 ANALYZE AN ISSUE ANSWERS AND EXPLANATIONS

SAMPLE ESSAY RESPONSES

Issue Essay Sample Response: Score of 6

At face value, the belief that "one should look upon any information described as 'factual' with skepticism since it may well be proven false in the future," seems ludicrous almost to the point of threatening anarchy. Yet not only does this belief prove well justified, it is also the linchpin around which our complex, highly technical society creates and consolidates its advances.

Science itself provides the best evidence and examples in support of this statement. One need look no further than contemporary medicine to see how far we have come from the days when illness was perceived as a sign of moral weakness or as a punishment from on high. In fact, the most outstanding characteristic of what we call "the scientific method" amounts to endless questioning of received theory in search of a more comprehensive explanation of what we perceive to be true. This iterative style of inquiry (and re-inquiry) perpetuates an ongoing scientific dialogue that catalyzes further breakthroughs in the developed world.

Furthermore, advances made through constant questioning are not limited to the scientific arena: The skeptical attitudes of ancient Greek philosophers, as well as those of Renaissance mariners, 19th century suffragists, and 20th century civil rights activists, have left the world a richer and more hopeful place. By refusing to accept the world as explained by contemporary "fact," these doubters helped give birth to societies and cultures in which human potential and accomplishment have been enabled to an unprecedented degree.

In contrast, those societies that cultivate adherence to received belief and a traditional non-skeptical approach have advanced very little over the centuries. In Tibet, for instance, the prayer wheels spin endlessly around a belief system as secure and unquestioning as the Himalayas themselves. While there may very well be things worth learning from such a society, Tibet has proven to lack adaptability and expansiveness and prefers to turn inward, away from the modern world. Such introspection has given Tibet neither immunity nor an array of defenses in the face of contemporary medical, social, and political problems. Thus, cultural inflexibility regarding received wisdom and convention comes with a price.

To conclude, it seems clear from the above discussion that a healthy skepticism remains the hallmark of Western epistemology as we face the future. A close look at the statement reveals that it is not advocating the wholesale rejection of orthodox thinking, but rather that we be open to redefining our assumptions. As the basis of our resiliency and creativity, this attitude offers the most positive prognosis for a society that revels in the solution of conundrums that its own constant questioning brings continually into view.

ANALYTICAL WRITING 2 ANALYZE AN ARGUMENT ANSWERS AND EXPLANATIONS

Argument Essay Sample Response: Score of 6

In this memo, the owner of the Juniper Café; concludes that cutting hours is the "best strategy for us to save money and remain in business without having to eliminate jobs." While the café 's employees are undoubtedly grateful for the intent of the memo, they may see that its logic is flawed. First, the memo does not provide enough supporting evidence to prove that the money saved by cutting hours would exceed the money lost by losing early-morning and weekend clients. Second, the owner does not seem to evaluate other options that would either cut back on overhead or change the café 's operation to bring in more revenue.

First, the owner relies on an unproven assumption about the cause of the overhead. He concludes, without justifying, that being open too many hours is causing too much overhead expense. There may be other causes, however, such as waste in other areas of management. While it is true that reducing café hours would save money spent on utilities, employee wages, and other operating costs, there is no evidence that those savings would outweigh the café's loss of business. The owner's message fails to give details of operating costs, wages, and utilities saved if the café is closed for the hours suggested by the memo. Perhaps the highest utility expenses are actually incurred between noon and 3 p.m., when the sun is the hottest and the café's air conditioning and refrigeration are most in use. The owner needs to do more research, including the habits and demography of the town. For example, since the café is located in the downtown area, perhaps *increasing* the number of hours the café is open would be a better solution.

Yes, it would cost more in overhead, but doing so might, in fact, make much more money for the café. Say, for instance, the Juniper becomes the only restaurant open on Friday and Saturday date nights, after the football games and movies let out. Second, the owner of the Juniper Caféis not considering that the café serves a small American city. Cutting early-morning hours at a café, in a downtown area, where businesspeople and city workers most likely stop for coffee or breakfast on their way to work, seems very short-sighted and ill-informed. Are there one or more other cafés that will gladly steal business from 6 a.m. to 8 a.m. weekdays and that will perhaps win the permanent loyalty of those customers for lunch and dinner?

Furthermore, the owner does not seem to have evaluated other options to save the café. There are other places where overhead costs could potentially be cut. Certainly the owner would benefit from a brainstorming session with all employees, to get other ideas on the table. Maybe a new, lower-rent freezer storage facility is nearby. Maybe employees can suggest cutting waste in the purchasing department or dropping services the café doesn't need. It stands to reason that there is a plurality of ways to decrease overhead, aside from simply cutting hours.

In conclusion, the memo as it stands now does not logically prove that reduction in those particular hours will result in financial and future success for the café. There are several unstated assumptions upon which the argument turns, principally the assertion that simply being open for a certain number of hours is causing crippling overhead expenses. The owner's argument would profit enormously from further research, which may affect the hours he chooses to cut. Customer polling could show that few people eat or want coffee in that part of town between 2 p.m. and 5 p.m., and the café could be closed between lunch and dinner, adding flex hours or overlapping shifts for the staff. The memo lacks outlining what other restaurant services are available in the area and how or if they affect the 6 a.m. to 8 a.m. block and weekend hours. Once the marketing research and brainstorming is complete, the owner of the Juniper Café will make a better informed choice for his café's operating hours.

ANALYTICAL WRITING SCORING RUBRIC

6: "Outstanding" Essay
- Insightfully presents and convincingly supports an opinion on the issue or a critique of the argument
- Communicates ideas clearly and is generally well organized; connections are logical
- Demonstrates superior control of language: grammar, stylistic variety, and accepted conventions of writing; minor flaws may occur

5: "Strong" Essay
- Presents well-chosen examples and strongly supports an opinion on the issue or a critique of the argument
- Communicates ideas clearly and is generally well organized; connections are logical
- Demonstrates solid control of language: grammar, stylistic variety, and accepted conventions of writing; minor flaws may occur

4: "Adequate" Essay
- Presents and adequately supports an opinion on the issue or a critique of the argument
- Communicates ideas fairly clearly and is adequately organized; logical connections are satisfactory
- Demonstrates satisfactory control of language: grammar, stylistic variety, and accepted conventions of writing; some flaws may occur

3: "Limited" Essay
- Succeeds only partially in presenting and supporting an opinion on the issue or a critique of the argument
- Communicates ideas unclearly and is poorly organized
- Demonstrates less than satisfactory control of language: contains significant mistakes in grammar, usage, and sentence structure

2: "Weak" Essay
- Shows little success in presenting and supporting an opinion on the issue or a critique of the argument
- Struggles to communicate ideas; essay shows a lack of clarity and organization
- Meaning is impeded by many serious mistakes in grammar, usage, and sentence structure

1: **"Fundamentally Deficient" Essay**

- Fails to present a coherent opinion and/or evidence on the issue or a critique of the argument
- Fails to communicate ideas; essay is seriously unclear and disorganized
- Lacks meaning due to widespread and severe mistakes in grammar, usage, and sentence structure

0: **"Unscorable" Essay**

- Completely ignores topic
- Attempts to copy the assignments
- Written in a foreign language or contains undecipherable text

PART SIX

Test Day and Beyond

CHAPTER 22

Take Control of the Test

Now that you're familiar with the content that makes up each section of the GRE, and are armed with the strategies and techniques you'll need to tackle all of the question types, you're ready to turn your attention to building the right mentality and attitude that will help you succeed on Test Day. Let's first go over the basic principles of good test mentality.

KAPLAN'S FOUR BASIC PRINCIPLES OF GOOD TEST MENTALITY

You are already armed with the weapons that you need to do well on the GRE. But you must wield those weapons with the right frame of mind and in the right spirit. This involves taking a certain stance toward the entire test and bolstering your stamina, confidence, and attitude.

TEST AWARENESS

To do your best on the GRE, keep in mind that the test is different from other tests you've taken before, both in terms of its content and in terms of its scoring system. If you took a test in high school or college and got a quarter of the questions wrong, you probably received a mediocre grade. But this is not necessarily true with the GRE. The test is geared so that even the very best test takers don't necessarily get every question right.

What does this mean for you? Well, just as you shouldn't let one tough Reading Comprehension passage ruin an entire section, you shouldn't let what you consider to be a subpar performance on one section ruin your performance on the entire test. If you allow that subpar section to rattle you, it sets in motion a downward spiral that could do serious damage to your score. Losing a few extra points won't do you in, but losing your head will. Keeping your composure is an important test-taking skill.

Also, you should remember that if you feel you've done poorly on a section, it could very well be the experimental section. You'll have the opportunity immediately after you've taken the test to think about whether you want to cancel your score. You might underestimate your performance, since you're more likely to remember the questions you thought were more difficult. The major takeaway is to stay confident throughout the test.

STAMINA

Overall, the GRE is a grueling experience. Remember, you'll be completing six full-length sections on Test Day (one Analytical Writing, two Verbal Reasoning, two Quantitative Reasoning, and one Experimental or Research). It is a true test of endurance, and some test takers run out of gas on the final few sections.

To avoid this, you must build up your test-taking stamina by taking as many full-length practice tests as possible several weeks before the test. If you do this, by Test Day, completing this test won't seem like such a daunting task.

You can download a free copy of the POWERPREP II software, including two multi-stage practice tests, directly from **gre.org**.

Another option, if you haven't already done so, would be to take a Kaplan course, either classroom-based or online. You could also set up special one-on-one tutoring sessions with Kaplan faculty. If you decide to go this route, visit **kaptest.com/GRE** or call 1-800-KAP-TEST for information on a Kaplan classroom or tutoring program.

CONFIDENCE

Confidence is self-sustaining, and unfortunately, so is its opposite—self-doubt. Confidence in your ability leads to quick, sure answers and an ease of concentration that translates into more points. If you lack confidence, you might lose concentration and end up reading sentences and answer choices two, three, or four times. This leads to timing difficulties, which only continue the downward spiral, causing anxiety and a tendency to rush. If you subscribe to the test-prep mindset that we've described, however, you'll be ready and able to take control of the test. Learn our techniques and then practice them over and over again. That's the way to score your best on the test.

ATTITUDE

Those who fear the test or consider it an extra hurdle in the long race toward graduate school usually don't fare as well as those who see the GRE as an opportunity to show off the reading and reasoning skills that graduate schools are looking for. In fact, consider this: the test is designed to reward you. Those who look forward to the GRE as a challenge—or, at least, who enjoy the opportunity to distinguish themselves from the rest of the applicant pack—tend to score better than do those who resent it.

It may sound a little dubious, but take our word for it: altering your approach is proven to raise scores. Here are a few steps you can take to make sure you develop the right GRE attitude:

- Look at the GRE as a challenge, but try not to obsess over it; you certainly don't want to psych yourself out of the game.
- Remember that, yes, the GRE is obviously important, but contrary to what some people think, this one test will not single-handedly determine the outcome of your life. In many cases, it's not even the most important piece of your graduate application.
- Since the test is predictable, think of the GRE as a reward for understanding the same core skills that show up all the time.
- Remember that you're more prepared than most people. You've trained with Kaplan. You have the tools you need, plus the know-how to use those tools.

Kaplan's basic principles of good test mentality are as follows:

- Be aware of the test and keep your composure even when you are struggling with a difficult question; missing one question won't ruin your score for a section.
- Build your stamina by taking as many practice tests as you can.
- Be confident; you are already well on your way to a great score!
- Stay positive; consider the GRE an opportunity rather than an obstacle.

THE KAPLAN ADVANTAGE™ STRESS-MANAGEMENT SYSTEM

Is it starting to feel as if your whole life is a buildup to the GRE? You've known about it for years, worried about it for months, and now spent at least a few weeks in solid preparation for it. As the test gets closer, you may find that your anxiety is on the rise. You shouldn't worry. Armed with the preparation strategies that you've learned from this book, you're in good shape for Test Day. To calm any pre-test jitters that you may have, however, let's go over a few strategies for the couple of days before the test.

TIPS FOR THE DAYS JUST BEFORE THE EXAM

- The best test takers do less and less as the test approaches. Taper off your study schedule and take it easy on yourself. Give yourself time off, especially the evening before the exam. By that time, if you've studied well, everything you need to know is firmly stored in your memory bank. In fact, it's in your best interest to marshal your physical and psychological resources for the last 24 hours or so before the test. Keep the test out of your consciousness; go to a movie, take a pleasant walk, or just relax. Eat healthy meals and steer clear of sugar and caffeine. And, of course, get plenty of rest that night, and also the night before. It's hard to fall asleep earlier than you're used to, and you don't want to lie there worrying about the test.

- Most importantly, make sure you know where the test will be held and the easiest, quickest way to get there. You'll have great peace of mind by knowing that all the little details are set before Test Day.
- Visit the test site a few days in advance, particularly if you are especially anxious.

HANDLING STRESS DURING THE TEST

The biggest source of stress will be the test itself. Fear not! The following are methods to relieve your stress during the test:

- Keep moving forward instead of getting bogged down in a difficult question. You don't have to get everything right to achieve a solid score. So don't linger out of desperation on a question that is going nowhere even after you've spent considerable time on it.
- Breathe! Weak test takers tend to share one major trait: they don't breathe properly as the test proceeds. They might hold their breath without realizing it or breathe irregularly. Improper breathing hurts confidence and accuracy. Just as importantly, it interferes with clear thinking.

TEST DAY

The night before Test Day, gather the following things together:

- ID
- admission ticket
- a watch
- a bottle of water
- aspirin or other painkiller, in case you get a headache
- a snack, such as fruit or an energy bar, to keep your energy up for the later sections of the test
- names of schools you'd like to receive your scores

Test Day should start with a moderate, high-energy breakfast. Cereal, fruit, bagels, or eggs are good. Avoid doughnuts, pastries, or anything else with a lot of sugar. Also, unless you are utterly catatonic without it, it's a good idea to stay away from coffee.

Yes, perhaps you drink two cups every morning and don't even notice it. But it's different during the test. Coffee won't make you alert (your adrenaline will do that much more effectively); it will just give you the jitters. Kaplan has done experiments in which test takers go into one exam having drunk various amounts of coffee and another exam without having drunk coffee. The results indicate that even the most caffeine-addicted test takers will lose their focus midway through the second section if they've had coffee, but they report no alertness problems without it.

When you get to the test center, you will be seated at a computer station. Some administrative questions will be asked before the test begins and, once you're done with those, you're set to go. While you're taking the test, a small clock will count down the time you have left in each section. The computer will tell you when you're done with each section and when you've completed the test.

Here are some last-minute reminders to help guide your work on the test:

- Take a few minutes now to look back over your preparation and give yourself credit for all the work you put into it. Confidence is far more useful than distress.
- Give all answer choices a fair shot in Verbal Reasoning (especially Reading Comprehension), time permitting. For the Quantitative Reasoning section, go with the clearly correct answer as soon as you find it and forget the rest of the answer choices.
- Don't bother trying to figure out which section is the experimental section. It can't help you, and you might make a tragic mistake if you guess wrong. Instead, just do your best on every section.
- Dress in layers for maximum comfort. This way, you can adjust to the room's temperature accordingly.
- During the exam, try not to fixate on what your score is or how you're doing so far. It's counterproductive to continue to think about questions you've already answered or ones you haven't gotten to yet. If you worry about the next section, or the one you've just completed, you'll just feel overwhelmed. Instead, focus on the question-by-question task of picking the correct answer choice. Try to take things one step at a time. Concentrate on each question, each passage, and each essay prompt—on the mechanics, in other words—and you'll avoid cognitive confusion.

After all the hard work that you've put in preparing for and taking the GRE, make sure you take time to celebrate afterward. Plan to get together with friends the evening after the test. You prepared for the test ahead of time. You did your best. You're going to get a great score.

CHAPTER 23

Where and When to Apply

You probably know what you want to study as a graduate student, but where should you apply? The answer to this question is dependent on two main factors: which programs would be best for you, and which of these programs you can actually get into. This chapter will help you answer these questions—and many more you may have about the process of choosing a school for postgraduate study.

WHAT PROGRAMS YOU SHOULD CONSIDER

Once you have made the decision to pursue graduate studies, you should take the decision about where to go to school seriously—it will have a major influence on your daily life for the next several years and will influence your academic and career paths for years to come. Many students allow themselves to be influenced by a professor, a mentor, or school rankings and then find they're unhappy in a certain program because of its location, its workload, its cost, or some other unforeseen factor. If you complete your own research, even if it takes time and hard work, you will be happier with your own choice. Let's take a look at some of the factors you'll need to consider when choosing a school.

YOUR GOALS

Keep your goals in mind when evaluating graduate programs. Before you take the leap, it's important that you have a pretty clear idea where your interests lie, what grad school life is like, and whether you're compatible with a particular program and its professors. Armed with this information, you should be able to successfully apply to the right programs, get accepted, and use your time in graduate school to help you get a head start on the post-graduation job search.

Students decide to enter master's and doctoral degree programs for a variety of reasons. Some want to pursue a career in academia. To teach at two-year colleges, you'll need at least a master's degree; to teach and do research at four-year colleges, universities, and graduate programs, you'll need a doctorate. Other people need graduate education to meet national and state licensing requirements in fields such as social work, engineering, and architecture. Some students want to change careers, while others expect an advanced degree to open up new opportunities in their current field.

Most master's programs are two years long, and master's students are generally one of two types: those on an academic track, where the degree program focuses on classical research and scholarship, and those on a practical track, where the degree program is actually a professional training course that qualifies people to enter or advance in a field such as social work or education.

Other options to consider if you're pursuing a master's degree are cooperative, joint, and interdisciplinary programs. In cooperative programs, you apply to, answer to, and graduate from one school, but you have access to classes, professors, and facilities at one or more cooperating schools. In joint- or dual-degree programs, you work toward two degrees simultaneously, either within the same school or at two neighboring schools. Interdisciplinary programs are generally run by a committee consisting of faculty from a number of different departments. You apply to, register with, and are graduated by only one of the departments; you and your faculty committee design your curriculum.

Doctoral programs are designed to create scholars capable of independent research that will add new and significant knowledge to their fields. At first, you'll be regarded as an apprentice in your field. Your first year or two in the program will be spent on coursework, followed by "field" or "qualifying" exams. Once you have passed those exams, demonstrating that you have the basic factual and theoretical knowledge of your field down cold, you'll be permitted to move on to independent research in the form of your doctoral dissertation. During most of this time, you can get financial aid in the form of stipends through teaching or research.

If you want to get a doctoral degree, you can get a master's and then apply to PhD programs, or you may enter directly into the doctoral program. The first method gives you flexibility but generally takes longer, costs more in the long run, and means reliving the application process. However, some doctoral programs in certain fields of study require a full master's degree for acceptance.

PROGRAM REPUTATION

Although you should not place too much stock in school and program rankings, you should consider a program's overall reputation. When you assess a program's reputation, don't just consider its national ranking but think about whether it fits your goals and interests. You can get information from a variety of sources, formal and informal.

Each year, various groups publish rankings of graduate programs: *U.S. News and World Report* on American graduate programs, *Maclean's* on Canadian programs, and many others. These rankings can give you a general sense of the programs in your field and may include profiles of distinguished professors, but they tell you nothing about departmental politics, job placement records, or financial aid possibilities.

You should find out which programs are highly regarded in the areas that interest you. You can learn these details through professional associations (such as the American Psychological Association for programs in psychology fields), comprehensive commercial directories of graduate programs (available through school or local libraries), and the Internet.

Don't forget to contact schools and departments directly. Most departments have a chairperson who is also the admissions contact; she can put you in touch with current students and alumni who are willing to discuss the program with you. The chair is usually willing to answer questions as well.

Try to speak to at least one current student and one alumnus from each program you're seriously considering. You'll find that many graduate students are quite outspoken about the strengths and weaknesses of professors, programs, and the state of the job market in their field.

If you're an undergraduate, or still have contacts from your undergraduate experience, ask your professors for their take on the various graduate programs. You'll often find that they have a great deal of inside information on academic and research trends, impending retirements, intellectual rivalries, and rising stars.

Remember, a program's reputation isn't everything, but the higher your school is regarded in the marketplace, the better your job prospects are likely to be upon graduation.

LOCATION

Two key questions you should consider regarding a school's location are: How will it affect the overall quality of your graduate school experience, and how will it affect your ability to be employed once you are done with your studies? Some students prefer an urban setting. Others prefer a more rustic environment. Cost of living can also be a factor.

Geography may be an important criterion for you. Perhaps your geographical choices are limited by a spouse's job or other family obligations. Perhaps you already know where you want to live after graduation. If you're planning on a career in academia, you'll probably want to choose a nationally known program, regardless of where it's located. If, on the other hand, your program involves a practice component (physician's assistant, social work, education, or some interdisciplinary programs), you may want to concentrate your school search on the area in which you hope to live and work, at least initially.

CURRICULUM

To maximize the value of your graduate school experience, be sure that a department's areas of concentration match up with your own interests. Knowing a program's particular theoretical bent and practical selling points can help ensure that you choose a school that reflects your own needs and academic leanings. Does one school of thought or one style of research predominate? If so, is there anyone else working in the department with a different theoretical framework? Will you have opportunities to work within a variety of theories and orientations? What special opportunities are available? How well are research programs funded? Do the professors have good records at rounding up grants? In field or clinical work, what are the options? Are programs available in your area of interest?

Find the environment that works best for you. Don't put yourself in a situation in which you don't have access to the courses or training you're seeking. It's your education. Your time. Your energy. Your investment in your future. By being proactive, you can help guarantee that you maximize your graduate school experience.

FACULTY

One of the most important decisions you make in your graduate school career will be your choice of adviser. This one person will help you with course selection as well as clinical, research, or field education opportunities; he can make or break the thesis/dissertation process. So when you investigate a department, look for a faculty member whose interests and personality are compatible with yours. Since this single person (your "dream adviser") may not be available, be sure to look for a couple of other professors with whom you might be able to work.

If one of your prime motivations in attending a certain program is to take classes from specific professors, make sure you'll have that opportunity. At the master's level, access to prominent professors is often limited to large, foundation-level lecture courses, where papers and exams are graded by the professor's graduate assistants or tutors. At the doctoral level, professors are generally much more accessible.

Is the department stable or changing? Find out whether the faculty is nearing retirement age. Impending retirements may not affect you in a two-year master's program, but this is a serious consideration in doctoral programs, which can (and often do) stretch on for over five years. If you have hopes of working with a distinguished professor, will she even be available for that time—or longer, if you get delayed? Will the department be large and stable enough to allow you to put together a good thesis or dissertation committee? Also, try to find out whether younger members of the department are established. Do they get sufficient funding? Have they settled in to the institution enough that there are not likely to be political controversies?

PLACEMENT

Although some people attend graduate school for the love of knowledge, most want to enhance their career prospects in some way. When you graduate with your hard-won degree, what are your chances of getting your desired job?

You'll want to ask what kind of track record a given program has in placing its alumni. With a highly competitive job market, it's especially important to find out when and where graduates have found work. If you're considering work in business, industry, local agencies, schools, health care facilities, or the government, find out whether these employers visit the campus to recruit. Major industries may visit science programs to interview prospective graduates. Some will even employ graduate students over the summer or part-time. If you're going into academia, find out whether recent grads have been able to find academic posts, how long the search took, and where they're working. Are they getting tenure-track positions, or are they shifting from temporary appointment to temporary appointment with little hope of finding a stable position? Don't just look at the first jobs that a school's graduates take. Where are they in 5, 10, or even 25 years?

Your career is more like a marathon than a sprint. So take the long view. A strong indicator of a program's strength is the accomplishments of its alumni.

STUDENT BODY

Some graduate catalogs contain profiles of or statements by current master's and PhD students. Sometimes this is an informal blurb on a few students—it's really marketing material—and sometimes it's a full listing of graduate students. Use this as a resource both to find out what everyone else in the program is up to and to find current students you can interview about the school and the program.

Because much of your learning will come from your classmates, consider the makeup of your class. A school with a geographically, professionally, and ethnically diverse student body will expose you to far more viewpoints than will a school with a more homogeneous group. If you're an older applicant, ask yourself how you'll fit in with a predominantly younger group of students. For many, the fit is terrific, but for others, the transition can be tougher. The answer depends on you, but it's something to consider.

The student body, as well as the faculty, will have varied philosophical and political orientations. The theories and perspectives considered liberal in one program can be deemed conservative in another, and where you fit among your peers can have a lot of influence on your image and your opportunities. If you plan on an academic career, remember that your student colleagues will someday likely be your professional colleagues.

NETWORKING

Forging relationships—with your classmates, your professors, and, in a larger sense, all the alumni—is a big part of the graduate school experience. One of the things you'll take with you when you graduate, aside from an education, a diploma, and debt, is that network. And whether you thrive on networking or tend to shy away from it, it's a necessity. At some point it may help you advance your career, in academia or outside.

QUALITY OF LIFE

Your graduate school experience will extend far beyond your classroom learning, particularly for full-time students. That's why it's so important to find out as much as you can about the schools that interest you. For example, what activities would you like to participate in? Perhaps convenient recreational facilities or an intramural sports program is appealing. If you'd like to be involved in community activities, perhaps there's a school volunteer organization. Regardless of your interests, your ability to maintain balance in your life in the face of a rigorous academic challenge will help you keep a healthy outlook.

Housing is another quality-of-life issue to consider. Is campus housing available? Is off-campus housing convenient? Is it affordable? Where do most of the students live?

Quality of life is another important consideration for significant others, especially if your school choice requires a move to a new city. When graduate school takes over your life, your partner may feel left out. Find out what kind of groups and activities there are for families and partners. For example, are there any services to help your spouse find employment? Is child care available? What sort of public transportation is available?

FULL-TIME VERSUS PART-TIME

In a full-time program, you can focus your energy on your studies to maximize your learning. You're also likely to meet more people and forge closer relationships with your classmates. Many programs are oriented toward the full-time student, and many top-tier programs don't offer part-time options. A part-time schedule may also make it difficult for you to take classes with the best professors.

There are, however, many compelling reasons for attending part-time. It may not be economically feasible for you to attend full-time. Or you may wish to continue gaining professional experience while earning the degree that will allow you to move on to the next level. If there's a possibility that you'll have to work while you're in school, particularly while you're in the coursework stage, check out the flexibility of any program that interests you. Are there night or weekend classes? When is the library open? What about the lab? Talk to students currently in the program, especially those who work. Part-time programs often take a long time to complete, which can be discouraging, especially when licensure or salary increases are at stake. However, there are some programs, especially master's programs, that are specifically designed for part-time students (for example, many business school and physical therapy programs). In such programs, classes can be taken on weekends or specific nights of the week. It can be worth seeking out these sorts of options.

Although many students in full-time graduate programs support themselves with part-time work, their primary allegiance is to the graduate degree. Many students who must work during graduate school are employed by their schools. This is an option worth exploring. Since graduate studies tend to become the focus of your life, if you can manage full-time or nearly full-time studies at the higher levels, do it. You can graduate earlier and start picking up the financial pieces that much sooner—often with a more secure base for your job search in the form of good support from your adviser.

Most master's programs are flexible about part-time studies, but doctoral programs are less so. Many doctoral programs expect a minimum amount of time "in residence"—that is, enrolled as a full-time student for a certain number of consecutive semesters. This requirement is usually listed in the catalog.

PROGRAM COSTS

Some graduate programs charge per credit or per hour, meaning that your tuition bill is calculated by the number of credits you take each semester. Other programs charge per semester or per year with a minimum and maximum number of credits you can take per semester for that flat fee. In general, per credit tuition makes sense for part-time students, while per semester tuition makes sense for full-time students. Generally speaking, the most expensive kind of graduate program (per semester) will be a master's degree at a private school. Loans are available to master's-level students, but grants, scholarships, and other forms of "free" financial assistance are harder to find. Furthermore, most private schools apply the same tuition rate to in-state and out-of-state residents. State colleges and universities usually give in-state residents a tuition break. Other forms of savings can come from finding the cheapest living and housing expenses and from working your way through the program as quickly as possible.

At the doctoral level, tuition remission (you don't pay any of it) and grants or stipends (they pay you) are common. Percentages of doctoral students in a program receiving full tuition remission plus stipend/grant money can range anywhere from 0 percent to 100 percent—every student in the program pays no tuition and receives some grant or stipend. In these programs, the major financial burden will be your living expenses over the years of coursework, language requirements, qualifying and field exams, research, and the dissertation.

WHERE YOU CAN GET IN

Once you've developed a list of schools that meet your needs, take an objective look at your chances of getting into them.

A good way to get a sense of how graduate schools will perceive you is to make up a fact sheet with your GRE scores (or projected scores), your overall grade point average (GPA), your GPA in your major, and your work experience. Outside activities and your personal statement will contribute to the overall "score" that admissions officers will use to evaluate you, but let's stick with the raw data for now.

The next step is to find a current source of information about graduate school programs. There are several guides published every year that provide data about acceptance rates for given years, as well as median GPA and GRE scores. You can also request this information directly from a given department. The school of your dreams may not care very much about your GPA, but it might be very interested in your GRE scores. Make sure you find out what your target school prioritizes in its search for worthy applicants.

One of the best ways to gauge whether you're in contention for a certain program is to compare your numbers to theirs. And remember that you needn't hit the nail on the head. Median is similar to average, so some applicants do better or worse than the GRE scores or GPA cited. And remember all the other factors that add up to make you a desirable applicant. Comparing numbers is merely a good way to get a preliminary estimate of your compatibility with the schools of your choice.

"SAFETY" SCHOOLS

Once you have some idea of where you fall in the applicant pool, you can begin to make decisions about your application strategy. No matter what your circumstances, it's wise to choose at least one school that is likely to accept you, a "safety" school. Make sure it's one that fits your academic goals and your economic circumstances. If your GRE scores and GPA are well above a school's median scores and you don't anticipate any problems with other parts of your record or application, you've probably found your safety school.

"WISHFUL THINKING" SCHOOLS

If your ideal program is one that you don't seem qualified for, apply to your "dream school" anyway. You may be surprised! GPA and GRE scores aren't the only criteria by which applicants are judged, and you may discover that you're admitted in spite of your academic background on the merits of your personal statement, work samples, or other criteria. It's always worth a try. Some people underestimate their potential and apply only to safety schools. This can often lead to disappointment when they end up at one of these schools and discover that it doesn't provide the rigorous training they want.

WHEN TO APPLY

With the number of graduate school applications received by institutions of higher learning on the rise, the issue of when to apply for admission has become very important. There are perfect times to begin and end the application process. You should begin at least a year before you plan to enter school (sooner if you're a nontraditional candidate or are changing fields). Find out the following essential dates as early as possible and incorporate them into your own personal application schedule:

- standardized test registration deadlines
- transcript deadlines (some schools send out transcripts only on particular dates)
- letters-of-recommendation due dates
- application deadlines (submit your application as early as possible to ensure that you get a fair and comprehensive review)
- financial aid forms deadlines (federal/state programs, universities, and independent sources of aid all have definite deadlines)

SETTING UP AN APPLICATION SCHEDULE

We've organized the following "seasonal" schedule to help you understand how to proceed through the admissions process.

Winter (18–20 months prior to start date)

- If you're a nontraditional applicant or plan to switch fields, begin investigating program requirements. Take courses to make up any missing portion of your background.

Spring (16–18 months prior to start date)

- Browse through program catalogs and collect information on different grants and loans. Create your own graduate school library.

Summer

- Request applications from schools. If they're not available yet, ask for last year's so you can get a feel for the questions you'll have to answer.
- Write a draft of your personal statement and show it to trusted friends and/or colleagues for feedback.
- Consider registering for the GRE in the fall. This will give you plenty of time to submit your scores with your application.
- Research your options for test preparation. Take the test included in this book to give you a good idea of where you stand with regard to the GRE.

Early Fall

- Ask for recommendations. Make sure that your recommenders know enough about you to write a meaningful letter. Ask them first if they would be willing to write you recommendations and then ask how much lead time they would need.

Once your recommenders have agreed to write recommendations, make sure to give them clear deadlines so you can avoid any timing conflicts.

Late Fall

- Take the GRE.
- Request applications from schools, if you haven't already done so.
- Request institutional, state, and federal financial aid materials from school aid offices.
- Request information on independent grants and loans.
- Order transcripts from your undergraduate (and any graduate) institution(s).
- Follow up with your recommenders, sending a thank-you note to those who have sent their recommendations in already.

Winter

- Fill out applications. Mail them as early as possible.
- Fill out financial aid applications. Mail these early as well.
- Make sure your recommendation writers have the appropriate forms and directions for mailing. Remind them of deadline dates.

Spring

- Sit back and relax (if you can). Most schools indicate how long it will take to inform you of their decision. This is also a crucial time to solidify your financial plans as you begin to receive offers of aid (with any luck).

The timing described here is approximate, and you needn't follow it exactly. The most important thing for you to do is make yourself aware of strict deadlines well in advance so that you'll be able to devote plenty of quality time to your application. In the next chapter, we'll go over the application process in detail.

CHAPTER 24

How to Apply to Graduate School

You've taken the GRE and you've researched schools that offer programs you want. Your next step in the application process is to get the application forms from the various schools you've selected. Some schools will require you to complete an online application, some will have PDF downloads of the application documents, and yet others will require that you request applications that will then be sent to you. Once you get the applications, you'll notice one thing quickly: no two applications are exactly alike. Some ask you to write one essay or personal statement, and others ask for three or more essays on various subjects. Some have very detailed forms requiring extensive background information; others are satisfied with your name and address and little else.

Despite these differences, most applications follow a general pattern with variations on the same kinds of questions. So read this section with the understanding that, although not all of it is relevant to every application, these guidelines will be valuable for just about any graduate school application you'll encounter.

HOW SCHOOLS EVALUATE APPLICANTS

Each graduate school has its own admissions policies and practices, but all programs evaluate your application based on a range of objective and subjective criteria. Regardless of which schools you are pursuing, understanding how admissions officers judge your candidacy can give you a leg up on the competition.

Generally, all admissions officers use the application process to measure your intellectual abilities, aptitude in your field of study, and personal characteristics. When you submit your application, admissions officers will evaluate the total package. Most admissions officers look for reasons to admit candidates, not reject them. Your challenge, therefore, is to distinguish yourself positively from the other candidates.

INTELLECTUAL ABILITY

To assess your intellectual ability, admissions officers look at two key factors: your academic record and your GRE scores.

Academic Record

Your grade point average (GPA) is important, but it's just part of your academic profile. Admissions officers will consider the reputation of your undergraduate institution and the difficulty of your courses. Admissions officers are well aware that comparing GPAs from different schools and even different majors from the same school is like comparing apples and oranges. So they'll look closely at your transcript. Do your grades show an upward trend? How did you perform in your major? How did you fare in courses related to the program you're applying to?

Admissions officers focus primarily on your undergraduate performance, but they will consider all graduate studies and non-degree coursework that you have completed. Be sure to submit those transcripts. Generally, the undergraduate GPA of an applicant who is about to complete or has recently completed an undergraduate degree is given much more weight than that of an applicant returning to school after several years.

If you have a poor academic record, it will be tougher to get into a top school, but it is by no means impossible. Your challenge is to find other ways to demonstrate your intellectual horsepower. High GRE scores, an intelligently written personal statement, and strong recommendations will help.

The GRE

You are already familiar with the GRE and are armed with strategies to score higher on the test. An integral part of the admissions process at virtually all schools, the GRE measures general verbal, quantitative, and analytical writing skills. Some programs, particularly in psychology and the sciences, require you to take one or more GRE Subject Tests as well. In addition to or instead of the GRE, some programs require the Miller Analogies Test (MAT). Be sure to check with the programs you're considering to see which tests they require.

When admissions officers review your GRE scores, they'll look at your Verbal Reasoning, Quantitative Reasoning, and Analytical Writing scores separately, particularly if they have any questions about your abilities in a certain area. Different programs give varying weight to each score. If you've taken the GRE more than once, schools will generally credit you with your highest score for each section, though some may average the scores or take the most recent.

Used by itself, the GRE may not be a perfect predictor of academic performance, but it is the single best one available. The GRE does not measure your intelligence, nor does it measure the likelihood of your success in your field. The revised GRE has been designed to predict with more certainty your success in graduate school. As with any standardized test, by preparing properly for the GRE, you can boost your score significantly. The strategies you practice and learn will also help you decipher difficult academic text you may encounter in your future studies.

One thing to note is that your essays from the Analytical Writing section are now sent to the schools to which you send a score report. Previously, schools would only receive your score report. Schools will know that these are GRE essays, completed under time limits. Still, it makes the Analytical Writing section even more important to complete well.

Fellowships and Assistantships

Some graduate programs award fellowships and assistantships partly on the basis of GRE scores. Because most programs have limited funds and therefore limited positions to offer, the awards process can be quite competitive. Not only should you take your scores seriously, you should also confirm the submission deadline with your department. The financial aid deadline is usually earlier than the application deadline.

RELEVANT EXPERIENCE AND SKILLS

When evaluating your application, admissions officers look at work experience and other activities related to the program in question. In fields like psychology, social work, and health, your research and practical experience will play a role in the admissions decision. If you're applying to film, writing, or other arts programs, you'll be asked to submit samples of your work. And if you're planning on an academic career, your research and publications will be of particular interest to the admissions committee. The way you present yourself and your achievements should be tailored to the programs you're applying to.

You can communicate some of your abilities through the straightforward "data" part of your application. Be sure to describe your job and internship responsibilities. Be aware that your job title alone will not necessarily communicate enough about what you do or the level of your responsibilities. If you are asked to submit a résumé or CV, make sure you illustrate your experience and on-the-job training in a way that highlights skills you already have and those you think will serve you well in your future field of study.

If you are working and applying to a graduate program in the same field, admissions officers will look at your overall career record. How have you progressed? Have you been an outstanding performer? What do your recommendation writers say about your performance? Have you progressed to increasingly higher levels of responsibility? If you have limited work experience, you will not be expected to match the accomplishments of an applicant with 10 years' experience, but you will be expected to demonstrate your abilities.

Extracurricular activities and community involvement also present opportunities for you to highlight your skills. For younger applicants, college activities play a more significant role than for more seasoned applicants. Your activities say a lot about who you are and what's important to you. Were you a campus leader? Did your activities require discipline and commitment? Did you work with a team? What did you learn from your involvement?

Active community involvement provides a way for you to demonstrate your skills and to impress admissions officers with your personal character. In fact, many applications ask directly about community activities. Getting involved in your community is a chance to do something worthwhile and enhance your application in the process.

PERSONAL CHARACTERISTICS

The third, and most subjective, criterion on which schools evaluate you is your personal character. Admissions officers judge you in this area primarily through your personal statement (and essays, if applicable), recommendations, and personal interview (if applicable). Although different schools emphasize different qualities, most seek candidates who demonstrate maturity, integrity, responsibility, and a clear sense of how they fit into their chosen field. The more competitive programs place special emphasis on these criteria because they have many qualified applicants for each available spot in the class.

WHO EVALUATES APPLICANTS

At most schools, the admissions board includes professional admissions officers and/or faculty from the department to which you're applying. At some schools, the authority to make admissions decisions lies with the graduate school itself—that is, with the central administration. At others, it lies with individual departments.

WHAT DECISIONS DO THEY MAKE?

Upon reviewing your application, the admissions board may make any number of decisions, including the following:

- *Admit:* Congratulations, you're in! But read the letter carefully. The board may recommend or, in some cases, require you to do some preparatory coursework to ensure that your quantitative or language skills are up to speed.
- *Reject:* At the top schools, there are far more qualified applicants than spaces in the class. Even though you were rejected, you can reapply at a later date. However, if you are considering reapplying, you need to understand why you

were rejected and whether you have a reasonable chance of being admitted the next time around. Some schools will speak with you about your application, but they often wait until the end of the admissions season, by which time you may have accepted another offer.

- *Waiting list:* Schools use the waiting list to manage class size, leaving the applicant with a mixed message. The good news is that you are a strong enough candidate to have made the list. The bad news is there is no way to know with certainty whether you'll be accepted. Take heart, though, that schools do tend to look kindly upon wait-listed candidates who reapply in a subsequent year. Similar to the waiting list is the *provisional admit.* You may be asked to retake the GRE or resend another part of your application in order to gain admission to your desired school.

- *Request for an interview:* Schools at which an interview is not required may request that you interview prior to making their final decision. Your application may have raised some specific issues that you can address in an interview, or perhaps the board feels your personal statement did not give them a complete enough picture to render a decision. Look at this as a positive opportunity to strengthen your case.

PREPARING YOUR APPLICATION

A key part of getting into the graduate school of your choice is to develop a basic application strategy so you can present yourself in the best light.

YOUR APPLICATION AS A MARKETING TOOL

When it comes to applying to graduate school, you are the product. Your application is your marketing document. Of course, marketing yourself doesn't mean that you should lie or even embellish; it just means that you need to make a tight presentation of the facts. Everything in your application should add up to a coherent whole and underscore the fact that not only are you qualified to be in the program but you should be in it.

Many application forms have a comforting and accepting tone. *Why would you like to come to our program?* they ask. They do want an answer to that question, but what's even more important—the subtext for the whole application process—is the question: *Why should we accept you?* This is the question that your application will answer. And with some effective marketing strategies, your answer will be clear, concise, coherent, and strong.

MAXIMIZING THE VARIOUS PARTS OF YOUR APPLICATION

Let's take a close look at how you should approach the specific parts of your application.

PERSONAL STATEMENT

Your personal statement is a critical part of your application. The personal statement is where you can explain why you're applying to graduate school, what interests you about this program, and what your future goals are. The situations you choose to write about and the manner in which you present them can have a major bearing on the strength of your candidacy.

Writing an effective personal statement requires serious self-examination and sound strategic planning. What major personal and professional events have shaped you? What accomplishments best demonstrate your abilities? Remember, admissions officers are interested in getting to know you as a complete person. What you choose to write about sends clear signals about what's important to you and what your values are. You want the readers to put your essay down and think, "Wow! That was really interesting and memorable," and, "Wow! This person really knows why he's going into this program and has real contributions to make to the field."

Creating Your Statement

Your statement should demonstrate the patterns in your life that have led you to apply to the program. Part of demonstrating why you are right for the program involves demonstrating that you understand what the program is and where it will lead you. A personal statement requires honesty and distinctiveness. If you are heading to graduate school straight from undergraduate school, what has made you so certain that you know what you want to do with your life? If you are returning to school, particularly if you are changing fields, what has led you to this decision? You can use vignettes from your personal history, academic life, work life, and extracurricular activities to explain. If you are applying to a doctoral program, indicate which ideas, fields of research, or problems intrigue you. It's always a good idea to demonstrate familiarity with the field you want to enter.

You should start compiling information for your statement three or four months before you fill out your application. Write a draft once you've narrowed your list of potential topics. Have it edited by someone who knows you well. After rewriting, have someone whose opinion and writing skills you trust read your final draft, make suggestions, and, above all, help you proofread.

General Personal Statement Tips

Once you've determined what you plan to write for your statement, keep the following tips in mind:

- *Length:* Schools are pretty specific about how long they want your statement to be. Adhere to their guidelines.
- *Spelling/typos/grammar:* Remember, your application is your marketing document. What would you think of a product that's promoted with sloppy materials containing typos, spelling errors, and grammatical mistakes?
- *Write in the active voice:* Candidates who write well have an advantage in the application process because they can state their case in a concise, compelling manner. Sentences in the passive voice tend to be unnecessarily wordy. For example:

  > Passive voice: *The essays were written by me.*
  > Active voice: *I wrote the essays.*

  Strong writing will not compensate for a lack of substance, but poor writing can torpedo an otherwise impressive candidate.

- *Tone:* On the one hand, you want to tout your achievements and present yourself as a poised, self-confident applicant. On the other hand, arrogance and self-importance do not go over well with admissions officers. Before you submit your application, be sure that you're comfortable with the tone as well as the content.
- *Creative approaches:* If you choose to submit a humorous or creative application, you are employing a high-risk, high-reward strategy. If you're confident you can pull it off, go for it. Be aware, though, that what may work for one admissions officer may fall flat with another. Admissions officers who review thousands of essays every year may consider your approach gimmicky or simply find it distracting. Remember, your challenge is to stand out in the applicant pool in a positive way. Don't let your creativity obscure the substance of your application.
- *Answer the question asked:* Schools do not want to receive a personal statement or other essay that seems to have been written generically or perhaps even for another school.

Making Your Statement Distinctive

Depending on the amount of time you have and the amount of effort you're willing to put in, you can write a personal statement that will stand out from the crowd. One of the first mistakes that some applicants make is in thinking that "thorough" and "comprehensive" are sufficient qualities for their personal statement. They try to include as much information as possible, without regard for length limitations or strategic intent. Application readers dread reading these bloated personal statements. So how do you decide what to include? There are usually clear length guidelines, and admissions officers prefer that you adhere to them. So get rid of the idea of "comprehensive" and focus more on "distinctive."

Unless they ask for it, don't dwell on your weak points. A strong personal statement, for example, about how much you learned in your current position and how the experience and knowledge you've gained inspired you to apply to graduate school will give readers what they want—a quick image of who you are, how you got that way, and why you want to go to their school. One of the best ways to be distinctive is to sell your image briefly and accurately, including real-life examples to back up your points.

The admissions team wants to know about you, but there is the potential for including too much personal information. Beware of sharing reasons for applying that include furthering personal relationships, improving finances, or proving someone wrong.

"Distinctive" means that your statement should answer the questions that admissions officers think about while reading personal statements: What's different about this applicant? Why should we pick this applicant over others? Authentic enthusiasm can be a plus, and writing about parts of your life or career that are interesting and relevant helps grab a reader's attention.

The Interview

In some programs, an interview with the department is conducted at the applicant's discretion: if you want one, you're welcome to ask. In other programs, only the most promising applicants are invited to interview. Whether or not a department can pay your travel expenses depends on its financial circumstances. If you have the opportunity, definitely go to interview at your first-choice departments. There's no substitute for face-to-face contact with your potential colleagues, and by visiting the school, you can check out the city or town where it is located. You should investigate cost-of-living and transportation options during your visit.

As you prepare for an interview, here are some tips:

- *Review your application:* If you've submitted your application prior to the interview, your interviewer is likely to use it as a guide and may ask specific questions about it. Be sure you remember what you wrote.

- *Be ready to provide examples and specifics:* Professionally trained interviewers are more likely to ask you about specific situations than to ask broad, open-ended questions. They can learn more by asking what you've done in situations than by asking what you think you'd do. Here are a few situations an interviewer may ask you to discuss: "Tell me about a recent accomplishment." "Discuss a recent situation in which you demonstrated leadership." "Give me an example of a situation where you overcame difficult circumstances." As you think about these situations, be prepared to discuss specifics—what you did and why you did it that way. You do not need to "script" or overrehearse your responses, but you should go into the interview confident that you can field any question.

- *Be open and honest:* Don't struggle to think of "right" answers. The only right answers are those that are right for you. By responding openly and honestly, you'll find the interview less stressful, and you'll come across as a more genuine, attractive candidate.

- *Ask questions:* The interview is as much an opportunity for you to learn about the school as for the school to learn about you. Good questions demonstrate your knowledge about a particular program and your thoughtfulness about the entire process.

- *Follow proper professional decorum:* Be on time, dress appropriately, and follow up with thank-you letters. Treat the process as you would a job interview, which in many respects it is.

- *Watch your nonverbal cues:* Nonverbal communication is much more important than people realize. Maintain eye contact, keep good posture, sustain positive energy, and avoid nervous fidgeting. It will help you come across as confident, poised, and mature.

- *Be courteous to the administrative staff:* These people are colleagues of the board members, and how you treat them can have an impact, either positive or negative.

- *Relax and have fun:* Interviews are inherently stressful. But by being well prepared, you can enhance your prospects for admission, learn about the school, and enjoy yourself in the process.

RECOMMENDATIONS

Graduate schools will require at least three recommendations. Choose recommenders who can write meaningfully about your strengths. One of the more common mistakes is to sacrifice an insightful recommendation from someone who knows you well for a generic recommendation from a celebrity or a prominent professor. Admissions officers are not impressed by famous names. So unless that individual knows you and can write convincingly on your behalf, it's not a strategy worth pursuing. Good choices for recommenders include current and past supervisors, professors, academic and nonacademic advisers, and people you work with in community activities.

Many schools will specifically request an academic recommendation. Professors in your major are ideal recommenders, as they can vouch for your ability to study at the graduate level. If you don't have a professor who can recommend you, use a TA who knows your work well. Similarly, if requesting a recommendation from your employer would create an awkward situation, look for someone else who can comment on your skills. Your recommendations will confirm your strengths and, in some cases, help you overcome perceived weaknesses in your application.

If you wish to submit an extra recommendation, it's generally not a problem. Most schools will include the letter in your file, and those that don't will not penalize you for it. You should, however, send a note explaining why you have requested an additional recommendation so it does not appear that you disregarded the instructions. It's also a good idea to check with the admissions department before submitting an extra recommendation.

Asking for Recommendations

There are two fundamental rules of requesting recommendations: ask early and ask nicely. As soon as you decide to go to graduate school, you should start sizing up potential recommendation writers and let them know that you may ask them for a recommendation. This will give them plenty of time to think about what to say. Once they've agreed, let them know about deadlines well in advance to avoid potential scheduling conflicts. The more time they have, the better the job they'll do recommending you. As for asking nicely, you should let these people know you think highly of their opinion and you'd be happy and honored if they would consider writing you a letter of recommendation. You can help your recommenders by scheduling brief appointments with them to discuss your background; providing a list of due dates for each application; providing any forms required by the program; listing which recommendations will be submitted in hard copy and which will be submitted online; providing any forms required by the program; supplying stamped, addressed envelopes for hard-copy submissions; and following up with the recommenders.

BEFORE YOU SUBMIT YOUR APPLICATION

When you've completed your personal statement and you're ready to submit your application, take two more steps to ensure that your application is as strong as it can be.

1. Be sure to read your personal statement in the context of your entire application.
    a. Does the total package make sense? Does it represent you favorably? Is everything consistent?
    b. Have you demonstrated your intellectual ability, relevant experience and skills, and personal characteristics?
    c. Most importantly, do you feel good about the application? After all, you don't want to be rejected on the basis of an application that you don't believe represents the real you.

2. Have someone you trust and respect review your application. Someone who has not been involved in writing the application may pick up spelling or grammatical errors that you've overlooked. In addition, because your application is an intensely personal document that requires significant self-examination, you may not be able to remain objective. Someone who knows you and can be frank will tell you whether your application has "captured" you most favorably. Note, however, that some schools prohibit you from using any outside help on your application. A last-minute once-over from a friend or family member is probably within reason, but you may want to directly ask the school what is permissible.

PUTTING IT ALL TOGETHER

There are no magic formulas that automatically admit you to, or reject you from, the school of your choice. Rather, your application is like a jigsaw puzzle. Each component—GPA, GRE scores, professional experience, school activities, recommendations—is a different piece of the puzzle.

Outstanding professional experience and personal characteristics may enable you to overcome a mediocre academic record. Conversely, outstanding academic credentials will not ensure your admission to a top-tier program if you do not demonstrate strong relevant skills and experience, as well as solid personal character. Your challenge in preparing your application is to convince the admissions board that all of the pieces in your background fit together to form a substantial and unique puzzle.

CONGRATULATIONS!

You have all of the tools you need to put together a stand-out application package, including a top GRE score. Best of luck, and remember, your Kaplan training will be with you each step of the way.

A SPECIAL NOTE FOR INTERNATIONAL STUDENTS

About a quarter of a million international students pursue advanced academic degrees at the master's or PhD level at US universities each year. This trend of pursuing higher education in the United States, particularly at the graduate level, is expected to continue. Business, management, engineering, and the physical and life sciences are popular areas of study for students coming to the United States from other countries. Along with these academic options, international students are also taking advantage of opportunities for research grants, teaching assistantships, and practical training or work experience in US graduate departments.

If you are not from the United States but are considering attending a graduate program at a university in the United States, here is what you'll need to get started.

- If English is not your first language, you will probably need to take the Test of English as a Foreign Language (TOEFL) or show some other evidence that you're proficient in English prior to gaining admission to a graduate program. Graduate programs will vary on what is an acceptable TOEFL score. For degrees in business, journalism, management, or the humanities, a minimum TOEFL score of 100 (600 on the paper-based TOEFL) or better is expected. For the hard sciences and computer technology, a TOEFL score of 79 (550 on the paper-based TOEFL) is a common minimum requirement.

- You may also need to take the GRE. The strategies in this book are designed to help you maximize your score on the computer-based GRE. However, many sites outside the United States and Canada offer only the paper-based version of the GRE. Fortunately, most strategies can be applied to the paper-based version as well. For additional paper-based GRE strategies, see Chapter 2.

- Because admission to many graduate programs is quite competitive, you may want to select three or four programs you would like to attend and complete applications for each program.

- Selecting the correct graduate school is very different from selecting a suitable undergraduate institution. You should research the qualifications and interests of faculty members teaching and doing research in your chosen field. Look for professors who share your specialty.

- You need to begin the application process at least a year in advance. Be aware that many programs offer only August or September start dates. Find out application deadlines and plan accordingly.

- Finally, you will need to obtain an I-20 Certificate of Eligibility in order to obtain an F-1 student visa to study in the United States.

KAPLAN ENGLISH INTERNATIONAL CENTERS

If you need more help with the complex process of graduate school admissions, assistance preparing for the TOEFL or GRE, or help building your English language skills in general, you may be interested in Kaplan's English language and test preparation for international students, available at Kaplan's International Centers/Colleges around the world.

Kaplan's English courses have been designed to help students and professionals from outside the United States meet their educational and career goals. At locations throughout the United States, international students take advantage of Kaplan's programs to help them improve their academic and conversational English skills; to raise their scores on the TOEFL, GRE, and other standardized exams; and to gain admission to the schools of their choice. Our staff and instructors give international students the individualized instruction they need to succeed. Here is a brief description of some of Kaplan's programs for international students.

General Intensive English

Kaplan's General Intensive English course is the fastest and most effective way for students to improve their English. This full-time program integrates the four key elements of language learning—listening, speaking, reading, and writing. The challenging curriculum and intensive schedule are designed for both the general language learner and the academically bound student.

TOEFL and Academic English (TAE)

Our world-famous TOEFL course prepares you for the TOEFL and teaches you the academic language and skills needed to succeed in a university. Designed for high-intermediate to proficiency-level English speakers, our course includes TOEFL-focused reading, writing, listening, speaking, vocabulary, and grammar instruction.

General English

Our General English course is a semi-intensive program designed for students who want to improve their listening and speaking skills without the time commitment of an intensive program. With morning or afternoon class times and flexible Structured Study hours throughout the week, our General English course is perfect for every schedule.

GRE FOR INTERNATIONAL STUDENTS

The GRE is required for admission to many graduate programs in the United States. Nearly a half-million people take the GRE each year. A high score can help you stand out from other test takers. This course, designed especially for nonnative English speakers, includes the skills you need to succeed on each section of the GRE, as well as access to Kaplan's exclusive computer-based practice materials and extra Verbal practice.

OTHER KAPLAN PROGRAMS

Since 1938, more than three million students have come to Kaplan to advance their studies, prepare for entry to American universities, and further their careers. In addition to the above programs, Kaplan offers courses to prepare for the SAT, GMAT, LSAT, MCAT, DAT, OAT, PCAT, USMLE, NCLEX, and other standardized exams at locations throughout the United States.

APPLYING TO KAPLAN ENGLISH PROGRAMS

To get more information, or to apply for admission to any of Kaplan's programs for international students and professionals, please visit our website at **kaplaninternational.com.**

PART SEVEN

GRE Resources

Kaplan's Word Groups

The following lists contain a lot of common GRE words grouped together by meaning. Make flashcards from these lists and look over your cards a few times a week from now until the day of the test. Look over the word group lists once or twice a week every week until the test. If you don't have much time until the exam date, look over your lists more frequently. Then, by the day of the test, you should have a rough idea of what most of the words on your lists mean.

Note: Words in each group are various parts of speech and not necessarily synonyms of one another. The categories in which these words are listed are *general* and should *not* be interpreted as the exact definitions of the words.

A

Abbreviated Communication

abridge
compendium
cursory
curtail
syllabus
synopsis
terse

Act Quickly

abrupt
apace
headlong
impetuous
precipitate

Assist

abet
advocate
ancillary
bolster
corroborate
countenance
espouse
mainstay
munificent
proponent
stalwart
sustenance

B

Bad Mood

bilious
dudgeon
irascible

pettish
petulant
pique
querulous
umbrage
waspish

Beginner/Amateur

dilettante
fledgling
neophyte
novitiate
proselyte
tyro

Beginning/Young

burgeoning
callow
engender
inchoate

incipient
nascent

Biting (as in wit or temperament)

acerbic
acidulous
acrimonious
asperity
caustic
mordacious
mordant
trenchant

Bold

audacious
courageous
dauntless
intrepid

Boring

banal
fatuous
hackneyed
insipid
mundane
pedestrian
platitude
prosaic
quotidian
trite

C

Carousal

bacchanalian
debauchery
depraved
dissipated
iniquity
libertine
libidinous
licentious
reprobate
ribald
salacious
sordid
turpitude

Changing Quickly

capricious
mercurial
volatile

Copy

counterpart
emulate
facsimile
factitious
paradigm
precursor
quintessence
simulate
vicarious

Criticize/Criticism

aspersion
belittle
berate
calumny
castigate
decry
defame/defamation

denounce
deride/derisive
diatribe
disparage
excoriate
gainsay
harangue
impugn
inveigh
lambaste
objurgate
obloquy
opprobrium
pillory
rebuke
remonstrate
reprehend
reprove
revile
tirade
vituperate

D

Death/Mourning

bereave
cadaver
defunct
demise
dolorous
elegy
knell
lament
macabre
moribund
obsequies
sepulchral
wraith

Denying of Self

abnegate
abstain
ascetic
spartan
stoic
temperate

Dictatorial

authoritarian
despotic
dogmatic
hegemonic/
  hegemony
imperious

peremptory
tyrannical

Difficult to Understand

abstruse
ambiguous
arcane
bemusing
cryptic
enigmatic
esoteric
inscrutable
obscure
opaque
paradoxical
perplexing
recondite
turbid

Disgusting/Offensive

defile
fetid
invidious
noisome
odious
putrid
rebarbative
malodorous

E

Easy to Understand

articulate
cogent
eloquent
evident
limpid
lucid
pellucid

Eccentric/Dissimilar

aberrant
anachronism
anomalous
discrete
eclectic
esoteric
iconoclast

Embarrass

abash
chagrin
compunction

contrition
diffidence
expiate
foible
gaucherie
rue

Equal

equitable
equity
tantamount

F

Falsehood

apocryphal
canard
chicanery
dissemble
duplicity
equivocate
erroneous
ersatz
fallacious
feigned
guile
mendacious/
  mendacity
perfidy
prevaricate
specious
spurious

Family

conjugal
consanguine
distaff
endogamous
filial
fratricide
progenitor
scion

Favoring/Not Impartial

ardent/ardor
doctrinaire
fervid
partisan
tendentious
zealot

Forgive/Make Amends

- absolve
- acquit
- ameliorate
- exculpate
- exonerate
- expiate
- palliate
- redress
- vindicate

Funny

- chortle
- droll
- facetious
- flippant
- gibe
- jocular
- levity
- ludicrous
- raillery
- riposte

G

Gaps/Openings

- abatement
- aperture
- fissure
- hiatus
- interregnum
- interstice
- lull
- orifice
- rent
- respite
- rift

Generous/Kind

- altruistic
- beneficent
- clement
- largess
- magnanimous
- munificent
- philanthropic
- unstinting

Greedy

- avaricious
- covetous
- mercenary
- miserly
- penurious
- rapacious
- venal

H

Hard-Hearted

- asperity
- baleful
- dour
- fell
- malevolent
- mordant
- sardonic
- scathing
- truculent
- vitriolic
- vituperation

Harmful

- baleful
- baneful
- deleterious
- inimical
- injurious
- insidious
- minatory
- perfidious
- pernicious

Harsh-Sounding

- cacophony
- din
- dissonant
- raucous
- strident

Hatred

- abhorrence
- anathema
- antagonism
- antipathy
- detestation
- enmity
- loathing
- malice
- odium
- rancor

Healthy

- beneficial
- salubrious
- salutary

Hesitate

- dither
- oscillate
- teeter
- vacillate
- waver

Hostile

- antithetic
- churlish
- curmudgeon
- irascible
- malevolent
- misanthropic
- truculent
- vindictive

I

Innocent/Inexperienced

- credulous
- gullible
- ingenuous
- naive
- novitiate
- tyro

Insincere

- disingenuous
- dissemble
- fulsome
- ostensible
- unctuous

Investigate

- appraise
- ascertain
- assay
- descry
- peruse

L

Lazy/Sluggish

- indolent
- inert
- lackadaisical
- languid
- lassitude
- lethargic
- phlegmatic
- quiescent
- slothful
- torpid

Luck

- adventitious
- amulet
- auspicious
- fortuitous
- kismet
- portentous
- propitiate
- propitious
- providential
- serendipity
- talisman

N

Nag

- admonish
- belabor
- cavil
- enjoin
- exhort
- harangue
- hector
- martinet
- remonstrate
- reproof

Nasty

- fetid
- noisome
- noxious

Not a Straight Line

- askance
- awry
- careen
- carom
- circuitous
- circumvent
- gyrate
- labyrinth
- meander
- oblique
- serrated
- sidle
- sinuous
- undulating
- vortex

O

Overblown/Wordy

bombastic
circumlocution
garrulous
grandiloquent
loquacious
periphrastic
prolix
rhetoric
turgid
verbose

P

Pacify/Satisfy

ameliorate
appease
assuage
defer
mitigate
mollify
placate
propitiate
satiate
slake
soothe

Pleasant-Sounding

euphonious
harmonious
melodious
sonorous

Poor

destitute
impecunious
indigent

Praise

acclaim
accolade
aggrandize
encomium
eulogize
extol
fawn
laud/laudatory
venerate/
  veneration

Predict

augur
auspice
fey
harbinger
portentous
presage
prescient
prognosticate

Prevent/Obstruct

discomfit
encumber
fetter
forfend
hinder
impede
inhibit
occlude
thwart

S

Smart/Learned

astute
canny
erudite
perspicacious

Sorrow

disconsolate
doleful
dolor
elegiac
forlorn
lament
lugubrious
melancholy
morose
plaintive
threnody

Stubborn

implacable
inexorable
intractable
intransigent
obdurate
obstinate
recalcitrant
refractory
renitent
untoward
vexing

T

Terse

compendious
curt
laconic
pithy
succinct
taciturn

Time/Order/Duration

anachronism
antecede
antedate
anterior
archaic
diurnal
eon
ephemeral
epoch
fortnight
millennium
penultimate
synchronous
temporal

Timid/Timidity

craven
diffident
pusillanimous
recreant
timorous
trepidation

Truth

candor/candid
fealty
frankness
indisputable
indubitable
legitimate
probity
sincere
veracious
verity

U

Unusual

aberration
anomaly
iconoclast
idiosyncrasy

W

Wandering

ambulatory
discursive
expatiate
forage
itinerant
meander
peregrination
peripatetic
sojourn

Weaken

adulterate
enervate
exacerbate
inhibit
obviate
stultify
undermine
vitiate

Wisdom

adage
aphorism
apothegm
axiom
bromide
dictum
epigram
platitude
sententious
truism

Withdrawal/Retreat

abeyance
abjure
abnegation
abortive
abrogate
decamp
demur
recant
recidivism
remission
renege
rescind
retrograde

Kaplan's Root List

While it is impossible to predict exactly which words will show up on your test, the testmakers favor certain words. The following Root List gives you the component parts of many of these typical GRE words, and knowing roots can help you in a couple of key ways. First, instead of learning one word at a time, you can learn a whole group of words that contain a certain root. They'll be related in meaning, so if you remember one, it will be easier for you to remember others. Second, roots can often help you decode an unknown GRE word. If you recognize a familiar root, you could get a good enough grasp of the word to answer the question.

This list is written with the GRE in mind and is not an exhaustive guide. Roots are given in their most common forms, with their most common or broadest definitions; often, other forms and meanings exist. Similarly, the definitions for the words given as examples may be incomplete, and other senses of those words may exist. Get into the habit of looking up unfamiliar words in a good, current dictionary—whether on paper or on the Internet—and be sure to check their etymologies while you're there.

A

A/AN: not, without

agnostic: one who believes the existence of God is not provable

amoral: neither moral nor immoral; having no relation to morality

anomaly: an irregularity

anonymous: of unknown authorship or origin

apathy: lack of interest or emotion

atheist: one who does not believe in God

atrophy: the wasting away of body tissue

atypical: not typical

AB: off, away from, apart, down

abdicate: to renounce or relinquish a throne

abduct: to take away by force

abhor: to hate, detest

abject: cast down; degraded

abnormal: deviating from a standard

abolish: to do away with, make void

abstinence: forbearance from any indulgence of appetite

abstract: conceived apart from concrete realities, specific objects, or actual instances

abstruse: hard to understand; secret, hidden

ABLE/IBLE: capable of, worthy of

changeable: able to be changed

combustible: capable of being burned; easily inflamed

inevitable: impossible to be avoided; certain to happen

presentable: suitable for being presented

AC/ACR: sharp, bitter, sour

acerbic: sour or astringent in taste; harsh in temper

acid: something that is sharp, sour, or ill-natured

acrimonious: caustic, stinging, or bitter in nature

acumen: mental sharpness; quickness of wit

acute: sharp at the end; ending in a point

exacerbate: to increase bitterness or violence; aggravate

ACT/AG: to do, to drive, to force, to lead

agile: quick and well coordinated in movement; active, lively

agitate: to move or force into violent, irregular action

litigate: to make the subject of a lawsuit

pedagogue: a teacher

prodigal: wastefully or recklessly extravagant

synagogue: a gathering or congregation of Jews for the purpose of religious worship

ACOU: hearing

acoustic: pertaining to hearing; sound made through mechanical, not electronic, means

AD: to, toward, near

(Often the *d* is dropped and the first letter to which *a* is prefixed is doubled.)

accede: to yield to a demand; to enter office

adapt: to adjust or modify fittingly

addict: to give oneself over, as to a habit or pursuit

address: to direct a speech or written statement to

adhere: to stick fast; cleave; cling

adjacent: near, close, or contiguous; adjoining

adjoin: to be close or in contact with

admire: to regard with wonder, pleasure, and approval

advocate: to plead in favor of

attract: to draw either by physical force or by an appeal to emotions or senses

AL/ALI/ALTER: other, another

alias: an assumed name; another name

alibi: the defense by an accused person that he was verifiably elsewhere at the time of the crime with which he is charged

alien: one born in another country; a foreigner

allegory: the figurative treatment of one subject under the guise of another

alter ego: the second self; a substitute or deputy

alternative: a possible choice

altruist: a person unselfishly concerned for the welfare of others

AM: love

amateur: a person who engages in an activity for pleasure rather than financial or professional gain

amatory: of or pertaining to lovers or lovemaking

amiable: having or showing agreeable personal qualities

amicable: characterized by exhibiting good will

amity: friendship; peaceful harmony

amorous: inclined to love, esp. sexual love

enamored: inflamed with love; charmed; captivated

inamorata: a female lover

AMBI/AMPHI: both, on both sides, around

ambidextrous: able to use both hands equally well

ambient: moving around freely; circulating

ambiguous: open to various interpretations

amphibian: any cold-blooded vertebrate, the larva of which is aquatic and the adult of which is terrestrial; a person or thing having a twofold nature

AMBL/AMBUL: to go, to walk

ambulance: a vehicle equipped for carrying sick people (from a phrase meaning "walking hospital")

ambulatory: of, pertaining to, or capable of walking

perambulator: one who makes a tour of inspection on foot

preamble: an introductory statement (originally: to walk in front)

ANIM: of the life, mind, soul, breath

animal: a living being

animosity: a feeling of ill will or enmity

equanimity: mental or emotional stability, especially under tension

magnanimous: generous in forgiving an insult or injury

unanimous: of one mind; in complete accord

ANNUI/ENNI: year

annals: a record of events, esp. a yearly record

anniversary: the yearly recurrence of the date of a past event

annual: of, for, or pertaining to a year; yearly

annuity: a specified income payable at stated intervals

perennial: lasting for an indefinite amount of time

ANT/ANTE: before

antebellum: before the war (especially the American Civil War)

antecedent: existing, being, or going before

antedate: precede in time

antediluvian: belonging to the period before the biblical flood; very old or old-fashioned

anterior: placed before

ANTHRO/ANDR: man, human

androgen: any substance that promotes masculine characteristics

androgynous: being both male and female

android: robot; mechanical man

anthropocentric: regarding humanity as the central fact of the universe

anthropology: the science that deals with the origins of humankind

misanthrope: one who hates humans or humanity

philanderer: one who carries on flirtations

ANTI: against, opposite

antibody: a protein naturally existing in blood serum that reacts to overcome the toxic effects of an antigen

antidote: a remedy for counteracting the effects of poison, disease, etc.

antipathy: aversion

antipodal: on the opposite side of the globe

antiseptic: free from germs; particularly clean or neat

APO: away

apocalypse: revelation; discovery; disclosure

apocryphal: of doubtful authorship or authenticity

apogee: the highest or most distant point

apology: an expression of one's regret or sorrow for having wronged another

apostasy: a total desertion of one's religion, principles, party, cause, etc.

apostle: one of the 12 disciples sent forth by Jesus to preach the Gospel

AQUA/AQUE: water

aquamarine: a bluish-green color

aquarium: a tank for keeping fish and other underwater creatures

aquatic: having to do with water

aqueduct: a channel for transporting water

subaqueous: underwater

ARCH/ARCHI/ARCHY: chief, principal, ruler

anarchy: a state or society without government or law

archenemy: chief enemy

architect: the devisor, maker, or planner of anything

monarchy: a government in which the supreme power is lodged in a sovereign

oligarchy: a state or society ruled by a select group

ARD: to burn
ardent: burning; fierce; passionate
ardor: flame; passion
arson: the crime of setting property on fire

AUTO: self
autocrat: an absolute ruler
automatic: self-moving or self-acting
autonomy: independence or freedom

B

BE: about, to make, to surround, to affect (often used to transform words into transitive verbs)
belie: to misrepresent; to contradict
belittle: to make small; to make something appear smaller
bemoan: to moan for; to lament
bewilder: to confuse completely (that is, to make one mentally wander)

BEL/BELL: beautiful
belle: a beautiful woman
embellish: to make beautiful; to ornament

BELL: war
antebellum: before the war (especially the American Civil War)
belligerent: warlike, given to waging war
rebel: a person who resists authority, control, or tradition

BEN/BENE: good
benediction: act of uttering a blessing
benefit: anything advantageous to a person or thing
benevolent: desiring to do good to others
benign: having a kindly disposition

BI/BIN: two
biennial: happening every two years
bilateral: pertaining to or affecting two or both sides
bilingual: able to speak one's native language and another with equal facility
binocular: involving two eyes
bipartisan: representing two parties
combination: the joining of two or more things into a whole

BON/BOUN: good, generous
bona fide: in good faith; without fraud
bonus: something given over and above what is due
bountiful: generous

BREV/BRID: short, small
abbreviate: to shorten
abridge: to shorten
brevet: an honorary promotion with no additional pay
breviloquent: laconic; concise in one's speech
brevity: shortness
brief: short

BURS: purse, money
bursar: treasurer
bursary: treasury
disburse: to pay
reimburse: to pay back

C

CAD/CID: to fall, to happen by chance
accident: happening by chance; unexpected
cascade: a waterfall descending over a steep surface
coincidence: a striking occurrence of two or more events at one time, apparently by chance
decadent: decaying; deteriorating
recidivist: one who repeatedly relapses, as into crime

CANT/CENT/CHANT: to sing
accent: prominence of a syllable in terms of pronunciation
chant: a song; singing
enchant: to subject to magical influence; to bewitch
incantation: the chanting of words purporting to have magical power
incentive: that which incites action
recant: to withdraw or disavow a statement

CAP/CAPIT/CIPIT: head, headlong
capital: the city or town that is the official seat of government
capitulate: to surrender unconditionally or on stipulated terms
caption: a heading or title

disciple: one who is a pupil of the doctrines of another

precipice: a cliff with a vertical face

precipitate: to hasten the occurrence of; to bring about prematurely

CAP/CIP/CEPT: to take, to get

anticipate: to realize beforehand; foretaste or foresee

capture: to take by force or stratagem

emancipate: to free from restraint

percipient: having perception; discerning; discriminating

precept: a commandment or direction given as a rule of conduct

susceptible: capable of receiving, admitting, undergoing, or being affected by something

CARD/CORD/COUR: heart

cardiac: pertaining to the heart

concord: agreement; peace, amity

concordance: agreement, concord, harmony

discord: lack of harmony between persons or things

encourage: to inspire with spirit or confidence

CARN: flesh

carnage: the slaughter of a great number of people

carnival: a traveling amusement show

carnivorous: eating flesh

incarnation: a being invested with a bodily form

reincarnation: rebirth of a soul in a new body

CAST/CHAST: to cut

cast: to throw or hurl; fling

caste: a hereditary social group, limited to people of the same rank

castigate: to punish in order to correct

chaste: free from obscenity; decent

chastise: to discipline, esp. by corporal punishment

CAUS/CAUT: to burn

caustic: burning or corrosive

cauterize: to burn or deaden

cautery: an instrument used for branding; branding

holocaust: a burnt offering; complete destruction by fire or other means

CED/CEED/CESS: to go, to yield, to stop

accede: to yield to a demand; to enter office

antecedent: existing, being, or going before

cessation: a temporary or complete discontinuance

concede: to acknowledge as true, just, or proper; admit

incessant: without stop

predecessor: one who comes before another in an office, position, etc.

CELER: speed

accelerant: something used to speed up a process

accelerate: to increase in speed

celerity: speed; quickness

decelerate: to decrease in speed

CENT: hundred, hundredth

bicentennial: two-hundredth anniversary

cent: a hundredth of a dollar

centigrade: a temperature system with one hundred degrees between the freezing and boiling points of water

centimeter: one hundredth of a meter

centipede: a creature with many legs

century: one hundred years

percent: in every hundred

CENTR: center

centrifuge: an apparatus that rotates at high speed and separates substances of different densities using centrifugal force (that is, force flying off from the center)

centrist: of or pertaining to moderate political or social ideas

concentrate: to bring to a common center; to converge, to direct toward one point

concentric: having a common center, as in circles or spheres

eccentric: off-center

CERN/CERT/CRET/CRIM/CRIT: to separate, to judge, to distinguish, to decide

ascertain: to make sure of; to determine

certitude: freedom from doubt

criterion: a standard of judgment or criticism

discreet: judicious in one's conduct of speech, esp. with regard to maintaining silence about something of a delicate nature

discrete: detached from others, separate

hypocrite: a person who pretends to have beliefs that she does not

CHROM: color

chromatic: having to do with color

chrome: a metallic element (chromium) used to make vivid colors, or something plated with chromium

chromosome: genetic material that can be studied by coloring it with dyes

monochromatic: having only one color

CHRON: time

anachronism: something that is out-of-date or belonging to the wrong time

chronic: constant, habitual

chronology: the sequential order in which past events occurred

chronometer: a highly accurate clock or watch

synchronize: to occur at the same time or agree in time

CIRCU/CIRCUM: around

circuit: a line around an area; a racecourse; the path traveled by electrical current

circuitous: roundabout, indirect

circumference: the outer boundary of a circular area

circumspect: cautious; watching all sides

circumstances: the existing conditions or state of affairs surrounding and affecting an agent

CIS: to cut

exorcise: to seek to expel an evil spirit by ceremony

incision: a cut, gash, or notch

incisive: penetrating, cutting

precise: definitely stated or defined

scissors: a cutting instrument for paper

CLA/CLO/CLU: to shut, to close

claustrophobia: an abnormal fear of enclosed places

cloister: a courtyard bordered with covered walks, esp. in a religious institution

conclude: to bring to an end; finish; to terminate

disclose: to make known, reveal, or uncover

exclusive: not admitting of something else; shutting out others

preclude: to prevent the presence, existence, or occurrence of

CLAIM/CLAM: to shout, to cry out

clamor: a loud uproar

disclaim: to deny interest in or connection with

exclaim: to cry out or speak suddenly and vehemently

proclaim: to announce or declare in an official way

reclaim: to claim or demand the return of a right or possession

CLI: to lean toward

climax: the most intense point in the development of something

decline: to cause to slope or incline downward

disinclination: aversion, distaste

proclivity: inclination, bias

recline: to lean back

CO/COL/COM/CON: with, together

coerce: to compel by force, intimidation, or authority

collaborate: to work with another, cooperate

collide: to strike one another with a forceful impact

commensurate: suitable in measure, proportionate

compatible: capable of existing together in harmony

conciliate: to placate, win over

connect: to bind or fasten together

COGN/CONN: to know

cognition: the process of knowing

incognito: with one's name or identity concealed

recognize: to identify as already known

CONTRA/CONTRO/COUNTER: against

contradict: to oppose; to speak against

contrary: opposed to; opposite

controversy: a disputation; a quarrel

counterfeit: fake; a false imitation

countermand: to retract an order

encounter: a meeting, often with an opponent

CORP/CORS: body

corporation: a company legally treated as an individual

corps: a body (an organized group) of troops

corpse: a dead body

corpulent: obese; having a lot of flesh

corset: a garment used to give shape and support to the body

incorporation: combining into a single body

COSM: order, universe, world

cosmetic: improving the appearance (making it look better ordered)

cosmic: relating to the universe

cosmology: a theory of the universe as a whole

cosmonaut: an astronaut; an explorer of outer space

cosmopolitan: worldly

cosmos: the universe; an orderly system; order

microcosm: a small system that reflects a larger whole

COUR/CUR: running, a course

concur: to accord in opinion, agree

courier: a messenger traveling in haste who bears news

curriculum: the regular course of study

cursive: handwriting in flowing strokes with the letters joined together

cursory: going rapidly over something; hasty; superficial

excursion: a short journey or trip

incursion: a hostile entrance into a place, esp. suddenly

recur: to happen again

CRE/CRESC/CRET: to grow

accretion: an increase by natural growth

accrue: to be added as a matter of periodic gain

creation: the act of producing or causing to exist

excrescence: an outgrowth

increase: to make greater in any respect

increment: something added or gained; an addition or increase

CRED: to believe, to trust

credentials: anything that provides the basis for belief

credit: trustworthiness

credo: any formula of belief

credulity: willingness to believe or trust too readily

incredible: unbelievable

CRYPT: hidden

apocryphal: of doubtful authorship or authenticity

crypt: a subterranean chamber or vault

cryptography: procedures of making and using secret writing

cryptology: the science of interpreting secret writings, codes, ciphers, and the like

CUB/CUMB: to lie down

cubicle: any small space or compartment that is partitioned off

incubate: to sit upon for the purpose of hatching

incumbent: holding an indicated position

recumbent: lying down; reclining; leaning

succumb: to give away to superior force; yield

CULP: fault, blame

culpable: deserving blame or censure

culprit: a person guilty of an offense

inculpate: to charge with fault

mea culpa: through my fault; my fault

D

DAC/DOC: to teach

didactic: intended for instruction

docile: easily managed or handled, tractable

doctor: someone licensed to practice medicine; a learned person

doctrine: a particular principle advocated, as of a government or religion

indoctrinate: to imbue a person with learning

DE: away, off, down, completely, reversal

decipher: to make out the meaning; to interpret

defame: to attack the good name or reputation of

deferential: respectful; to yield to judgment

defile: to make foul, dirty, or unclean

delineate: to trace the outline of; sketch or trace in outline

descend: to move from a higher to a lower place

DELE: to erase

delete: to erase; to blot out; to remove

indelible: impossible to erase; lasting

DEM: people

democracy: government by the people

demographics: vital and social statistics of populations

endemic: peculiar to a particular people or locality

epidemic: affecting a large number of people at the same time and spreading from person to person

pandemic: general, universal

DEXT: right hand, right side, deft

ambidextrous: equally able to use both hands

dexter: on the right

dexterity: deftness; adroitness

DI: day

dial: a device for seeing the hour of the day; a clock face; rotatable discs or knobs used as a control input

diary: a record of one's days

dismal: gloomy (from "bad days")

diurnal: daily

meridian: a direct line from the North Pole to the South Pole; the highest point reached by the sun; noon

quotidian: everyday; ordinary

DI/DIA: in two, through, across

diagnose: to identify disease or fault from symptoms

dialogue: a conversation between two or more persons

diameter: a line going through a circle, dividing it in two

dichotomy: division into two parts, kinds, etc.

DI/DIF/DIS: away from, apart, reversal, not

diffuse: to pour out and spread, as in a fluid

dilate: to make wider or larger; to cause to expand

dilatory: inclined to delay or procrastinate

disperse: to drive or send off in various directions

disseminate: to scatter or spread widely; promulgate

dissipate: to scatter wastefully

dissuade: to deter by advice or persuasion

DIC/DICT/DIT: to say, to tell, to use words

dictionary: a book containing a selection of the words of a language

interdict: to forbid; prohibit

predict: to tell in advance

verdict: a judgment or decision

DIGN: worth

condign: well deserved; fitting; adequate

deign: to think fit or in accordance with one's dignity

dignitary: a person who holds a high rank or office

dignity: nobility or elevation of character; worthiness

disdain: to look upon or treat with contempt

DOG/DOX: opinion

dogma: a system of tenets, as of a church

orthodox: sound or correct in opinion or doctrine

paradox: an opinion or statement contrary to accepted opinion

DOL: to suffer, to pain, to grieve

condolence: an expression of sympathy with one who is suffering

doleful: sorrowful, mournful

dolorous: full of pain or sorrow, grievous

indolence: a state of being lazy or slothful

DON/DOT/DOW: to give

anecdote: a short narrative about an interesting event

antidote: something that prevents or counteracts ill effects

donate: to present as a gift or contribution

endow: to provide with a permanent fund

pardon: kind indulgence, forgiveness

DORM: sleep

dormant: sleeping; inactive

dormitory: a place for sleeping; a residence hall

DORS: back

dorsal: having to do with the back

endorse: to sign on the back; to vouch for

DUB: doubt

dubiety: doubtfulness

dubious: doubtful

indubitable: unquestionable

DUC/DUCT: to lead

abduct: to carry off or lead away

conducive: contributive, helpful

conduct: personal behavior, way of acting

induce: to lead or move by influence

induct: to install in a position with formal ceremonies

produce: to bring into existence; give cause to

DULC: sweet

dulcet: sweet; pleasing

dulcified: sweetened; softened

dulcimer: a musical instrument

DUR: hard, lasting

dour: sullen, gloomy (originally: hard, obstinate)

durable: able to resist decay

duration: the length of time something exists

duress: compulsion by threat, coercion

endure: to hold out against; to sustain without yielding

obdurate: stubborn, resistant to persuasion

DYS: faulty, abnormal

dysfunctional: poorly functioning

dyslexia: an impairment of the ability to read

dyspepsia: impaired digestion

dystrophy: faulty or inadequate nutrition or development

E

E/EX: out, out of, from, former, completely

efface: to rub or wipe out; surpass, eclipse

evade: to escape from, avoid

exclude: to shut out; to leave out

exonerate: to free or declare free from blame

expire: to breathe out; to breathe one's last; to end

extricate: to disentangle, release

EGO: self

ego: oneself; the part of oneself that is self-aware

egocentric: focused on oneself

egoism/egotism: selfishness; self-absorption

EM/EN: in, into

embrace: to clasp in the arms; to include or contain

enclose: to close in on all sides

EPI: upon

epidemic: affecting a large number of people at the same time and spreading from person to person

epidermis: the outer layer of the skin

epigram: a witty or pointed saying tersely expressed

epilogue: a concluding part added to a literary work

epithet: a word or phrase added to—or replacing—a name, to describe or insult its bearer

EQU: equal, even

adequate: equal to the requirement or occasion

equation: the act of making equal

equidistant: equally distant

iniquity: gross injustice; wickedness

ERR: to wander

arrant: notorious; downright (originally: wandering)

err: to go astray in thought or belief, to be mistaken

erratic: deviating from the proper or usual course in conduct

error: a deviation from accuracy or correctness

ESCE: becoming

adolescent: between childhood and adulthood

convalescent: recovering from illness

incandescent: glowing with heat, shining

obsolescent: becoming obsolete

reminiscent: reminding or suggestive of

EU: good, well

eugenics: improvement of qualities of race by control of inherited characteristics

eulogy: speech or writing in praise or commendation

euphemism: a pleasant-sounding term for something unpleasant

euphony: pleasantness of sound

euthanasia: killing a person painlessly, usually one who has an incurable, painful disease

EXTRA: outside, beyond

extract: to take out, obtain against a person's will

extradite: to hand over (person accused of crime) to the state where the crime was committed

extraordinary: beyond the ordinary

extrapolate: to estimate (unknown facts or values) from known data

extrasensory: derived by means other than known senses

F

FAB/FAM: to speak

affable: friendly, courteous

defame: to attack the good name of

fable: a fictional tale, esp. legendary

famous: well known, celebrated

ineffable: too great for description in words; that which must not be uttered

FAC/FIC/FIG/FAIT/FEIT/FY: to do, to make

configuration: manner of arrangement, shape
counterfeit: imitation, forgery
deficient: incomplete or insufficient
effigy: a sculpture or model of a person
faction: a small dissenting group within a larger one, esp. in politics
factory: a building for the manufacture of goods
prolific: producing many offspring or much output
ratify: to confirm or accept by formal consent

FAL: to err, to deceive

default: to fail
fail: to be insufficient; to be unsuccessful; to die out
fallacy: a flawed argument
false: not true; erroneous; lying
faux pas: a false step; a social gaffe
infallible: incapable of being wrong or being deceived

FATU: foolish

fatuity: foolishness; stupidity
fatuous: foolish; stupid
infatuated: swept up in a fit of passion, impairing one's reason

FER: to bring, to carry, to bear

confer: to grant, bestow
offer: to present for acceptance, refusal, or consideration
proffer: to offer
proliferate: to reproduce; produce rapidly
referendum: to vote on a political question open to the entire electorate

FERV: to boil, to bubble

effervescent: with the quality of giving off bubbles of gas
fervid: ardent, intense
fervor: passion, zeal

FI/FID: faith, trust

affidavit: a written statement on oath
confide: to entrust with a secret
fidelity: faithfulness, loyalty
fiduciary: of a trust; held or given in trust
infidel: a disbeliever in the supposed true religion

FIN: end

confine: to keep or restrict within certain limits; imprison
definitive: decisive, unconditional, final
final: at the end; coming last
infinite: boundless; endless
infinitesimal: infinitely or very small

FLAGR/FLAM: to burn

conflagration: a large, destructive fire
flagrant: blatant, scandalous
flambeau: a lighted torch
inflame: to set on fire

FLECT/FLEX: to bend, to turn

deflect: to bend or turn aside from a purpose
flexible: able to bend without breaking
genuflect: to bend one knee, esp. in worship
inflect: to change or vary the pitch of
reflect: to throw back

FLU/FLUX: to flow

confluence: merging into one
effluence: flowing out of (light, electricity, etc.)
fluctuation: something that varies, rising and falling
fluid: substance, esp. gas or liquid, capable of flowing freely
mellifluous: pleasing, musical

FORE: before

foreshadow: to be a warning or indication of (future event)
foresight: care or provision for the future
forestall: to prevent by advance action
forthright: straightforward, outspoken, decisive

FORT: chance

fortuitous: happening by luck
fortunate: lucky, auspicious
fortune: chance or luck in human affairs

FORT: strength

forte: strong point; something a person does well
fortify: to provide with fortifications; strengthen
fortissimo: very loud

FRA/FRAC/FRAG/FRING: to break

fractious: irritable, peevish

fracture: breakage, esp. of a bone

fragment: a part broken off

infringe: to break or violate (a law, etc.)

refractory: stubborn, unmanageable, rebellious

FUG: to flee, to fly

centrifugal: flying off from the center

fugitive: on the run; someone who flees

fugue: a musical composition in which subsequent parts imitate or pursue the first part; a psychological state in which one flies from one's own identity

refuge: a haven for those fleeing

refugee: a fleeing person who seeks refuge

subterfuge: a deception used to avoid a confrontation

FULG: to shine

effulgent: shining forth

refulgent: radiant; shining

FUM: smoke

fume: smoke; scented vapor; to emit smoke or vapors

fumigate: to treat with smoke or vapors

perfume: scents, from burning incense or other sources of fragrance

FUS: to pour

diffuse: to spread widely or thinly

fusillade: continuous discharge of firearms or outburst of criticism

infusion: the act of permeating or steeping; liquid extract so obtained

profuse: lavish, extravagant, copious

suffuse: to spread throughout or over from within

G

GEN: birth, creation, race, kind

carcinogenic: producing cancer

congenital: existing or as such from birth

gender: classification roughly corresponding to the two sexes and sexlessness

generous: giving or given freely

genetics: study of heredity and variation among animals and plants

progeny: offspring, descendants

GN/GNO: to know

agnostic: one who believes that the existence of God is not provable

diagnose: to identify disease or fault from symptoms

ignoramus: a person lacking knowledge, uninformed

ignore: to refuse to take notice of

prognosis: to forecast, especially of disease

GRAD/GRESS: to step

aggressive: given to hostile acts or feelings

degrade: to humiliate, dishonor, reduce to lower rank

digress: to depart from the main subject

egress: going out; the way out

progress: forward movement

regress: to move backward, revert to an earlier state

GRAM/GRAPH: to write, to draw

diagram: a figure made by drawing lines; an illustration

epigram: a short poem; a pointed statement

grammar: a system of language and its rules

graph: a diagram used to convey mathematical information

graphite: a mineral used for writing, as the "lead" in pencils

photograph: a picture, originally made by exposing chemically treated film to light

GRAT: pleasing

gracious: kindly, esp. to inferiors; merciful

grateful: thankful

gratuity: money given for good service

ingratiate: to bring oneself into favor

GREG: flock

aggregate: a number of things considered as a collective whole

congregate: to come together in a group

egregious: remarkably bad; standing out from the crowd

gregarious: sociable; enjoying spending time with others

segregate: to separate from the crowd

H

HAP: by chance

haphazard: at random

hapless: without luck

happen: occur (originally: to occur by chance)

happily: through good fortune

happy: pleased, as by good fortune

mishap: an unlucky accident

perhaps: a qualifier suggesting something might (or might not) take place

HEMI: half

hemisphere: half a sphere; half of the Earth

hemistich: half a line of poetry

HER/HES: to stick

adherent: able to adhere; believer or advocate of a particular thing

adhesive: tending to remain in memory; sticky; an adhesive substance

coherent: logically consistent; having waves in phase and of one wavelength

inherent: involved in the constitution or essential character of something

(H)ETERO: different, other

heterodox: different from the acknowledged standard; holding unorthodox opinions or doctrines

heterogeneous: of other origin; not originating in the body

heterosexual: of or pertaining to sexual orientation toward members of the opposite sex; relating to different sexes

HOL: whole

catholic: universal

holocaust: a burnt offering; complete destruction by fire or other means

hologram: a sort of three-dimensional image

holograph: a document written entirely by the person whose name it's in

holistic: considering something as a unified whole

(H)OM: same

anomaly: deviation from the common rule

homeostasis: a relatively stable state of equilibrium

homogeneous: of the same or a similar kind of nature; of uniform structure of composition throughout

homonym: one of two or more words spelled and pronounced alike but different in meaning

homosexual: of, relating to, or exhibiting sexual desire toward a member of one's own sex

HUM: earth

exhume: unearth

humble: down-to-earth

humility: the state of being humble

HYPER: over, excessive

hyperactive: excessively active

hyperbole: purposeful exaggeration for effect

hyperglycemia: an abnormally high concentration of sugar in the blood

HYPO: under, beneath, less than

hypochondriac: one affected by extreme depression of mind or spirits, often centered on imaginary physical ailments

hypocritical: pretending to have beliefs one does not

hypodermic: relating to the parts beneath the skin

hypothesis: an assumption subject to proof

I

ICON: image, idol

icon: a symbolic picture; a statue; something seen as representative of a culture or movement

iconic: being representative of a culture or movement

iconoclast: one who attacks established beliefs; one who tears down images

iconology: symbolism

IDIO: one's own

idiom: a language, dialect, or style of speaking particular to a people

idiosyncrasy: peculiarity of temperament; eccentricity

idiot: an utterly stupid person

IN/IM: in, into

(Often the *n* or *m* is dropped and the first letter to which *i* is prefixed is doubled.)

implicit: not expressly stated; implied

incarnate: given a bodily, esp. a human, form

indigenous: native; innate, natural

influx: the act of flowing in; inflow

intrinsic: belonging to a thing by its very nature

IN/IM: not, without
(Often the *n* or *m* is dropped and the first letter to which *i* is prefixed is doubled.)
immoral: not moral; evil
impartial: not partial or biased; just
inactive: not active
indigent: deficient in what is requisite
indolence: showing a disposition to avoid exertion; slothful
innocuous: not harmful or injurious

INTER: between, among
interim: a temporary or provisional arrangement; meantime
interloper: one who intrudes in the domain of others
intermittent: stopping or ceasing for a time
intersperse: to scatter here and there
interstate: connecting or jointly involving states

INTRA: inside, within
intramural: within a school; inside a city
intrastate: within a state
intravenous: inside the veins

IT/ITER: way, journey
ambition: strong desire to achieve (from "going around" for votes)
circuit: a line around an area; a racecourse; the path traveled by electrical current
itinerant: traveling
itinerary: travel plans
reiterate: to repeat
transit: traveling; means of transportation

J

JECT: to throw, to throw down
abject: utterly hopeless, humiliating, or wretched
conjecture: formation of opinion on incomplete information
dejected: sad, depressed
eject: to throw out, expel
inject: to place (quality, etc.) where needed in something

JOC: joke
jocose: given to joking; playful
jocular: in a joking manner; funny
jocund: merry; cheerful

joke: a witticism; a humorous anecdote; something funny

JOIN/JUG/JUNCT: to meet, to join
adjoin: to be next to and joined with
conjugal: related to marriage
conjunction: joining; occurring together; a connecting word
injunction: a command; an act of enjoining
junction: the act of joining; combining; a place where multiple paths join
junta: a group of military officers who join together to run a country; a council
rejoinder: a reply, retort
subjugate: to make subservient; to place under a yoke

JOUR: day
adjourn: to close a meeting; to put off further proceedings for another day
journal: a record of one's days
journey: a trip (originally: a day's travel)

JUD: to judge
adjudicate: to act as a judge
judiciary: a system of courts; members of a court system
judicious: having good judgment
prejudice: a previous or premature judgment; bias

JUR: law, to swear
abjure: to renounce on oath
adjure: to beg or command
jurisprudence: a system of law; knowledge of law
perjury: willful lying while on oath

JUV: young
juvenile: young; immature
juvenilia: writings or art produced in one's youth
rejuvenate: to refresh; to make young again

L

LANG/LING: tongue
bilingual: speaking two languages
language: a system of (usually spoken) communication
linguistics: the study of language

LAUD: praise, honor

cum laude: with honors

laudable: praiseworthy

laudatory: expressing praise

LAV/LAU/LU: to wash

ablution: act of cleansing

antediluvian: before the biblical flood; extremely old

deluge: a great flood of water

dilute: to make thinner or weaker by the addition of water

laundry: items to be, or that have been, washed

lavatory: a room with equipment for washing hands and face

LAX/LEAS/LES: loose

lax: loose; undisciplined

laxative: medicine or food that loosens the bowels

lease: to rent out (that is, to let something loose for others' use)

leash: a cord used to hold an animal while giving it some freedom to run loose

relax: to loosen; to be less strict; to calm down

release: to let go; to set free

LEC/LEG/LEX: to read, to speak

dialect: a manner of speaking; a regional variety of a language

lectern: a reading desk

lecture: an instructional speech

legend: a story; a written explanation of a map or illustration

legible: readable

lesson: instruction (originally: part of a book or oral instruction to be studied and repeated to a teacher)

lexicographer: a writer of dictionaries

lexicon: a dictionary

LECT/LEG: to select, to choose

collect: to gather together or assemble

eclectic: selecting ideas, etc. from various sources

elect: to choose; to decide

predilection: preference, liking

select: to choose with care

LEV: to lift, to rise, light (weight)

alleviate: to make easier to endure, lessen

levee: embankment against river flooding

levitate: to rise in the air or cause to rise

levity: humor, frivolity, gaiety

relevant: bearing on or pertinent to information at hand

relieve: to mitigate; to free from a burden

LI/LIG: to tie, to bind

ally: to unite; one in an alliance

league: an association; a group of nations, teams, etc. that have agreed to work for a common cause

liable: legally responsible; bound by law

liaison: a connection; one who serves to connect

lien: the right to hold a property due to an outstanding debt

ligament: a band holding bones together; a bond

ligature: a connection between two letters; a bond

oblige: to obligate; to make indebted or form personal bonds by doing a favor

rely: to depend upon (originally: to come together; to rally)

LIBER: free

deliver: to set free; to save; to hand over

liberal: generous; giving away freely

liberality: generosity

liberate: to set free

libertine: one who follows one's own path, without regard for morals or other restrictions

liberty: freedom

livery: a uniform; an emblem indicating an owner or manufacturer (originally: an allowance of food or other provisions given to servants)

LITH: stone

acrolith: a statue with a stone head and limbs (but a wooden body)

lithography: a printing process that originally involved writing on a flat stone

lithology: the study of rocks and stones

lithotomy: an operation to remove stones from the body

megalith: a very big stone

monolith: a single block of stone, often shaped into a monument

LOC/LOG/LOQU: word, speech, thought

colloquial: of ordinary or familiar conversation

dialogue: a conversation, esp. in a literary work

elocution: the art of clear and expressive speaking

eulogy: a speech or writing in praise of someone

grandiloquent: pompous or inflated in language

loquacious: talkative

prologue: an introduction to a poem, play, etc.

LUC/LUM/LUS: light (brightness)

illuminate: to supply or brighten with light

illustrate: to make intelligible with examples or analogies

illustrious: highly distinguished

lackluster: lacking brilliance or radiance

lucid: easily understood, intelligible

luminous: bright, brilliant, glowing

translucent: permitting light to pass through

LUD/LUS: to play

allude: to refer casually or indirectly

delude: to mislead the mind or judgment of, deceive

elude: to avoid capture or escape defection by

illusion: something that deceives by producing a false impression of reality

ludicrous: ridiculous, laughable

prelude: a preliminary to an action, event, etc.

M

MACRO: great, long

macro: broad; large; a single computer command that executes a longer set of commands

macrobiotics: a system intended to prolong life

macrocephalous: having a large head

macrocosm: the universe; a large system that is reflected in at least one of its subsets

macroscopic: large enough to be visible to the naked eye

MAG/MAJ/MAX: big, great

magnanimous: generous in forgiving an insult or injury

magnate: a powerful or influential person

magnify: to increase the apparent size of

magnitude: greatness of size, extent, or dimensions

maxim: an expression of general truth or principle

maximum: the highest amount, value, or degree attained

MAL/MALE: bad, ill, evil, wrong

maladroit: clumsy, tactless

malady: a disorder or disease of the body

malapropism: humorous misuse of a word

malediction: a curse

malfeasance: misconduct or wrongdoing often committed by a public official

malfunction: failure to function properly

malicious: full of or showing malice

malign: to speak harmful untruths about, to slander

MAN/MANU: hand

emancipate: to free from bondage

manifest: readily perceived by the eye or the understanding

manual: operated by hand

manufacture: to make by hand or machinery

MAND/MEND: to command, to order, to entrust

command: to order; an order; control

commend: to give something over to the care of another; to praise

countermand: to retract an order

demand: to strongly ask for; to claim; to require

mandatory: commanded; required

recommend: to praise and suggest the use of; to advise

remand: to send back

MEDI: middle

immediate: nearest; having nothing in between

intermediate: in the middle

mean: average; in the middle

mediate: to serve as a go-between; to try to settle an argument

medieval: related to the Middle Ages

mediocre: neither good nor bad; so-so

medium: size between small and large; a substance or agency that things travel through (as, for example, light travels through air, and news is conveyed by television and newspapers)

MEGA: large, great

megalith: a very big stone

megalomania: a mental condition involving delusions of greatness; an obsession with doing great things

megalopolis: a very large city

megaphone: a device for magnifying the sound of one's voice

megaton: explosive power equal to 1,000 tons of TNT

MICRO: very small

microbe: a very small organism

microcosm: a small system that reflects a larger whole

micron: a millionth of a meter

microorganism: a very small organism

microscope: a device that magnifies very small things for viewing

MIN: small

diminish: to lessen

diminution: the act or process of diminishing

miniature: a copy or model that represents something in greatly reduced size

minute: a unit of time equal to one-sixtieth of an hour

minutiae: small or trivial details

MIN: to project, to hang over

eminent: towering above others; projecting

imminent: about to occur; impending

preeminent: superior to or notable above all others

prominent: projecting outward

MIS: bad, wrong, to hate

misadventure: bad luck; an unlucky accident

misanthrope: one who hates people or humanity

misapply: to use something incorrectly

mischance: bad luck; an unlucky accident

mischief: bad or annoying behavior

misconstrue: to take something in a way that wasn't intended; to understand something incorrectly

misfit: somebody or something that doesn't fit in

MIS/MIT: to send

emissary: a messenger or agent sent to represent the interests of another

intermittent: stopping and starting at intervals

remission: a lessening of intensity or degree

remit: to send money

transmit: to send from one person, thing, or place to another

MISC: mixed

miscellaneous: made up of a variety of parts or ingredients

promiscuous: consisting of diverse and unrelated parts or individuals; indiscriminate

MOB/MOM/MOT/MOV: to move

automobile: a vehicle that moves under its own power; a motorized car

demote: to move downward in an organization

immovable: incapable of being moved; unyielding

locomotion: moving from place to place; the ability to do so

mob: the rabble; a disorderly group of people (from the Latin *mobile vulgus*, meaning "the movable crowd")

mobile: movable

mobilize: to make ready for movement; to assemble

moment: an instant; importance

momentous: of great importance (originally: having the power to move)

momentum: the force driving a moving object to keep moving; a growing force

motion: movement

motive: a reason for action; what moves a person to do something

motor: a device that makes something move

mutiny: rebellion against authority, esp. by sailors

promote: to move to a higher rank in an organization

remove: to take away; to move away

MOLL: soft

emollient: something that softens or soothes (e.g., a lotion)

mild: gentle; kind

mollify: soothe; soften; calm

mollusk: a phylum of invertebrate animals—including octopuses, squids, oysters, clams, and slugs—with soft bodies

MON/MONIT: to remind, to warn

admonish: to counsel against something; caution

monitor: one that admonishes, cautions, or reminds

monument: a structure, such as a building, tower, or sculpture, erected as a memorial

premonition: forewarning, presentiment

remonstrate: to say or plead in protest, objection, or reproof

summon: to call together; convene

MON/MONO: one

monarchy: rule by a single person

monk: a man in a religious order living apart from society (originally: a religious hermit)

monochord: a musical instrument with a single string

monogram: a design combining multiple letters into one

monograph: a scholarly study of a single subject

monologue: a speech or other dramatic composition recited by one person

monomania: an obsession with a single subject

monotonous: boring; spoken using only one tone

MOR/MORT: death

immortal: not subject to death

morbid: susceptible to preoccupation with unwholesome matters

moribund: dying, decaying

MORPH: shape

amorphous: without definite form; lacking a specific shape

anthropomorphism: attribution of human characteristics to inanimate objects, animals, or natural phenomena

metamorphosis: a transformation, as by magic or sorcery

MULT: many

multiple: many, having many parts; a number containing some quantity of a smaller number without remainder

multiplex: having many parts; a movie theater or other building with many separate units

multiply: to increase; to become many

multitudinous: very many; containing very many; having very many forms

MUT: to change

commute: to substitute; exchange; interchange

immutable: unchangeable, invariable

mutation: the process of being changed

permutation: a complete change; a transformation

transmute: to change from one form into another

N

NAT/NAS/NAI/GNA: birth

cognate: related by blood; having a common ancestor

naive: lacking worldliness and sophistication; artless

nascent: starting to develop

native: belonging to one by nature; inborn; innate

natural: present due to nature, not to artificial or man-made means

renaissance: rebirth, esp. referring to culture

NAU/NAV: ship, sailor

astronaut: one who travels in outer space

circumnavigate: to sail all the way around

cosmonaut: one who travels in outer space

nauseous: causing a squeamish feeling (originally: seasickness)

nautical: related to sailing or sailors

naval: related to the navy

nave: the central portion of a church (which resembles the shape of a ship)

navy: a military force consisting of ships and sailors

NIHIL: nothing, none

annihilate: to wipe out; to reduce to nothing

nihilism: denial of all moral beliefs; denial that existence has any meaning

NOC/NOX: harm

innocent: uncorrupted by evil, malice, or wrongdoing

innocuous: not harmful or injurious

noxious: injurious or harmful to health or morals

obnoxious: highly disagreeable or offensive

NOCT/NOX: night

equinox: one of two times in a year when day and night are equal in length

noctambulant: walking at night; sleepwalking

nocturnal: related to the night; active at night

nocturne: a dreamlike piece of music; a painting set at night

NOM: rule, order

astronomy: the scientific study of the universe beyond Earth

autonomy: independence, self-governance

economy: the careful or thrifty use of resources, as of income, materials, or labor

gastronomy: the art or science of good eating

taxonomy: the science, laws, or principles of classification

NOM/NYM/NOUN/NOWN: name

acronym: a word formed from the initial letters of a name

anonymous: having an unknown or unacknowledged name

nomenclature: a system of names; systematic naming

nominal: existing in name only; negligible

nominate: to propose by name as a candidate

noun: a word that names a person, place, or thing

renown: fame; reputation

synonym: a word having a meaning similar to that of another word of the same language

NON: not

nonconformist: one who does not conform to a church or other societal institution

nonentity: something that doesn't exist; something that is unimportant

nonpareil: something with no equal

nonpartisan: not affiliated with a political party

NOUNC/NUNC: to announce

announce: to proclaim

pronounce: to articulate

renounce: to give up, especially by formal announcement

NOV/NEO/NOU: new

innovate: to begin or introduce something new

neologism: a newly coined word, phrase, or expression

neophyte: a beginner; a new convert; a new worker

neoplasm: a new growth in the body; a tumor

nouveau riche: one who has lately become rich

novice: a person new to any field or activity

renovate: to restore to an earlier condition

NULL: nothing

annul: to cancel; to make into nothing

nullify: to cancel; to make into nothing

nullity: the condition of being nothing

O

OB: toward, to, against, over

obese: extremely fat, corpulent

obfuscate: to render indistinct or dim; darken

oblique: having a slanting or sloping direction

obsequious: overly submissive

obstinate: stubbornly adhering to an idea, inflexible

obstreperous: noisily defiant, unruly

obstruct: to block or fill with obstacles

obtuse: not sharp, pointed, or acute in any form

OMNI: all

omnibus: an anthology of the works of one author or of writings on related subjects

omnipotent: all powerful

omnipresent: everywhere at one time

omniscient: having infinite knowledge

ONER: burden

exonerate: to free from blame (originally: to relieve of a burden)

onerous: burdensome; difficult

onus: a burden; a responsibility

OSS/OSTE: bone

ossify: to become bone; to harden; to become callous

ossuary: a place where bones are kept; a charnel house

osteopathy: a medical system based on the belief that many illnesses can be traced to issues in the skeletal system

P

PAC/PEAC: peace

appease: to bring peace to

pacifier: something or someone that eases the anger or agitation of

pacify: to ease the anger or agitation of

pact: a formal agreement, as between nations

PALP: to feel

palpable: capable of being felt; tangible

palpate: to feel; to examine by feeling

palpitate: to beat quickly, as the heart; to throb

PAN/PANT: all, everyone

pandemic: widespread, general, universal

panegyric: formal or elaborate praise at an assembly

panoply: a wide-ranging and impressive array or display

panorama: an unobstructed and wide view of an extensive area

pantheon: a public building containing tombs or memorials of the illustrious dead of a nation

PAR: equal

apartheid: any system or caste that separates people according to race, etc.

disparage: to belittle, speak disrespectfully about

disparate: essentially different

par: an equality in value or standing

parity: equally, as in amount, status, or character

PARA: next to, beside

parable: a short, allegorical story designed to illustrate a moral lesson or religious principle

paragon: a model of excellence

parallel: extending in the same direction

paranoid: suffering from a baseless distrust of others

parasite: an organism that lives on or within a plant or animal of another species, from which it obtains nutrients

parody: to imitate for purposes of satire

PAS/PAT/PATH: feeling, suffering, disease

compassion: a feeling of deep sympathy for someone struck by misfortune, accompanied by a desire to alleviate suffering

dispassionate: devoid of personal feeling or bias

empathy: the identification with the feelings or thoughts of others

impassive: showing or feeling no emotion

pathogenic: causing disease

sociopath: a person whose behavior is antisocial and who lacks a sense of moral responsibility

sympathy: harmony or agreement in feeling

PAU/PO/POV/PU: few, little, poor

impoverish: to deplete

paucity: smallness of quantity; scarcity; scantiness

pauper: a person without any personal means of support

poverty: the condition of being poor

puerile: childish, immature

pusillanimous: lacking courage or resolution

PEC: money

impecunious: having no money; penniless

peculation: embezzlement

pecuniary: relating to money

PED: child, education

encyclopedia: book or set of books containing articles on various topics, covering all branches of knowledge or of one particular subject

pedagogue: a teacher

pedant: one who displays learning ostentatiously

pediatrician: a doctor who primarily has children as patients

PED/POD: foot

antipodes: places that are diametrically opposite each other on the globe

expedite: to speed up the progress of

impede: to retard progress by means of obstacles or hindrances

pedal: a foot-operated lever or part used to control

pedestrian: a person who travels on foot

podium: a small platform for an orchestra conductor, speaker, etc.

PEL: to drive, to push

compel: to force; to command

dispel: to drive away; to disperse

expel: to drive out; to banish; to eject

impel: to force; to drive forward

propel: to drive forward

PEN/PENE: almost

peninsula: a landmass that is mostly surrounded by water, making it almost an island

penultimate: second-to-last

penumbra: a shaded area between pure shadow and pure light

PEN/PUN: to pay, to compensate

penal: of or pertaining to punishment, as for crimes

penalty: a punishment imposed for a violation of law or rule

penance: a punishment undergone to express regret for a sin

penitent: contrite

punitive: serving for, concerned with, or inflicting punishment

PEND/PENS: to hang, to weight, to pay

appendage: a limb or other subsidiary part that diverges from the central structure

appendix: supplementary material at the end of a text

compensate: to counterbalance, offset

depend: to rely; to place trust in

indispensable: absolutely necessary, essential, or requisite

stipend: a periodic payment; fixed or regular pay

PER: completely

perforate: to make a way through or into something

perfunctory: performed merely as routine duty

perplex: to cause to be puzzled or bewildered over what is not understood

persistent: lasting or enduring tenaciously

perspicacious: shrewd, astute

pertinacious: resolute, persistent

peruse: to read with thoroughness or care

PERI: around

perimeter: the border or outer boundary of a two-dimensional figure

peripatetic: walking or traveling about; itinerant

periscope: an optical instrument for seeing objects in an obstructed field of vision

PET/PIT: to go, to seek, to strive

appetite: a desire for food or drink

centripetal: moving toward the center

compete: to strive to outdo another

impetuous: characterized by sudden or rash action or emotion

petition: a formally drawn request soliciting some benefit

petulant: showing sudden irritation, esp. over some annoyance

PHIL: love

bibliophile: one who loves or collects books

philatelist: one who loves or collects postage stamps

philology: the study of literary texts to establish their authenticity and determine their meaning

philosophy: the rational investigation of the truths and principles of being, knowledge, or conduct

PHOB: fear

claustrophobia: fear of enclosed places

hydrophobia: fear of water, which is a symptom of rabies; rabies

phobia: fear; an irrational fear

xenophobia: fear of foreigners; hatred of foreigners

PHON: sound

euphony: the quality of sounding good

megaphone: a device for magnifying the sound of one's voice

phonetics: the study of the sounds used in speech

polyphony: the use of simultaneous melodic lines to produce harmonies in musical compositions

telephone: a device for transmitting sound at a distance

PHOTO: light

photograph: a picture, originally made by exposing chemically treated film to light

photon: a packet of light or other electromagnetic radiation

photosynthesis: a process by which plants create carbohydrates when under light

PLAC: to please

complacent: self-satisfied, unconcerned

complaisant: inclined or disposed to please

implacable: unable to be pleased

placebo: a substance with no pharmacological effect that acts to placate a patient who believes it to be a medicine

placid: pleasantly calm or peaceful

PLE/PLEN: to fill, full

complete: having all parts or elements

deplete: to decrease seriously or exhaust the supply of

implement: an instrument, tool, or utensil for accomplishing work

plenitude: fullness

plethora: excess, overabundance

replete: abundantly supplied

supplement: something added to supply a deficiency

PLEX/PLIC/PLY: to fold, twist, tangle, or bend

complex: composed of many interconnected parts

duplicity: deceitfulness in speech or conduct, double-dealing

implicate: to show to be involved, usually in an incriminating manner

implicit: not expressly stated, implied

replica: any close copy or reproduction

supplicate: to make humble and earnest entreaty

POLY: many

polyandry: the practice of having multiple husbands

polygamy: the practice of having multiple wives

polyglot: someone who speaks many languages

polygon: a figure with many sides

polytheism: the belief in many gods

PON/POS/POUND: to put, to place

component: a constituent part; elemental ingredient

expose: to lay open to danger, attack, or harm

expound: to set forth in detail

juxtapose: to place close together or side by side

repository: a receptacle or place where things are deposited

PORT: to carry

deportment: conduct, behavior

disport: to divert or amuse oneself

export: to transmit abroad

import: to bring in from a foreign country

importune: to urge or press with excessive persistence

portable: easily carried

POST: behind, after

post facto: after the fact

posterior: situated at the rear

posterity: future generations

posthumous: after death

POT: to drink

potable: drinkable; safe to drink; a drink

potation: drinking; a drink

potion: a drinkable medicine, poison, or other concoction

PRE: before, in front

precarious: dependent on circumstances beyond one's control

precedent: an act that serves as an example for subsequent situations

precept: a commandment given as a rule of action or conduct

precocious: unusually advanced or mature in mental development or talent

premonition: a feeling of anticipation over a future event

presentiment: foreboding

PREHEND/PRISE: to take, to get, to seize

apprehend: to take into custody

comprise: to include or contain

enterprise: a project undertaken

reprehensible: deserving rebuke or censure

reprisals: retaliation against an enemy

surprise: to strike with an unexpected feeling of wonder or astonishment

PRI/PRIM: first

primal: original; most important

primary: first; most important

prime: first in quality; best

primeval: ancient; going back to the first age of the world

pristine: original; like new; unspoiled; pure

PRO: in front, before, much, for

problem: a difficult question (originally: one put before another for solution)

proceed: to go forward

profuse: spending or giving freely

prolific: highly fruitful

propound: to set forth for consideration

proselytize: to convert or attempt to recruit

provident: having or showing foresight

PROB: to prove, to test

approbation: praise, consideration

opprobrium: the disgrace incurred by shameful conduct

probe: to search or examine thoroughly

probity: honesty, high-mindedness

reprobate: a depraved or wicked person

PROP/PROX: near

approximate: very near; close to being accurate

proximate: nearby; coming just before or just after

proximity: nearness; distance

PROT/PROTO: first

protagonist: the main character in a play or story

protocol: diplomatic etiquette; a system of proper conduct; the original record of a treaty or other negotiation

prototype: the first version of an invention, on which later models are based

protozoan: belonging to a group of single-celled animals, which came before more complex animals

PSEUD/PSEUDO: false
pseudonym: a false name; a pen name

pseudopod: part of a single-celled organism that can be stuck out (like a foot) and used to move around

pseudoscience: false science; something believed to be based on the scientific method but that actually is not

PUG: to fight
impugn: to challenge as false

pugilist: a fighter or boxer

pugnacious: to quarrel or fight readily

repugnant: objectionable or offensive

PUNC/PUNG/POIGN: to point, to prick, to pierce
compunction: a feeling of uneasiness for doing wrong

expunge: to erase; to eliminate completely

point: a sharp or tapering end

punctilious: strict or exact in the observance of formalities

puncture: the act of piercing

pungent: caustic or sharply expressive

PYR: fire
pyre: a bonfire, usually for burning a dead body

pyromania: an urge to start fires

pyrosis: heartburn

pyrotechnics: fireworks

Q

QUAD/QUAR/QUAT: four
quadrant: a quarter of a circle; a 90-degree arc

quadrille: a square dance involving four couples

quadruple: four times as many

quadruplets: four children born in one birth

quart: one-fourth of a gallon

quaternary: the number four; the fourth in a series

QUE/QUIS: to seek
acquire: to come into possession of

conquest: the act of gaining control by force

exquisite: of special beauty or charm

inquisitive: given to research, eager for knowledge

perquisite: a gratuity, tip

querulous: full of complaints

query: a question, inquiry

QUIE/QUIT: quiet, rest
acquiesce: to comply, give in

disquiet: lack of calm or peace

quiescence: the condition of being at rest, still, inactive

quiet: making little or no sound

tranquil: free from commotion or tumult

QUIN/QUINT: five
quinquennial: a five-year period; a fifth anniversary

quintessence: the essential part of something (originally: the "fifth essence," which was believed to permeate everything and be what stars and planets were made of)

quintuple: five times as many

R

RACI/RADI: root
deracinate: to uproot

eradicate: to uproot; to wipe out

radical: pertaining to roots; questioning everything, even basic beliefs; going to root causes; thorough

radish: a root vegetable

RAMI: branch
ramification: a branch; an offshoot; a collection of branches; a consequence

ramiform: branchlike

RE: back, again
recline: to lean back; to lie down

regain: to gain again; to take back

remain: to stay behind; to be left; to continue to be

reorganize: to organize again

request: to ask (originally: to seek again)

RECT: straight, right
correct: to set right

direct: to guide; to put straight

erect: upright; standing up straight

rectangle: a four-sided figure in which every angle is a right angle

rectitude: moral uprightness; moral straightness

REG: king, rule
interregnum: a period between kings

realm: a kingdom; a domain

regal: kingly; royal

regent: one who serves on behalf of a king; one who rules

regicide: killing a king; one who kills a king

regiment: a body of troops in an army; to form into such a body; to subject to strict rule

regular: having a structure following some rule; orderly; normally used; average

RETRO: backward

retroactive: extending to things that happened in the past

retrofit: to install newer parts into an older device or structure

retrograde: moving backward; appearing to move backward

retrospective: looking back at the past

RID/RIS: to laugh

derision: the act of mockery

risible: causing laughter

ROG: to ask

abrogate: to abolish by formal means

arrogant: making claims to superior importance or rights

arrogate: to claim unwarrantably or presumptuously

derogatory: belittling, disparaging

interrogate: to ask questions of, esp. formally

surrogate: a person appointed to act for another

RUB/RUD: red

rouge: a red powder used as makeup

rubella: German measles; a disease marked by red spots

rubicund: reddish; rosy-cheeked

rubric: a rule; a guide for scoring tests; a heading in a book set in red letters

russet: reddish-brown; a coarse cloth, usually reddish-brown; a type of apple or pear, typically reddish-brown

RUD: crude

erudite: scholarly; learned (that is, trained out of crudeness)

rude: uncivilized; impolite

rudimentary: undeveloped; related to rudiments

rudiments: first principles; imperfect first step of one's training

S

SACR/SANCT: holy

execrable: abominable

sacrament: something regarded as possessing sacred character

sacred: devoted or dedicated to a deity or religious purpose

sacrifice: the offering of some living or inanimate thing to a deity in homage

sacrilege: the violation of anything sacred

sanctify: to make holy

sanction: authoritative permission or approval

SAG/SAP/SAV: taste, thinking, discerning

insipid: tasteless

sagacious: perceptive; discerning; insightful

sage: wise

sapient: wise

savant: a learned person

savor: to taste; to enjoy flavors

SAL: salt

salary: payment for services (originally: money for Roman soldiers to buy salt)

saline: containing salt; salty

SAL/SIL/SAULT/SULT: to leap, to jump

assault: a sudden or violent attack

desultory: at random, unmethodical

exult: to show or feel triumphant joy

insolent: boldly rude or disrespectful

insult: to treat with contemptuous rudeness

resilient: able to spring back to an original form after compression

salient: prominent or conspicuous

somersault: to roll the body end over end, making a complete revolution

SALU: health

salubrious: healthful

salutary: healthful

salute: to greet; a gesture of greeting (originally: to wish good health)

SALV: to save

salvage: to save; something saved or recovered

salvation: being saved

savior: one who saves

SAN: healthy

sane: mentally healthy

sanitarium: a place of healing

sanitary: promoting health; related to conditions that affect health, such as cleanliness

SANG: blood

consanguinity: being related by blood

sanguinary: bloody; bloodthirsty

sanguine: hopeful; confident (from the "sanguine humor," which was believed to be associated with those traits)

SAT: enough

assets: property; possessions (originally: enough property to cover one's debts)

dissatisfied: feeling that one does not have enough

sate: to fill

satisfy: to meet one's desires; to meet an obligation; to provide with enough

saturate: to fill completely; to entirely satisfy

SCI: to know

conscience: the inner sense of what is right or wrong, impelling one toward right action

conscious: aware of one's own existence

omniscient: knowing everything

prescient: having knowledge of things before they happen

unconscionable: unscrupulous

SCRIBE/SCRIPT: to write

ascribe: to credit or assign, as to a cause or course

circumscribe: to draw a line around

conscription: draft

describe: to tell or depict in words

postscript: any addition or supplement

proscribe: to condemn as harmful or odious

scribble: to write hastily or carelessly

script: handwriting

transcript: a written or typed copy

SE: apart, away

secede: to withdraw formally from an association

sedition: incitement of discontent or rebellion against a government

seduce: to lead astray

segregate: to separate or set apart from others

select: to choose in preference to another

separate: to keep apart, divide

sequester: to remove or withdraw into solitude or retirement

SEC/SEQU/SUE/SUI: to follow

non sequitur: an inference or a conclusion that does not follow from the premises

obsequious: fawning

prosecute: to seek to enforce by legal process

pursue: to chase after

second: next after the first

sequence: the following of one thing after another

suite: a series; a set (originally: a train of followers)

SED/SESS/SID: to sit, to settle

assiduous: diligent, persistent, hardworking (literally, "sitting down" to business)

dissident: disagreeing, as in opinion or attitude (literally, "sitting apart")

insidious: intended to entrap or beguile; lying in wait to entrap

preside: to exercise management or control; to sit in the leader's chair

resident: a person who lives in a place

residual: remaining, leftover

sediment: the matter that settles to the bottom of a liquid

session: a meeting at which people sit together in discussion

SEM: seed, to sow

disseminate: to spread; to scatter around

semen: seed (of male animals)

seminary: a school, esp. for religious training (originally: a place for raising plants)

SEMI: half

semicircle: half a circle

semiconscious: only partly conscious; half awake

SEN: old

senate: the highest legislative body (from "council of elders")

senescent: getting old

senile: relating to old age; experiencing memory loss or other age-related mental impairments

sire: a title for a king; a father (originally: an important person, an old man)

SENS/SENT: to feel, to be aware

dissent: to differ in opinion, esp. from the majority

insensate: without feeling or sensitivity

presentiment: a feeling that something is about to happen

resent: to feel or show displeasure

sense: any of the faculties by which humans and animals perceive stimuli originating outside the body

sensory: of or pertaining to the senses or sensation

sentiment: an attitude or feeling toward something

sentinel: a person or thing that stands watch

SIN/SINU: bend, fold, curve

insinuate: to introduce in sneaky or winding ways

sinuous: moving in a bending or wavy manner

sinus: a curved or irregularly shaped cavity in the body, such as those related to the nostrils

SOL: alone

desolate: deserted; laid waste; left alone

isolate: to set apart from others

soliloquize: talk to oneself; talk onstage as if to oneself

solipsism: the belief that the only thing that really exists, or can really be known, is oneself

solitude: the state of being alone

SOL: sun

parasol: an umbrella that protects from the sun

solar: related to the sun

solarium: a sunroom; a room with windows for taking in the sun

solstice: one of two days when the sun reaches its highest point at noon and seems to stand still

SOL: to loosen, to free

absolution: forgiveness for wrongdoing

dissolute: indifferent to moral restraints

dissolution: the act or process of dissolving into parts or elements

dissolve: to make a solution of, as by mixing in a liquid

resolution: a formal expression of opinion or intention made

soluble: capable of being dissolved or liquefied

SOMN: sleep

insomnia: inability to sleep

somnambulist: a sleepwalker

somniferous: sleep-inducing

somniloquist: one who talks while asleep

somnolent: sleep-inducing; sleepy; drowsy

SOPH: wisdom

philosopher: one who studies logic, beauty, truth, etc.; one who seeks wisdom

sophism: a superficially appealing but fallacious argument

sophisticated: complex; worldly; experienced

SOURC/SURG/SURRECT: to rise

insurgent: rising up in revolution; rushing in

insurrection: rising up in armed rebellion

resurrection: coming back to life; rising again

source: where something comes from (such as spring water rising out of the ground)

surge: to rise up forcefully, as ocean waves

SPEC/SPIC: to look, to see

circumspect: watchful and discreet, cautious

conspicuous: easily seen or noticed; readily observable

perspective: one's mental view of facts, ideas, and their interrelationships

perspicacious: having keen mental perception and understanding

retrospective: contemplative of past situations

specious: deceptively attractive

spectrum: a broad range of related things that form a continuous series

speculation: the contemplation or consideration of some subject

SPIR: breath

aspire: to desire; to pant for (originally: to breathe on)

expire: to breathe out; to breathe one's last; to come to an end

spirit: the breath of life; the soul; an incorporeal supernatural being; an outlook; a lively quality

STA/STI: to stand, to be in place

apostasy: the renunciation of an object of one's previous loyalty

constitute: to make up

destitute: without means of subsistence

obstinate: stubbornly adhering to a purpose, opinion, or course of action

stasis: the state of equilibrium or inactivity caused by opposing equal forces

static: of bodies or forces at rest or in equilibrium

STRICT/STRING/STRAN: to tighten, to bind

astringent: causing to tighten

constrain: to confine; to bind within certain limits

restriction: a limitation

strangle: to kill by suffocation, usually by tightening a cord or one's hand around the throat

SUA: sweet, pleasing, to urge

assuage: to make less severe, ease, relieve

dissuade: to deter; to advise against

persuade: to encourage; to convince

suave: smoothly agreeable or polite; sweet

SUB/SUP: below, under

subliminal: existing or operating below the threshold of confidence

submissive: inclined or ready to submit

subsidiary: serving to assist or supplement

subterfuge: an artifice or expedient used to evade a rule

subtle: thin, tenuous, or rarefied

suppose: to put down as a hypothesis; to use as the underlying basis of an argument; to assume

SUMM: highest, total

consummate: highly qualified; complete; perfect

sum: total; amount of money

summary: concise statement of the total findings on a subject; comprehensive

summit: highest point

SUPER/SUR: over, above

supercilious: arrogant, haughty, condescending

superfluous: extra, more than necessary

superlative: the highest kind or order

supersede: to replace in power, as by another person or thing

surmount: to get over or across, to prevail

surpass: to go beyond in amount, extent, or degree

surveillance: a watch kept over someone or something

SYM/SYN: together

symbiosis: living together in a mutually beneficial relationship

symmetry: balanced proportions; having opposite parts that mirror one another

sympathy: affinity; feeling affected by what happens to another

symposium: a meeting at which ideas are discussed (originally: a party at which people drink together)

synonym: a word that means the same thing as another

synthesis: combining things to create a new whole

T

TAC/TIC: to be silent

reticent: disposed to be silent or not to speak freely

tacit: unspoken understanding

taciturn: uncommunicative

TACT/TAG/TAM/TANG: to touch

contact: to touch; to get in touch

contagious: able to spread by contact, as disease

contaminate: to corrupt, taint, or otherwise damage the integrity of something by contact or mixture

contiguous: directly touching; sharing a boundary

intact: untouched; whole

intangible: unable to be touched

tactile: pertaining to touch; touchable

TAIN/TEN/TENT/TIN: to hold

abstention: the act of refraining voluntarily

detain: to keep from proceeding

pertain: to have reference or relation

pertinacious: persistent, stubborn

sustenance: nourishment, means of livelihood

tenable: capable of being held, maintained, or defended

tenacious: holding fast

tenure: the holding or possessing of anything

TEND/TENS/TENT/TENU: to stretch, to thin

attenuate: to weaken or reduce in force

contentious: quarrelsome, disagreeable, belligerent

distend: to expand by stretching

extenuating: making less serious by offering excuses

tendentious: having a predisposition toward a point of view

tension: the act of stretching or straining

tentative: experimental; uncertain; hesitant

TEST: to bear witness

attest: to bear witness

contest: to dispute (from bringing a lawsuit by calling witnesses)

detest: to despise; to hate (originally: to curse something by calling upon God to witness it)

protest: a dissent; a declaration, esp. of disagreement

testament: a statement of a person's wishes for the disposal of his or her property after death; a will

testify: bear witness

THEO: god

apotheosis: glorification, glorified ideal

atheist: one who does not believe in a deity or divine system

theocracy: a form of government in which a deity is recognized as the supreme ruler

theology: the study of divine things and the divine faith

THERM: heat

thermal: relating to heat; retaining heat

thermometer: a device for measuring heat

thermonuclear: relating to a nuclear reaction that takes place at high temperatures

thermostat: a device for regulating heat

TIM: fear

intimidate: to strike fear into; to make fearful

timid: fearful; shy

TOR/TORQ/TORT: to twist

contort: to twist; to distort

distort: to pull out of shape, often by twisting; to twist or misrepresent facts

extort: to wring money, property, or services out of somebody using threats or force

torch: a portable flame used for light (perhaps derived from hemp twisted around sticks, then dipped in pitch)

torque: twisting force; a force that creates rotation

tort: a wrongful act (other than breach of contract) that legally entitles one to damages

torture: to inflict pain (including by twisting instruments like the rack or wheel)

TORP: stiff, numb

torpedo: a explosive weapon used to sink ships (originally: a fish—the electric ray—that could shock victims to numbness)

torpid: numbed; sluggish

torpor: numbness; listlessness; apathy

TOX: poison

antitoxin: an antibody that counteracts a given poison

intoxication: being poisoned; drunkenness

toxic: poisonous

TRACT: to drag, to pull, to draw

abstract: to draw or pull away, remove

attract: to draw either by physical force or by an appeal to emotions or senses

contract: a legally binding document

detract: to take away from, esp. a positive thing

protract: to prolong, draw out, extend

tractable: easily managed or controlled

tractor: a powerful vehicle used to pull farm machinery

TRANS: across, beyond

intransigent: refusing to agree or compromise

transaction: the act of carrying on or conduct to a conclusion or settlement

transcendent: going beyond ordinary limits

transgress: to violate a law, command, or moral code

transition: a change from one way of being to another

transparent: easily seen through, recognized, or detected

U

ULT: last, beyond

penultimate: second-to-last

ulterior: beyond what is immediately present; future; beyond what is stated; hidden

ultimate: last; final

ultimatum: final offer; final terms

ultraviolet: beyond the violet end of the spectrum

UMBR: shadow

adumbrate: to foreshadow; to sketch; to over-shadow

penumbra: a shaded area between pure shadow and pure light

somber: gloomy; darkened

umbrage: shade; shadow; displeasure; resentment

umbrella: a device providing shade from the sun or protection from rain

UN: not

unseen: not seen

unusual: not usual; exceptional; strange

UND: wave

abound: to be plentiful; to overflow (from water flowing in waves)

inundate: to flood

undulate: to move in a wavelike way

UNI/UN: one

reunion: a meeting that brings people back together

unanimous: of one mind; in complete accord

unicorn: a mythical animal with a single horn

uniform: of one kind; consistent

universe: all things considered as one whole

URB: city

suburb: a residential area just outside a city; an outlying area of a city

urban: relating to a city

urbane: polite; refined; polished (considered characteristic of those in cities)

urbanization: the process of an area becoming more like a city

US/UT: to use

abuse: to use wrongly or improperly

usage: a customary way of doing something

usurp: to seize and hold

utilitarian: efficient, functional, useful

V

VAIL/VAL: strength, use, worth

ambivalent: being caught between contradictory feelings of equal power or worth

avail: to have force; to be useful; to be of value

convalescent: recovering strength; healing

equivalent: of equal worth, strength, or use

evaluate: to determine the worth of

invalid: having no force or strength; void

valediction: a farewell (from wishing that someone be well; i.e., that someone have strength)

valid: having force; legally binding; effective; useful

value: worth

VEN/VENT: to come or to move toward

adventitious: accidental

contravene: to come into conflict with

convene: to assemble for some public purpose

intervene: to come between disputing factions, mediate

venturesome: showing a disposition to undertake risks

VER: truth

aver: to affirm, to declare to be true

veracious: habitually truthful

verdict: a judgment or decision

verisimilitude: the appearance or semblance of truth

verity: truthfulness

VERB: word

proverb: an adage; a byword; a short, commonly known saying

verbatim: exactly as stated; word-for-word

verbiage: excessive use of words; diction

verbose: wordy

VERD: green

verdant: green with vegetation; inexperienced

verdure: fresh, rich vegetation

VERS/VERT: to turn

aversion: dislike

avert: to turn away from

controversy: a public dispute involving a matter of opinion

diverse: of a different kind, form, character

extrovert: an outgoing person

inadvertent: unintentional

introvert: a person concerned primarily with inner thoughts and feelings

revert: to return to a former habit

VI: life

convivial: sociable

joie de vivre: joy of life (French expression)

viable: capable of living

vivacity: the quality of being lively, animated, spirited

vivid: strikingly bright or intense

VID/VIS: to see

adviser: one who gives counsel

evident: plain or clear to the sight or understanding

survey: to view in a general or comprehensive way

video: elements pertaining to the transmission or reception of an image

vista: a view or prospect

VIL: base, mean

revile: to criticize with harsh language

vile: loathsome, unpleasant

vilify: to slander, to defame

VIRU: poison

virulent: acrimonious; very bitter; very poisonous

viruliferous: containing a virus

virus: a submicroscopic agent that infects an organism and causes disease

VOC/VOK: call, word

advocate: to support or urge by argument

avocation: something one does in addition to a principle occupation

convoke: to call together

equivocate: to use ambiguous or unclear expressions

invoke: to call on a deity

vocabulary: the stock of words used by or known to a particular person or group

vocation: a particular occupation

vociferous: crying out noisily

VOL: wish

benevolent: characterized by or expressing goodwill

malevolent: characterized by or expressing bad will

volition: free choice, free will; act of choosing

voluntary: undertaken of one's own accord or by free choice

VOLU/VOLV: to roll, to turn

convolution: a twisting or folding

evolve: to develop naturally; literally, to unfold or unroll

revolt: to rebel; to turn against those in authority

revolve: to rotate; to turn around

voluble: easily turning; fluent; changeable

volume: a book (originally: a scroll); size or dimensions (originally: of a book)

VOR: to eat

carnivorous: meat-eating

omnivorous: eating or absorbing everything

voracious: having a great appetite

Top GRE Words in Context

The GRE tests the same kinds of words over and over again. Here you will find the most popular GRE words with their definitions in context to help you to remember them. If you see a word that's unfamiliar to you, take a moment to study the definition and, most importantly, reread the sentence with the word's definition in mind.

Remember: Learning vocabulary words in context is one of the best ways for your brain to retain the words' meanings. A broader vocabulary will serve you well on all four GRE Verbal question types and will also be extremely helpful in the Analytical Writing section.

A

ABATE: to reduce in amount, degree, or severity

As the hurricane's force ABATED, the winds dropped and the sea became calm.

ABSCOND: to leave secretly

The patron ABSCONDED from the restaurant by sneaking out the back door without paying his bill.

ABSTAIN: to choose not to do something

She ABSTAINED from choosing a mouthwatering dessert from the tray.

ABYSS: an extremely deep hole

The submarine dove into the ABYSS to chart the previously unseen depths.

ADULTERATE: to make impure

The chef made his ketchup last longer by ADULTERATING it with water.

ADVOCATE: to speak in favor of

The vegetarian ADVOCATED a diet containing no meat.

AESTHETIC: concerning the appreciation of beauty

Followers of the AESTHETIC Movement regarded the pursuit of beauty as the only true purpose of art.

AGGRANDIZE: to increase in power, influence, and reputation

The supervisor sought to AGGRANDIZE herself by claiming that the achievements of her staff were actually her own.

ALLEVIATE: to make more bearable

Taking aspirin helps to ALLEVIATE a headache.

AMALGAMATE: to combine; to mix together

Giant Industries AMALGAMATED with Mega Products to form Giant-Mega Products Incorporated.

AMBIGUOUS: doubtful or uncertain; able to be interpreted several ways

The directions she gave were so AMBIGUOUS that we disagreed on which way to turn.

AMELIORATE: to make better; to improve

The doctor was able to AMELIORATE the patient's suffering using painkillers.

ANACHRONISM: something out of place in time

The aged hippie used ANACHRONISTIC phrases like *groovy* and *far out* that had not been popular for years.

ANALOGOUS: similar or alike in some way; equivalent to

In the Newtonian construct for explaining the existence of God, the universe is ANALOGOUS to a mechanical timepiece, the creation of a divinely intelligent "clockmaker."

ANOMALY: deviation from what is normal

Albino animals may display too great an ANOMALY in their coloring to attract normally colored mates.

ANTAGONIZE: to annoy or provoke to anger

The child discovered that he could ANTAGONIZE the cat by pulling its tail.

ANTIPATHY: extreme dislike

The ANTIPATHY between the French and the English regularly erupted into open warfare.

APATHY: lack of interest or emotion

The APATHY of voters is so great that less than half the people who are eligible to vote actually bother to do so.

ARBITRATE: to judge a dispute between two opposing parties

Since the couple could not come to an agreement, a judge was forced to ARBITRATE their divorce proceedings.

ARCHAIC: ancient; old-fashioned

Her ARCHAIC Commodore computer could not run the latest software.

ARDOR: intense and passionate feeling

Bishop's ARDOR for the landscape was evident when he passionately described the beauty of the scenic Hudson Valley.

ARTICULATE: able to speak clearly and expressively

She is such an ARTICULATE defender of labor that unions are among her strongest supporters.

ASSUAGE: to make something unpleasant less severe

Serena used aspirin to ASSUAGE her pounding headache.

ATTENUATE: to reduce in force or degree; to weaken

The Bill of Rights ATTENUATED the traditional power of governments to change laws at will.

AUDACIOUS: fearless and daring

Her AUDACIOUS nature allowed her to fulfill her dream of skydiving.

AUSTERE: severe or stern in appearance; undecorated

The lack of decoration makes military barracks seem AUSTERE to the civilian eye.

B

BANAL: predictable; clichéd; boring

He used BANAL phrases like *Have a nice day*, or *Another day, another dollar.*

BOLSTER: to support; to prop up

The presence of giant footprints BOLSTERED the argument that Sasquatch was in the area.

BOMBASTIC: pompous in speech and manner

The ranting of the radio talk-show host was mostly BOMBASTIC; his boasting and outrageous claims had no basis in fact.

C

CACOPHONY: harsh, jarring noise

The junior-high orchestra created an almost unbearable CACOPHONY as they tried to tune their instruments.

CANDID: impartial and honest in speech

The observations of a child can be charming since they are CANDID and unpretentious.

CAPRICIOUS: changing one's mind quickly and often

Queen Elizabeth I was quite CAPRICIOUS; her courtiers could never be sure which of their number would catch her fancy.

CASTIGATE: to punish or criticize harshly

Many Americans are amazed at how harshly the authorities in Singapore CASTIGATE perpetrators of what would be considered minor crimes in the United States.

CATALYST: something that brings about a change in something else

The imposition of harsh taxes was the CATALYST that finally brought on the revolution.

CAUSTIC: biting in wit

Dorothy Parker gained her reputation for CAUSTIC wit from her cutting, yet clever, insults.

CHAOS: great disorder or confusion

In many religious traditions, God created an ordered universe from CHAOS.

CHAUVINIST: someone prejudiced in favor of a group to which one belongs

The attitude that men are inherently superior to women and therefore must be obeyed is common among male CHAUVINISTS.

CHICANERY: deception by means of craft or guile

Dishonest used car salespeople often use CHICANERY to sell their beat-up old cars.

COGENT: convincing and well reasoned

Swayed by the COGENT argument of the defense, the jury had no choice but to acquit the defendant.

CONDONE: to overlook, pardon, or disregard

Some theorists believe that failing to prosecute minor crimes is the same as CONDONING an air of lawlessness.

CONVOLUTED: intricate and complicated

Many people bought *A Brief History of Time* because it took CONVOLUTED scientific theories and made them easier to understand.

CORROBORATE: to provide supporting evidence

Fingerprints CORROBORATED the witness's testimony that he saw the defendant in the victim's apartment.

CREDULOUS: too trusting; gullible

Although some four-year-olds believe in the Easter Bunny, only the most CREDULOUS nine-year-olds also believe in him.

CRESCENDO: steadily increasing volume or force

The CRESCENDO of tension became unbearable as Evel Knievel prepared to jump his motorcycle over the school buses.

D

DECORUM: appropriateness of behavior or conduct; propriety

The countess complained that the vulgar peasants lacked the DECORUM appropriate for a visit to the palace.

DEFERENCE: respect; courtesy

The respectful young law clerk treated the Supreme Court justice with the utmost DEFERENCE.

DERIDE: to speak of or treat with contempt; to mock

The awkward child was often DERIDED by his classmates.

DESICCATE: to dry out thoroughly

After a few weeks of lying on the desert's baking sands, the cow's carcass became completely DESICCATED.

DESULTORY: jumping from one thing to another; disconnected

Diane had a DESULTORY academic record; she had changed majors 12 times in three years.

DIATRIBE: an abusive, condemnatory speech

The trucker bellowed a DIATRIBE at the driver who had cut him off.

DIFFIDENT: lacking self-confidence

Steve's DIFFIDENT manner during the job interview stemmed from his nervous nature and lack of experience in the field.

DILATE: to make larger; to expand

When you enter a darkened room, the pupils of your eyes DILATE to let in more light.

DILATORY: intended to delay

The congressman used DILATORY measures to delay the passage of the bill.

DILETTANTE: someone with an amateurish and superficial interest in a topic

Jerry's friends were such DILETTANTES that they seemed to have new jobs and hobbies every week.

DIRGE: a funeral hymn or mournful speech

Melville wrote the poem "A DIRGE for James McPherson" for the funeral of a Union general who was killed in 1864.

DISABUSE: to set right; to free from error

Galileo's observations DISABUSED scholars of the notion that the sun revolved around the Earth.

DISCERN: to perceive; to recognize

It is easy to DISCERN the difference between butter and butter-flavored topping.

DISPARATE: fundamentally different; entirely unlike

Although the twins appear to be identical physically, their personalities are quite DISPARATE.

DISSEMBLE: to present a false appearance; to disguise one's real intentions or character

The villain could DISSEMBLE to the police no longer—he admitted the deed and tore up the floor to reveal the body of the old man.

DISSONANCE: a harsh and disagreeable combination, often of sounds

Cognitive DISSONANCE is the inner conflict produced when long-standing beliefs are contradicted by new evidence.

DOGMA: a firmly held opinion, often a religious belief

Linus's central DOGMA was that children who believed in the Great Pumpkin would be rewarded.

DOGMATIC: dictatorial in one's opinions

The dictator was DOGMATIC—he, and only he, was right.

DUPE: to deceive; a person who is easily deceived

Bugs Bunny was able to DUPE Elmer Fudd by dressing up as a lady rabbit.

E

ECLECTIC: selecting from or made up from a variety of sources

Budapest's architecture is an ECLECTIC mix of Eastern and Western styles.

EFFICACY: effectiveness

The EFFICACY of penicillin was unsurpassed when it was first introduced; the drug completely eliminated almost all bacterial infections for which it was administered.

ELEGY: a sorrowful poem or speech

Although Thomas Gray's "ELEGY Written in a Country Churchyard" is about death and loss, it urges its readers to endure this life and to trust in spirituality.

ELOQUENT: persuasive and moving, especially in speech

The Gettysburg Address is moving not only because of its lofty sentiments but also for its ELOQUENCE.

EMULATE: to copy; to try to equal or excel

The graduate student sought to EMULATE his professor in every way, copying not only how she taught but also how she conducted herself outside of class.

ENERVATE: to reduce in strength

The guerrillas hoped that a series of surprise attacks would ENERVATE the regular army.

ENGENDER: to produce, cause, or bring about

His fear and hatred of clowns was ENGENDERED when he witnessed the death of his father at the hands of a clown.

ENIGMA: a puzzle; a mystery

Speaking in riddles and dressed in old robes, the artist gained a reputation as something of an ENIGMA.

ENUMERATE: to count, list, or itemize

Moses returned from the mountain with tablets on which the commandments were ENUMERATED.

EPHEMERAL: lasting a short time

The lives of mayflies seem EPHEMERAL to us, since the flies' average life span is a matter of hours.

EQUIVOCATE: to use expressions of double meaning in order to mislead

When faced with criticism of her policies, the politician EQUIVOCATED and left all parties thinking she agreed with them.

ERRATIC: wandering and unpredictable

The plot seemed predictable until it suddenly took a series of ERRATIC turns that surprised the audience.

ERUDITE: learned; scholarly; bookish

The annual meeting of philosophy professors was a gathering of the most ERUDITE, well-published individuals in the field.

ESOTERIC: known or understood by only a few

Only a handful of experts are knowledgeable about the ESOTERIC world of particle physics.

ESTIMABLE: admirable

Most people consider it ESTIMABLE that Mother Teresa spent her life helping the poor of India.

EULOGY: speech in praise of someone

His best friend gave the EULOGY, outlining his many achievements and talents.

EUPHEMISM: use of an inoffensive word or phrase in place of a more distasteful one

The funeral director preferred to use the EUPHEMISM *resting* instead of the word *dead*.

EXACERBATE: to make worse

It is unwise to take aspirin to try to relieve heartburn; instead of providing relief, the drug will only EXACERBATE the problem.

EXCULPATE: to clear from blame; prove innocent

The adversarial legal system is intended to convict those who are guilty and to EXCULPATE those who are innocent.

EXIGENT: urgent; requiring immediate action

The patient was losing blood so rapidly that it was EXIGENT to stop the source of the bleeding.

EXONERATE: to clear of blame

The fugitive was EXONERATED when another criminal confessed to committing the crime.

EXPLICIT: clearly stated or shown; forthright in expression

The owners of the house left a list of EXPLICIT instructions detailing their house sitter's duties, including a schedule for watering the houseplants.

F

FANATICAL: acting excessively enthusiastic; filled with extreme, unquestioned devotion

The storm troopers were FANATICAL in their devotion to the emperor, readily sacrificing their lives for him.

FAWN: to grovel

The understudy FAWNED over the director in the hopes of being cast in the part on a permanent basis.

FERVID: intensely emotional; feverish

The fans of Maria Callas were unusually FERVID, doing anything to catch a glimpse of the great opera singer.

FLORID: excessively decorated or embellished

The palace had been decorated in a FLORID style; every surface had been carved and gilded.

FOMENT: to arouse or incite

The protesters tried to FOMENT feeling against the war through their speeches and demonstrations.

FRUGALITY: a tendency to be thrifty or cheap

Scrooge McDuck's FRUGALITY was so great that he accumulated enough wealth to fill a giant storehouse with money.

G

GARRULOUS: tending to talk a lot

The GARRULOUS parakeet distracted its owner with its continuous talking.

GREGARIOUS: outgoing; sociable

She was so GREGARIOUS that when she found herself alone, she felt quite sad.

GUILE: deceit or trickery

Since he was not fast enough to catch the road-runner on foot, the coyote resorted to GUILE in an effort to trap his enemy.

GULLIBLE: easily deceived

The con man pretended to be a bank officer so as to fool GULLIBLE bank customers into giving him their account information.

H

HOMOGENOUS: of a similar kind

The class was fairly HOMOGENOUS, since almost all of the students were senior journalism majors.

I

ICONOCLAST: one who opposes established beliefs, customs, and institutions

His lack of regard for traditional beliefs soon established him as an ICONOCLAST.

IMPERTURBABLE: not capable of being disturbed

The counselor had so much experience dealing with distraught children that she seemed IMPERTURBABLE, even when faced with the wildest tantrums.

IMPERVIOUS: impossible to penetrate; incapable of being affected

A good raincoat will be IMPERVIOUS to moisture.

IMPETUOUS: quick to act without thinking

It is not good for an investment broker to be IMPETUOUS, since much thought should be given to all the possible options.

IMPLACABLE: unable to be calmed down or made peaceful

His rage at the betrayal was so great that he remained IMPLACABLE for weeks.

INCHOATE: not fully formed; disorganized

The ideas expressed in Nietzsche's mature work also appear in an INCHOATE form in his earliest writing.

INGENUOUS: showing innocence or childlike simplicity

She was so INGENUOUS that her friends feared her innocence and trustfulness would be exploited when she visited the big city.

INIMICAL: hostile, unfriendly

Even though the children had grown up together, they were INIMICAL to each other at school.

INNOCUOUS: harmless

Some snakes are poisonous, but most species are INNOCUOUS and pose no danger to humans.

INSIPID: lacking interest or flavor

The critic claimed that the painting was INSIPID, containing no interesting qualities at all.

INTRANSIGENT: uncompromising; refusing to be reconciled

The professor was INTRANSIGENT on the deadline, insisting that everyone turn the assignment in at the same time.

INUNDATE: to overwhelm; to cover with water

The tidal wave INUNDATED Atlantis, which was lost beneath the water.

IRASCIBLE: easily made angry

Attila the Hun's IRASCIBLE and violent nature made all who dealt with him fear for their lives.

L

LACONIC: using few words

She was a LACONIC poet who built her reputation on using words as sparingly as possible.

LAMENT: to express sorrow; to grieve

The children continued to LAMENT the death of the goldfish weeks after its demise.

LAUD: to give praise; to glorify

Parades and fireworks were staged to LAUD the success of the rebels.

LAVISH: to give unsparingly (v.); extremely generous or extravagant (adj.)

She LAVISHED the puppy with so many treats that it soon became overweight and spoiled.

LETHARGIC: acting in an indifferent or slow, sluggish manner

The clerk was so LETHARGIC that, even when the store was slow, he always had a long line in front of him.

LOQUACIOUS: talkative

She was naturally LOQUACIOUS, which was a problem in situations in which listening was more important than talking.

LUCID: clear and easily understood

The explanations were written in a simple and LUCID manner so that students were immediately able to apply what they learned.

LUMINOUS: bright; brilliant; glowing

The park was bathed in LUMINOUS sunshine, which warmed the bodies and the souls of the visitors.

M

MALINGER: to evade responsibility by pretending to be ill

A common way to avoid the draft was by MALINGERING—pretending to be mentally or physically ill so as to avoid being taken by the Army.

MALLEABLE: capable of being shaped

Gold is the most MALLEABLE of precious metals; it can easily be formed into almost any shape.

METAPHOR: a figure of speech comparing two different things; a symbol

The METAPHOR "a sea of troubles" suggests a lot of troubles by comparing their number to the vastness of the sea.

METICULOUS: extremely careful about details

To find all the clues at the crime scene, the investigators METICULOUSLY examined every inch of the area.

MISANTHROPE: a person who dislikes others

The character Scrooge in *A Christmas Carol* is such a MISANTHROPE that even the sight of children singing makes him angry.

MITIGATE: to soften; to lessen

A judge may MITIGATE a sentence if she decides that a person committed a crime out of need.

MOLLIFY: to calm or make less severe

Their argument was so intense that it was difficult to believe any compromise would MOLLIFY them.

MONOTONY: lack of variation

The MONOTONY of the sound of the dripping faucet almost drove the research assistant crazy.

N

NAIVE: lacking sophistication or experience

Having never traveled before, the elementary-school students were more NAIVE than their high-school counterparts on the field trip.

O

OBDURATE: hardened in feeling; resistant to persuasion

The president was completely OBDURATE on the issue, and no amount of persuasion would change his mind.

OBSEQUIOUS: overly submissive and eager to please

The OBSEQUIOUS new associate made sure to compliment her supervisor's tie and agree with him on every issue.

OBSTINATE: stubborn; unyielding

The OBSTINATE child could not be made to eat any food that he disliked.

OBVIATE: to prevent; to make unnecessary

The river was shallow enough to wade across at many points, which OBVIATED the need for a bridge.

OCCLUDE: to stop up; to prevent the passage of

A shadow is thrown across the Earth's surface during a solar eclipse, when the light from the sun is OCCLUDED by the moon.

ONEROUS: troublesome and oppressive; burdensome

The assignment was so extensive and difficult to manage that it proved ONEROUS to the team in charge of it.

OPAQUE: impossible to see through; preventing the passage of light

The heavy buildup of dirt and grime on the windows almost made them OPAQUE.

OPPROBRIUM: public disgrace

After the scheme to embezzle the elderly was made public, the treasurer resigned in utter OPPROBRIUM.

OSTENTATION: excessive showiness

The OSTENTATION of the Sun King's court is evident in the lavish decoration and luxuriousness of his palace at Versailles.

P

PARADOX: a contradiction or dilemma

It is a PARADOX that those most in need of medical attention are often those least able to obtain it.

PARAGON: model of excellence or perfection

She is the PARAGON of what a judge should be: honest, intelligent, hardworking, and just.

PEDANT: someone who shows off learning

The graduate instructor's tedious and excessive commentary on the subject soon gained her a reputation as a PEDANT.

PERFIDIOUS: willing to betray one's trust

The actress's PERFIDIOUS companion revealed all of her intimate secrets to the gossip columnist.

PERFUNCTORY: done in a routine way; indifferent

The machine-like bank teller processed the transaction and gave the waiting customer a PERFUNCTORY smile.

PERMEATE: to penetrate

This miraculous new cleaning fluid is able to PERMEATE stains and dissolve them in minutes!

PHILANTHROPY: charity; a desire or effort to promote goodness

New York's Metropolitan Museum of Art owes much of its collection to the PHILANTHROPY of private collectors who willed their estates to the museum.

PLACATE: to soothe or pacify

The burglar tried to PLACATE the snarling dog by saying, "Nice doggy," and offering it a treat.

PLASTIC: able to be molded, altered, or bent

The new material was very PLASTIC and could be formed into products of vastly different shapes.

PLETHORA: excess

Assuming that more was better, the defendant offered the judge a PLETHORA of excuses.

PRAGMATIC: practical, as opposed to idealistic

While daydreaming gamblers think they can get rich by frequenting casinos, PRAGMATIC gamblers realize that the odds are heavily stacked against them.

PRECIPITATE: to throw violently or bring about abruptly; lacking deliberation

Upon learning that the couple married after knowing each other only two months, friends and family members expected such a PRECIPITATE marriage to end in divorce.

PREVARICATE: to lie or deviate from the truth

Rather than admit that he had overslept again, the employee PREVARICATED and claimed that heavy traffic had prevented him from arriving at work on time.

PRISTINE: fresh and clean; uncorrupted

Since concerted measures had been taken to prevent looting, the archeological site was still PRISTINE when researchers arrived.

PRODIGAL: lavish; wasteful

The PRODIGAL son quickly wasted all of his inheritance on a lavish lifestyle devoted to pleasure.

PROLIFERATE: to increase in number quickly

Although she only kept two guinea pigs initially, they PROLIFERATED to such an extent that she soon had dozens.

PROPITIATE: to conciliate; to appease

The management PROPITIATED the irate union by agreeing to raise wages for its members.

PROPRIETY: correct behavior; obedience to rules and customs

The aristocracy maintained a high level of PROPRIETY, adhering to even the most minor social rules.

PRUDENCE: wisdom, caution, or restraint

The college student exhibited PRUDENCE by obtaining practical experience along with her studies, which greatly strengthened her resume.

PUNGENT: sharp and irritating to the senses

The smoke from the burning tires was extremely PUNGENT.

Q

QUIESCENT: motionless

Many animals are QUIESCENT over the winter months, minimizing activity in order to conserve energy.

R

RAREFY: to make thinner or sparser

Since the atmosphere RAREFIES as altitudes increase, the air at the top of very tall mountains is too thin to breathe.

REPUDIATE: to reject the validity of

The old woman's claim that she was Russian royalty was REPUDIATED when DNA tests showed she was not related to them.

RETICENT: silent; reserved

Physically small and RETICENT in her speech, Joan Didion often went unnoticed by those upon whom she was reporting.

RHETORIC: effective writing or speaking

Lincoln's talent for RHETORIC was evident in his beautifully expressed Gettysburg Address.

S

SATIATE: to satisfy fully or overindulge

His desire for power was so great that nothing less than complete control of the country could SATIATE it.

SOPORIFIC: causing sleep or lethargy

The movie proved to be so SOPORIFIC that soon loud snores were heard throughout the theater.

SPECIOUS: deceptively attractive; seemingly plausible but fallacious

The student's SPECIOUS excuse for being late sounded legitimate but was proved otherwise when her teacher called her home.

STIGMA: a mark of shame or discredit

In *The Scarlet Letter*, Hester Prynne was required to wear the letter *A* on her clothes as a public STIGMA for her adultery.

STOLID: unemotional; lacking sensitivity

The prisoner appeared STOLID and unaffected by the judge's harsh sentence.

SUBLIME: lofty or grand

The music was so SUBLIME that it transformed the rude surroundings into a special place.

T

TACIT: done without using words

Although not a word had been said, everyone in the room knew that a TACIT agreement had been made about which course of action to take.

TACITURN: silent, not talkative

The clerk's TACITURN nature earned him the nickname "Silent Bob."

TIRADE: long, harsh speech or verbal attack

Observers were shocked at the manager's TIRADE over such a minor mistake.

TORPOR: extreme mental and physical sluggishness

After surgery, the patient experienced TORPOR until the anesthesia wore off.

TRANSITORY: temporary; lasting a brief time

The reporter lived a TRANSITORY life, staying in one place only long enough to cover the current story.

V

VACILLATE: to sway physically; to be indecisive

The customer held up the line as he VACILLATED between ordering chocolate chip or rocky road ice cream.

VENERATE: to respect deeply

In a traditional Confucian society, the young VENERATE their elders, deferring to the elders' wisdom and experience.

VERACITY: filled with truth and accuracy

She had a reputation for VERACITY, so everyone trusted her description of events.

VERBOSE: wordy

The professor's answer was so VERBOSE that his student forgot what the original question had been.

VEX: to annoy

The old man who loved his peace and quiet was VEXED by his neighbor's loud music.

VOLATILE: easily aroused or changeable; lively or explosive

His VOLATILE personality made it difficult to predict his reaction to anything.

W

WAVER: to fluctuate between choices

If you WAVER too long before making a decision about which testing site to register for, you may not get your first choice.

WHIMSICAL: acting in a fanciful or capricious manner; unpredictable

The ballet was WHIMSICAL, delighting the children with its imaginative characters and unpredictable sets.

Z

ZEAL: passion; excitement

She brought her typical ZEAL to the project, sparking enthusiasm in the other team members.

COMMONLY CONFUSED WORDS

Already—by this or that time; previously
He already completed his work.
All ready—completely prepared
The students were all ready to take their exam.

Altogether—entirely; completely
I am altogether certain that I turned in my homework.
All together—in the same place
She kept the figurines all together on her mantle.

Capital—a city containing the seat of government; the wealth or funds owned by a business or individual; resources
Atlanta is the capital of Georgia.
The company's capital gains have diminished in recent years.
Capitol—the building in which a legislative body meets
Our trip included a visit to the Capitol building in Washington, D.C.

Coarse—rough, not smooth; lacking refinement
The truck's large wheels enabled it to navigate the coarse, rough terrain.
His coarse language prevented him from getting hired for the job.
Course—path; series of classes or studies
James's favorite course is biology.
The doctor suggested that Amy rest and let the disease run its course.

Here—in this location
George Washington used to live here.
Hear—to listen to or to perceive by the ear
Did you hear the question?

Its—a personal pronoun that shows possession
Please put the book back in its place.
It's—the contraction of "it is" or "it has"
It's snowing outside.
It's been too long.

Lead—to act as a leader, to go first, or to take a superior position
The guide will lead us through the forest.
Led—past tense of "lead"
The guide led us through the forest.
Lead—a metal
It is dangerous to inhale fumes from paint containing lead.

Loose—free; to set free; not tight
She always wears loose clothing when she does yoga.
Lose—to become without
Use a bookmark so you don't lose your place in your book.

Passed—the past tense of "pass"; a euphemism for someone dying
We passed by her house on Sunday.
Past—that which has gone by or elapsed in time
In the past, Abby never used to study.
We drove past her house.

Principal—the head of a school; main or important
The quarterback's injury is the principal reason the team lost.
The principal of the school meets with parents regularly.
Principle—a fundamental law or truth
The laws of motion are among the most important principles in physics.

Stationary—fixed, not moving
Thomas rode a stationary bicycle at the gym.
Stationery—paper used for letter writing
The principal's stationery has the school's logo on the top.

Their—possessive of "they"
Paul and Ben studied for their test together.
There—a place; in that matter or respect
There are several question types on the GRE.
Please hang up your jacket over there.
They're—contraction of "they are"
Be careful of the bushes as they're filled with thorns.

Your—possessive of "you"
With practice, your vocabulary will increase.
You're—contraction of "you" and "are"
You're likely to encounter new words in practice exams.

Math Reference

The math on the GRE covers a lot of ground—from number properties and arithmetic to basic algebra and symbol problems to geometry and statistics. Don't let yourself be intimidated.

We've highlighted the 100 most important concepts that you need to know and divided them into three levels. The GRE Quantitative sections test your understanding of a relatively limited number of mathematical concepts, all of which you will be able to master.

Level 1 consists of foundational math topics. Though these topics may seem basic, review this list so that you are aware that these skills may play a part in the questions you will answer on the GRE. Look over the Level 1 list to make sure you're comfortable with the basics.

Level 2 is where most people start their review of math. Level 2 skills and formulas come into play quite frequently on the GRE. If the skills needed to handle Level 1 or 2 topics are keeping you from feeling up to the tasks expected on the GRE Quantitative section, you might consider taking the Kaplan GRE Math Refresher course.

Level 3 represents the most challenging math concepts you'll find on the GRE. Don't spend a lot of time on Level 3 if you still have gaps in Level 2, but once you've mastered Level 2, tackling Level 3 can put you over the top.

LEVEL 1

1. How to add, subtract, multiply, and divide WHOLE NUMBERS

You can check addition with subtraction.

$$17 + 5 = 22 \qquad 22 - 5 = 17$$

You can check multiplication with division.

$$5 \times 28 = 140 \qquad 140 \div 5 = 28$$

2. How to add, subtract, multiply, and divide FRACTIONS

Find a common denominator before adding or subtracting fractions.

$$\frac{4}{5} + \frac{3}{10} = \frac{8}{10} + \frac{3}{10} = \frac{11}{10} \text{ or } 1\frac{1}{10}$$

$$2 - \frac{3}{8} = \frac{16}{8} - \frac{3}{8} = \frac{13}{8} \text{ or } 1\frac{5}{8}$$

To multiply fractions, multiply the numerators first and then multiply the denominators. Simplify if necessary.

$$\frac{3}{4} \times \frac{1}{6} = \frac{3}{24} = \frac{1}{8}$$

You can also reduce before multiplying numerators and denominators. This keeps the products small.

$$\frac{5}{8} \times \frac{2}{15} = \frac{\overset{1}{\cancel{5}}}{\underset{4}{\cancel{8}}} \times \frac{\overset{1}{\cancel{2}}}{\underset{3}{\cancel{15}}} = \frac{1}{12}$$

To divide by a fraction, multiply by its reciprocal. To write the reciprocal of a fraction, flip the numerator and the denominator.

$$5 \div \frac{1}{3} = \frac{5}{1} \times \frac{3}{1} = 15 \qquad \frac{1}{3} \div \frac{4}{5} = \frac{1}{3} \times \frac{5}{4} = \frac{5}{12}$$

3. How to add, subtract, multiply, and divide DECIMALS

To add or subtract, align the decimal points and then add or subtract normally. Place the decimal point in the answer directly below existing decimal points.

$$\begin{array}{r} 3.25 \\ +\,4.4 \\ \hline 7.65 \end{array} \qquad \begin{array}{r} 7.65 \\ -\,4.4 \\ \hline 3.25 \end{array}$$

To multiply with decimals, multiply the digits normally and count off decimal places (equal to the total number of places in the factors) from the right.

$$2.5 \times 2.5 = 6.25$$
$$0.06 \times 2{,}000 = 120.00 = 120$$

To divide by a decimal, move the decimal point in the divisor to the right to form a whole number; move the decimal point in the dividend the same number of places. Divide as though there were no decimals, then place the decimal point in the quotient.

$$6.25 \div 2.5$$
$$= 62.5 \div 25 = 2.5$$

4. How to convert FRACTIONS TO DECIMALS and DECIMALS TO FRACTIONS

To convert a fraction to a decimal, divide the numerator by the denominator.

$$\frac{4}{5} = 0.8 \qquad \frac{4}{50} = 0.08 \qquad \frac{4}{500} = 0.008$$

To convert a decimal to a fraction, write the digits in the numerator and use the decimal name in the denominator.

$$0.003 = \frac{3}{1{,}000} \qquad 0.03 = \frac{3}{100} \qquad 0.3 = \frac{3}{10}$$

5. How to add, subtract, multiply, and divide POSITIVE AND NEGATIVE NUMBERS

When addends (the numbers being added) have the same sign, add their absolute values; the sum has the same sign as the addends. But when addends have different signs, subtract the absolute values; the sum has the sign of the greater absolute value.

$$3 + 9 = 12, \text{ but } -3 + (-9) = -12$$
$$3 + (-9) = -6, \text{ but } -3 + 9 = 6$$

In multiplication and division, when the signs are the same, the product/quotient is positive. When the signs are different, the product/quotient is negative.

$6 \times 7 = 42$ and $-6 \times (-7) = 42$
$-6 \times 7 = -42$ and $6 \times (-7) = -42$
$96 \div 8 = 12$ and $-96 \div (-8) = 12$
$-96 \div 8 = -12$ and $96 \div (-8) = -12$

6. How to plot points on the NUMBER LINE

To plot the point 4.5 on the number line, start at 0, go right to 4.5, halfway between 4 and 5.

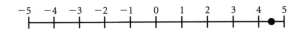

To plot the point −2.5 on the number line, start at 0, go left to −2.5, halfway between −2 and −3.

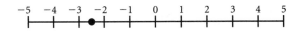

7. How to plug a number into an ALGEBRAIC EXPRESSION

To evaluate an algebraic expression, choose numbers for the variables or use the numbers assigned to the variables.

Evaluate $4np + 1$ when $n = -4$ and $p = 3$.

$4np + 1 = 4(-4)(3) + 1 = -48 + 1 = -47$

8. How to SOLVE a simple LINEAR EQUATION

Use algebra to isolate the variable. Do the same steps to both sides of the equation.

$$
\begin{aligned}
28 &= -3x - 5 \\
28 + 5 &= -3x - 5 + 5 \quad \text{Add 5.} \\
33 &= -3x \\
\frac{33}{-3} &= \frac{-3x}{-3} \quad\quad\quad \text{Divide by } -3. \\
-11 &= x
\end{aligned}
$$

9. How to add and subtract LINE SEGMENTS

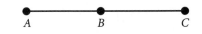

If $AB = 6$ and $BC = 8$, then $AC = 6 + 8 = 14$.
If $AC = 14$ and $BC = 8$, then $AB = 14 - 8 = 6$.

10. How to find the THIRD ANGLE of a TRIANGLE, given the other two angles

Use the fact that the sum of the measures of the interior angles of a triangle always equals 180°.

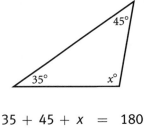

$$
\begin{aligned}
35 + 45 + x &= 180 \\
80 + x &= 180 \\
x &= 100
\end{aligned}
$$

LEVEL 2

11. How to use PEMDAS

When you're given a complex arithmetic expression, it's important to know the order of operations. Just remember PEMDAS (as in "Please Excuse My Dear Aunt Sally"). What PEMDAS means is this: Clean up **Parentheses** first (nested sets of parentheses are worked from the innermost set to the outermost set); then deal with **Exponents** (or **Radicals**); then do the **Multiplication** and **Division** together, going from left to right; and finally do the **Addition** and **Subtraction** together, again going from left to right.

Example:

$$9 - 2 \times (5 - 3)^2 + 6 \div 3 =$$

Begin with the parentheses:

$$9 - 2 \times (2)^2 + 6 \div 3 =$$

Then do the exponent:

$$9 - 2 \times 4 + 6 \div 3 =$$

Now do multiplication and division from left to right:

$$9 - 8 + 2 =$$

Finally, do addition and subtraction from left to right:

$$1 + 2 = 3$$

12. How to use the PERCENT FORMULA

Identify the part, the percent, and the whole.

$$Part = Percent \times Whole$$

Find the part.

Example:

What is 12 percent of 25?

Setup:

$$Part = \frac{12}{100} \times 25 = \frac{300}{100} = 3$$

Find the percent.

Example:

45 is what percent of 9?

Setup:

$$45 = \frac{Percent}{100} \times 9$$
$$4,500 = Percent \times 9$$
$$500 = Percent$$

Find the whole.

Example:

15 is $\frac{3}{5}$ percent of what number?

Setup:

$$15 = \frac{3}{5}\left(\frac{1}{100}\right) \times Whole$$
$$15 = \frac{3}{500} \times Whole$$
$$Whole = 15\left(\frac{500}{3}\right) = \frac{7,500}{3} = 2,500$$

13. How to use the PERCENT INCREASE/DECREASE FORMULAS

Identify the original whole and the amount of increase/decrease.

$$Percent\ increase = \frac{Amount\ of\ increase}{Original\ whole} \times 100\%$$

$$Percent\ decrease = \frac{Amount\ of\ decrease}{Original\ whole} \times 100\%$$

Example:

The price goes up from $80 to $100. What is the percent increase?

Setup:

$$Percent\ increase = \frac{20}{80} \times 100\%$$
$$= 0.25 \times 100\% = 25\%$$

14. How to predict whether a sum, difference, or product will be ODD or EVEN

Don't bother memorizing the rules. Just take simple numbers like 2 for even numbers and 3 for odd numbers and see what happens.

Example:

If m is even and n is odd, is the product mn odd or even?

Setup:

Say $m = 2$ and $n = 3$.
$2 \times 3 = 6$, which is even, so mn is even.

15. How to recognize MULTIPLES OF 2, 3, 4, 5, 6, 9, 10, and 12

2: Last digit is even.

3: Sum of digits is a multiple of 3.

4: Last two digits are a multiple of 4.

5: Last digit is 5 or 0.

6: Sum of digits is a multiple of 3, and last digit is even.

9: Sum of digits is a multiple of 9.

10: Last digit is 0.

12: Sum of digits is a multiple of 3, and last two digits are a multiple of 4.

16. How to find a COMMON FACTOR of two numbers

Break both numbers down to their prime factors to see which they have in common. Then multiply the shared prime factors to find all common factors.

Example:

What factors greater than 1 do 135 and 225 have in common?

Setup:

First find the prime factors of 135 and 225; $135 = 3 \times 3 \times 3 \times 5$, and $225 = 3 \times 3 \times 5 \times 5$. The numbers share $3 \times 3 \times 5$ in common. Thus, aside from 3 and 5, the remaining common factors can be found by multiplying 3, 3, and 5 in every possible combination: $3 \times 3 = 9$, $3 \times 5 = 15$, and $3 \times 3 \times 5 = 45$. Therefore, the common factors of 135 and 225 are 3, 5, 9, 15, and 45.

17. How to find a COMMON MULTIPLE of two numbers

The product of two numbers is the easiest common multiple to find, but it is not always the least common multiple (LCM).

Example:

What is the least common multiple of 28 and 42?

Setup:

$$28 = 2 \times 2 \times 7$$
$$42 = 2 \times 3 \times 7$$

The LCM can be found by finding the prime factorization of each number, then seeing the greatest number of times each factor is used. Multiply each prime factor the greatest number of times it appears.

In 28, 2 is used twice. In 42, 2 is used once. In 28, 7 is used once. In 42, 7 is used once, and 3 is used once.

So you multiply each factor the greatest number of times it appears in a prime factorization:

$$LCM = 2 \times 2 \times 3 \times 7 = 84$$

18. How to find the AVERAGE or ARITHMETIC MEAN

$$Average = \frac{Sum\ of\ terms}{Number\ of\ terms}$$

Example:

What is the average of 3, 4, and 8?

Setup:

$$Average = \frac{3 + 4 + 8}{3} = \frac{15}{3} = 5$$

19. How to use the AVERAGE to find the SUM

$$Sum = (Average) \times (Number\ of\ terms)$$

Example:

17.5 is the average (arithmetic mean) of 24 numbers.

What is the sum of the 24 numbers?

Setup:

$$Sum = 17.5 \times 24 = 420$$

20. How to find the AVERAGE of CONSECUTIVE NUMBERS

The average of evenly spaced numbers is simply the average of the smallest number and the largest number. The average of all the integers from 13 to 77, for example, is the same as the average of 13 and 77:

$$\frac{13 + 77}{2} = \frac{90}{2} = 45$$

21. How to COUNT CONSECUTIVE NUMBERS

The number of integers from A to B inclusive is $B - A + 1$.

Example:

How many integers are there from 73 through 419, inclusive?

Setup:

$$419 - 73 + 1 = 347$$

22. How to find the SUM OF CONSECUTIVE NUMBERS

$$Sum = (Average) \times (Number\ of\ terms)$$

Example:

What is the sum of the integers from 10 through 50, inclusive?

Setup:

Average: $\dfrac{10 + 50}{2} = 30$

Number of terms: $50 - 10 + 1 = 41$

Sum: $30 \times 41 = 1{,}230$

23. How to find the MEDIAN

Put the numbers in numerical order and take the middle number.

Example:

What is the median of 88, 86, 57, 94, and 73?

Setup:

First, put the numbers in numerical order, then take the middle number:

$$57, 73, 86, 88, 94$$

The median is 86.

In a set with an even number of numbers, take the average of the two in the middle.

Example:

What is the median of 88, 86, 57, 73, 94, and 100?

Setup:

First, put the numbers in numerical order.

$$57, 73, 86, 88, 94, 100$$

Because 86 and 88 are the two numbers in the middle:

$$\frac{86 + 88}{2} = \frac{174}{2} = 87$$

The median is 87.

24. How to find the MODE

Take the number that appears most often. For example, if your test scores were 88, 57, 68, 85, 98, 93, 93, 84, and 81, the mode of the scores would be 93 because it appears more often than any other score. (If there's a tie for most often, then there's more than one mode. If each number in a set is used equally often, there is no mode.)

25. How to find the RANGE

Take the positive difference between the greatest and least values. Using the example under "How to find the MODE" above, if your test scores were 88, 57, 68, 85, 98, 93, 93, 84, and 81, the range of the scores would be 41, the greatest value minus the least value ($98 - 57 = 41$).

26. How to use actual numbers to determine a RATIO

To find a ratio, put the number associated with *of* on the top and the number associated with *to* on the bottom.

$$Ratio = \frac{of}{to}$$

The ratio of 20 oranges to 12 apples is $\dfrac{20}{12}$, or $\dfrac{5}{3}$.

Ratios should always be reduced to lowest terms. Ratios can also be expressed in linear form, such as 5:3.

27. How to use a ratio to determine an ACTUAL NUMBER

Set up a proportion using the given ratio.

Example:

The ratio of boys to girls is 3 to 4. If there are 135 boys, how many girls are there?

Setup:

$$\frac{3}{4} = \frac{135}{g}$$
$$3 \times g = 4 \times 135$$
$$3g = 540$$
$$g = 180$$

28. How to use actual numbers to determine a RATE

Identify the quantities and the units to be compared. Keep the units straight.

Example:

Anders typed 9,450 words in $3\frac{1}{2}$ hours. What was his rate in words per minute?

Setup:

First convert $3\frac{1}{2}$ hours to 210 minutes. Then set up the rate with words on top and minutes on bottom (because "per" means "divided by"):

$$\frac{9,450 \text{ words}}{210 \text{ minutes}} = 45 \text{ words per minute}$$

29. How to deal with TABLES, GRAPHS, AND CHARTS

Read the question and all labels carefully. Ignore extraneous information and zero in on what the question asks for. Take advantage of the spread in the answer choices by approximating the answer whenever possible and choosing the answer choice closest to your approximation.

30. How to count the NUMBER OF POSSIBILITIES

You can use multiplication to find the number of possibilities when items can be arranged in various ways.

Example:

How many three-digit numbers can be formed with the digits 1, 3, and 5 each used only once?

Setup:

Look at each digit individually. The first digit (or, the hundreds digit) has three possible numbers to plug in: 1, 3, or 5. The second digit (or, the tens digit) has two possible numbers, since one has already been plugged in. The last digit (or, the ones digit) has only one remaining possible number. Multiply the possibilities together: $3 \times 2 \times 1 = 6$.

31. How to calculate a simple PROBABILITY

$$Probability = \frac{Number\ of\ desired\ outcomes}{Number\ of\ total\ possible\ outcomes}$$

Example:

What is the probability of throwing a 5 on a fair six-sided die?

Setup:

There is one desired outcome—throwing a 5. There are 6 possible outcomes—one for each side of the die.

$$Probability = \frac{1}{6}$$

32. How to work with new SYMBOLS

If you see a symbol you've never seen before, don't be alarmed. It's just a made-up symbol whose operation is uniquely defined by the problem. Everything you need to know is in the question stem. Just follow the instructions.

33. How to SIMPLIFY BINOMIALS

A binomial is a sum or difference of two terms. To simplify two binomials that are multiplied together, use the **FOIL** method. Multiply the **F**irst terms, then the **O**uter terms, followed by the **I**nner terms and the **L**ast terms. Lastly, combine like terms.

Example:

$$(3x + 5)(x + 1) =$$
$$3x^2 + 3x + 5x + 5 =$$
$$3x^2 + 2x + 5$$

34. How to FACTOR certain POLYNOMIALS

A polynomial is an expression consisting of the sum of two or more terms, where at least one of the terms is a variable.

Learn to spot these classic polynomial equations.

$$ab + ac = a(b + c)$$
$$a^2 + 2ab + b^2 = (a + b)^2$$
$$a^2 - 2ab + b^2 = (a - b)^2$$
$$a^2 - b^2 = (a - b)(a + b)$$

35. How to solve for one variable IN TERMS OF ANOTHER

To find x "in terms of" y, isolate x on one side, leaving y as the only variable on the other.

36. How to solve an INEQUALITY

Treat it much like an equation—adding, subtracting, multiplying, and dividing both sides by the same thing. Just remember to reverse the inequality sign if you multiply or divide by a negative quantity.

Example:

Rewrite $7 - 3x > 2$ in its simplest form.

Setup:

$$7 - 3x > 2$$

First, subtract 7 from both sides:

$$7 - 3x - 7 > 2 - 7$$

$$-3x > -5$$

Now divide both sides by -3, remembering to reverse the inequality sign:

$$x < \frac{5}{3}$$

37. How to handle ABSOLUTE VALUES

The *absolute value* of a number n, denoted by $|n|$, is defined as n if $n \geq 0$ and $-n$ if $n < 0$. The absolute value of a number is the distance from zero to the number on the number line. The absolute value of a number or expression is always positive.

$$|-5| = 5$$

If $|x| = 3$, then x could be 3 or -3.

Example:

If $|x - 3| < 2$, what is the range of possible values for x?

Setup:

Represent the possible range for $x - 3$ on a number line.

$|x - 3| < 2$, so $(x - 3) < 2$ and $(x - 3) > -2$
$x - 3 < 2$ and $x - 3 > -2$
$x < 2 + 3$ and $x > -2 + 3$
$x < 5$ and $x > 1$
So $1 < x < 5$.

38. How to TRANSLATE ENGLISH INTO ALGEBRA

Look for the key words and systematically turn phrases into algebraic expressions and sentences into equations.

Here's a table of key words that you may have to translate into mathematical terms:

Operation	Key Words
Addition	sum, plus, and, added to, more than, increased by, combined with, exceeds, total, greater than
Subtraction	difference between, minus, subtracted from, decreased by, diminished by, less than, reduced by
Multiplication	of, product, times, multiplied by, twice, double, triple, half
Division	quotient, divided by, per, out of, ratio __ of __ to
Equals	equals, is, was, will be, the result is, adds up to, costs, is the same as

39. How to find an ANGLE formed by INTERSECT-ING LINES

Vertical angles are equal. Angles along a line add up to 180°.

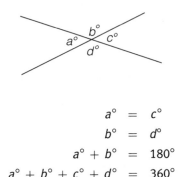

$$a° = c°$$
$$b° = d°$$
$$a° + b° = 180°$$
$$a° + b° + c° + d° = 360°$$

40. How to find an angle formed by a TRANSVER-SAL across PARALLEL LINES

When a transversal crosses parallel lines, all the acute angles formed are equal, and and all the obtuse angles formed are equal. Any acute angle plus any obtuse angle equals 180°.

Example:

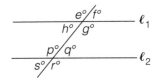

$$e° = g° = p° = r°$$
$$f° = h° = q° = s°$$
$$e° + q° = g° + s° = 180°$$

41. How to find the AREA of a TRIANGLE

$$Area = \frac{1}{2}(Base)(Height)$$

Base and height must be perpendicular to each other. Height is measured by drawing a perpendicular line segment from the base—which can be any side of the triangle—to the angle opposite the base.

Example:

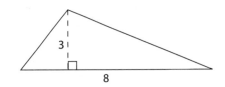

Setup:

$$Area = \frac{1}{2}(8)(3) = 12$$

42. How to work with ISOSCELES TRIANGLES

Isosceles triangles have at least two equal sides and two equal angles. If a GRE question tells you that a triangle is isosceles, you can bet that you'll need to use that information to find the length of a side or a measure of an angle.

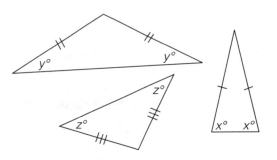

43. How to work with EQUILATERAL TRIANGLES

Equilateral triangles have three equal sides and three 60° angles. If a GRE question tells you that a triangle is equilateral, you can bet that you'll need to use that information to find the length of a side or the measure of an angle.

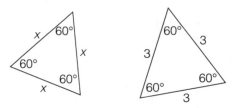

44. How to work with SIMILAR TRIANGLES

In similar triangles, corresponding angles are equal, and corresponding sides are proportional. If a GRE question tells you that triangles are similar, use the properties of similar triangles to find the length of a side or the measure of an angle.

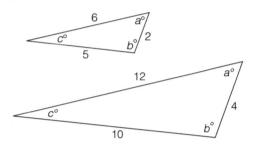

45. How to find the HYPOTENUSE or a LEG of a RIGHT TRIANGLE

For all right triangles, the Pythagorean theorem is $a^2 + b^2 = c^2$, where a and b are the legs and c is the hypotenuse.

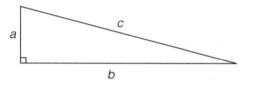

46. How to spot SPECIAL RIGHT TRIANGLES

Special right triangles are ones that are seen on the GRE with frequency. Recognizing them can streamline your problem solving.

$$3:4:5$$
$$5:12:13$$

These numbers (3, 4, 5 and 5, 12, 13) represent the ratio of the side lengths of these triangles.

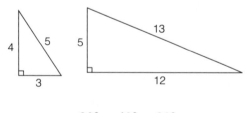

$$30° - 60° - 90°$$
$$45° - 45° - 90°$$

In a $30 - 60 - 90$ triangle, the side lengths are multiples of 1, $\sqrt{3}$, and 2, respectively. In a $45 - 45 - 90$ triangle, the side lengths are multiples of 1, 1, and $\sqrt{2}$, respectfully.

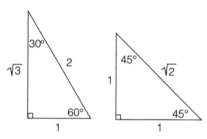

47. How to find the PERIMETER of a RECTANGLE

$$Perimeter = 2(Length + Width)$$

Example:

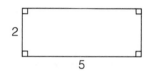

Setup:

$$Perimeter = 2(2 + 5) = 14$$

48. How to find the AREA of a RECTANGLE

$$Area = (Length)(Width)$$

Example:

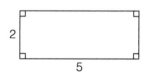

Setup:

$$Area = 2 \times 5 = 10$$

49. How to find the AREA of a SQUARE

$$Area = (Side)^2$$

Example:

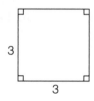

Setup:

$$Area = 3^2 = 9$$

50. How to find the AREA of a PARALLELOGRAM

$$Area = (Base)(Height)$$

Example:

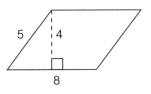

Setup:

$$Area = 8 \times 4 = 32$$

51. How to find the AREA of a TRAPEZOID

A trapezoid is a quadrilateral having only two parallel sides. You can always drop a perpendicular line or two to break the figure into a rectangle and a triangle or two triangles. Use the area formulas for those familiar shapes. Alternatively, you could apply the general formula for the area of a trapezoid:

$$Area = (Average\ of\ parallel\ sides) \times (Height)$$

Example:

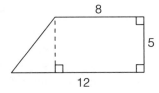

Setup:

$$Area\ of\ rectangle = 8 \times 5 = 40$$
$$Area\ of\ triangle = \frac{1}{2}(4 \times 5) = 10$$
$$Area\ of\ trapezoid = 40 + 10 = 50$$
$$Area\ of\ trapezoid = \left(\frac{8+12}{2}\right) \times 5 = 50$$

52. How to find the CIRCUMFERENCE of a CIRCLE

$Circumference = 2\pi r$, *where* r *is the radius*
$Circumference = \pi d$, *where* d *is the diameter*

Example:

Setup:

$$Circumference = 2\pi(5) = 10\pi$$

53. How to find the AREA of a CIRCLE

$Area = \pi r^2$ *where* r *is the radius*

Example:

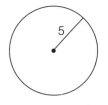

Setup:

$$Area = \pi \times 5^2 = 25\pi$$

54. How to find the DISTANCE BETWEEN POINTS on the coordinate plane

If two points have the same x coordinates or the same y coordinates—that is, they make a line segment that is parallel to an axis—all you have to do is subtract the numbers that are different. Just remember that distance is always positive.

Example:

What is the distance from (2, 3) to (−7, 3)?

Setup:

The y's are the same, so just subtract the x's: $2 − (−7) = 9$.

If the points have different *x* coordinates and different *y* coordinates, make a right triangle and use the Pythagorean theorem or apply the special right triangle attributes if applicable.

Example:
What is the distance from (2,3) to (−1,−1)?

Setup:

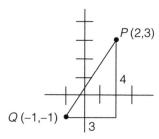

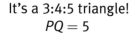

It's a 3:4:5 triangle!
$PQ = 5$

55. How to find the SLOPE of a LINE

$$Slope = \frac{Rise}{Run} = \frac{Change\ in\ y}{Change\ in\ x}$$

Example:
What is the slope of the line that contains the points (1,2) and (4,−5)?

Setup:

$$Slope = \frac{-5-2}{4-1} = \frac{-7}{3} = -\frac{7}{3}$$

LEVEL 3

56 How to determine COMBINED PERCENT INCREASE/DECREASE when no original value is specified
Start with 100 as a starting value.

Example:
A price rises by 10 percent one year and by 20 percent the next. What's the combined percent increase?

Setup:
Say the original price is $100.

Year one:
$100 + (10% of 100) = 100 + 10 = 110

Year two:
110 + (20% of 110) = 110 + 22 = 132

From 100 to 132 is a 32 percent increase.

57. How to find the ORIGINAL WHOLE before percent increase/decrease
Think of a 15 percent increase over *x* as 1.15*x* and set up an equation.

Example:
After decreasing by 5 percent, the population is now 57,000. What was the original population?

Setup:
0.95 × (*Original population*) = 57,000
Divide both sides by 0.95.
Original population = 57,000 ÷ 0.95 = 60,000

58. How to solve a SIMPLE INTEREST problem
With simple interest, the interest is computed on the principal only and is given by

$$Interest = Principle \times rt$$

In this formula, *r* is defined as the interest rate per payment period, and *t* is defined as the number of payment periods.

Example:
If $12,000 is invested at 6 percent simple annual interest, how much interest is earned after 9 months?

Setup:
Since the interest rate is annual and we are calculating how much interest accrues after 9 months, we will express the payment period as $\frac{9}{12}$.

$$(12,000) \times (0.06) \times \frac{9}{12} = \$540$$

59. How to solve a COMPOUND INTEREST problem

If interest is compounded, the interest is computed on the principal as well as on any interest earned. To compute compound interest:

$$(\textit{Final balance}) = (\textit{Principal}) \times \left(1 + \frac{\textit{interest rate}}{c}^{(time)(c)}\right)$$

where c = the number of times the interest is compounded annually.

Example:

If $10,000 is invested at 8 percent annual interest, compounded semiannually, what is the balance after 1 year?

Setup:

Final balance

$$= (10,000) \times \left(1 + \frac{0.08}{2}^{(1)(2)}\right)$$

$$= (10,000) \times (1.04)^2$$

$$= \$10,816$$

Semiannual interest is interest that is distributed twice a year. When an interest rate is given as an annual rate, divide by 2 to find the semiannual interest rate.

60. How to solve a REMAINDERS problem

Pick a number that fits the given conditions and see what happens.

Example:

When n is divided by 7, the remainder is 5. What is the remainder when $2n$ is divided by 7?

Setup:

Find a number that leaves a remainder of 5 when divided by 7. You can find such a number by taking any multiple of 7 and adding 5 to it. A good choice would be 12. If $n = 12$, then $2n = 24$, which when divided by 7 leaves a remainder of 3.

61. How to solve a DIGITS problem

Use a little logic—and some trial and error.

Example:

If A, B, C, and D represent distinct digits in the addition problem below, what is the value of D?

$$\begin{array}{r} AB \\ + BA \\ \hline CDC \end{array}$$

Setup:

Two 2-digit numbers will add up to at most something in the 100s, so $C = 1$. B plus A in the units column gives a 1, and since A and B in the tens column don't add up to C, it can't simply be that $B + A = 1$. It must be that $B + A = 11$, and a 1 gets carried. In fact, A and B can be any pair of digits that add up to 11 (3 and 8, 4 and 7, etc.), but it doesn't matter what they are: they always give you the same value for D, which is 2:

$$\begin{array}{r} 47 \\ + 74 \\ \hline 121 \end{array} \qquad \begin{array}{r} 83 \\ + 38 \\ \hline 121 \end{array}$$

62. How to find a WEIGHTED AVERAGE

Give each term the appropriate "weight."

Example:

The girls' average score is 30. The boys' average score is 24. If there are twice as many boys as girls, what is the overall average?

Setup:

$$\textit{Weighted avg.} = \frac{(1 \times 30) + (2 \times 24)}{3} = \frac{78}{3} = 26$$

HINT: Don't just average the averages.

63. How to find the NEW AVERAGE when a number is added or deleted

Use the sum of the terms of the old average to help you find the new average.

Example:

Michael's average score after four tests is 80. If he scores 100 on the fifth test, what's his new average?

Setup:

Find the original sum from the original average:

$$Original\ sum = 4 \times 80 = 320$$

Add the fifth score to make the new sum:

$$New\ sum = 320 + 100 = 420$$

Find the new average from the new sum:

$$New\ average = \frac{420}{5} = 84$$

64. How to use the ORIGINAL AVERAGE and NEW AVERAGE to figure out WHAT WAS ADDED OR DELETED

Use the sums.

Number added = (*New sum*) − (*Original sum*)
Number deleted = (*Original sum*) − (*New sum*)

Example:

The average of five numbers is 2. After one number is deleted, the new average is −3. What number was deleted?

Setup:

Find the original sum from the original average:

$$Original\ sum = 5 \times 2 = 10$$

Find the new sum from the new average:

$$New\ sum = 4 \times (-3) = -12$$

The difference between the original sum and the new sum is the answer.

Number deleted = 10 − (−12) = 22

65. How to find an AVERAGE RATE

Convert to totals.

$$Average\ A\ per\ B = \frac{Total\ A}{Total\ B}$$

Example:

If the first 500 pages have an average of 150 words per page, and the remaining 100 pages have an average of 450 words per page, what is the average number of words per page for the entire 600 pages?

Setup:

$$
\begin{aligned}
Total\ pages &= 500 + 100 = 600 \\
Total\ words &= (500 \times 150) + (100 \times 450) \\
&= 75{,}000 + 45{,}000 \\
&= 120{,}000
\end{aligned}
$$

$$Average\ words\ per\ page = \frac{120{,}000}{600} = 200$$

To find an average speed, you also convert to totals.

$$Average\ speed = \frac{Total\ distance}{Time}$$

Example:

Rosa drove 120 miles one way at an average speed of 40 miles per hour and returned by the same 120-mile route at an average speed of 60 miles per hour. What was Rosa's average speed for the entire 240-mile round trip?

Setup:

To drive 120 miles at 40 mph takes 3 hours. To return at 60 mph takes 2 hours. The total time, then, is 5 hours.

$$Average\ speed = \frac{240\ miles}{5\ hours} = 48\ mph$$

66. How to solve a COMBINED WORK PROBLEM

In a combined work problem, you are given the rate at which people or machines perform work individually and you are asked to compute the rate at which they work together (or vice versa). The work formula states: *The inverse of the time it would take everyone working together equals the sum of the inverses of the times it would take each working individually.* In other words:

$$\frac{1}{r} + \frac{1}{s} = \frac{1}{t}$$

where r and s are, for example, the number of hours it would take Rebecca and Sam, respectively, to complete a job working by themselves, and t is the number of hours it would take the two of them working together. Remember that all these variables must stand for units of TIME and must all refer to the amount of time it takes to do the same task.

Example:

If it takes Joe 4 hours to paint a room and Pete twice as long to paint the same room, how long would it take the two of them, working together, to paint the same room, if each of them works at his respective individual rate?

Setup:

Joe takes 4 hours, so Pete takes 8 hours; thus:

$$\frac{1}{4} + \frac{1}{8} = \frac{1}{t}$$

$$\frac{2}{8} + \frac{1}{8} = \frac{1}{t}$$

$$\frac{3}{8} = \frac{1}{t}$$

$$t = \frac{1}{\left(\frac{3}{8}\right)} = \frac{8}{3}$$

So it would take them $\frac{8}{3}$ hours, or 2 hours and 40 minutes, to paint the room together.

67. How to determine a COMBINED RATIO

Multiply one or both ratios by whatever you need in order to get the terms they have in common to match.

Example:

The ratio of a to b is 7:3. The ratio of b to c is 2:5. What is the ratio of a to c?

Setup:

Multiply each member of a:b by 2 and multiply each member of b:c by 3, and you get a:$b = 14$:6 and b:$c = 6$:15. Now that the values of b match, you can write a:b:$c = 14$:6:15 and then say a:$c = 14$:15.

68. How to solve a DILUTION or MIXTURE problem

In dilution or mixture problems, you have to determine the characteristics of a resulting mixture when different substances are combined. Or, alternatively, you have to determine how to combine different substances to produce a desired mixture. There are two approaches to such problems—the straightforward setup and the balancing method.

Example:

If 5 pounds of raisins that cost $1 per pound are mixed with 2 pounds of almonds that cost $2.40 per pound, what is the cost per pound of the resulting mixture?

Setup:

The straightforward setup:

($1)(5) + ($2.40)(2) = $9.80 = total cost for 7 pounds of the mixture

The cost per pound is $\frac{\$9.80}{7} = \$1.40$.

Example:

How many liters of a solution that is 10 percent alcohol by volume must be added to 2 liters of a solution that is 50 percent alcohol by volume to create a solution that is 15 percent alcohol by volume?

Setup:

The balancing method: Make the weaker and stronger (or cheaper and more expensive, etc.) substances balance. That is, (percent difference between the weaker solution and the desired solution) × (amount of weaker solution) = (percent difference between the stronger solution and the desired solution) × (amount of stronger solution).

Make n the amount, in liters, of the weaker solution.

$$n(15 - 10) = 2(50 - 15)$$
$$5n = 2(35)$$
$$n = \frac{70}{5} = 14$$

So 14 liters of the 10 percent solution must be added to the original, stronger solution.

69. How to solve an OVERLAPPING SETS problem involving BOTH/NEITHER

Some GRE word problems involve two groups with overlapping members and possibly elements that belong to neither group. It's easy to identify this type of question because the words *both* and/or *neither* appear in the question. These problems are quite workable if you just memorize the following formula:

Group 1 + Group 2 + Neither − Both = Total

Example:

Of the 120 students at a certain language school, 65 are studying French, 51 are studying Spanish, and 53 are studying neither language. How many are studying both French and Spanish?

Setup:

$$65 + 51 + 53 - Both = 120$$
$$169 - Both = 120$$
$$Both = 49$$

70 How to solve an OVERLAPPING SETS problem involving EITHER/OR CATEGORIES

Other GRE word problems involve groups with distinct "either/or" categories (male/female, blue-collar/white-collar, etc.). The key to solving this type of problem is to organize the information in a grid.

Example:

At a certain professional conference with 130 attendees, 94 of the attendees are doctors, and the rest are dentists. If 48 of the attendees are women and $\frac{1}{4}$ of the dentists in attendance are women, how many of the attendees are male doctors?

Setup:

To complete the grid, use the information in the problem, making each row and column add up to the corresponding total:

	Doctors	Dentists	Total
Male	55	27	82
Female	39	9	48
Total	94	36	130

After you've filled in the information from the question, use simple arithmetic to fill in the remaining boxes until you get the number you are looking for—in this case, that 55 of the attendees are male doctors.

71. How to work with FACTORIALS

You may see a problem involving factorial notation, which is indicated by the ! symbol. If n is an integer greater than 1, then n factorial, denoted by $n!$, is defined as the product of all the integers from 1 to n. For example:

$$2! = 2 \times 1 = 2$$
$$3! = 3 \times 2 \times 1 = 6$$
$$4! = 4 \times 3 \times 2 \times 1 = 24, etc$$

By definition, $0! = 1$.

Also note: $6! = 6 \times 5! = 6 \times 5 \times 4!$, etc. Most GRE factorial problems test your ability to factor and/or cancel.

Example:

$$\frac{8!}{6! \times 2!} = \frac{8 \times 7 \times 6!}{6! \times 2 \times 1} = 28$$

72: How to solve a PERMUTATION problem

Factorials are useful for solving questions about permutations (i.e., the number of ways to arrange elements sequentially). For instance, to figure out how many ways there are to arrange 7 items along a shelf, you would multiply the number of possibilities for the first position times the number of possibilities remaining for the second position, and so on—in other words: $7 \times 6 \times 5 \times 4 \times 3 \times 2 \times 1$, or $7!$.

If you're asked to find the number of ways to arrange a smaller group that's being drawn from a larger group, you can either apply logic, or you can use the permutation formula:

$$_nP_k = \frac{n!}{(n-k)!}$$

where n = (the number in the larger group) and k = (the number you're arranging).

Example:

Five runners run in a race. The runners who come in first, second, and third place will win gold, silver, and bronze medals, respectively. How many possible outcomes for gold, silver, and bronze medal winners are there?

Setup:

Any of the 5 runners could come in first place, leaving 4 runners who could come in second place, leaving 3 runners who could come in third place, for a total of $5 \times 4 \times 3 = 60$ possible outcomes for gold, silver, and bronze medal winners. Or, using the formula:

$$_5P_3 = \frac{5!}{(5-3)!} = \frac{5!}{2!} = \frac{5 \times 4 \times 3 \times \cancel{2} \times \cancel{1}}{\cancel{2} \times \cancel{1}}$$
$$= 5 \times 4 \times 3 = 60$$

73: How to solve a COMBINATION problem

If the order or arrangement of the smaller group that's being drawn from the larger group does NOT matter, you are looking for the numbers of combinations, and a different formula is called for:

$$_nC_k = \frac{n!}{k!(n-k)!}$$

where n = (the number in the larger group) and k = (the number you're choosing).

Example:

How many different ways are there to choose 3 delegates from 8 possible candidates?

Setup:

$$_nC_k = \frac{8!}{3!(8-3)!} = \frac{8!}{3! \times 5!}$$
$$= \frac{8 \times 7 \times \cancel{6} \times \cancel{5} \times \cancel{4} \times \cancel{3} \times \cancel{2} \times \cancel{1}}{\cancel{3} \times \cancel{2} \times 1 \times \cancel{5} \times \cancel{4} \times \cancel{3} \times \cancel{2} \times \cancel{1}}$$
$$= 8 \times 7 = 56$$

So there are 56 different possible combinations.

74. How to solve PROBABILITY problems where probabilities must be multiplied

Suppose that a random process is performed. Then there is a set of possible outcomes that can occur. An event is a set of possible outcomes. We are concerned with the probability of events.

When all the outcomes are all equally likely, the basic probability formula is this:

$$Probability = \frac{Number\ of\ desired\ outcomes}{Number\ of\ total\ possible\ outcomes}$$

Many more difficult probability questions involve finding the probability that several events occur. Let's consider first the case of the probability that two events occur. Call these two events A and B. The probability that both events occur is the probability that event A occurs multiplied by the probability that event B occurs given that event A

occurred. The probability that B occurs given that A occurs is called the conditional probability that B occurs given that A occurs. Except when events A and B do not depend on one another, the probability that B occurs given that A occurs is not the same as the probability that B occurs.

The probability that three events A, B, and C occur is the probability that A occurs multiplied by the conditional probability that B occurs given that A occurred multiplied by the conditional probability that C occurs given that both A and B have occurred.

This can be generalized to any number of events.

Example:

If 2 students are chosen at random to run an errand from a class with 5 girls and 5 boys, what is the probability that both students chosen will be girls?

Setup:

The probability that the first student chosen will be a girl is $\frac{5}{10} = \frac{1}{2}$, and since there would be 4 girls and 5 boys left out of 9 students, the probability that the second student chosen will be a girl (given that the first student chosen is a girl) is $\frac{4}{9}$. Thus the probability that both students chosen will be girls is $\frac{1}{2} \times \frac{4}{9} = \frac{2}{9}$. There was conditional probability here because the probability of choosing the second girl was affected by another girl being chosen first. Now let's consider another example where a random process is repeated.

Example:

If a fair coin is tossed 4 times, what's the probability that at least 3 of the 4 tosses will be heads?

Setup:

There are 2 possible outcomes for each toss, so after 4 tosses, there are $2 \times 2 \times 2 \times 2 = 16$ possible outcomes.

We can list the different possible sequences where at least 3 of the 4 tosses are heads. These sequences are

$$HHHT$$
$$HHTH$$
$$HTHH$$
$$THHH$$
$$HHHH$$

Thus, the probability that at least 3 of the 4 tosses will come up heads is:

$$\frac{Number\ of\ desired\ outcomes}{Number\ of\ total\ possible\ outcomes} = \frac{5}{16}$$

We could have also solved this question using the combinations formula. The probability of a head is $\frac{1}{2}$, and the probability of a tail is $\frac{1}{2}$. The probability of any particular sequence of heads and tails resulting from 4 tosses is $\frac{1}{2} \times \frac{1}{2} \times \frac{1}{2} \times \frac{1}{2}$, which is $\frac{1}{16}$.

Suppose that the result each of the four tosses is recorded in each of the four spaces.

$$\underline{\qquad} \quad \underline{\qquad} \quad \underline{\qquad} \quad \underline{\qquad}$$

Thus, we would record an H for head or a T for tails in each of the 4 spaces.

The number of ways of having exactly 3 heads among the 4 tosses is the number of ways of choosing 3 of the 4 spaces above to record an H for heads.

The number of ways of choosing 3 of the 4 spaces is

$$_4C_3 = \frac{4!}{3!\,(4-3)!} = \frac{4!}{3!\,(1)!} = \frac{4 \times 3 \times 2 \times 1}{3 \times 2 \times 1 \times 1} = 4$$

The number of ways of having exactly 4 heads among the 4 tosses is 1.

If we use the combinations formula, using the definition that $0! = 1$, then

$$_4C_4 = \frac{4!}{4!(4-4)!} = \frac{4!}{4!(0)!}$$

$$= \frac{4 \times 3 \times 2 \times 1}{4 \times 3 \times 2 \times 1 \times 1} = 1$$

Thus, $_4C_3 = 4$ and $_4C_4 = 1$. So the number of different sequences containing at least 3 heads is $4 + 1 = 5$.

The probability of having at least 3 heads is $\frac{5}{16}$.

75. How to deal with STANDARD DEVIATION

Like the terms *mean*, *mode*, *median*, and *range*, *standard deviation* is a term used to describe sets of numbers. Standard deviation is a measure of how spread out a set of numbers is (how much the numbers deviate from the mean). The greater the spread, the higher the standard deviation. You'll rarely have to calculate the standard deviation on Test Day (although this skill may be necessary for some high-difficulty questions). Here's how standard deviation is calculated:

- Find the average (arithmetic mean) of the set.
- Find the differences between the mean and each value in the set.
- Square each of the differences.
- Find the average of the squared differences.
- Take the positive square root of the average.

In addition to the occasional question that asks you to calculate standard deviation, you may also be asked to compare standard deviations between sets of data or otherwise demonstrate that you understand what standard deviation means. You can often handle these questions using estimation.

Example:
High temperatures, in degrees Fahrenheit, in two cities over five days:

September	1	2	3	4	5
City A	54	61	70	49	56
City B	62	56	60	67	65

For the five-day period listed, which city had the greater standard deviation in high temperatures?

Setup:
Even without trying to calculate them out, one can see that City A has the greater spread in temperatures and, therefore, the greater standard deviation in high temperatures. If you were to go ahead and calculate the standard deviations following the steps described above, you would find that the standard deviation in high temperatures for

City A $= \sqrt{\dfrac{254}{5}} \approx 7.1$ while the standard deviation for City

B $= \sqrt{\dfrac{74}{5}} \approx 3.8$.

76. How to MULTIPLY/DIVIDE VALUES WITH EXPONENTS

Add/subtract the exponents.

Example:

$$x^a \times x^b = x^{a+b}$$
$$2^3 \times 2^4 = 2^7$$

Example:

$$\frac{x^a}{x^b} = x^{a-b}$$
$$\frac{2^8}{2^2} = 2^{8-2} = 2^6$$

77. How to handle a value with an EXPONENT RAISED TO AN EXPONENT

Multiply the exponents.

Example:

$$(x^a)^b = x^{ab}$$
$$(3^4)^5 = 3^{20}$$

78. How to handle EXPONENTS with a base of ZERO and BASES with an EXPONENT of ZERO

Zero raised to any nonzero exponent equals zero.

Example:

$$0^4 = 0^{12} = 0^1 = 0$$

Any nonzero number raised to the exponent 0 equals 1.

Example:

$$3^0 = 15^0 = (0.34)^0 = (-345)^0 = \pi^0 = 1$$

The lone exception is 0 raised to the 0 power, which is *undefined*.

79. How to handle NEGATIVE POWERS

A number raised to the exponent $-x$ is the reciprocal of that number raised to the exponent x.

Example:

$$n^{-1} = \frac{1}{n}, \ n^{-2} = \frac{1}{n^2}, \text{ and so on.}$$

$$5^{-3} = \frac{1}{5^3} = \frac{1}{5 \times 5 \times 5} = \frac{1}{125}$$

80. How to handle FRACTIONAL POWERS

Fractional exponents relate to roots. For instance, $x^{\frac{1}{2}} = \sqrt{x}$.

Likewise, $x^{\frac{1}{3}} = \sqrt[3]{x}$, $x^{\frac{2}{3}} = \sqrt[3]{x^2}$, and so on.

Example:

$$\sqrt{x^{-2}} = (x^{-2})^{\frac{1}{2}} = x^{(-2)\frac{1}{2}} = x^{-1} = \frac{1}{x}$$

$$4^{\frac{1}{2}} = \sqrt{4} = 2$$

81. How to handle CUBE ROOTS

The cube root of x is just the number that when used as a factor 3 times (i.e., cubed) gives you x. Both positive and negative numbers have one and only one cube root, denoted by the symbol $\sqrt[3]{\ }$, and the cube root of a number is always the same sign as the number itself.

Example:

$$(-5) \times (-5) \times (-5) = -125, \text{ so } \sqrt[3]{-125} = -5$$

$$\frac{1}{2} \times \frac{1}{2} \times \frac{1}{2} = \frac{1}{8}, \text{ so } \sqrt[3]{\frac{1}{8}} = \frac{1}{2}$$

82. How to ADD, SUBTRACT, MULTIPLY, and DIVIDE ROOTS

You can add/subtract roots only when the parts inside the $\sqrt{\ }$ are identical.

Example:

$$\sqrt{2} + 3\sqrt{2} = 4\sqrt{2}$$

$$\sqrt{2} - 3\sqrt{2} = -2\sqrt{2}$$

$$\sqrt{2} + \sqrt{3} \quad \text{cannot be combined.}$$

To multiply/divide roots, deal with what's inside the $\sqrt{\ }$ and outside the $\sqrt{\ }$ separately.

Example:

$$(2\sqrt{3})(7\sqrt{5}) = (2 \times 7)(\sqrt{3 \times 5}) = 14\sqrt{15}$$

$$\frac{10\sqrt{21}}{5\sqrt{3}} = \frac{10}{5}\sqrt{\frac{21}{3}} = 2\sqrt{7}$$

83. How to SIMPLIFY A RADICAL

Look for factors of the number under the radical sign that are perfect squares; then find the square root of those perfect squares. Keep simplifying until the term with the square root sign is as simplified as possible, that is, when there are no other perfect square factors (4, 9, 16, 25, 36, ...) inside the $\sqrt{\ }$. Write the perfect squares as separate factors and "unsquare" them.

Example:

$$\sqrt{48} = \sqrt{16}\ \sqrt{3} = 4\sqrt{3}$$

$$\sqrt{180} = \sqrt{36}\ \sqrt{5} = 6\sqrt{5}$$

84. How to solve certain QUADRATIC EQUATIONS

Manipulate the equation (if necessary) so that it is equal to 0, factor the left side (reverse FOIL by finding two numbers whose product is the constant and whose sum is the coefficient of the term without the exponent), and break the quadratic into two simple expressions. Then find the value(s) for the variable that make either expression $= 0$.

Example:

$$
\begin{aligned}
x^2 + 6 &= 5x \\
x^2 - 5x + 6 &= 0 \\
(x - 2)(x - 3) &= 0 \\
x - 2 &= 0 \text{ or } x - 3 = 0 \\
x &= 2 \text{ or } 3
\end{aligned}
$$

Example:

$$
\begin{aligned}
x^2 &= 9 \\
x &= 3 \text{ or } -3
\end{aligned}
$$

85. How to solve MULTIPLE EQUATIONS

When you see two equations with two variables on the GRE, they're probably easy to combine in such a way that you get something closer to what you're looking for.

Example:

If $5x - 2y = -9$ and $3y - 4x = 6$, what is the value of $x + y$?

Setup:

The question doesn't ask for x and y separately, so don't solve for them separately if you don't have to. Look what happens if you just rearrange a little and "add" the equations:

$$
\begin{aligned}
5x - 2y &= -9 \\
+[-4x + 3y &= 6] \\
\hline
x + y &= -3
\end{aligned}
$$

86. How to solve a SEQUENCE problem

The notation used in sequence problems scares many test takers, but these problems aren't as bad as they look. In a sequence problem, the nth term in the sequence is generated by performing an operation, which will be defined for you, on either n or on the previous term in the sequence. The term itself is expressed as a_n. For instance, if you are referring to the fourth term in a sequence, it is called a_4 in sequence notation. Familiarize yourself with sequence notation and you should have no problem.

Example:

What is the positive difference between the fifth and fourth terms in the sequence 0, 4, 18, . . . whose nth term is $n^2(n - 1)$?

Setup:

Use the definition given to come up with the values for your terms:

$$
\begin{aligned}
a_5 &= 5^2(5 - 1) = 25(4) = 100 \\
a_4 &= 4^2(4 - 1) = 16(3) = 48
\end{aligned}
$$

So the positive difference between the fifth and fourth terms is $100 - 48 = 52$.

87. How to solve a FUNCTION problem

You may see function notation on the GRE. An algebraic expression of only one variable may be defined as a function, usually symbolized by f or g, of that variable.

Example:

What is the minimum value of x in the function $f(x) = x^2 - 1$?

Setup:

In the function $f(x) = x^2 - 1$, if x is 1, then $f(1) = 1^2 - 1 = 0$. In other words, by inputting 1 into the function, the output $f(x) = 0$. Every number inputted has one and only one output (although the reverse is not necessarily true). You're asked to find the minimum value, so how would you minimize the expression $f(x) = x^2 - 1$?

Since x^2 cannot be negative, in this case $f(x)$ is minimized by making $x = 0$: $f(0) = 0^2 - 1 = -1$, so the minimum value of the function is -1.

88. How to handle GRAPHS of FUNCTIONS

You may see a problem that involves a function graphed onto the xy-coordinate plane, often called a "rectangular coordinate system" on the GRE. When graphing a function, the output, $f(x)$, becomes the y-coordinate. For example, in the previous example, $f(x) = x^2 - 1$, you've already determined 2 points, $(1,0)$ and $(0,-1)$. If you were to keep plugging in numbers to determine more points and then plotted those points on the xy-coordinate plane, you would come up with something like this:

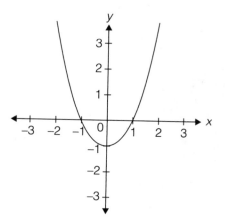

This curved line is called a *parabola*. In the event that you should see a parabola on the GRE (it could be upside down or narrower or wider than the one shown), you will most likely be asked to choose which equation the parabola is describing. These questions can be surprisingly easy to answer. Pick out obvious points on the graph, such as $(1,0)$ and $(0,-1)$ above, plug these values into the answer choices, and eliminate answer choices that don't jibe with those values until only one answer choice is left.

89. How to handle LINEAR EQUATIONS

You may also encounter linear equations on the GRE. A linear equation is often expressed in the form

$y = mx + b$, where

$m =$ the slope of the line $= \dfrac{rise}{run}$

$b =$ the y-intercept (the point where the line crosses the y-axis)

Example:

The graph of the linear equation

$$y = -\frac{3}{4}x + 3 \text{ is this:}$$

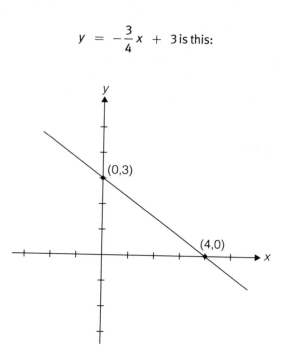

Note:

The equation could also be written in the form $3x + 4y = 12$, but this form does not readily describe the slope and y-intercept of the line.

To get a better handle on an equation written in this form, you can solve for y to write it in its more familiar form. Or, if you're asked to choose which equation the line is describing, you can pick obvious points, such as $(0,3)$ and $(4,0)$ in this example, and use these values to eliminate answer choices until only one answer is left.

90. How to find the x- and y-INTERCEPTS of a line

The x-intercept of a line is the value of x where the line crosses the x-axis. In other words, it's the value of x when $y = 0$. Likewise, the y-intercept is the value of y where the line crosses the y-axis (i.e., the value of y when $x = 0$). The y-intercept is also the value b when the equation is in the form $y = mx + b$. For instance, in the line shown in the previous example, the x-intercept is 4 and the y-intercept is 3.

91. How to find the MAXIMUM and MINIMUM lengths for a SIDE of a TRIANGLE

If you know the lengths of two sides of a triangle, you know that the third side is somewhere between the positive difference and the sum of the other two sides.

Example:

The length of one side of a triangle is 7. The length of another side is 3. What is the range of possible lengths for the third side?

Setup:

The third side is greater than the positive difference ($7 - 3 = 4$) and less than the sum ($7 + 3 = 10$) of the other two sides.

92. How to find the sum of all the ANGLES of a POLYGON and one angle measure of a REGULAR POLYGON

Sum of the interior angles in a polygon with n sides:

$$(n - 2) \times 180$$

The term *regular* means all angles in the polygon are of equal measure.

Degree measure of one angle in a regular polygon with n sides:

$$\frac{(n - 2) \times 180}{n}$$

Example:

What is the measure of one angle of a regular pentagon?

Setup:

Since a pentagon is a five-sided figure, plug $n = 5$ into the formula:

Degree measure of one angle:

$$\frac{(5 - 2) \times 180}{5} = \frac{540}{5} = 108$$

93. How to find the LENGTH of an ARC

Think of an arc as a fraction of the circle's circumference. Use the measure of an interior angle of a circle, which has 360 degrees around the central point, to determine the length of an arc.

$$\text{Length of arc} = \frac{n}{360} \times 2\pi r$$

94. How to find the AREA of a SECTOR

Think of a sector as a fraction of the circle's area. Again, set up the interior angle measure as a fraction of 360, which is the degree measure of a circle around the central point.

$$\text{Area of sector} = \frac{n}{360} \times \pi r^2$$

95. How to find the dimensions or area of an INSCRIBED or CIRCUMSCRIBED FIGURE

Look for the connection. Is the diameter the same as a side or a diagonal?

Example:

If the area of the square is 36, what is the circumference of the circle?

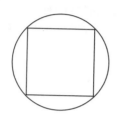

Setup:

To get the circumference, you need the diameter or radius. The circle's diameter is also the square's diagonal. The diagonal of the square is $6\sqrt{2}$. This is because the diagonal of the square transforms it into two separate $45° - 45° - 90°$ triangles (see #46). So, the diameter of the circle is $6\sqrt{2}$.

$$Circumference = \pi(Diameter) = 6\pi\sqrt{2}.$$

96. How to find the VOLUME of a RECTANGULAR SOLID

$$Volume = Length \times Width \times Height$$

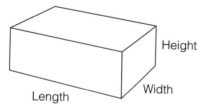

97. How to find the SURFACE AREA of a RECTANGULAR SOLID

To find the surface area of a rectangular solid, you have to find the area of each face and add the areas together. Here's the formula:

Let l = length, w = width, h = height:

$$Surface\ area = 2(lw) + 2(wh) + 2(lh)$$

98. How to find the DIAGONAL of a RECTANGULAR SOLID

Use the Pythagorean theorem twice, unless you spot "special" triangles.

Example:

What is the length of *AG*?

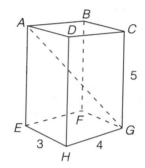

Setup:

Draw diagonal *AC*.

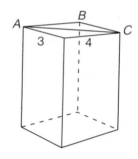

ABC is a 3:4:5 triangle, so $AC = 5$. Now look at triangle *ACG*:

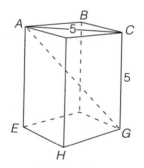

ACG is another special triangle, so you don't need to use the Pythagorean theorem. *ACG* is a $45° - 45° - 90°$ triangle, so $AG = 5\sqrt{2}$.

99. How to find the VOLUME of a CYLINDER

Volume = Area of the base × Height $= \pi r^2 h$

Example:

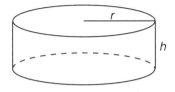

Let $r = 6$ and $h = 3$.

Setup:

$$Volume = \pi r^2 h = \pi(6^2)(3) = 108\pi$$

100. How to find the SURFACE AREA of a CYLINDER

Surface area $= 2\pi r^2 + 2\pi rh$

Example:

Let $r = 3$ and $h = 4$.

Setup:

$$
\begin{aligned}
Surface\ area &= 2\pi r^2 + 2\pi rh \\
&= 2\pi(3)^2 + 2\pi(3)(4) \\
&= 18\pi + 24\pi = 42\pi
\end{aligned}
$$